OXFORD MONOGRAPHS IN INTERNATIONAL
HUMANITARIAN AND CRIMINAL LAW

General Editors

SUZANNAH LINTON

Distinguished Professor at the Law School of Zhejiang Gongshang University, China

ROBERT CRYER

Professor of International and Criminal Law at the University of Birmingham Law School, UK

SALVATORE ZAPPALÀ

Professor of International Law at the University of Catania

Detention in Non-International Armed Conflict

OXFORD MONOGRAPHS IN INTERNATIONAL
HUMANITARIAN AND CRIMINAL LAW

The aim of this series is to publish original and innovative books on fundamental, topical, or cutting-edge issues in international humanitarian law and international criminal justice. The primary purpose of the series is to publish books which, in addition to critically surveying existing law, also suggest new avenues for improving the law.

Special attention will be given to works by young scholars.

Detention in Non-International Armed Conflict

LAWRENCE HILL-CAWTHORNE

OXFORD
UNIVERSITY PRESS

OXFORD
UNIVERSITY PRESS

Great Clarendon Street, Oxford, OX2 6DP,
United Kingdom

Oxford University Press is a department of the University of Oxford.
It furthers the University's objective of excellence in research, scholarship,
and education by publishing worldwide. Oxford is a registered trade mark of
Oxford University Press in the UK and in certain other countries

© Lawrence Hill-Cawthorne 2016
© Preface to Paperback Edition: Lawrence Hill-Cawthorne 2020

The moral rights of the author have been asserted

First published 2016
First published in paperback 2020

All rights reserved. No part of this publication may be reproduced, stored in
a retrieval system, or transmitted, in any form or by any means, without the
prior permission in writing of Oxford University Press, or as expressly permitted
by law, by licence or under terms agreed with the appropriate reprographics
rights organization. Enquiries concerning reproduction outside the scope of the
above should be sent to the Rights Department, Oxford University Press, at the
address above

You must not circulate this work in any other form
and you must impose this same condition on any acquirer

Published in the United States of America by Oxford University Press
198 Madison Avenue, New York, NY 10016, United States of America

British Library Cataloguing in Publication Data

Data available

Library of Congress Cataloging in Publication Data

Data available

ISBN 978–0–19–874992–9 (Hbk.)
ISBN 978–0–19–884309–2 (Pbk.)

Links to third party websites are provided by Oxford in good faith and
for information only. Oxford disclaims any responsibility for the materials
contained in any third party website referenced in this work.

Preface to Paperback Edition

When this book was originally published in March 2016, the subject of detention in armed conflict, and particularly in non-international armed conflict, was extremely topical. At that time, for example, the much discussed *Serdar Mohammed* and *Al-Waheed* cases, on UK detentions during the non-international armed conflicts in Afghanistan and Iraq, were progressing through the English courts.[1] The 32nd International Conference of the Red Cross and Red Crescent held in December 2015 had also just recommended in Resolution 1 that the International Committee of the Red Cross (ICRC) develop concrete outcomes following the ICRC's three year consultation process with States and other actors on strengthening protections for conflict-related detainees.[2] And just two years earlier, both the European Court of Human Rights (ECtHR) and the Human Rights Committee (HRC) had explicitly set out their views on the relationship between international humanitarian law and the Convention and Covenant regarding detention.[3]

The subject has continued to dominate much academic debate and practice. For example, there remains considerable debate over the regulation of detentions by non-State armed groups,[4] the legal basis for detentions by States and non-State groups,[5] and the interaction between international humanitarian law and human rights law.[6] Regarding practice, the controversy of this topic is reflected in the inability of States to reach agreement on taking forward the call in Resolution 1 of the 32nd International Conference to develop concrete proposals for strengthening protections for detainees.[7] Furthermore, the litigation concerning UK detention operations culminated in a Supreme Court judgment in January 2017,[8] which has since been applied at the trial level.[9] Given that this Supreme Court

---

1 *Serdar Mohammed v Ministry of Defence* [2014] EWHC 1369 (QB); *Serdar Mohammed et al v Secretary of State for Defence* [2015] EWCA Civ 843; *Abd Ali Hameed Ali Al-Waheed v The Ministry of Defence* [2014] EWHC 2714 (QB).
2 Resolution 1: Strengthening international humanitarian law protecting persons deprived of their liberty, 32IC/15/R1.
3 *Hassan v United Kingdom*, App No 29750/09, Judgment (Grand Chamber), 16 September 2014; HRC, General Comment No 35: Article 9 (Liberty and security of person), CCPR/C/GC/35, 16 December 2014.
4 See, eg, A Clapham, 'Detention by Armed Groups under International Law' (2017) 93 Intl L Stud 1.
5 See, eg, D Murray, 'Non-State Armed Groups, Detention Authority in Non-International Armed Conflict, and the Coherence of International Law: Searching for a Way Forward' (2017) 30 Leiden J Intl L 435.
6 See, eg, Y Shany, 'A Human Rights Perspective to Global Battlefield Detention: Time to Reconsider Indefinite Detention' (2017) 93 Intl L Stud 102.
7 See ICRC, 'Strengthening IHL protecting persons deprived of their liberty in relation to armed conflict', 1 April 2017 <https://www.icrc.org/en/document/detention-non-international-armed-conflict-icrcs-work-strengthening-legal-protection-0> accessed 16 July 2019.
8 *Abd Ali Hameed Al-Waheed and Serdar Mohammed v Ministry of Defence* [2017] UKSC 2.
9 *Kamil Najim Abdullah Alseran, Abd Ali Hameed Al-Waheed, MRE and KSU v Ministry of Defence* [2017] EWHC 3289 (QB).

judgment engages squarely with the topic of this book, the remainder of this preface will focus principally on analysing the approach taken by the Court and its relationship with the approach adopted in this book. The aim is not to explore this recent jurisprudence exhaustively, but rather to provide an important update to the original monograph. A few other recent developments are also noted along the way.

The Legal Basis for Detention in Non-International Armed Conflict

The High Court and Court of Appeal judgments in the *Serdar Mohammed* case were discussed in the book, notably for their rejection of the UK government's argument that IHL provided a legal basis to detain in non-international armed conflicts.[10] The UK again made this argument in its appeal to the Supreme Court. Unlike the courts below, however, the majority in the Supreme Court did not take a final position on this question, though Lord Sumption, in the majority, was 'inclined to agree' with that part of Lord Reed's dissent which concluded that no legal basis exists under conventional or customary IHL.[11] The majority instead agreed with the government that relevant Security Council resolutions, which in Afghanistan authorized Member States simply to take 'all necessary measures' to fulfil the 'International Security Assistance Force's mandate', constituted a sufficient legal basis for detaining persons on grounds of imperative reasons of security.[12] I continue to take the position that such a general authorization under a Security Council resolution, focused on legality under the *ius ad bellum*, cannot operate as a sufficient legal basis for detention.[13] This is because, without specifying any clear grounds on which detention may be based, the general authorization found in Security Council resolutions cannot satisfy the requirements of predictability and certainty under international human rights law, applicable in non-international armed conflicts.[14] To say that a vague authorization to take 'all necessary measures' can constitute a legal basis for detention that satisfies international human rights law is to negate the *raison d'être* of the very requirement of a legal basis.

---

10 See section 3.1.
11 *Al-Waheed/Mohammed* (n 8) [14] (Lord Sumption). See also ibid at [16] (Lord Sumption) ('[t]here is no doubt that practice in international and non-international armed conflicts is converging, and it is likely that this will eventually be reflected in *opinio juris*. It is, however, clear from the materials before us that a significant number of state participating in non-international armed conflicts, including the United Kingdom, do not yet regard detention as being authorised in such conflicts by customary international law.')
12 Ibid, [30] (Lord Sumption).
13 See the discussion on this in section 3.1. The relevant Iraq resolutions were different, with the annexed letters referring explicitly to internment for imperative reasons of security, which might constitute a sufficient legal basis.
14 On the requirement of predictability under international human right law, see section 4.2.1; see also General Comment No 35 (n 3) [22].

Before the Supreme Court, the government relied on some recent examples of practice that it claimed supported its assertion that a legal basis to detain in non-international armed conflicts could be found in either treaty or customary IHL. Most significantly, it pointed to the preamble of Resolution 1 of the 32nd International Conference of the Red Cross and Red Crescent,[15] which states that 'deprivation of liberty is an ordinary and expected occurrence in armed conflict, and that under IHL States have, in all forms of armed conflict, both the power to detain, and the obligation to provide protection and to respect applicable legal safeguards'.[16] The language of this preamble is, however, unclear and fully reconcilable with the view, taken in this book, that the most that can be said is that IHL *does not prohibit* (non-arbitrary) detention in non-international armed conflict.

What is more, even had the language been clear, a preambular paragraph in such a resolution that is actually concerned with enhancing the protections for detainees cannot constitute sufficient evidence of customary international law. To show this, one might draw an analogy to the debate over the relevance of General Assembly resolutions to customary law formation. Though such resolutions may indicate States' views as to the existence of custom,[17] caution has been advised in assuming an intention to indicate an *opinio iuris* in such a political forum (and in the case of the International Conference of the Red Cross and Red Crescent, comprised of both States and non-State entities, such caution is even more important).[18] What is clear is that such resolutions cannot replace the need for State practice that is supported by *opinio iuris*, and they must not be used 'as a short cut to ascertaining international practice in its entirety on a matter—practice in the larger world arena is still the relevant canvas'.[19] Importantly in this context, the stark absence of practice of States detaining in non-international armed conflicts on the grounds of a presumed legal basis under custom (as opposed to domestic law, for example)[20] significantly undermines the degree to which any normative weight can be given to the preamble in this resolution.[21]

---

15 See discussion in *Al-Waheed/Mohammed* (n 8) [272] (Lord Reed).
16 Resolution 1 (n 2) preambular [1].
17 *Legality of the Threat or Use of Nuclear Weapons*, Advisory Opinion [1996] ICJ Rep 226, [70] ('[t]he Court notes that General Assembly resolutions, even if they are not binding, may sometimes have normative value. They can, in certain circumstances, provide evidence important for establishing the existence of a rule or the emergence of an opinio juris').
18 MD Öberg, 'The Legal Effects of Resolutions of the UN Security Council and General Assembly in the Jurisprudence of the ICJ' (2006) 16 EJIL 879, at 902 ('[h]owever, the GA is also a political organ, which does not make it an ideal forum for establishing the law. States may indeed have reasons other than legal ones for voting the way they do, such as moral, political, or pragmatic'); ILC, Third Report on Identification of Customary International Law by Michael Wood, Special Rapporteur, A/CN.4/682, 27 March 2015, [47].
19 R Higgins, *Problems and Process: International Law and How We Use It* (Clarendon Press 1994) 28.
20 See section 3.1.
21 E Suy, 'Innovation in International Law-Making Processes' in R St John Macdonald et al (eds), *The International Law and Policy of Human Welfare* (Sitjhoff & Noordhoff 1978) 190 ('the most one could say is that overwhelming (or even unanimous) approval is an indication of *opinio juris sive necessitatis*, but this does not create law without any concomitant practice'); P Tomka, 'Custom and the International Court of Justice' (2013) 12 The Law & Practice of International

It should finally be noted that the ICRC has set out its view on the legal basis of detention in its revised commentaries to the Geneva Conventions, the first two of which were published in 2016 and 2017 respectively.[22] There, the ICRC asserts that

> both customary and international humanitarian treaty law contain an inherent power to detain in non-international armed conflict. However, additional authority related to the grounds and procedure for deprivation of liberty in non-international armed conflict must in all cases be provided, in keeping with the principle of legality.[23]

In light of the qualification in the second sentence, it is unclear what the consequence of such a 'power' would be. Indeed, it is submitted that the use of terms such as 'power' or 'right' in this area are obfuscatory and cloud the fact that what we are asking is whether a legal basis to detain exists that would satisfy the requirement for such a basis in international human rights law. In any event, once again, this view of the ICRC must be tested against the traditional criteria for establishing custom. As noted above, and as set out more fully in section 3.1 of this book, that test confirms that custom continues to be silent as to the legal basis for detention in non-international armed conflict. Custom is, of course, subject to change in light of practice, and one can certainly see a trend towards recognizing a legal basis to detain under custom at least amongst certain States; should this practice and *opinio iuris* expand and become shared by States more generally, the conclusions here may need to be revised.[24]

The Procedural Safeguards for Detainees in Non-International Armed Conflict

In addition to its relevance to the debate over the legal basis for detention, this UK case law is also noteworthy for its assessment of the application more generally of the European Convention on Human Rights to detentions in non-international armed conflicts. As noted above, the majority in *Al-Waheed/Mohammed* took the view that the applicable Security Council resolutions constituted a sufficient legal basis for detention in non-international armed conflicts on the basis of 'imperative

---

Courts and Tribunals 195, 211 ('[t]he resolution does not have any legal force of its own, and it must be considered whether there is indeed a general view, held by States, that the resolution expresses a binding rule of international law, such that instances of State practice in accordance with that rule could be said to be motivated by that rule').

22 ICRC, *Commentary on the First Geneva Convention: Convention (I) for the Amelioration of the Condition of the Wounded and Sick in Armed Forces in the Field* (CUP 2016); ICRC, *Commentary on the Second Geneva Convention: Convention (II) for the Amelioration of the Condition of Wounded, Sick and Shipwrecked Members of Armed Forces at Sea* (CUP 2017).

23 ICRC, *Commentary on the Second Geneva Convention*, ibid, [750] (footnotes omitted).

24 Similarly, see *Al-Waheed/Mohammed* (n8) [16] (Lord Sumption); ibid, [275] (Lord Reed).

reasons of security'.[25] In his judgment, Lord Sumption, with whom other members of the majority agreed, then considered what impact this might have on the applicability of Article 5 ECHR, and his approach was to draw by analogy from the ECtHR's *Hassan v UK* judgment, thereby not requiring derogation by States.[26] Though *Hassan* appears to be authority solely for the interaction between the internment regime in GCIV (governing civilians in international armed conflict) and Article 5 ECHR,[27] in Lord Sumption's view, *Hassan* is authority for a more general floor below which procedural safeguards for detainees must not fall if they are to comply with Article 5.[28] As such, he held that, where detention in a non-international conflict is authorized by a Security Council resolution (eg where the resolution authorizes 'all necessary measures'), that detention complies with Article 5(1).[29] In addition, since *Hassan* made clear that the procedural safeguards in Articles 43 and 78 GCIV comply with Article 5(4) ECHR in an international armed conflict, those provisions also represent the minimum procedures required by Article 5(4) in a non-international armed conflict.[30]

The advantage of Lord Sumption's approach is its consistency and certainty—the GCIV internment regime would reflect the minimum applicable (for those not protected by GCIII) in both international and non-international armed conflicts, and Council of Europe States would know what minimum procedures must be provided to detainees in a non-international armed conflict in order to comply with Article 5 ECHR. Indeed, the outcome of this approach is similar to the proposals made in this book regarding the content of an internment regime for non-international armed conflicts.[31] However, those proposals are for an internment regime that is accessible by States only where they explicitly derogate (from either Article 5(1) and (4) ECHR or Article 9(4) of the International Covenant on Civil and Political Rights).[32]

In my view, derogation, in contrast to the approach of the majority in *Al-Waheed/Mohammed*, is preferable for four reasons. First, *ex ante* derogation, in which a clear legal regime is established from the outset, in contrast to *ex post facto* attempts at reconciling international humanitarian law and international human rights law, is more likely to ensure a consistent and non-arbitrary approach to detention throughout a conflict. Second, by making clear from the outset the legal regime governing detention as part of a State's derogation, the law is likely

---

25 *Al-Waheed/Mohammed* (n 8) [28] (Lord Sumption).
26 On *Hassan v UK*, see section 5.1.2.
27 Ibid, [104] ('[i]t can only be in cases of international armed conflict, where the taking of prisoners of war and the detention of civilians who pose a threat to security are accepted features of international humanitarian law, that Article 5 could be interpreted as permitting the exercise of such broad powers.')
28 *Al-Waheed/Mohammed* (n 8) [68] (Lord Sumption).
29 Ibid [65].
30 Ibid [66]–[67].
31 See chapter 7.
32 See section 5.1.2 for a discussion of the extent of possible interpretive harmonisation of the IHL internment regimes in international armed conflicts and Article 5 ECHR and Article 9 ICCPR.

to be more predictable, as individuals will be on notice as to what legal regime will be applied to them. Third, States should be permitted to rely on detention regimes that meet only these minimum standards (and thus depart from the usual understanding of Article 5 ECHR or Article 9 ICCPR) only where this can be shown actually to be necessary in the circumstances, which would be the case was derogation a prerequisite. This would help to counter the increasing phenomenon of States relying on IHL as a permissive body of law.[33] This is preferable to *assuming* the need for lower human rights protections in the context of armed conflict, which would be the consequence of the majority's approach in *Al-Waheed/Mohammed*.[34]

Fourth, and finally, Lord Sumption's legal reasoning is not free from controversy. First, in drawing on *Hassan*, one is faced with the problem that the reasoning of the Strasbourg Court that explained the approach in *Hassan* does not apply in the context of non-international armed conflicts.[35] Thus, neither Article 31(3)(b) nor (c) of the Vienna Convention on the Law of Treaties, on which the ECtHR relied in reasoning that Article 5 ECHR must be read down in light of IHL, lead to the same conclusion in non-international armed conflicts.[36] Subsequent practice, under Article 31(3)(b), cannot be said to indicate a clear view amongst Council of Europe States that Article 5 ECHR can be read down in the context of a non-international armed conflict without the need for derogation.[37] Similarly, whereas the IHL internment regimes in international armed conflicts provide 'other relevant rules of international law' that might inform the interpretation of Article 5 ECHR in such contexts (under Article 31(3)(c) VCLT), the absence of any such rules that applied in *Al-Waheed/Mohammed* (under either IHL or relevant Security Council resolutions) seems to count against reading down Article 5 in that case.

The second limitation in Lord Sumption's reasoning, noted in Lord Reed's dissent,[38] concerns the question of the correct Strasbourg case law to apply. Based on the majority's view of where the legal basis for detention lies, the issue in *Al-Waheed/Mohammed* concerned the interaction between the ECHR and Security Council resolutions. However, rather than applying the Strasbourg case law on that particular relationship,[39] Lord Sumption applied *Hassan*, which con-

---

33 I have explored this elsewhere: L Hill-Cawthorne, 'Humanitarian Law, Human Rights Law and the Bifurcation of Armed Conflict' (2015) 64 ICLQ 293; L Hill-Cawthorne, 'Rights under International Humanitarian Law' (2017) 28 EJIL 1187.
34 I have argued for a move away from such assumptions elsewhere: L Hill-Cawthorne, 'The Role of Necessity in International Humanitarian and Human Rights Law' (2014) 47 Isr L Rev 225.
35 The reasoning in *Hassan* is explored in section 5.1.2.
36 *Hassan* (n 3) [100]–[103].
37 See, eg, the derogations by Ukraine, of which the first was dated 5 June 2015, in respect of certain parts of eastern Ukraine, in order to introduce, inter alia, a law on preventive detention of members of suspected terrorists, available at <https://www.coe.int/en/web/conventions/full-list/-/conventions/treaty/005/declarations?p_auth=VO4BT17M> accessed 18 July 2019.
38 *Al-Waheed/Mohammed* (n 8) [298] (Lord Reed).
39 *Al-Jedda v United Kingdom*, App No 27021/08, Judgment (Grand Chamber), 7 July 2011; *Nada v Switzerland*, App No 10593/08, Judgment (Grand Chamber), 12 September 2012; *Al-Dulimi and Montana Managment Inc. v. Switzerland*, App No 5809/08, Judgment (Grand Chamber), 21 June 2016.

cerned the interaction between the ECHR and IHL. The result is a very different approach to that usually adopted by Strasbourg when reading the ECHR in light of Security Council resolutions. On both grounds, it is submitted that *Hassan* was not an appropriate analogy in this case. Thus, States wishing to apply a detention regime in non-international armed conflicts that mirrors that applicable to civilians in international armed conflicts should still be required to derogate from Article 5 ECHR.

Further Developments Concerning Article 5 ECHR in International Armed Conflicts

Another recent UK case is also noteworthy here, in part because it follows Lord Sumption's approach of invoking *Hassan* as a basis for a uniform approach to detention in international and non-international armed conflicts. The case of *Alseran* was the first full trial of civil compensation claims for UK detention operations during the Iraq conflict.[40] Amongst the many issues arising in that case was the long-standing problem of a person interned in an international armed conflict as prisoner of war but who challenges that status (and thus that internment).[41] Simply put, the Third Geneva Convention does not provide a review mechanism for such a person. Mr Justice Leggatt (as he then was) held, however, that the Supreme Court's treatment of *Hassan* in *Al-Waheed/Mohammed* confirmed that

> the duty of review imposed by articles 43 and 78 of Geneva IV represents a minimum standard which must be met in all cases in the context of an armed conflict in order to comply with article 5 of the European Convention. As further established by those cases, this minimum standard requires: (1) an initial review shortly after the person is detained, followed by further reviews at frequent intervals; and (2) that the reviews should be conducted by an impartial body in accordance with a fair procedure.[42]

Just as the Supreme Court invoked *Hassan* as a basis for harmonizing (to an extent) the rules on detention in international and non-international armed conflicts, Mr Justice Leggatt invoked both *Hassan* and *Al-Waheed/Mohammed* as a basis for harmonizing the rules on detention of prisoners of war and civilians in international armed conflicts. In both cases, Articles 42–3 and 78 GCIV were seen as the minimum standard required in order to comply with Article 5 ECHR.

---

40 *Alseran* (n 9).
41 Ibid, [290]. On this issue, see the discussion in this book at section 2.3.2. See also Y Naqvi, 'Doubtful Prisoner-of-War Status' (2002) 84 IRRC 571; N Mercer, 'The Future of Article 5 Tribunals in the Light of Experiences in the Iraq War, 2003' in N White et al (eds), *Contemporary Challenges to the Laws of War* (CUP, 2014).
42 *Alseran* (n 9) [290].

Series Editors' Preface

This book, *Detention in Non-International Armed Conflict* by Lawrence Hill-Cawthorne, is the second step in 2016 of the 'cultural project' that is the establishment of the Series of *Oxford Monographs in International Humanitarian and Criminal Law*. The main goal of the series is to broaden and deepen the analysis in these two areas of law through the publication of thought provoking publications. Even in an area of law as well researched and studied as international humanitarian law (IHL), it is nevertheless necessary to continually confront new challenges linked to the changing realities of armed conflicts, with a particular focus on the renewed relevance of this body of law in a world increasingly torn apart by armed violence (with issues revolving around asymmetric warfare, drone wars, detentions, and so forth). On the other hand, as far as international criminal law is concerned, there is a need for further studies in an area of law which has boomed after the establishment of the UN ad hoc tribunals in the 1990s and the International Criminal Court (ICC) in 1998; this has become a "new" area of law which has now entered a stage of maturity that requires scholars today, more than ever, to follow the operation of international institutions with a critical eye.

The main idea underlying this series has always been to support publications from younger scholars that address topical issues in a critical and original manner.

Detention in Non-International Armed Conflict is paradigmatic in this respect. It is an excellent book that tackles a topical issue. We agreed with enthusiasm to publish it in this series because it is a solid and in-depth analysis of a topic of great relevance in current international affairs, which poses unresolved challenges; and it is the result of the research work of a promising scholar, which makes it even more coherent with the overall project of the series.

The author offers his approach in a constructive manner based on solid legal work. We are sure it will contribute to the debate in this area. The book emphasizes the status of traditional international law in assessing detention in the course of armed conflict, pointing out the traditional differences between the law of international and non-international armed conflict. It tackles the gaps in regulation and analyzes the problems in the light of recent practice, including notably the conflicts in Iraq and Afghanistan, as well as those in Colombia, Sri Lanka, and Nepal.

The book examines the *procedural* guarantees for detainees in armed conflicts, examining both IHL and international human rights law, in search of a constructive way to analyze the relationship between the two bodies of law. It is confirmed that certain (minimal) guarantees must be applied in any case, confirming that detention in non-international armed conflict is not unregulated by international law. The book is additionally to be praised for offering concrete ideas on how to develop the law in this area, an aspect that we found particularly in the spirit of the initiator of this series.

The editors
Paola Gaeta and Salvatore Zappala

Acknowledgements

As is so often the case, this book began life as a doctoral thesis, which was submitted to the Law Faculty at the University of Oxford in February 2014. The process of writing a doctorate is a journey marked with hugely diverging emotions, ranging from great satisfaction and enjoyment to extraordinary stress and anxiety. The final thesis is, in a way, just a small part of this process, a roadmap of one's personal and academic development. Support is essential if one is to get through this process. I was extremely fortunate during my DPhil to have as my supervisor and mentor Professor Dapo Akande, who provided excellent support and advice, reading not only lengthy, and no doubt often rambling, early drafts of chapters of the thesis, but also drafts of articles and conference abstracts. It was Dapo who first introduced me to the topic of this book, and it is through discussing these issues with him that the ideas found here developed. It is only really now, when I appreciate the great pressures on an academic's time, that I realize just how generous Dapo was in giving his, and for that I am truly grateful.

I was also very fortunate to have Professors Guy Goodwin-Gill and Sandesh Sivakumaran as my DPhil examiners. The viva, though tough and challenging, was a considerably rewarding experience as a result of their deep engagement with the thesis. Their questions and comments forced me to build upon the thesis for the book and have, as a result, strengthened it.

The journey of writing a doctoral thesis can, if one is not careful, quite easily become an isolating and lonely experience. I have a lot of people to thank, for ensuring that this was not the case for me. First are my closest friends from home, David, Matthew, and Ric, who throughout my life have provided the kind of nourishment of the soul that only close friends can. Next are the friends I made in Oxford. Particular mention should be made of Eirik Bjorge, Seth Estrin, Monic Gupta, Kubo Mačák, Greg Messenger, Martins Paparinskis, and Ruvi Ziegler. Moreover, the Oxford public international law community provided a wonderful setting for research students. Weekly research seminars led by Professors Vaughan Lowe and Guy Goodwin-Gill offered a great place not just for intellectual development but also for meeting other research students who would quickly become close friends. Vaughan and Sally Lowe added to this with their great BBQs for students and staff in public international law. It is these things that made this journey so fulfilling and enjoyable. Finally, at Merton College, Professor Jennifer Payne and Mindy Chen-Wishart offered extraordinary support and guidance throughout my postgraduate studies, and I am extremely grateful to them.

I had the enormous privilege of funding throughout the DPhil from the Arts and Humanities Research Council (AHRC). Needless to say, it simply would not have been possible to work on this project for four years without this generous support. The AHRC also kindly granted me further funding to take up a four-month fellowship at the Kluge Center in the Library of Congress, Washington, DC, where I was able to build upon my research and discuss the project with policymakers. It was in Washington that I met a number of fellow researchers that have become close friends of mine, in particular Patrick Andelic, Kevin Crosby, Pete Mills, Iain Rowley, and Peter West-Oram.

Of course, the final product of the research that is captured in these pages is a result of the brilliant support I have had from OUP, and I must especially thank Emma Endean and Merel Alstein for their help and guidance along the way. The reviewers of my original manuscript must also be thanked for their thoughtful and constructive comments.

The final words of thanks must, of course, go to my family, for it is they that have throughout my life offered me comfort and unwavering support. My parents, Tina and Tony, and my step-parents, Peter and Sue, have always encouraged me to find my own path in life and pursue it without fear, whilst always remembering to value the truly important things. I must not fail to mention my grandparents, June, David, Bill, Daphne, and James, and my two brothers, Josh and Grant, for each has helped and influenced me in significant ways. Teresa, for proof-reading the entirety of my doctoral thesis, and Averil, for being such a welcoming and kind host when I was in India writing part of the thesis, have also helped me more than they could imagine in completing this research. Finally, I must thank my wife and best friend, Anne-Marie. If completing a doctoral thesis is challenging, being the person on whom you rely when doing so is far more challenging. Writing a doctoral thesis is about as far from a 9 to 5 job as one can get, and the book then extended this for a further nine months. Yet at every point along the way, Anne-Marie has supported me without reservation and, just as importantly, kept me grounded and reminded me that there is far more to life than work alone. It is to her, and my whole family, that this book is dedicated.

Table of Contents

Tables of Cases	xxiii
Tables of Legislation	xxxi
Introduction	1

PART I. CONTEXT

1. The Distinction between International and Non-International Armed Conflicts	11

PART II. INTERNATIONAL HUMANITARIAN LAW

2. Internment in International Armed Conflict under IHL	33
3. Internment in Non-International Armed Conflict under IHL	66

PART III. INTERNATIONAL HUMAN RIGHTS LAW

4. Detention under IHRL	111
5. Detention and the Relationship between IHL and IHRL	144
6. The Practical Application of IHRL to Detention in Non-International Armed Conflict	192

PART IV. DEVELOPING THE LAW

7. Conclusion: Developing an Internment Regime for Non-International Armed Conflicts	225
Select Bibliography	245
Index	269

Detailed Table of Contents

Tables of Cases	xxiii
Tables of Legislation	xxxi
Introduction	1
I.1 Aims and Scope of Enquiry	4
I.2 Methodology	6

PART I. CONTEXT

1. The Distinction between International and Non-International Armed Conflicts	11
1.1 Overview and Historical Basis	11
1.2 Criticisms of the Distinction	19
1.2.1 IHL's claim to pragmatism	19
1.2.2 IHL's claim to humanitarianism	21
1.3 Reasons for Preserving the Distinction	22
1.3.1 Sovereignty concerns	23
1.3.2 Humanitarian concerns	27
1.4 Conclusions	30

PART II. INTERNATIONAL HUMANITARIAN LAW

2. Internment in International Armed Conflict under IHL	33
2.1 Status	34
2.1.1 Combatants/POWs	34
2.1.2 Civilians	37
2.1.3 A third category?—'unlawful combatants'	37
2.2 Standard for Internment	39
2.2.1 Civilians	39
2.2.2 Combatants	47
2.3 Review of Internment	51
2.3.1 Civilians	51
2.3.1.1 Initial review	51
2.3.1.2 Periodic review	56
2.3.2 Combatants	56
2.4 Release	59
2.4.1 Civilians	59
2.4.2 Combatants	60
2.5 Article 5 GCIV	62
2.6 Conclusions	65

3. Internment in Non-International Armed Conflict under IHL — 66
3.1 The Legal Basis to Intern in Non-International Armed Conflicts — 66
3.2 Procedural Rules under Conventional IHL — 76
3.2.1 Common Article 3 — 76
3.2.2 Additional Protocol II — 83
3.3 Procedural Rules under Customary IHL — 85
3.3.1 Prohibition of arbitrary deprivation of liberty — 91
3.3.2 The end-point of internment — 95
3.3.3 Conclusions on customary IHL — 98
3.4 The Binding Nature of IHL for Non-State Armed Groups — 99
3.4.1 Do common Article 3 and APII bind non-state groups? — 100
3.4.2 On what basis do common Article 3 and APII bind non-state groups? — 101
3.4.3 On what basis does customary IHL bind non-state groups? — 104
3.4.4 Conclusion on the binding nature of IHL — 105
3.5 Conclusions — 107

PART III. INTERNATIONAL HUMAN RIGHTS LAW

4. Detention under IHRL — 111
4.1 Applicability of IHRL in Armed Conflict — 111
4.2 The Procedural Rules Applicable to Detention under Human Rights Treaties — 116
4.2.1 Standard for detention — 117
4.2.1.1 The conformity of internment with the IHRL standard — 120
4.2.2 Reasons for detention — 122
4.2.3 Initial review (*habeas corpus*) — 124
4.2.3.1 'Without delay' — 124
4.2.3.2 The nature and procedures of the review body — 125
4.2.3.3 Scope of review and the meaning of 'lawfulness' — 127
4.2.3.4 Comparing *habeas corpus* and the IHL review procedures — 128
4.2.4 Periodic review — 130
4.2.5 Release from detention — 131
4.2.6 Conclusions on the rules under IHRL — 132
4.3 The Procedural Rules Applicable to Detention under Customary International Law — 132
4.3.1 The prohibition of arbitrary deprivation of liberty — 133
4.3.2 Release where the justifications cease — 139
4.3.3 Reasons for detention and *habeas corpus* — 139
4.4 Conclusions — 142

5. Detention and the Relationship between IHL and IHRL — 144
5.1 The Relationship between IHL and IHRL — 144
5.1.1 The ICJ's case law — 147
5.1.2 Detention in international armed conflict — 152
5.1.3 Detention in non-international armed conflict — 159
5.2 State Practice in Specific Non-International Armed Conflicts — 164

	5.2.1 Traditional non-international armed conflicts	165
	5.2.1.1 Colombia	165
	5.2.1.2 Sri Lanka	167
	5.2.1.3 Nepal	168
	5.2.1.4 Democratic Republic of the Congo	170
	5.2.1.5 Conclusions on traditional non-international armed conflicts	172
	5.2.2 Extraterritorial non-international armed conflicts	174
	5.2.2.1 Iraq (from 2003)	174
	5.2.2.2 Afghanistan (post-2001)	179
	5.2.2.3 Conclusions on extraterritorial non-international armed conflicts	183
	5.2.3 Transnational armed conflicts	185
	5.2.3.1 US conflict with al-Qaeda	185
5.3	Conclusions on State Practice	189

6. The Practical Application of IHRL to Detention in Non-International Armed Conflict   192

6.1	The Practice of Human Rights Treaty Bodies	192
	6.1.1 Human Rights Committee (HRC)	194
	6.1.2 European Court of Human Rights (ECtHR)	196
	6.1.3 Inter-American institutions	201
	6.1.4 African Commission on Human and Peoples' Rights (ACiHPR)	205
	6.1.5 Conclusions on treaty body practice: a proposal for reconciling their approaches	207
6.2	Extraterritorial Application of IHRL	212
	6.2.1 Extraterritorial derogation from human rights treaties	216
6.3	Human Rights Obligations of Non-State Armed Groups	217
	6.3.1 Concluding remarks: the inadequacy of IHRL	221

PART IV. DEVELOPING THE LAW

7. Conclusion: Developing an Internment Regime for Non-International Armed Conflicts   225

7.1	Building on the Current Law	226
	7.1.1 Eliminate the distinction between categories of armed conflict?	227
	7.1.2 Developing an internment regime for non-international armed conflicts	228
7.2	Analogizing to GCIII	230
7.3	Analogizing to GCIV	234
	7.3.1 Standard for internment	234
	7.3.2 Reasons for internment	238
	7.3.3 Review of internment	239
	7.3.4 Release	241
7.4	Concluding Remarks	242

Select Bibliography   245
Index   269

Tables of Cases

INTERNATIONAL COURTS AND TRIBUNALS

Permanent Court of International Justice (PCIJ)

Jurisdiction of the Courts of Danzig (1928) PCIJ Series B, No 15 .... 26, 103
'Lotus' Judgment No 9 (1927) PCIJ Series A, No 10 .... 67, 70, 77
The Mavrommatis Palestine Concessions, PCIJ Ser A, No 2 (1924) 150
The Oscar Chinn Case, PCIJ Series A/B, No 63, 1934 164

International Court of Justice (ICJ)

Application of the Convention on the Prevention and Punishment of the Crime of Genocide (Bosnia and Herzegovina v Yugoslavia), Preliminary Objections, Judgment [1996]
ICJ Rep 595 163
Case Concerning Ahmadou Sadio Diallo (Republic of Guinea v Democratic Republic of Congo),
Merits Judgment [2010] ICJ Rep 639 .... 7, 193
Case Concerning Armed Activities on the Territory of the Congo (DRC v Uganda)
[2005] ICJ Rep 116 .... 28, 69, 113, 147, 148, 149, 190, 205, 214–215
Case Concerning Military and Paramilitary Activities in and Against Nicaragua (Nicaragua v United States) [1986] ICJ Rep 14 .... 6, 8, 41–42, 55, 76, 91, 104, 135, 137
Case Concerning Oil Platforms (Islamic Republic of Iran v United States of America),
Preliminary Objections [1996] ICJ Rep 803 .... 79, 83
Case Concerning the Arrest Warrant of 11 April 2000 (Democratic Republic of the Congo v Belgium), Judgment [2002] ICJ Rep 3 8
Case Concerning The Barcelona Traction, Light and Power Company, Limited (Belgium v Spain), Second Phase, Judgment [1970] ICJ Rep 3 163
Case Concerning the Continental Shelf (Tunisia/Libyan Arab Jamahiriya) [1982] ICJ Rep 38 150
Case Concerning the Gabčikovo-Nagymaros Project (Hungary v Slovakia), Judgment [1997]
ICJ Rep 7 .... 83, 150
Case Concerning United States Diplomatic and Consular Staff in Tehran (United States of America v Iran) [1980] ICJ Rep 3 137
Dispute Regarding Navigational and Related Rights (Costa Rica v Nicaragua) (Judgment)
[2009] ICJ Rep 213 79
Kasikili/Sedudu Island (Botswana/Namibia) (Judgment) [1999] ICJ Rep 1045 150
Legal Consequences of the Construction of a Wall in the Occupied Palestinian Territory,
Advisory Opinion [2004] ICJ Rep 136 .... 8, 113, 148, 149, 152, 153, 162, 190, 213
Legality of the Threat or Use of Nuclear Weapons, Advisory Opinion [1996] ICJ Rep 226 ... 8, 28, 79,
113, 135, 146, 148–150, 153–154, 155, 156, 194, 201
North Sea Continental Shelf Cases (Federal Republic of Germany/Denmark; Federal Republic of Germany/Netherlands) [1969] ICJ Rep 3 .... 8, 73
Nuclear Tests (Australia v France) [1974] ICJ Rep 253 106
Questions Relating to the Obligation to Prosecute or Extradite (Belgium v Senegal), Judgment
[2012] ICJ Rep 422 163
Reparation for Injuries Suffered in the Service of the United Nations (Reparations),
Advisory Opinion, [1949] ICJ Rep 174 .... 104, 219
Reservations to the Convention on the Prevention and Punishment of the Crime of Genocide,
Advisory Opinion [1951] ICJ Rep 15 .... 14, 150

UN Human Rights Committee

A v Australia, CCPR/C/59/D/560/93, 3 April 1997 ....119, 126, 127, 130, 235
Baban et al v Australia, CCPR/C/78/D/1014/2001, 18 September 2003 ....127, 131, 139, 241
Berry v Jamaica, CCPR/C/50/D/330/1988, 26 April 1994 127
C v Australia, CCPR/C/76/D/900/1999, 28 October 2002............127, 128, 130, 131, 241
Celiberti de Casariego v Uruguay, CCPR/C/OP/1, 29 July 1981......................214, 215
Drescher Caldas v Uruguay, CCPR/C/OP/2, 21 July 1983 123
Lopez Burgos v Uruguay, CCPR/C/13/D/52/1979, 29 July 1981 ....213, 214, 215
Macado de Cámpora v Uruguay, CCPR/C/OP/2, 12 October 1982 121
Maharjan v Nepal, CCPR/C/105/D/1863/2009, 2 August 2012..........................195
Mansour Ahani v Canada, CCPR/C/80/D/1051/2002, 15 June 2004 ....122, 125
Sarma v Sri Lanka, CCPR/C/78/D/950/2000, 31 July 2003........................115, 195
Suarez de Guerrero v Colombia, UN Doc Supp No 40 (A/37/40), 9 April 1981 29
Torres v Finland, CCPR/C/38/D/291/1988, 5 April 1990..........................124, 125
Traoré v Côte d'Ivoire, CCPR/C/103/D/1759/2008, 17 January 2011 195
Van Alphen v The Netherlands, CCPR/C/39/D/305/1988, 15 August 1990 ....119, 120
Vuolanne v Finland, CCPR/C/35/D/265/1987, 2 May 1989............................125

UN Working Group on Arbitrary Detention

Obaidullah v United States, A/HRC/WGAD/2013/10, 12 June 2013..........131, 140, 195, 242

World Trade Organization (WTO) Dispute Settlement Body

EC—Computer Equipment, Appellate Body Report, WT/DS62/AB/R, WT/DS67/AB/R,
WT/DS68/AB/R, 5 June 1998...150

Arbitrations

*Arbitral Award Rendered pursuant to the Compromis signed at London, March 4, 1930,
between France and the United Kingdom of Great Britain and Northern Ireland, In the
Matter of the Claim of Madame Chevreau Against the United Kingdom* (1933) 27 AJIL 153...68
Civilians Claims, Ethiopia's Claim 5 (Ethiopia/Eritrea), Partial Award, 17 December 2004,
135 ILR 427..46, 55, 236
Civilians Claims, Ethiopia's Claim 15, 16, 23 and 27-32 (Ethiopia/Eritrea), Partial Award,
17 December 2004, 135 ILR 374 46
CMS Gas Transmission Co v Argentine Republic, ICSID Case No ARB/01/08, Award,
12 May 2005 83
*Interpretation of the Air Transport Services Agreement between the United States of America
and France* (1963) 16 RIAA 5..150
Southern Bluefin Tuna case (Australia and New Zealand/Japan) (Jurisdiction and
Admissibility) UNRIAA vol XXIII (2004) 157

REGIONAL COURTS AND TRIBUNALS

European Commission on Human Rights

Greek case (1969) 12 YB 1 193

European Court of Human Rights (ECtHR)

A and others v United Kingdom, App No 3455/05, Judgment (Grand Chamber),
19 February 2009 ......118, 119, 121, 126, 127, 141, 199, 200, 201, 207, 208, 210, 229, 238
Aksoy v Turkey, App No 21987/93, Judgment (Merits), 18 December 1996.............127, 141
Al-Jedda v United Kingdom, App No 27021/08, Judgment (Grand Chamber),
7 July 2011....................71, 115, 121, 145, 177, 178, 179, 198–199, 215, 217
Al-Saadoon and Mufdhi v United Kingdom, App No 61498/08, Admissibility Decision,
30 June 2009 ....214, 215

Al-Skeini v United Kingdom, App No 55721/07, Judgment (Grand Chamber),
 7 July 2011..114, 214–215
Assenov and others v Bulgaria, App No 24760/94, Judgment, 28 October 1998..............130
Bankovic v United Kingdom, App No 52207/99, Admissibility Decision,
 12 December 2001..214, 215
Behrami and Behrami v France, Saramati v France, Germany and Norway, App Nos 71412/0
 and 78166/01, Admissibility Decision (Grand Chamber), 2 May 2007..................6
Bezicheri v Italy, App No 11400/85, Judgment, 25 October 1989........................130
Brannigan and McBride v United Kingdom, App Nos 14553/89 and 14554/89, Judgment,
 25 May 1993..126, 141
Brogan and others v United Kingdom, App Nos 11209/84, 11234/84, 11266/84 and
 11386/85, Judgment, 29 November 1988......................................127
Case of Ilascu and others v Moldova and Russia, App No 48787/99, Judgment
 (Grand Chamber), 8 July 2004...220
Çetinkaya and Çağlayan v Turkey, App Nos 3921/02, 35003/02, and 17261/03, Judgment,
 23 January 2007..124
Chahal v United Kingdom, App No 22414/93, Judgment (Grand Chamber),
 15 November 1996..126, 127, 200, 208
Ergi v Turkey, App No 23818/94, Judgment (Merits), 28 July 1998......................197
Fox, Campbell and Hartley v United Kingdom, App Nos 12244/86 and 12245/86,
 Judgment, 30 August 1990..123, 124
Hassan v United Kingdom, App No 29750/09, Judgment (Grand Chamber),
 16 September 2014....................114, 149, 155, 156, 158–159, 196, 199, 201
Ireland v United Kingdom, App No 5310/71, Judgment, 18 January 1978.........121, 199–201,
 207, 208, 210, 211, 229, 239
Isayeva, Yusupova and Bazayeva v Russia, App Nos 57947/00, 57948/00, and 57949/00,
 Judgment (Merits), 24 February 2005...197
Isayeva v Russia, App No 57950/00, Judgment (Merits), 24 February 2005.................197
Issa v Turkey, App No 31821/96, Judgment, 16 November 2004........................214
Kadem v Malta, App No 55263/00, Judgment, 9 January 2003.........................125
Kerr v United Kingdom, App No 40451/98, Admissibility Decision, 7 December 1999....123, 210
Khudyakova v Russia, App No 13476/04, Judgment, 8 January 2009..........124, 125, 126, 211
Lawless v Ireland (No 3), App No 332/57, Judgment (Plenary), 1 July 1961..............121, 141
Lebedev v Russia, App No 4493/04, Judgment, 25 October 2007........................130
Loizidou v Turkey, App No 15318/89, Judgment (Grand Chamber), 18 December 1996...114, 215
Luberti v Italy, App No 9019/80, Judgment, 23 February 1984..........................130
Mamedova v Russia, App No 7064/05, Judgment, 1 June 2006.........................125
McCann and others v United Kingdom, App No 18984/91, 27 September 1995..........29, 197
Medvedyev and others v France, App No 3394/03, Judgment (Grand Chamber),
 29 March 2010...119, 121, 169, 215, 235
Nada v Switzerland, App No 10593/08, Judgment (Grand Chamber), 12 September 2012.....157
Neumeister v Austria, App No 1936/63, Judgment, 27 June 1968........................126
Öcalan v Turkey, App No 46221/99, Judgment, 12 May 2005..................127, 214, 215
Othman v United Kingdom, App No 8139/09, Judgment, 17 January 2012...................6
Saadi v United Kingdom, App No 13229/03, Judgment, 29 January 2008.........119–120, 123,
 132, 235, 242
Sakik and others v Turkey, App Nos 23878/94, 23879/94, 23880/94, 23881/94, 23882/94,
 23883/94, Judgment, 26 November 1997......................................193
Sanchez-Reisse v Switzerland, App No 9862/82, Judgment, 21 October 1986............125, 127
Singh v United Kingdom, App No 23389/94, Judgment, 21 February 1996.................126
Smith & Grady v United Kingdom, App Nos 33985/96 and 33986/96, Judgment,
 27 September 1999...45
Steel and others v United Kingdom, App No 24838/94, Judgment,
 23 September 1998..119, 122, 236

Stephens v Malta (No 1), App No 11956/07, Judgment, 21 April 2009....................126
Storck v Germany, App No 62603/00, Judgment, 16 June 2005..........................118
Toth v Austria, App No 11894/85, Judgment, 12 December 1991.........................127
Van der Leer v Netherlands, App No 11509/85, Judgment, 21 February 1990....123, 124, 210, 238
Weeks v United Kingdom, App No 9787/82, Judgment, 2 March 1987......................126
Włoch v Poland, App No 27785/95, Judgment, 19 October 2000.........................127
X v United Kingdom, App No 7215/75, Judgment, 5 November 1981......................127

European Court of Justice (ECJ)
Commission v Spain [1999] ECR I-5585..45

Inter-American Commission on Human Rights (IACiHR)
Abella v Argentina, Report No 55/97, 18 November 1997.........................115, 201
Alejandre v Cuba, Report No 86/99, 29 September 1999..........................114, 214
Ameziane v United States, Report No 17/12, Admissibility Decision, 20 March 2012..........202
Caizales Dogenesama (Luis and Leonardo) v Colombia, Report No 152/11, 2 November 2011...203
Coard et al v United States, Report No 109/99, 22 September 1999.......53, 114, 121, 156, 202, 203, 208, 214, 215, 239
Extrajudicial Executions and Forced Disappearances of Persons (Peru), Report No 101/01,
    11 October 2001..203
Ferrer-Mazorra v United States, Report No 51/01, 4 April 2001.........................127
Franklin Guillermo Aisalla Molina (Ecuador v Colombia), Inter-State Petition IP-02
    (Admissibility), Report No 112/10, 21 October 2010.........................202, 214
Levoyer Jiménez v Ecuador, Report No 66/01, 14 June 2001......................119, 235
Nativi & Martinez v Honduras, Report No 4/87, 28 March 1987.........................125
Request for Precautionary Measures Concerning the Detainees at Guantanamo Bay, Cuba,
    Decision of 12 March 2002..114, 202

Inter-American Court of Human Rights (IACtHR)
Alvarez and Iniguez v Ecuador, Judgment, IACtHR (Series C) No 170 (2007)...118, 120, 125, 235
Case of Ituango Massacres v Colombia, Judgment, IACtHR (Series C) No 148 (2006)..........203
Case of Osorio Rivera and Family Members v Peru, Judgment, IACtHR (Series C)
    No 274 (2013)..205
Case of Rodríguez Vera et al (The Disappeared from the Palace of Justice) v Colombia,
    Judgment (Series C) No 287 (2014).......................................202, 203
Case of the Santo Domingo Massacre v Colombia, Judgment, IACtHR (Series C)
    No 259 (2012)..202
Durand and Ugarte v Peru, Judgment, IACtHR (Series C) No 68 (2000)..................204
*Habeas Corpus in Emergency Situations (Arts. 27(2) and 7(6) of the American Convention
    on Human Rights)*, Advisory Opinion OC-8/87, IACtHR (Series A) No 8 (1987)...125, 126, 127, 204, 205, 208
*Judicial Guarantees in States of Emergency (Arts. 27(2), 25 and 8 of the American Convention
    on Human Rights)*, Advisory Opinion OC-9/87, IACtHR (Series A) No 9 (1987)........205
Las Palmeras v Colombia, Judgment (Preliminary Objections), IACtHR (Ser C) No 67 (2000)....202
Sanchez v Honduras, Judgment, IACtHR (Series C) No 99 (2003).....................124, 238
Serrano-Cruz Sisters v El Salvador, Judgment (Preliminary Objections), IACtHR
    (Series C) No 118 (2004)...202
Tibi v Ecuador, Judgment, IACtHR (Series C) No 114, (2004)..........119, 126, 127, 208, 211
Velasquez v Guatemala, Judgment, IACtHR (Series C) No 70 (2000)...............114, 115, 203

African Commission on Human and Peoples' Rights (ACiHPR)
Amnesty International and others v Sudan, Communication Nos 48/90, 50/91, 52/91,
    and 89/93 (2003)..........................115, 119, 125, 205, 206, 208, 209, 235–236

Tables of Cases xxvii

Commission nationale des droits de l'Homme et des libertés v Chad, Communication
  No 74/92 (1995) 205, 206
Constitutional Rights Project, Civil Liberties Organisation and Media Rights Agenda v Nigeria,
  Communication Nos 140/94, 141/94, and 145/95 (1999) 205, 206, 211
DRC v Burundi, Uganda and Rwanda, Communication No 227/99 (2003)........... 162, 190,
                                                                        205, 206, 214
Huri-Laws v Nigeria, Communication No 225/98 (2000) 205, 206, 208
Kazeem Aminu v Nigeria, Communication No 205/97 (2000).........................205
*Sudan Human Rights Organisation & Centre on Housing Rights and Evictions (COHRE) v
  Sudan,* Communication Nos 279/03 and 296/05 (2009)..........................205

INTERNATIONAL AND HYBRID CRIMINAL TRIBUNALS

International Criminal Tribunal for the Former Yugoslavia (ICTY)

Prosecutor v Aleksovski (Trial Judgment) ICTY-95-14/1 (25 June 1999) 78
Prosecutor v Delalić et al (Trial Judgment) ICTY-96-21 (16 November 1998)....... 41, 42, 44, 46,
                                                              52, 64, 98, 129, 130, 208, 236, 237
Prosecutor v Delalić et al (Appeals Judgment) ICTY-96-21-A (20 February 2001).... 41, 44, 46, 53,
                                                              54–55, 98, 168, 177, 182, 204, 236, 240
Prosecutor v Furundzija (Trial Judgment) IT-95-17/1-T (10 December 1998) 163
Prosecutor v Galić (Appeals Judgment) IT-98-29-A (30 November 2006) 103
Prosecutor v Kordić and Čerkez (*Trial* Judgment) ICTY-95-14/2-T
  (26 February 2001) 41, 42, 44, 46, 52, 63, 64, 81, 236, 237
Prosecutor v Kordić and Čerkez (Appeals Judgment) ICTY-95-14/2 (17 December 2004)....39, 103
Prosecutor v Krnojelac (Trial Judgment) ICTY-97-25 (15 March 2002)........42, 59, 92, 138, 237
Prosecutor v Kunarac et al (Appeals Judgment) IT-96-23&23/1 (12 June 2002) 47
Prosecutor v Kunarac et al (Trial Judgment) IT-96-23-T and IT-96-23/1-T
  (22 February 2001) 217
Prosecutor v Kupreškić et al (Trial Judgment) ICTY-95-16 (14 January 2000) 7
Prosecutor v Limaj et al (Prosecution's Final Brief (Redacted Public Version)) ICTY-03-66
  (26 July 2005) 77–78
Prosecutor v Simić, Tadić and Zarić (Trial Judgment) ICTY-95-9-T (17 October 2003) 59
Prosecutor v Tadić (Decision on the Defence Motion Motion for Interlocutory Appeal
  on Jurisdiction) ICTY-94-1 (2 October 1995) 5, 17, 18, 20, 22, 27, 37, 91, 96, 228

International Criminal Tribunal for Rwanda (ICTR)

Prosecutor v Akayesu (Trial Judgment) ICTR-96-4 (2 September 1998) 91, 106
Prosecutor v Ntagerura et al (Trial Judgment) ICTR-99-46T (25 February 2004) 67, 138

Extraordinary Chambers in the Courts of Cambodia

KAING Guek Eav alias Duch, Case File 001/18-07-2007/ECCC/TC (Trial Judgment)
  (26 July 2010) 67, 94, 138

Special Court for Sierra Leone

Prosecutor v Kallon and Kamara (Decision on Challenge to Jurisdiction, Lomé
  Accord Amnesty) SCSL-2004-15-AR72(E) (13 March 2004) 91, 104, 106

NATIONAL COURTS

Bosnia and Herzegovina

Lučić case, Court of Bosnia and Herzegovina, Judgment, 19 September 2007, 67–8,
  cited in ICRC, Customary IHL Database 84, 94

Canada

Canada (Justice) v Khadr [2008] 2 SCR 125 (Canadian Supreme Court) 188

Chile

Contreras Sepúlveda, Case No 2182-98, Judgment, 17 November 2004
  (Chilean Supreme Court) 94

Colombia

Constitutional Case No C-291/07, Constitutional Court Judgment, 25 April 2007, 112, cited in
  ICRC, Customary IHL Database 93

Israel

A and B v State of Israel, CrimA 3261/08 (11 June 2008) (Israel Supreme Court) 38, 41,
  42, 43, 44, 45, 232, 237
Abu Bakr v Judge of the Military Court in Schechem, HCJ 466/86, 40(3) PD 649 .... 55, 240
*Ajuri and others v IDF Commander in the West Bank, IDF Commander in the Gaza Strip
  and others,* HCJ 7015/02 and 7019/02 [2002] 125 ILR 537
  (Israeli Supreme Court) 41, 120, 122, 208
Al-Ahmar case, Israel High Court of Justice, Judgment, 26 February 2004, cited in ICRC,
  Customary IHL Database 56
Anonymous v Minister of Defence, ADA 10/94, 53(1) PD 97 46
Anonymous v Minister of Defence, CFH 7048/97, 54(1) PD 721 .... 46, 56, 242
Issawi case, Jerusalem District Court, Judgment, 21 April 2010, cited in ICRC,
  Customary IHL Database 56
Jamal Mustafa Yusef 'Abdullah (Hussin) v Commander of IDF Forces in the West Bank,
  HCJ 7607/05, (2005) 8 YIHL 443 (Israel Supreme Court) 140
Mar'ab et al v IDF Commander of Judea and Samaria et al, HCJ 3239/02, 57(2) PD 349
  (Israel Supreme Court) 42, 53, 94, 154
Public Committee Against Torture in Israel et al v The Government of Israel et al, HCJ 769/02,
  57(6) PD 285 (Israel Supreme Court) 38
Salame et al v IDF Commander of Judea and Samaria et al, HCJ 5784/03,
  57(6) PD 721 122

Malaysia

Malek case, Judgment, High Court (Kuala Lumpur) 18 October 2007, cited in ICRC,
  Customary IHL Database 135, 140

Nepal

Bajracharya case, Supreme Court, Division Bench, Order, 31 August 2007, cited in ICRC,
  Customary IHL Database 92
*Rabindra Prasad Dhakal on Behalf of Rajendra Prasad Dhakal v Government of Nepal,
  Ministry of Home Affairs and others* (Divisional Bench of the Supreme Court of Nepal),
  1 June 2002 (2008) 14 Asian YBIL 170

Russia

Re Khodorkovskiy, Case No KAS06-129, Russian Supreme Court (Cassation Chamber),
  133 ILR 365 140

Sweden

Public Prosecutor (On Behalf of Behrem (Hussein) and ors) v Arklöf (Jackie), Judgment, Case
  No B 4084–04, ILDC 633 (SE 2006), 18 December 2006 (Stockholm District Court) 89

United Kingdom

A and others v Secretary of State for the Home Department [2002] EWCA Civ 1502............136
Abbasi v Secretary of State for Foreign and Commonwealth Affairs et al [2002]
  EWCA Civ 1598..188
Al-Jedda v Secretary of State for Defence [2005] EWHC 1809 (Admin) 52, 53, 174
*GS (Existence of Internal Armed Conflict) Afghanistan v Secretary of State for the
  Home Department*, CG [2009] UKAIT 00010....................................179
HM, RM, HF v the Secretary of State for the Home Department [2012] UKUT 409 (IAC).......174
Liversidge v Anderson [1942] AC 206 40
Netz v Chuter Ede [1946] 1 All ER 628 40
*R (Abbasi) v Secretary of State for Foreign and Commonwealth Affairs & Secretary of State for
  the Home Department* [2002] EWCA Civ 1598 140
R (Al-Jedda) v Secretary of State for Defence [2007] UKHL 58.......................175, 216
R (Al-Skeini and others) v Secretary of State for Defence (The Redress Trust and others intervening)
  [2005] EWCA Civ 1609 214
R (Al-Skeini and others) v Secretary of State for Defence (The Redress Trust and others intervening)
  [2007] UKHL 26...214
R (Evans) v Secretary of State for Defence [2010] EWHC 1445 (Admin) 74
R (Smith and others) v The Ministry of Defence [2013] UKSC 41..........................216
R (Smith) v Secretary of State for Defence [2010] UKSC 29 216
R v Bottrill, ex p Kuechenmeister [1946] 2 All ER 434...............................40, 155
R v Gul [2012] EWCA Crim 280..174, 179
R v Halliday ex p Zadig [1917] AC 260 40
R v Superintendent of Vine Street Police Station, ex p Liebmann [1916] 1 KB 268............155
*Rahmatullah and the Iraqi Civilian Claimants v Ministry of Defence and Foreign and
  Commonwealth Office* [2015] EWCA Civ 843 ....71, 160
*Secretary of State for Foreign and Commonwealth Affairs and another (Appellants) v
  Rahmatullah* [2012] UKSC 48..155, 157
Serdar Mohammed v Ministry of Defence [2014] EWHC 1369 (QB)............. 71, 74, 75, 145,
                                                                                179, 180, 182, 216
Serdar Mohammed et al v Secretary of State for Defence [2015] EWCA Civ 843.........71, 74, 75,
                                                                            87, 89, 160, 177, 179, 180, 182

United States

Al-Bihani v Obama and others, 590 F.3d 866 (2010) (DC Cir Ct) 189, 233
Aldana v Del Monte Fresh Produce NA Inc (2005) 416 F.3d 1242 93
Ali Saleh Kahlah Al-Marri and Mark A Berman v Commander John Pucciarelli,
  534 F.3d 213 (2008) 74
Awad v Obama, 608 F 3d 1 (DC Cir 2010)..233
Basardh v Obama, 612 F Supp 2d 30 (DDC 2009) 233
Boumediene et al v Bush et al, 553 US 723 (2008)........................189, 212, 243
Fadi Al Maqaleh et al v Robert Gates et al (21 May 2010) (DC Cir Ct)....................182
Gherebi v Obama, 609 F Supp 2d 43 (DDC 2009) 57......................2, 70, 185, 232
In re Guantanamo Bay Detainee Litigation, Misc No 08-442 (TFH)
  (DDC 13 March 2009) 159, 232
In re Guantanamo Detainee Cases, 355 F Supp 2d 443 (DDC 2005) 122, 233
Hamdan v Rumsfeld et al, 548 US 557 (2006), 521 (US Supreme Court)................55, 189
Hamdi et al v Rumsfeld et al, 542 US 507 (2004), 521 (US Supreme Court) 46, 97, 186
Hamlily v Obama, 616 F Supp 2d 63 (DDC 2009) 73.....................2, 70, 185, 232, 233
Medellin v Texas, 552 US 491 (2008) (US Supreme Court) 128, 133

Mehinovic et al v Vuckovic (2002) 198 F Supp 2d 1322 (US District Ct for the
   Northern District of Georgia) 93, 136
Minotto v Bradley (1918) 252 Fed 600 40
Padilla v CT Hanft, 423 F.3d 386 (2005) 122
Rasul v Bush, 542 US 466 (2004) 186, 189, 237
Sexual Minorities Uganda v Lively (2013) 960 F.Supp.2d 304 93
Sosa v Alvarez-Machain, 542 US 692 (2004) 2769 ....93, 137

Tables of Legislation

INTERNATIONAL TREATIES

Charter of the United Nations
 (26 June 1945, entered into force
 24 October 1945)
 Art 1(3) 14
 Art 51 .... 75, 180
 Art 103 179
Convention on the Prevention and
 Punishment of the Crime of
 Genocide (9 December 1948, entered
 into force 12 January 1951,
 78 UNTS 277). 14
Convention on the Prohibition of the
 Development, Production, Stockpiling
 and Use of Chemical Weapons and on
 their Destruction (13 January 1993,
 entered into force 29 April 1997
 [1997] ATS 3) 17
Convention on the Prohibition of the
 Development, Production and
 Stockpiling of Bacteriological
 (Biological) and Toxin Weapons and
 on their Destruction (10 April 1972,
 entered into force 26 March 1975
 1015 UNTS 163). 17
Convention on the Prohibition of the
 Use, Stockpiling, Production and
 Transfer of Anti-Personnel Mines and
 on their Destruction (18 September
 1997, entered into force 1 March
 1999 [1999] ATS 3). 17
General Agreement on Tariffs and
 Trade (GATT)
 Art XXI 41–42
Geneva Convention I for the Amelioration
 of the Condition of the Wounded
 and Sick in Armed Forces in the Field
 (12 August 1949, entered into force
 21 October 1950, 75 UNTS 31) 11
 Arts 1-3 *see* Geneva Conventions:
  Common Articles
 Art 28 34
Geneva Convention II for the Amelioration
 of the Condition of the Wounded, Sick
 and Shipwrecked Members of the Armed
 Forces at Sea (12 August 1949, entered
 into force 21 October 1950,
 75 UNTS 85). 11
 Arts 1-3 *see* Geneva Conventions:
  Common Articles
 Art 37 11
Geneva Convention III Relative to the
 Treatment of Prisoners of War
 (12 August 1949, entered into force
 21 October 1950, 75 UNTS 135) 11,
    228, 230–234
 Arts 1-3 *see* Geneva Conventions:
  Common Articles
 Art 4 .... 35, 48, 50, 58
 Art 4A(1) 35, 41, 49
 Art 4A(2) 35, 36, 49
 Art 4A(3) 35, 49
 Art 4A(4) 35, 49–50
 Art 4A(5) 35, 50, 51
 Art 4A(6) 35, 49
 Art 4B(1) 35, 50–51
 Art 4B(2) 35, 50–51
 Art 5 .... 57, 58, 176, 188
 Art 5(2) 56–57
 Art 21 .... 67, 117, 230
 Art 21(1) 48, 49
 Art 109 60
 Art 109(1) 61
 Art 118 61- 62, 230
 Art 118(1) 60
Geneva Convention IV Relative to the
 Protection of Civilian Persons in
 Time of War (12 August 1949,
 entered into force 21 October 1950,
 75 UNTS 287). 11, 228, 234, 242
 Arts 1-3 *see* Geneva Conventions:
  Common Articles
 Art 4 .... 37, 38, 84
 Art 4(1) 37
 Art 4(2) 37, 84
 Art 4(2)(b) 84
 Art 5 .... 38, 62, 84
 Art 5(1) 62
 Art 5(2) 62
 Art 5(3) 62
 Art 6 84–85
 Art 27 80–81
 Art 27(1) 80–81

Geneva Convention IV Relative to the
   Protection of Civilian Persons in
   Time of War (12 August 1949,
   entered into force 21 October 1950,
   75 UNTS 287) (*cont.*):
Art 27(2) 81
Art 27(3) 81
Art 27(4) ... 41, 43, 46, 49, 67, 81, 83, 235
Art 41 40–41
Art 42 ... 1, 40–41, 42, 46, 47, 49, 63, 68,
   74, 83, 108, 117, 172
Art 42(1) 41, 44, 44–45, 234, 240
Art 43 .... 1, 40–41, 58, 63, 68, 108,
   129, 130, 172, 204, 232
Art 43(1) 51, 56, 56, 234, 239
Art 78 .... 41, 42, 45, 46, 47, 49, 58,
   63, 83, 108, 117, 129, 130, 154,
   155, 158, 172, 203–204, 232, 239
Art 78(1) 41, 44–45, 234, 236
Art 78(2) 51, 56, 234
Art 118(1) 97
Art 1321, ... 56, 108
Art 132(1) 59–60, 97, 131, 234, 242
Art 132(2) 60
Art 13397 108
Art 133(1) 60, 131, 242
Art 14739
Part II........................... 84
Part III, Section II 40
Part III, Section III.................. 40
Geneva Conventions: Common Articles
Art 2 13–14
Art 3 .... 1, 6, 13–14,15–16, 23, 47,
   68–69, 76–83, 84, 85, 91, 95,
   100–105, 106, 107, 231
Art 3(1) 78
Art 3(1)(d) 84
Hague Convention II with Respect to the
   Laws and Customs of War on Land
   with Annex: Regulations respecting
   the laws and customs of war on land
   (29 July 1899, entered into force
   September 1900, 187 CTS)
Art 2 12
Hague Convention IV Respecting the
   Laws and Customs of War on Land
   (18 October 1907, entered into
   force 26 January 2010) 205 CTS
Art 13 50
Hague Convention V respecting the
   Rights and Duties of Neutral Powers
   and Persons in Case of War on Land,
   18 October 1907
Art 11 50

International Covenant on Civil and Political
   Rights (ICCPR) (16 December 1966,
   entered into force 23 March 1976,
   99 UNTS 171)...................134
Art 2(1) 213, 219
Art 4 .... 10–11, 115, 173, 209
Art 4(1) 193, 216, 243
Art 4(2) 193
Art 6 .... 149, 194
Art 6(1) 3, 73, 149
Art 9 .... 3, 89, 119, 121, 122,
   187, 160, 166, 168, 169, 172,
   173, 178, 184, 194–196, 200
Art 9(1) 67, 78, 177, 119, 127–128,
   154, 173, 196
Art 9(2) 123, 168, 195
Art 9(3) 168, 172, 173
Art 9(4) 3, 124, 125, 127–128,
   130, 155, 189, 195, 210
Protocol I to the Geneva Conventions
   of 12 August 1949, and Relating to
   the Protection of Victims of
   International Armed Conflicts
   (12 December 1977, entered into
   force 7 December 1978, 1125
   UNTS 3) 16–17, 113
Art 1(2) 85
Art 1(4) 17
Art 43 .... 48, 49, 58
Art 43(1) 35
Art 43(2) 18, 36
Art 44 .... 36–37, 58
Art 44(1) 35
Art 44(3) 36
Art 44(4) 36
Art 44(7) 36
Art 45(1) 57–58
Art 50(1) 49
Art 51 149
Art 51(3) 46–47, 74
Art 72 113
Art 75 55
Art 75(1) 55
Art 75(3) 238
Part III........................... 34
Part IV........................... 34
Protocol II to the Geneva Conventions of
   12 August 1949, and Relating to the
   Protection of Victims of
   Non-International Armed Conflicts
   (12 December 1977, entered into
   force 7 December 1978, 1125 UNTS
   609) 1, 16–17, 22, 23–24, 69,
   83–85, 100–105, 113

Tables of Legislation

Preamble 85, 113
Art 1(1) 17, 85
Art 2(2) 97
Art 3 25
Art 3(1) 23–24
Art 3(2) 24
Art 3(4) 25, 26
Art 5 .... 70, 77, 97
Art 5(1) 69, 111
Art 6 .... 70, 97
Art 6(1) 84
Art 6(5) 27
Art 13(3) 46–47
'Martens Clause'.................. 85
St Petersburg Declaration Renouncing the Use, in Time of War, of Explosive Projectiles under 400 Grammes in Weight (11 December 1868, 138 CTS)......................12
Vienna Convention on Succession of States in Respect of Treaties, 1946 UNTS 3 (23 August 1978, entered into force 6 November 1996)
   Art 11 219
   Art 12 219
Vienna Convention on the Law of Treaties (23 May 1969, entered into force 28 January 1980, 1155 UNTS 331) 7, 102
   Art 3 107
   Art 26 99
   Art 31(1) 7, 149, 208
   Art 31(3)(b) 7, 82, 158, 158, 162
   Art 31(3)(c) 149, 152, 158
   Art 31(4) 149
   Art 32 7
   Art 34 102
   Art 35 102
   Art 41(1)(b)(i) 164
Vienna Convention on the Law of Treaties between States and International Organizations (21 March 1986), UN Doc A/CONF.129/15 107

OTHER INTERNATIONAL INSTRUMENTS

Body of Principles for the Protection of All Persons under Any Form of Detention or Imprisonment, UNGA Res 43/173, 9 December 1988......140
   Principle 10 238
   Principle 17 241
   Principle 32(1).................. 239
Hague Regulations 1899
   Art 20 60
Rome Statute of the International Criminal Court (17 July 1998, entered into force 1 July 2002, 2187 UNTS 3)
   Art 8(2) 18
   Art 12(2) 103
Statute of the International Court of Justice (26 June 1945, entered into force 24 October 1945)
   Art 1(3) 14
   Art 38(1) 68
   Art 38(1)(c) 140
UN Commission on Human Rights Resolution 2004/39, 19 April 2004...................140
UN General Assembly Resolution 804 (VIII) (1953) (Korea)............113
UN General Assembly Resolution 1312 (XIII) (1958) (Hungary)......113
UN General Assembly Resolution 2444 (XXIII) (1968) 113
UN General Assembly Resolution 2546 (XXIV) (1969) 113
UN General Assembly Resolution 2675 (XXV) (1970) 113
UN General Assembly Resolution 3525 A (XXX) (1975) (territories occupied by Israel) 113
UN General Assembly Resolution 40/161 A (1985) (Israel).......136, 137
UN General Assembly Resolution 46/135 (1991) (Kuwait under Iraqi occupation) 113
UN General Assembly Resolution 48/153 (1993) (former Yugoslavia) ... 218
UN General Assembly Resolution 50/193 (1995) (the former Yugoslavia)......113
UN General Assembly Resolution 52/145 (1997) (Afghanistan) 113
UN General Assembly Resolution 53/160 (1998) 218
UN General Assembly Resolution 54/182 (1999) (Sudan)..................218
UN General Assembly Resolution 55/112 (2000) (Myanmar).........136
UN General Assembly Resolution 55/116 (2000) (Sudan) 77
UN General Assembly Resolution 57/230 (2002) 218

UN General Assembly Resolution
  59/199 (2004) 136
UN General Assembly Resolution
  60/166 (2005) 120
UN General Assembly Resolution
  61/161 (2006) 136, 139
UN General Assembly Resolution
  61/171 (2006) 136
UN General Assembly Resolution
  62/159 (2007) 136
UN General Assembly Resolution
  66/230 (2011) (Myanmar) 136, 139
UN General Assembly Resolution
  67/233 (2012) (Myanmar) 136
UN General Assembly Resolution
  67/262 (2013) (Syria) 113, 116, 218
UN Human Rights Council
  Resolution 6/4, 28 September 2007 . . . 140
UN Security Council Resolution
  237 (1967) 113
UN Security Council Resolution
  417 (1977) (South Africa) 136
UN Security Council Resolution
  473 (1980) (South Africa) 136
UN Security Council Resolution
  569 (1985) 137
UN Security Council
  Resolution 827 (1993) 138
UN Security Council Resolution
  1034 (1995) 113
UN Security Council Resolution
  1127 (1997) (UNITA) 107
UN Security Council Resolution
  1213 (1998) (Angola) 218
UN Security Council Resolution
  1417 (2002) 218
UN Security Council Resolution
  1464 (2003) (Côte d'Ivoire) 218
UN Security Council Resolution
  1468 (2003) 218
UN Security Council Resolution
  1546 (2004) 174, 175, 180, 198
UN Security Council Resolution
  1574 (2004) (Sudan) 115
UN Security Council Resolution
  1635 (2005) (DRC) 113
UN Security Council Resolution
  1637 (2005) 174
UN Security Council Resolution 1653
  (2006) (Great Lakes region) 113
UN Security Council Resolution
  1707 (2006) 180
UN Security Council Resolution
  1723 (2006) 174
UN Security Council Resolution
  1790 (2007) 174
UN Security Council Resolution 1814
  (2008) (Somalia) 218
UN Security Council Resolution 1834
  (2008) (Chad) 218
UN Security Council Resolution 1877
  (2009) 138
UN Security Council Resolution 2093
  (2013) (Somalia) 115–116
UN Security Council Resolution 2095
  (2013) (Libya) 113
UN Security Council Resolution 2100
  (2013) (Mali) 77
UN Security Council Resolution 2111
  (2013) (Somalia) 113
UN Security Council Resolution 2139
  (2014) (Syria) 77
UN Security Council Resolution 2227
  (2015) (Mali) 113
UN Security Council Resolution 4569
  (1985) (South Africa) 136
Universal Declaration of Human
  Rights, UN General Assembly
  Resolution 217 A(III), UN
  Doc A/810 (1948) 14, 112
  Art 3 117
  Art 9 . . . . 78, 117, 119

REGIONAL AGREEMENTS

African Charter on Human and Peoples'
  Rights (27 June 1981, entered
  into force 21 October 1986) 21
  ILM 58 (ACHPR) . . . 117, 134, 193, 214
  Art 6 . . . . 67, 78, 117, 154, 205–206
  Part I, ch II 219
American Convention on Human
  Rights (ACHR) (22 Nov1969,
  entry into force 11 July 1978) . . . 113–114,
              116–117, 134, 201–202, 202–203
  Art 1(1) 213, 219
  Art 7 . . . . 121, 203
  Art 7(1) 117
  Art 7(2) 117, 118
  Art 7(3) 117, 154

Art 7(4) 123
Art 7(6) 124–125, 204
Art 27(1) 115, 193
Art 27(2) 193
American Declaration on the Rights
  and Duties of Man (ADRDM)
  1948.......... 114, 116, 201, 203, 214
Art I........................... 117
Art XXV........ 117, 124, 203, 203–204
Arab Charter on Human and Peoples'
  Rights (ArCHR) (22 May 2004,
  entry into force 2008) 116–117, 134
Art 3(1) 213
Art 4(1) 193
Art 4(2) 193
Art 14(1) 117, 154
Art 14(2) 117
Art 14(3) 123
European Convention for the Protection
  of Human Rights and Fundamental
  Freedoms 1950 (ECHR)... 117–118, 134
Art 1 .... 162, 213, 219
Art 2 73
Art 2(2)(a) 197–198
Art 5 ...... 118, 121, 122, 158, 166, 179,
           182, 188, 196–197, 198–201, 207
Art 5(1) 67, 78, 117, 121, 155, 162,
                 198, 199, 200, 201,
                 207, 210, 229
Art 5(2) 123, 198, 199, 200, 201
Art 5(4) 124, 125–126, 126, 130, 158,
                 198, 199, 200, 200, 201, 210
Art 15 .... 201, 209
Art 15(1) 114, 193, 243
Art 15(2) 193

BILATERAL TREATIES

Friendship, Commerce and Navigation
  Treaty between the United States
  and Nicaragua
  Art XXI 42
Treaty of Amity and Commerce between
  the United States and Prussia 1785.... 12

NATIONAL LEGISLATION

Angola
Peace Accords between the Government
  of Angola and UNITA 1991 95

Armenia
Penal Code 2003
  Art 390.2(4)..................... 91

Azerbaijan
Criminal Code 1999
  Art 112 92
  Art 116 92

Belgium
Law concerning the Repression of
  Grave Breaches of the Geneva
  Conventions and their Additional
  Protocols as amended (1993)
  Art 1(1)(6) 91
  Art 1(2)(5) 91

Bosnia and Herzegovina
Criminal Code 1998
  Art 154(1) 92

China
Constitution 1982 (amended 2004)
  Art 37 135

Ethiopia
Penal Code 1957
  Art 282(c) 92

Georgia
Criminal Code 1999
  Art 411(2) 91

Moldova
Penal Code 2002 91

Myanmar
Defence Services Act 1959
  s 49(a) 135, 140

Nepal
Communist Party of Nepal-Maoist, Public
  Legal Code 2060 (2003/04) 237
Public Security (2nd Amendment)
  Act 1991 ....89, 169
Terrorist and Disruptive Activities
  (Control and Punishment)
  Act 2002 ....70, 169
Terrorist and Disruptive Activities
  (Control and Punishment)
  Ordinance 2004...............89, 169

Nicaragua
Draft Penal Code 1999
    Art 461 91

Portugal
Penal Code 1996
    Art 241(1)(g) 91, 92

Sierra Leone
Abidjan Peace Agreement between the Government of Sierra Leone and the Revolutionary United Front, 30 November 1996
    Art 2 106

Sri Lanka
Prevention of Terrorism Act
    1979......................71, 167
    s 9(1) 167
    s 13(2) 167
    s 13(3) 167
Tamil Eelam Child Protection Act
    (Act No 3 of 2006)...............237

Slovenia
Penal Code 1994
    Art 374(1) 92

Sudan
Darfur Peace Agreement between the Government of the Sudan, the Sudan Liberation Movement/Army and the Justice and Equality Movement 2006...............95–96

United Kingdom
Anti-Terrorism, Crime and Security
    Act 2001 188

United States
Act on Restitution for World War II Internment of Japanese-Americans and Aleuts 1988
    s 1989a.......................... 46
Authorization for Use of Military Force (AUMF), Pub. L. 107–40, 115 Stat 224 (18 September 2001)
    s 2(a) 185
Detainee Treatment Act 2005...........189
Executive Order 13,567 (7 March 2011), 'Periodic Review of Individuals Detained at Guantanamo Bay Naval Station Pursuant to the Authorization for Use of Military Force'
    s 3(c) 240
Military Commissions Act 2006.........189
National Defense Authorization Act 2012
    s 1023(b)(1)..................... 187
    s 1023(b)(2)..................... 187
    s 1024 182

Uruguay
Law on Cooperation with the ICC 2006
    Art 26.2......................... 92
    Art 26.3.7 92

Yugoslavia, Federal Republic of
Penal Code 1994
    Art 142(1) 92

Introduction

Since its earliest elaborations, international humanitarian law (IHL) has treated international and non-international armed conflicts differently.[1] The consequence of this difference is that the former (conflicts between two or more states) have traditionally been regulated far more comprehensively than the latter (conflicts between states and non-state armed groups, or between such groups).[2] In light of the post-1945 shift that has seen non-international conflicts become the norm, this distinction seems particularly anachronistic.[3]

This differentiated approach to the regulation of armed conflict is particularly stark with respect to preventive, security detention or 'internment', defined as a deprivation of liberty ordered by the executive on the basis of future security threat without criminal charge.[4] Whereas the law of international armed conflict explicitly sets out 'procedural' rules on who may be interned, what processes must be provided to review their internment, and when they must be released, the treaty law of non-international armed conflict is silent on these matters.[5] Consequently, conventional wisdom holds that IHL 'contains no indication of how [internment] is to be regulated'.[6] In addition, whilst international human rights law (IHRL)

---

[1] The distinction between the two categories of armed conflict in IHL is discussed in detail in chapter 1, and for that reason the coverage here is very brief.

[2] E Crawford, *The Treatment of Combatants and Insurgents under the Law of Armed Conflict* (OUP, Oxford 2010) 1. The term 'non-state armed group/party' will be adopted throughout this book to refer to the non-state party to non-international armed conflicts, whereas the terms 'non-state armed forces/fighters' will be used to refer specifically to the military wing of the non-state party.

[3] E Crawford, 'Unequal before the Law: The Case for the Elimination of the Distinction between International and Non-international Armed Conflicts' (2007) 20 Leiden J Intl L 441, 442.

[4] J Pejic, 'Procedural Principles and Safeguards for Internment/Administrative Detention in Armed Conflict and Other Situations of Violence' (2005) 87 IRRC 375, 375–6. References to 'internment' and 'detention' are used throughout this book interchangeably and should be interpreted according to the definition here, unless stated otherwise.

[5] See, eg, Geneva Convention Relative to the Protection of Civilian Persons in Time of War (adopted 12 August 1949, opened for signature 12 August 1949, entered into force 21 October 1950) 75 UNTS 287 (hereinafter 'GCIV'), arts 42–3 and 132 (on civilian internment in international armed conflict); art 3 GCIV and Protocol Additional to the Geneva Conventions of 12 August 1949, and Relating to the Protection of Victims of Non-International Armed Conflicts (Protocol II) (adopted 8 June 1977, opened for signature 12 December 1977, entered into force 7 December 1978) 1125 UNTS 609 (hereinafter 'APII') (the principal treaty rules applicable in non-international armed conflict).

[6] LM Olson, 'Guantánamo Habeas Review: Are the D.C. District Court's Decisions Consistent with IHL Internment Standards?' (2009) 42 Case W Res J Intl L 197, 208.

also stipulates certain procedural safeguards that must be adhered to whenever detaining, disagreement exists over the application of those rules in armed conflict,[7] as well as the relationship between IHL and IHRL.[8]

These controversies regarding the legal rules applicable to detention in non-international armed conflicts are particularly worrying, for not only is it recognized in applicable treaty provisions that internment will occur in non-international armed conflicts,[9] but reports of arbitrary deprivations of liberty in such situations are common, for example, in Colombia,[10] Nepal,[11] Haiti,[12] Syria,[13] and Mali.[14] Indeed, this lack of clarity has triggered fears over so-called 'legal black holes',[15] battlefields in which states detain unconstrained by both domestic and international law. It is this which lies at the heart of some of the most controversial practices and intractable debates in IHL in the post-9/11 era, with states increasingly engaging in non-international armed conflicts abroad. The detention practices of the United States in its conflict with al-Qaeda, as well as those of multi-national forces in Afghanistan and Iraq, are a few, prominent examples of the controversy surrounding detention in non-international conflicts.[16] One can see in these cases considerable divergence in the views of the various actors involved regarding the applicable legal framework governing detention operations. For example, in the US' military operations against al-Qaeda, considered by that state to constitute a non-international armed conflict,[17] the US government has argued that the

---

[7] See, eg, UN Human Rights Committee (HRC), 'Second Periodic Report: Israel', CCPR/C/ISR/2001/2, 4 December 2001, [8]; HRC, 'Concluding Observations: United States of America', CCPR/C/US/CO/3/Rev.1, 18 December 2006, [10].

[8] The literature on this is vast: see, eg, R Provost, *International Human Rights and Humanitarian Law* (CUP, Cambridge 2002); N Prud'homme, '*Lex Specialis*: Oversimplifying a More Complex and Multifaceted Relationship?' (2007) 40 Isr L Rev 356; MJ Dennis, 'Non-Application of Civil and Political Rights Treaties Extraterritorially During Times of International Armed Conflict' (2007) 40 Isr L Rev 453; F Ni Aolain, 'The No Gaps Approach to Parallel Application in the Context of the War on Terror' (2007) 40 Isr L Rev 563; BA Schabas, '*Lex Specialis*? Belt and Suspenders? The Parallel Operation of Human Rights Law and the Law of Armed Conflict, and the Conundrum of *Jus Ad Bellum*' (2007) 40 Isr L Rev 592; C Droege, 'Elective Affinities? Human Rights and Humanitarian Law' (2008) 90 IRRC 501; I Scobbie, 'Principle or Pragmatics? The Relationship between Human Rights Law and the Laws of Armed Conflict' (2009) 14 JCSL 449; M Milanović, 'A Norm Conflict Perspective on the Relationship between International Humanitarian Law and Human Rights Law' (2009) 14 JCSL 459; LM Olson, 'Practical Challenges of Implementing the Complementarity between International Humanitarian and Human Rights Law—Demonstrated by the Procedural Regulation of Internment in Non-International Armed Conflict' (2009) 40 Case W Res J Intl L 437.

[9] See, eg, art 5 APII.

[10] Inter-American Commission on Human Rights, 'Third Report on the Human Rights Situation in Colombia' (26 February 1999) OEA/Ser.L/V/II.102 Doc 9 rev 1, ch IV, [120]–[132] <http://www.cidh.org/countryrep/colom99en/table%20of%20contents.htm> accessed 7 August 2015.

[11] PJC Schimmelpenninck van der Oije, 'International Humanitarian Law from a Field Perspective—Case Study: Nepal' (2006) 9 YIHL 394, 406.

[12] UNSC Res 1576 (2004) preamble [9].   [13] UNGA Res 69/189 (2014) [3].

[14] UNSC Res 2227 (2015) preambular [21].

[15] J Steyn, 'Guantanamo Bay: The Legal Back Hole' (2004) 53 ICLQ 1.

[16] These and other examples are explored in detail in chapter 5.

[17] US Department of Justice White Paper, 'Lawfulness of a Lethal Operation Directed Against a U.S. Citizen Who is a Senior Operational Leader of Al-Qa'ida or An Associated Force' (undated; made public on 4 February 2013) 3, available at <http://msnbcmedia.msn.com/i/msnbc/sections/

detention authority conferred upon the President by Congress must be elaborated by drawing an analogy from the law of international armed conflict:

> The laws of war have evolved primarily in the context of international armed conflicts between the armed forces of nation states. This body of law, however, is less well-codified with respect to our current, novel type of armed conflict against armed groups such as al-Qaida and the Taliban. Principles derived from law-of-war rules governing international armed conflicts, therefore, must inform the interpretation of the detention authority Congress has authorized for the current armed conflict.[18]

The UN Human Rights Committee, on the other hand, considers Article 9 of the International Covenant on Civil and Political Rights (ICCPR), setting out the key procedural safeguards for detainees under IHRL, to be the governing legal framework in such situations.[19] This offers a more robust set of protections than drawing by analogy from the law of international armed conflict, seen, for example, in the Committee's demand that Guantánamo detainees be provided access to *habeas corpus*, in accordance with Article 9(4) ICCPR.[20] Others have gone further, arguing that these supposed gaps in the current law of non-international armed conflict are, in fact, sufficiently filled by domestic *criminal* law, and that it is only on this basis that detentions in such situations should be carried out.[21] These disagreements regarding the current *lex lata* have led to a number of proposals in recent years on how the current rules applicable to detention in non-international conflicts might be developed. These have included proposals by commentators,[22] international organizations,[23] and states.[24]

---

news/020413_DOJ_White_Paper.pdf> accessed 7 August 2015. US federal courts similarly view the conflict as a non-international armed conflict: *Gherebi v Obama*, 609 F Supp 2d 43 (DDC 2009) 57, fn 8; *Hamlily v Obama*, 616 F Supp 2d 63 (DDC 2009) 73.

[18] 'Respondents' Memorandum Regarding the Government's Detention Authority Relative to Detainees Held at Guantanamo Bay', *In Re: Guantanamo Bay Detainee Litigation*, Misc No 08-442 (TFH) (DDC 13 March 2009) 1 <http://www.justice.gov/opa/documents/memo-re-det-auth.pdf> accessed 7 August 2015.

[19] HRC, 'Concluding Observations: United States' (n 7) [18].   [20] Ibid.

[21] See, eg, DN Pearlstein, 'Avoiding an International Law Fix for Terrorist Detention' (2008) 41 Creighton L Rev 663. Such arguments have been criticized, however, for their alleged impracticalities, eg regarding evidence collection: MC Waxman, 'Administrative Detention of Terrorists: Why Detain and Detain Whom?' (2009) 3 J Nat Sec L & Pol 1, 10–11; JB Bellinger and VM Padmanabhan, 'Detention Operations in Contemporary Conflicts: Four Challenges for the Geneva Conventions and Other Existing Law' (2011) 105 AJIL 201, 212.

[22] See, eg, Chatham House and the International Committee of the Red Cross (ICRC), 'Meeting Summary: Procedural Safeguards for Security Detention in Non-International Armed Conflict', London, 22–23 September 2008 <http://www.chathamhouse.org/sites/files/chathamhouse/public/Research/International%20Law/il220908summary.pdf> accessed 7 August 2015; Olson (n 8); J Pejic, 'Conflict Classification and the Law Applicable to Detention and the Use of Force' in Elizabeth Wilmshurst (ed), *International Law and the Classification of Conflicts* (OUP, Oxford 2012).

[23] See, eg, Pejic (n 4) (adopted by the ICRC as their official policy); 31st International Conference of the Red Cross and Red Crescent 2011, 'Resolution 1: Strengthening Legal Protection for Victims of Armed Conflict', [6] <http://www.icrc.org/eng/resources/documents/resolution/31-international-conference-resolution-1-2011.htm> accessed 7 August 2015 (placing on the ICRC's agenda the formulation of new guidance on detention in non-international conflicts).

[24] See, eg, 'The Copenhagen Process on the Handling of Detainees in International Military Operations, The Copenhagen Process: Principles and Guidelines' (October 2012) <http://um.dk/

It is on these issues that this book focuses, providing the first in-depth analysis of the present state of international law regarding the procedural rules applicable to security detention or 'internment' in non-international armed conflict. In so doing, a comprehensive examination of the relevant rules under both IHL (chapters 2 and 3) and IHRL (chapter 4), as well as their interaction and practical application in situations of non-international armed conflict (chapters 5 and 6), is undertaken so as to demonstrate where the law currently stands in this area. The focus here is on the primary rules applicable to *both* states and non-state armed groups that are party to non-international conflicts.[25] That examination is then utilized to conclude the book in chapter 7 with a set of proposals for how the law might most appropriately be developed.

Importantly, the book begins in chapter 1 with a discussion of the context within which the problem being addressed falls, that is, the general distinction between international and non-international armed conflicts. This will be explored from an historical perspective, considering how the distinction has developed over time and its appropriateness in contemporary international law. In so doing, a greater understanding of IHL's differentiated approach to the regulation of detention is then possible, which will prove especially important in chapter 7 when considering how the law should develop. Before that, however, a few words should be said about the scope of the present enquiry and the methodology adopted.

I.1 Aims and Scope of Enquiry

The aim of the current book is twofold. First, it seeks to provide the first comprehensive examination of the current *lex lata* regarding the procedural rules applicable to internment in non-international armed conflict. Second, after highlighting the deficiencies in the current law, it offers a proposal for developing the law in a manner that builds upon, rather than replaces, the current legal rules.

A number of points must be highlighted regarding the scope of enquiry of this book. First, the enquiry is not into substantive treatment standards for internees nor the conditions of detention, but rather the deprivation of liberty itself. Thus, the terms 'procedural regulation' and 'procedural rules' are used throughout, in contradistinction to substantive treatment standards, to refer to the grounds justifying internment, the mechanisms for reviewing internment, and the point at which internment must cease.[26] Whilst there has been much controversy in practice with the substantive treatment of detainees in non-international armed conflicts,[27]

---

en/-/media/UM/English-site/Documents/Politics-and-diplomacy/Copenhangen%20Process%20 Principles%20and%20Guidelines.pdf> accessed 7 August 2015.

[25] The rules governing internment by non-state armed groups are often given insufficient attention: see, eg, Bellinger and Padmanabhan (n 21).

[26] Chapter 2 will demonstrate that this framework of rules is set out in the relevant IHL provisions in international armed conflicts.

[27] Indeed, at the time of writing, the ICRC's ongoing process on strengthening the protection of detainees in non-international conflicts covers substantive treatment standards: see, eg, ICRC,

I.1 Aims and Scope of Enquiry

it is with regard to the procedural rules that the key legal questions exist, as it is here where IHL treaty law provides no explicit rules. Second, as noted above, this book concerns internment (ie preventive, security detention ordered by the executive), as opposed to other forms of detention that may occur in non-international conflicts, such as detention on criminal charges. Once again, it is here that the principal legal questions exist.

Third, the enquiry is restricted to internment in *non-international armed conflicts*, which can be defined primarily as 'protracted armed violence between governmental authorities and organized armed groups or between such groups within a State'.[28] However, it is important to note that the precise contours of this category of conflicts are unclear. Jelena Pejic, for example, notes that the following seven scenarios have all, validly or not, been categorized as non-international armed conflicts: traditional intra-state conflicts between the state and non-state armed groups; conflicts between two or more non-state groups in a single territory; traditional intra-state conflicts between a state and non-state group that 'spill over' into an adjacent state; conflicts in which multinational forces assist a 'host state' in countering non-state groups on the latter's territory; conflicts in which forces acting under the aegis of the United Nations (UN) or another international organization assist in 'stabilizing' the host state against non-state forces; conflicts between states and non-state armed groups which operate from the territory of an adjacent state, without the latter state's authority or control; and global conflicts between states and transnational non-state groups that are not confined to particular territories.[29] Some of these scenarios are more widely recognized than others as situations that can constitute non-international armed conflicts,[30] subject to the thresholds established in jurisprudence being met.[31] The precise contours of the category of non-international armed conflict and the appropriateness of classifying as such the scenarios above are beyond the scope of the present work. Instead, for the purposes of this enquiry, it is sufficient that, when examining state practice in a particular situation, the state(s) involved considered it to constitute a non-international armed conflict to which IHL applied or at least did not contest that characterization. Moreover, when examining other practice, such as that of human rights treaty bodies, it is sufficient that either the treaty body itself considered the situation to constitute a non-international conflict, or that the situation was generally recognized as such.

Strengthening Legal Protection for Persons Deprived of their Liberty in Relation to Non-International Armed Conflict, Regional Consultations 2012–13: Background Paper (undated), 6–10.

[28] *Prosecutor v Duško Tadić* (Decision on the Defence Motion Motion for Interlocutory Appeal on Jurisdiction) ICTY-94-1 (2 October 1995), [70].
[29] J Pejic, 'The Protective Scope of Common Article 3: More Than Meets the Eye' (2011) 93 IRRC 189, 193–5.
[30] See, eg, ibid, 196–7 (noting the ICRC's rejection of the US' claim that the final scenario can constitute a single, global non-international armed conflict).
[31] *Prosecutor v Duško Tadić* (Trial Judgment) IT-94-1-T (7 May 1997), [562] (stating that the two thresholds that must be met in order for a particular situation to be classified as a non-international armed conflict relate to 'the intensity of the conflict and the organisation of the parties to the conflict').

6 *Introduction*

Fourth, given that many contemporary military operations involve multinational forces operating under the aegis of an international organization, complex questions increasingly arise surrounding the issue of attribution of particular conduct, including detention operations.[32] Such considerations, however, are excluded from the present enquiry, which is limited to an examination of the primary rules applicable to states and non-state groups.[33]

Finally, there are a number of issues that do not directly fall within the scope of 'procedural rules' applicable to detention, as defined here, but are closely linked to the rules explored in this book. For example, whilst the regulation of the point of release of internees does form part of the scope of enquiry, issues concerning transfer of internees are not addressed.[34] Questions relating to transfer, *non-refoulement*, and procedures for determining whether a real risk of rights violations exists are, however, of increasing importance in contemporary armed conflicts, where states frequently assist 'host' states against non-state armed groups on the latter's territory.[35] Moreover, as noted, the book deals with the procedural rules applicable to internment, defined as the grounds permitting internment, the review mechanisms provided, and the point at which internment must cease. A number of other indirect safeguards that protect persons from arbitrary deprivations of liberty cannot, for reasons of space, also be addressed. These include, inter alia, requirements relating to the place of detention, access of the International Committee of the Red Cross to detainees, and information for members of the detainee's family.[36]

I.2 Methodology

The majority of this book is dedicated to determining the current rules of international law that apply in this area, looking especially at IHL and IHRL. It is in these areas in particular that commentators and tribunals have at times adopted methodologies that seem to depart from the traditional positivist, consent-based model of international legal obligation.[37] Without passing judgement on the

---

[32] See, eg, Chatham House and ICRC (n 22) 8. This issue was faced by the European Court of Human Rights (ECtHR) in *Behrami and Behrami v France, Saramati v France, Germany and Norway*, App Nos 71412/0 and 78166/01, Admissibility Decision (Grand Chamber), 2 May 2007; on this case, see M Milanović and T Papić, 'As Bad As It Gets: The European Court of Human Rights' (ECtHR) *Behrami and Saramati* Decision and General International Law' (2009) 58 ICLQ 267.

[33] On the issue of whether multinational forces can become parties to armed conflicts and thus regulated directly by IHL, see T Ferraro, 'The Applicability and Application of International Humanitarian Law to Multinational Forces' (2013) 95 IRRC 561.

[34] On this, see, eg, ECtHR, *Othman v UK*, App No 8139/09, 17 January 2012, [231]–[235]; E-C Gillard, 'There's No Place Like Home: States' Obligations in Relation to Transfers of Persons' (2008) 90 IRRC 703; C Droege, 'Transfers of Detainees: Legal Framework, *Non-Refoulement* and Contemporary Challenges' (2008) 90 IRRC 669; RM Chesney, 'Leaving Guantanamo: The Law of International Detainee Transfers' (2006) 40 U Rich L Rev 657; J Yoo, 'Transferring Terrorists' (2004) 79 Notre Dame L Rev 1183.

[35] Pejic (n 22) 97.   [36] Pejic (n 4) 384–5 and 389–91.

[37] See, eg, *Case Concerning Military and Paramilitary Activities in and Against Nicaragua (Nicaragua v United States)* [1986] ICJ Rep 14, [218]–[219] (finding common Article 3 of the 1949 Geneva Conventions

validity of such approaches, this book seeks to adhere to the more traditional tests for establishing the existence and content of international legal norms. It is hoped that this will help to ensure a balanced approach and thus reduce any concerns of bias. Indeed, by dealing in chapters 2 to 6 with the *lex lata* and chapter 7 with the *lex ferenda*, the book specifically aims to maintain a separation between the two. Thus, in interpreting applicable treaty provisions, the test applied throughout the book is grounded in the rules codified in the Vienna Convention on the Law of Treaties, that is, in good faith in accordance with the ordinary meaning to be given to the terms in their context and in light of their object and purpose.[38] Reliance is also placed on the subsequent practice of the states parties as well as the *travaux préparatoires* of the provisions,[39] in order to discern 'what was the intention of the parties'.[40] International jurisprudence will also be referred to in interpreting treaty provisions. For example, when interpreting IHL treaties, the jurisprudence of international criminal tribunals is important, offering the first recent elaborations of the rules of IHL on which many of the international crimes within their jurisdiction are based.[41] Similarly, when interpreting human rights treaties, reference is made to the jurisprudence of human rights treaty bodies. This is not only because those bodies offer authoritative interpretations of their respective treaties, but also because it is before those bodies that the detention operations of states in non-international conflicts will in practice often be judged.[42] Indeed, notwithstanding the variations in the binding character of decisions of human rights treaty bodies,[43] there is a clear trend towards relying on the authoritative interpretations by those bodies of their respective treaties.[44]

---

to reflect custom without reference to state practice or *opinio iuris*); *Prosecutor v Zoran Kupreškić et al* (Trial Judgment) ICTY-95-16 (14 January 2000), [527] (stating that customary IHL can form with scant practice by virtue of the Martens Clause, relying on *opinio iuris* as the decisive element where the 'imperatives of humanity or public conscience' so dictate); T Meron, 'The Geneva Conventions as Customary Law' (1987) 81 AJIL 361 (noting the trend in jurisprudence towards greater reliance on *opinio iuris* in the absence of state practice); FL Kirgis, 'Custom on a Sliding Scale' (1987) 81 AJIL 146 (similarly recognizing the same trend in jurisprudence, based on the ICJ's *Nicaragua* judgment); J Dingwall, 'Unlawful Confinement as a War Crime: The Jurisprudence of the Yugoslav Tribunal and the Common Core of International Humanitarian Law Applicable to Contemporary Armed Conflicts' (2004) 9 JCSL 133, 136–8 (arguing in favour of a less stringent test for the emergence of customary IHL).

[38] Vienna Convention on the Law of Treaties (adopted 23 May 1969, opened for signature 23 May 1969, entered into force 28 January 1980) (hereinafter 'VCLT'), art 31(1).

[39] Art 31(3)(b) VCLT (subsequent practice) and art 32 VCLT (*travaux*).

[40] Sir H Lauterpacht, *The Development of International Law by the International Court* (reissue, CUP, Cambridge 1982) 27.

[41] See, eg, G Mettraux, *International Crimes and the Ad Hoc Tribunals* (OUP, Oxford 2005) (for general discussions of the development of IHL by the ad hoc tribunals); S Sivakumaran, 'Re-Envisaging the International Law of Internal Armed Conflict' (2011) 22 EJIL 219, 232–3 (on the importance of international criminal law in developing the law of non-international armed conflict).

[42] See section 6.1.

[43] Compare, eg, the binding nature of judgments of the European Court of Human Rights, with the non-binding nature of 'views' and general comments of the UN Human Rights Committee, 'Selected Decisions of the Human Rights Committee under the Optional Protocol: Volume II' (1985), CCPR/C/OP/1, 1–2, [8].

[44] See, eg, *Case Concerning Ahmadou Sadio Diallo (Republic of Guinea v Democratic Republic of Congo)*, Merits Judgment [2010] ICJ Rep 639, [66]–[68]; S Ghandhi, 'Human Rights and the

When discussing whether particular norms have crystallized as custom, the traditional, cumulative test of state practice and *opinio iuris* is adhered to.[45] In conformity with the International Court of Justice's (ICJ) approach to custom, it is 'sufficient that the conduct of states should, in general, be consistent' with the purported customary rule, and that inconsistent practice is treated by other states as a breach of the rule and defended by the offending state 'by appealing to exceptions or justifications contained within the rule itself'.[46] For the purposes of finding state practice and *opinio iuris*, a number of different sources are taken into account. For example, when considering state practice, in addition to actual operational practice, official statements of the executive, domestic legislation, domestic judicial decisions, and military manuals are also taken into account. Doctrine and jurisprudence confirms the validity of such sources of state practice.[47] Indeed, these sources are especially important in this area, given the often scant publicly available information regarding actual operational practice in armed conflict.[48] Moreover, reliance is also placed on a number of different sources for evidence of *opinio iuris*, including, for example, UN resolutions, where these are clearly phrased as a statement as to the current legal norms applicable in a particular situation.[49]

The aim is, therefore, to adhere to the traditional rules applicable to treaty interpretation and the emergence of custom, whilst taking account of the wide range of processes and fora in which states and authoritative bodies now frequently express their views regarding the state of the law. Further discussion of the methodology adopted will be engaged with at various points throughout the book.

International Court of Justice: The *Ahmadou Sadio Diallo* Case' (2011) 11 HRLR 527, 533–8; N Rodley, 'The International Court of Justice and Human Rights Treaty Bodies' in M Andenas and E Bjorge (eds), *A Farewell to Fragmentation: Reassertion and Convergence in International Law* (CUP, Cambridge 2015) 94–6.

[45] *North Sea Continental Shelf Cases (Federal Republic of Germany/Denmark; Federal Republic of Germany/Netherlands)* [1969] ICJ Rep 3, [74].

[46] *Nicaragua* (n 37) [186].

[47] See, eg, *North Sea Continental Shelf Cases* (n 45) [47]; *Nicaragua* (n 37) [190]; *Case Concerning the Arrest Warrant of 11 April 2000 (Democratic Republic of the Congo v Belgium)*, Judgment [2002] ICJ Rep 3, [56]–[58]; Report of the International Law Commission to the General Assembly on its Second Session, 5 June–29 July 1950, Document A/1316 [1950] Ybk of the International Law Commission (ILC), Vol II, 369–72; M Akehurst, 'Custom as a Source of International Law' (1975) 47 BYIL 1, 1–3; MN Shaw, *International Law* (CUP, Cambridge 2012) 81–4. For a minority view that state practice is restricted to physical acts of states, see AA D'Amato, *The Concept of Custom in International Law* (Cornell University Press, Ithaca 1971) 88.

[48] *Tadić* (n 28) [99].

[49] *Nicaragua* (n 37) [188]; *Legality of the Threat or Use of Nuclear Weapons*, Advisory Opinion [1996] ICJ Rep 226, [70]; *Legal Consequences of the Construction of a Wall in the Occupied Palestinian Territory*, Advisory Opinion [2004] ICJ Rep 136, [86]–[88]; Shaw (n 47) 88–9.

PART I
CONTEXT

1

The Distinction between International and Non-International Armed Conflicts

Before moving on to the central enquiry of this book, the present chapter will consider the historical basis and justification for the general distinction in international law between international and non-international armed conflict.[1] This is necessary for two reasons. First, as will be shown, the lack of clarity regarding the procedural rules applicable to internment in non-international armed conflicts arises out of the general distinction between the two categories of armed conflict. This chapter therefore provides the context for the remainder of the book. Second, whether the distinction *should* exist with regard to internment will be considered in chapter 7. As such, the reasons for, as well as the arguments in favour of and against, the distinction generally must be examined first; only then can its desirability in the specific area of internment be assessed.

The first section below (1.1) will give a brief historical overview of this distinction in international law. Section 1.2 will then note the main criticisms that have been made of it, with section 1.3 then considering the various justifications advanced for its preservation.

1.1 Overview and Historical Basis

Until the adoption of the four Geneva Conventions of 1949,[2] the distinction between international and non-international armed conflicts arose from the fact

---

[1] Parts of this chapter were originally published in L Hill-Cawthorne, 'Humanitarian Law, Human Rights Law and the Bifurcation of Armed Conflict' (2015) 64 ICLQ 293.
[2] Geneva Convention for the Amelioration of the Condition of the Wounded and Sick in Armed Forces in the Field (adopted 12 August 1949, opened for signature 12 August 1949, entered into force 21 October 1950) 75 UNTS 31 (hereinafter 'GCI'); Geneva Convention for the Amelioration of the Condition of the Wounded, Sick and Shipwrecked Members of the Armed Forces at Sea (adopted 12 August 1949, opened for signature 12 August 1949, entered into force 21 October 1950) 75 UNTS 85 (hereinafter 'GCII'); Geneva Convention Relative to the Treatment of Prisoners of War (adopted 12 August 1949, opened for signature 12 August 1949, entered into force 21 October 1950) 75 UNTS 135 (hereinafter 'GCIII'); Geneva Convention Relative to the Protection of Civilian Persons in Time of War (adopted 12 August 1949, opened for signature 12 August 1949, entered into force 21 October 1950) 75 UNTS 287 (hereinafter 'GCIV'). These abbreviations will be used throughout this book.

that treaty law was concerned only with conflicts between states and did not regulate civil conflicts within a state.[3] Although there have long existed customary rules on the laws of war, the project of codifying those rules in multilateral treaties did not begin until the mid-nineteenth century.[4] At this point in history, international law was presumed to regulate only the reciprocal relationships between states, and treaties generally dealt only with questions relevant to this subject matter; *intra*-state issues tended to be excluded, as these were seen as belonging to the realm of domestic, as opposed to international law.[5] Early treatises confirmed this inter-state focus, with the first editions of *Oppenheim* containing the classic formulation: 'International Law is a law between States only and exclusively.'[6] The *Oppenheim* formula certainly glossed over many of the nuances concerning the position of non-state actors within international law at the time, and one might note here as examples the international minimum standard on the treatment of aliens and direct access of individuals to international tribunals. However, as a formal description, it was for the most part accurate, for whilst individuals were directly engaged by international law in these areas, the principal relationship at issue remained inter-state.[7] Thus, the international minimum standard concerned the treatment of *foreign* nationals,[8] whilst individual access to international tribunals was restricted to claims against a *foreign* state.[9] This helps to explain why, with the adoption of the early conventions on the law of armed conflict, the question of their application to civil (intra-state) conflict did not arise.[10] Instead, they

---

[3] See, eg, Declaration Renouncing the Use, in Time of War, of Explosive Projectiles under 400 Grammes in Weight, Signed at St Petersburg (opened for signature 11 December 1868, entered into force 11 December 1868) 138 CTS (1868–9) 297–9 (French) [6]; 1899 Hague Convention (II) with Respect to the Laws and Customs of War on Land with Annex: Regulations respecting the laws and customs of war on land (opened for signature 29 July 1899, entered into force September 1900) 187 CTS (1898–9) 429–43, Art 2.

[4] Y Dinstein, *The Conduct of Hostilities under the Law of International Armed Conflict* (2nd edn, CUP, Cambridge 2010) 14. Note, however, certain bilateral treaties before that period included provisions relating to the conduct of hostilities, such as the 1785 Treaty of Amity and Commerce between the United States and Prussia: see A Roberts and R Guelff, *Documents on the Laws of War* (3rd edn, OUP, Oxford 2000) 4.

[5] For a historical assessment of the origins of the inter-state nature of international law, see K Parlett, *The Individual in the International Legal System* (CUP, Cambridge 2011) 10–16.

[6] L Oppenheim, *International Law, A Treatise: Volume II, War and Neutrality* (Longmans, Green & Co, London 1906) 266. Similarly, see J Westlake, *Chapters on the Principles of International Law* (CUP, Cambridge 1894) 1 ('[i]nternational law is the body of rules prevailing between states').

[7] There were possible exceptions to this, for example, in the case of minority protection, which has a long pedigree in international law, albeit being defined differently over time: P Thornberry, *International Law and the Rights of Minorities* (OUP, Oxford 1991); JE Nijman, 'Minorities and Majorities' in B Fassbender and A Peters (eds), *The Oxford Handbook of the History of International Law* (OUP, Oxford 2012).

[8] AH Roth, *The Minimum Standard of International Law Applied to Aliens* (AW Sijthoff's Uitgeversmaatschappij NV, Leiden 1949) 23 ('[c]ontrary to the national, whom we have discovered to be practically at the mercy of his own State, the alien enjoys a much more favourable situation').

[9] See, eg, MO Hudson, 'The Central American Court of Justice' (1932) 26 AJIL 759, 765; E Borchard, 'The Access of Individuals to International Courts' (1930) 24 AJIL 359; M Paparinskis, *The International Minimum Standard and Fair and Equitable Treatment* (OUP, Oxford 2013) 34–6.

[10] Similarly, see Y Sandoz, C Swinarski, and B Zimmerman (eds), *Commentary on the Additional Protocols of 8 June 1977 to the Geneva Conventions of 12 August 1949* (ICRC/Martinus Nijhoff, Geneva 1987) [4342]; E Crawford, 'Unequal Before the Law: The Case for the Elimination of the

were generally applicable only in situations of 'war',[11] which did not include conflicts between states and their subjects: '[t]o be considered war, the contention must be going on *between States*'.[12]

The nineteenth century did, however, witness the emergence in customary international law of the doctrines of insurgency and belligerency, each of which addressed, to differing degrees, civil war.[13] The effectiveness of these doctrines, however, remained constrained by the inter-state focus of international law. In particular, they tended to be relevant mainly to those internal conflicts that affected the interests of third states, being invoked by such states to regulate their relations with the parties to the conflict.[14] Moreover, even according to the doctrine of belligerency, whereby insurgents could be recognized as belligerents either by the state against which they were fighting (leading to the application of the *ius in bello* between them) or by a third state (leading to the application of the law of neutrality), recognition remained entirely at the discretion of the particular state.[15] Humanitarian concerns were, therefore, somewhat marginal. Indeed, recognition of belligerency fell into desuetude in the twentieth century, and it was the refusal by states in particularly atrocious civil wars, such as that in Spain, to recognize the belligerent status of their opponents, which highlighted the need for a more robust method by which to regulate these conflicts; the consequence was a renewed demand, particularly by the International Committee of the Red Cross (ICRC), for treaty rules in this area.[16]

It was, therefore, only in 1949 that non-international armed conflicts explicitly became subject to treaty-based regulation under Article 3 common to the four Geneva Conventions ('common Article 3').[17] At the same time, the distinction between international and non-international armed conflicts was codified. Thus,

---

Distinction between International and Non-International Armed Conflicts' (2007) 20 Leiden J Intl L 441, 443–4; R Bartels, 'Timelines, Borderlines and Conflicts: The Historical Evolution of the Legal Divide between International and Non-International Armed Conflicts' (2009) 91 IRRC 35, 47–8; D Kretzmer, 'Rethinking Application of IHL in Non-International Armed Conflicts' (2009) 42 Isr L Rev 8, 11–13; D Akande, 'Classification of Armed Conflicts: Relevant Legal Concepts' in E Wilmshurst (ed), *International Law and the Classification of Conflicts* (OUP, Oxford 2012) 32–3.

[11] See above, n 3. It is noteworthy that a few of the earliest treaties on the law of armed conflict were silent with regard to their scope of application, and certain authorities used this as a basis for arguing that they applied equally in internal conflicts: S Sivakumaran, *The Law of Non-International Armed Conflict* (OUP, Oxford 2012) 30–1.

[12] Oppenheim (n 6) 58 (emphasis in original; footnotes omitted). Similarly, see R Phillimore, *Commentaries upon International Law: Volume III* (T & JW Johnson & Co, Philadelphia 1857) 67.

[13] SC Neff, *War the Law of Nations: A General History* (CUP, Cambridge 2005) 258–75.

[14] RA Falk, 'Janus Tormented: The International Law of Internal War' in JN Rosenau (ed), *International Aspects of Civil Strife* (Princeton University Press, Princeton 1964) 208. Similarly see AP Higgins (ed), *Hall's Treatise on International Law* (8th edn, Clarendon Press, Oxford 1924) 39.

[15] There was some disagreement as to whether states were bound to recognize belligerency once the factual conditions for it were satisfied, although a consensus seems to have arisen for the view that it was within their discretion: Neff (n 13) 264–6; WE Hall, *A Treatise on International Law* (3rd edn, Clarendon Press 1890) 34; H Lauterpacht, *Recognition in International Law* (CUP, Cambridge 1947) 246.

[16] L Moir, *The Law of Internal Armed Conflict* (CUP, Cambridge 2002) 19–21.

[17] Ibid, 30.

whilst Article 2 common to the four Geneva Conventions ('common Article 2') states that the Conventions apply in armed conflicts 'between two or more of the High Contracting Parties' (international armed conflicts),[18] the single common Article 3 sets out the entire regime applicable in 'armed conflict[s] not of an international character' (non-international armed conflicts).[19] Although marking the first time that treaty law had been applied to non-international conflicts, and thus an important development in international humanitarian law (IHL), the brevity of common Article 3 exemplifies the limited degree to which such conflicts have traditionally been regulated by international law.[20]

As the first treaty provision on non-international armed conflicts, common Article 3 was one of a number of developments at the time that reflected the expansion of the subject matter of international law to include purely intrastate matters. Other developments included the emergence of international human rights law (IHRL), reflected in provisions of the UN Charter,[21] the 1948 Universal Declaration of Human Rights (UDHR),[22] and the 1948 Convention on the Prevention and Punishment of the Crime of Genocide.[23] Lea Brilmayer has opined that these post-war developments represented a shift in international law from traditional contractual notions of legal obligation to the rise of non-reciprocal 'pledges' by states to conform to morality.[24] Importantly, these 'pledges' were intra-state in the strictest sense, in that the obligations thereunder rested on states vis-à-vis their own nationals (and, of course, non-nationals within their jurisdiction). The novelty therefore laid in the absence of any necessary inter-state element, in contrast to those previous developments in international law noted above that directly engaged individuals, such as the treatment of aliens.[25]

---

[18] Common Art 2(1) GCI–IV.   [19] Common Art 3, *chapeau*, GCI–IV.
[20] E Crawford, *The Treatment of Combatants and Insurgents under the Law of Armed Conflict* (OUP, Oxford 2010) 1–2.
[21] Charter of the United Nations and Statute of the International Court of Justice (adopted 26 June 1945, entered into force 24 October 1945), Art 1(3).
[22] Universal Declaration of Human Rights, UN General Assembly Resolution 217 A(III), UN Doc A/810 at 71 (1948). Although non-binding, the UDHR had important 'moral authority': H Lauterpacht, 'The Universal Declaration of Human Rights' (1948) 25 BYIL 354, 370–5.
[23] Convention on the Prevention and Punishment of the Crime of Genocide (adopted 9 December 1948, opened for signature 9 December 1948, entered into force 12 January 1951) 78 UNTS 277. The International Court of Justice soon recognized the non-traditional character of the obligations under the Genocide Convention: *Reservations to the Convention on the Prevention and Punishment of the Crime of Genocide*, Advisory Opinion [1951] ICJ Rep 15, 23.
[24] L Brilmayer, 'From "Contract" to "Pledge": The Structure of International Human Rights Agreements' (2007) 77 BYIL 163. Others have similarly noted the non-traditional structure of human rights obligations: see, eg, GG Fitzmaurice, 'The Law and Procedure of the International Court of Justice 1951–4: Treaty Interpretation and Other Treaty Points' (1957) 33 BYIL 203, 277; B Simma, 'From Bilateralism to Community Interest in International Law' (1994) 250 *Recueil des Cours* 217, 242–3; O Hathaway, 'Do Human Rights Treaties Make a Difference?' (2002) 11 Yale LJ 1935, 1938; J Crawford, 'Multilateral Rights and Obligations in International Law' (2006) 319 *Recueil des Cours* 325.
[25] As noted already, however, certain earlier developments in specialized fields did, to different degrees, address intra-state relationships, such as the rules on the protection of minorities in particular states: see above, n 7. The post-1945 developments were, however, still unique in their attempt to lay down *general* human rights standards to apply to *all states*.

The adoption of common Article 3 in 1949 must be seen as part of this broader trend in international law, with the consolidation of intra-state structures of obligation providing the necessary foundations for the adoption of a treaty provision on non-international armed conflicts. The premise underpinning both IHRL and the law of non-international armed conflict is, after all, that it is the relationship between a state and those within its jurisdiction that is to be regulated.[26] Indeed, Theodor Meron has highlighted this close relationship between the post-war emergence of human rights law and the adoption of common Article 3:

> This Article [common Article 3] is a clear demonstration of the influence of human rights law on humanitarian law. The inclusion in the United Nations Charter of the promotion of human rights as a basic purpose of the Organization, the recognition of crimes against humanity as international crimes, the conclusion of the 1948 Genocide Convention and the regulation by a multilateral treaty of non-international armed conflicts for the first time in 1949, all stemmed from this influence.[27]

The novelty of these broader developments, however, meant that common Article 3 would prove the most contentious article during the 1949 diplomatic conference.[28] Indeed, at the heart of many of the debates regarding draft common Article 3 was not so much concern with extending *humanitarian law* to internal conflicts but rather more generally with extending *international law* to intra-state matters. This is evidenced by the comments of the Burmese delegation, unofficial representative of the Asian bloc,[29] which objected to the inclusion of any provision relating to non-international armed conflicts.[30] A central concern of the Burmese delegation was that '[i]nternal matters cannot be ruled by international law or Conventions...It is not the object of the Conference to intervene in matters essentially within the domestic jurisdiction of any State.'[31] Such objections did not prevail, however, largely because they ignored the contemporaneous development of intra-state structures of obligation in international law. Indeed, in response to similar objections by the United Kingdom,[32] the Soviet delegate made clear the

---

[26] H Krieger, 'A Conflict of Norms: The Relationship between Humanitarian Law and Human Rights Law in the ICRC Customary Law Study' (2006) 11 JCSL 265, 275; Kretzmer (n 10) 9. Admittedly, the growth of the category of 'non-international armed conflict' has seen a number of examples that do not fit this model, such as those involving two or more non-state armed groups, with no central government involvement.
[27] T Meron, *The Humanization of International Law* (The Hague Academy of International Law, Martinus Nijhoff, The Hague 2006) 7 (footnotes omitted). Whilst Meron also refers to the prosecution of crimes against humanity, at the time these could only be prosecuted where linked to an inter-state conflict: E Schwelb, 'Crimes Against Humanity' (1946) 23 BYIL 178, 207; A Cassese, *International Criminal Law* (2nd edn, OUP, Oxford 2008) 104.
[28] B de Schutter and C Van Der Wyngaert, 'Coping with Non-International Armed Conflicts: The Borderline Between National and International Law' (1983) 13 Ga J Intl & Comp L 279, 284 (noting that common Art 3 was the most debated provision at the conference).
[29] DA Elder, 'The Historical Background of Common Article 3 of the Geneva Conventions of 1949' (1979) 11 Case W Res J Intl L 37, 50 (referring to Burma as the 'self-styled Asian representative' at the conference).
[30] The main objections of Burma can be found in *Final Record of the Diplomatic Conference of Geneva of 1949: Volume II, Section B* (ICRC, 1963) 327–30.
[31] Ibid, 330.   [32] Ibid, 10.

importance of recent developments in laying the foundation for the adoption of common Article 3:

> This theory [that international law does not regulate internal matters] was not convincing, since although the jurists themselves were divided in opinion on this point, some were of the view that civil war was regulated by international law. Since the creation of the Organization of the United Nations, this question seemed settled. Article 2 of the Charter provided that Member States must ensure peace and world security. They could therefore not be indifferent to the cessation of hostilities, no matter the character or localization of the conflict. Colonial and civil wars therefore came within the purview of international law.[33]

The post-war consolidation of intra-state structures of obligation thus played an important role in the adoption of common Article 3. In this sense, although it is true that, generally, there was no cross fertilization between IHL and IHRL at this time,[34] there was an important structural relationship between IHRL and the law of non-international armed conflict.[35] As reflected in the quote by Meron above, these post-war developments in IHL and IHRL were not coincidental but intimately connected.[36] The extension of international law to intra-state matters rendered anachronistic the historical basis for differentiating between international and non-international armed conflicts.

Importantly, common Article 3 was based on the proposed (but eventually unsuccessful) preamble to the Geneva Conventions.[37] The new treaty law of non-international armed conflict was, therefore, modelled on the law applicable in international armed conflict, with the result that, whilst codifying the distinction, the Geneva Conventions partially narrowed it. This provenance of common Article 3 helps to explain why it lays down only the most basic and open-ended norms. Of course, the uniqueness of these broader developments in international law meant that any provision regarding internal conflicts was necessarily going to be very limited, as many states were concerned as to the consequence that legislating for such conflicts would have on their sovereignty.[38]

Developments since the adoption of common Article 3 have further narrowed the distinction between international and non-international armed conflicts. Most notably, in 1977, two Additional Protocols to the 1949

---

[33] Ibid, 14.
[34] R Kolb, 'The Relationship between International Humanitarian Law and Human Rights Law: A Brief History of the 1948 Universal Declaration of Human Rights and the 1949 Geneva Conventions' (1998) 38 IRRC 409.
[35] Similarly, see Kretzer (n 10) 9. [36] See above, text to n 27.
[37] JS Pictet (ed), *Commentary to Geneva Convention I for the Amelioration of the Condition of the Wounded and Sick in Armed Forces in the Field* (ICRC, Geneva 1952) 23. A brief look at some of the proposals for the preambles reveals their similarity to common Art 3: see, eg, *Final Record of the Diplomatic Conference of Geneva of 1949: Volume II, Section A* (ICRC, Geneva 1963) 366 (Soviet Union); *Final Record of the Diplomatic Conference of Geneva of 1949: Volume I* (ICRC, Geneva 1963) 113 (Stockholm draft).
[38] See section 1.3.1 below on these sovereignty concerns.

1.1 Overview and Historical Basis

Geneva Conventions were adopted, the first developing further rules to apply in international conflicts,[39] the second doing the same for non-international conflicts.[40] These had important implications for the distinction between types of armed conflict. First, Article 1(4) of Additional Protocol I (API) lifted 'armed conflicts in which peoples are fighting against colonial domination and alien occupation and against racist regimes in the exercise of their right of self-determination' out of the category of non-international conflicts and brought them under the umbrella of international armed conflicts.[41] Second, a number of the rules in Additional Protocol II (APII) were based on those applicable in international armed conflicts.[42] However, it comprises only fifteen substantive provisions, compared with the seventy contained in API. Moreover, it applied only to non-international armed conflicts between a state and those non-state groups that, 'under responsible command, exercise such control over a part of [the state's] territory as to enable them to carry out sustained and concerted military operations' and to implement the Protocol.[43]

The law of non-international armed conflict has continued to develop under both conventional and customary law since the adoption of the Additional Protocols. Regarding conventional law, a number of weapons treaties, for example, now apply equally in all armed conflicts (and peacetime).[44] At the level of custom, it has also increasingly been argued that a large number of rules of IHL now apply in non-international conflicts, most notably by the International Criminal Tribunal for the former Yugoslavia (ICTY) and the ICRC.[45]

---

[39] Protocol Additional to the Geneva Conventions of 12 August 1949, and Relating to the Protection of Victims of International Armed Conflicts (Protocol I) (adopted 8 June 1977, opened for signature 12 December 1977, entered into force 7 December 1978) 1125 UNTS 3 (hereinafter 'API').

[40] Protocol Additional to the Geneva Conventions of 12 August 1949, and Relating to the Protection of Victims of Non-International Armed Conflicts (Protocol II) (adopted 8 June 1977, opened for signature 12 December 1977, entered into force 7 December 1978) 1125 UNTS 609 (hereinafter 'APII').

[41] Such conflicts were previously considered non-international in character: D Schindler, 'The Different Types of Armed Conflicts According to the Geneva Conventions and Protocols' (1979) 163 *Recueil des Cours* 117, 133.

[42] Sivakumaran (n 11) 64.   [43] Art 1(1) APII.

[44] See, eg, Convention on the Prohibition of the Development, Production and Stockpiling of Bateriological (Biological) and Toxin Weapons and on their Destruction (opened for signature 10 April 1972, entered into force 26 March 1975) 1015 UNTS 163; Convention on the Prohibition of the Development, Production, Stockpiling and Use of Chemical Weapons and on their Destruction (opened for signature 13 January 1993, entered into force 29 April 1997) [1997] ATS 3; Convention on the Prohibition of the Use, Stockpiling, Production and Transfer of Anti-Personnel Mines and on the Destruction (opened for signature 18 September 1997, entered into force 1 March 1999) [1999] ATS 3.

[45] Regarding the ICTY, see, eg, *Prosecutor v Duško Tadić* (Decision on the Defence Motion for Interlocutory Appeal on Jurisdiction) ICTY-94-1 (2 October 1995) [127] (noting that certain rules on the means and methods of warfare previously applicable only in international conflicts now also apply under custom in non-international conflicts). Regarding the ICRC, see J-M Henckaerts and L Doswald-Beck, *Customary International Humanitarian Law Volumes I & II: Rules & Practice* (CUP, Cambridge 2005).

The latter, for example, in its Study on *Customary International Humanitarian Law*, recognized 161 core customary rules, with 147 applicable in all armed conflicts.[46]

These developments notwithstanding, important differences remain between the law applicable in international and non-international armed conflicts, and states have consistently expressed their desire to preserve the general distinction.[47] Indeed, notwithstanding its finding that a number of rules now apply under custom in all armed conflicts, the ICTY confirmed that the distinction remains relevant, stating that 'only a number of rules and principles governing international armed conflicts have gradually been extended to apply in internal conflicts' and that 'this extension has not taken place in the form of a full and mechanical transplant of those rules to internal conflicts; rather, the general essence of those rules, and not the detailed regulation they may contain' have been extended.[48]

Whilst the (more recent) Study by the ICRC suggests that the rules applicable in each category of armed conflict have continued to converge since the decision in *Tadić*, the distinction can still be seen to operate with regard to specific areas of regulation. One example where the difference between the law of international and non-international armed conflict remains stark relates to combatant status and immunity from domestic prosecution for 'ordinary' (ie IHL-compliant) acts of war, which is granted to combatants in international armed conflicts.[49] A non-state fighter in a non-international armed conflict, by contrast, may be prosecuted under domestic law merely for participating in hostilities, even if in full compliance with IHL.[50] This remains the case under customary international law.[51] As will be shown in chapter 3, the distinction also remains important for the procedural rules applicable to internment, where the law of international and non-international armed conflict continues to diverge. Notwithstanding developments in IHL, therefore, how an armed conflict is categorized can still have important consequences.

---

[46] J Pejić, 'Status of Armed Conflicts' in E Wilmshurst and SC Breau (eds), *Perspectives on the ICRC Study on Customary International Humanitarian Law* (CUP, Cambridge 2007) 78–9.

[47] See, eg, Rome Statute of the International Criminal Court (adopted 17 July 1998, opened for signature 17 July 1998, entered into force 1 July 2002) 2187 UNTS 3 (arts 8(2)(a) and (b) give the Court jurisdiction over specific war crimes committed in international conflicts, whilst the much shorter arts 8(2)(c) and (e) relate to war crimes in non-international conflicts). Noting the continued importance of the distinction, see, eg, GH Aldrich, 'The Laws of Wars on Land' (2000) 84 AJIL 42, 61–2; S Boelart-Suominen, 'Grave Breaches, Universal Jurisdiction and Internal Armed Conflict: Is Customary Law Moving Towards a Uniform Mechanism for all Armed Conflicts?' (2000) 5 JCSL 63, 103; C Byron, 'Armed Conflicts: International or Non-International?' (2001) 6 JCSL 63, 65–6; Crawford (n 20) 47.

[48] *Tadić* (n 45) [126].   [49] Art 43(2) API; Dinstein (n 4) 37.

[50] JS Pictet (ed), *Commentary to Geneva Convention III Relative to the Treatment of Prisoners of War* (ICRC, Geneva 1960) 40; Crawford (n 20) 68–76; Y Dinstein, *Non-International Armed Conflicts in International Law* (CUP, Cambridge 2014) 12–13; *United States v Marilyn Buck* [1988] 690 F Supp 1291 (US District Ct for the Southern District of New York).

[51] Henckaerts, *Vol I* (n 45) 12–13. This is discussed further below: see section 1.3.1.

1.2 Criticisms of the Distinction

The partial convergence of the law applicable in international and non-international armed conflicts has in part been encouraged by the significant criticism to which the distinction has long been subjected. It is on two grounds especially that the distinction has been challenged, summed up well by Alison Duxbury:

First, it undermines international humanitarian law's claim that it is a pragmatic body of law. Second, it creates silences about other types of conflict and violence that are not defined as armed conflicts or are excluded from the ambit of international armed conflict. This... undermines the law's claim to humanity.[52]

In light of these challenges, a number of commentators have argued in favour of the elimination of what remains of the distinction between the two categories of armed conflict.[53] Each of these grounds for criticizing the distinction will be examined in turn.

1.2.1 IHL's claim to pragmatism

IHL depends for its effectiveness on being a pragmatic body of law. The legal distinction between categories of armed conflict, however, undermines this, which in turn risks non-compliance. There are two grounds in particular on which this claim can be made. First, IHL's distinction between international and non-international armed conflict and its focus on the former seem outdated. It is clear that at the time of the drafting of the 1949 Geneva Conventions, inter-state war dominated the focus of the negotiations, with the Second World War still very much at the forefront of the minds of the delegates.[54] In the post-1945 period, however, non-international armed conflicts have become the norm rather than the exception: of the 225 armed conflicts that occurred between 1946 and 2001, only forty-two were inter-state.[55] The result is that the majority of (treaty) rules of IHL

---

[52] A Duxbury, 'Drawing Lines in the Sand – Characterising Conflicts for the Purposes of Teaching International Humanitarian Law' (2007) 8 MJIL 259, 268. Duxbury invokes these two grounds of critique in order to challenge not only IHL's distinction between international and non-international armed conflict, but also its distinction between armed conflict and other situations of violence, that is, the point below which IHL does not apply.

[53] JG Stewart, 'Towards a Single Definition of Armed Conflict in International Humanitarian Law: A Critique of Internationalized Armed Conflict' (2003) 85 IRRC 313; RE Brooks, 'War Everywhere: Rights, National Security Law, and the Law of Armed Conflict in the Age of Terror' (2004) 153 U Pa L Rev 675, 755–6; D Wilmott, 'Removing the Distinction between International and Non-International Armed Conflict in the *Rome Statute of the International Criminal Court*' (2004) 5 MJIL 196; Crawford (n 10); K Mastorodimos, 'The Character of the Conflict in Gaza: Another Argument Towards Abolishing the Distinction between International and Non-International Armed Conflicts' (2010) 12 ICLR 437.

[54] G Best, *War and Law Since 1945* (OUP, Oxford 1994) 89–90 (on the relevance of the United Kingdom's experience in the Second World War to its approach at the 1949 diplomatic conference, including its objection to the extension of the Conventions to non-international armed conflict).

[55] NP Gleditsch et al, 'Armed Conflict 1946–2001: A New Dataset' (2002) 39 J of Peace Research 615, cited in Crawford (n 20) 14 (fn 30–1). Similarly, see *Tadić* (n 45) [96]–[97].

apply only in a minority of situations.[56] Indeed, this was acknowledged already during the drafting of the 1977 Additional Protocols.[57] This notwithstanding, the delegates at the 1974–7 diplomatic conference adopted only minimal rules for such conflicts, and, as noted above, the continued evolution of the law of non-international armed conflict has not entirely eliminated this distinction in IHL.

The second way in which the distinction undermines IHL's claim to pragmatism lies in the falsity of rigidly bifurcating armed conflicts into the categories of inter-state and intra-state:

> Armed conflicts are in reality not as clearly defined as the legal categories. Some of them may not exactly tally with any of the concepts envisaged in international humanitarian law. This raises the question of whether those categories need to be supplemented or adapted with a view to ensuring that these situations do not end up in a legal vacuum.[58]

By establishing two categories of armed conflict and stipulating different rules for each, IHL requires us to classify conflicts before we can determine the relevant legal rules, and yet many situations have both international and non-international aspects. Indeed, this difficulty was faced by the ICTY when attempting to classify the conflicts arising out of the dissolution of the former Yugoslavia.[59] There is, therefore, a significant divergence between war in practice and war as it is conceived in law. For IHL to succeed in limiting abuses during armed conflict, the legal conception of war must reflect war as it exists in practice. Indeed, the history of IHL reflects an acknowledgement of this need to align legal concept with actual practice, seen, for example, in the substitution of the legal concept of 'war' for the practical concept of 'armed conflict' in 1949.[60]

A topical example of the difficulty with classifying particular armed conflicts according to one of the two legal categories can be seen in so-called 'transnational armed conflicts' between states and non-state armed groups that transcend the borders of a single state.[61] Whether to treat such situations as single armed conflicts and, if so, of what character has been the subject of significant debate. On the one hand, one might consider these to be regulated most effectively as extraterritorial law enforcement operations. On the other hand, they might be considered either international armed conflicts, due to their transnational nature, or

---

[56] Crawford (n 10) 442.

[57] See, eg, *Official Records of the Diplomatic Conference on the Reaffirmation and Development of International Humanitarian Law Applicable in Armed Conflicts (Geneva 1974–77): Volume V* (Federal Political Department, Bern 1978) 131–2 (Federal Republic of Germany); ibid, 184 (Canada).

[58] S Vité, 'Typology of Armed Conflicts in International Humanitarian Law: Legal Concepts and Actual Situations' (2009) 91 IRRC 69, 83.

[59] *Prosecutor v Duško Tadić* (Appeals Judgment), IT-94-1-A (15 July 1999) [83]–[162]. For different views on this, see, eg, T Meron, 'International Criminalization of Internal Atrocities' (1995) 89 AJIL 554; C Greenwood, 'International Humanitarian Law and the *Tadic* Case' (1996) 7 EJIL 265; T Meron, 'Classification of Armed Conflict in the Former Yugoslavia: *Nicaragua*'s Fallout' (1998) 92 AJIL 236.

[60] C Greenwood, 'The Concept of War in Modern International Law' (1987) 36 ICLQ 283, 295, and 303–4. Similarly, see *Conference of Government Experts on the Reaffirmation and Development of International Humanitarian Law Applicable in Armed Conflicts, Volume V: Protection of Victims of Non-International Armed Conflicts* (ICRC, Geneva 1971) 13.

[61] On these, see Vité (n 58) 88–93.

non-international armed conflicts, due to the parties involved. The United States, for example, has taken the view that it is in a single, global armed conflict with al-Qaeda,[62] and that this conflict is non-international in character, due to the nature of the parties involved.[63] These claims have, however, been refuted on various grounds by commentators.[64] The lack of clarity in this area has led some to advocate for the recognition of a third category of 'transnational' armed conflict under IHL.[65] Indeed, one particularly noteworthy concern that has been expressed with this current state of affairs is the possibility of so-called 'legal black holes' emerging into which these hard cases fall, with no accountability for those involved.[66]

The case of transnational armed conflicts exemplifies the difficulty with applying the legal distinction between international and non-international armed conflicts in practice. This difficulty arises not because all armed conflicts are identical, but rather because they operate along a spectrum, involving different actors, levels of violence and geographical reach. As Michael Reisman argues, 'the terms "international" and "noninternational" conflict import a bipartite universe that authorizes only two reference points on the spectrum of factual possibilities.'[67] This also has consequences for the enforcement of IHL via international criminal law, seen in the example above of the difficulty faced by the ICTY regarding the conflicts in the former Yugoslavia.[68] Deidre Wilmott criticizes the distinction on this basis, calling for its elimination so as to free international tribunals from having to consider complex questions of conflict characterization.[69]

1.2.2 IHL's claim to humanitarianism

In addition to pragmatic concerns, the legal bifurcation of armed conflict also raises concerns regarding IHL's goal of humanizing armed conflict. First, as noted,

[62] UN Human Rights Council, 'Universal Periodic Review: United States of America (National Report)', A/HRC/WG.6/9/USA/1 (23 August 2010) [82]; HH Koh, 'The Obama Administration and International Law', Remarks at the Annual Meeting of ASIL, Washington, DC, 25 March 2010 <http://www.state.gov/s/l/releases/remarks/139119.htm> accessed 20 July 2015.
[63] US Department of Justice White Paper, 'Lawfulness of a Lethal Operation Directed Against a U.S. Citizen Who is a Senior Operational Leader of Al-Qa'ida or An Associated Force' (undated; made public on 4 February 2013) 3, available at <http://msnbcmedia.msn.com/i/msnbc/sections/news/020413_DOJ_White_Paper.pdf> accessed 20 July 2015.
[64] See, eg, UN Human Rights Council, 'Report of the Special Rapporteur on Extrajudicial, Summary or Arbitrary Executions, Philip Alston: Study on Targeted Killings', A/HRC/14/24/Add.6, 28 May 2010, [53]; N Lubell, 'The War (?) Against Al-Qaeda' in E Wilmshurst (ed), *International Law and the Classification of Conflicts* (OUP, Oxford 2012) 430–7.
[65] See, eg, RS Schöndorf, 'Extra-State Armed Conflicts: Is there a Need for a New Legal Regime?' (2004) 37 NYU J Intl L & Pol 1; GS Corn, 'Hamdan, Lebanon, and the Regulation of Armed Conflict: The Need to Recognise a Hybrid Category of Armed Conflict' (2007) 40 Vand J Transnat L 295. Other commentators argue that such conflicts can be addressed by the current categories: compare Akande (n 10) 70–9 and Lubell (n 64).
[66] J Steyn, 'Guantanamo Bay: The Legal Black Hole' (2004) 53 ICLQ 1; Vité (n 58) 83.
[67] WM Reisman, 'Application of Humanitarian Law in Noninternational Armed Conflicts' (1991) 85 ASIL Proc 83, 85; Crawford (n 10) 450. A similarly false dichotomy arguably exists in IHL's distinction between non-international conflicts and internal tensions not reaching the level of armed conflict: Duxbury (n 52); F Bugnion, '*Jud Ad Bellum, Jus In Bello* and Non-International Armed Conflicts' (2003) 6 YIHL 167, 183 (fn 53).
[68] See above, text to n 59. [69] Wilmott (n 53) 205.

non-international armed conflicts are now far more common than international armed conflicts. Second, due to the fratricidal hatred they often engender, internal conflicts can be more atrocious than their inter-state counterparts.[70] Thus, by focusing its attention on international armed conflicts, rather than these potentially more destructive, and certainly more common, non-international conflicts, IHL's claim to protect the victims of armed conflict is undermined.

These humanitarian concerns have been a catalyst for many of the developments in the law of non-international armed conflict mentioned in section 1.1 above, which have reduced the extent to which international and non-international conflicts are treated differently. The ICTY, for example, in holding that a number of treaty rules originally designed for international armed conflict now apply under custom also in non-international armed conflict, made the following observation:

> A State-sovereignty-oriented approach has been gradually supplanted by a human-being-oriented approach... It follows that in the area of armed conflict the distinction between inter-State wars and civil wars is losing its value as far as human beings are concerned. Why protect civilians from belligerent violence, or ban rape, torture or the wanton destruction of hospitals, churches, museums or private property, as well as proscribe weapons causing unnecessary suffering when two sovereign States are engaged in war, and yet refrain from enacting the same bans or providing the same protection when armed violence has erupted 'only' within the territory of a sovereign State?[71]

The ICTY was clearly of the view that the distinction between international and non-international armed conflicts should be reduced in order better to protect victims of the latter. This approach of drawing on the law applicable in international armed conflict to supplement the few treaty rules applicable in non-international armed conflict has been the principal means to date by which the latter has been humanized.[72] As noted above, however, there nonetheless remain important differences between the rules applicable in each type of armed conflict. Indeed, as will be demonstrated in the following section, one of the reasons more recently put forward for preserving what remains of the distinction is, in fact, that eliminating it is *no longer* the best means of humanizing non-international armed conflicts.

1.3 Reasons for Preserving the Distinction

It is clear from the above discussion that not only has the historical basis for the distinction between international and non-international armed conflicts fallen away, but also that the distinction itself has been challenged continuously since its

---

[70] Pictet, *GCI* (n 37) 39; R Müllerson, 'International Humanitarian Law in Internal Conflicts' (1997) 2 JACL 109, 109.
[71] *Tadić* (n 45) [97]. Similarly, see Meron (n 27) 4.
[72] See, eg, Sivakumaran (n 11) 64 (noting that, regarding the drafting of APII, drawing on the law of international armed conflict was considered the self-evident means of regulating non-international armed conflicts).

codification in 1949 on pragmatic and humanitarian grounds. It must therefore be asked why it continues to exist, even if in an emasculated form. It to this question that we now turn in the final sections of this chapter.

1.3.1 Sovereignty concerns

It was explained in section 1.1 that the historical basis for the distinction between types of armed conflict lies in the traditional limitation of international law to the regulation of inter-state relations. It was also noted that the adoption of common Article 3 was part of a more general expansion in the applicability of international law to intra-state matters. This development continued over subsequent decades, encouraging the further evolution in the law of non-international armed conflict, itself based on that applicable in international armed conflict. Notwithstanding this clear trend, states have continued to reject the complete unification of the law of armed conflict, guarding their discretion over particular aspects of the way in which non-international armed conflicts are regulated. Various arguments have been advanced for preserving what remains of the distinction, most of which can be considered to fall under the general category of 'sovereignty concerns': states are of the view that 'equating non-international and international armed conflicts would undermine State sovereignty'.[73] Indeed, Theodor Meron has described APII, constrained as it was by the general reluctance of states to legislate for non-international armed conflicts, as 'an apex in the glorification of non-intervention.'[74]

The decisive role played by sovereignty concerns is clear from the *travaux* of the 1949 Geneva Conventions and the 1977 Additional Protocols. In 1949, for example, the UK delegate made clear its objection to what would become common Article 3, arguing that it would 'strike at the root of *national sovereignty*'.[75] France raised similar objections to a proposal by the Soviet Union, which would have applied a large number of the provisions of the Conventions to non-international armed conflicts.[76] Sovereignty concerns also played a significant role at the 1974–7 diplomatic conference during the drafting of APII.[77] Indeed, certain newly independent states that saw their stability as threatened by insurgencies were especially concerned.[78] These concerns resulted in Article 3(1) APII, which confirms

---

[73] Akande (n 10) 37. Similarly, see WA Solf, 'Problems with the Application of Norms Governing Interstate Armed Conflict to Non-International Armed Conflict' (1983) 13 Ga J of Intl & Comp L 291, 291; Stewart (n 53) 316–17; Wilmott (n 53) 200–201; Duxbury (n 52) 268–9.

[74] T Meron, 'Application of Humanitarian Law in Noninternational Armed Conflicts' (1991) 85 ASIL Proc 83, 84.

[75] *Final Record: Vol II-B* (n 30) 10 (my emphasis).   [76] Ibid, 98–9.

[77] See, eg, *Official Records of the Diplomatic Conference on the Reaffirmation and Development of International Humanitarian Law Applicable in Armed Conflicts, Geneva (1974–1977): Volume VIII* (Federal Political Department, Bern 1978) 205 (Argentina); ibid, 206 (German Democratic Republic); ibid, 208 (Belgium); ibid, 230 (Yugoslavia); *Official Records of the Diplomatic Conference on the Reaffirmation and Development of International Humanitarian Law Applicable in Armed Conflicts, Geneva (1974–1977): Volume VII* (Federal Political Department, Bern 1978) 81 (India); ibid, 71 (Indonesia); ibid, 72 (Chile); *Official Records: Vol V* (n 57) 103 (Romania).

[78] See, eg, *Official Records: Vol VII* (n 77) 80 (Ghana); ibid, 81 (India); *Official Records: Vol V* (n 57) 197 (Senegal).

that '[n]othing in this Protocol shall be invoked for the purpose of affecting the sovereignty of a State'. Article 3(2) APII then emphasizes that '[n]othing in this Protocol shall be invoked as a justification for intervening, directly or indirectly, for any reason whatever, in the armed conflict or in the internal or external affairs of the High Contracting Party'. The *travaux* of these provisions reflect the concern of states that bringing internal armed conflicts within the realm of international legal regulation would undermine their sovereignty.[79]

In many instances, both in 1949 and 1974–7, sovereignty concerns were invoked in a very general, abstract way, simply stating, for example, that legislating for non-international armed conflicts 'would constitute interference in the internal affairs of that State'.[80] However, these concerns have also manifested in more specific objections to the drafting of rules for internal conflicts. In particular, states have consistently expressed concern at two alleged consequences of developing international legal rules for these situations. First, it has been argued that attempting to regulate non-international armed conflicts at the international level would unduly restrict the latitude a state has in quelling internal rebellion.[81] This fear was expressed by certain states during the 1949 diplomatic conference in response to the Stockholm draft proposing the application of the Conventions *in toto* to non-international conflicts.[82] Indeed, it was recorded that the various proposals that sought to limit the kinds of non-international armed conflicts to which the Conventions would be extended had a shared concern

... that it would be dangerous to weaken the State when confronted by movements caused by disorder, anarchy and banditry, by compelling it to apply to them, in addition to its peacetime legislation, Conventions which were intended for use in a state of declared or undeclared war.[83]

This concern is also reflected in APII, Article 3(1) of which states that nothing in the Protocol restricts the state's responsibility, 'by all legitimate means, to maintain or re-establish law and order in the State or to defend the national unity and territorial integrity of the State'.

It is submitted that this specific concern cannot justify the general distinction between international and non-international armed conflict, particularly in light of the criticisms of it discussed above. First, whilst this argument *may* justify the exclusion of certain rules from application in non-international conflicts, it cannot justify the exclusion of many other rules. For example, extending combatant immunity to all non-international conflicts might enable rebels continuously to return to hostilities, given that states would not be able to prosecute them for rebellion (though the not uncommon practice of offering amnesties

---

[79] See, eg, *Official Records: Vol VIII* (n 77) 301 (Belgium).
[80] See, eg, *Official Records: Vol VII* (n 77) 72 (Chile); *Official Records: Vol VIII* (n 77) 205 (Argentina); *Official Records: Vol V* (n 57) 103 (Romania).
[81] JS Pictet (ed), *Commentary to Geneva Convention IV Relative to the Protection of Civilian Persons in Time of War* (ICRC, Geneva 1958) 44.
[82] See, eg, *Final Record: Volume II-B* (n 30) 13 (Canada); ibid, 10 (France); ibid, 10–11 (Greece).
[83] *Final Record: Volume II-B* (n 30) 121.

1.3 Reasons for Preserving the Distinction 25

in internal conflicts suggests that even this argument is not always accurate[84]). However, with regard to the rules on which the current book focuses—those relating to detention—the same argument cannot justify their exclusion from non-international armed conflicts, for it cannot reasonably be claimed that a state's ability to respond to a rebellion would be undermined by requiring them to apply these rules. This is particularly the case given that, as will be shown in chapter 2, the procedural rules applicable to internment in international armed conflicts leave considerable discretion to states.

Second, as will be discussed in more detail below, far from restricting a state's ability to respond to rebellion, extending IHL *in toto* to non-international armed conflicts could serve to broaden the scope of permissible state action, given the nature of many of the rules of IHL and their implications for otherwise applicable rules of IHRL.[85] In consequence, this argument cannot justify the general distinction between international and non-international armed conflicts but, at best, can justify the exclusion of only certain rules of IHL from the latter.

A second specific objection frequently voiced by states to eliminating the distinction between the two categories of armed conflict is that, as a result of IHL's equal application to all parties to a conflict,[86] the non-state armed group will obtain an elevated status that, if only implicitly, appears to legitimize their actions.[87] This can be seen in the UK delegate's comments at the 1949 diplomatic conference regarding draft common Article 3, when he noted that 'the application of the Conventions [to internal conflicts] would appear to give the status of belligerents to insurgents, whose right to wage war could not be recognized.'[88] Indeed, these concerns are reflected in common Article 3(4), which makes clear that the legal status of the parties to the conflict is not altered by IHL. David Elder referred to this 'non-effect' clause as 'the *sine qua non* of any reference to non-international conflicts in the Geneva Conventions.'[89] Similar concerns were also expressed at the 1974–7 diplomatic conference during the drafting of APII.[90] It is useful to separate this concern into the status of non-state armed groups under international law and under municipal law. Regarding the former, it must be noted that the mere adoption of international rules binding on non-state armed groups need not in any way affect the status of those groups under international law, for it is not any inherent legal personality of those groups that enables international law directly to bind them, but rather the legislative jurisdiction of states that have determined that such groups shall be bound directly by certain treaty

---

[84] See below at text to n 100.   [85] See section 1.3.2.
[86] On this, see C Greenwood, 'Historical Development and Legal Basis' in D Fleck (ed), *The Handbook of International Humanitarian Law* (2nd edn OUP, Oxford 2008) 10–11.
[87] This is frequently invoked as one of the major reasons for IHL's distinction between international and non-international conflicts: Pictet, *GCI* (n 37) 43–4; Reisman (n 67) 87; Aldrich (n 47) 59; D Fleck, 'The Law of Non-International Armed Conflict' in D Fleck (ed), *The Handbook of International Humanitarian Law* (3rd edn, OUP, Oxford 2013) 590.
[88] *Final Record: Volume II-B* (n 30) 10. Similarly, see ibid, 330 (Burma).
[89] Elder (n 29) 68. Similarly, see S Junod, 'Additional Protocol II: History and Scope' (1983) 33 Am U L Rev 29, 30.
[90] See, eg, *Official Records: Vol VIII* (n 77) 212 (Indonesia); ibid, 335 (Iraq).

rules.[91] Indeed, this is the ultimate expression of the special standing of states in international law and the subordination of non-state groups thereto, for the former are able to create obligations directly binding on the latter without their consent.[92]

Regarding states' concerns with the status of non-state groups under domestic law, common Article 3(4) renders this moot for the current law of non-international armed conflict, with states left free to prosecute insurgents for their acts of rebellion. However, that would not be the case were IHL extended *in toto* to non-international armed conflict, for the principle of combatant status/immunity would carry over and, assuming they satisfied the conditions for this, the position of non-state fighters vis-à-vis domestic law would be affected, as they would enjoy immunity from domestic prosecution for their 'ordinary' acts of war.[93] As Emily Crawford notes, the 'accepted wisdom' behind the refusal to grant immunity to non-state fighters is that this 'is fundamentally at odds with the modern system of the international law of sovereign states.'[94] As the Pakistani delegate's comments at the 1974–7 diplomatic conference are recorded: 'In his [the Pakistani delegate's] country insurgents would be executed, and any attempt to impose international legislation…would, in his opinion, constitute interference with the sovereign right of States.'[95] Importantly, however, this objection can only justify the exclusion of combatant status and immunity from non-international armed conflicts; it cannot justify the general distinction between the two categories of armed conflict for the purposes of other rules of IHL.

Various considerations are at play in the question of whether to extend combatant immunity to non-state fighters in non-international armed conflicts. First, it was argued by the Burmese delegate to the 1949 diplomatic conference that offering non-state fighters combatant immunity could eliminate a disincentive against revolt and thus promote internal rebellion.[96] It is not at all clear, however, that this argument is empirically sound.[97] Indeed, one can equally argue that offering such immunity creates an incentive, currently lacking in the law, for non-state fighters to adhere to IHL; presently, the prospect of prosecution under domestic law for mere participation in hostilities risks undermining any deterrent effect that might come from the threat of prosecutions (domestic or international) for violations of IHL.[98] Thus, in treating members of the National Liberation Army in Algeria as combatants and avoiding prosecutions thereof except where they committed

---

[91] S Sivakumaran, 'Binding Armed Opposition Groups' (2006) 55 ICLQ 369. See the discussion on this in section 3.4.
[92] *Jurisdiction of the Courts of Danzig* (1928) PCIJ Series B, No 15, 17–18.
[93] See above, text to nn 49–51.
[94] Crawford (n 20) 154. Some states have, nevertheless, advocated extending combatant status to non-international conflicts: see, eg, *Official Records: Vol VIII* (n 77) 359 (Sweden).
[95] *Official Records: Vol VIII* (n 77) 360. Similarly, see ibid, 362 (Spain).
[96] *Final Record: Volume II-B* (n 30) 330.
[97] N Berman, 'Privileging Combat? Contemporary Conflict and the Legal Construction of War' (2004) 43 Colum J Transnat L 1, 12.
[98] Bugnion (n 67) 194–5; Stewart (n 52) 346–7; Crawford (n 20) 157–8.

atrocities, the commander-in-chief of the French Forces in Algeria acknowledged that the alternative often meant rebels fought with greater ferocity.[99]

Second, as Emily Crawford has noted, the practice of offering *ex post facto* immunity via amnesties for domestic law violations (eg rebellion) following internal conflicts is becoming increasingly common.[100] An *ex ante* immunity would not, therefore, necessarily constitute a fundamental change in practice. Indeed, amnesties can often help with post-conflict reconciliation, particularly where tied to transitional justice mechanisms such as truth and reconciliation commissions.[101] This was recognized by the drafters of APII, with Article 6(5) requiring that, '[a]t the end of hostilities, the authorities in power shall endeavour to grant the broadest possible amnesty'. Of course, from the perspective of states, the gap between *ex ante* immunity and *ex post facto* amnesty remains significant, with the former eliminating the discretion that states currently enjoy in this area.

There are, therefore, a number of complex considerations that arise when considering whether to extend combatant status and immunity to non-state fighters in non-international armed conflicts. In any event, as noted, the concern that eliminating the distinction between the two categories of armed conflict could elevate the status of non-state fighters can only justify the exclusion of combatant status from non-international armed conflict; it cannot justify the exclusion of other rules, such as those relating to the procedural regulation of internment.

1.3.2 Humanitarian concerns

The preceding section discussed the main sovereignty-based concerns with eliminating the distinction between international and non-international armed conflict. This final section will now discuss a more recent argument advanced by certain commentators, whereby the preservation of what remains of IHL's distinction is considered essential in safeguarding the rights of the victims in such conflicts. It was noted earlier that a major criticism of the distinction has been its inconsistency with the humanitarian premise of IHL: by focusing on international armed conflict, and marginalizing non-international armed conflict, IHL has failed sufficiently to protect victims of the latter.[102] The solution to this problem that traditionally has been adopted both in practice and jurisprudence is gradually to eliminate the distinction between the two categories of armed conflict by extending the rules applicable in international armed conflicts to non-international armed conflicts.[103] This has similarly been the approach advocated

---

[99] Superior Army Command, 10th Military Region, Memorandum of 19 March 1958, ICRC Archives, file 225 (12), cited in Bugnion (n 67) at 195 (fn 80).
[100] Crawford (n 20) 104–9.   [101] Crawford (n 20) 111–12.   [102] Section 1.2.2.
[103] See, eg, *Tadić* (n 45) [97]; Sivakumaran (n 11) 61–5. Those states that have sought to increase the protections for victims in internal conflicts have similarly advocated extending most or all of the rules of IHL to them: see, eg, *Final Record: Volume II-B* (n 30) 326 (Soviet Union); *Final Record: Volume I* (n 37) 47 (ICRC); *Official Records: Vol V* (n 57) 91 (Norway); *Official Records: Vol VII* (n 77) 321–2 (Holy See).

by commentators that are concerned to increase the protections afforded to victims of internal conflicts.[104]

That humanitarian concerns with non-international armed conflicts have traditionally been addressed by drawing from the rules applicable in international armed conflicts arose from the assumption that, but for IHL, no other rules of international law applied to regulate the conduct of states in internal situations.[105] However, the emergence of IHRL has now changed this.[106] Although this has been a topic of some dispute in the past, it is now trite to note the mainstream view that IHRL, absent derogation, continues to apply in armed conflict, including non-international armed conflict.[107] Were the distinction between international and non-international conflicts eliminated, the entirety of IHL would then apply alongside IHRL in non-international conflicts, raising the question of how these rules would interact. The precise relationship between IHL and IHRL will be discussed in detail in chapter 5; suffice it to say here that the ICJ has demonstrated how the human right not arbitrarily to be deprived of one's life may be interpreted in armed conflict such that what is 'arbitrary' is determined not according to the usual IHRL standards developed in jurisprudence, but rather the IHL rules on the conduct of hostilities as the *lex specialis*.[108] Those IHL rules, however, are more permissive than IHRL as the latter has been elaborated in jurisprudence. Thus, it is generally accepted that IHL permits the lethal targeting of combatants at any time on the basis of status alone, without the requirement that it actually be necessary in the prevailing circumstances.[109] This status-based approach to combatant targeting is premised on the presumed threat that is posed by the *group*, 'whether or not he or she *personally* endangers the lives or interests of the other party to the conflict.'[110] Indeed, when the ICRC argued that the force used against otherwise legitimate targets (including combatants) 'must not exceed what is actually necessary to accomplish a legitimate military purpose in the prevailing circumstances',[111] it was heavily criticized for its alleged failure to reflect the *lex lata* accurately.[112]

---

[104] See, eg, Crawford (n 10); Mastorodimos (n 53).   [105] Kretzmer (n 10) 18–21.
[106] Ibid, 21.
[107] This is discussed in detail in section 4.1. See, eg, C Droege, 'Elective Affinities? Human Rights and Humanitarian Law' (2008) 90 IRRC 501, 503–9; N Lubell, *Extraterritorial Use of Force Against Non-State Actors* (OUP, Oxford 2010) 237–40; *Legality of the Threat of Use of Nuclear Weapons* (Advisory Opinion) [1996] ICJ Rep 226, [25]; *Legal Consequences of the Construction of a Wall in the Occupied Palestinian Territory*, Advisory Opinion [2004] ICJ Rep 136, [106]; *Case Concerning Armed Activities on the Territory of the Congo (DRC v Uganda)* [2005] ICJ Rep 116, [216]–[217].
[108] *Legality of Nuclear Weapons* (n 108), [25].
[109] See, eg, G Solis, 'Targeted Killing and the Law of Armed Conflict' (2007) 60 NWCR 127, 130; Dinstein (n 4) 34.
[110] D Kretzmer, 'Targeted Killing of Suspected Terrorists: Extra-Judicial Executions or Legitimate Means of Defence?' (2005) 16 EJIL 171, 190–1 (emphasis in original).
[111] N Melzer, *Interpretive Guidance on the Notion of Direct Participation in Hostilities under International Humanitarian Law* (ICRC, Geneva 2009) Section IX. For similar views, see, eg, JS Pictet, *Development and Principles of International Humanitarian Law* (Martinus Nijhoff, Dordrecht 1985) 75; N Melzer, *Targeted Killing in International Law* (OUP, Oxford 2008) 288–96; R Goodman, 'The Power to Kill or Capture Enemy Combatants' (2013) 24 EJIL 819.
[112] See, eg, WJ Fenrick, 'ICRC Guidance on Direct Participation in Hostilities' (2009) 12 YIHL 287, 298–9; D Akande, 'Clearing the Fog of War? The ICRC's Interpretive Guidance on Direct Participation in Hostilities' (2010) 59 ICLQ 180, 191–2; WH Parks, 'Part IX of the ICRC's "Direct Participation in Hostilities": No Mandate, No Expertise and Legally Incorrect' (2010) 42 NYU J of

1.3 Reasons for Preserving the Distinction

This liberal approach to targeting under IHL contrasts starkly with the equivalent rules in IHRL as they have been developed in jurisprudence. There, it is required that the use of lethal force only be employed where it is necessary in the prevailing circumstances for the achievement of a legitimate aim, such as in self-defence, and where proportionate to that aim.[113] Thus, unlike in IHL, under IHRL nobody may be targeted solely on the grounds of their status.

By virtue of the ICJ's *lex specialis* approach, extending more of the rules of IHL to non-international armed conflicts could, therefore, be invoked as a justification for significantly curtailing the protections otherwise afforded by the applicable rules of IHRL. As will become clear in later chapters, this more permissive approach of IHL compared with IHRL can similarly be seen with regard to the procedural regulation of internment. Consequently, the long-held view that eliminating the distinction in IHL would improve the protections afforded to victims of non-international conflicts now faces a powerful counterargument.[114] This will prove an important consideration when discussing how the law should develop in this area in chapter 7. Whereas various arguments were put forward above that supported the complete elimination of the distinction between the two categories of armed conflict, this section has demonstrated that there exists a strong humanitarian argument for preserving the distinction.

Of course, depending on the perspective one takes, the argument in this section could be invoked both in favour of and against eliminating the distinction between the two categories of armed conflict. From a humanitarian perspective, in order to protect victims of internal armed conflicts better, one should be cautious in proposing the extension of more rules of IHL to such conflicts. However, from the perspective of states wishing to preserve their discretion, eliminating the distinction could offer various advantages that they may not enjoy were IHRL the sole governing regime. Clauss Kreß has pointed to this advantage for states, noting that 'the resort to the armed conflict model offers the advantage of applying, as the *lex specialis*, a targeting and detention regime that is appreciably more permissive than that under international human rights law'.[115]

Intl L & Pol 769; MN Schmitt, 'The Interpretive Guidance on the Notion of Direct Participation in Hostilities: A Critical Analysis' (2010) 1 Harv Nat Sec J 5, 39–43; JK Kleffner, 'Section IX of the ICRC Interpretive Guidance on Direct Participation in Hostilities: The End of Jus in Bello Proportionality as We Know It?' (2012) 45 Isr L Rev 35.

[113] See, eg, Human Rights Committee, *Suarez de Guerrero v Colombia*, UN Doc Supp No 40 (A/37/40), 9 April 1981, [13.2]–[13.3]; European Court of Human Rights (ECtHR), *McCann and others v UK*, App No 18984/91, 27 September 1995, [145]–[214]. See also UNGA, Report of the Special Rapporteur on Extrajudicial, Summary or Arbitrary Executions (Christof Heyns), A/68/382, 13 September 2013, [32]–[37].

[114] Kretzmer (n 10) 39.

[115] C Kreß, 'Some Reflections on the International Legal Framework Governing Transnational Armed Conflicts' (2010) 15 JCSL 245, 260–1.

1.4 Conclusions

This chapter has served two purposes. First, it has explored the general context within which the topic to be addressed in this book falls. As will become clear in subsequent chapters, whilst IHL contains procedural rules applicable to internment in international armed conflict, the relevant treaty provisions applicable in non-international armed conflict are silent on such matters. This is a specific manifestation of the general distinction drawn between the two categories of armed conflict. Second, this chapter has considered the reasons for and arguments against preserving the general distinction in IHL, enabling an informed discussion in later chapters of whether the distinction should be preserved with regard to the procedural regulation of internment. Importantly for our purposes, it was shown that the traditional view that eliminating the distinction between the two types of armed conflict was the most appropriate means of humanizing non-international conflicts is no longer necessarily valid, given the development of IHRL. Such considerations could have important consequences for the line of enquiry pursued in the present work and will be returned to in chapter 7 when considering the desirability of eliminating the distinction in this area. Before that, however, a full examination of the current *lex lata* is needed. This will begin in the next chapter with a consideration of the procedural rules applicable to internment in international armed conflict under IHL, so as to develop a frame of reference for judging the rules applicable in non-international conflicts in the subsequent chapters.

PART II

INTERNATIONAL HUMANITARIAN LAW

2
Internment in International Armed Conflict under IHL

The previous chapter introduced the context for this book by examining the historical basis of, as well as arguments in favour of and against, the distinction drawn in international humanitarian law (IHL) between international and non-international armed conflict. With that in mind, the present chapter introduces the focus of the current book, that is, the procedural rules applicable to internment. As noted in the introduction, 'procedural' in this sense is used in contradistinction to treatment standards and conditions of detention; the focus instead is on the deprivation of liberty itself. In particular, three categories of rules are explored, relating to the standard for internment (ie the grounds justifying internment), the availability of review procedures, and the point at which internment must cease. In so doing, the focus of this chapter is on the relevant rules that apply under IHL in international armed conflict. Given the view that, 'with regard to the law of war, states are bound by a reasonably robust set of procedural rules when they administratively detain [or "intern"] protected persons during international armed conflict',[1] it is important to examine what these rules are, in order to proceed in the next chapter to a comparison with the degree of regulation in non-international armed conflicts. As such, this chapter will create a frame of reference for subsequent chapters by elaborating on the categories of procedural rules which will be discussed throughout the book.

In addition, by examining the rules applicable to internment in international armed conflicts, any deficiencies therein can be highlighted. This is especially important for the discussion in chapter 7 regarding how the law of non-international armed conflict might appropriately be developed in this area. The previous chapter demonstrated that the traditional means by which the law of non-international armed conflict has developed has been to draw by analogy from the rules in international conflicts. Whether this should also be the case with regard to the procedural regulation of internment requires, first, examining the adequacy of those rules. Indeed, it will be argued that the claim that the procedural rules applicable in international conflicts are 'robust' significantly overstates

---

[1] AS Deeks, 'Administrative Detention in Armed Conflict' (2009) 40 Case W Res J Intl L 403, 414.

the case, for whilst the relevant IHL treaties do specify certain rules, they remain vague. For this reason, the elaboration of these treaty rules through practice will also be discussed, which will then be drawn on in chapter 7.

The present chapter will be structured according to the different categories of procedural rules in international armed conflict, exploring the standard for internment (section 2.2), the review process for challenging internment (section 2.3), and the point at which internment must cease (section 2.4). In each of these sections a comparison will be made between the different rules that apply to civilian and combatant internees.[2] These different rules regulating civilian and combatant internment are seen by some as disconnected.[3] It will, however, be shown that the same basic rule may be seen to underlie each internment regime,[4] such that internment is permitted only where necessary for security reasons.

The chapter will begin with an examination of the statuses of combatant and civilian in section 2.1. This is not only a necessary precursor to comparing the rules on internment applicable to each, but it will also provide further information for the discussion in the following chapters regarding the rules applicable in non-international conflicts and the degree to which the distinction between the two categories of armed conflict should be eliminated in this area.

2.1 Status

The law of international armed conflict differentiates between two key categories of protected persons, those of 'combatant' and 'civilian'.[5] For each, a separate set of rules exists, including those regulating internment. Each status will be examined in turn to consider who qualifies and, thus, which set of procedural rules on internment applies.

2.1.1 Combatants/POWs

The rules regulating the treatment of combatants are found in the Third Geneva Convention (GCIII) and Additional Protocol I (API). As Knut Ipsen explains, the primary status of combatant gives rise to the secondary status of prisoner of

---

[2] Retention of medical and religious personnel under Art 28 GCI and Art 37 GCII on the basis of the medical or spiritual needs of prisoners of war is outside the scope of the present book, not being 'internment' as defined above.

[3] LM Olson, 'Guantánamo Habeas Review: Are the D.C. District Court's Decisions Consistent with IHL Internment Standards' (2009) 42 Case W Res J Intl L 197, 202 (referring to 'the reasoning behind the basis for internment of prisoners of war under IHL' as 'unique' and not extending to civilians).

[4] The expression 'internment regime' is used throughout the book to describe the collection of procedural rules regulating the grounds, procedural safeguards, and end-points of internment.

[5] See, eg, Part III of API relating to combatants/POWs and Part IV of API relating to the civilian population. See also K Ipsen, 'Combatants and Non-Combatants' in D Fleck (ed), *The Handbook of International Humanitarian Law* (3rd edn OUP, Oxford 2013) 79.

war (POW) when the combatant falls into the power of the enemy.[6] Article 4 GCIII specifies upon whom POW status, and thus the protections of GCIII, are conferred. According to this provision, POWs are persons that have fallen into the power of the enemy and belong to one of the following:

1. The armed forces and the militias and volunteer corps forming part of the forces of a party to the conflict (Article 4A(1))
2. Other militias or volunteer corps belonging to a party to the conflict, where commanded by a person responsible for subordinates, wear a fixed, distinctive emblem, carry arms openly, and adhere to IHL (Article 4A(2))
3. Regular forces professing allegiance to an authority not recognized by the detaining power (Article 4A(3))
4. Non-members authorized to accompany the armed forces (Article 4A(4))
5. Members of crews of merchant marine and civil aircraft of the parties to the conflict where no greater protection is offered under international law (Article 4A(5))
6. Members of a *levée en masse* (Article 4A(6))

Article 4B GCIII specifies two further categories of persons to be *treated as* POWs:

7. Demobilized members of the armed forces of occupied territory, if the occupier considers it necessary to intern them, for example where they have attempted to rejoin the enemy forces, or where they do not comply with a summons for internment, so long as hostilities continue outside the occupied territory (Article 4B(1))
8. Those falling into one of the above categories who are in neutral or non-belligerent states and whom such states are obligated under international law to intern (Article 4B(2))

For those states that subsequently have ratified API, the rules on combatant/POW status have changed.[7] Article 44(1) states that the armed forces of a Party to a conflict are entitled to POW status where they fall into the hands of the enemy, with Article 43(1) API defining 'armed forces' as:

...all organized armed forces, groups and units which are under a command responsible to that Party for the conduct of its subordinates, even if that Party is represented by a government or an authority not recognized by an adverse Party. Such armed forces shall be subject to an internal disciplinary system which, *inter alia*, shall enforce compliance with the rules of international law applicable in armed conflict.

API thus brings regular armed forces, as well as organized groups and units, previously dealt with separately under Articles 4A(1) and (2) GCIII, under this

---

[6] Ipsen (n 5) 79.
[7] Y Dinstein, *The Conduct of Hostilities under the Law of International Armed Conflict* (2nd edn CUP, Cambridge 2010) 51.

single paragraph. The requirements for *all* such forces are now simply that they be organized, operate under a command responsible to a party to the conflict, and have an internal disciplinary system to enforce IHL.[8] Article 43(2) then confirms that members of the armed forces are combatants, and thus have a right to participate directly in hostilities; they cannot, therefore, be prosecuted for their mere participation in hostilities when acting in compliance with IHL ('combatant immunity').[9] These rules, together with those in GCIII, confirm that only those *lawfully* participating in hostilities (as opposed to civilians taking up arms) may be considered combatants and subject to internment as a POW.[10]

Finally, Article 44(3) API, after confirming that 'combatants are obliged to distinguish themselves from the civilian population while they are engaged in an attack or in a military operation preparatory to an attack', states that a combatant shall, nevertheless, retain his combatant status if he cannot so distinguish himself, as long as he carries his arms openly during each military engagement and when visible to the enemy whilst deploying for an attack. Article 44(4) then states that failure to honour these requirements shall lead to a forfeiture of POW status, although such persons 'shall, nevertheless, be given protections equivalent in all respects to those accorded to prisoners of war'. The requirement of a fixed, distinctive emblem for combatant/POW status, originally in Article 4A(2)(b) GCIII, has thus been relaxed by Article 44(3).[11] Yoram Dinstein argues that this change is to the detriment of the civilian population, for whom the principle of distinction is so essential.[12] However, Article 44(3)'s purpose was to bring the increasingly common phenomenon of guerilla warfare within the POW framework,[13] rather than to change the tradition of the wearing of uniforms by the regular state armed forces.[14]

It was this controversy regarding Article 44 API which was invoked by certain states, including the United States, as a reason for not ratifying API.[15] Indeed, the International Committee of the Red Cross (ICRC) noted how controversial this provision continues to be, preventing it, as yet, from crystallizing as custom.[16] Commentators too consider Article 44 API as binding only states parties.[17] Given

---

[8] Ipsen (n 5) 85.
[9] E Crawford, *The Treatment of Combatants and Insurgents under the Law of Armed Conflict* (OUP, Oxford 2010) 52–3. See the discussion on this in section 1.1.
[10] The issue of whether those participating in hostilities but not subject to POW status are protected elsewhere is discussed below in section 2.1.3.
[11] LC Green, *The Contemporary Law of Armed Conflict* (3rd edn Manchester University Press, Manchester 2008) 135.
[12] Dinstein (n 7) 53–4. Similarly, see GB Roberts, 'The New Rules for Waging War: The Case Against Ratification of Additional Protocol I' (1985–6) 26 VJIL 109, 129; AD Sofaer, 'The Rationale for the United States Decision' (1988) 82 AJIL 784, 786.
[13] Y Sandoz, C Swinarski, and B Zimmerman (eds), *Commentary on the Additional Protocols of 8 June 1977 to the Geneva Conventions of 12 August 1949* (ICRC/Martinus Nijhoff, Geneva 1987) 520–1.
[14] Art 44(7) API.   [15] Sofaer (n 12) 786.
[16] J-M Henckaerts and L Doswald-Beck, *Customary International Humanitarian Law Volume I: Rules* (CUP, Cambridge 2005) 387–9.
[17] Dinstein (n 7) 54–5. Similarly, see C Greenwood, 'The Law of War (International Humanitarian Law)' in MD Evans (ed), *International Law* (2nd edn OUP, Oxford 2006) 790.

that, unlike the 1949 Geneva Conventions, the Additional Protocols do not enjoy universal ratification, this has important consequences on the applicable law in particular conflicts.[18] Thus, as Christopher Greenwood has argued, whereas states parties to API are bound by the more relaxed requirements in Article 44, '[o]ther States continue to be bound by the stricter rule in the Hague Regulations and the Geneva POW Convention. The highly unsatisfactory result is that there are currently two different standards of what constitutes lawful combatancy'.[19]

2.1.2 Civilians

Whilst combatants are protected by GCIII, civilians are protected by the Fourth Geneva Convention (GCIV), together with API. Article 4 GCIV defines those protected by GCIV in negative terms,[20] that is, those that are in the hands of the enemy and are not protected by the first three Geneva Conventions. Further limitations, however, are placed on GCIV's application: first, it apparently only applies where the individual is in the hands of a party to the conflict of which they are not a national;[21] second, it only applies where the individual's national state is bound by the Convention;[22] third, it does not apply to nationals of neutral states in the territory of a belligerent state, and nationals of co-belligerent states, as long as their states maintain normal diplomatic relations with the state in whose hands they are.[23] GCIV consequently protects only a subset of what might normally be referred to as 'civilians'.[24]

Finally, even if an individual satisfies the conditions in Article 4 GCIV, they may be stripped of some of their rights under the Convention by virtue of the derogation provision in Article 5 GCIV. So as to examine this provision's relevance for the procedural rules applicable to civilian internment that are to be examined in the following sections, Article 5 GCIV is discussed at the end of this chapter in section 2.5.

2.1.3 A third category?—'unlawful combatants'

Before moving on to a discussion of the different categories of procedural rules applicable to civilian and combatant internment in international armed conflict, it

---

[18] As of 29 June 2015, 196 states are party to the 1949 Geneva Conventions, 174 are party to API, and 168 are party to APII: <https://www.icrc.org/applic/ihl/ihl.nsf/> accessed 7 July 2015.
[19] Greenwood (n 17) 790.
[20] It should be noted that GCIV does not define 'civilian' as such, but instead those persons protected by the Convention.
[21] Art 4(1) GCIV. The ICTY Appeals Chamber in *Prosecutor v Duško Tadić* (Appeals Judgment) ICTY-94-1-A (15 July 1999) at [166]–[169], however, stated that the drafting history and object and purpose of GCIV, together with the trend in modern warfare that now sees conflicts as being inter-*ethnic* rather than primarily inter-*state*, necessitate a reading of the test for the applicability of GCIV as being based not on nationality but allegiance.
[22] Art 4(2) GCIV.   [23] Art 4(2) GCIV.
[24] However, for convenience, and unless stated otherwise, reference to 'civilians' in the context of detention will mean persons protected by GCIV.

is worth briefly considering debates regarding a possible third category of persons under IHL—so-called 'unlawful combatants' or 'unprivileged belligerents'— who directly participate in hostilities without being entitled to combatant/POW status. This is important to the present discussion, for it raises the question of whether the legality of internment of such individuals is to be assessed under the regime for POWs in GCIII, civilians in GCIV, or neither. This debate was revived in light of the so-called 'war on terror' and resulting detentions at Guantánamo Bay, Cuba, by the US Department of Defence of those that the latter considered 'unlawful enemy combatants' (including members of the Taliban and al-Qaeda), falling outside both GCIII and GCIV.[25] In examining the status of the Taliban and al-Qaeda, Christopher Greenwood implied that they fall outside both GCIII and GCIV.[26] Dinstein similarly argued that, '[a] person who engages in military raids by night, while purporting to be an innocent civilian by day, is neither a civilian nor a lawful combatant. He is an unlawful combatant'.[27]

Such arguments, however, are difficult to reconcile with the text of the Geneva Conventions. As Knut Dörmann argues, the text makes it clear that no third category of person exists, since the scope of GCIV is defined negatively, as protecting those not protected by the other Conventions.[28] Moreover, given that Article 5 GCIV, examined below, was designed as a derogation provision for those individuals who may be characterized as unlawful combatants, it is clear that GCIV was intended to cover such persons.[29] Indeed, state practice, much of which has been in response to post-9/11 US detention practices, similarly confirms the non-existence of this alleged third category.[30] Thus, Emily Crawford notes that, '[g]iven the almost uniform resistance to US attempts to proclaim a "Geneva" status of "unlawful enemy combatant", it is doubtful such a legal category exists'.[31] Consequently, where not entitled to POW status, if its Article 4 conditions are met, an individual is protected by GCIV, albeit subject to Article 5 GCIV.[32]

---

[25] Crawford (n 9) 56–61; Ipsen (n 5) 83. The US' detention practice here is explored in detail in section 5.2.3.1.

[26] CJ Greenwood, 'International Law and the "War Against Terrorism"' (2002) 78 Intl Affairs 301, 316.

[27] Dinstein (n 7) 36. For a slightly different approach, see J Callen, 'Unlawful Combatants and the Geneva Conventions' (2004) 44 VJIL 1025 (arguing that GCIV applies to unlawful combatants in enemy territory but not to unlawful combatants on the battlefield, invoking the distinction drawn in RR Baxter, 'So-Called 'Unprivileged Belligerency': Spies, Guerrillas, and Saboteurs' (1951) 28 BYIL 323).

[28] K Dörmann, 'The Legal Situation of "Unlawful/Unprivileged Combatants"' (2003) 85 IRRC 45, 49.

[29] Ibid, 50.

[30] See, eg, PC Tange, 'Netherlands State Practice' (2007) 38 NYIL 263, 290; HCJ 769/02, *Public Committee Against Torture in Israel et al v The Government of Israel et al*, 57(6) PD 285 (Israel Supreme Court) [26]–[28]; *A and B v State of Israel*, CrimA 3261/08 (11 June 2008) (Israel Supreme Court) [12]; UK Ministry of Defence, *Joint Doctrine Publication 1-10: Captured Persons (CPERS)* (3rd edn, Ministry of Defence, Shrivenham 2015) 1–16 [141].

[31] Crawford (n 9) 60.

[32] Similarly, see JS Pictet (ed), *Commentary to Geneva Convention IV Relative to the Protection of Civilian Persons in Time of War* (ICRC, Geneva 1958) 51; Dörmann (n 28) 49; D Jinks, 'The Declining Significance of POW Status' (2004) 45 Harvard Intl LJ 367, 381–6; M Sassòli, 'The

2.2 Standard for Internment

Having discussed the different statuses under IHL, the procedural rules applicable to internment in international armed conflict can now be examined. These rules give content to the international crime of unlawful confinement, which constitutes a grave breach of GCIV.[33] As such, failure to observe them might, where the further conditions for the crime are met, entail the individual criminal responsibility of the perpetrator (in addition to the responsibility of the state).[34]

The first category of procedural rules to consider are those that specify in what circumstances a person may be interned. In exploring these, this section will look in turn at the grounds justifying civilian and combatant internment.

2.2.1 Civilians

GCIV represented the first IHL treaty on the protection of civilian persons. Prior to 1949, the only rules regarding when 'enemy' civilians could be interned were those found in custom and, as a result, they were unclear and susceptible to change in light of new practice.[35] For example, many writers during the early twentieth century considered customary international law to have developed so as to prohibit automatic internment of enemy nationals residing in a belligerent state's territory.[36] This was, to a large extent, a result of the gradual development in the preceding centuries of the notion that war represented a conflict between states and not between entire populations.[37] However, by virtue of compulsory military service during the First World War, together with the intricate networks of espionage and widespread public opinion in favour of detention (particularly in Britain, where mob violence against German nationals soon erupted), a change

---

Status of Persons Held in Guantánamo under International Humanitarian Law' (2004) 2 JICJ 96, 100–2; Crawford (n 9) 60–1.

[33] Art 147 GCIV.

[34] *Prosecutor v Dario Kordić and Mario Čerkez* (Appeals Judgment) ICTY-95-14/2 (17 December 2004) [69]–[70]; K Dörmann, *Elements of War Crimes under the Rome Statute of the International Criminal Court: Sources and Commentary* (CUP, Cambridge 2003) 112–23.

[35] See, eg, AS Hershey, 'Treatment of Enemy Aliens' (1918) 12 AJIL 156, 156 ('…there has never been a clearly defined rule of international law governing the treatment of enemy aliens').

[36] J Westlake, *International Law Part II: War* (CUP, Cambridge 1907) 42; AS Herschey, *Essentials of International Public Law* (Macmillan, New York 1912) 362; N Bentwich, 'International Law as Applied by England in the War: The Treatment of Alien Enemies' (1915) 9 AJIL 642, 646; JW Garner, 'Treatment of Enemy Aliens: Measures in Respect to Personal Liberty' (1918) 12 AJIL 27, 27. Cf other writers who took a slightly different view as to the relevant customary rule, instead considering it to require a belligerent state to allow resident enemy aliens the opportunity to leave the territory at the outbreak of war, based on the widespread practice of concluding treaties to that effect: see, eg, L Oppenheim, *International Law, A Treatise: Volume II, War and Neutrality* (Longmans, Green & Co, London 1906) 109; EJ Cohn, 'Legal Aspects of Internment' (1941) 4 MLR 200, 201.

[37] Westlake (n 36) 32–8; Bentwich (n 36) 646.

seemed to occur to the effect that general internment of resident enemy aliens, or at least those males subject to military service, was considered acceptable (and apparently even necessary for their protection).[38] In the UK, for example, a general policy of internment, particularly of the adult male German population, was adopted in May 1915, with an 'internment committee', presided over by a High Court judge, established to hear appeals by enemy aliens against their internment.[39] By the Second World War, it was suggested that no custom restricted states in this area.[40] In the UK, the authority to detain enemy aliens was seen as an element of the royal prerogative and, as in the United States, was considered unfettered by both international law and domestic judicial control.[41] This trend towards a more permissive view of international law during the first half of the twentieth century was described clearly by Georg Schwarzenberger soon after the end of the Second World War:

There was a tendency in the nineteenth century to draw a dividing line between civilians and the armed forces and to leave the former as much as possible undisturbed. The development, however, since the First World War tends to revert to the original practice of identifying the individual with his home State... Civilians who are resident in the country of a belligerent and are of enemy nationality may, therefore, be interned like prisoners of war, or be subjected to other restrictions, as may be required in the interest of national security.[42]

In light of this precarious position in which civilians found themselves by the end of the Second World War, the drafting of GCIV and its rules regulating civilian internment were an important, progressive development.

GCIV deals separately with the protection of civilians in the territory of a party to the conflict (Part III, Section II of GCIV) and those in occupied territory (Part III, Section III of GCIV), establishing for each slightly different rules on

---

[38] Bentwich (n 36) 646–7; Garner (n 36); Hershey (n 35). In the 1921 edition of *Oppenheim*, Roxburgh, whilst noting the policy of general internment during the First World War, continues the previous editions' claims regarding custom noted above at n 36: R Roxburgh, *Oppenheim's International Law, A Treatise: Volume II, War and Neutrality* (3rd edn Longman's, Green & Co, London 1921) 147–8 (on the state of custom) and 149 (on contrary practice during the First World War).
[39] Garner (n 36) 40–2. The committee was discussed, and the Order authorizing internment of enemy aliens declared valid by the House of Lords in *R v Halliday ex p Zadig* [1917] AC 260.
[40] Cohn (n 36) 202 ('...it is safe to assume that international law as such does not contain any rule which renders the wholesale arrest and internment of the resident enemy alien population clearly illegal...').
[41] *Liversidge v Anderson* [1942] AC 206; *R v Bottrill, ex p Kuechenmeister* [1946] 2 All ER 434; *Netz v Chuter Ede* [1946] 1 All ER 628 (UK); *Minotto v Bradley* (1918) 252 Fed 600 (US); M Brandon, 'Legal Control over Resident Enemy Aliens in Time of War in the United States and in the United Kingdom' (1950) 44 AJIL 382, 384–5.
[42] G Schwarzenberger, *A Manual of International Law* (Stevens & Sons, London 1947) 80. Interestingly, in the 1940 edition of *Oppenheim*, Lauterpacht, now also noting this practice during the Second World War of general internment, continued to reiterate the view of custom from the first and second editions: H Lauterpacht, *Oppenheim's International Law, A Treatise: Volume II, War and Neutrality* (6th edn Longman's, Green & Co, London 1940) 247 (on the state of custom) and 249 (on practice during the Second World War).

internment (Articles 41–3 and 78, respectively). The basic norm governing all civilian internments, however, is found in Article 27(4) GCIV, which states that 'the Parties to the conflict may take such measures of control and security in regard to protected persons as may be necessary as a result of the war'. Article 41 GCIV notes that internment is the most severe measure of control permissible, which can only be resorted to where the grounds and procedures in Articles 42–3 or 78 GCIV are adhered to. Thus, Article 27(4) may be seen as establishing the authority to intern civilians, with Articles 41–3 and 78 giving content to this authorization and detailing the limits thereof.[43] This is confirmed in the jurisprudence of the International Criminal Tribunal for the former Yugoslavia (ICTY):

Article 41... specifies that the internment of civilians is the most severe measure of control permitted under Article 27, paragraph 4, of the Convention. However, such extreme measures are subject to strict conditions, primarily set out in Articles 42 and 43 of Geneva Convention IV.[44]

In the Israeli Supreme Court's words, '[t]hese parameters create a "zone" of situations—a kind of "zone of reasonableness"—within which the military commander may act'.[45]

Regarding the grounds for internment, Article 42(1) stipulates that civilian internment in the territory of a party to the conflict is permitted, 'only if the security of the Detaining Power makes it absolutely necessary', whilst Article 78(1) permits internment in occupied territory only where the 'Occupying Power considers it necessary, for imperative reasons of security'. The ICRC Commentary argues that the phrase 'imperative reasons of security' indicates that internment in occupied territory 'should be even more exceptional than it is inside the territory of the Parties to the conflict'.[46] However, it is not clear why this should be the case; indeed, the reference to 'absolute' necessity in Article 42(1) could equally suggest a more stringent test. Moreover, Article 78(1) permits internment where the detaining power *considers* it necessary, whereas Article 42(1) does so only where it *is* necessary. The ordinary meaning of this additional word in Article 78(1) would suggest that, whilst in occupied territory the test for necessity of internment is self-judging, in the territory of a party to the conflict it is objective, ie internment must *actually* be necessary for security reasons.[47]

---

[43] Pictet, *GCIV* (n 32) 207; H-P Gasser and K Dörmann, 'Protection of the Civilian Population' in D Fleck (ed), *The Handbook of International Humanitarian Law* (3rd edn OUP, Oxford 2013) 283; *Prosecutor v Zejnil Delalić et al* (Trial Judgment) ICTY-96-21 (16 November 1998) [574]; *Prosecutor v Dario Kordić and Mario Čerkez* (Trial Judgment) ICTY-95-14/2-T (26 February 2001) [281]–[283]; *A and B v Israel* (n 30) [17].
[44] *Kordić and Čerkez* (n 43) [283]. Similarly see *Delalić* (n 43) [574].
[45] HCJ 7015/02 and 7019/02, *Ajuri and others v IDF Commander in the West Bank, IDF Commander in the Gaza Strip and others* [2002] 125 ILR 537, [29].
[46] Pictet, *GCIV* (n 32) 367.
[47] Suggesting the objective nature of the test in Article 42(1), see *Prosecutor v Zejnil Delalić et al* (Appeals Judgment) ICTY-96-21-A (20 February 2001) [320] ('...the involuntary confinement of a civilian where the security of the Detaining Power does not make this absolutely necessary will be unlawful.') Similar *a contrario* reasoning to that applied here has been adopted in other areas of international law: see, eg, *Case Concerning Military and Paramilitary Activities in and*

Notwithstanding the difference in language between Articles 42 and 78 GCIV, it is clear that these standards share two key elements: first, the individual in question must pose a threat to the detaining power's security; second, that threat must have reached the point of rendering internment of that particular individual necessary (whether actually or in the view of the detaining power), such that the threat cannot be avoided by a less restrictive measure:

> ...the relevant norms of international humanitarian law have been developed such that only absolute necessity, based on the requirements of State security, can justify recourse to these measures [ie internment], and only then if security cannot be safeguarded by other, less severe means.[48]

It will be noticed that the above two elements are expressed in terms of the particular individual. This is because civilian internment can never be taken as a collective measure. As the ICTY has held, internment is 'to be taken only after careful consideration of each individual case. Such measures are never to be taken on a collective basis'.[49] Notwithstanding support for this view,[50] the issue is not without controversy, however. The ICRC Commentary to Article 42 GCIV, for example, states that 'a belligerent may intern people or place them in assigned residence if it has serious and legitimate reason to think that they are members of organizations whose object is to cause disturbances'.[51] This might be read as to suggest that civilian internment may be based solely on membership of certain organizations, without the need for an *individual* threat determination. The text of Articles 42 and 78 GCIV sheds no light on this question, for nothing in either provision reveals whether or not the drafters intended collective decisions to be permissible. The *travaux* also offers little help here, with different delegations at the 1949 diplomatic conference taking different views. On the one hand, the United States argued strongly in favour of the permissibility of collective internment, with the initial review procedure (to be examined below) providing the opportunity to correct any mistakes.[52] Other delegations, however, opposed this as they were concerned with the risks it posed of mass, arbitrary internment.[53] It is

---

Against Nicaragua (Nicaragua v United States) (Merits) [1986] ICJ Rep 14, [222] (comparing the self-judging provision in Article XXI of the GATT with the objective test in Article XXI of the 1956 FCN Treaty between the United States and Nicaragua). Similarly, see D Akande and S Williams, 'International Adjudication on National Security Issues: What Role for the WTO?' (2003) 43 VJIL 365, 388 (following the ICJ's suggestion in the aforementioned case as to the self-judging nature of Article XXI GATT).

[48] *Delalić* (n 43) [571].
[49] *Delalić* (n 43) [578]. Similarly, see *Kordić and Čerkez* (n 43) [285]; *Prosecutor v Milorad Krnojelac* (Trial Judgment) ICTY-97-25 (15 March 2002) [123]; HCJ 3239/02, *Mar'ab et al v IDF Commander of Judea and Samaria et al*, 57(2) PD 349, [23] (Israel Supreme Court); *A and B v Israel* (n 30) [18]–[19]; Pictet, *GCIV* (n 32) 258; J Pejic, 'Procedural Principles and Safeguards for Internment/Administrative Detention in Armed Conflict and Other Situations of Violence' (2005) 87 IRRC 375, 381.
[50] See above at n 49.   [51] Pictet, *GCIV* (n 32) 258.
[52] *Final Record of the Diplomatic Conference of Geneva of 1949: Vol III* (ICRC, 1963) 126.
[53] *Final Record of the Diplomatic Conference of Geneva of 1949: Vol II, Section A* (ICRC, 1963) 756 (Italy and Austria).

submitted that this latter view (which is consistent with the ICTY's interpretation of these provisions) is the more accurate, as more in keeping with the object and purpose of these rules, which seek to give content to the basic principle in Article 27(4) GCIV, permitting internment only where *necessary* as a result of the war.[54] Collective internment is likely to undermine this principle by increasing the possibility of detention of individuals that pose no security threat themselves and for whom internment is therefore unnecessary.

It may reasonably be argued that internment on the basis of status and internment on the basis of individual security threat are not necessarily incompatible, for being a member of an armed organization could in itself render one a security threat.[55] However, permitting pure status-based internment under GCIV would leave the detaining state free to define the parameters of internment, for it would likely be that state which determines what constitutes 'membership' of the particular organization (and what constitutes the organization itself).[56] Indeed, these issues have arisen with regard to the US' post-9/11 military operations against al-Qaeda.[57] It is submitted that a reasonable compromise might be based on the Israeli Supreme Court's approach to this question in *A and B v Israel*.[58] Here, the Court stated that a domestic law permitting administrative security detention should be interpreted 'with reference to the security purpose of the law and in accordance with the constitutional principles and international humanitarian law...*which require the proof of an individual threat as a ground for administrative detention*'.[59] Where an individual is a member of a terrorist organization, the Court stated that 'we should consider the detainee's connection and the nature of his contribution to the cycle of hostilities of the organization in the broad sense of this concept'.[60] Whilst recognizing the importance of status/membership, the Court therefore made clear that the state is not free to define membership and then detain accordingly, but must consider the individual's role within the organization and whether that role renders them a security threat.[61] In this sense, membership or status is not the end in itself, but rather a means for determining whether the individual truly does pose such a security threat as to render their internment necessary.

The discussion above demonstrates that the parameters of the internment authority under IHL are controversial. This arises in large part from the

---

[54] See above, text to n 43.
[55] Indeed, as is shown below, that assumption underpins combatant internment: see section 2.2.2.
[56] The difficulties with applying status-based internment to non-state armed groups are explored in detail in chapter 7.
[57] N Lubell, 'The War (?) Against Al-Qaeda' in E Wilmshurst (ed), *International Law and the Classification of Conflicts* (OUP, Oxford 2012) 424–8.
[58] *A and B v Israel* (n 30).   [59] Ibid, [21] (emphasis added).   [60] Ibid.
[61] Though the Israeli law under interpretation also contained a (rebuttable) presumption of the necessity of internment for members of hostile forces fighting against Israel, which cannot be consistent with the need to demonstrate necessity for the duration of the internment: E Debuf, *Captured in War: Lawful Internment in Armed Conflict* (Editions A Pedone/Hart, Paris/Oxford 2013) 357–8.

indeterminacy of the GCIV internment standards and their broad nature. As noted above, Articles 42(1) and 78(1) contain two common elements: first, the individual must pose a threat to the detaining power's security; second, internment must be the only means (or, in occupied territory, be considered the only means) of protecting against that threat. Regarding the first element, the ICTY has conceded that '"[s]ecurity"...does not appear susceptible to more concrete definition. The measure of activity deemed prejudicial to the...security of the State...is left largely to the authorities of that State itself'.[62] The Appeals Chamber has gone further and argued that some deference to the state is *appropriate*, leaving a certain degree of discretion in determining what constitutes a threat to its own security.[63] To an extent, this is true. The state and its military commanders should be well-informed regarding security threats and are, thus, arguably well placed to make decisions on the necessity of an internment. Moreover, attempting to develop a definition of 'security' *in abstracto* would be doomed to failure, as any such definition would be either under- or overinclusive, omitting certain characteristics that may reasonably be considered a security threat, or avoiding such omissions by casting a net so wide as to capture those not reasonably considered a threat.

Nevertheless, the ICTY has offered some general comments on what is required by these provisions, stating that 'the party must have good reason to think that the person concerned, by his activities, knowledge or qualifications, represents a real threat to its present or future security'.[64] More specifically:

Subversive activity carried on inside the territory of a party to the conflict, or actions which are of direct assistance to an opposing party, may threaten the security of the former, which may, therefore, intern people or place them in assigned residence if it has *serious and legitimate reasons* to think that they may seriously prejudice its security by means such as sabotage or espionage.[65] (emphasis in original)

Little more, however, can be said about the GCIV standards *in abstracto*. Rather, preference in jurisprudence appears to be for a case-by-case assessment.[66] The Israeli Supreme Court, for example, has stated that, 'it is not possible to define the nature of such a [threat] precisely and exhaustively, and the matter will be examined on a case by case basis according to the circumstances'.[67] Indeed, states have similarly not elaborated a clear list of circumstances justifying internment.[68] Instead, the tendency is to quote verbatim from the open standards from Articles 42(1) and 78(1) GCIV in military manuals, listing examples of situations in

---

[62] *Delalić* (n 43) [574]. Similarly, see *Kordić and Čerkez* (n 43) [284]; Pictet, *GCIV* (n 32) 257; Olson (n 3) 203–4; Y Dinstein, *The International Law of Belligerent Occupation* (CUP, Cambridge 2009) 172.
[63] *Delalić* (n 47) [323].
[64] *Delalić* (n 43) [577]. This standard was originally included in Pictet, *GCIV* (n 32) at 257–8 and has been adopted in the UK's Ministry of Defence, *The Manual of the Law of Armed Conflict* (OUP, Oxford 2004) at 230.
[65] *Delalić* (n 43) [576]. [66] See, eg, the cases at ibid, [1133].
[67] *A and B v Israel* (n 30) [21]. [68] Debuf (n 61) 370–7.

which internment would be justified only in particular operations, with such lists remaining outside the public domain.[69]

It is important to note that this difficulty with defining 'security' *in abstracto* is not limited to IHL, but exists in many areas of international law by virtue of the ubiquity of state security considerations and the inclusion of security exception clauses in many treaties, itself a consequence of the fact that such matters are intimately connected with the concept of the sovereign state.[70] We may, therefore, make reference to these other areas when addressing the issue at hand. Dapo Akande and Sope Williams, for example, when discussing national security exceptions under the General Agreement on Tariffs and Trade, refer to the jurisprudence of the ICJ, European Court of Human Rights (ECtHR) and European Court of Justice (ECJ) that addresses similar national security exceptions. Akande and Williams emphasize that these tribunals address separately the questions of whether security interests are engaged and the necessity of the measures adopted, with the result that, whilst deference is given to the state in defining what constitutes a threat to its security, the necessity element is an objective standard susceptible to judicial review.[71] The same approach might be adopted here, with the necessity element of the GCIV internment standards acting as a counter to the subjective security element. This approach is useful even regarding the necessity test in Article 78 GCIV, which, as was noted above, appears to be self-judging, for as Akande and Williams argue, under such provisions the state must nonetheless *actually* consider such a measure necessary for its security.[72]

In addition, notwithstanding the difficulty in defining the GCIV internment standards *in abstracto*, practice and doctrine have confirmed certain limits on states' internment authority. First, as the text of these provisions makes clear, internment must never be used as a punishment for past acts, but only where necessary to prevent a present or future security threat arising.[73] Second, as noted, the ICTY has confirmed that internment must be based on an individual threat determination.[74] This requirement not only limits in itself the internment powers conferred by GCIV, but it also helps to explain a number of further, more specific limits that have been recognized. To this end, the ICTY has confirmed a third limit, that simply being 'a national of, or aligned with, an enemy

---

[69] For examples where military doctrine merely quotes the GCIV standards, see US Army Field Manual, *FM 27-10: The Law of Land Warfare* (Department of the Army, Washington, DC 1956) 110 [281]; US Army Regulation 190–8, *Enemy Prisoners of War, Retained Personnel, Civilian Internees and Other Detainees* (Departments of the Army, Navy, Air Force and Marine Corps, Washington, DC 1997) s 5-1(b); Canada, *Joint Doctrine Manual: Law of Armed Conflict at the Operational and Tactical Levels* (Office of the Judge Advocate General, Ottawa, 2001) 11–7 [1125]; UK Ministry of Defence, *Joint Doctrine Publication 1-10* (n 30) 1–16 [142].

[70] HL Schloemann and S Ohlhoff, '"Constitutionalization" and Dispute Settlement in the WTO: National Security as an Issue of Competence' (1999) 93 AJIL 424, 443–4.

[71] Akande and Williams (n 47) 382–3, citing, inter alia, ECJ, *Commission v Spain* [1999] ECR I-5585; ECtHR, *Smith & Grady v United Kingdom* (2000) 29 EHRR 493.

[72] Akande and Williams (n 47) 389–90.

[73] *A and B v Israel* (n 30) [22]; Pejic (n 49) 381; Debuf (n 61) 322–6.

[74] See above, text to n 49.

party cannot be considered as threatening the security of the opposing party... and is not, therefore, a valid reason for interning him'.[75] This is now recognized as a restriction on internment authority under IHL in state practice.[76] For the same reason, the ICTY has also confirmed a fourth limit, that merely being of military age cannot justify internment.[77] Fifth, there is both academic and judicial support for the view that intelligence value alone is insufficient to warrant internment; simply because an individual has knowledge of an act to be committed by another person that *would* constitute a security threat, does not render *that knowledge itself* a threat.[78] Sixth, political or religious opinions and practices should not be considered sufficient to constitute a security threat permitting internment; only where translated into action that does constitute such a threat could internment be justified.[79] Seventh, practice has also confirmed that the internment of persons solely as 'bargaining chips' for negotiating the release of prisoners held by the opposing side is impermissible and constitutes the proscribed act of hostage taking.[80]

Finally, it is clear that the security basis for internment must have a nexus to the armed conflict. The basic principle underpinning Articles 42 and 78 GCIV confirms this. As noted, this principle, found in Article 27(4) GCIV, permits states to take such measures of control 'as may be necessary as a result of the war'; acts of individuals which have no link to the armed conflict cannot, therefore, justify internment for it would not be 'necessary *as a result of the war*'.[81] Indeed, in other areas too it is clear that one cannot rely on the laws of armed conflict as a basis for particular actions unless those actions have a nexus to the armed conflict. For example, in the context of considering what constitutes 'direct participation in

---

[75] *Delalić* (n 43) [577]; *Delalić* (n 47) [327]; *Kordić and Čerkez* (n 43) [284]. Similarly, see Pictet, *GCIV* (n 32) 258; Eritrea Ethiopia Claims Commission (EECC), *Civilians Claims, Ethiopia's Claim 5 (Ethiopia/Eritrea)*, Partial Award, 17 December 2004, 135 ILR 427, [102]–[104].
[76] UK Ministry of Defence (n 64) 230. Similarly, see US, *Act on Restitution for World War II Internment of Japanese-Americans and Aleuts* (1988), s 1989a. There do, however, remain apparent instances of internment solely on the basis of nationality: see, eg, F Hampson, 'The Geneva Conventions and the Detention of Civilians and Alleged Prisoners of War' [1991] PL 507; G Risius, 'Prisoners of War in the United Kingdom' and B Walsh, 'Detention and Deportation of Foreign Nationals in the United Kingdom during the Gulf Conflict' in P Rowe (ed), *The Gulf War 1990–91 in International and English Law* (Routledge, Oxford 1993).
[77] *Delalić* (n 43) [577]; *Kordić and Čerkez* (n 43) [284]; Pictet, *GCIV* (n 32) 258. Although cf EECC, *Civilians Claims, Eritrea's Claims 15, 16, 23 and 27–32 (Eritrea/Ethiopia)*, Partial Award, 17 December 2004, 135 ILR 374, [115]–[117].
[78] *Hamdi et al v Rumsfeld et al*, 542 US 507 (2004), 521 (US Supreme Court); Pejic (n 49) 380; T Davidson and K Gibson, 'Experts Meeting on Security Detention Report' (2009) 40 Case W Res J Intl L 323, 343–4.
[79] Similarly, see Israel, Ministry of Justice, Fact Sheet on Administrative Detention (2003) 3, cited in Debuf (n 61) 406; Sandoz et al (n 13) 871.
[80] See, eg, the development in the Israeli Supreme Court's case law from ADA 10/94, *Anonymous v Minister of Defence*, 53(1) PD 97 (holding that Lebanese nationals could be interned as bargaining chips in negotiations with Hezbollah) to CFH 7048/97, *Anonymous v Minister of Defence*, 54(1) PD 721, 742 (holding that such internment is unlawful and amounts to hostage-taking), both cited in Dinstein (n 62) 153. On the illegality of hostage-taking under IHL, see common Art 3 GCI–IV; Art 34 GCIV; Pejic (n 49) 380 (fn 20).
[81] Similarly, see Debuf (n 61) 314.

hostilities' by civilians, at which point they become lawful targets,[82] the ICRC has emphasized the need for a 'belligerent nexus':

> ...armed violence which is not designed to harm a party to an armed conflict, or which is not designed to do so in support of another party, cannot amount to any form of 'participation' in hostilities taking place between these parties...such violence...must be addressed through law enforcement measures.[83]

More fundamentally, the ICTY Appeals Chamber has employed a notion that is similar to belligerent nexus in its treatment of the geographical scope of application of IHL; in determining whether actions beyond the traditional battlefield fall under the purview of IHL, the question is thus whether an armed conflict exists and whether the particular act to be regulated occurs in relation to that armed conflict.[84] The same principle of belligerent nexus can be applied here, *mutatis mutandis*, to limit the situations that can be considered a security threat necessitating internment.

It is therefore clear that, whilst Articles 42 and 78 GCIV specify the grounds on which civilians protected by GCIV may be interned, these provisions leave considerable discretion to the detaining state. Certain limits on states' detention authority, however, can be discerned from practice. Whilst the remaining indeterminacy of the detention standards leaves room for arbitrary decisions by the detaining power, two points must be borne in mind. First, as noted, having a pre-determined, exhaustive list of circumstances in which internment is justified would risk being either over- or under-inclusive. Second, it will be shown below that GCIV recognizes this initial discretion left to states and provides a safeguard in the form of review to help remedy mistakes. Whether this *post hoc* remedy is sufficient to counter the risks posed to the civilian population arising from the discretion left to states will be discussed below.

2.2.2 Combatants

POWs have always been in a precarious position. Historically subject to summary execution, the principles underpinning the contemporary framework on the protection of POWs developed in the seventeenth and eighteenth centuries, as it became accepted that captured enemies were held on behalf of the state rather than by the individual captor.[85] Prior to the nineteenth century, however, long-term internment of enemy combatants was the exception rather than the rule; instead, captured enemy combatants were often either induced into joining the

---

[82] Art 51(3) API and Art 13(3) APII.
[83] N Melzer, *Interpretive Guidance on the Notion of Direct Participation in Hostilities under International Humanitarian Law* (ICRC, Geneva 2009) 59.
[84] *Prosecutor v Kunarac et al* (Appeals Judgment) IT-96-23&23/1 (12 June 2002) [55]–[60]. Similarly, see N Lubell and N Derejko, 'A Global Battlefield? Drones and the Geographical Scope of Armed Conflict' (2013) 11 JICJ 65.
[85] GIAD Draper, 'The Geneva Conventions of 1949' (1965) 114 *RdC* 59, 101; HS Levie, *Prisoners of War in International Armed Conflict* (Intl L Stud Vol 59, US Naval War College, Newport 1978) 5.

detaining power's forces, released on parole, or exchanged on a 'man-for-man' and 'grade-for-grade' basis.[86] As these methods of dealing with captured enemy combatants became rarer, due, for example to the inability to conclude agreements on exchange (as was the case regarding Britain and France in the French Revolutionary Wars), indefinite internment was increasingly used, necessitating rules on the treatment of POWs.[87] It was not until the mid-nineteenth century that the codification of the rules regulating their treatment began (and indeed the codification of the law of armed conflict more generally),[88] with the Third Geneva Convention of 1949 and Additional Protocol I embodying the current legal framework. Even since 1949, however, POWs have been 'continually subjected to poor treatment, abuse and were genuinely used as political tools in a global ideological struggle'.[89] It has been argued that, whilst historically it was disadvantageous to be considered a POW, lest one be subjected to lengthy internment, the First World War saw a shift in this regard as a result of the abuses committed against civilians together with the development of protections for POWs.[90] In light of the adoption of GCIV, the first IHL treaty on the protection of civilians, this preference for POW status is arguably less clear now, the exception being for those participating in hostilities who wish to claim combatant immunity, a privilege to which only lawful combatants/POWs are entitled.[91]

The differences between the GCIII and GCIV internment regimes illustrate this point well. As argued above, GCIV permits the internment of civilians only if the particular civilian poses a security threat rendering internment necessary, requiring an *individual* threat determination (typically shown by conduct).[92] GCIII, on the other hand, permits internment of enemy forces by virtue of their *status* as combatants ('status-based internment'), with no requirement of an individual threat determination. This is seen in Article 21(1) GCIII, which confers the power to intern combatants on parties to international armed conflicts, stating that, '[t]he Detaining Power may subject prisoners of war to internment'; it was shown in section 2.1.1 that enemy combatants become POWs (and thus subject to internment) when they fall into the hands of the opposing forces, without any further requirement of an individual threat determination.[93] Notwithstanding

---

[86] SC Neff, 'Prisoners of War in International Law: The Nineteenth Century' in S Scheipers (ed), *Prisoners in War* (OUP, Oxford 2010).
[87] Ibid, 62.
[88] See, eg, Project of an International Declaration concerning the Laws and Customs of War (Brussels, 27 August 1874), arts 23–34, in D Schindler and J Toman, *The Laws of Armed Conflicts* (Martinus Nijhoff, The Hague 1988) 22. Although the Brussels Declaration never came into force, its provisions influenced subsequent codifications that did come into force: Levie (n 85) 8.
[89] S Carvin, 'Caught in the Cold: International Humanitarian Law and Prisoners of War During the Cold War' (2006) 11 JCSL 67, 67.
[90] R Stone, 'American-German Conference on Prisoners of War' (1919) 13 AJIL 406, 436. Though others argue that, notwithstanding *legal* standards for treatment developing, *actual* treatment standards for POWs during the First World War were much worse than is commonly thought: AR Kramer, 'Prisoners in the First World War' in S Scheipers (ed), *Prisoners in War* (OUP, Oxford 2010).
[91] Jinks (n 32) (demonstrating that the traditional preference for POW status is declining).
[92] Section 2.2.1.   [93] Arts 4 GCIII and 43 API.

this difference between the civilian and combatant internment regimes, however, it is submitted that both are premised on the same rule that permits internment only where necessary as a result of the war (ie for security reasons). Section 2.2.1 explained that the basis for civilian internment is found in Article 27(4) GCIV, permitting measures of control and security that are necessary as a result of the war. It was shown that the internment standards in Articles 42 and 78 build upon this provision, permitting internment only where necessary to prevent a present or future security threat arising. Similarly, with combatants (ie those listed in Articles 4A(1), (2), (3), and (6) GCIII and Article 43 API), '[t]he purpose of captivity is to exclude enemy soldiers from further military operations... [P]risoners of war shall only be considered as captives detained for reasons of security'.[94] Hence, combatants are interned on the same basis as civilians, that is, where necessary to prevent a security threat arising. With civilians, the existence of such a threat must be established on a case-by-case basis; with combatants, that risk is assumed to exist by virtue of their status, given that they may rejoin hostilities if released. Indeed, as explained in chapter 1, this same assumption of threat posed by the *group* similarly underpins the status-based approach to the targeting of combatants.[95]

It must be noted, however, that GCIII permits internment of persons as POWs that are not combatants and thus for whom the above argument would not seem to apply. Section 2.1.1 explored those categories of persons that qualify for POW status and are thus subject to internment under Article 21(1) GCIII. These should be compared with the following definition of 'civilian' for the purposes of targeting in Article 50(1) API:

A civilian is any person who does not belong to one of the categories of persons referred to in Article 4 A (1), (2), (3) and (6) of the Third [Geneva] Convention and in Article 43 of this Protocol [ie combatants].

Read alongside GCIII, Article 50(1) API demonstrates that there is a point at which the statuses of combatant and POW diverge, with those persons falling within Articles 4A(4) and 4A(5) qualifying as POWs, subject to internment *ipso facto*, but not as combatants. It is worth quoting these provisions in full. Article 4A(4) confers POW status on:

Persons who accompany the armed forces without actually being members thereof, such as civilian members of military aircraft crews, war correspondents, supply contractors, members of labour units or of services responsible for the welfare of the armed forces, provided that they have received authorization from the armed forces which they

---

[94] H Fischer, 'Protection of Prisoners of War' in D Fleck (ed), *The Handbook of International Humanitarian Law* (2nd edn OUP, Oxford 2008) 372. Similarly, see Oppenheim (n 36) 131; Stone (n 90) 414; L Doswald-Beck, 'Introduction: Background Paper' in The University Centre for International Humanitarian Law, 'Expert Meeting on the Supervision of the Lawfulness of Detention During Armed Conflict' (Geneva, 24–5 July 2004) 2 <http://www.geneva-academy.ch/docs/expert-meetings/2004/4rapport_detention.pdf> accessed 29 July 2015; Dinstein (n 7) 34–5.
[95] See section 1.3.2.

accompany, who shall provide them for that purpose with an identity card similar to the annexed model.

Article 4A(5) further confers POW status on:

Members of crews, including masters, pilots and apprentices, of the merchant marine and the crews of civil aircraft of the Parties to the conflict, who do not benefit by more favourable treatment under any other provisions of international law.

Unlike the other categories of POW, those falling into the above two categories are not members of opposing armed forces and thus do not pose the risk of rejoining hostilities if released. The question therefore arises as to why GCIII permits internment of such individuals. Regarding Article 4A(4), it appears that those falling within this provision were included in the POW category solely to ensure that such persons benefit from the protections in GCIII applicable to POWs. Indeed, given that such persons accompany the armed forces, there is an increased risk of their internment along with those forces; Article 4A(4) merely recognized this fact and brought them within the protective POW regime.[96] This interpretation is supported by the *travaux* of this provision, with the ICRC delegate at the 1949 diplomatic conference explaining that draft Article 4A(4) 'was designed to extend the *protection* of the Convention to the new units to which modern warfare had given rise, such as welfare units'.[97] This is not to suggest that the other categories of POWs listed under Article 4 GCIII were not also included in part for the purpose of extending the protections of GCIII to them; like IHL generally, GCIII contains both protective rules and permissive rules, such that those labelled as POWs are both exposed to the risk of very lengthy internment but also protected by the detailed rules in GCIII. The point being made, however, is that, whilst many of those under Article 4 GCIII are subject to internment due to their perceived security threat, but then also enjoy the protections of the Convention, those falling within Article 4A(4) pose no security threat and thus were included *solely* in order to offer them the protections of the Convention, on the assumption that they would also be interned. This interpretation would also seem to apply to Article 4B(2), which, as noted, requires neutral or non-belligerent powers to treat as POWs any person falling in another paragraph of Article 4 GCIII who is on their territory and whom they are required to intern under international law.[98]

---

[96] Levie (n 85) 60–2. Indeed, this would seem to be the interpretation in *Oppenheim* of Art 13 of the 1907 Hague Convention IV Respecting the Laws and Customs of War on Land (adopted 18 October 1907, entered into force 26 January 2010) 205 CTS (1907) 277–98, on which Art 4A(4) GCIII was partly based: Oppenheim (n 36) 133.
[97] *Final Record: Vol II-A* (n 53) 238 (emphasis added).
[98] Demonstrating that this provision was adopted with a view to extending the protections of GCIII, see JS Pictet (ed), *Commentary to Geneva Convention III Relative to the Treatment of Prisoners of War* (ICRC, Geneva 1960) 70. It is Article 11 of Hague Convention V of 1907, requiring a neutral state to intern troops that enter its territory to avoid capture by the enemy, to which Art 4B(2) GCIII refers when speaking of an obligation to intern under international law: see Levie (n 85) 68–9. Internment under Art 4B(1) GCIII, on the other hand, which similarly calls for certain

Indeed, this provision was necessitated by the practice of certain states during the Second World War that refused to extend POW status to such persons.[99]

Regarding Article 4A(5), which also labels as POWs, and thus subject to internment *ipso facto*, certain persons that are not entitled to combatant status, this can in fact be reconciled with the argument that internment is permitted only where necessary for security reasons. This is because merchant seamen had been known in the past to participate in military operations, posing a security threat to the opposing power.[100] The assumption underlying Article 4A(5) is still, therefore, that the persons subject thereto pose a security threat necessitating internment, with the protections of GCIII then applying to those internees.

2.3 Review of Internment

Having explored the rules relating to when internment may occur in international armed conflict, this section will now consider those governing the review of internment. Again, it will look in turn at the relevant rules applicable to civilians and combatants.

2.3.1 Civilians

Once a civilian protected by GCIV has been interned, that Convention specifies that they must enjoy both an initial review of the internment decision as well as periodic reviews thereafter, should internment continue. Each type of review will be examined in turn.

2.3.1.1 Initial review

For internees that are held by a party to the conflict in its own territory, Article 43(1) GCIV requires that the internee be entitled to have the internment decision 'reconsidered as soon as possible by an appropriate court or administrative board designated by the Detaining Power for that purpose'. For those interned in occupied territory, Article 78(2) states:

Decisions regarding...assigned residence or internment shall be made according to a regular procedure to be prescribed by the Occupying Power in accordance with the provisions of the present Convention. This procedure shall include the right of appeal for the parties concerned. Appeals shall be decided with the least possible delay.

---

persons to be treated as POWs, can be considered as accepting internment for security reasons, since it concerns members or former members of the armed forces of occupied territory whom the occupying power 'considers it necessary by reason of such allegiance to intern'.

[99] See Levie (n 85) 68–70.   [100] Pictet, *GCIII* (n 98) 65.

The obligations under Articles 43(1) and 78(2) are, strictly speaking, to provide a *right* of review and appeal, respectively, which the internee may or may not opt to exercise.[101] Failure to honour these provisions will render unlawful any internment.[102]

The text of Article 78(2) appears to be less prescriptive than that of Article 43(1), stipulating simply a 'regular procedure' and 'right of appeal' as opposed to 'an appropriate court or administrative board'. Given this difference in language, one might infer an intention of the drafters that the rules in occupied territory are to be less demanding than those in a state's own territory. Indeed, this seems to be confirmed by the *travaux*, which indicates a clear rejection of proposals to equate the two provisions 'owing to the difference which existed between the situation in an occupied territory and that in national territory'.[103] Nonetheless, it is argued in the ICRC Commentary that Article 78 requires the same procedures as Article 43.[104] Moreover, certain state practice seems to support such a view.[105] It is submitted that this latter interpretation is the better one, as more supportive of the object and purpose of the review procedures under both Articles 43(1) and 78. Thus, the purpose of initial review is to ensure that the grounds for internment specified in GCIV (as explored in the previous section) are met in a particular case, that is, to ensure that internment is necessary for the security of the detaining power: 'if these measures were inspired by other considerations, the reviewing body would be bound to vacate them.'[106] These procedures are, therefore, the key safeguards against the arbitrary exercise of the internment authority under IHL. It was shown in section 2.2.1 that the detaining power has significant discretion when deciding whether to intern a civilian; these review mechanisms are designed to provide a check on this discretion.[107] Indeed, it may be argued that the concerns raised in the previous section regarding the indeterminacy of the initial internment standard, and the resulting risk of arbitrariness, are sufficiently answered by these review mechanisms.

However, Articles 43(1) and 78(2) GCIV themselves also leave some discretion to the detaining power. First, neither provision specifies a maximum length of time before which an internee's request for initial review must be honoured;

---

[101] Pictet, *GCIV* (n 32) 260; ICRC, Report of the 31st International Conference of the Red Cross and Red Crescent, 'IHL and the Challenges of Contemporary Armed Conflicts', October 2011, 17; Gasser and Dörmann (n 43) 313.

[102] *Delalić* (n 43) [583].

[103] *Final Record: Vol II-A* (n 53) 772. The relevant drafting history can be found at ibid, 772–3 and 790. For an example of a state in favour of bringing the two provisions closer together, see *Final Record of the Diplomatic Conference of Geneva of 1949: Vol II, Section B* (ICRC, 1963) 441 (Belgium).

[104] Pictet, *GCIV* (n 32) 368.

[105] *Al-Jedda v Secretary of State for Defence* [2005] EWHC 1809 (Admin) [139] ('...there is no warrant for departing from the views expressed by Pictet, who does provide a reasoned basis for linking Article 78 with Articles 35(2) and 43 and for interpreting the reference to a "competent body" in Article 78 as being a reference to a court or administrative board'); The Baha Mousa Public Inquiry, 'Closing Submissions on Modules 1–3 on Behalf of the Ministry of Defence', 25 June 2010, [10.28].

[106] *Delalic* (n 43) [581]; *Kordić and Čerkez* (n 43) [287]; Pictet, *GCIV* (n 32) 261.

[107] *Delalić* (n 43) [580].

rather, they simply state that this must be 'as soon as possible' and 'with the least possible delay', respectively. The Israeli Supreme Court considered that a period of twelve days before which a person is given access to review proceedings would be too long.[108] The ICTY Appeals Chamber has highlighted the context-dependent nature of this requirement:

... the reasonable time which is to be afforded to a detaining power to ascertain whether detained civilians pose a security risk must be the *minimum* time necessary to make enquiries to determine whether a view that they pose a security risk has any objective foundation such that it would found a 'definite suspicion' of the nature referred to in Article 5 of Geneva Convention IV.[109]

This demonstrates that any delay must be justifiable. This is confirmed by the Inter-American Commission on Human Rights' case of *Coard v United States*, in which it held a delay of six to nine days to be a breach of Article 78 GCIV because it was 'not attributable to a situation of active hostilities or explained by other information on the record'.[110]

Second, very few rules regarding the composition of the review bodies are specified, and no requirement as such of independence is laid down in the treaty provisions. The only clear rule regarding composition is found in the reference in Article 43(1) to 'administrative *board*', which confirms that the decision cannot rest with a single person;[111] based on the interpretation above, this same requirement applies under Article 78(2).[112] However, it is clear that, under both Articles 43(1) and 78(2), review can be by an administrative, rather than judicial, authority, and there is no requirement that, in addition to military officers, civilian members of the judiciary be present. Consequently, military interests may appear over-represented, potentially undermining the impartiality (real or perceived) of the review process.

Third, the procedures to be followed by the review bodies are not prescribed.[113] For example, rules relating to evidentiary standards and on whom the burden of proof falls are not elaborated, apparently leaving such issues to the discretion of the detaining power. Indeed, were a detaining power to decide that the burden of proof is to fall on the internee and that a low evidentiary standard for confirming the necessity of internment is to be sufficient, the effectiveness of such review procedures in containing the detaining power's discretion would be significantly undermined.[114] This is exacerbated by the absence of any guarantee in Articles 43(1) or 78(2) GCIV of standard due process requirements, such as legal representation for internees, the right to appear, and the right to call and challenge witnesses.

---

[108] *Mar'ab* (n 49) [32]–[34]. Although the Court was specifically referring to judicial intervention under domestic administrative detention laws, it referred to the GCIV internment regimes by analogy at ibid, [28].
[109] *Delalić* (n 47) [328] (emphasis in original).
[110] *Coard et al v United States*, IACiHR, Rep No 109/99, 22 September 1999, [57].
[111] Pictet, *GCIV* (n 32) 260; Pejic (n 49) 387.
[112] *Al-Jedda* (n 105) [140]; Baha Mousa (n 105) [10.28].
[113] Gasser and Dörmann (n 43) 313; Deeks (n 1) 409–10.
[114] See references below to case law in which rules on the burden of proof have been elaborated: n 125.

Finally, there is no guidance on the standard of review to be applied, that is, whether the reviewing authority will adopt a *de novo* or deferential approach to the detaining authorities. It is useful at this point to remember that the GCIV standards for internment comprise the two elements of security threat and necessity. As noted above, whilst deference may be given to the state in defining what constitutes a threat to its security, the reviewing authority could ensure a full, objective review of the necessity of internment, judging whether there genuinely was no other, less rights-restrictive means of countering that threat.[115] As noted, even for review under Article 78, which requires only that the detaining authority 'consider' internment necessary, a review that the determination of necessity was made in good faith would apply at a minimum.[116]

The GCIV provisions on initial review, therefore, remain vague. Indeed, this was very much intended by the drafters, demonstrated by the rejection of the Canadian proposal at the 1949 diplomatic conference to include more detailed rules in these provisions.[117] However, these vague provisions have been elaborated in practice, with certain states developing more detailed policy guidance that helps to address some of the shortcomings noted above. The UK's *Joint Doctrine Publication on Captured Persons*, for example, requires that the review tribunal be independent of those involved in the initial decision to intern and that it include the head of detention operations, the chief of staff, a policy adviser and the Commander Legal.[118] Moreover, the review tribunal is to make an initial determination no later than forty-eight hours after capture, with periodic reviews at least every twenty-eight days; these reviews include a consideration of whether it is possible to transfer the internee to criminal jurisdiction.[119] The United States has similarly elaborated on the GCIV procedures, albeit in less detail. For example, under US military doctrine, decisions on internment are to be made by 'a responsible commissioned officer',[120] with reviews carried out 'by a board of officers'.[121]

These elaborations in UK and US military doctrine appear to be policy-based rather than indications of *opinio iuris*.[122] However, the content of Articles 43(1) and 78(2) GCIV has, to some extent, also been elaborated *de lege lata*. First, the ICTY Appeals Chamber in *Delalić* held that the Military Investigative Commission, established by the defendants to review civilian detentions, failed to satisfy the requirements of Article 43(1), 'as it did not have the power to decide *finally* on the release of prisoners whose detention could not be considered as justified for any serious reason'.[123] Thus, the bodies reviewing the decision to intern must have the final say on whether internment should continue. This seems in keeping with the object and purpose of both Article 43(1) and 78(2),

---

[115] See the discussion above at text to nn 70–72.   [116] Ibid.
[117] *Final Record: Vol III* (n 52) 127.
[118] UK Ministry of Defence, *Joint Doctrine Publication 1-10* (n 30) Annex 1B [1B3].
[119] Ibid, [1B5].   [120] US Army Regulation 190–8 (n 69) s 5.1(c)(1)(a).
[121] Ibid, s 5.1(g)(1).
[122] RM Chesney, 'Iraq and the Military Detention Debate: Firsthand Perspectives from the Other War, 2003–2010' (2011) 51 VJIL 549, 561 (referring to the US Army Regulations as 'policy').
[123] *Delalić* (n 47) [329] (emphasis added).

for only then can the review body effectively protect persons against unnecessary internment.[124] In the same case, the ICTY also held that the burden of proof for establishing that internment is necessary for security reasons must lie with the detaining authority, thus ensuring that the review process is not rendered ineffective by placing the burden on the internee to prove that internment is unnecessary.[125] Third, the ICRC Commentary states that, if these review procedures are to serve their roles as checks on the exercise of detention power, they must operate impartially and independently from the authority that ordered detention.[126] These elaborations thus help to ensure that the review procedures offer a robust mechanism for challenging the necessity of civilian internment.

Before moving on to periodic review, an additional right must be mentioned here that is closely related to the review process, namely the right of civilian internees to know the reasons for their internment. The requirement to give reasons forms an essential aspect of the right to have the internment decision reviewed, for without knowing the reason for internment, one cannot effectively challenge it.[127] Article 75 API, which is generally considered to reflect customary international law and thus applies even to those not party to API,[128] stipulates in paragraph 3 that internees 'shall be informed promptly...of the reasons' for their internment. Although Article 75(1) limits that article's applicability to those 'who do not benefit from more favourable treatment' under the Geneva Conventions or API, given that it is designed to embody 'minimum rules of protection',[129] the rules contained therein must *a fortiori* apply where persons are protected by the more comprehensive IHL regimes.[130] Indeed, military doctrine confirms that civilian internees must be given the reasons for their internment.[131]

---

[124] See above, text to nn 106–7 (confirming that the purpose of these review procedures is to ensure persons are interned only where so permitted by IHL).
[125] *Delalić* (n 47) [329]. Similarly, see EECC, *Civilians Claims, Ethiopia's Claim 5* (n 75) [104]; HCJ 466/86, *Abu Bakr v Judge of the Military Court in Schechem*, 40(3) PD 649, 650–1, cited in Dinstein (n 62) 176.
[126] Pictet, *GCIV* (n 32) 260. Similarly, see Pejic (n 49) 386–7.
[127] Chatham House and ICRC, 'Meeting Summary: Procedural Safeguards for Security Detention in Non-International Armed Conflict', London, 22–3 September 2008, 10–11 <https://www.icrc.org/eng/assets/files/other/security-detention-chatham-icrc-report-091209.pdf> accessed 29 July 2015; Deeks (n 1) 412.
[128] EECC, *Civilians Claims, Ethiopia's Claim 5* (n 75) [29]; Dörmann (n 28) 70; Pejic (n 49) 377; S Krähenmann, 'Protection of Prisoners in Armed Conflict' in D Fleck (ed), *The Handbook of International Humanitarian Law* (3rd edn, OUP, Oxford 2013) 368. The US, for example, has recognized the customary status of Art 75 API: The White House (Office of the Press Secretary), 'Fact Sheet: New Actions on Guantanamo and Detainee Policy' (7 March 2011); *Hamdan v Rumsfeld et al*, 548 US 557 (2006) 633–5 (US Supreme Court); WH Taft, IV, 'The Law of Armed Conflict After 9/11: Some Salient Features' (2003) 28 Yale J Intl L 319, 321–2.
[129] Sandoz et al (n 13) 865.
[130] Similarly, see Dörmann (n 28) 73. This reasoning is similar to the ICJ's conclusion in *Nicaragua* (n 47) at [218], that common Article 3, as it is the minimum applicable in non-international armed conflicts, must necessarily also apply in international conflicts, the rules for the latter being much more comprehensive than those for the former. This logical approach to the structure of IHL is similarly adopted in R Goodman, 'The Detention of Civilians in Armed Conflict' (2009) 103 AJIL 48, 50 (fn 10).
[131] US Army Regulation 190–8 (n 69) s 5.1(c)(2)(b); UK Ministry of Defence (n 64) 216–17; Canada, *Joint Doctrine Manual* (n 69) 11–10 [1135(3)].

2.3.1.2 Periodic review

Where the decision to intern is upheld following the initial review procedure, Article 43(1) goes on to specify:

…the court or administrative board [that provided the initial review] shall periodically, and at least twice yearly, give consideration to his or her case, with a view to the favourable amendment of the initial decision, if circumstances permit.

Similarly, Article 78(2) requires periodic review 'if possible every six months, by a competent body set up by the [Occupying] Power'. Once again, the language of Article 78 seems more liberal than that of Article 43, and it makes no reference to a bias in favour of release, as does Article 43(1). In practice, certain occupying states have offered periodic reviews much more frequently than Article 78 requires. Thus, during its occupation of Iraq following the 2003 invasion, the United Kingdom gave periodic reviews of civilian internment at the ten, twenty-eight and ninety day intervals, and every ninety days thereafter.[132]

The purpose of periodic review is to re-examine the original basis for internment in light of changing circumstances, so as to ensure that no person is interned 'for a longer time than the security of the Detaining State demands'.[133] It also acts, therefore, as an enforcement mechanism for Article 132 GCIV, discussed below, requiring the release of internees as soon as the reasons justifying internment cease.[134] In light of this, it has been suggested that, as the period of internment increases, so the burden required to prove the continued necessity for internment similarly increases.[135]

However, these provisions on periodic review suffer from the same shortcomings as those on initial review noted above, such as an absence of any guidance on the composition or procedures of the review bodies. The only rule of procedure specified in Article 43(1) is that there is a bias in favour of release 'if circumstances permit', confirming that the burden of proof falls on the detaining power to demonstrate the continued necessity of internment. Beyond this, however, discretion once again appears to have been left to the detaining authority.

2.3.2 Combatants

At first sight, GCIII appears to provide an initial review procedure similar to that in GCIV. Article 5(2) GCIII stipulates that:

Should any doubt arise as to whether persons, having committed a belligerent act and having fallen into the hands of the enemy, belong to any of the categories enumerated in

---

[132] UK, House of Commons, Written Answer by the Minister of State for the Armed Forces, Ministry of Defence, *Hansard* HC, vol 415 (8 December 2003), Written Answers, Col 269W, cited in ICRC, Customary IHL Database: Practice Relating to Rule 99 Deprivation of Liberty (British Red Cross/ICRC) <https://www.icrc.org/customary-ihl/eng/docs/v2_rul_rule99> accessed 29 July 2015.
[133] Pictet, *GCIV* (n 32) 261.   [134] Pictet, *GCIV* (n 32) 261; *Delalić* (n 43) [581].
[135] Pejic (n 49) 382; CFH 7048/97, *Anonymous v Minister of Defence* (n 80) [25]; *Issawi* case, Jerusalem District Court, Judgment, 21 April 2010, [11], cited in ICRC, Customary IHL Database (n 132); though cf *Al-Ahmar* case, Israel High Court of Justice, Judgment, 26 February 2004, cited in ICRC, Customary IHL Database (n 132).

Article 4, such persons shall enjoy the protection of the present Convention until such time as their status has been determined by a competent tribunal.[136]

However, Article 5(2) was not designed for the purpose of providing a review mechanism for those *contesting their internment*; instead, it was meant for those that have committed a belligerent act who *assert their right* to POW status in order to claim combatant immunity and the protections under GCIII.[137] This is clear from Article 5(2)'s requirement that such persons 'shall enjoy' POW status until otherwise determined by a competent tribunal; Geoffrey Corn argues that this demonstrates that the 'operative presumption' underlying that provision is that the individual has been captured on suspicion of participation in hostilities and, therefore, desires combatant/POW status in order to enjoy immunity from domestic prosecution.[138] Indeed, the provision was proposed by the ICRC to address the practice during the Second World War whereby adversaries would refuse to recognize certain national forces as POWs, instead treating them as *francs-tireurs*.[139] The article thus seeks to ensure that POW status is granted to such persons, notwithstanding the negative consequence of that status, that is, internment for the duration of hostilities.[140]

Similarly, Article 45(1) API, which 'updates' Article 5 GCIII to include the new definitions of combatant in API, requires that a 'person who takes part in hostilities and falls into the power of an adverse party shall be presumed to be a prisoner of war' until a competent tribunal has determined otherwise. As with Article 5 GCIII, the presumption underlying this article is that the individual claims that they qualify for POW status (and are thus subject to internment). Indeed, Article 45(1) sought to bring a greater number of persons within the POW regime, by stipulating that POW status shall be presumed whenever the individual, or his national state, claims such status or where they appear to be entitled thereto. As the ICRC Commentary explains, this paragraph is 'intended to reduce to a minimum those cases in which a captor could *arbitrarily deny* the status of prisoner of war'.[141] This is indicative of the traditional presumption, noted above, that POW

---

[136] States have elaborated procedures here: see, eg, US Army Regulation 190–8 (n 69) s 1.6 (requiring a panel of 3 commissioned officers, before which the detainee has a right to testify and call witnesses); Canada, Prisoner of War Status Determination Regulations, SOR/91-134, 25 January 1991 (a tribunal of one officer of the Legal Branch of the Canadian Forces, which can call witnesses, with the detainee having a right to representation by an appointed officer or non-commissioned member, with a right of review by the authority that directed the creation of the tribunal).

[137] K Dörmann, 'To What Extent Does International Humanitarian Law provide for the Supervision of the Lawfulness of Detention?: Presentation' in The University Centre for International Humanitarian Law, 'Expert Meeting on the Supervision of the Lawfulness of Detention During Armed Conflict' (Geneva, 24–5 July 2004) 13 <http://www.geneva-academy.ch/docs/expert-meetings/2004/4rapport_detention.pdf> accessed 29 July 2015.

[138] GS Corn, 'Enemy Combatants and Access to *Habeas Corpus*: Questioning the Validity of the Prisoner of War Analogy' (2007) 5 Santa Clara J Intl L 236, 258–9.

[139] Sandoz et al (n 13) 544; Corn (n 138) 258.

[140] Similarly, see *Final Record: Vol II-A* (n 53) 563.

[141] Sandoz et al (n 13) 553 (emphasis added).

status is beneficial; however, as also noted there, and as shown throughout this chapter regarding the procedural regulation of internment, POW status is not necessarily advantageous compared with civilian status.[142]

Consequently, the tribunals required by Articles 5 GCIII and 45 API are not comparable to those required by Articles 43 and 78 GCIV; the former are reviews of the *status* of internees, for those wishing to claim POW status and combatant immunity, whereas the latter are reviews of the *internment* itself, for those challenging their deprivation of liberty. In reality, GCIII does not provide initial or periodic review comparable to that in GCIV. This may be explained by the different assumptions underpinning these two internment regimes. As explained above, the basic norm regulating civilian internment— that it must be necessary for security—may be seen equally to underlie combatant internment.[143] For civilians, it was shown that significant discretion is left to the detaining power when deciding whether to intern a particular individual, requiring an initial review as a check against the exercise of this discretion (although, as noted, the review procedures also leave discretion to the state). Moreover, the need for periodic review of civilian internment demonstrates that an individual may cease to pose a security threat during their internment, rendering continued internment no longer necessary. For combatants, on the other hand, Article 4 GCIII and Articles 43 and 44 API, in defining the categories of persons subject to POW status, already list those for whom internment is presumed necessary. It is thus assumed that limited discretion will be exercised under GCIII, rendering any initial review procedure without purpose. Moreover, as explained in section 2.4.2 below, it is also assumed that POWs will remain a security threat for the duration of hostilities by virtue of the possibility of them rejoining hostilities if released.[144] Consequently, no periodic review is provided.

Whilst these assumptions help to explain the absence of review procedures for those interned under GCIII, they may, at times, be ill-founded. To illustrate this, a distinction must be drawn between defining those categories of persons subject to internment and determining whether a particular individual falls within one of those categories. Thus, although GCIII, unlike GCIV, clearly defines those categories of persons for whom internment is considered necessary, discretion may still be exercised at the second stage, when determining whether a particular individual falls into one of those categories. This may be the case, for example, where the individual in question is not in uniform, yet is alleged to be a member of the enemy armed forces. Indeed, as noted in section 2.1.1, Article 44 API brought irregular guerilla forces within the combatant/POW framework.[145] As such forces may lack a distinctive emblem by which they may clearly be identified, the detaining power will likely need to exercise some discretion in determining whether the particular individual is a combatant and thus subject to internment. Such cases

---

[142] See above, text to nn 90–1.   [143] See section 2.2.2.
[144] Dörmann (n 137) 10; Doswald-Beck (n 94) 2 (fn 2).   [145] See above, text to nn 11–14.

could result in mistakes being made, with an individual being incorrectly labelled a combatant. It is submitted that this reflects a flaw in GCIII and API, for they allow a detaining state to exercise discretion when interning certain persons, without requiring a review for those challenging their internment. The presumption is that POW status will be desired; however, that presumption is arguably no longer well-founded, in light of the lengthy internment that follows and the more protective internment regimes in GCIV.[146] Indeed, the ICTY was faced with such a case in *Prosecutor v Krnojelac*, which involved the detention of Muslim men as POWs, based on the fact that some of them were carrying weapons.[147] The Trial Chamber held such evidence to be insufficient to raise a reasonable doubt as to civilian status, and thus, for the detentions to be lawful, compliance with the procedural rules in GCIV was necessary.[148] Certain states have addressed these problems by employing Article 5(2) GCIII tribunals as a mechanism for individuals to challenge their internment as POWs; this appeared to be the practice of the United States in both the 1990–91 Gulf War and the initial international armed conflict in Iraq following the 2003 invasion.[149] However, this seems to remain a matter of policy rather than of legal obligation.

2.4 Release

The final set of procedural rules relates to the point at which internees must be released. This section will demonstrate that, whilst the precise rules on release from civilian and combatant internment differ, the same principle can be seen operating with respect to both.

2.4.1 Civilians

For civilian internees, whether in 'enemy' territory or occupied territory, Article 132(1) GCIV requires release 'as soon as the reasons which necessitated his internment no longer exist'. Thus, the UK, following the 2003 invasion of Iraq, stated that persons interned 'will be held until it is assessed that their internment is no longer necessary for reasons of security'.[150] The ICRC Commentary notes that Article 132(1) GCIV forms the 'counterpart to the principle stated in Article 42',

---

[146] See above, text to nn 90–1.   [147] *Krnojelac* (n 49).
[148] *Krnojelac* (n 49) [117]. Similarly, see also *Prosecutor v Blagoje Simić, Miroslav Tadić and Simo Zarić* (Trial Judgment) ICTY-95-9-T (17 October 2003) [659]; Hampson (n 76) 514–17 (noting a similar assumption by the United Kingdom regarding resident Iraqis in the United Kingdom).
[149] MC Waxman, 'The Law of Armed Conflict and Detention Operations in Afghanistan' in MN Schmitt (ed), *The War in Afghanistan: A Legal Analysis* (2009) (Vol 85, US Naval War College International Law Studies) 348 (fn 27) (on US practice in the Gulf War); M Schmitt, 'Iraq (2003 onwards)' in E Wilmshurst (ed), *International Law and the Classification of Conflicts* (OUP, Oxford 2012) 376 (on US practice following the 2003 invasion of Iraq).
[150] United Kingdom, House of Lords, Written Answer by the Parliamentary Under-Secretary of State for Defence, *Hansard* HL vol 652 (8 September 2003), Written Answers, Col WA45, cited in ICRC, Customary IHL Database (n 132).

permitting internment only where necessary for security.[151] In other words, internment is permitted only if, *and for so long as*, it is necessary for security reasons. Article 132(2) additionally requires, for humanitarian reasons, that the parties to a conflict endeavour to conclude agreements for the early release of particular internees, such as those that have been detained for a long period.

Article 133(1) then establishes an absolute end-point for internment, requiring that it cease, if not before, 'as soon as possible after the close of hostilities'. Article 133(1) is closely related to Article 132(1): 'Since hostilities are the main cause for internment, internment should cease when hostilities cease.'[152] It should be noted that this refers to 'a state of fact rather than the legal situation covered by laws or decrees fixing the date of cessation of hostilities'; a peace treaty is therefore not necessary.[153] The purpose of this factual test for the end-point of internment is to ensure release at the earliest possible moment, preventing political difficulties in reaching a formal settlement from unnecessarily prolonging internment.

2.4.2 Combatants

For POWs, absent special circumstances,[154] Article 118(1) GCIII states the basic rule that '[p]risoners of war shall be released and repatriated without delay after the cessation of active hostilities'. Like Article 133 GCIV, the reference to 'active hostilities' demonstrates that this is a factual, rather than legal standard, without the need for an armistice or peace treaty.[155] This factual test sought to address problems arising from previous treaty provisions which conditioned POW repatriation on the conclusion of peace.[156] Indeed, it was the long delays in the repatriation of POWs by all sides following the Second World War that prompted this change in the law.[157] However, this turn from the legal to the factual in the point of POW release has not prevented claims in conflicts since 1949 that attempt to undercut this factual basis with political motives.[158]

At first sight, GCIII appears to regulate the point of release to a lesser degree than GCIV regarding civilians. Thus, it was shown above that GCIV requires release of civilian internees as soon as the reasons for internment cease and, if not before, at the close of hostilities. GCIII, on the other hand, seems to stipulate only the second (generally later) of these two end-points. However, once again, the difference between the GCIII and GCIV internment regimes is not as stark

---

[151] Pictet, *GCIV* (n 32) 510–11; *Kordić and Čerkez* (n 43) [288].
[152] Pictet, *GCIV* (n 32) 515.   [153] Ibid, 514.
[154] See, eg, Art 109 GCIII (early release of wounded or sick POWs).
[155] Pictet, *GCIV* (n 32) 514–15. In the context of occupation this is especially important, such that any continuation of an occupation cannot justify extending internment of POWs beyond the factual close of hostilities: Krähenmann (n 128) 409.
[156] See, eg, Art 20 of the 1899 Hague Regulations. On this development, see Pictet, *GCIII* (n 98) 541.
[157] Levie (n 85) 418–19 (fn 116) (on delays by the US, UK, France, and (especially) the Soviet Union).
[158] See, eg, HS Levie, 'Legal Aspects of the Continued Detention of the Pakistani Prisoners of War by India' (1973) 67 AJIL 512.

as it appears. Thus, although GCIII does not explicitly require release as soon as the reasons justifying internment cease, this reflects the assumption that the reasons necessitating combatant internment, that is, the threat posed by their possible return to the battlefield, co-exist with the hostilities, and thus cease only when hostilities do. As such, '[t]he *length of detention* is limited to what is necessary (until the end of active hostilities…)'.[159] This interpretation is confirmed by the provisions on early release. Article 109(1), for example, requires early repatriation of seriously wounded and sick POWs. In addition to promoting humanitarian ends, this reflects the fact that such persons, by virtue of being wounded, are not likely to rejoin the hostilities; hence, their internment is no longer necessary. As the ICRC Commentary to this article makes clear, '[t]he main objection raised by the Detaining Power against early repatriation is that repatriated prisoners of war might return to active service. This danger does not exist in the case of wounded and sick'.[160] Nevertheless, that internment for the duration of the hostilities is the presumption for combatants reflects once again the more robust procedural rules in the GCIV internment regime compared with those in the GCIII regime.

Finally, Article 118 GCIII raises the question of what happens where the POW does not wish to be repatriated. The text of the provision suggests repatriation should take place regardless of the POW's wishes.[161] Previous practice, notably found in the many agreements made at the conclusion of the First World War, recognized that repatriation should not occur against the will of the POW.[162] The agreements following the Second World War did not appear to continue this practice, however,[163] and a proposal by the Austrian delegate to the 1949 diplomatic conference that would have allowed a POW to apply for transfer to a state other than that of their nationality was rejected.[164] This issue arose at the end of the Korean War, where North Korea asserted its right under Article 118 to have its forces returned to it, contrary to the wishes of many of the POWs.[165] The West disagreed with North Korea's interpretation of the law, and in December 1952 the UN General Assembly adopted a resolution confirming that force must not be used to repatriate POWs.[166] The ICRC Commentary to Article 118 consequently states that '[p]risoners of war have an inalienable right to be repatriated once active hostilities have ceased'.[167] This demonstrates that Article 118 is now seen not as giving *states* a right to have their nationals repatriated, but rather as giving *POWs* a

---

[159] Dörmann (n 137) 10; Dowald-Beck (n 94) 2; Pictet, *GCIII* (n 98) 515.
[160] Pictet, *GCIII* (n 98) 515.
[161] Though some have read the apparently absolute language in Art 118 GCIII as simply indicating the desire of the drafters to ensure that there was no possibility of undermining a POW's right of repatriation: see, eg, JAC Gutteridge, 'The Repatriation of Prisoners of War' (1953) 2 ICLQ 207, 213.
[162] Levie (n 85) 421–2.   [163] Ibid, 422–3.   [164] *Final Record: Vol II-A* (n 53) 462.
[165] Pictet, *GCIII* (n 98) 543.   [166] UNGA Res 610 (VII) (1952) preambular [2].
[167] Pictet, *GCIII* (n 98) 546–7. Similarly, see Krähenmann (n 128) 410 (noting that, following the second Gulf War, the United States passed the names of POWs that did not wish to be repatriated on to the ICRC).

right to repatriation, which they are free not to exercise. This development should be seen in the context of the evolution of IHL generally, which in the post-Second World War era has been seen less as comprising *state* rights and more as protecting *individual* rights, a process Theodor Meron has termed 'the humanization of humanitarian law'.[168] The ICRC now considers it a norm of customary international law that states involve them in any intended repatriations, to ensure POWs are not repatriated against their will.[169]

2.5 Article 5 GCIV

The final issue to be discussed in this chapter concerns the possibility of derogation from particular provisions of GCIV under Article 5. Article 5(1) states that a protected person in enemy territory 'definitely suspected of or engaged in activities hostile to the security of the State' shall not be entitled to such rights and privileges under GCIV as would, if granted, be 'prejudicial to the security' of the state. Article 5(2), referring to occupied territory, states that a protected person shall, 'where absolute military security so requires, be regarded as having forfeited rights of communication' under GCIV where they are 'detained as a spy or saboteur, or as a person under definite suspicion of activity hostile to the security of the Occupying Power'. Article 5(3) then confirms that the principle of humane treatment and the rights to fair and regular trial in GCIV are non-derogable. Moreover, paragraph 3 requires that such persons, 'shall also be granted the full rights and privileges of a protected person...at the earliest date consistent with the security of the State or Occupying Power'. In his consideration of the drafting of GCIV and the historical context surrounding the 1949 diplomatic conference, Geoffrey Best notes that Article 5, forming part of what he calls the 'security- and order-maintaining parts' of GCIV, constituted a counterpart to the 'civilian-protecting parts, which otherwise and on their own must be considered pure fantasy'.[170] Indeed, the Australian delegate to the 1949 diplomatic conference proposed draft Article 5 of GCIV because, '[i]n his opinion, the rights of the State in relation to certain persons such as spies, saboteurs, fifth columnists and traitors, had been insufficiently defined'.[171]

---

[168] T Meron, 'The Humanization of Humanitarian Law' (2000) 94 AJIL 239, 251–6 (also referring to this example of POW repatriation). Stephen Neff has made the argument that the substantive rules of protection for POWs that developed in the nineteenth century were a precursor to this, in that such protective rules were seen no longer as being based on military necessity, as they had been by Vattel, for example, but rather human dignity: Neff (n 86) 70.

[169] Henckaerts, *Vol I* (n 16) 455. Though see the more cautious reading of this practice and of the ICRC's view in International Law Commission (ILC), 'Second Report on Subsequent Agreements and Subsequent Practice in Relation to the Interpretation of Treaties by Georg Nolte, Special Rapporteur', A/CN.4/671, 26 March 2014, [16]–[18].

[170] G Best, *War and Law since 1945* (OUP, Oxford 1994) 124.

[171] *Final Record: Vol II-A* (n 53) 622.

2.5 Article 5 GCIV

The existence of Article 5 GCIV begs the question of whether that provision might limit the applicability of the procedural rules on internment explored in this chapter. Indeed, those subject to internment under GCIV and those falling within Article 5 would seem to overlap considerably. It might be argued, therefore, that such persons may not enjoy the procedural safeguards in Articles 42, 43, and 78 GCIV where the state considers it necessary to derogate. Indeed, during the drafting of Article 5 GCIV, certain states expressed the concern that it was too broad and could undermine the protections that had already been agreed upon, including the procedural rules on internment.[172] However, limits are clearly placed on a state's authority to derogate under Article 5. First, the subset of activities to which Article 5 applies arguably is not broad. As Hans-Peter Gasser and Knut Dörmann argue, 'it can be assumed that this rule refers primarily to acts of espionage or sabotage'.[173] The ICTY similarly adopts a limited view of the acts that can trigger Article 5 GCIV:

> Although the language of this provision may suggest a broad application of Article 5…the Chamber observes nevertheless that 'activities hostile to the security of the State', are above all espionage, sabotage and intelligence with the enemy Government or enemy nationals and exclude, for example, a civilian's political attitude towards the State.[174]

Moreover, as Derek Jinks notes, in determining whether individuals fall within Article 5, the article requires individualized assessments both of the activities of the individual and whether derogation is necessary.[175] It cannot, therefore, operate as the basis for collective actions.[176] This is consistent with the *travaux* of Article 5, seen in the statement by the Australian delegation, which had proposed the provision, that it 'had been carefully worded so as to ensure that only *individual* measures should be taken against *individual* persons'.[177]

Second, both in the territory of a party to the conflict and in occupied territory, Article 5 requires a necessity test, limiting derogation in the former to situations where non-derogation would be prejudicial to state security and in the latter to situations where 'absolute military security so requires'. Jinks argues that '[t]his requirement [of necessity] limits sharply the range of permissible derogations'.[178] Indeed, the ICRC considers that, given this necessity test, the range of rights from which derogation is permitted is very limited, even in the territory of a party to the conflict (where the right to derogate seems broadest), comprising:

> …the right to correspond, the right to receive individual or collective relief, the right to spiritual assistance from ministers of their faith and the right to receive visits from

---

[172] *Final Record: Vol II-A* (n 53) 797 (Bulgaria); *Final Record: Vol II-B* (n 103) 378 (Soviet Union). Similarly, see Draper (n 85) 131.
[173] Gasser and Dörmann (n 43) 254.   [174] *Kordić and Čerkez* (n 43) [280].
[175] Jinks (n 32) 390.
[176] Similarly, see RW Gehring, 'Loss of Civilian Protections under the Fourth Geneva Convention and Protocol I' (1980) 19 MLLWR 11, 81; Pejic (n 49) 381–2.
[177] *Final Record: Vol II-A* (n 53) 796 (emphasis added). Similarly, see ibid, 798 (France). No delegation at the conference disagreed with this interpretation of Art 5.
[178] Jinks (n 32) 390.

representatives of the Protecting Power and the International Committee of the Red Cross. *The security of the State could not conceivably be put forward as a reason for depriving such persons of the benefit of other provisions.*[179]

In light of this necessity requirement, it is submitted that the procedural rules explored in this chapter could not be the subject of derogation, for the granting of those safeguards could never be prejudicial to state security (particularly given how minimalist their requirements are), and thus derogation therefrom would be unnecessary. In occupied territory in particular, derogation is permitted only with regard to rights of communication (ie with the outside world), a category into which the procedural rules regulating internment do not fall.[180] This interpretation of Article 5 is buttressed by the fact that to hold otherwise would be to render ineffective the procedural rules explored in this chapter, for were a significant subset of those subject to internment *ipso facto* to lose the procedural safeguards under GCIV, the protective purpose of those safeguards would be lost.[181] Indeed, this interpretation has been confirmed by the ICTY, which has held that even those subject to Article 5 GCIV must still enjoy the safeguards under Article 43 GCIV.[182] The same approach regarding the non-derogability of Article 78 GCIV finds support in the literature.[183]

These restrictive interpretations of Article 5 GCIV are not universally held, however. Dinstein, for example, has argued that so-called 'unlawful combatants', discussed in section 2.1.3, do not 'enjoy the benefits of civilian status: Article 5...specifically permits derogations from the rights of such a person.'[184] In suggesting that such persons do not enjoy the benefits of civilian status due to the operation of Article 5, Dinstein might be read as implying that the provision's scope is much broader than that suggested above.[185] The present author cannot accept such a reading. Not only is this inconsistent with the jurisprudence examined above, it is also contrary to the ordinary meaning even of the wider authorization in Article 5(1), which still permits derogation only 'from such rights and privileges...as would...be prejudicial to the security of the State'. A broad reading of the scope of Article 5 must, therefore, be rejected.

[179] Pictet, *GCIV* (n 32) 56, cited in Jinks (n 32) 390–1 (emphasis added).
[180] Jinks (n 32) 391–2.
[181] As noted above at text to n 172, this concern was raised during the drafting of Art 5.
[182] *Delalić* (n 43) [579] ('[i]n case the internment of civilian persons can be justified according to articles 5, 27 or 42 of Geneva Convention IV, the persons so detained must still be granted some basic procedural rights. These rights are entrenched in article 43 of Geneva Convention IV...'). Similarly, see *Kordić and Čerkez* (n 43) [286].
[183] Y Arai-Takahashi, *The Law of Occupation: Continuity and Change of International Humanitarian Law, and its Interaction with International Human Rights Law* (Martinus Nijhoff, Leiden 2009) 276–7.
[184] Y Dinstein, *The Conduct of Hostilities under the Law of International Armed Conflict* (CUP, Cambridge 2004) 29–30.
[185] Though he does note the limitation on derogation under paragraph 3: ibid, 32.

2.6 Conclusions

This chapter has examined the procedural regulation of internment under IHL in international armed conflict. In so doing, it has explored the three key sets of procedural rules found in IHL: the grounds on which internment may be based; the review mechanisms that must be provided to internees; and the point at which an internee must be released. In addition, it was shown that internees are entitled to know the reasons for their internment, so as to enable them to challenge it. Having shown this, we are now better prepared to move on to an examination of the degree to which international law stipulates equivalent rules in non-international armed conflict. This chapter thus provides a frame of reference for the subsequent chapters. It will also prove essential to the discussion in chapter 7 regarding how the law should develop in this area and, in particular, whether the rules explored in this chapter should be extended to non-international conflicts.

Two themes have been explored in this chapter. First, notwithstanding the distinct regimes for combatant and civilian internment, certain common principles underlie each. For example, it was shown that the same basic premise underpins both internment regimes, namely, that internment is permitted only where necessary for security. Notwithstanding such common denominators between the two internment regimes, it was also made clear that there are many advantages to internment under GCIV compared with that under GCIII, most notably the fact that, whilst the former is an exceptional measure based on individualized threat, the latter is presumed for any combatant and entails internment for the duration of hostilities without any right of review. Indeed, the absence of review for POWs constitutes a key difference between the civilian and combatant internment regimes, which was explained on the basis of the different assumptions that underpin each.

The second theme explored related to the inadequacies of these internment regimes as they appear in the treaties. Importantly, it was shown that considerable discretion is left to the detaining power under each regime. Whilst a certain amount of discretion is necessary, it was argued that this could undermine the extent to which these regimes effectively protect against the arbitrary exercise of detention power. To repeat a quote referenced at the start of this chapter, 'with regard to the law of war, states are bound by a reasonably robust set of procedural rules when they administratively detain...during international armed conflict'.[186] This chapter has demonstrated that, whilst it is true that IHL establishes certain procedural rules for internees in international armed conflict, one should be cautious in viewing them as a benchmark towards which the law of non-international armed conflict should aim. This will become particularly clear in chapter 4, when comparing these rules to the equivalent provisions in international human rights law.

---

[186] Deeks (n 1) 414.

3
Internment in Non-International Armed Conflict under IHL

The previous chapter examined the procedural rules applicable to internment in international armed conflict, regulating the grounds for internment, the availability of review procedures, and the point at which internees must be released. Those rules will now be used as a frame of reference for examining the extent to which equivalent rules exist for non-international armed conflicts.

This chapter is divided into four parts. Section 3.1 begins by considering whether international humanitarian law (IHL) provides a legal basis for internment in non-international armed conflict. It will be argued that no such legal basis exists but must instead be sought elsewhere, for example in domestic law or, potentially, a Security Council resolution. Sections 3.2 and 3.3 will then examine the degree to which treaty and customary IHL, respectively, provide rules on the procedural regulation of internment in non-international armed conflict. It will be shown that, contrary to the views of certain commentators,[1] IHL is not silent here, but instead can be read to contain a basic prohibition of internment that is not necessary as a result of the war. However, it will also be demonstrated that the trend towards the general convergence of the law of international and non-international armed conflict at the level of custom cannot be seen in this area, and thus the distinction between the two categories of armed conflict remains important here. Section 3.4 will then examine the binding nature of IHL vis-à-vis non-state armed groups. This is necessary in order to confirm that the (minimal) rules examined in this chapter regulate detentions by both states and armed groups.

3.1 The Legal Basis to Intern in Non-International Armed Conflicts

It is important at the outset to consider as a preliminary matter whether IHL provides a legal basis to intern in non-international armed conflict.[2] This may seem

---

[1] See, eg, L Lopez, 'Uncivil Wars: The Challenge of Applying International Humanitarian Law to Internal Armed Conflicts' (1994) 69 NYU L Rev 916, 935; LM Olson, 'Guantánamo Habeas Review: Are the D.C. District Court's Decisions Consistent with IHL Internment Standards' (2009) 42 Case W Res J Intl L 197, 208.

[2] This section has benefited considerably from discussions with Professor Dapo Akande, Dr Kubo Mačák and Dr Aurel Sari on the *EJIL:Talk!* blog, and many of the points below are

3.1 The Legal Basis to Intern

a strange question with which to begin our analysis, given that one traditionally would conceive of international law as prohibitive in nature, leaving states free to act (at least as a matter of law) absent a prohibition to the contrary.[3] This would suggest that our question should be what *limits* international law imposes on internment in non-international conflicts. Whilst this will be the focus of the present book, as a preliminary matter it remains necessary to ask whether IHL contains a legal basis to intern. This question arises for two reasons. First, the existence of other rules in international law that restrict the power of states to detain, specifically under international human rights law (IHRL), means that the background normative position is not freedom of action. In particular, IHRL requires, inter alia, that any deprivation of liberty be based on grounds established in law, in addition to being non-arbitrary in a broader sense.[4] It will be shown in chapter 5 that this rule of IHRL continues to apply in non-international armed conflicts, and, consequently, without a legal basis, internment would violate IHRL.[5] The importance of having a legal basis on which to ground detention in any situation is also highlighted by the fact that the crime against humanity of imprisonment, applicable in both peacetime and armed conflict, is defined, inter alia, as a deprivation of liberty without a legal basis.[6] Second, it is important to consider whether such a legal basis can be found in *international humanitarian law*, given that it is IHL that provides a legal basis to intern in international armed conflicts. Though some would argue that IHL is purely prohibitive in nature and does not provide authorization to act even in international armed conflicts,[7] chapter 2 demonstrated that the treaty provisions on internment clearly provide legal authority to intern POWs and civilians in certain circumstances.[8]

---

based on two posts co-authored with Professor Dapo Akande: L Hill-Cawthorne and D Akande, 'Does IHL Provide a Legal Basis for Detention in Non-International Armed Conflict?', *EJIL:Talk!*, 7 May 2014; L Hill-Cawthorne and D Akande, 'Locating the Legal Basis for Detention in Non-International Armed Conflicts: A Rejoinder to Aurel Sari', *EJIL:Talk!*, 2 June 2014.

[3] *'Lotus' Judgment No 9* (1927) PCIJ Series A, No 10, 19; though cf the more modern view in R Jennings and A Watts, *Oppenheim's International Law: Volume I, Peace* (9th edn, Longman, London 1992) 12.

[4] See, eg, International Covenant on Civil and Political Rights (adopted 16 December 1966, entered into force 23 March 1976) 999 UNTS 171 (ICCPR), Art 9(1); Convention for the Protection of Human Rights and Fundamental Freedoms (European Convention on Human Rights, as amended) (ECHR), Art 5(1); African Charter on Human and Peoples' Rights (adopted 27 June 1981, entered into force 21 October 1986) (1982) 21 ILM 58 (ACHPR), Art 6. These IHRL rules will be explored in detail in chapter 4.

[5] Similarly, see J Pejic, 'Procedural Principles and Safeguards for Internment/Administrative Detention in Armed Conflict and Other Situations of Violence' (2005) 87 IRRC 375, 383 (noting the need for internment to adhere to the principle of legality).

[6] *Prosecutor v Milorad Krnojelac* (Trial Judgment) ICTY-97-25 (15 March 2002) [114]; *Prosecutor v Blagoje Simić, Miroslav Tadić and Simo Zarić* (Trial Judgment) ICTY-95-9-T (17 October 2003) [63]; *Prosecutor v Ntagerura et al* (Trial Judgment) ICTR-99-46T (25 February 2004) [702]; Case File 001/18-07-2007/ECCC/TC, *KAING Guek Eav alias Duch* (Trial Judgment) (26 July 2010) [348].

[7] RR Baxter, 'So-Called Unprivileged Belligerency: Spies, Guerillas, and Saboteurs' (1951) 28 BYIL 323, 324 (arguing that IHL is purely prohibitive in nature); D Jinks, 'International Human Rights Law in Times of Armed Conflict' in A Clapham and P Gaeta (eds), *The Oxford Handbook of International Law in Armed Conflict* (OUP, Oxford 2014) 666–9 (stating that IHL 'does not provide affirmative authorization' to parties to an armed conflict).

[8] See, eg, Art 21 GCIII; Art 27(4) GCIV.

Indeed, it was necessary to specify when enemy aliens could be interned even before the advent of IHRL, as the international minimum standard provided the background normative position with respect to the treatment of foreign nationals, and it was clear that this provided protection against arbitrary deprivation of liberty.[9] The consequence, as Susan Marks and Andrew Clapham note, is that one instance in which the basic requirements of legality and non-arbitrariness under IHRL are met is where detention is authorized by GCIII or GCIV.[10] Moreover, with respect to the crime against humanity of imprisonment, jurisprudence confirms that it will not have been committed where Articles 42–3 GCIV have been complied with in an international armed conflict.[11] Against this background, before considering whether IHL limits the detention authority of states and non-state groups in non-international conflicts, it must first be examined whether it confers that authority.

As with any purported rule of international law, a legal basis to intern would need to be located firmly in either treaty or custom. The possibility of finding a legal basis as a general principle of law in the sense of Article 38(1)(c) of the Statute of the International Court of Justice (ICJ) will not be considered here. First, the nature of general principles of law is contested, and, perhaps as a result of this, it is extremely rare that they are relied upon as an independent source of law.[12] Second, it seems intuitively problematic to rely on the notion of a general principle as opposed to a concrete rule for the purpose of a legal basis to detain.[13] Regarding

---

[9] JB Moore, *History and Digest of the International Arbitrations to which the United States has been a Party: Volume IV* (Government Printing Office, Washington 1898) 3278–311 (referring to cases before the British-American Claims Commission brought by individuals relating to arrests and detentions); *Arbitral Award Rendered pursuant to the Compromis signed at London, March 4, 1930, between France and the United Kingdom of Great Britain and Northern Ireland, In the Matter of the Claim of Madame Chevreau Against the United Kingdom* (1933) 27 AJIL 153, 160 ('[t]he arbitrary arrest, detention or deportation of a foreigner may give rise to a claim in international law. But the claim is not justified if these measures were taken in good faith and upon reasonable suspicion, especially if a zone of military operations is involved…As to the foregoing principles, there do not seem to be any serious differences between the parties'); MO Hudson, 'The Central American Court of Justice' (1932) 26 AJIL 759 (referring to cases brought by individuals before the Court of Justice concerning, inter alia, alleged cases of arbitrary arrest and detention); AH Roth, *The Minimum Standard of International Law Applied to Aliens* (AW Sijthoff's Uitgeversmaatschappij NV, Leiden 1949) 144–51.
[10] S Marks and A Clapham, *International Human Rights Lexicon* (OUP, Oxford 2005) 75. Similarly, see N Rodley and M Pollard, *The Treatment of Prisoners under International Law* (3rd edn OUP, Oxford 2009) 490; J Pejic, 'Conflict Classification and the Law Applicable to Detention and the Use of Force' in E Wilmshurst (ed), *International Law and the Classification of Conflicts* (OUP, Oxford 2012) 87; W Kalin, 'Human Rights Law Relating to Arbitrary Detention During Armed Conflict: The Covenant on Civil and Political Rights and its Relationship with International Humanitarian Law' in The University Centre for International Humanitarian Law, 'Expert Meeting on the Supervision of the Lawfulness of Detention During Armed Conflict' (Geneva, 24–25 July 2004) 31–2 <http://www.geneva-academy.ch/docs/expert-meetings/2004/4rapport_detention.pdf> accessed 31 July 2015. The relationship between these rules under IHL and IHRL is considered in more detail in section 5.1.2.
[11] *Krnojelac* (n 6) [111].
[12] H Thirlway, *The Sources of International Law* (OUP, Oxford 2014) 93–104.
[13] G Fitzmaurice, 'The General Principles of International Law Considered from the Standpoint of the Rule of Law' (1957) 92 *RdC* 1, 7 ('[b]y a principle, or a general principle, as opposed to a rule,

conventional IHL, it is clear that none of those provisions applicable in non-international armed conflicts, comprising (principally) common Article 3 and Additional Protocol II (APII), provides an explicit legal basis for internment.[14] Nonetheless, applicable treaty rules recognize that parties to non-international conflicts will intern, regulating various aspects thereof, including treatment standards for detainees.[15] Certain commentators argue that this recognition in treaty provisions should be read as conferring an implicit legal basis to intern.[16] This is a misreading of these provisions, however. Whilst it is true that common Article 3 and APII refer to detention/internment, this merely recognizes the fact of detention in non-international armed conflict and seeks to regulate particular aspects thereof, such as substantive treatment standards. Thus, although these references confirm that internment is not prohibited by IHL, one cannot thereby conclude that this recognition and regulation itself creates a legal basis for detention, much less one that could satisfy the IHRL requirement of legality, which, it will be shown in the next chapter, demands a clear and predictable legal basis.[17] This difference between *regulating* and *authorizing* particular action is a common feature of international law and may be illustrated with a few examples. First, it lies at the heart of IHL itself, which, whilst regulating all aspects of armed conflict, does not in any way affect its legality under the *ius ad bellum*.[18] Second, a similar distinction in a different context was acknowledged by the ICJ in *DRC v Uganda*. Here, the ICJ held that the Lusaka Agreement between the two parties, in laying down a timetable for the withdrawal of foreign forces from DRC territory, did not thereby constitute DRC consent to the presence of Ugandan forces on its soil for the remainder of the timetable; rather, the Agreement simply took as its starting point the realities on the ground and established a *modus operandi* for their cessation, but it did not make lawful the continued presence of Ugandan troops.[19] The same approach is taken here, such that the fact of internment is recognized by IHL and regulated, but a legal basis is not thereby created.

even a general rule, of law is meant chiefly something which is not itself a rule, but which underlies a rule, and explains or provides the reason for it').

[14] LM Olson, 'Practical Challenges of Implementing the Complementarity between International Humanitarian and Human Rights Law—Demonstrated by the Procedural Regulation of Internment in Non-International Armed Conflict' (2009) 40 Case W Res J Intl L 437, 452.

[15] See, eg, references to 'interned' persons in Art 5(1) APII.

[16] Pejic (n 10) 94 ('...both treaty and customary international humanitarian law contain an inherent power to intern and may in that sense be said to provide a legal basis for internment in non-international armed conflict'); International Committee of the Red Cross (ICRC), 'Internment in Armed Conflict: Basic Rules and Challenges' (Opinion Paper, Nov 2014) 7 <https://www.icrc.org/en/document/internment-armed-conflict-basic-rules-and-challenges> accessed 30 July 2015 ('...treaty IHL contain[s] an inherent power to intern and may in this respect be said to provide a legal basis for internment in NIAC').

[17] See section 4.2.1.

[18] L Oppenheim, *International Law, A Treatise: Volume II, War and Neutrality* (Longmans, Green & Co, London 1906) 56 ('[w]ar is a fact recognised, and with regard to many points regulated, but not established, by International Law'); Y Dinstein, *The Conduct of Hostilities under the Law of International Armed Conflict* (2nd edn, CUP, Cambridge 2010) 3–4.

[19] *Case Concerning Armed Activities on the Territory of the Congo (DRC v Uganda)* (Judgment) [2005] ICJ Rep 168, [98]–[105].

It has, contrarily, been suggested that the *travaux* of the treaty provisions that regulate particular aspects of internment in non-international armed conflict confirm that those provisions were intended to provide an implicit legal basis to intern. Kubo Mačák, for example, refers to the *travaux* of Articles 5 and 6 APII, discussed below in section 3.2.2, in which delegates acknowledged the existence of detentions in non-international armed conflict, including by non-state armed groups, without suggesting that such detention would necessarily be unlawful.[20] However, such references do not take the argument any further, for all that this confirms is that detention in non-international conflicts is *not prohibited* by IHL; it was simply recognized as a matter of fact, rendering it necessary to regulate such actions. This is very different from claiming that it is *explicitly authorized* by IHL. Importantly, there is nothing in the *travaux* of common Article 3 or Additional Protocol II that expresses a view that the legal basis to intern in such situations is to be found in IHL.

In principle, a legal basis to intern in non-international armed conflict could equally be located in customary international law. Indeed, it is also on this source that a number of commentators have relied for such a legal basis.[21] Robert Barnsby, for example, argues that there is overwhelming practice of states interning in non-international conflicts, suggesting that a legal basis exists in custom.[22] However, similarly to the arguments noted above concerning an implicit basis in treaty law, this practice demonstrates no more than the fact that IHL *does not prohibit* internment. To establish a rule of custom, one would need to demonstrate not only the existence of such practice but also accompanying *opinio iuris* to the effect that the relevant states rely on customary international law as providing the legal authority to intern in such situations.[23] Similarly, those arguments referred to above, that IHL treaty provisions provide an implicit legal basis to intern in non-international conflicts, require support from subsequent practice, such that states rely *on IHL* as the basis for detentions in such situations. Importantly, however, states generally rely on sources other than treaty-based IHL or customary international law, primarily domestic law, for providing the legal basis to intern in non-international conflicts.[24] Even in those situations where often no domestic

---

[20] K Mačák, 'Needle in a Haystack? Locating the Legal Basis for Detention in Non-International Armed Conflict' (2015) IYHR (forthcoming).
[21] See, eg, RE Barnsby, 'Yes We Can: The Authority to Detain as Customary International Law' (2009) 202 Mil L Rev 53; Pejic (n 10) 94; ICRC (n 16) 7.
[22] Barnsby (n 21). [23] *Lotus* (n 3) 28.
[24] Similarly, see E Debuf, *Captured in War: Lawful Internment in Armed Conflict* (Hart/Pedone, Oxford/Paris 2014) 471–2. See, eg, UN Commission on Human Rights, 'Report of the Working Group on Involuntary or Enforced Disappearances: Mission to Nepal', E/CN.4/2005/65/Add.1 (28 January 2005) [45] (on the Nepalese government's reliance on the 2002 Terrorist and Disruptive Activities (Control and Punishment) Act as the basis for internment); 'Respondents' Memorandum Regarding the Government's Detention Authority Relative to Detainees Held at Guantanamo Bay', *In Re: Guantanamo Bay Detainee Litigation*, Misc No 08-442 (TFH) (DDC 13 March 2009) 1 (demonstrating that the Obama Administration relies on domestic law as providing the authority to detain in its conflict with al-Qaeda); *Gherebi v Obama*, 609 F Supp 2d 43 (DDC 2009) 61–2 and *Hamlily v Obama*, 616 F Supp 2d 63 (DDC 2009) 71–2 (also relying on domestic law as providing a legal basis for detentions in the US' conflict with al-Qaeda); AS Deeks, 'Administrative Detention

3.1 The Legal Basis to Intern

law can be relied upon, such as certain extraterritorial non-international armed conflicts, states still tend to look to sources other than IHL or custom to provide the legal basis to intern.[25] As a result, the *opinio iuris* of states does not support the view that IHL, under either treaty or custom, provides a legal basis for internment in non-international conflicts.

It must be conceded, however, that at the time of writing there have been some recent expressions of *opinio iuris* here, and some writers have relied on these to support the view that a legal basis to intern in non-international conflicts lies in treaty and/or customary IHL.[26] The UK government, for example, in the case of *Serdar Mohammed v Ministry of Defence* relied, in part, on both treaty and custom as providing the legal basis for Serdar Mohammed's detention in the non-international armed conflict in Afghanistan.[27] Two points suggest that this expression of *opinio iuris* is of limited value, however. First, both claims were rejected at first instance and on appeal, with both the High Court of England and Wales and the Court of Appeal concluding that neither treaty nor customary law applicable in non-international armed conflict provide a legal basis to detain.[28] This is relevant practice and *opinio iuris* for the United Kingdom and, whilst at the time of writing it is unclear whether the case will further be appealed, it suggests that the position of the United Kingdom is yet to be settled.[29] Second, this claim by the United Kingdom represents a very recent change from its previous practice, in which it did not recognize a legal basis under IHL to intern in non-international armed conflicts.[30]

---

in Armed Conflict' (2009) 40 Case W Res J Intl L 403, 425 (on the Sri Lankan government's reliance on the 1979 Prevention of Terrorism Act as the basis for internment).

[25] Germany, Bundestag, Reply by the Federal Government to the Minor Interpellation by the Members Winfried Nachtwei, Alexander Bonde, Volker Beck (Cologne), further Members and the Parliamentary Group Bündis 90/Die Grünen—BT-Drs 16/6174, Basic Law and International Law in Deployments Abroad of the Federal Armed Forces: Treatment of Persons Taken into Custody, BT-Drs, 16/6282, 29 August 2007, 5–13 (relying on self-defence under Art 51 UNC and SCRs), cited in ICRC, Customary IHL Database: Practice Relating to Rule 99 Deprivation of Liberty (British Red Cross/ICRC) <https://www.icrc.org/customary-ihl/eng/docs/v2_rul_rule99> accessed 30 July 2015; United States, Speech by the Legal Advisor, US Department of State, 'The Obama Administration and International Law', ASIL, Washington, DC, 25 March 2010 (relying on self-defence, Afghan government consent and SCRs, as a matter of international law, and the Authorization for Use of Military Force (AUMF) as a matter of domestic law) <http://www.state.gov/s/l/releases/remarks/139119.htm> accessed 30 July 2015; ECtHR, *Al-Jedda v United Kingdom*, App No 27021/08, Judgment (Grand Chamber), 7 July 2011, [16] (the UK government relying on SCR 1546 in Iraq).

[26] Mačák (n 20).

[27] *Serdar Mohammed v Ministry of Defence* [2014] EWHC 1369 (QB), [239] (on implying a legal basis from the treaty provisions) and [254] (on custom).

[28] Ibid, [239]–[251] (rejecting the treaty-based argument) and [254]–[261] (rejecting the customary law argument); *Serdar Mohammed et al v Secretary of State for Defence; Yanus Rahmatullah and the Iraqi Civilian Claimants v Ministry of Defence and Foreign and Commonwealth Office* [2015] EWCA Civ 843, [200]–[219] (on implication from the treaty provisions) and [220]–[244] (on the customary law argument).

[29] International Law Commission (ILC), Second Report on Identification of Customary International Law by Michael Wood, Special Rapporteur, A/CN4/672, 22 May 2014, 36 [50] (stating that, where the state does not speak with one voice, 'its practice is ambivalent, and such conflict may well weaken the weight to be given to the practice concerned').

[30] *Serdar Mohammed* (n 27) [40] and [44] (UK statements reflecting the view that no legal basis to intern in Afghanistan existed). Similarly, compare UK Ministry of Defence, *Joint Doctrine*

It has also been suggested that the United States has similarly expressed an *opinio iuris* to the effect that custom (or at least IHL generally) provides a legal basis to intern in non-international conflicts.[31] Whilst certain statements by the US executive might be interpreted in such a manner,[32] their practice here is extremely equivocal, and they seem equally to rely on US domestic law as the basis for detention operations in their conflict with al-Qaeda,[33] which, as explained in section 5.2.3.1, is deemed by them to be a non-international armed conflict. Even more than the example of the United Kingdom above, therefore, the US' position here seems ambiguous. As a result, this very limited practice and *opinio iuris* suggesting that a legal basis to intern in non-international conflicts is to be found in either treaty-based IHL or custom cannot be considered sufficient either to confirm such an interpretation of the treaty provisions or to found a customary rule to that effect. Whilst it has been argued that this limited practice and *opinio iuris* is supported by the absence of 'any protest or denunciation from other members of the international community',[34] this is not sufficient for meeting the threshold required for the creation of a customary rule. First, it is rather misleading, as whilst the specific claim as to the location of a legal basis to intern in non-international conflicts may not itself have been challenged, the detention practices more generally of, for example, the United Kingdom and the United States in recent extraterritorial military operations have been criticized heavily.[35] Second, to require that other states specifically dissent from these legal claims that have only recently been made explicitly is surely unrealistic and incompatible with more conventional approaches to custom formation and treaty interpretation. In particular, whilst inaction or acquiescence can in some cases certainly be relevant to the formation of custom, whether as a form of practice itself[36] or

---

Publication 1-10: Prisoners of War, Internees and Detainees (Ministry of Defence, Shrivenham 2006) 1–7 [113a] and UK Ministry of Defence, *Joint Doctrine Publication 1-10: Captured Persons (CPERS)* (3rd edn, Ministry of Defence, Shrivenham 2015) 1–18 [148] (only the latter suggesting a legal basis to intern could be found in IHL); UK Ministry of Defence, *The Manual of the Law of Armed Conflict* (OUP, Oxford 2004) 403 ('[i]nternal armed conflicts, since they are principally governed by domestic law, will inevitably lead to an increase in detentions and other restrictions being imposed *by that law* for security reasons related to the conflict' (emphasis added))).

[31] Mačák (n 20).

[32] See, eg, Committee Against Torture, Second Periodic Report of States Parties: United States of America, CAT/C/48/Add.3/Rev.1, 13 January 2006, Annex I, [1] ('[t]here is no question that under the law of armed conflict, the United States has the authority to detain persons who have engaged in unlawful belligerence until the cessation of hostilities', cited in Mačák (n 20).

[33] 'Respondents' Memorandum' (n 24). Suggesting some other legal bases, but still not IHL or custom, see United States, Speech by the Legal Advisor (n 25) (relying on self-defence, Afghan consent, and Security Council authorization).

[34] Mačák (n 20).

[35] See the discussion of different practice in the context of Iraq and Afghanistan in section 5.2.2.

[36] M Akehurst, 'Custom As a Source of International Law' (1975) 47 BYIL 1, 18 ('[a] practice followed by a very small number of States can create a rule of customary law if there is no practice which conflicts with the rule'); GM Danilenko, 'The Theory of International Customary Law' (1988) 31 GYIL 9, 28 (suggesting that 'passive' customary practice 'increases the precedent value of active practice and thus becomes a major factor in the process of creating generally accepted customary rules'); R Kolb, 'Selected Problems in the Theory of Customary International Law' (2003) 50 NYIL 119, 135–6; ILC (n 29) 28–9 [42] ('[i]naction by States may be central to the development

3.1 The Legal Basis to Intern

as *opinio iuris*,[37] in the present case those states that have not expressly objected to this practice may have remained silent for various reasons. One must, therefore, be cautious in drawing normative inferences from such silence. Indeed, such caution is especially warranted here, where the practice invoked in support of the purported rule is not such as to demand a response from other states, given that the rights of other states are not directly and explicitly engaged. This not only undermines the value of this silence as relevant state practice,[38] but it also means it cannot, in itself, provide evidence of *opinio iuris*, for 'absence of protest implies acquiescence only if practice affects interests and rights of an inactive state'.[39]

A final argument that has been made is that, since IHL contains a legal basis to kill in non-international armed conflicts, it must also contain the lesser power to detain.[40] This argument is, of course, premised on the view that IHL contains a legal basis to use lethal force in non-international armed conflicts. This premise, however, is incorrect. As with internment, IHL simply does not prohibit the targeting of certain individuals (ie those directly participating in hostilities); it does not thereby create a legal basis to target such persons. Indeed, this argument misunderstands why we are asking for a legal basis to detain in non-international armed conflict. Such a legal basis is necessary as it is required by IHRL for detention to be lawful; with regard to the use of lethal force, however, IHRL does not require a legal basis as such but rather prohibits arbitrary deprivation of life.[41] It would be a strange thing indeed for a domestic law specifically to authorize

---

and ascertainment of rules of customary international law, in particular when it qualifies (or is perceived) as acquiescence' (footnotes omitted)).

[37] K Wolfke, *Custom in Present International Law* (2nd edn, Martinus Nijhoff 1993) 48 ('toleration of a practice by other states, considering all relevant circumstances, justifies the presumption of its acceptance as law'); ILC (n 29) 69 [77].

[38] ILC, 'Report of the Work of its Sixty-Sixth Session (5 May to 6 June and 7 July to 8 August 2014)', Official Records, Sixty-Ninth Session, Supp No 10 (A/69/10) 245 ('As to the inclusion of "inaction" as a form of practice, there was a general view that the issue needed to be further explored and clarified. Several members considered that the precise conditions by which inaction becomes of interest should be examined, indicating that silence or inaction may only be relevant when the circumstances call for some reaction'). For specific examples in the ILC debates, see eg, ILC, Provisional Summary Record of the 3225th Meeting (17 July 2014), A/CN.4/SR.3225, 18 September 2014, 6 (Mr Forteau) ('[o]nly certain types of inaction could constitute practice'); ibid, 10 (Mr Kittichaisaree) ('[s]ilence in the absence of an obligation to speak should not necessarily imply consent'). Debates in the Sixth Committee on the ILC's work on custom revealed a repeated concern that the relevance of inaction depended on the circumstances: see, eg, UNGA, Sixth Committee Summary Record of the 27th Meeting (5 November 2014), A/C.6/69/SR.27, 4 [17] (United States); ibid, 7–8 [37] (Jamaica); ibid, 13–14 [72] (Republic of Korea).

[39] GM Danilenko, *Law-Making in the International Community* (Martinus Nijhoff, Dordrecht 1993) 108. Similarly, see *North Sea Continental Shelf cases (Federal Republic of Germany/Denmark; Federal Republic of Germany/Netherlands)* [1969] ICJ Rep 3, [73] ('[t]hat non-ratification may sometimes be due to factors other than active disapproval of the convention concerned can hardly constitute a basis on which positive acceptance of its principles can be implied: the reasons are speculative, but the facts remain'); ILC (n 29) 69 [77].

[40] See, eg, S Aughey and A Sari, 'Targeting and Detention in Non-International Armed Conflict: *Serdar Mohammed* and the Limits of Human Rights Convergence' (2015) 91 Intl L Stud 60, 103–8. This argument was also made by the MoD in *Serdar Mohammed* (n 27) [252].

[41] Art 6(1) ICCPR; Art 2 ECHR (containing an exhaustive list of grounds on which deprivation of life would be permissible).

killing; rather, such laws generally specify in what circumstances killing is prohibited. A final problem with this argument is that it assumes parity between those persons subject to targeting and those subject to internment. Such parity, however, does not exist, with the category of persons subject to internment in an international armed conflict, for example, being far broader than those subject to targeting.[42]

Thus, whilst IHL recognizes that the parties to a non-international armed conflict will intern, it does not provide a legal basis for such actions; rather, it merely accepts that internment will occur and regulates it. This interpretation finds broad support in both scholarship and jurisprudence.[43] Indeed, this appears to be the general approach taken under the law of non-international armed conflict, which, whilst having developed by analogy to the law of international armed conflict, has done so by drawing only on prohibitive rules, without also incorporating those rules that grant specific legal authority for particular actions. As Sandesh Sivakumaran states in his treatise on the law of non-international armed conflict:

> It should also be recalled that the law of non-international armed conflict does not provide the parties to the conflict with a right to undertake certain actions. Rather, it prohibits certain actions and regulates other conduct should the parties choose to engage in particular endeavours.[44]

That this should be the case is to be expected: given that IHL applies without distinction to all parties to an armed conflict,[45] in extending rules to non-international conflicts, states have been keen to ensure that nothing in those rules could be read as authorizing the non-state party to engage in rebellious acts.[46]

---

[42] Compare, eg, Art 42 GCIV (permitting internment of civilians where absolutely necessary for reasons of security) with Art 51(3) API (permitting targeting of civilians only where and for so long as they directly participate in hostilities).

[43] See, eg, UN Commission on Human Rights, 'Report of the Working Group on Arbitrary Detention', E/CN.4/2006/7, 12 December 2005, [72]; G Rona, 'An Appraisal of US Practice Relating to "Enemy Combatants"' (2007) 10 YIHL 232, 240–1; Deeks (n 24) 404–5; M Hakimi, 'International Standards for Detaining Terrorism Suspects: Moving Beyond the Armed Conflict-Criminal Divide' (2009) 40 Case W Res J Intl L 593, 607; Olson (n 14) 452; Rodley and Pollard (n 11) 491; P Rowe, 'Is There a Right to Detain Civilians by Foreign Armed Forces During a Non-International Armed Conflict' (2011) 61 ICLQ 697; Debuf (n 24); *Ali Saleh Kahlah Al-Marri and Mark A Berman v Commander John Pucciarelli*, 534 F.3d 213 (2008), 234; *Serdar Mohammed* (n 27); *Serdar Mohammed* (n 28) [251]–[253]. As one possible (unreasoned) exception, see *R (Evans) v Secretary of State for Defence* [2010] EWHC 1445 (Admin), [17] (implying there is a 'right' under international law to intern in non-international conflicts, though without any elaboration or supporting authority).

[44] S Sivakumaran, *The Law of Non-International Armed Conflict* (OUP, Oxford 2012) 71. Similarly, see Rowe (n 43) 702 (in non-international armed conflicts, 'IHL is generally stated in negative, rather than in positive, terms. It prohibits acts, such as attacking those who do not take a direct part in hostilities or who have ceased to do so. It does not, of itself, give a legal power to attack those who do take a direct part in hostilities').

[45] C Greenwood, 'Scope of Application of Humanitarian Law' in D Fleck (ed), *The Handbook of International Humanitarian Law* (2nd edn, OUP, Oxford 2008) 56. The basis on which IHL binds non-state armed groups is explored below in section 3.4.

[46] See, eg, *Official Records of the Diplomatic Conference on the Reaffirmation and Development of International Humanitarian Law Applicable in Armed Conflicts, Geneva (1974–1977): Volume VII*

3.1 The Legal Basis to Intern

Consequently, the legal basis for internment during a non-international armed conflict must lie elsewhere, primarily in domestic law,[47] allowing states to adopt legislation permitting *state agents* to intern, whilst leaving non-state groups open to prosecution under domestic law.[48] Examples are cited above to states relying on other (non-IHL) sources to provide a legal basis to detain in extra-territorial non-international armed conflicts, notably Security Council resolutions and the right of self-defence under Article 51 UNC.[49] With regard to Security Council resolutions with simply a general authorization to 'take all necessary measures', given that they are designed to provide an exception to the general prohibition on the use of force, and thus speak principally to legality under the *ius ad bellum*, it is questionable whether they could in principle provide a sufficient legal basis for specific actions such as internment.[50] In any event, however, the vagueness of the general authorization in Chapter VII resolutions to 'take all necessary measures' would seem insufficiently precise to satisfy the principle of legality in human rights law.[51] This scepticism would appear even stronger for the argument that an exercise of self-defence under Article 51 of the Charter of the United Nations (UNC) could confer a legal basis to intern. Article 51 UNC speaks only to the inter-state relationship, acting as an exception to the prohibition on the use of force between states. It has no bearing, however, on the conduct of hostilities or other applicable rules of international law, and it is certainly not sufficiently precise to constitute a legal basis to detain.[52]

To conclude this section, though it is clear that IHL does not prohibit internment in non-international armed conflict, states can rely on neither treaty-based IHL nor custom for a *legal basis* to intern in non-international armed conflict. The temptation to say that IHL does not simply *not prohibit* internment but actually *authorizes* it is no doubt influenced by the interaction between IHL and IHRL in this area: if IHL explicitly authorizes internment, it is easier then to argue that that authorization operates as the *lex specialis* relative to applicable norms of

---

(Federal Political Department, Bern 1978) 132 (the US delegate objecting that draft Art 24 APII, on the protection of civilians from attack, 'even in its revised form, implied that rebels were allowed to choose their objectives. He was therefore against the article').

[47] Rowe (n 43) 702–3; Debuf (n 24) 459–60; G Rona, 'Is There a Way Out of the Non-International Armed Conflict Detention Dilemma?' (2015) 91 Intl L Stud 32, 37. See the references above at n 24 to domestic laws.

[48] See the discussion in section 1.3.1 on the challenges posed by this lack of combatant immunity in non-international conflicts. The requirement under IHRL that detentions have a legal basis, and the absence of any such basis for non-state groups, raises the question of whether such groups violate IHRL when detaining. This will be explored in chapter 6.

[49] See above at n 25.

[50] Both the High Court and Court of Appeal, though to different degrees, took the view that the general authorization to 'take all necessary measures' in SCRs can function as a legal basis for detention: *Serdar Mohammed* (n 27) at [218]–[219]; *Serdar Mohammed* (n 28) [146]–[157].

[51] See section 4.2.1 (on the need for clarity and predictability to satisfy the IHRL requirement of a legal basis for detention).

[52] Similarly, see Chatham House and ICRC, 'Expert Meeting on Procedural Safeguards for Security Detention in Non-International Armed Conflict' (2009) 91 IRRC 859, 867.

IHRL.[53] But it is important to keep these two issues separate. The question with which we are dealing here is whether IHL contains a legal basis for certain actions (in particular, detention) in non-international armed conflict. Its interaction with other applicable rules of international law (including IHRL) is a separate, secondary question.[54] To be consistent with IHRL, any such internment would thus need to be based on legal grounds established elsewhere, for example in domestic law. Thus, unlike in international armed conflicts, where IHL confers detention authority on states, in non-international conflicts, IHL presumes such powers already exist in domestic law and regulates them. The degree to which it so regulates internment is the subject of the remainder of this chapter.

3.2 Procedural Rules under Conventional IHL

Chapter 2 demonstrated that treaty-based IHL establishes a framework of rules regulating the grounds, procedures, and end-point of internment in international armed conflicts. This section will now examine whether any equivalent treaty rules exist under IHL applicable in non-international armed conflict. Common Article 3 and APII will be examined in turn.

3.2.1 Common Article 3

Chapter 1 introduced common Article 3, the provision specifically designed for application in non-international armed conflict and the 'minimum yardstick' below which no conduct may fall in any armed conflict.[55] Due to its basic character, the rules therein are very general. However, one of the key features of common Article 3 is the principle of humane treatment in the *chapeau* of paragraph one.[56] The *chapeau* reads:

> Persons taking no active part in the hostilities, including members of armed forces who have laid down their arms and those placed *hors de combat* by sickness, wounds, detention, or any other cause, *shall in all circumstances be treated humanely*, without any adverse distinction founded on race, colour, religion or faith, sex, birth or wealth, or any other similar criteria. (emphasis added)

The principle of humane treatment is then followed by four specific examples of treatment necessarily inconsistent therewith: violence to life and person, in particular murder, cruel treatment, mutilation, and torture; the taking of hostages; outrages upon personal dignity; and the passing of sentences or carrying out of executions without due process.[57]

---

[53] On the notion of *lex specialis*, see section 5.1.
[54] This secondary question is addressed in chapter 5.
[55] *Case Concerning Military and Paramilitary Activities in and Against Nicaragua (Nicaragua v United States)* [1986] ICJ Rep 14, [218].
[56] H Lauterpacht, 'The Problem of the Revision of the Law of War' (1952) 29 BYIL 360, 361.
[57] Common Art 3(1)(a)–(d).

3.2 Rules under Conventional IHL

Two points must be noted at the outset. First, the reference in paragraph one to 'detention' (which can be assumed to include preventive, security detention or 'internment') is a clear acknowledgement that it may occur in non-international armed conflict.[58] Indeed, as noted, APII refers explicitly to 'internment'.[59] Second, this recognition notwithstanding, common Article 3 contains no explicit rules specifying the grounds on which internment must be based, the procedures that must be followed, nor the point at which internment must end. Consequently, in what appears to be an application of the *Lotus* principle, Laura Lopez has concluded that, in non-international conflicts, 'innocent civilians may be detained arbitrarily'.[60] Practice, however, confirms that detentions in non-international armed conflicts are not unregulated by international law generally, and thus this view, to the extent that it makes such a claim, cannot be valid.[61] Whilst some acknowledge the relevance of other areas of international law (the most relevant being IHRL), many continue to view conventional IHL as silent in this area, arguing that it merely 'indicates that internment occurs in non-international conflicts but contains no indication of how it is to be regulated'.[62]

Conversely, whilst acknowledging that common Article 3 contains no explicit procedural rules applicable to internment, certain commentators are of the view that it is not silent here. Joanna Dingwall, for example, has argued that it prohibits 'unlawful confinement', seeing it as simply 'self-evident' that such acts would be inconsistent with the principle of humane treatment.[63] Others take a similar view, considering common Article 3 to prohibit either 'unlawful confinement' or 'arbitrary deprivation of liberty'.[64] Moreover, as Dingwall noted,[65] the Prosecutor of the International Criminal Tribunal for the former Yugoslavia (ICTY) has stated

---

[58] Deeks (n 24) 413.   [59] Art 5 APII; Pejic (n 5) 377.   [60] Lopez (n 1) 935.

[61] See UN resolutions condemning arbitrary arrests and detentions in non-international armed conflicts as violations of IHL and IHRL: eg, UNGA Res 55/116 (2000) (Sudan) [2(ii)]; UNSC Res 2100 (2013) (Mali) preambular [9]; UNSC Res 2139 (2014) (Syria) [1].

[62] Olson (n 1) 208. Similarly, see K Dörmann, 'To What Extent Does International Humanitarian Law provide for the Supervision of the Lawfulness of Detention?: Presentation' in The University Centre for International Humanitarian Law (n 10) 15; L Doswald-Beck, 'Introduction: Background Paper' in The University Centre for International Humanitarian Law (n 10) 3; Pejic (n 5) 377; A Jachec-Neale, 'Status and Treatment of Prisoners of War and Other Persons Deprived of Their Liberty' in E Wilmshurst and S Breau (eds), *Perspectives on the ICRC Study on Customary International Humanitarian Law* (CUP, Cambridge 2007) 313; M Sassòli and LM Olson, 'The Relationship between International Humanitarian and Human Rights Law Where It Matters: Admissible Killing and Internment of Fighters in Non-International Armed Conflicts' (2008) 90 IRRC 599, 618; T Davidson and K Gibson, 'Experts Meeting on Security Detention Report' (2009) 40 Case W Res J Intl L 323, 337; Deeks (n 24) 413; Hakimi (n 43) 607.

[63] J Dingwall, 'Unlawful Confinement as a War Crime: The Jurisprudence of the Yugoslav Tribunal and the Common Core of International Humanitarian Law Applicable to Contemporary Armed Conflicts' (2004) 9 JCSL 133, 150.

[64] See, eg, GS Corn, 'Enemy Combatants and Access to *Habeas Corpus*: Questioning the Validity of the Prisoner of War Analogy' (2007) 5 Santa Clara J Intl L 236, 260–1; C Droege, '"In truth the leitmotiv": The Prohibition of Torture and Other Forms of Ill-Treatment in International Humanitarian Law' (2007) 89 IRRC 515, 537; R Goodman, 'Rationales for Detention: Security Threats and Intelligence Value' in MN Schmitt (ed), *The War in Afghanistan: A Legal Analysis* (2009) (Vol 85, US Naval War College International Law Studies) 373–4.

[65] Dingwall (n 63) 142–3.

that 'arbitrary deprivation of liberty, without due process of law, inherently constitutes a serious attack on human dignity within the meaning of Cruel Treatment' in common Article 3.[66] Similarly, the ICRC has stated that 'common Article 3... require[s] that all civilians and persons *hors de combat* be treated humanely... whereas arbitrary deprivation of liberty is not compatible with this requirement'.[67] Indeed, the Inter-American Commission on Human Rights has held that, during the non-international conflict in Colombia, certain detentions by paramilitary groups constituted 'arbitrary deprivations of liberty, in violation of international humanitarian law'.[68] Finally, this view appears to have been endorsed at a 2002 conference of the African Parliamentary Union, comprising twenty-one African states, which declared that arbitrary detention, inter alia, in any armed conflict 'seriously violate[s] the rules of International Humanitarian Law'.[69]

These views are not unreasonable interpretations of the humane treatment requirement in common Article 3, as the ordinary meaning of that principle certainly allows for arbitrary deprivations of liberty to be covered. Indeed, the broad scope of the principle has been highlighted by the ICTY:

...while there are four sub-paragraphs [in common Article 3(1)] which specify the absolutely prohibited forms of inhuman treatment from which there can be no derogation, the general guarantee of humane treatment is not elaborated, except for the guiding principle underlying the Convention, that its object is the humanitarian one of protecting the individual *qua* human being and, therefore, it must safeguard the entitlements which flow therefrom.[70]

International law has long recognized that liberty, and freedom from the arbitrary deprivation thereof, constitutes one of the 'entitlements which flow' from being a human being.[71] As such, arbitrary deprivation of this right could qualify as

---

[66] *Prosecutor v Fatmir Limaj et al* (Prosecution's Final Brief (Redacted Public Version)) ICTY-03-66 (26 July 2005) [391]–[392]. It should be noted, however, that, since Dingwall's article, the ICTY Trial Chamber in *Prosecutor v Fatmir Limaj et al* (Trial Judgment) ICTY-03-66 (30 November 2005) acquitted the defendants of the charge of unlawful detention as a war crime, which the Prosecutor argued violated the common Article 3 prohibition of cruel treatment, concluding at [232] that 'in the circumstances of this case, these acts in and of themselves do not amount to a serious attack on human dignity within the meaning of cruel treatment' (emphasis in original). It did not reject the principle that such acts *might* as such constitute a violation of common Art 3, however.
[67] J-M Henckaerts and L Doswald-Beck, *Customary International Humanitarian Law, Volume I: Rules* (CUP, Cambridge 2005) 344 (Rule 99).
[68] Inter-American Commission on Human Rights, 'Third Report on the Human Rights Situation in Colombia' (26 February 1999) OEA/Ser.L/V/II.102 Doc 9 rev 1, ch IV [300] <http://www.cidh.org/countryrep/Colom99en/table of contents.htm> accessed 31 July 2015. See also ibid [122] (noting that IHL prohibits internment of civilians except for imperative reasons of security, finding at [120]–[132] violations of this rule by non-state armed groups in Colombia).
[69] African Parliamentary Conference on International Humanitarian Law for the Protection of Civilians during Armed Conflict, Niamey, 18–20 February 2002, Final Declaration, preamble <http://www.ipu.org/splz-e/niamey02.htm> accessed 31 July 2015.
[70] *Prosecutor v Zlatko Aleksovski* (Trial Judgment) ICTY-95-14/1 (25 June 1999) [49] (footnotes omitted). Similarly, see JS Pictet (ed), *Commentary to Geneva Convention IV Relative to the Protection of Civilian Persons in Time of War* (ICRC, Geneva 1958) 204.
[71] Art 9(1) ICCPR; Art 5(1) ECHR; Art 6 ACHPR; Universal Declaration of Human Rights, UNGA Res 217 A(III) (1948), Art 9.

inhumane treatment. Moreover, the open-endedness of the 'humane treatment' requirement helps to avoid problems of inter-temporality that might otherwise restrict our ability to interpret it with reference to subsequent developments in international law.[72]

It might be questioned, however, whether the humane treatment requirement is too vague to yield such a norm. Indeed, overly broad treaty terms have been found by the ICJ to undermine the extent to which they are capable of yielding specific rights and obligations.[73] This is particularly the case where the object and purpose of the treaty does not support the specific obligation which is argued to arise from the vague provision.[74] However, common Article 3 is clearly intended as the source of specific obligations for belligerents, evidenced by the explicit enumeration of certain acts prohibited by the humane treatment requirement.[75] Moreover, interpreting the humane treatment requirement in common Article 3 as prohibiting arbitrary or unlawful detention would seem perfectly consistent with the object and purpose of the Geneva Conventions. Thus, it is generally argued that IHL, including the Geneva Conventions, serves two purposes, those of humanity and military necessity;[76] although the balance has, arguably, shifted towards the former since the Second World War.[77] Whilst interpreting common Article 3 as prohibiting *all* deprivations of liberty would no doubt be inconsistent with the military necessity prong of IHL, viewing it as excluding *arbitrary* deprivations of liberty, for example, would not. Not only would such a rule advance the humanitarian goals of the Conventions, but to prohibit arbitrary detention would, it is submitted, also be consistent with the principle of military necessity, for detaining a person arbitrarily (ie without reason) could never be militarily necessary. This is not to suggest that the principle of military necessity sits above the positive rules applicable in armed conflict as an additional constraining element, but rather that military necessity could not be invoked to justify arbitrary deprivations of liberty.

One could, therefore, reasonably reach the conclusion that common Article 3, by virtue of its humane treatment requirement, prohibits arbitrary detention. The difficulty with the approach taken above, however, is that it is unclear what the

---

[72] *Dispute regarding Navigational and Related Rights (Costa Rica v Nicaragua)* (Judgment) [2009] ICJ Rep 213, [64] ('...there are situations in which the parties' intent upon conclusion of the treaty was...to give the terms used...a meaning or content capable of evolving, not one fixed once and for all, so as to make allowance for, among other things, developments in international law').

[73] *Case Concerning Oil Platforms (Islamic Republic of Iran v United States of America)* (Preliminary Objections) [1996] ICJ Rep 803, [24]–[31]; Sir F Berman, 'Treaty "Interpretation" in a Judicial Context' (2004) Yale J Intl L 315, 317.

[74] *Oil Platforms* (Preliminary Objections) (n 73) [28].

[75] Ibid, [27] (noting the importance of such explicit enumerations as evidence that a broadly-phrased provision is capable of yielding specific rights and obligations).

[76] C Greenwood, 'Historical Development and Legal Basis' in D Fleck (ed), *The Handbook of International Humanitarian Law* (2nd edn, OUP, Oxford 2008) 37–8; Dinstein (n 18) 4–6; MN Schmitt, 'Military Necessity and Humanity in International Humanitarian Law: Preserving the Delicate Balance' (2010) 50 VJIL 795, 798; GD Solis, *The Law of Armed Conflict: International Humanitarian Law in War* (CUP, Cambridge 2010) 258.

[77] *Legality of the Threat or Use of Nuclear Weapons* (Advisory Opinion) [1996] ICJ Rep 226, [95]; T Meron, 'The Humanization of Humanitarian Law' (2000) 94 AJIL 239; Schmitt (n 76) 807–11.

content of such a rule would be; indeed, as noted, certain commentators refer to the prohibition in terms of 'unlawful' rather than 'arbitrary' detention.[78] It is submitted, however, that an examination of the context of common Article 3 not only supports the view that arbitrary detention is itself prohibited, but also makes clear what the content of that rule might be. To demonstrate this, a brief detour into the *travaux* of the provision is necessary. Thus, whilst common Article 3 is often labelled a 'Convention in miniature', given its apparent self-containment,[79] its drafting history reveals an intimate relationship with the other provisions in the 1949 Geneva Conventions.[80] This becomes clear when one recognizes that the content of common Article 3 is based on the various proposals that were made for preambles to the Conventions (which, for unrelated reasons, were never adopted).[81] Common Article 3 may, therefore, be considered to embody the principles, including that of humane treatment, from which the specific rules of the Conventions are derived.[82]

Based on this drafting history, the ICRC Commentary views the principle of humane treatment in common Article 3 as the 'leitmotiv' of the Geneva Conventions.[83] Indeed, it can be seen not only in common Article 3 itself, but also as an explicit principle in each Convention applicable in international armed conflict,[84] which, the ICRC argues, reflects the fact that the principle constitutes the 'basic theme' of the Conventions.[85] For example, Article 27(1) GCIV contains the humane treatment principle for the purposes of GCIV, and the Commentary notes that that article is 'the central point in relation to which all other provisions [of the Conventions] must be considered'.[86] Importantly, the principle is 'identical' in each provision in which it appears throughout the Conventions.[87] In interpreting the principle in common Article 3, we may, therefore, make reference to

---

[78] See, eg, Dingwall (n 63) 150.

[79] *Final Record of the Diplomatic Conference of Geneva of 1949: Volume II, Section B* (ICRC, 1963) 35; JS Pictet (ed), *Commentary to Geneva Convention I for the Amelioration of the Condition of the Wounded and Sick in Armed Forces in the Field* (ICRC, Geneva 1952) 48.

[80] A similar argument is made in Dingwall (n 63) 148–52.

[81] Pictet, *GCI* (n 79) 23. See, eg, the various proposals for preambles, clearly mirroring what became common Art 3: *Final Record of the Diplomatic Conference of Geneva of 1949: Volume II, Section A* (ICRC, 1963) 366 (Soviet proposal); ibid, 366–7 (Swiss proposal); *Remarks and Proposals Submitted by the International Committee of the Red Cross: Documents for the Consideration of Governments Invited by the Swiss Federal Council to Attend the Diplomatic Conference at Geneva (April 21, 1949)* (ICRC, Geneva 1949) 8 (ICRC proposal); *Final Record of the Diplomatic Conference of Geneva of 1949: Volume III* (ICRC, 1963) 97 (French proposal).

[82] See *Report on the Work of the Conference of Government Experts for the Study of the Conventions for the Protection of War Victims: Geneva, April 14–26, 1947* (ICRC, Geneva 1947) 8, 103, 272 (calling for the application in non-international armed conflicts of the 'principles' underlying what would become GCI, GCII, and GCIII); *Final Record: Vol II-B* (n 79) 123 (French proposal calling for the application of the 'provisions of the preamble to the [Civilians] Convention' to non-international armed conflicts).

[83] Pictet, *GCIV* (n 70) 204.

[84] Art 12(2) GCI; Art 12(2) GCII; Art 13(1) GCIII; Art 27(1) GCIV.

[85] JS Pictet (ed), *Commentary to Geneva Convention III Relative to the Treatment of Prisoners of War* (ICRC, Geneva 1960) 140.

[86] Pictet, *GCIV* (n 70) 201. [87] Ibid, 38.

understandings of it elsewhere, for these references may be seen as part of the context of common Article 3.[88] In this regard, it is important to note that Article 27 GCIV draws a clear relationship between humane treatment on the one hand and internment on the other. Thus, whereas Articles 27(1)–(3) GCIV lay down the basic humanitarian principles of GCIV (including humane treatment), paragraph four then reads: 'However, the Parties to the conflict may take such measures of control and security in regard to protected persons as may be necessary as a result of the war.' It was shown in chapter 2 that such 'measures of control and security' include internment and that Article 27(4) GCIV underpins the more detailed civilian internment regimes in GCIV.[89] Article 27 GCIV, therefore, makes clear that operating alongside the principle of humane treatment (as well as the other basic guarantees in Articles 27(1)–(3)) is the notion that parties may intern where necessary as a result of the war. The precise relationship between humane treatment and internment is alluded to in the ICRC Commentary to Article 27, which states that the requirement of humane treatment is,

...valid 'in all circumstances' and 'at all times', and appl[ies], for example, to cases where a protected person is the *legitimate* object of strict measures, since the dictates of humanity and measures of security or repression, even when they are severe, are not necessarily incompatible.[90]

From this, it is clear that the humane treatment requirement is non-derogable. It is also clear that measures of control, such as internment, when *legitimate*, are compatible with the humane treatment requirement. It is therefore submitted that the notion of necessity in Article 27(4) can be considered to inform the content of the principle of humane treatment in Article 27(1), such that a measure of control or security (internment) is consistent with humane treatment only where it is 'necessary as a result of the war'; where not necessary, internment in itself (that is, the deprivation of liberty as such, without reference to standards of treatment or conditions of detention) will be inhumane.

Whilst Article 27 GCIV itself does not apply in non-international armed conflict, it does offer an understanding of what the humane treatment principle requires. Given its identical meanings in common Article 3 and Article 27, that understanding may be applied when interpreting the former. On this basis, a

---

[88] Art 31(1) VCLT; J-M Sorel and V Boré Eveno, '1969 Vienna Convention, Article 31: General Rule of Intepretation' in O Corten and P Klein (eds), *The Vienna Conventions on the Law of Treaties: A Commentary, Volume I* (OUP, Oxford 2011) 824 (noting that 'context' includes the treaty text itself).

[89] See section 2.2.1.

[90] Pictet, *GCIV* (n 70) 205 (emphasis added). Similarly, see *Final Record: Vol II-A* (n 81) 712 (the Swiss delegate commenting that the fourth paragraph 'did not, however, restore to Governments the right to take arbitrary action, nor did it affect the general prohibitions resulting from the humanitarian principles of the Convention'); ibid, 821 (Committee III noting that draft Art 27(4) 'does not re-establish arbitrary governmental power... it leaves intact the general prohibitions imposed by the humanitarian principles of the Convention'); *Prosecutor v Dario Kordić and Mario Čerkez* (Trial Judgment) ICTY-95-14/2-T (26 February 2001) [281] (noting that even where security measures are resorted to pursuant to Art 27(4), 'the treatment of protected persons must in all circumstances meet the standards set forth in paragraphs 1, 2 and 3 of Article 27').

strong argument may be made that common Article 3 prohibits internment that is not necessary as a result of the war. In so doing, it is possible to move beyond stating that it is simply 'self-evident' that the principle of humane treatment in common Article 3 prohibits arbitrary detention; the Conventions themselves make clear that this is the case and confirm that what is 'arbitrary' is any deprivation of liberty that is not 'necessary as a result of the war'. Importantly, as section 3.3.1 will demonstrate, this interpretation of IHL as prohibiting arbitrary detention in non-international armed conflict finds support in the practice of states and international bodies.[91] Whilst it is true, therefore, that common Article 3 does not contain explicit procedural rules on internment, it is not the case that it is entirely silent in this area.

It is clear, nevertheless, that the degree to which common Article 3 regulates internment is very limited. In particular, whereas chapter 2 demonstrated that, in international conflicts, IHL builds upon this basic prohibition of internment that is not necessary as a result of the war, by, for example, requiring initial and periodic review, this is not the case in non-international conflicts. Here, the basic prohibition is all that common Article 3 may be considered to stipulate. The argument above is premised on the structure of Article 27 GCIV and its relationship to common Article 3; to go further, for example by also claiming that the review procedures apply via the humane treatment principle, might no longer reflect a good faith interpretation. Nonetheless, one can discern certain cases that would fall on either side of the line of what is necessary as a result of the conflict. For example, it is clear that the internment of a member of a non-state armed group that is known personally to carry out attacks continuously against the state is not likely to be considered a breach of this basic rule of IHL. Similarly, for the non-state armed group, the internment of a member of the state armed forces would likely not be in violation of this rule.[92] On the other hand, the detention of a civilian with no clear evidence that they pose a threat to state security necessitating their internment would be unlawful. Indeed, one can reasonably draw on the elaborations of the internment standards applicable under IHL in international armed conflicts that were discussed in chapter 2 to help inform the parameters of this rule in non-international armed conflicts, though chapter 7 will demonstrate the limits of such analogical reasoning here.[93] It should be emphasized, however, that this all speaks only to whether a particular detention *is in violation of*

---

[91] Subsequent practice is, of course, an important reference when interpreting treaties: Art 31(3)(b) VCLT.
[92] Inter-American Commission on Human Rights, 'Third Report on the Human Rights Situation in Colombia' (n 68) Ch IV [131]–[132] ('[t]he Commission deems it necessary to clarify why it does not condemn, as violative of international law, the acts of armed dissident groups in capturing members of the Army and security forces where the captives are not converted into hostages…International humanitarian law does not prohibit the capture of combatants. It simply treats such captures as a situation of deprivation of liberty which may, in practice, occur in armed conflict'). The binding nature of this rule for non-state armed groups is confirmed in section 3.4 below.
[93] For similar arguments based on analogies to the law of international armed conflict, see R Goodman, 'The Detention of Civilians in Armed Conflict' (2009) 103 AJIL 48; Debuf (n 24) 508–14. Relevant case law, notably that of the United States, attempting to construct a detention standard

IHL applicable in non-international armed conflict; other applicable rules of international law may further limit when states can detain in such situations, and this will be explored in subsequent chapters.

Finally, as noted in section 2.2.1 regarding civilian internment in international armed conflict, whereas the test for determining the necessity of internment under Article 42 GCIV is objective, the test under Article 78 GCIV appears subjective, referring to the requirement that the state 'consider' internment necessary for security. The reference in Article 27(4) to 'measures of control...as may be necessary', rather than 'as may be *considered* necessary', demonstrates that this test, like that in Article 42 GCIV, is objective, and, since we are drawing on Article 27(4), the test for non-international armed conflicts may also be considered objective. Indeed, Nils Melzer views Article 27(4) as an expression of the principle of military necessity,[94] and he argues that, '[i]t would contradict the nature of military necessity as an abstract principle of law, and as a decisive restraint on military action, to leave its assessment entirely to the operating party to the conflict'.[95] More generally, it is clear from other areas of international law in which necessity features as a basis for particular acts, that such tests, absent clear indication to the contrary, set objective standards.[96] Without the need for some degree of reasonableness in the claim of necessity, the prohibition of internment that is not necessary as a result of the war could be rendered meaningless, for what is necessary would be left entirely to the whim of each commander. Moreover, this necessity test includes within it a proportionality assessment, such that internment can only be necessary as a result of the conflict where there are no other less restrictive means for containing the threat. That this is an essential element of the necessity test was shown in section 2.2.1 in the case of civilian internment in international armed conflicts, and it applies equally here.

3.2.2 Additional Protocol II

The relevance of APII for the procedural regulation of internment can be addressed swiftly. As noted in chapter 1, the field of application of APII is more narrowly

---

for the US conflict with al-Qaeda, will be discussed in chapter 7 when considering this issue *de lege ferenda*.

[94] N Melzer, *Targeted Killing in International Law* (OUP, Oxford 2008) 291 (fn 263).

[95] Ibid, 291–2. Whether one agrees or not with Melzer's view of military necessity as a 'decisive restraint on military action' does not detract from the point that necessity entails an objective test.

[96] *Case Concerning Oil Platforms (Islamic Republic of Iran v United States of America)* Judgment [2003] ICJ Rep 161, [73] ('the requirement of international law that measures taken avowedly in self-defence must have been necessary for that purpose is strict and objective, leaving no room for any "measure of discretion"'); *Case Concerning the Gabčikovo-Nagymaros Project (Hungary v Slovakia)* Judgment [1997] ICJ Rep 7, [51] (with regard to the invocation of necessity as a circumstance precluding wrongfulness under the law of state responsibility, the ICJ noted that 'the State concerned is not the sole judge of whether those conditions [that must be met for a valid necessity plea] have been met'); *CMS Gas Transmission Co v Argentine Republic*, ICSID Case No ARB/01/08, Award, 12 May 2005, [370] (regarding necessity as a basis for non-precluded measures under a bilateral investment treaty, the tribunal held that, 'when States intend to create for themselves a right to determine unilaterally the legitimacy of extraordinary measures importing non-compliance with obligations assumed in a treaty, they do so expressly').

defined than that of common Article 3.[97] Thus, Christopher Greenwood notes that APII is applicable only to those non-international armed conflicts that we might label a civil war.[98]

As with common article 3, APII recognizes that internment will occur in non-international conflicts by specifying minimum treatment standards for internees.[99] Once again, however, APII lacks any explicit reference to procedural rules on internment. Part II, comprising Articles 4–6, elaborates the principle of humane treatment in common Article 3, but focuses on treatment standards and the conditions of internment rather than on grounds or procedural safeguards.[100] First, Article 4 contains 'fundamental guarantees' applicable to those who are not, or no longer, taking a direct part in hostilities, including internees. As with common Article 3, it sets out the humane treatment principle in paragraph one and then gives examples of treatment that would be inconsistent therewith.[101] However, rather than addressing the act of internment itself, this article prescribes certain substantive standards of treatment, such as a prohibition on acts of terrorism.[102] That said, Article 4(2)(b) prohibits collective punishments, which 'concerns not only penalties imposed in the normal judicial process, but also any other kind of sanction'.[103] Certain commentators and courts have argued on this basis that internment of one person cannot be justified solely by another's acts; the justification necessitating internment, so the argument goes, must apply to each internee.[104] However, the language of Article 4(2)(b) APII demonstrates that it applies to sanctions or punishments; internment, on the other hand, is a preventive measure, based on future security threat.[105] It is submitted that the same end can be reached via the prohibition of unnecessary internment, shown in the previous section to apply under common Article 3. Thus, internment could not reasonably be necessary if based solely on the actions of another individual.[106]

The remainder of Part II of APII is similarly without relevance to the procedural regulation of internment. Thus, Article 5 APII, entitled '[p]ersons whose liberty has been restricted', is concerned not with procedural rules but rather with the conditions of and treatment during internment.[107] Finally, Article 6 elaborates the requirement in common Article 3(1)(d) that sentences and executions be passed only after judgment by a 'regularly constituted court' offering essential standards of due process. As with that provision, Article 6, being concerned with 'prosecution and punishment of criminal offences,'[108] is not relevant to the non-penal measure of internment.

---

[97] Y Sandoz, C Swinarski, and B Zimmerman (eds), *Commentary on the Additional Protocols of 8 June 1977 to the Geneva Conventions of 12 August 1949* (ICRC/Martinus Nijhoff, Geneva 1987) 1349–50.
[98] Greenwood (n 45) 55.   [99] Art 5 APII.   [100] Deeks (n 24) 414.
[101] Arts 4(2)(a)–(h) APII.   [102] Art 4(2)(d) APII.   [103] Sandoz et al (n 97) 1374.
[104] Pejic (n 5) 381–2; Davidson and Gibson (n 62) 340; Bosnia and Herzegovina, Court of Bosnia and Herzegovina, *Lučić case*, Judgment, 19 September 2007, 67–8, cited in ICRC, Customary IHL Database (n 25).
[105] Pejic (n 5) 375–6.
[106] Similarly, see the discussion in section 2.2.1 on the need for individual determinations of security threat under the GCIV internment regimes.
[107] Sandoz et al (n 97) 1384.   [108] Art 6(1) APII.

Notwithstanding its fleshing out of common Article 3, APII therefore adds nothing to the procedural regulation of internment. Given that APII was designed to 'develop and supplement' common Article 3, this is disappointing.[109] Indeed, there was recognition before 1977 that common Article 3 provided insufficient procedural safeguards for internees. Richard Baxter, for example, commenting in 1974 on the future development of the law of non-international armed conflict, stated:

> The internment of individuals who have not engaged in hostilities but are thought to represent a threat to the security of the state should... be subject to procedural and substantive safeguards.[110]

No further developments in this area have since occurred under treaty law. As a result, the only relevant norm that arguably may be distilled from the treaty rules applicable in non-international conflicts is a prohibition of internment that is not necessary as a result of the conflict, for example for security reasons. This is in contrast to the treaty rules applicable in international armed conflicts, which define who may be interned, what review mechanisms must be provided, and the point at which they must be released.[111] In light of this clear gap in conventional IHL, the next section will examine the extent to which customary IHL might be of relevance here.

3.3 Procedural Rules under Customary IHL

At the time of the adoption of the Additional Protocols in 1977, it was thought that the international regulation of non-international armed conflicts was too novel for customary rules to have crystallized, hence the Martens Clause in APII making no reference to custom.[112] Chapter 1 noted, however, that customary rules have subsequently emerged that extend the norms traditionally applicable only in international armed conflicts to non-international conflicts, contributing to the partial erosion of the distinction between the two categories of armed conflict.[113] This section examines whether this is true regarding the procedural regulation of internment. In so doing, it is important to note that we are concerned here with what might be termed 'customary *IHL*'. By using this term, it is not suggested that customary international law is naturally divided into categories according to its subject matter; rather, as is also the case with treaty law, the various categories to which we refer (such as 'IHL', 'international environmental law', and 'international economic law') are merely useful descriptors of those rules

---

[109] Art 1(1) APII; Sandoz et al (n 97) 1324.
[110] RR Baxter, 'Ius in Bello Interno: The Present and Future Law' in JN Moore (ed), *Law and Civil War in the Modern World* (The Johns Hopkins University Press, Baltimore 1974) 535.
[111] See, generally, chapter 2.
[112] Compare APII, preambular [4], and Art 1(2) API; Sandoz et al (n 97) 1341.
[113] See section 1.1.

that share certain common features.[114] This is important to remember because, as will become clear, much of the practice in this area is very general, particularly regarding the situations to which it refers. Ashley Deeks, for example, notes that, notwithstanding states introducing administrative detention laws, it is often unclear whether they are intended for, or apply in, armed conflict situations.[115] In addition, as will be demonstrated in the next chapter, there is much state practice supporting a general prohibition of arbitrary detention in international law, but without any indication as to its application in armed conflict. The focus in this section, however, is on custom arising from practice specifically in the context of non-international armed conflict, and it is in this sense that the term 'customary IHL' is used. More general practice, not specific to non-international conflicts, will be examined in chapter 4,[116] where it will be shown that there exist generally applicable rules of customary international law that regulate detention in all situations.

One might reasonably question whether such an assessment of the state of custom is valid (or at least necessary), given the potentially artificial nature of this categorization and the fact that there is much practice that is not specific to non-international armed conflict. A better approach, it might be argued, is to examine state practice with respect to detention generally, both within and without armed conflict, with the scope of any resulting customary rules flowing naturally from that practice and its accompanying *opinio iuris*. The present author, however, feels that a separate examination of 'customary IHL' is useful for three principal reasons. First, the goal here is, in part, to consider whether the distinction between international and non-international armed conflict has been eroded in this area by custom, in common with other areas. Such erosion follows from the general extension of rules applicable in international armed conflicts to non-international conflicts. This requires looking at the practice of states in the specific situation of a non-international armed conflict. Second, whilst such views are shown in section 4.1 to be invalid, certain states consider operations conducted during any armed conflict to be regulated by IHL alone, to the exclusion of other areas of international law (specifically IHRL).[117] Other states have claimed more specifically that certain procedural rules do apply that regulate detention in non-international conflicts to a similar degree as exist in international conflicts, which then displace otherwise applicable rules of IHRL.[118] This is illustrative of the point made in section 1.3.2,

---

[114] Similarly, see F Hampson, 'Other Areas of Customary Law in Relation to the Study' in E Wilmshurst and S Breau (eds), *Perspectives on the ICRC Study on Customary International Humanitarian Law* (CUP, Cambridge 2007) 54–8; Report of the Study Group of the International Law Commission, 'Fragmentation of International Law: Difficulties Arising from the Diversification and Expansion of International Law', Finalized by Martti Koskenniemi, 13 April 2006, A/CN.4/L.682, [129]–[133].
[115] Deeks (n 24) 422. [116] Section 4.3.
[117] See, eg, UN Human Rights Committee (HRC), Fourth Periodic Reports of States Parties due in 2013: Israel, CCPR/C/ISR/4, 12 December 2013, [45]–[49].
[118] Australia Permanent Mission to the UN Geneva, Australian Response to UN Working Group on Arbitrary Detention's Draft Principles and Guidelines on remedies and procedures on

3.3 Rules under Customary IHL

that the convergence of the law of international and non-international armed conflict, contrary to its traditionally humanizing purpose, might now serve to weaken protections in non-international armed conflicts, such convergence raising the possibility that more protective rules of IHRL will be displaced by more permissive rules of IHL. Considering what customary IHL in particular has to say on this topic is, therefore, important. Finally, whereas the binding nature of IHRL vis-à-vis non-state actors is controversial,[119] it is reasonable to presume, in common with IHL generally, that customary rules that emerge from state practice specifically in non-international conflicts are intended to bind both states and non-state groups equally. That said, such a presumption must remain rebuttable by state practice and *opinio iuris* to the contrary.[120] There is, therefore, value in examining state practice and *opinio iuris* in the specific context of non-international armed conflicts, before an examination of customary international law more generally is carried out in chapter 4.

It should be noted at the outset that there is some state practice that provides support for the contention that the law of international and non-international armed conflict have converged with respect to detention. For example, the military doctrine of certain states suggests that no distinction is drawn between the rules they apply to the regulation of detention in international and non-international armed conflicts.[121] Moreover, in the Copenhagen Principles on the Handling of Detainees, adopted by a number of states in October 2012,[122] a set of procedural guidelines for application in 'international military operations' (intended to

---

the right of anyone deprived of his or her liberty, Note 23/2015, 17 March 2015, [9] (referring to the Copenhagen Principles, discussed below, as embodying the principles that, in Australia's view, govern detention in non-international conflicts); *Serdar Mohammed* (n 28) [174] ('[i]t was also the Secretary of State's case that there were procedural safeguards for noninternational armed conflicts in substance similar to the principles expressly provided for international armed conflicts in Geneva III and IV, which could be derived from the nature of international humanitarian law and customary international law').

[119] This is discussed in section 6.3.
[120] The binding nature of customary IHL for non-state groups is discussed below in section 3.4.3.
[121] See, with regard to detention specifically, UK, *CPERS* (n 30) [1-18] and Annex 1B (respectively, that persons can be interned for imperative reasons of security in non-international armed conflict and specifying the review procedures for internees, without differentiating between international and non-international armed conflicts). With regard to applying IHL generally (including, presumably, rules on detention) in any armed conflict, see, The United States Army Judge Advocate General's Legal Center and School, *Law of Armed Conflict Deskbook* (Charlottesville 2014) 27–8 ('DoD policy requires that all "[m]embers of the DoD Components comply with the law of war during all armed conflicts, however such conflicts are characterized, and in all other military operations"'); Judge Advocate General (Canada), *Law of Armed Conflict at the Operational and Tactical Levels* (Office of the Judge Advocate General, Ottawa 2001) 17–1 ('...the law applicable to such conflicts [non-international] is limited. It is CF [Canadian Forces'] policy, however, that the CF will, as a minimum, apply the spirit and principles of the LOAC [law of armed conflict] during all operations other than domestic operations'); Netherlands Ministry of Defence, Netherlands Defence Doctrine (2013) 49 ('[e]ven if IHL does not apply, Dutch and NATO policy is to use IHL restrictions as a safety margin for operations by the Netherlands armed forces') <http://www.defensie.nl/binaries/defence/documents/publications/2013/11/20/defence-doctrine-en/defensie-doctrine_en.pdf> accessed 2 August 2015.
[122] 'The Copenhagen Process on the Handling of Detainees in International Military Operations, The Copenhagen Process: Principles and Guidelines' (October 2012) (hereinafter 'Copenhagen

include extraterritorial non-international armed conflicts and peace operations[123]) was drafted in a manner that clearly mirrors the internment regime under GCIV.[124] One might take this to indicate a general practice on the part of states that they do not differentiate between international and non-international armed conflicts with respect to detention, thereby supporting the claim that the procedural rules explored in the previous chapter apply equally under custom in non-international armed conflicts.[125] However, it is made explicit in the Copenhagen Principles, and the Chairman's Commentary annexed thereto, that not only did the states involved not intend to create new legal obligations or authorizations via the Principles,[126] they also did not intend for any normative inferences to be drawn from the Principles more generally: 'Since the *Copenhagen Process Principles and Guidelines* were not written as a restatement of customary international law, the mere inclusion of a practice in the *Copenhagen Process Principles and Guidelines* should not be taken as evidence that States regard the practice as required out of a sense of legal obligation.'[127] The Copenhagen Principles cannot, therefore, be invoked as evidence of an *opinio iuris* to the effect that the procedural rules applicable to internment in international armed conflict now also apply under custom in non-international armed conflict. Indeed, this is supported by the fact that the Copenhagen Principles are also intended to apply in peace operations outside the context of armed conflict; here, there could be no suggestion that the relevant rules of IHL apply.[128] Moreover, in the case of military doctrine that applies the internment regimes under GCIII and/or GCIV equally in both international and non-international armed conflict, the same general lack of *opinio iuris* suggests that this too is considered a matter of policy rather than legal obligation.[129]

Principles') <http://um.dk/en/~/media/UM/English-site/Documents/Politics-and-diplomacy/Copenhangen%20Process%20Principles%20and%20Guidelines.pdf> accessed 2 August 2015. Annexed thereto is the 'Chairman's Commentary to the Copenhagen Process: Principles and Guidelines' (hereinafter 'Chairman's Commentary'). The twenty-four states are listed there in the preamble as: Argentina, Australia, Belgium, Canada, China, Denmark, Finland, France, Germany, India, Malaysia, New Zealand, Nigeria, Norway, Pakistan, Russia, South Africa, Sweden, Tanzania, the Netherlands, Turkey, Uganda, the United Kingdom, and the United States. It should be noted that this number is a little lower than the twenty-eight states that reportedly attended the Second Copenhagen Conference in June 2009: T Winkler, 'The Copenhagen Process on Detainees: A Necessity' (2010) 78 Nordic J Intl L 489, 497.

[123] Copenhagen Principles (n 122) preambular [9].
[124] See, eg, Copenhagen Principles (n 122) Principle 12 (on the need for initial and periodic administrative review). See generally L Hill-Cawthorne, 'The Copenhagen Principles on the Handling of Detainees: Implications for the Procedural Regulation of Internment' (2013) 18 JCSL 481.
[125] See references above at n 118.
[126] Copenhagen Principles (n 122) preambular [2].
[127] Chairman's Commentary (n 122) [16.2].
[128] Whilst in certain peace operations detention regimes have been applied that appear similar to IHL, relevant rules of IHRL have also been drawn on: see, eg, B Oswald, 'The Law on Military Occupation: Answering the Challenges of Detention During Contemporary Peace Operations?' (2007) 8 Melb J Intl L 311.
[129] UK, *CPERS* (n 30) 1–10 ('[c]ategories of CPERS will differ depending on the legal nature of the conflict. It is, therefore, essential to distinguish between international armed conflict, non-international armed conflict and other operations') and 1–18 (making clear that the *legal* requirements concerning handling of internees differ in international and non-international armed conflict, and noting that '[d]uring non-international armed conflict, the law governing the treatment of

3.3 Rules under Customary IHL

Whilst it must be conceded that there is some evidence of an *opinio iuris* amongst a few states that the internment regimes applicable in international armed conflicts apply as a matter of custom also in non-international armed conflicts, this appears insufficiently dense to lead to a different conclusion to that drawn here.[130]

Turning to state practice in specific non-international armed conflicts, it is clear that many states have adopted and applied internment regimes. This is the case, for example, in traditional non-international conflicts (eg Sri Lanka), so-called extra-territorial non-international conflicts (eg Iraq post-2003 and Afghanistan post-2001), and transnational conflicts between states and non-state groups that some consider to constitute non-international armed conflicts (eg the US conflict with al-Qaeda).[131] To different degrees, these internment regimes resemble those applicable in international armed conflicts, again raising the question of whether such practice has contributed to an elimination of the distinction between the two categories of armed conflict in this area.[132] However, it is submitted that no such conclusion may validly be made. First, this practice, as will be shown in chapter 5, varies considerably from state to state, making it difficult to extrapolate general customary rules.[133] Second, and most importantly, once again there is no *opinio iuris* to suggest that those states considered themselves to be applying mandatory rules of IHL in adopting those internment regimes. Rather, as will be made clear in chapter 5, those internment regimes were generally grounded in domestic law, and no claim was made that they were based on customary international law.[134] Similarly, in Iraq, the internment regime in GCIV was extended to the non-international armed conflict phase of the hostilities not by custom but rather a Security Council resolution.[135] Moreover, it will also be demonstrated in chapter 5 that those states that have adopted such regimes generally do so on the assumption that the relevant normative environment is IHRL, which defines the parameters within which the internment regime must operate.[136]

CPERS detained by our Armed Forces differs markedly from that described above [in international armed conflict]').

[130] *Public Prosecutor (On Behalf of Behrem (Hussein) and ors) v Arklöf (Jackie)*, Judgment, Case No B 4084–04, ILDC 633 (SE 2006), 18 December 2006 (Stockholm District Court) [133] (holding that Article 78 GCIV applied in the non-international armed conflict in Bosnia-Herzegovina as a matter of custom, relying on Rule 99 of the ICRC Study on Customary International Humanitarian Law, discussed in detail below, but without any reference to state practice or *opinio iuris*); Australia Permanent Mission to the UN Geneva (n 118); *Serdar Mohammed* (n 28) [174].

[131] State practice in each of these conflicts is discussed in detail in section 5.2, and, to avoid repetition, the reader is directed to that section for more information.

[132] See, eg, section 5.2.1.2 (Sri Lanka) and section 5.2.2.1 (Iraq), demonstrating that, in each, the states involved adopted internment regimes with both grounds and review procedures similar to those applicable under GCIII and GCIV.

[133] Compare, eg, the approaches taken in Colombia (section 5.2.1.1) and Afghanistan (section 5.2.2.2).

[134] See, eg, section 5.2.1.3 (demonstrating that Nepal's internment regimes were based on its domestic Public Security (2nd Amendment) Act 1991 and Terrorist and Disruptive Activities (Control and Punishment) Ordinance 2004).

[135] UNSC Res 1546 (2004). Similarly, see RM Chesney, 'Iraq and the Military Detention Debate: Firsthand Perspectives from the Other War, 2003–2010' (2011) 51 VJIL 549, 575.

[136] See, eg, section 5.2.1.2 (demonstrating that Sri Lanka derogated from certain provisions of Art 9 ICCPR, indicating its acknowledgement that that provision governed its detention operations).

It cannot therefore be said that custom has eliminated the distinction between international and non-international armed conflict in this area. In this respect, the procedural regulation of internment is one of the few areas that remains immune to the general convergence of the law of international and non-international armed conflict.[137] However, that is not to say that custom is silent here. To demonstrate this, the remainder of this section will evaluate the relevant conclusions in the ICRC's 2005 Study on *Customary International Humanitarian Law*.[138] The importance of the Study for our purposes is demonstrated by Theodor Meron's comment that 'the principal driving force behind the project...was the desire to remedy the scarcity of rules applicable to noninternational armed conflicts'.[139] As such, reference will be made below to the Study, particularly Volume II thereof, comprising the collection of state practice.[140] Additionally, more recent practice will also be included.[141]

Whilst a general examination of the ICRC Study is beyond the scope of this chapter, it is important to note that it was not uncontroversial. First, its methodology was criticized on a number of grounds, including its use of military manuals and its general approach to the application of the traditional test for identifying customary international law.[142] Second, the Study has been criticized for particular rules that it determined to be custom (although none of those with which this section deals).[143] The authors of the Study have, however, responded cogently to many of these criticisms.[144]

Importantly, supporting the conclusions above, the ICRC Study does not take the view that the internment regimes applicable in international armed conflicts

---

[137] See also E Crawford, *The Treatment of Combatants and Insurgents under the Law of Armed Conflict* (OUP, Oxford 2011) (demonstrating that the other principal areas that remain immune to convergence are combatant immunity and POW status, which continue to apply only in the context of international armed conflicts).
[138] Henckaerts, *Vol I* (n 67); J-M Henckaerts and L Doswald-Beck, *Customary International Humanitarian Law Volume II: Practice* (CUP, Cambridge 2005).
[139] T Meron, 'Revival of Customary Humanitarian Law' (2005) 99 AJIL 817, 833.
[140] Henckaerts, *Vol II* (n 138).
[141] The task of updating the Study's collection of state practice has been taken up by the British Red Cross in conjunction with the Lauterpacht Centre for International Law, University of Cambridge, and its findings are uploaded onto the website: <https://www.icrc.org/customary-ihl/eng/docs/home> accessed 2 August 2015. Where practice is taken from the ICRC Study or the online database, it is cited as such.
[142] See, eg, JB Bellinger, III and WJ Haynes, II, 'A US Government Response to the International Committee of the Red Cross Study *Customary International Humanitarian Law*' (2007) 89 IRRC 443, 444–8; D Bethlehem, 'The Methodological Framework of the Study' in E Wilmshurst and S Breau (eds), *Perspectives on the ICRC Study on Customary International Humanitarian Law* (CUP, Cambridge 2007); I Scobbie, 'The Approach to Customary International Law in the Study' in E Wilmhurst and S Breau (eds), *Perspectives on the ICRC Study on Customary International Humanitarian Law* (CUP, Cambridge 2007); The Baha Mousa Public Inquiry, Closing Submissions on Modules 1–3 on Behalf of the Ministry of Defence, 25 June 2010, [12]. The use of military manuals as state practice and *opinio iuris* is discussed below at text to nn 154–5.
[143] Bellinger and Haynes (n 142) 448–71; G Aldrich, 'Customary International Humanitarian Law—An Interpretation on Behalf of the International Committee of the Red Cross' (2005) 76 BYIL 503, 508–22.
[144] See, eg, J-M Henckaerts, '*Customary International Humanitarian Law*: A Response to US Comments' (2007) 89 IRRC 473.

extend under custom to non-international conflicts.[145] However, the Study does conclude that two customary rules of IHL that are of relevance to the present work may be distilled from practice: first, a prohibition of arbitrary deprivation of liberty; second, a requirement of release where the reasons justifying internment cease. Beyond this, however, customary IHL appears not (at present) to fill the gaps left by treaty law in this area. Chapters 4 to 6 will examine the relevance and role of IHRL here. Before that, however, the remainder of this section will look in more detail at these two customary rules advanced by the ICRC.

3.3.1 Prohibition of arbitrary deprivation of liberty

It should first be noted that, in addition to common Article 3 *qua* treaty law, common Article 3 is also widely considered to reflect customary law.[146] As such, based on the interpretation of that provision in section 3.2.1 above, both conventional and customary humanitarian law, through the principle of humane treatment, may be considered to prohibit internment that is not actually necessary as a result of the conflict.

The ICRC Study refers to the practice of states and other actors to support the claim that customary IHL prohibits the 'arbitrary deprivation of liberty' in non-international conflicts.[147] First, the Study notes that all states have legislation specifying the grounds on which individuals may be detained, suggesting an acceptance that deprivation of liberty generally must be grounded in law and is not to be seen as unfettered.[148] Moreover, of the more than seventy states that criminalize the unlawful deprivation of liberty during armed conflicts, most do so equally in international and non-international conflicts.[149] There are also examples of military manuals that either apply in, or have been applied in, non-international conflicts that confirm that unlawful confinement is a grave breach of IHL.[150] Similarly, much of the national legislation prohibiting arbitrary or

---

[145] Henckaerts, *Vol I* (n 67) 347–52 (demonstrating that the content of the arbitrary deprivation of liberty prohibition, which, as explained below, the Study does find to be customary in all armed conflicts, differs depending on the character of the conflict).

[146] *Nicaragua* (n 55) [218]; *Prosecutor v Duško Tadić* (Decision on the Defence Motion for Interlocutory Appeal on Jurisdiction) ICTY-94-1 (2 October 1995) [98]; *Prosecutor v Jean-Paul Akayesu* (Judgment) ICTR-96-4 (2 September 1998) [608]; *Prosecutor v Morris Kallon and Brima Bazzy Kamara* (Decision on Challenge to Jurisdiction, Lomé Accord Amnesty) SCSL-2004-15-AR72(E) (13 March 2004) [47]; Baha Mousa Inquiry (n 142) [10.2].

[147] Henckaerts, *Vol I* (n 67) 344 (Rule 99). [148] Ibid, 347.

[149] Ibid, 347. See, eg, Armenia, *Penal Code* (2003), Art 390.2(4), cited in Henckaerts, *Vol II* (n 138) 2331 [2555]; Belgium, *Law concerning the Repression of Grave Breaches of the Geneva Conventions and their Additional Protocols as amended* (1993), arts 1(1)(6) and 1(2)(5), cited in Henckaerts, *Vol II* (n 138) 2331 [2562]; Georgia, *Criminal Code* (1999), Art 411(2)(f), cited in Henckaerts, *Vol II* (n 138) 2333 [2580]; Moldova, *Penal Code* (2002), Art 391, cited in Henckaerts, *Vol II* (n 138) 2334 [2593]; Nicaragua, *Draft Penal Code* (1999), Art 461, cited in Henckaerts, *Vol II* (n 138) 2335 [2599]; Portugal, *Penal Code* (1996), Art 241(1)(g), cited in Henckaerts, *Vol II* (n 138) 2336 [2607]. References to other national legislation criminalizing unlawful deprivation of liberty in non-international conflicts are made in Henckaerts, *Vol I* (n 67) at 347 (fn 290).

[150] Henckaerts, *Vol I* (n 67) 347. See, eg, Australia, *Commanders' Guide* (1994), s 1305(d), cited in Henckaerts, *Vol II* (n 138) 2329 [2536]; Croatia, *LOAC Compendium* (1991) Annex 9, p 56,

unlawful detention in both international and non-international conflicts to which the ICRC Study refers explicitly states that such detention is a 'war crime' and thus a violation of IHL.[151] Other state practice further endorses the notion that arbitrary or unlawful detention is considered to be impermissible in non-international armed conflict.[152] The ICRC Study concludes that this practice endorses a customary prohibition of 'arbitrary' deprivation of liberty in non-international armed conflict (in addition to international armed conflict).[153]

However, in order for the above practice to establish a customary rule, as opposed to reflecting policy or obligations under domestic law and/or human rights treaty law, it must be accompanied by evidence of *opinio iuris*. In this regard, it should be noted that the use of military manuals in the ICRC Study has been criticized on the ground that these often reflect policy rather than legal considerations.[154] On the one hand, it is true that the extent to which military manuals can contribute

cited in Henckaerts, *Vol II* (n 138) 2329 [2539]; Germany, *Military Manual* (1992), s 1209, cited in Henckaerts, *Vol II* (n 138) 2330 [2543]; South Africa, *LOAC Manual* (1996), s 40, cited in Henckaerts, *Vol II* (n 138) 2330 [2549].

[151] See, eg, *Azerbaijan's Criminal Code* (1999), arts 112 and 116.0.18 (referring to deprivation of liberty 'contrary to the norms of international law' and 'deprivation of procedural rights'), cited in Henckaerts, *Vol II* (n 138) 2331 [2559]; *Bosnia and Herzegovina's Criminal Code* (1998), Art 154(1) (referring simply to 'illegal arrests and detention'), cited in Henckaerts, *Vol II* (n 138) 2332 [2563]; *Ethiopia's Penal Code* (1957), Art 282(c), cited in Henckaerts, *Vol II* (n 138) 2333 [2579] (referring to 'illegal detention in concentration camps' of civilians); *Portugal's Penal Code* (1996), Art 241(1)(g), cited in Henckaerts, *Vol II* (n 138) 2336 [2607] (referring to 'prolonged and unjustified restriction' of liberty); *Slovenia's Penal Code* (1994), Art 374(1), cited in Henckaerts, *Vol II* (n 138) 2336 [2611] (referring to 'unlawful confinements of civilian persons' as a war crime); *Socialist Federal Republic of Yugoslavia's Penal Code* (1976), Art 142(1) ('unlawful confinement of civilian persons is a war crime'), cited in Henckaerts, *Vol II* (n 138) 2337 [2624]; *Uruguay, Law on Cooperation with the ICC*, 2006, arts 26.2 and 26.3.7, cited in ICRC, Customary IHL Database (n 25).

[152] See, eg, Sri Lanka, Statement by the President of Sri Lanka, Directions Issued by Her Excellency the President, Commander-in-Chief of the Armed Forces and Minister of Defence, Colombo, 31 July 1997, s 2, cited in ICRC, Customary IHL Database (n 25) ('[n]o person shall be arrested or detained under any Emergency Regulation or the Prevention of Terrorism Act No. 48 of 1979 except in accordance with the law and proper procedure and by a person who is authorised by law to make such arrest or order such detention'); Uganda, Initial Report to the Human Rights Committee, UN Doc CCPR/C/UGA/2003/1, 25 February 2003, [232] ('[a] clear pattern emerged indicating that the army had arrested a number of people, detained them for long periods, and released them without trial. This is contrary to the law'); Germany, Bundestag (n 25) (explaining the legal basis for detentions in Afghanistan during the non-international armed conflict there, thus suggesting that such a basis is necessary); Nepal, Supreme Court, Division Bench, *Bajracharya case*, Order, 31 August 2007, cited in ICRC, Customary IHL Database (n 25) (finding that the detention by the army of an individual suspected of Maoist involvement was unlawful given the absence of a legal basis to detain); Chad, Initial Report to the Committee Against Torture, UN Doc CAT/C/TCD/1, 22 September 2008, [10]–[11] (referring to secret detentions in the context of civil war and stating that 'illegal arrests [and] arbitrary detentions...are prohibited'); United States, Speech by the Legal Advisor (n 25) ('[t]his Administration and I personally have spent much of the last year seeking to revise those [detention] practices [of the Bush Administration] to ensure their full compliance with domestic and international law...[including] by ensuring that all detained individuals are being held pursuant to lawful authorities', and proceeding to explain the legal basis for detentions in Guantanamo and Bagram).

[153] Henckaerts, *Vol I* (n 67) 344 (Rule 99).

[154] Bellinger and Haynes (n 142) 446–7. Similarly see C Garraway, 'The Use and Abuse of Military Manuals' (2004) 7 YIHL 425, 440 (arguing that the law-making function of military manuals should not be overstated).

to the process of custom formation will often be undermined by the fact that they may not reflect the *opinio iuris* of the state. However, that is not to say that they necessarily cannot be taken into consideration as a form of state practice where *opinio iuris* is not clearly excluded. Indeed, military manuals are among the most illustrative sources of state practice in IHL, for they reflect the considered general policy of the state, whereas actual operational practice, for example, might often reflect a particular commander's approach or the policy adopted for a specific situation.[155] With regard to the particular rule at issue, the existence of *opinio iuris* is supported by the fact that '[n]o official contrary practice was found with respect to either international or non-international armed conflicts. Alleged cases of unlawful deprivation of liberty have been condemned'.[156] The value of this is significant. The lack of *official* contrary practice demonstrates that, where arbitrary detentions occur, those accused will seek to rely not on extra-legal arguments (eg that there is no rule prohibiting arbitrary detentions) but, rather, will proffer a response within the legal framework (eg that a particular detention was not arbitrary).[157]

The existence of *opinio iuris* in this area is also evidenced by a number of other sources. First, as noted above, the ICRC Study states that practice in this area includes military manuals and national legislation that treat arbitrary detention in non-international conflicts *as a violation of IHL*, suggesting that such practice is not merely reflective of policy.[158] Second, certain domestic case law that has dealt with these issues has confirmed the existence of *opinio iuris* here. In a 2007 case, for example, the Colombian Constitutional Court stated:

Taking into account...the development of customary international humanitarian law applicable in internal armed conflicts, the Constitutional Court notes that the fundamental guarantees stemming from the principle of humanity, some of which have attained *ius cogens* status,... [include] the prohibition of arbitrary deprivation of liberty.[159]

Similarly, in the 2002 case of *Mehinovic v Vuckovic*, a US District Court held that:

Acts of torture, inhuman treatment, and arbitrary detention of civilians committed in the course of hostilities violate the international law of war as codified in the Geneva Conventions... Such acts, whether committed in an international or a non-international armed conflict, violate customary international law.[160]

---

[155] See also the discussion in the introductory chapter regarding the more general debate over the use of statements, in addition to actions, in finding customary international law.

[156] Henckaerts, *Vol I* (n 67) 347.

[157] The ICJ has accepted that such practice confirms, rather than negates, the existence of a customary rule: *Nicaragua* (n 55) [186].

[158] See above, text to nn 150–1.

[159] *Constitutional Case No C-291/07*, Judgment, 25 April 2007, 112, cited in ICRC, Customary IHL Database (n 25).

[160] *Kemal Mehinovic et al v Nikola Vuckovic* (2002) 198 F Supp 2d 1322 (US District Ct for the Northern District of Georgia) 1350. Whilst subsequent US case law has not favoured the conclusions in *Mehinovic* (see, eg, *Aldana v Del Monte Fresh Produce NA Inc* (2005) 416 F.3d 1242, 1247; *Sexual Minorities Uganda v Lively* (2013) 960 F.Supp.2d 304, 317), the major objection has been to the notion that 'a single illegal detention of less than a day, followed by the transfer of custody

Other case law further supports this view.[161] The UK Ministry of Defence has also made clear that the United Kingdom considers Rule 99 of the ICRC Study, prohibiting arbitrary deprivation of liberty in all armed conflicts, to reflect customary international law accurately.[162]

Whilst clearly rejecting the notion of unfettered detention power in non-international armed conflict, the above practice varies considerably in the terminology used (eg 'unlawful'/'arbitrary' detention) and the permissible grounds for detention. This notwithstanding, the ICRC Study concludes that one can nonetheless discern a general prohibition of 'arbitrary deprivation of liberty' in any armed conflict.[163] This is, indeed, supported by the sources of *opinio iuris* referred to above, which seem on the whole to recognise 'arbitrariness' as the appropriate standard.[164] The question then arises as to what constitutes 'arbitrariness' in this context. Whilst considering this customary rule to apply in both international and non-international armed conflicts, the ICRC Study suggests a different content depending on the character of the conflict. With regard to international armed conflicts, the Study refers to the IHL internment regimes explored in chapter 2,[165] whereas for non-international conflicts it refers to human rights treaty obligations, explored in chapter 4.[166] This differentiated approach is consistent with the argument above that the distinction between international and non-international armed conflicts has not yet been eliminated with respect to detention. In addition, it will be demonstrated in subsequent chapters that the human rights treaty obligations of states continue to apply to detention operations carried out in the context of non-international armed conflicts.[167] However, for the reasons explained at the outset of this section, there is value in exploring 'customary IHL' here independently of applicable IHRL. It is

---

to lawful authorities and a prompt arraignment' violates a 'norm of customary international law so well defined as to support the creation of a federal remedy' that is actionable under the Alien Torts Claims Act: *Sosa v Alvarez-Machain*, 542 US 692 (2004) 2769; *Sexual Minorities Uganda v Lively* (2013) 960 F.Supp.2d 304,317.

[161] In the context of a non-international armed conflict, see *Contreras Sepúlveda case*, Case No 2182-98, Judgment, 17 November 2004 (Chilean Supreme Court) [26] ('the irregular detention of civilians may not be considered to fall within the competence of the military'), cited in ICRC, Customary IHL Database (n 25). See also, albeit not specifically in the context of non-international armed conflicts, HCJ 3239/02, *Mar'ab et al v IDF Commander of Judea and Samaria et al*, 57(2) PD 349, [20] (stating that in both peace and war, '[t]here is no authority to detain arbitrarily'); *Lučić* (n 104) 67 (implying that for internment to be lawful in any armed conflict, it must be 'absolutely necessary for the State security [sic]', albeit not specifying whether such a limitation flows from IHL, IHRL or customary international law); *Duch* (n 6) [347] (in the context of imprisonment as a crime against humanity, applicable in any armed conflict and peacetime, the Trial Chamber noted that '[t]he customary status of the prohibition of arbitrary imprisonment under international law initially developed from the laws of war and is supported by human rights instruments').
[162] Baha Mousa Inquiry (n 142) [12] and [12.12] ('...in relation to the rules described below the Government accepts that they reflect CIL...Arbitrary deprivation of liberty is prohibited').
[163] Henckaerts, *Vol I* (n 67) 344 (Rule 99).   [164] See above at nn 159–62.
[165] Henckaerts, *Vol I* (n 67) 344–6.
[166] Ibid, 349–52. On the IHRL rules, see section 4.2.
[167] Though see Olson (n 14) 451–3 (discussing a number of problems with the ICRC's use of IHRL to elaborate the customary IHL rule).

therefore submitted that the content of this customary rule in the specific context of non-international armed conflicts might reasonably be drawn from the interpretation above of common Article 3, ie that internment is 'arbitrary', and thus prohibited, when it is not actually necessary as a result of the conflict, eg for security reasons. This approach is supported by the fact that common Article 3 exists in both treaty and customary law, as explained above, which suggests a certain logic in interpreting these rules coherently. Indeed, the ICRC Study suggests that, at its most basic, the arbitrary deprivation of liberty prohibition in customary IHL requires '[t]he need for a valid reason for the deprivation of liberty'.[168] It may, therefore, be concluded that, in non-international armed conflicts, both treaty-based IHL and custom prohibit internment that is not actually necessary as a result of the conflict.

3.3.2 The end-point of internment

The ICRC Study argues that one further relevant norm has crystallized as custom. Rule 128, comprising three parts, A to C, relates to the release of internees. Rule 128C applies to non-international conflicts, stating that, unless detained on penal grounds, '[p]ersons deprived of their liberty in relation to a non-international armed conflict must be released as soon as the reasons for the deprivation of their liberty cease'.[169] Interestingly, the practice referred to in the ICRC Study as evidence for this rule on the whole relates to release of internees at the cessation of hostilities, rather than specifically when the reasons justifying internment cease. Indeed, much of the practice comprises ceasefire agreements requiring the release of internees, such as that between the government of Angola and the National Union for the Total Independence of Angola (UNITA):

The ceasefire entails the release of all civilian and military prisoners who were detained as a consequence of the conflict between the Government of the People's Republic of Angola and UNITA.[170]

More recently, the Darfur Peace Agreement similarly required the parties to the conflict to 'unconditionally release all persons detained in relation to the armed conflict in Darfur'.[171] It should be noted that it is the state's practice in forming

---

[168] Henckaerts, *Vol I* (n 67) 348.
[169] Ibid, 451. Similarly, see Pejic (n 5) 382–3.
[170] Peace Accords between the Government of Angola and UNITA (Bicesse Accords), annexed to Letter dated 17 May 1991 from the Chargé d'affaires a.i. of the Permanent Mission of Angola to the UN addressed to the UN Secretary General, UN Doc S/22609 (17 May 1991) [II.3], cited in Henckaerts, *Vol II* (n 138) 2863 [627]. The ICRC Study cited many other such ceasefire agreements with similar provisions requiring release of all military detainees: Henckaerts, *Vol I* (n 67) 454 (fn 161).
[171] Darfur Peace Agreement between the Government of the Sudan, the Sudan Liberation Movement/Army and the Justice and Equality Movement (done at Abuja, Nigeria, 5 May 2006) [364] <http://www.sudantribune.com/IMG/pdf/Darfur_Peac_Agreement-2.pdf> accessed 2 August 2015.

such agreements which is relevant. Although they also represent the practice of non-state groups, due to the uncertainty of its relevance, this was not taken into account by the ICRC.[172]

The ICRC Study also refers to actual operational practice in which military detainees have been released during non-international conflicts, such as in Rwanda, although this practice does not specifically stipulate that the end-point of internment must be when the reasons for it cease.[173] Finally, certain states have publicly called for the release of detainees during particular non-international conflicts, including Bangladesh,[174] France,[175] Philippines,[176] India,[177] and the United States,[178] although, again, these calls do not refer specifically to release where the reasons for detention cease.

The practice referred to, therefore, cannot by itself lead to the conclusion that custom requires the release of internees in non-international conflicts as soon as the reasons justifying their internment cease. Indeed, Agnieszka Jachec-Neale questions whether Rule 128C reflects custom, by virtue of the limited supporting practice; she does, however, concede that, whilst 'perhaps not yet fully matured, this customary norm may well be developing'.[179] Moreover, there is no sign that the practice referenced is accompanied by *opinio iuris*, and states may well argue that it is merely policy-based. It is submitted, however, that the requirement of release when the reasons for internment cease may simply be seen as a component of the prohibition of internment that is not necessary as a result of the conflict.[180] The latter will be infringed whenever a person is interned unnecessarily, be it initially or at some subsequent point by virtue of the original justification ceasing to apply.[181]

---

[172] Henckaerts, *Vol I* (n 67) xxxvi. The ICTY has been more open to taking into account the practice of non-state armed groups in examining customary IHL: *Tadić* (n 146) [108]. Arguing in favour of a law-making role for non-state armed groups, see A Roberts and S Sivakumaran, 'Lawmaking by Non-State Actors: Engaging Armed Groups in the Creation of International Humanitarian Law' (2012) 37 YJIL 107. This issue is discussed in more detail below in section 3.4.

[173] Association Rwandaise pour la défense des droits de la personne et des libertés puliques, *Rapport sur les droits de l'homme au Rwanda* (Kigali, 1993) 45 and 51, cited in Henckaerts, *Vol II* (n 138) 2873 [712]. Similarly, see ICRC, *Report on the Practice of Colombia* (1998) ch 1.8, cited in Henckaerts, *Vol II* (n 138) 2872 [702]; ICRC, *Report on the Practice of Nigeria* (1997) ch 5.4, cited in Henckaerts, *Vol II* (n 138) 2873 [710].

[174] UNSC Verbatim Record, Statement by Bangladesh (16 November 1992) UN Doc S/PV.3137, 111, cited in Henckaerts, *Vol II* (n 138) 2872 [700].

[175] ICRC, *Report on the Practice of France* (1999) ch 5.4, cited in Henckaerts, *Vol II* (n 138) 2872 [704].

[176] Philippines 10th Congress, House of Representatives Res No 27 (28 November 1995), cited in Henckaerts, *Vol II* (n 138) 2873 [711].

[177] ICRC, *Report on the Practice of India* (1997) ch 5.4, cited in Henckaerts, *Vol II* (n 138) 2873 [707].

[178] ICRC, *Report on US Practice* (1997), chs 5.3 and 5.4, cited in Henckaerts, *Vol II* (n 138) 2873–4 [713].

[179] Jachec-Neale (n 62) 334.

[180] This point was made with regard to the same rule on release of civilian internees in international conflicts: section 2.4.1.

[181] Similarly, see Henckaerts, *Vol I* (n 67) 452; Pejic (n 5) 382–3.

However, there appears to remain a significant gap in the regulation of the end-point of internment in non-international conflicts. Chapter 2 explained that in international conflicts the release of civilian internees must take place as soon as the reasons for internment cease or, if not before, *as soon as possible after the close of hostilities*.[182] Similarly, POWs must be released 'without delay after the cessation of active hostilities'.[183] IHL therefore establishes the point at which hostilities cease as the definite end-point for internment in international conflicts. In contrast, Rule 128C in the ICRC Study suggests that custom requires release only once the reasons for internment cease, with no absolute end-point corresponding to the cessation of hostilities. As noted, most of the practice referred to does in fact relate to the end of hostilities; however, this arguably is not sufficiently dense or supported by *opinio iuris* for a customary norm to have formed. The ICRC may simply have viewed the cessation of hostilities as the latest point at which the reasons justifying internment cease, extrapolating a more general rule from the practice. However, these two points in time arguably may not converge, and thus the consequence of the ICRC's conclusion seems to be that internment may continue beyond the cessation of hostilities, for a seemingly indefinite period, if the initial reason for internment continues. Indeed, after the cessation of hostilities, certain individuals are more likely to pose a security threat in non-international conflicts than in international conflicts, at the end of which POWs, for example, are generally repatriated and thus pose no immediate security risk to the detaining state. Moreover, whilst the legal basis to intern in international armed conflicts is found in IHL and is thus subject to the scope of application of that body of law (ie only during an armed conflict), it was shown above that the legal basis to intern in a non-international armed conflict must be found elsewhere, primarily domestic law, which is unlikely to be restricted to application only during the armed conflict proper.

These concerns were raised with regard to Article 2(2) APII, which, in requiring that the treatment and trial standards in Articles 5 and 6 APII be applied to detentions that continue beyond the cessation of hostilities, recognized that internment may continue thereafter. The ICRC Commentary sought to address this by stating that, '[i]n principle, measures restricting a person's liberty, taken for reasons related to the conflict, should cease at the end of active hostilities'.[184] However, this problem is exacerbated by the uncertain end of hostilities in non-international conflicts, highlighted by the US Supreme Court in *Hamdi v Rumsfeld*:

If the Government does not consider this unconventional war won for two generations, and if it maintains during that time that Hamdi might, if released, rejoin forces fighting against the United States, then the position it has taken throughout the litigation of this case suggests that Hamdi's detention could last for the rest of his life.[185]

---

[182] Arts 132(1) and 133 GCIV. [183] Art 118(1) GCIII.
[184] Sandoz et al (n 97) 1360.
[185] *Hamdi v Rumsfeld* (2004) 542 US 507, 520 (US Supreme Court). This issue is discussed *de lege ferenda* in chapter 7.

Of course, if interned beyond the cessation of hostilities, an individual will remain protected by IHRL, which more broadly protects the right not to be deprived arbitrarily of one's liberty.[186] Moreover, as will be shown in chapter 4, under IHRL criminal prosecution is preferred to preventive, security detention, and thus one would expect persons detained as a result of the conflict either to be released or transferred to the criminal justice system following the cessation of hostilities.

3.3.3 Conclusions on customary IHL

In light of the above, it can reasonably be said that customary international humanitarian law prohibits arbitrary deprivation of liberty in non-international armed conflict, defined as a deprivation of liberty that is not actually necessary as a result of the conflict. However, beyond this, it has been demonstrated that little more may confidently be claimed. In particular, whereas custom has filled many gaps in the treaty law applicable in non-international armed conflict by extending rules previously applicable only in international armed conflict, the same is not true for detention. Whilst the basic prohibition of arbitrary deprivation of liberty can be said to apply in any armed conflict, the more detailed procedural rules applicable to internment explored in chapter 2 continue to apply exclusively in international armed conflicts. Of course, it is unlikely that that basic norm could be honoured if there is no mechanism for initially and periodically reviewing the existence of a justification for internment. Indeed, in order to adhere to the requirement of release where the reasons cease, in practice there must be a system for ensuring that release is not delayed, and it would seem that the only suitable mechanism is some form of periodic review. As noted by the ICTY, this is precisely the role played by periodic review in international armed conflict.[187] However, this would still result in initial and periodic review being only a corollary obligation under IHL in non-international conflicts, rather than a free-standing obligation. As such, although failure to review internment in international conflicts periodically is itself a violation of IHL,[188] in non-international conflicts this would not be the case; the violation would only occur if the internee is held beyond the point at which the reasons for their internment cease to exist. In light of these apparent gaps in the protections afforded by IHL, the following chapters will consider the relevance of IHRL here and the ability of that body of law to address, in particular, this lack of procedural safeguards for internees in non-international armed conflicts. Before that, however, the next section will close the discussion of IHL with a consideration of its scope of application and, specifically, the degree to which it binds non-state armed groups that are party to a non-international armed conflict.

---

[186] See section 4.2.1.
[187] *Prosecutor v Zejnil Delalić et al* (Trial Judgment) ICTY-96-21 (16 November 1998) [581]; Pictet, *GCIV* (n 70) 261; Deeks (n 24) 410. See section 2.3.1.2.
[188] *Prosecutor v Zejnil Delalić* et al (Appeals Judgment) ICTY-96-21 (20 February 2001) [322].

3.4 The Binding Nature of IHL for Non-State Armed Groups

This chapter has shown that IHL is not silent with respect to the procedural regulation of internment in non-international armed conflict, though it is extremely limited, with the distinction between the two categories of armed conflict not having converged in this area. It was argued that both treaty and customary IHL can be interpreted as prohibiting internment that is not necessary as a result of the conflict. This brings us to the question of upon whom this obligation falls. In international armed conflicts, since the parties are states, each state is bound to apply the IHL treaties which they have ratified by virtue of the principle of *pacta sunt servanda*.[189] In addition, those obligations that exist under custom bind states as a consequence of the latter's inherent international legal personality. However, in a non-international armed conflict, where (at least) one party is a non-state armed group, the question arises as to whether and, if so, how the applicable rules of IHL bind such groups (and, more specifically, the individual members). This has proved a controversial matter for scholars.[190]

The importance of this issue for the present book is emphasized by the frequency with which non-state groups detain in non-international armed conflicts. In the Colombian conflict, for example, the *Feurzas Armadas Revolucionarias de Colombia* (FARC) has routinely detained individuals, including members of the Colombian armed forces.[191] Such a detention took place in January 2013, when the FARC detained two police officers, stating that they were held as 'prisoners of war', in order to make clear that they had ended their previous policy of kidnappings for ransom.[192] Similarly, members of the *Rassemblement Congolais pour la Democratie* (RCD) group that was party to a non-international armed conflict in the Democratic Republic of Congo detained, inter alia, 'persons suspected of not supporting the RCD authorities... because of acts they might commit'.[193] In the 2008 South Ossetia conflict, South Ossetian forces, likewise, detained a number of individuals, including civilians and members of the Georgian armed forces, as hostages.[194] In order comprehensively to examine the extent to which

---

[189] Art 26 VCLT.
[190] Compare, eg, A Cassese, 'The Status of Rebels Under the 1977 Geneva Protocol on Non-international Armed Conflicts' (1981) 30 ICLQ 416 and S Sivakumaran, 'Binding Armed Opposition Groups' (2006) 55 ICLQ 369.
[191] F Szesnat and A Bird, 'Colombia' in E Wilmshurst (ed), *International Law and the Classification of Conflicts* (OUP, Oxford 2012) 231–2.
[192] 'Captive Policemen are "POWs": FARC', *IOL News* (South Africa), 30 January 2013, <http://www.iol.co.za/news/world/captive-policemen-are-pows-farc-1.1461429#.UgDMRJLVCSo> accessed 2 August 2015.
[193] UN Commission on Human Rights, 'Report on the situation of human rights in the Democratic Republic of the Congo, submitted by the Special Rapporteur, Mr Roberto Garretón, in accordance with Commission on Human Rights resolution 2000/15', E/CN.4/2001/40, 1 February 2001, [114].
[194] 'Report of the Independent International Fact-Finding Mission on the Conflict in Georgia: Volume II', September 2009, 360–2; Human Rights Watch, 'Up in Flames: Humanitarian Law Violations and Civilian Victims in the Conflict Over South Ossetia', 1-56432-427-3, January 2009, 170–3.

IHL regulates internment in non-international armed conflict, the relevance of the rules discussed in this chapter for these detentions must be considered. Moreover, it has been shown that the legitimacy of international legal rules will often influence compliance therewith, such that explaining how, if at all, IHL binds non-state armed groups might improve the protections afforded to victims of non-international conflicts.[195]

In examining this issue, this section will begin by demonstrating that common Article 3 and APII are clearly considered by states and commentators to be binding on non-state armed groups. It will then consider on what basis these treaty provisions bind non-state groups, concluding that the general authority of states to create rights and obligations directly for individuals at the international level offers the best explanation. The final part will then argue that non-state groups may also be bound by customary IHL, by virtue of their limited legal personality in this area.

3.4.1 Do common Article 3 and APII bind non-state groups?

The text of these instruments reflects the clear intention of the states parties that they bind states and non-state groups in non-international conflicts equally. Regarding common Article 3, the reference to 'each Party to the conflict', when defining to whom that provision applies, makes clear that it binds insurgents, along with government armed forces.[196] Unlike common Article 3, APII does not refer to its provisions as binding 'each Party to the conflict'. Indeed, this has been suggested as evidence that APII does not bind non-state armed groups.[197] This was not, however, intended to demonstrate that APII does not bind armed groups. Rather, the reluctance of many delegates at the 1974–7 diplomatic conference to legislate for non-international conflicts led to the Pakistani delegation introducing a shorter draft Protocol, as it became clear that a more detailed version could not be adopted by consensus.[198] It was at this stage that all references to 'parties to the conflict' were deleted so as to address the concern that such terms suggested recognition of non-state groups; there was no suggestion, however, that they would not thereby be bound.[199]

Liesbeth Zegveld has demonstrated that '[w]ide international practice' confirms the binding nature of common Article 3 and APII for non-state armed

---

[195] Sivakumaran (n 190) 374–5 and 394. The notion of legitimacy is contested, with many viewing process as an essential component of it, such that a norm cannot be legitimate unless 'those addressed believe that the rule or institution has come into being and operated in accordance with generally accepted principles of right process': TM Franck, *The Power of Legitimacy Among Nations* (OUP, Oxford 1990) 24.

[196] Common Art 3, *chapeau*.

[197] See, eg, GIAD Draper, 'Humanitarian Law and Human Rights' in MA Meyer and H McCoubrey (eds), *Reflections on Law and Armed Conflicts* (Kluwer, The Hague 1998) 146 (suggesting this to be a significant difference between APII and common Art 3).

[198] Sandoz et al (n 97) 1335.

[199] Ibid, 1338–9; *Official Records: Vol VII* (n 46) 61. See the discussion in section 1.3.1 on this concern with IHL more generally.

groups, referring, inter alia, to the practice of the ICJ, the UN Security Council, and international criminal tribunals.[200] The large majority of commentators support this conclusion.[201] As Christopher Greenwood has stated, 'common article 3 and the Protocol [II] apply with equal force to all parties to an armed conflict, government and rebels alike'.[202]

3.4.2 On what basis do common Article 3 and APII bind non-state groups?

Having thus shown that both common Article 3 and APII are considered binding on non-state armed groups, it must now be considered how a non-signatory, non-state group can be so bound. During the drafting of the Geneva Conventions, doubt was expressed as to how a non-state group could be bound by common Article 3.[203] The ICRC Commentary suggests that if the group exercises effective control over part of the territory, it is bound by the fact that it claims to represent a part of the state.[204] This, however, fails to explain how groups without territorial control are bound by common Article 3, which does not condition its applicability on such control.[205] Moreover, whilst the application of APII *is* conditioned on territorial control, this explanation assumes that the non-state group claims to represent the state, which is not the case with many such groups.[206]

The ICRC Commentary to GCII offers another explanation as to how common Article 3 binds non-state groups: '[B]y the fact of ratification, an international Convention becomes part of law and is therefore binding upon all the individuals of that country.'[207] However, as the Commentary acknowledges, this concept of the self-executing treaty, which then binds those within the jurisdiction of the state party *qua* domestic law, is not universal, and thus it cannot explain the generally binding nature of common Article 3 and APII for non-state groups.[208]

---

[200] L Zegveld, *Accountability of Armed Opposition Groups in International Law* (CUP, Cambridge 2002) 10–11, citing, inter alia, *Nicaragua* (n 55) [219]; UNSC Res 1193 (1998) [12] (Afghanistan); UNSC Res 794 (1992) [4] (Somalia); *Akayesu* (n 146) [611].
[201] GIAD Draper, *The Red Cross Conventions* (Stevens & Sons, London 1958) 102–3 (regarding common Art 3); M Bothe, 'Article 3 and Protocol II: Case Studies of Nigeria and El Salvador' (1982) 31 Am U L Rev 899, 907; L Moir, *The Law of Internal Armed Conflict* (CUP, Cambridge 2002) 52; Zegveld (n 200) 10–11; Sivakumaran (n 190); Greenwood (n 45) 56; D Fleck, 'The Law of Non-International Armed Conflicts' in D Fleck (ed), *The Handbook of International Humanitarian Law* (3rd edn, OUP, Oxford 2013) 585–6.
[202] Greenwood (n 45) 56.
[203] Pictet, *GCI* (n 79) 51.   [204] Ibid.   [205] Sivakumaran (n 190) 380.
[206] Moir (n 201) 55–6; Sivakumaran, ibid, 380; M Milanović, 'Is the Rome Statute Binding on Individuals? (And Why We Should Care)' (2011) 9 JICJ 25, 41 (giving as examples the KLA and LTTE as non-state groups that did not wish to represent the state).
[207] JS Pictet (ed), *Commentary to Geneva Convention II for the Amelioration of the Condition of Wounded, Sick and Shipwrecked Members of Armed Forces at Sea* (ICRC, Geneva 1960) 34.
[208] Ibid. Whether a treaty ratified by a state automatically becomes part of the domestic law of that state depends on the approach taken by that state to the relationship between international and municipal law. The United Kingdom, for example, requires incorporation of a treaty via an Act of Parliament in order for the provisions to take effect in domestic law (and then only *qua* the Act and

Antonio Cassese offered an alternative explanation for the binding nature of IHL, employing the framework in the Vienna Convention on the Law of Treaties (VCLT) governing the effect of treaties on third states (although Cassese's article dealt specifically with APII, his arguments apply equally to common Article 3).[209] This framework comprises Articles 34–5 VCLT, with Article 34 containing the general rule that non-parties remain unaffected by treaties and Article 35 VCLT containing an exception where, first, the parties to the treaty so intend and, second, the third state consents in writing. That the *pacta tertiis* rule can be extended as a matter of law from states to non-state armed groups is far from clear.[210] However, even assuming it can, the rule cannot explain the binding nature of IHL treaties for non-state groups. Whilst the preceding section demonstrated that common Article 3 and APII certainly show an intention on the part of the drafters to bind non-state armed groups, it is submitted that Cassese's argument fails due to the second condition in Article 35 VCLT (that the non-state group consents). This cannot be a condition for the application of APII (or common Article 3). First, neither common Article 3 nor APII suggests that this is the case. It is true that Article 1(1) APII limits its application to cases where the non-state group controls such territory 'as to enable [it]... to implement [the] Protocol', but this confirms that the Protocol applies not where the group is *committed* to implement it, but rather where it is *able* to implement it.[211] Second, the result of Cassese's argument is that 'it would be necessary to determine in each civil war whether rebels are ready and willing to accept the Protocol'.[212] Aside from practical problems in obtaining consent, this would leave non-state groups free to determine what rules apply to their actions, a conclusion that is inconsistent with a key tenet of humanitarian law, that is, that IHL regulates all conduct by all parties equally in situations objectively reaching the level of an armed conflict.[213]

It is submitted that the best explanation for the binding nature of common Article 3 and APII for non-state groups is that which recognizes that when a state ratifies a treaty, it does so on behalf of its population. The result is that, where intended by the states parties, individuals within their territory are bound by its provisions under international law. Indeed, this is the view that was put forward in the ICRC Commentary to APII:

...the commitment made by a state not only applies to the government but also to any established authorities and private individuals within the national territory of that

---

not *qua* the treaty): J Crawford, *Brownlie's Principles of Public International Law* (8th edn, OUP, Oxford 2012) 63–7.

[209] Cassese (n 190). Similarly, see Moir (n 201) 96–9.

[210] Sivakumaran (n 190) 377; Milanović (n 206) 39 ('[a]lthough the *pacta tertiis* rule has been extended to international organizations, at least those classically defined as inter-state entities and thus thought to be sufficiently analogous to states to benefit from the rule, its application to individuals and non-state actors is not straightforward' (footnotes omitted)).

[211] Moir (n 201) 107–9.

[212] Cassese (n 190) 428. Others too have taken the view that the treaties bind only where the group consents: RT Yingling and RW Ginnane, 'The Geneva Conventions of 1949' (1952) 46 AJIL 393, 395–6.

[213] C Greenwood, 'The Concept of War in Modern International Law' (1987) 36 ICLQ 283, 304.

state and certain obligations are therefore imposed upon them. The extent of rights and duties of private individuals is therefore the same as that of the rights and duties of the state.[214]

Two points must be elaborated here. First, only those provisions of a treaty that are intended to bind non-state groups directly (as well as the states parties) are capable of doing so.[215] The Permanent Court of International Justice (PCIJ) made clear in *Jurisdiction of the Courts of Danzig* that, whilst the presumption is that treaties cannot directly create rights and obligations for individuals, where the states parties intend for that treaty to bind individuals, this presumption is rebutted.[216] As shown above in section 3.4.1, it is clear that both common Article 3 and APII were intended to bind non-state armed groups, and hence this threshold is met for both.

The second point relates to which states may bind which non-state groups and their members. This might be seen as a matter of prescriptive and adjudicative jurisdiction, that is the right of a state to legislate, whether via national or international law, as well as their courts to adjudicate over, particular matters. It is well established that states can exercise prescriptive and adjudicative jurisdiction on the basis of territoriality and nationality.[217] The territoriality principle permits states to adopt laws that bind those present in their territory, whilst the nationality principle allows states to legislate for their nationals, whether present in their territory or abroad.[218] It is submitted that states may legislate for individuals directly via treaties on both of these bases of jurisdiction. Together they ensure that, in the event of a non-international armed conflict, the non-state group would be bound by common Article 3 and APII if *either* the state on whose territory they operate *or*, if different, their state of nationality has ratified them. Indeed, it is on these two bases that the International Criminal Court may (in cases other than Security Council referral) exercise jurisdiction over individuals suspected of committing crimes within the Court's jurisdiction.[219] Given that the territoriality and nationality principles have been incorporated into international criminal law as the two key bases of jurisdiction, it would seem appropriate for them also to operate as the bases on which common Article 3 and APII bind non-state groups.

---

[214] Sandoz et al (n 97) 1345. Similarly, see Sivakumaran (n 190) 381–93; Fleck (n 201) 586; Milanović (n 206) 47; D Murray, 'How International Humanitarian Law Treaties Bind Non-State Armed Groups' (2015) 20 JCSL 101.

[215] Milanović (n 206) 45.

[216] *Jurisdiction of the Courts of Danzig* (1928) PCIJ Series B, No 15, 17–18. That treaties can directly bind individuals has been upheld by the ICTY: see, eg, *Prosecutor v Dario Kordić and Mario Čerkez* (Appeals Judgment) ICTY-95-14/2 (17 December 2004) [40]–[46]; *Prosecutor v Galić* (Appeals Judgment) IT-98-29-A (30 November 2006) [85].

[217] AV Lowe, 'Jurisdiction' in MD Evans (ed), *International Law* (2nd edn, OUP, Oxford 2006) 342.

[218] Ibid.

[219] Art 12(2) of the Rome Statute; Milanović (n 206) 48; D Akande, 'The Jurisdiction of the International Criminal Court over Nationals of Non-Parties: Legal Basis and Limits' (2003) 1 JICJ 618.

3.4.3 On what basis does customary IHL bind non-state groups?

It was argued above that the prohibition of arbitrary deprivation of liberty is part of customary IHL applicable in non-international armed conflict. It has been accepted that customary IHL binds non-state armed groups,[220] and thus this norm can be considered binding on such groups under both treaty law and custom.[221] However, it must now be asked *how* customary IHL can bind non-state groups.

The best explanation lies in the legal personality of non-state armed groups in this area. In the *Reparations* advisory opinion, the ICJ made clear that, like all legal systems, in the international legal system what constitutes an actor with legal personality, and the rights and duties derived therefrom, varies depending on the needs of the community, and that 'the progressive increase in the collective activities of States has already given rise to instances of action upon the international plane by certain entities which are not States'.[222] Sandesh Sivakumaran has shown that the needs of the international community demand that non-state armed groups, by organizing themselves to such a degree as to become party to a non-international conflict, are capable of having sufficient legal personality as to have vested in them certain rights and obligations under custom.[223] The nature of this legal personality, however, is not identical to that of states, nor are the rights and duties emanating therefrom the same as those of states.[224] For example, it seems at present that non-state groups are incapable of contributing to the practice that enables a norm to crystallize under custom; this practice remains the practice of states alone.[225] For

---

[220] E Castren, *Civil War* (Suomalainen Tiedeakatemia, Helsinki 1966) 86–8; *Nicaragua* (n 55) [217]–[219] (noting the binding nature of common Art 3 for the *contras* after relying on its customary status); Moir (n 201) 56–8; *Kallon and Kamara* (n 146) [47]; Henckaerts, *Vol I* (n 67) 495 (Rule 139); Sivakumaran (n 190) 371–2 (referring to the Special Court for Sierra Leone and the International Commission of Inquiry on Darfur as relying on the customary status of rules for their binding quality vis-à-vis non-state groups).

[221] The binding nature of this specific customary norm for non-state groups has received very little attention, with a few exceptions: see, eg, UN Commission on Human Rights, Situation of Human Rights in Sudan, E/CN.4/1994/48, 1 February 1994, [3] (calling upon 'all parties to the hostilities to respect fully the applicable provisions of international humanitarian law, to halt the use of weapons against the civilian population and to protect all civilians from violations, including...arbitrary detention'); Inter-American Commission on Human Rights, 'Third Report on the Human Rights Situation in Colombia' (n 68) [120]–[132] (finding violations of IHL on the basis of arbitrary detentions by armed groups); D Casalin, 'Taking Prisoners: Reviewing the International Humanitarian Law Grounds for Deprivation of Liberty by Armed Opposition Groups' (2011) 93 IRRC 743, 748–9 ('it is clear that the customary prohibition on arbitrary deprivation of liberty is applicable to armed opposition groups').

[222] *Advisory Opinion Concerning Reparation for Injuries Suffered in the Service of the United Nations (Reparations)* ICJ Rep 1949, 178.

[223] Sivakumaran (n 190) 373–4. Similarly, see Draper (n 201) 102–3.

[224] *Reparations* (n 222) 179.

[225] Henckaerts, *Vol I* (n 67) xxxvi; Sivakumaran (n 190) 374; Fleck (n 201) 586. This is disputed by some commentators: see, eg, HA Wilson, *International Law and the Use of Force by National Liberation Movements* (OUP, Oxford 1998) 51 (distinguishing between custom for states and custom for non-state actors); Zegveld (n 200) 26. As noted, certain tribunals and commentators are open to a law-making role for non-state armed groups: see above at n 170.

the same reason, armed groups cannot avail themselves of the persistent objector principle as a means of preventing a customary norm from binding them.[226]

Finally, it should be noted that, just as treaties must indicate an intention that they bind non-state armed groups, so the state practice and *opinio iuris* contributing to the formation of a customary rule must point to such an effect. As argued in section 3.3, for practice specific to non-international armed conflicts, it might reasonably be presumed that the customary rule is intended to bind both states and non-state parties alike, in keeping with the general rule that IHL binds all parties to an armed conflict.[227] However, this presumption would be rebuttable by state practice and *opinio iuris* to the contrary.

3.4.4 Conclusion on the binding nature of IHL

To conclude this discussion, it has been argued that both common Article 3 and APII bind non-state groups that are party to non-international armed conflicts. Both can do so by virtue of a state's right to create obligations, via national and international law, binding on its nationals and those within its territory. Moreover, non-state groups are also bound by customary IHL as a result of their limited legal personality in this area. As such, the prohibition of internment that is not actually necessary as a result of the conflict, shown to be embodied in both treaty and customary IHL, binds states and non-state groups alike.

It should, however, be borne in mind that answering the question of how common Article 3 and APII bind non-state groups is not the end of the matter. It was stated at the outset of this section that the greater the legitimacy of a norm, the more likely there will be compliance therewith. However, legitimacy is not synonymous with legality, and the explanations given above, although legally sound, do not recognize a role of any kind for non-state armed groups in determining their legal obligations. This may well reduce the likelihood of compliance, particularly given that the applicable rules have been agreed by the state whose authority they question.[228] Indeed, Richard Baxter commented that explanations of the kind given above are not likely to induce compliance with IHL by non-state groups, demonstrated by the Viet Cong's refusal to adhere to common Article 3 on the ground that it had not consented to this obligation.[229] For practical reasons,

---

[226] Indeed, the existence and content of the persistent objector principle are controversial even for states: see, eg, TL Stein, 'The Approach of the Different Drummer: The Principle of the Persistent Objector in International Law' (1985) 26 Harv Intl LJ 457; P Dumberry, 'Incoherent and Ineffective: the Concept of Persistent Objector Revisited' (2010) 59 ICLQ 779.
[227] Greenwood (n 76) 10–11.
[228] Sivakumaran (n 190) 386.
[229] Baxter (n 110) 528. Though cf M Sassòli, 'Taking Armed Groups Seriously: Ways to Improve Compliance with International Humanitarian Law' (2010) 1 J Intl Human L Studies 12, 21 ('[i]n the 1970s, several guerrilla movements declared that they would not feel bound by new rules of IHL which they could not participate in developing. Today, in my experience, armed groups are more concerned that the law applies to them equally and that it is realistic than that they may contribute to its development').

therefore, states and non-governmental organizations such as the ICRC should continue to engage with these groups, for this opens up the discursive space, making it more likely to yield rules that insurgents consider legitimate and are thus willing to follow.[230]

Finally, it should be noted that non-state groups can also become bound by additional rules of IHL through both bilateral agreements with states (envisaged by common Article 3) and unilateral declarations.[231] Indeed, both have been used to incorporate the internment regimes applicable under GCIII and GCIV into specific non-international conflicts.[232] The normative status of commitments by non-state armed groups, and particularly their character under public international law, is, however, disputed.[233] It is submitted that, at least in certain situations, these two types of commitment can create international legal obligations binding on non-state groups.[234] Regarding unilateral commitments, just as unilateral declarations by states under certain circumstances can create binding obligations for the state concerned,[235] so there is no reason why a commitment by a non-state group could not be considered binding on that group under international law, particularly given that their limited legal personality in this area allows them to be bound by customary IHL.[236] Indeed, UN and other bodies have referred to such commitments as binding non-state groups.[237] Regarding bilateral agreements between states and non-state groups, both the Security Council and

---

[230] Sivakumaran (n 190) 394; Roberts and Sivakumaran (n 172); S Rondeau, 'Participation of Armed Groups in the Development of the Law Applicable to Armed Conflicts' (2011) 93 IRRC 649. There are organizations that seek to do this: see, eg, Geneva Call <http://www.genevacall.org> visited 2 August 2015. These dialogues appear to have effected an increase in rule compliance: P Bongard and J Somer, 'Monitoring Armed Non-State Actor Compliance with Humanitarian Norms: A Look at International Mechanisms and the Geneva Call *Deed of Commitment*' (2011) 93 IRRC 673.

[231] S Sivakumaran, 'Lessons from the Law of Armed Conflict from Commitments of Armed Groups: Identification of Legitimate Targets and Prisoners of War' (2011) 93 IRRC 463.

[232] Unilateral declarations drawing on the GCIII regime were made, eg, by the armed groups in the conflicts in Biafra, Eritrea, El Salvador, Turkey, and Libya: see Sivakumaran (n 232) 478–9. As an example of a bilateral agreement incorporating rules of IHL generally, see, eg, Abidjan Peace Agreement between the Government of Sierra Leone and the Revolutionary United Front, 30 November 1996, Art 21, <http://www.sierra-leone.org/abidjanaccord.html> accessed 2 August 2015.

[233] See, eg, *Kallon and Kamara* (n 146) [36]–[50] (finding that the Lomé Agreement between the central government and the RUF did not constitute a treaty as one of its parties was a non-state group that lacked treaty-making capacity). This aspect of the decision has been criticized: C Bell, 'Peace Agreements: Their Nature and Legal Status' (2006) 100 AJIL 373, 387–8; see more generally A Cassese, 'The Special Court and International Law: The Decision Concerning the Lomé Agreement Amnesty' (2004) 2 JICJ 1130.

[234] Similarly, see Roberts and Sivakumaran (n 172) 141–3 (on unilateral declarations) and 143–6 (on bilateral agreements).

[235] On the binding character of unilateral declarations by states, see *Nuclear Tests (Australia v France)* [1974] ICJ Rep 253, [43]; ILC, 'Guiding Principles Applicable to Unilateral Declarations of States Capable of Creating Legal Obligations with Commentaries Thereto' [2006] Ybk of the ILC, Volume II, Part II.

[236] See above, section 3.4.3.

[237] See, eg, Report of the Special Rapporteur on Extrajudicial, Summary or Arbitrary Executions, Mission to Sri Lanka, E/CN.4/2006/53/Add.5, 27 March 2006, [30], cited in Sivakumaran (n 44) 109; *Akayesu* (n 146) [627].

other international bodies have held these also to bind the groups party thereto.[238] It has been argued that there is no reason why an agreement between a state and non-state armed group could not constitute a treaty.[239] As a result, non-state groups are able to commit themselves to additional rules of IHL through unilateral declarations and bilateral agreements with states and international bodies.

3.5 Conclusions

This chapter has explored the current state of IHL regarding the procedural regulation of internment in non-international armed conflict. Section 3.1 demonstrated that, unlike in international armed conflicts, in non-international armed conflicts neither treaty-based IHL nor custom provides a legal basis for internment but, rather, assumes such a basis exists elsewhere, for example in domestic law. Section 3.2 then explored the regulation of internment by treaty-based IHL, challenging traditional arguments that it is silent in this area. It was argued that common Article 3 could reasonably be interpreted as prohibiting internment that is not necessary as a result of the conflict, for example for security reasons, which includes a requirement of release as soon as the reasons cease. Whilst a vague formulation, this is nonetheless an important finding, not least of all because IHL is the key body of international law that directly binds non-state groups party to non-international armed conflicts. Consequently, this chapter has demonstrated that there does exist a universal rule, applicable to both states and non-state groups, that regulates internment in such situations. None of the other procedural rules applicable in international armed conflicts applies, however. Furthermore, section 3.3 confirmed the ICRC's view that customary IHL prohibits 'arbitrary deprivations of liberty'. It was argued that this should be read as having the same content as the rule in common Article 3, such that internment will be 'arbitrary' where it cannot be shown to be necessary as a result of the conflict. Importantly, however, custom has not gone further in eliminating the distinction between international and non-international conflicts in this area. Finally, section 3.4 demonstrated that these rules bind both states and non-state armed groups.

It should be reiterated at this point that there is nothing incompatible between the finding in section 3.1 that IHL does not provide a legal basis to intern in non-international conflicts and that in sections 3.2 and 3.3 that IHL prohibits internment that is not necessary as a result of the conflict. It might be argued that, once it is accepted that IHL regulates the act of internment itself (as opposed to

---

[238] See, eg, UNSC Res 1127 (1997) (UNITA); Report of the International Commission of Inquiry on Darfur to the Secretary-General, S/2005/60, 1 February 2005, [174], both cited in Sivakumaran (n 44) 109.

[239] Bell (n 233) 380 (arguing that Art 3 VCLT and the 1986 Vienna Convention on the Law of Treaties between States and International Organizations or between International Organizations (21 March 1986), UN Doc A/CONF.129/15, confirm that agreements between states and non-state entities can constitute treaties under international law).

treatment standards or conditions of detention), it must thereby *authorize* internment in certain situations. Thus, by claiming that IHL prohibits unnecessary internment, so the argument goes, it must follow that IHL permits internment that *is* necessary, for example for reasons of security. However, as explained in detail in section 3.1, a distinction must be drawn between *not prohibiting* and *authorizing* acts under international law: whilst IHL *does not prohibit* internment where it is necessary as a result of the conflict, it does not thereby create a legal basis for internment for the purposes of satisfying the requirement of such a basis under IHRL. Importantly, this was confirmed in section 3.1 with reference to state practice: states tend to rely not on treaty or customary IHL but rather domestic law or Security Council resolutions as providing the legal basis for their detention operations in non-international armed conflicts.

Whilst this chapter has shown that IHL is not silent in this area, it is clear that it remains very under-developed. Chapter 2 demonstrated that, in international armed conflicts, civilian internment is permitted in the territory of a party to the conflict 'only if the security of the Detaining Power makes it absolutely necessary' or, in occupied territory, where necessary 'for imperative reasons of security'.[240] Moreover, such internment must be subject both to initial and periodic reviews,[241] and release must occur as soon as the reasons justifying internment cease or, at the latest, at the cessation of hostilities.[242] Combatant internment, whilst not subject to the same review procedures, is limited to defined categories of person who, by virtue of their status, are presumed to pose such a security threat as to render their internment necessary *ipso facto*.[243] IHL applicable in non-international conflicts is, therefore, significantly less detailed in this area than in international conflicts. The subsequent chapters will now consider the relevance of IHRL and the extent to which that body of law provides further procedural safeguards to internees in non-international armed conflicts.

---

[240] Arts 42 and 78 GCIV.   [241] Arts 43 and 78 GCIV.   [242] Arts 132–3 GCIV.
[243] Section 2.2.2.

PART III
INTERNATIONAL HUMAN RIGHTS LAW

4
Detention under IHRL

The previous chapters examined the regulation of internment under conventional and customary international humanitarian law (IHL). Chapter 3 demonstrated that IHL applicable in non-international armed conflict is very limited here, requiring simply that internment actually be necessary (and continue to be necessary) as a result of the conflict, for example for security reasons, without providing for any form of review mechanism for challenging one's internment. This was shown to lack even more detail than the rules applicable in international armed conflicts, which themselves were revealed in chapter 2 to have shortcomings. This is notwithstanding the fact that IHL recognizes that internment may occur in non-international armed conflict.[1]

A significant gap therefore exists in IHL,[2] with the question arising as to what other rules of international law might apply here. This is the aim of chapters 4 to 6, which will examine the relevance of the other key body of international law concerned with the protection of individuals, international human rights law (IHRL). The present chapter will offer a general examination of the procedural rules applicable to detention under IHRL, with chapters 5 and 6 exploring the application of those rules to non-international armed conflict. This chapter is divided into three sections. The first addresses a preliminary issue bearing on the relevance of IHRL for this study. Thus, section 4.1 considers the prima facie applicability of IHRL in armed conflict, including non-international armed conflict. After confirming that IHRL prima facie applies in such situations, section 4.2 then examines the procedural rules applicable to detention under IHRL, drawing comparisons to those under IHL. Section 4.3 then concludes the chapter with an examination of the extent to which these IHRL rules have crystallized as custom.

4.1 Applicability of IHRL in Armed Conflict

Before examining the IHRL rules on detention, the preliminary issue of the applicability of IHRL in armed conflict must first be addressed. This section will

---

[1] See, eg, Art 5(1) APII.
[2] I am using the word 'gap' in the sense employed by Sir Hersch Lauterpacht, that is, 'gaps from the point of view of the logical unity and consistency of the law, of its actual effectiveness in meeting emergencies, and of the moral and social ends of the international legal system': Sir H Lauterpacht, *The Function of Law in the International Community* (reissue with foreword and introduction, OUP, Oxford 2011) 109.

demonstrate that IHRL continues prima facie to apply in armed conflict and, more specifically, non-international armed conflict. The purpose of this section is merely to address the general, prima facie applicability of IHRL to the situations with which this book is concerned, in order to justify examining the relevant rules under that body of law in the following sections. The relationship between IHRL and IHL, as well as the practical application of the specific IHRL rules on detention in non-international armed conflict, will then be addressed in chapters 5 and 6.

It is often claimed that, traditionally, IHRL was thought not to be relevant to the actions of states in the context of armed conflict. Rather, the law of war and the law of peace (the latter of which IHRL was considered a part) were posited as entirely separate.[3] Accordingly, it has been said that '[i]t was probably not assumed, at the time [of the drafting of the Universal Declaration of Human Rights (UDHR)] that human rights would apply to situations of armed conflict, at least not to situations of international armed conflict'.[4] Katharine Fortin, however, has shown that this common claim is in fact misplaced and that even during the drafting of the UDHR it was accepted that international human rights obligations would continue to apply in armed conflict.[5] A more nuanced reading of the history than the traditional war/peace bifurcation is offered by David Kretzmer, who argues that:

...the original assumption was that human rights treaties continue to apply in times of war, but only to the relationship which is the concern of those treaties, namely, that between governors and governed. There is no indication that States which drew up the conventions considered that declaration of a state of emergency and derogation from certain of the rights would be required in order to open the path for a State to resort to the laws and customs of war in an armed conflict with another State.[6]

One can probably go further than this, for, as is shown below, the drafting of the derogation provisions in the various human rights treaties in fact supports the view that those treaties were assumed to apply even to the relationships regulated by IHL.[7] In any case, Kretzmer goes on to note that, following the adoption of treaty rules on non-international armed conflicts in 1949, the distinction he

---

[3] GIAD Draper, 'The Relationship between the Human Rights Regime and the Law of Armed Conflicts' (1971) 1 Isr Ybk Human Rights 191, 191–6; K Suter, 'An Inquiry into the Meaning of the Phrase "Human Rights in Armed Conflicts"' (1976) 15 *Revue de Droit Pénal Militaire et de Droit de la Guerre* 393.

[4] C Droege, 'Elective Affinities? Human Rights and Humanitarian Law' (2008) 90 IRRC 501, 504. Similarly, see R Kolb, 'The Relationship between International Humanitarian Law and Human Rights Law: a Brief History of the 1948 Universal Declaration of Human Rights and the 1949 Geneva Conventions' (1998) 38 IRRC 409.

[5] K Fortin, 'Complementarity between the ICRC and the United Nations and International Humanitarian Law and International Human Rights Law, 1948–1968' (2012) 94 IRRC 1433.

[6] D Kretzmer, 'Rethinking the Application of IHL in Non-International Armed Conflict' (2009) 42 Isr L Rev 8, 15. Similarly, see UN Human Rights Committee (HRC), 'Fourth Periodic Report: United States of America', CCPR/C/USA/4, 22 May 2012, [506]–[507].

[7] See below at text to nn 21–3.

4.1 Applicability of IHRL in Armed Conflict

advances between the relationships to which the two bodies of law applied began to unravel; the relationship regulated by IHL in such situations is precisely the same as that regulated by IHRL.[8]

Furthermore, practice since the Second World War has confirmed that IHRL, prima facie, is applicable to the actions of states in the context of armed conflict, including those relationships which, on Kretzmer's account, were traditionally the exclusive domain of IHL.[9] For example, from the 1950s onwards, the UN, in both the General Assembly and Security Council, has consistently invoked the continued relevance of IHRL during armed conflict.[10] The 1968 Tehran International Conference on Human Rights marked a significant milestone in this development, affirming the applicability of IHRL during armed conflict.[11] The General Assembly thereafter confirmed in a resolution that '[f]undamental human rights, as accepted in international law and laid down in international instruments, continue to apply fully in situations of armed conflict'.[12] This trend was continued at the 1974–7 International Conference on the Reaffirmation and Development of International Humanitarian Law, with the resulting Additional Protocols of 1977 confirming the applicability of human rights in armed conflict.[13]

The jurisprudence of international tribunals also confirms the continued applicability of IHRL to the actions of states during armed conflict. Thus, the ICJ held in its *Nuclear Weapons* Advisory Opinion that:

The Court observes that the protection of the International Covenant of Civil and Political Rights does not cease in times of war, except by operation of Article 4 of the Covenant whereby certain provisions may be derogated from in a time of national emergency.[14]

In that case, the Court held that the right not arbitrarily to be deprived of one's life continues to apply even for persons who are lawful targets under IHL.[15]

---

[8] Kretzmer (n 6) 17. This argument is less applicable to those non-international armed conflicts that involve two or more non-state armed groups in opposition, with no central government involvement.

[9] The structure of the following discussion was inspired by Droege (n 4) 504–9.

[10] See, eg, UNGA Res 804 (VIII) (1953) [2] (Korea); UNGA Res 1312 (XIII) (1958) [7] (Hungary); UNSC Res 237 (1967), preambular [2], UNGA Res 2546 (XXIV) (1969) [4], UNGA Res 3525 A (XXX) (1975) [11] (territories occupied by Israel); UNGA Res 46/135 (1991) preamble (Kuwait under Iraqi occupation); UNSC Res 1034 (1995) [1], UNGA Res 50/193 (1995) [3] (the former Yugoslavia); UNGA Res 52/145 (1997) [3] (Afghanistan); UNSC Res 1635 (2005) [7] (DRC); UNSC Res 1653 (2006) [6] (Great Lakes region); UNGA Res 67/262 (2013) [2] (Syria); UNSC Res 2111 (2013) preambular [6] (Somalia); UNSC Res 2095 (2013) [3] (Libya); UNSC Res 2227 (2015) preambular [21] and OP [33] (Mali).

[11] See, eg, *Final Act of the International Conference on Human Rights*, UN Doc A/Conf.32/41, 22 April–13 May 1968, 5 (Resolution I on 'Respect for and Implementation of Human Rights in Occupied Territories') and 18 (Resolution XXIII on 'Human Rights in Armed Conflict'); confirming this see UNGA Res 2444 (XXIII) (1968).

[12] UNGA Res 2675 (XXV) (1970) [1].

[13] Art 72 API; preamble of APII; Y Sandoz, C Swinarski, and B Zimmerman (eds), *Commentary on the Additional Protocols of 8 June 1977 to the Geneva Conventions of 12 August 1949* (ICRC/Martinus Nijhoff, Geneva 1987) [4429].

[14] *Legality of the Threat or Use of Nuclear Weapons*, Advisory Opinion [1996] ICJ Rep 226, [25].

[15] Ibid. Similarly, see *Legal Consequences of the Construction of a Wall in the Occupied Palestinian Territory*, Advisory Opinion [2004] ICJ Rep 136, [106]; *Case Concerning Armed Activities on the*

Moreover, the European Court of Human Rights (ECtHR) has applied the European Convention on Human Rights (ECHR) in international armed conflicts, including situations of occupation.[16] Similarly, the Inter-American Commission (IACiHR) and Court of Human Rights (IACtHR) have recognized the applicability of the American Declaration on the Rights and Duties of Man (ADRDM) and the American Convention on Human Rights (ACHR) to situations of armed conflict.[17]

It should be noted that there is some contrary practice in this area, most notably from the United States and Israel, both of which have, at times, contested the application of IHRL in armed conflict.[18] Louise Doswald-Beck, however, notes that '[t]hese are minority views which are contradicted by extensive practice to the contrary', and that, '[i]n addition, because of their lack of consistency, neither the United States nor Israel can be seen as persistent objectors to this rule'.[19] Indeed, the United States has now accepted the prima facie applicability of IHRL in armed conflict, subject to IHL as the *lex specialis*.[20]

It is clear, therefore, that states' IHRL obligations continue prima facie to apply during armed conflict, even with regard to those relationships for which IHL was traditionally designed. This is consistent with the text of the main human rights treaties, which, by including provisions permitting derogation in situations of emergency, demonstrate a general expectation on the part of the states parties that they will continue to apply in such situations *absent* derogation.[21] This is especially clear in the case of the ECHR and ACHR, which specifically refer to 'war' in their

---

Territory of the Congo (DRC v Uganda) [2005] ICJ Rep 116, [216]–[217]. The Court's approach to the relationship between IHL and IHRL in this area will be explored in section 5.1.1.

[16] See eg *Loizidou v Turkey*, App No 15318/89, Judgment (Grand Chamber), 18 December 1996; *Al-Skeini v United Kingdom*, App No 55721/07, Judgment (Grand Chamber), 7 July 2011; *Hassan v United Kingdom*, App No 29750/09, Judgment (Grand Chamber), 16 September 2014.

[17] IACiHR, *Coard et al v United States*, Report No 109/99, 29 September 1999; IACiHR, *Alejandre v Cuba*, Report No 86/99, 29 September 1999; *Bamaca Velasquez v Guatemala*, Judgment, IACtHR (Series C) No 70 (2000); IACiHR, *Request for Precautionary Measures Concerning the Detainees at Guantanamo Bay, Cuba*, Decision of 12 March 2002, all cited in Droege (n 4) 508.

[18] See, eg, HRC, 'Second Periodic Report: Israel', CCPR/C/ISR/2001/2, 4 December 2001, [8]; HRC, 'Third Periodic Report: United States of America', CCPR/C/USA/3, 28 November 2005, [130]; HRC, Concluding Observations: United States of America, CCPR/C/US/CO/3/Rev.1, 18 December 2006, [10]. Similarly, see MJ Dennis, 'Non-Application of Civil and Political Rights Treaties Extraterritorially During Times of International Armed Conflict' (2007) 40 Isr L Rev 453.

[19] L Doswald-Beck, *Human Rights in Times of Conflict and Terrorism* (OUP, Oxford 2012) 8. Similarly, see W Kälin, 'Universal Human Rights Bodies and International Humanitarian Law' in R Kolb and G Gaggioli (eds), *Research Handbook on Human Rights and Humanitarian Law* (Edward Elgar, Cheltenham 2013) 450 (fn 78) (referring to US practice in the Human Rights Council supporting resolutions calling for respect for human rights in armed conflict).

[20] HRC, Fourth Periodic Report (n 6). The notion of *lex specialis* is explored in detail in chapter 5.

[21] See, eg, Art 4 ICCPR; Art 15 ECHR; Art 27 ACHR. Similarly, see Fortin (n 5); H Krieger, 'A Conflict of Norms: The Relationship between Humanitarian Law and Human Rights Law in the ICRC Customary Law Study' (2006) 11 JCSL 265, 267; Droege (n 4) 507; M Milanović, 'The Lost Origins of Lex Specialis: Rethinking the Relationship between Human Rights and International Humanitarian Law,' in J Ohlin (ed), *Theoretical Boundaries of Armed Conflict and Human Rights* (CUP, Cambridge 2016, forthcoming) 16 <http://papers.ssrn.com/sol3/papers.cfm?abstract_id=2463957> accessed 4 August 2015.

4.1 Applicability of IHRL in Armed Conflict

derogation provisions.[22] Notwithstanding the absence of a reference to 'war' in the final text of Article 4 of the International Covenant on Civil and Political Rights (ICCPR), the drafting history of that provision confirms that that treaty too was foreseen as applying in armed conflict.[23] Moreover, in the situations relevant to this research, that is, non-international armed conflicts, it would seem even more self-evident that IHRL continues prima facie to apply absent derogation. First, the controversy that often arises regarding the applicability of IHRL in international armed conflicts, that is, concerning the extraterritoriality of those obligations, does not arise in traditional internal conflicts involving a state and non-state group on the former's territory.[24] Second, as the quote above by Kretzmer demonstrates, the relationship that is at the heart of IHRL is also at the heart of the law of non-international armed conflict, that is, that between a state and its own nationals (at least where the opposing parties are the state and a domestic non-state group).[25] Other commentators agree that it is in non-international conflicts, especially, that the continued applicability of IHRL alongside IHL is most clear.[26] Indeed, even those generally sceptical of the applicability of IHRL in armed conflict accept its applicability in internal armed conflicts.[27] That a state remains bound by its obligations under IHRL in non-international armed conflicts has been confirmed both in international jurisprudence[28] and UN practice.[29]

---

[22] Art 15(1) ECHR; Art 27(1) ACHR.

[23] M Milanović, 'Extraterritorial Derogations from Human Rights Treaties in Armed Conflict' in N Bhuta (ed), *The Frontiers of Human Rights: Extraterritoriality and its Challenges* (Collected Courses of the Academy of European Law, OUP, Oxford 2016, forthcoming) 9 <http://papers.ssrn.com/sol3/papers.cfm?abstract_id=2447183> accessed 4 August 2015; M Bossuyt, *Guide to the Travaux Préparatoires of the International Covenant on Civil and Political Rights* (Brill, Leiden 1987) 83 (referring to discussions on draft Art 4 ICCPR that noted that in times of war, for example, states could not be bound by the strict rules in the Covenant, confirming that the drafters considered war to constitute a ground for derogation) and 86 ('...it was recognized that one of the most important public emergencies was the outbreak of war').

[24] On extraterritoriality, see section 6.2.

[25] See above at text to nn 6–8. Similarly, see Krieger (n 21) 275.

[26] See, eg, K Watkin, 'Controlling the Use of Force: A Role for Human Rights Norms in Contemporary Armed Conflict' (2004) 98 AJIL 1, 25; J Cerone, 'Jurisdiction and Power: The Intersection of Human Rights Law & The Law of Non-International Armed Conflict in an Extraterritorial Context' (2007) 40 Isr L Rev 396, 401; S Sivakumaran, 'Re-envisaging the International Law of Internal Armed Conflict' (2011) 22 EJIL 219, 234.

[27] See, eg, Dennis (n 18) 455 ('[t]he majority of states do appear to accept the view that the provisions of the international human rights treaties may continue to apply *domestically* during an internal armed conflict'); NK Modirzadeh, 'The Darks Side of Convergence: A Pro-Civilian Critique of the Extraterritorial Application of Human Rights Law in Armed Conflict' in RA Pedrozo (ed), *The War in Iraq: A Legal Analysis* (2010) (Vol 86, US Naval War College International Law Studies) 396–8.

[28] See, eg, IACiHR, *Juan Carlos Abella v Argentina*, Report No 55/97, 18 November 1997, [160] ('[i]t is...during situations of internal armed conflict that these two branches of international law [IHL and IHRL] most converge and reinforce each other'); IACtHR, *Bamaca Velasquez v Guatemala* (n 17) [208]–[214]; ACiHPR, *Amnesty International and others v Sudan*, Communication Nos 48/90, 50/91, 52/91, and 89/93 (2003); HRC, *Sarma v Sri Lanka*, CCPR/C/78/D/950/2000, 31 July 2003; HRC, Concluding Observations: Democratic Republic of the Congo, CCPR/C/COD/CO/3, 26 April 2006 (generally applying the ICCPR notwithstanding the existence of non-international armed conflicts; see especially at [16], reminding the state of their positive obligations to investigate abuses by rebel groups); ECtHR, *Al-Jedda v UK*, App No 27021/08, 7 July 2011.

[29] See, eg, UNSC Res 1574 (2004), preambular [11] (calling for the respect of human rights law in the conflict in Sudan); UNSC Res 2120 (2013), preambular [24] (calling for compliance

IHRL continues, therefore, prima facie to apply in situations of armed conflict, including non-international armed conflicts. That default view might, however, be modified in specific cases, for example through permissible derogation or as a result of the applicability of other relevant rules of international law; these issues will be addressed in chapters 5 and 6. Thus, whilst making clear that '[t]oday, it is widely accepted that international human rights law applies in situations of armed conflict', Sandesh Sivakumaran goes on to say that '[f]ar more difficult than the applicability of international human rights law to situations of...armed conflict is its actual application therein'.[30] Before that, however, having demonstrated this preliminary point, we can now examine the procedural rules that apply to detention under IHRL.

4.2 The Procedural Rules Applicable to Detention under Human Rights Treaties

Although there are a number of international and regional human rights instruments, each specifying their own range of rights, certain norms can be discerned that are common to most or all such treaties. This is true of the procedural protections afforded to persons deprived of their liberty, which can be divided into the following categories: the standard for detention (ie when detention is permissible); the right to know the reasons for one's detention; the right to initial and periodic judicial review of detention (*habeas corpus*); and the requirement of release where the reasons justifying detention cease. It is according to these categories that the following sections are divided, and, as each set of rules is discussed, comparisons will be drawn to the IHL rules applicable in international and non-international conflicts. It is important to note that the goal here is not to provide a general overview of all aspects of these rules, but rather to highlight the key points that are of particular pertinence to the present work and will be drawn on in subsequent chapters.

These sets of rules are best reflected in the ICCPR, with most other instruments containing similar or identical provisions. Consequently, as these rules are explored below, reference is made in the first instance to the ICCPR, with the equivalent provisions of the other general human rights treaties referenced therewith. Where other instruments differ, this is noted. The instruments on which this chapter draws are the ICCPR, ECHR, ACHR, ADRDM, Universal Declaration

---

with IHRL by all parties to the conflict in Afghanistan); UNSC Res 2093 (2013) preambular [15] (condemning violations of IHRL in Somalia, including extrajudicial killings and arbitrary detentions); UNSC, Statement by the President of the Security Council, S/PRST/2013/15, 2 October 2013, [5] (condemning violations of IHL and IHRL by the Syrian authorities); UNGA Res 67/262 (2013) preambular [3] (condemning 'the continuation of grave violations of human rights by the Syrian authorities using heavy weapons, warplanes and Scud missiles to bomb neighbourhoods and populated areas').

[30] S Sivakumaran, *The Law of Non-International Armed Conflict* (OUP, Oxford 2012) 83 and 87.

of Human Rights (UDHR), Arab Charter of Human Rights (ArCHR), and the African Charter on Human and Peoples' Rights (ACHPR). It should be noted that the relevant provision of the ACHPR, Article 6, is very general, simply stating:

> Every individual shall have the right to liberty and to the security of his person. No one may be deprived of his freedom except for reasons and conditions previously laid down by law. In particular, no one may be arbitrarily arrested or detained.

It does not contain the more specific procedural rules found in the other human rights treaties (such as *habeas corpus*). However, the African Commission on Human and Peoples' Rights (ACiHPR) has elaborated Article 6, most comprehensively in its *Principles and Guidelines on the Right to a Fair Trial and Legal Assistance in Africa*, which develops the rules laid down, inter alia, in Article 6.[31] Reference will therefore be made to these *Principles and Guidelines* in the sections below.

4.2.1 Standard for detention

As shown in chapter 2, IHL applicable in international armed conflict permits internment only where necessary for security reasons.[32] Whereas civilians can only be interned on the basis of an individual threat determination, combatants are assumed to constitute a security threat necessitating internment.[33] Chapter 3 then argued that, whilst the treaty provisions applicable in non-international armed conflict do not contain explicit equivalent rules, they may be interpreted as prohibiting internment that is not necessary as a result of the conflict.[34] However, unlike in international conflicts, IHL provides no legal basis for interning in non-international conflicts, generally leaving this to domestic law.[35]

The two basic procedural rules on detention under IHRL are that everyone has the right to liberty,[36] and that nobody shall be subjected to arbitrary arrest or detention.[37] From this, it is clear that the right to liberty is not absolute, but can be curtailed in certain circumstances.[38] Thus, from these two basic rules flows the requirement that '[n]o one shall be deprived of his liberty except on such grounds and in accordance with such procedures as are established by law'.[39]

The ECHR differs here, as rather than simply prohibiting arbitrary detention, it lays out an exhaustive list of the bases on which a person may be deprived of their

---

[31] ACiHPR, *Principles and Guidelines on the Right to a Fair Trial and Legal Assistance in Africa*, adopted at 33rd session in Niamey, Niger, 29 May 2003, preamble <http://www.achpr.org/instruments/principles-guidelines-right-fair-trial/> accessed 4 August 2015.
[32] See section 2.2.   [33] Compare Arts 42 and 78 GCIV with Art 21 GCIII.
[34] See section 3.2.1.   [35] See section 3.1.
[36] Art 9(1) ICCPR; Art 5(1) ECHR; Art 7(1) ACHR; Art I ADRDM; Art 3 UDHR; Art 6 ACHPR; Art 14(1) ArCHR.
[37] Art 9(1) ICCPR; Art 7(3) ACHR; Art 9 UDHR; Art 6 ACHPR; Art 14(1) ArCHR.
[38] HRC, General Comment No 35: Article 9 (Liberty and security of person), CCPR/C/GC/35, 10 December 2014, [10].
[39] Art 9(1) ICCPR; Art 5(1), *chapeau*, ECHR; Art 7(2) ACHR; Art XXV ADRDM; Art 6 ACHPR; Art 14(2) ArCHR.

liberty.[40] Within this list there is no basis permitting preventive, security detention (ie internment), and consequently derogation is necessary for such measures to be employed by a state party to the ECHR.[41] The ECtHR has, however, confirmed that the list of permissible grounds for detention in Article 5 ECHR is a manifestation of the underlying principle prohibiting arbitrary deprivation of liberty.[42] This may, therefore, be seen as a universal rule of IHRL, underpinning the regimes regulating detention in each of the key treaties. Importantly, this right not only has a negative aspect (ie states may not arbitrarily detain) but also a positive aspect (ie states must protect persons within their jurisdiction from being arbitrarily deprived of their liberty by others).[43] Positive obligations under human rights treaties are not absolute, but rather require states 'to exercise due diligence, i.e. to take all measures reasonably within their power in order to prevent violations of human rights.'[44]

The structure and content of the detention standards in IHL and IHRL therefore differ in important respects. Whilst IHL prohibits (in all armed conflicts) internment that is not necessary as a result of the war, for example for security reasons, IHRL prohibits unlawful or arbitrary detention more generally. This difference between IHL and IHRL is explained by the fact that the IHL norm applies only in armed conflict and to deprivations of liberty with a nexus thereto, whereas IHRL applies at all times, governing primarily 'everyday' situations.[45] Consequently, rather than focusing on deprivations of liberty for a specific purpose (eg security reasons), IHRL (with the exception of the ECHR) simply sets out the two requirements of lawfulness and non-arbitrariness.[46]

Regarding the requirement of lawfulness under IHRL, the UN Working Group on Arbitrary Detention has suggested a strict interpretation:

The requirement, which a 'law' has to meet, is that the national legislation must set down all permissible restrictions and conditions thereof. Therefore, the word 'law' has to be understood in the strict sense of a parliamentary statute, or an equivalent unwritten norm of common law accessible to all individuals subject to the relevant jurisdiction...[47]

---

[40] Arts 5(1)(a)–(f) ECHR.
[41] ECtHR, *A and others v UK*, App No 3455/05, Judgment (Grand Chamber), 19 February 2009, [172].
[42] *A and others v UK* (n 41) [164]; ECtHR, *Guide on Article 5: Right to Liberty and Security* (Council of Europe/ECtHR 2012) [1] (the aim of Art 5 'is to ensure that no one should be deprived of [their] liberty in an arbitrary fashion').
[43] ECtHR, *Storck v Germany*, App No 62603/00, Judgment, 16 June 2005, [102]; ECtHR, *Guide on Article 5* (n 42) [15]; HRC (n 38) [7].
[44] M Milanović, *Extraterritorial Application of Human Rights Treaties: Law, Principles, and Policy* (OUP, Oxford 2011) 210.
[45] Droege (n 4) 521.   [46] See above, text to nn 36–9.
[47] UN Commission on Human Rights, Report of the Working Group on Arbitrary Detention, E/CN.4/2005/6, 1 December 2004, [54(a)]. Similarly, see *Chaparro Alvarez and Lapo Iniguez v Ecuador*, Judgment, IACtHR (Series C) No 170 (2007) [56] (adopting a similarly strict interpretation of 'law' for the purposes of Art 7(2) ACHR).

4.2 Rules under Human Rights Treaties

The broader requirement of non-arbitrariness has been elaborated in jurisprudence. For example, the HRC has stated:

The drafting history of article 9, paragraph 1 [of the ICCPR], confirms that 'arbitrariness' is not to be equated with 'against the law', but must be interpreted more broadly to include elements of inappropriateness, injustice and lack of predictability. This means that remand in custody pursuant to a lawful arrest must not only be lawful but reasonable in all the circumstances.[48]

Indeed, the prohibition of arbitrary detention in Article 9 UDHR, on which Article 9 ICCPR was based, was drafted with this in mind, employing the term 'arbitrary' instead of 'unlawful', lest it restrict the protections thereunder.[49] The jurisprudence of the other human rights treaty bodies confirms these requirements of legality and non-arbitrariness in the broader sense.[50] The consequence of this dual requirement of a legal basis *and* non-arbitrariness is demonstrated in the HRC's Concluding Observations on Trinidad and Tobago, in which the Committee advised that a domestic statute granting the police wide discretion in arresting individuals should be 'confined' so as to bring it into conformity with Article 9 ICCPR.[51] Similarly, the ECtHR in *Medvedyev v France* held:

...where deprivation of liberty is concerned it is particularly important that the general principle of legal certainty be satisfied. It is therefore essential that the conditions for deprivation of liberty...be clearly defined and that the law itself be foreseeable in its application.[52]

Importantly, as part of this non-arbitrariness standard, jurisprudence has also confirmed the need for a proportionality assessment. The HRC, for example, has held that any deprivation of liberty must be 'necessary in all the circumstances of the case',[53] requiring an examination of the proportionality of detention.[54] The ECtHR, too, has noted this requirement:

The detention of an individual is such a serious measure that it is justified only as a last resort where other, less severe measures have been considered and found to be insufficient

---

[48] HRC, *Van Alphen v The Netherlands*, CCPR/C/39/D/305/1988, 15 August 1990, [5.8]. Similarly, see HRC (n 38) [12].

[49] L Marcoux Jr, 'Protection from Arbitrary Arrest and Detention under International Law' (1982) 5 Boston College Intl & Comp L Rev 345, 351–5.

[50] ECtHR, *Steel and others v UK*, App No 24838/94, Judgment, 23 September 1998, [54]; ECtHR, *Saadi v UK*, App No 13229/03, Judgment, 29 January 2008, [67]–[74]; *A and others v UK* (n 41) [164]; *Tibi v Ecuador*, Judgment, IACtHR (Series C) No 114, 7 September 2004, [98]; *Amnesty International and others v Sudan* (n 28) [58]–[59].

[51] HRC, Concluding Observations: Trinidad and Tobago, CCPR/CO/70/TTO, 10 November 2000, [16]. Similarly, see HRC (n 38) [22].

[52] *Medvedyev and others v France*, App No 3394/03, Judgment (Grand Chamber) 29 March 2010, [80]. Similarly, see ECtHR, *Guide on Article 5* (n 42) [22]; IACiHR, *Dayra María Levoyer Jiménez v Ecuador*, Report No 66/01, 14 June 2001, [37]; *Amnesty International and others v Sudan* (n 28) [58]–[59].

[53] *A v Australia*, CCPR/C/59/D/560/93, 3 April 1997, [9.2].

[54] Ibid. Similarly, see S Shah, 'Administration of Justice' in D Moeckli, S Shah, and S Sivakumaran (eds), *International Human Rights Law* (OUP, Oxford 2010) 308.

to safeguard the individual or public interest which might require that the person concerned be detained... The principle of proportionality further dictates that where detention is to secure the fulfilment of an obligation provided by law, a balance must be struck between the importance in a democratic society of securing the immediate fulfilment of the obligation in question, and the importance of the right to liberty... The duration of the detention is a relevant factor in striking such a balance...[55]

The IACtHR has similarly emphasized this proportionality requirement and, in so doing, has noted that the purpose for which detention is claimed necessary must itself be legitimate.[56] Related to this, jurisprudence also confirms that detention will be arbitrary if taken for reasons related to the legitimate exercise of another right under IHRL, such as freedom of expression.[57]

4.2.1.1 *The conformity of internment with the IHRL standard*

Having introduced the IHRL standard governing detention, the compatibility with that standard of the type of detention with which we are concerned in this book, that is, preventive, security detention, or 'internment', must be considered. It will be shown that, with the exception of the ECHR, internment is not necessarily in violation of IHRL, and a state may thus intern in a manner that is consistent with its human rights obligations.

Internment clearly constitutes one form of detention to which the relevant rules of IHRL apply. It will be remembered that internment was defined in the introduction as a deprivation of liberty ordered by the executive, without criminal charge, for the purpose of preventing a security threat from materializing.[58] This may be compared to the language of a 1964 UN Study of the Right of Everyone to be Free from Arbitrary Arrest, Detention and Exile, in which detention for the purposes of IHRL was defined as:

... the act of confining a person to a certain place, whether or not in continuation of arrest, and under restraints which prevent him from living with his family or carrying out his normal occupational or social activities.[59]

---

[55] *Saadi v UK* (n 50) [70]. Similarly, see HCJ 7015/02 and 7019/02, *Ajuri and others v IDF Commander in the West Bank, IDF Commander in the Gaza Strip and others* [2002] 125 ILR 537, [25] (Israeli Supreme Court).
[56] *Chaparro Alvarez and Lapo Iniguez v Ecuador* (n 47) [93]. Similarly recognizing the need for a legitimate reason for detention, see *Van Alphen v Netherlands* (n 48) [5.8]; UN Working Group on Arbitrary Detention, 'Fact Sheet 26' <http://www.ohchr.org/Documents/Publications/FactSheet26en.pdf> accessed 4 August 2015. That detention must be based on legitimate grounds is inherent in Art 5(1) ECHR's exhaustive list.
[57] See, eg, HRC (n 38) [17]; UN Working Group on Arbitrary Detention, 'Fact Sheet 26' (n 56); Shah (n 54) 309. Similarly, see UNGA Res 60/166 (2005) [4(f)] (condemning detention on the basis of religion or belief).
[58] J Pejic, 'Procedural Principles and Safeguards for Internment/Administrative Detention in Armed Conflict and Other Situations of Violence' (2005) 87 IRRC 375, 375–6.
[59] UN Department of Economics and Social Affairs, *Study of the Right of Everyone to be Free from Arbitrary Arrest, Detention and Exile*, UN Doc E/CN 4/826 Rev 1 (1964) [21].

Internment, being a deprivation of liberty and involving the confinement of a person to a particular place, would clearly satisfy this definition and would, therefore, be subject to the human rights law rules on detention. Indeed, this is confirmed by jurisprudence. The HRC, for example, has made clear that, 'if so-called preventive detention is used, for reasons of public security, it must be controlled by these same provisions [Article 9 ICCPR]'.[60] Similarly, the ECtHR has applied the Article 5 ECHR rules to cases of internment in situations of emergency.[61] Moreover, in their commentary on the jurisprudence of the IACtHR, Laurence Burgogue-Larsen and Amaya Ubeda de Torres state that 'the text [of Article 7 ACHR on detention] includes every type of deprivation of liberty...so as to give as broad a scope as possible to protection under the Convention'.[62]

Given that internment constitutes detention for the purposes of IHRL, its compatibility with the IHRL standard must be examined. As noted above, for states party to the ECHR, internment is not provided for as a permissible ground for detention under Article 5(1) ECHR, and derogation is therefore necessary for states wishing to adopt an internment regime.[63] Under the other human rights treaties, since they contain an 'open' standard for detention (legality and non-arbitrariness), as opposed to a closed list of permissible grounds, internment is not necessarily unlawful. First, the requirement of a legal basis will be satisfied if it can be shown that a particular internment is based on 'such grounds and in accordance with such procedures established by law'.[64] Such a legal basis can, in principle, be located not only in domestic law but also international law, including treaties or, potentially, Security Council resolutions.[65] As noted in chapter 3, GCIII and GCIV provide the legal basis for combatant and civilian internment in international conflicts.[66] In non-international conflicts, however, neither IHL nor customary international law were shown to contain a legal basis to detain, requiring that one be found elsewhere.[67]

Second, there is nothing in the nature of internment that would necessarily breach the non-arbitrariness requirement under the IHRL standard. For example, as explained above, the HRC has interpreted the non-arbitrariness element as requiring that detention be appropriate, just, and predictable.[68] Preventive,

---

[60] HRC, General Comment No 8: Right to Liberty and Security of Persons, 30 June 1982, [4], <http://www.unhchr.ch/tbs/doc.nsf/(Symbol)/f4253f9572cd4700c12563ed00483bec?Opendocument> accessed 4 August 2015. Similarly, see HRC, *Macado de Cámpora v Uruguay*, CCPR/C/OP/2, 12 October 1982, [18.1].

[61] See, eg, *Lawless v Ireland (No 3)*, App No 332/57, Judgment (Plenary), 1 July 1961; *Ireland v UK*, App No 5310/71, Judgment, 18 January 1978; *A and others v UK* (n 41) [172]; *Al-Jedda v UK* (n 28).

[62] L Burgorgue-Larsen and AU De Torres, *The Inter-American Court of Human Rights: Case Law and Commentary* (OUP, Oxford 2011) [478].

[63] *Ireland v UK* (n 61) [194]–[196]; *A and others v UK* (n 41) [172].

[64] Art 9(1) ICCPR.

[65] *Coard v US* (n 17) [52]; *Medvedyev v France* (n 52) [79]. The UK relied on a Security Council resolution as the basis for its internment of Al-Jedda: *Al-Jedda* (n 28) [16]. As noted in chapter 3, more controversial is the reliance on the general language ('all necessary measures') of a Chapter VII resolution.

[66] See section 3.1.   [67] Ibid.   [68] See above at text to n 48.

security detention ordered by the executive is not inherently at odds with these requirements. However, were the law permitting internment to be considered overly broad or vague, this would likely fail to meet the IHRL standard. Indeed, as noted above, international tribunals have held detention to be unlawful where it is based on domestic laws that are framed too broadly.[69] It is therefore important that the legal basis for internment, whether it be found in domestic or international law, be framed in a clear, predictable way.[70]

It should finally be noted, however, that, under IHRL, preference is often expressed for criminal, rather than administrative detention. Thus, there is an 'assumption [in IHRL] that the criminal justice system is able to deal with persons suspected of representing a danger to State security'.[71] Indeed, certain authorities take the same view regarding internment under IHL.[72]

To conclude this section, internment, whilst incompatible with Article 5 ECHR, is not as such prohibited by the other human rights treaties. Rather, in each case it would need to satisfy the elements of the IHRL standard, as developed in jurisprudence.[73] Indeed, the HRC takes the same view, permitting internment but requiring its compliance with Article 9 ICCPR in each case.[74]

4.2.2 Reasons for detention

Chapter 2 explained that, where a person is interned for reasons of security in an international armed conflict, IHL requires the detaining authority to inform them of the reasons for their internment.[75] It was shown that this is a *conditio sine qua non* to the effective exercise of the right to initial (and periodic) review, required by GCIV.[76] Chapter 3, however, demonstrated that no equivalent IHL treaty rule

---

[69] See above at text to nn 51–2.

[70] Similarly, see *In re Guantanamo Detainee Cases*, 355 F Supp 2d 443 (DDC 2005) 474–8 (cautioning that the definition of 'enemy combatant' developed by the US for the purposes of defining who may be detained might be overly broad). Although note *Steel v UK* (n 50) [54]–[55] (the Court held that the ground for detention of 'breach of the peace' was not overly vague as its content had been elaborated in domestic jurisprudence).

[71] Pejic (n 58) 380. Similarly, see HRC, Concluding Observations: United States, CCPR/C/USA/CO/3, 15 September 2006, [19]; Chatham House and ICRC, 'Meeting Summary: Procedural Safeguards for Security Detention in Non-International Armed Conflict', London, 22–3 September 2008, 5 <http://www.chathamhouse.org/sites/files/chathamhouse/public/Research/International%20Law/il220908summary.pdf> accessed 4 August 2015; HRC (n 38) [14].

[72] Y Dinstein, *The International Law of Belligerent Occupation* (CUP, Cambridge 2009) 173, citing HCJ 5784/03, *L Salame et al v IDF Commander of Judea and Samaria et al*, 57(6) PD 721, [6]. Similarly, see *Ajuri v IDF Commander* (n 55) [26]; Y Arai-Takahashi, *The Law of Occupation: Continuity and Change of International Humanitarian Law, and its Interaction with International Human Rights Law* (Martinus Nijhoff, Leiden 2009) 275. Although cf *Jose Padilla v CT Hanft*, 423 F.3d 386 (2005) 394–5 (rejecting the view that the availability of the penal process rendered detention in relation to the US conflict with al-Qaeda unnecessary within the meaning of the domestic law authorization).

[73] Similarly, see Doswald-Beck (n 19) 263; N Rodley and M Pollard, *The Treatment of Prisoners under International Law* (OUP, Oxford 2009) 467.

[74] HRC (n 60) [4]; *Mansour Ahani v Canada*, CPR/C/80/D/1051/2002, 15 June 2004, [10.2].

[75] See section 2.3.1.1.   [76] Ibid.

exists for non-international conflicts, with custom appearing not to eliminate this distinction between the two categories of armed conflict in this area.

Like IHL applicable in international conflicts, IHRL similarly requires that all persons deprived of their liberty be informed of the reasons justifying their detention: 'Anyone who is arrested shall be informed, at the time of arrest, of the reasons for his arrest and shall be promptly informed of any charges against him.'[77] Notwithstanding the reference to 'arrest' and 'charges against him', this provision applies to all forms of detention, criminal or otherwise.[78]

The treaties require that reasons be given either at the time of the initial detention or 'promptly' thereafter.[79] The ECtHR has stated the following regarding the 'promptness' standard in Article 5(2):

While this information must be conveyed 'promptly'... it need not be related in its entirety by the arresting officer at the very moment of the arrest. Whether the content and promptness of the information conveyed were sufficient is to be assessed in each case according to its special features.[80]

In one case, the Court held an interval of up to six and a half hours as not 'falling outside the constraints of time imposed by the notion of promptness',[81] whereas in another, involving immigration detention, the Court found a delay of seventy-six hours to breach Article 5(2) ECHR.[82]

Finally, the degree of information that must be imparted to the detainee is not specified. However, importantly for the present enquiry, the HRC has confirmed that it is insufficient to be told that one is arrested 'under prompt security measures without any indication of the substance' of the reasons for detention.[83] Furthermore, the ECtHR has held that simply stating the legal basis of the detention is insufficient, and instead the factual basis must also be conveyed.[84] It is submitted that the purpose served by this particular right sheds light on the extent of information required. Thus, as is the case with the equivalent right under IHL, knowing the reasons for one's detention is a *sine qua non* to challenging effectively the legality of that detention as part of *habeas corpus* proceedings (discussed

---

[77] Art 9(2) ICCPR; Art 5(2) ECHR; Art 7(4) ACHR; Art 14(3) ArCHR; Principles and Guidelines (n 31) Principle M.2(a).

[78] HRC (n 38) [24]; ECtHR, *Van der Leer v Netherlands*, App No 11509/85, Judgment, 21 February 1990, [27]; Doswald-Beck (n 19) 265. The criminal law connotation does not exist in the case of Art 7(4) ACHR, which requires simply that '[a]nyone who is *detained* shall be informed of the reasons for his detention' (my emphasis).

[79] Specifically, the ICCPR and ArCHR require that the reasons be conveyed at the time of arrest; the ECHR states that the reasons must be conveyed 'promptly'; the ACHR states that '[a]nyone who is detained shall be informed of the reasons for his detention'; Principle M.2(a) of the ACiHPR's Principles and Guidelines (n 31) refers to notification of the reasons 'at the time of arrest'.

[80] *Kerr v UK*, App No 40451/98, Admissibility Decision, 7 December 1999.

[81] *Fox, Campbell and Hartley v UK*, App Nos 12244/86 and 12245/86, Judgment, 30 August 1990, [42].

[82] *Saadi v UK* (n 50) [81]–[85].

[83] HRC, *Adolfo Drescher Caldas v Uruguay*, CCPR/C/OP/2, 21 July 1983, [13.2].

[84] *Kerr v UK* (n 80).

immediately below).[85] The degree of (legal and factual) detail required must, therefore, be the minimum necessary to challenge the basis of detention.

4.2.3 Initial review (*habeas corpus*)

Chapter 2 demonstrated that civilian internees in international armed conflicts must receive an initial review by a court or administrative board to ensure that their internment is necessary for security reasons.[86] POW internment, on the other hand, is subject to no such review, given the assumption that their status as enemy combatants *ipso facto* renders their internment necessary for security reasons.[87] Chapter 3 then showed that, in non-international conflicts, treaty law is silent here and custom does not appear to have eliminated this distinction between the two categories of armed conflict.

The third procedural rule applicable to detention under IHRL similarly relates to review and requires that any person detained be given the right of access to *habeas corpus*:

> …[a]nyone who is deprived of his liberty by arrest or detention shall be entitled to take proceedings before a court, in order that that court may decide without delay on the lawfulness of his detention and order his release if the detention is not lawful.[88]

The various aspects of this right as developed in jurisprudence will briefly be examined.

4.2.3.1 'Without delay'

As Louise Doswald-Beck notes, there are two aspects to the requirement that a decision be made 'without delay' on the lawfulness of detention, 'the first being when a court is seised of the application and begins the inquiry, and the second being when a decision is reached'.[89] Regarding the first, the HRC has held a delay of seven days before which the detainee could challenge their detention to breach Article 9(4) ICCPR.[90] Applying the equivalent requirement in Article 5(4) ECHR, that a decision be made 'speedily', the ECtHR's jurisprudence confirms that this 'depends on all the circumstances.'[91] The Court has, however, held that six days 'sits ill with the notion of "speedily"'.[92] Similarly, the IACiHR held five days to be

---

[85] Similarly making this point, see HRC (n 38) [25]; *Van der Leer v Netherlands* (n 78) [28]; *Fox, Campbell and Hartley* (n 81) [40]; *Juan Humberto Sanchez v Honduras*, Judgment, IACtHR (Series C) No 99 (2003) [82].
[86] See section 2.3.1.1.   [87] See section 2.3.2.
[88] Art 9(4) ICCPR; Art 5(4) ECHR; Art 7(6) ACHR; Art XXV ADRDM; Art 14(6) ArCHR; Principles and Guidelines (n 31) Principle M.4.
[89] Doswald-Beck (n 19) 270. Similarly, see *Khudyakova v Russia*, App No 13476/04, Judgment, 8 January 2009, [97].
[90] HRC, *Torres v Finland*, CCPR/C/38/D/291/1988, 5 April 1990, [7.2].
[91] RCA White and C Ovey, *Jacobs, White & Ovey: The European Convention on Human Rights* (5th edn, OUP, Oxford 2010) 239.
[92] *Çetinkaya and Çağlayan v Turkey*, App Nos 3921/02, 35003/02, and 17261/03, Judgment, 23 January 2007, [43].

a 'very long delay' and incompatible with the requirement in Article 7(6) ACHR that the court decide 'without delay' on the lawfulness of detention.[93]

Regarding the second aspect of this temporal requirement, 'the test is whether the court acted with due diligence to make a decision as speedily as possible'.[94] Once again, the ECtHR has confirmed that the acceptable length of time for a decision to be made depends on the circumstances of each case.[95] Thus, in *Khudyakova v Russia*, it held an unjustified delay of fifty-four days to be impermissible, and in *Kadem v Malta* a delay of seventeen days before which a decision on the legality of detention was rendered was considered a breach of Article 5(4).[96] In *Mansour Ahani v Canada*, the HRC was faced with a more extreme case involving a delay of nine and a half months, which was held to be a violation of this requirement.[97] The Committee has confirmed more generally that '[t]he adjudication of the case should take place as expeditiously as possible'.[98]

4.2.3.2 *The nature and procedures of the review body*

It is important that each human rights treaty requires that the detention review be carried out by 'nothing less than a formally constituted court'.[99] The HRC has found violations of Article 9(4) ICCPR where the review procedures do not employ formal judicial bodies. Thus, in *Torres v Finland*, the HRC stated that the possibility of applying to the Ministry of the Interior to review the legality of immigration detention,

... while providing for some measure of protection and review of the legality of detention, does not satisfy the requirements of article 9, paragraph 4, which envisages that the legality of detention will be determined by a court so as to ensure a higher degree of objectivity and independence in such control.[100]

The other treaty bodies too have held that *habeas corpus* proceedings must be before a court that is independent of the executive authority that ordered the detention.[101] The ECtHR, whilst noting that the 'court' for the purposes of Article 5(4) does

---

[93] *Nativi & Martinez v Honduras*, Report No 4/87, 28 March 1987.
[94] Doswald-Beck (n 19) 271; *Khudyakova v Russia* (n 89) [97].
[95] *Sanchez-Reisse v Switzerland*, App No 9862/82, Judgment, 21 October 1986, [55].
[96] *Khudyakova v Russia* (n 89) [99]; ECtHR, *Kadem v Malta*, App No 55263/00, Judgment, 9 January 2003, [44]–[45]. See also *Mamedova v Russia*, App No 7064/05, Judgment, 1 June 2006, [96] (twenty-six days considered a violation).
[97] *Mansour Ahani v Canada* (n 74) [10.3].   [98] HRC (n 38) [47].
[99] Rodley and Pollard (n 73) 466.
[100] *Torres v Finland* (n 90) [7.2]. Similarly, see *Vuolanne v Finland*, CCPR/C/35/D/265/1987, 2 May 1989, [9.6] (holding that a superior military officer does not satisfy this requirement of review by a court, in the context of military disciplinary detention). Although note HRC (n 38) [45] (the 'court' in Art 9(4) 'should ordinarily be a court within the judiciary. Exceptionally, for some forms of detention, legislation may provide for proceedings before a specialized tribunal, which must be established by law and must either be independent of the executive and legislative branches or enjoy judicial independence in deciding legal matters in proceedings that are judicial in nature').
[101] *Habeas Corpus in Emergency Situations (Arts. 27(2) and 7(6) of the American Convention on Human Rights)*, Advisory Opinion OC-8/87, IACtHR (Series A) No 8 (1987), [30]; *Chaparro Alvarez and Lapo Iniguez v Ecuador* (n 47) [128] (noting that the review must be by a 'judge' or 'court');

not have to be a 'court of law of the classic kind integrated within the standard judicial machinery of the country',[102] has confirmed that 'the authority called upon...must possess a judicial character, that is to say, be independent both of the executive and of the parties to the case'.[103] That the body must be judicial, that is, objective and independent from the executive and the parties to the case, is consistent with the object and purpose of these provisions, which is to provide a check on the executive's detention authority and enforce the prohibition of arbitrary detention.[104]

In addition to the requirements of independence and objectivity, jurisprudence has also confirmed that the reviewing court must have the power to order release where detention is found to be unlawful.[105] In *Chahal v UK*, for example, the ECtHR held that an advisory panel, which made recommendations to the Home Secretary regarding security detention pending deportation, did not satisfy Article 5(4) ECHR as it could not make binding decisions.[106] This interpretation is consistent with the text of the relevant provisions, which require that the court 'order' release where detention is found to be unlawful.[107]

The procedures required in *habeas corpus* hearings have also been elaborated in case law. Thus, the ECtHR has held that:

> ...the requirement of procedural fairness under Article 5 § 4 does not impose a uniform, unvarying standard to be applied irrespective of the context, facts and circumstances. Although it is not always necessary that an Article 5 § 4 procedure be attended by the same guarantees as those required under Article 6 for criminal or civil litigation, it must have a judicial character and provide guarantees appropriate to the type of deprivation of liberty in question.[108]

Importantly, in that case, which concerned indefinite administrative detention (ie the kind with which we are dealing here), the Court stated that:

> ...in view of the dramatic impact of the lengthy—and what appeared at the time to be indefinite—deprivation of liberty on the applicant's fundamental rights, Article 5 paragraph 4 must import substantially the same fair trial guarantees as Article 6 paragraph 1 in its criminal aspect.[109]

Amnesty International and others v Sudan (n 28) [60]; Principles and Guidelines (n 31) Principles A.4(g) (requiring independence from the executive branch) and A.5 (requiring that the judicial officer has played no role in the particular case).

[102] *Weeks v UK*, App No 9787/82, Judgment, 2 March 1987, [61].

[103] *Neumeister v Austria*, App No 1936/63, Judgment, 27 June 1968, [24] of 'The Law'; *Weeks v UK* (n 102); *Stephens v Malta (No 1)*, App No 11956/07, Judgment, 21 April 2009, [95].

[104] Confirming that this is the object and purpose of these provisions, see *Brannigan and McBride v UK*, App No 14553/89 and 14554/89, Judgment, 25 May 1993, [63]; *Khudyakova v Russia* (n 89) [93]; *Tibi v Ecuador* (n 50) [129]; *Habeas Corpus in Emergency Situations* (n 101) [33]; HRC (n 38) [41].

[105] Doswald-Beck (n 19) 272.

[106] *Chahal v UK*, App No 22414/93, Judgment (Grand Chamber), 15 November 1996, [130]–[131]. Similarly, see *Singh v United Kingdom*, App No 23389/94, Judgment, 21 February 1996, [65]; *A v Australia* (n 53) [9.5]; HRC (n 38) [41].

[107] See above at n 88.   [108] *A and others v UK* (n 41) [203].

[109] Ibid, [216]–[217].

More specifically, tribunals have often suggested that, as part of the right to *habeas corpus*, detainees must appear before the court, in adversarial proceedings.[110] In addition, the HRC has also confirmed the importance of providing detainees with legal advice and representation as a *sine qua non* to the effective exercise of the right to *habeas corpus*:[111] 'In practice, it is virtually impossible for people to challenge their detention without legal representation.'[112] Indeed, in its Concluding Observations on Australia, the Committee went further and noted that, not only must this right to legal representation not be inhibited, it must also be brought to the attention of the detainee to enable them to avail themselves of it.[113] The other treaty bodies have similarly condemned cases in which detainees did not have access to a lawyer.[114]

4.2.3.3 Scope of review and the meaning of 'lawfulness'

The final issue regarding *habeas corpus* relates to the scope of review and, specifically, the meaning of 'lawfulness' in the *habeas* provisions. The HRC takes the view that, to satisfy Article 9(4) ICCPR, the court must examine not only the lawfulness of detention vis-à-vis domestic law, but also its lawfulness vis-à-vis international law, and specifically its compliance with Article 9(1) ICCPR (which, it will be remembered, requires both lawfulness and non-arbitrariness in the broader sense).[115] Thus, in *A v Australia*, which involved administrative immigration detention, the Committee found there to be a violation of Article 9(4) as the court 'was, in fact, limited to a formal assessment of the self-evident fact that [the detainee] was indeed a "designated person" within the meaning of the Migration Amendment Act' (and therefore subject automatically to detention).[116] The other human rights treaty bodies have taken similar approaches regarding the scope of *habeas* review under their treaties.[117]

---

[110] *Habeas Corpus in Emergency Situations* (n 101) [35]; ECtHR, *Toth v Austria*, App No 11894/85, Judgment, 12 December 1991, [84]; ECtHR, *Włoch v Poland*, App No 27785/95, Judgment, 19 October 2000, [125]–[131]; ECtHR, *Öcalan v Turkey*, App No 46221/99, Judgment, 12 May 2005, [68]; *Sanchez-Reisse v Switzerland* (n 95) [51] ('[t]he possibility for a detainee "to be heard either in person or, where necessary, through some form of representation"...features in certain instances among the "fundamental guarantees of procedure applied in matters of deprivation of liberty"').

[111] *Berry v Jamaica*, CCPR/C/50/D/330/1988, 26 April 1994, [11.1]; HRC (n 38) [46] (requiring 'prompt and regular access to counsel').

[112] S Joseph, J Schultz, and M Castan, *The International Covenant on Civil and Political Rights: Cases, Materials, and Commentary* (2nd edn OUP, Oxford 2005) 334.

[113] HRC, Concluding Observations: Australia, UN Doc A/55/40 (2000) [526]–[527]; Joseph et al (n 112) 335–6.

[114] ECtHR, *Aksoy v Turkey*, App No 21987/93, Judgment (Merits), 18 December 1996, [81]–[84]; *Chahal v UK* (n 106) [130]; Principles and Guidelines (n 31) Principles M.2(b) and M.2(f); *Tibi v Ecuador* (n 50) [112].

[115] *A v Australia* (n 53) [9.5]; *C v Australia*, CCPR/C/76/D/900/1999, 28 October 2002, [8.3]; *Baban et al v Australia*, CCPR/C/78/D/1014/2001, 18 September 2003, [7.2]; HRC (n 38) [44].

[116] *A v Australia* (n 53) [9.5].

[117] See, eg, ECtHR case law: *X v UK*, App No 7215/75, Judgment, 5 November 1981, [57]; *Brogan and others v UK*, App Nos 11209/84, 11234/84, 11266/84 and 11386/85, Judgment, 29 November 1988, [65]; *Chahal v UK* (n 106) [127]; *A and others v UK* (n 41) [202]. Similarly, see inter-American case law: IACiHR, *Ferrer-Mazorra v United States*, Report No 51/01, 4 April 2001, [235].

This interpretation of Article 9(4) ICCPR was criticized by Sir Nigel Rodley in his individual opinions in the HRC.[118] In his view, there is nothing in the text of Article 9(4) nor in the *travaux* that suggests 'legality' includes the requirement of conformity with the non-arbitrariness standard in Article 9(1);[119] indeed, the HRC's previous case law confirming that 'arbitrary' is wider than 'unlawful' suggests that the latter catches a smaller group of cases.[120] Rodley argues instead that those cases in which the review is limited to an examination of conformity with an arbitrary domestic law should be treated as being incompatible with Article 9(1) rather than Article 9(4).[121]

It is clear that the majority's approach in the HRC offers greater protections to detainees than Rodley's, and, for this reason, the majority's approach is supported by certain commentators.[122] However, requiring domestic courts to judge the compliance of detention with Article 9(1) ICCPR assumes that the Covenant applies directly in domestic law. As such, it fails to account for the diversity in domestic approaches to the incorporation of rules of international law, as only certain states will consider their international obligations as justiciable before domestic courts without further incorporation.[123] Notwithstanding the normative advantages of the majority opinion in the HRC, therefore, it seems that Rodley's criticisms accurately reflect the current law. That said, given that the other treaty bodies follow the same approach, it seems that in practice this approach will be required of states parties.

4.2.3.4 Comparing habeas corpus *and the IHL review procedures*

Habeas corpus serves the purpose of protecting against arbitrary deprivation of liberty.[124] It thus plays a very similar role to the initial review procedure required under IHL for civilian internees in international armed conflicts. As section 2.3.1 explained, GCIV provides for an initial review of the legality of civilian internment by an 'appropriate court or administrative board' (in enemy territory) and a 'regular procedure' and 'right of appeal' (in occupied territory).[125] These review procedures serve to ensure civilian internment falls within the legal authority

---

[118] See, eg, *C v Australia* (n 115), Individual Opinion of Committee Member Mr Nigel Rodley. Similarly, see HRC, 'Periodic Report of States Parties: Australia', CCPR/C/AUS/5, 19 February 2008, [12].
[119] *C v Australia* (n 115), Individual Opinion of Committee Member Mr Nigel Rodley.
[120] On that case law, see above at text to n 48.
[121] *C v Australia* (n 115), Individual Opinion of Committee Member Mr Nigel Rodley.
[122] Joseph et al (n 112) 344.
[123] See, eg, J Crawford, *Brownlie's Principles of Public International Law* (8th edn, OUP, Oxford 2012) 63–4 (on the dualist approach in the United Kingdom to unincorporated treaties); *Medellin v Texas*, 552 US 491 (2008) (US Supreme Court) (concluding, inter alia, that the UN Charter had not been incorporated into US law and was not, therefore, justiciable). It is conceivable that the argument could be based on customary law, which is directly applicable in many domestic jurisdictions that otherwise adopt a dualist approach to the incorporation of ratified treaties.
[124] See above at n 104.   [125] Arts 43 and 78 GCIV.

conferred on states by GCIV (ie that internment is necessary for the security of the detaining power), similarly protecting against arbitrariness.[126]

Both IHL and IHRL thus serve to protect against arbitrary deprivations of liberty, in part, by requiring that review procedures be provided. Moreover, in certain respects, jurisprudence has developed a similar content to the IHL review mechanisms and the IHRL requirement of *habeas corpus*. It was explained in section 2.3.1.1, for example, that the International Criminal Tribunal for the Former Yugoslavia (ICTY) considers GCIV to require that the review body has the power to order release;[127] this, as noted above, is similarly required for courts carrying out *habeas* reviews.[128] It also seems self-evident that, in order properly to perform their function as checks on the detention authority of states, the IHL review procedures must operate impartially and independently from the authority that ordered internment.[129] This is inherent in the *habeas corpus* procedure, which must be performed by a court, situated outside the executive branch.[130] In these respects, the review procedures under IHL and IHRL are similar.

However, significant differences remain between the two, both on the text of the provisions and as they have been developed in jurisprudence. First, unlike *habeas corpus*, it is clear that GCIV does not require a court, and instead a non-judicial, administrative board (that is not outside the executive branch) appears to suffice.[131] Second, case law has not elaborated on the procedures required in GCIV review proceedings, in contrast to IHRL, where, for example, legal counsel and the right to challenge the evidence against the detainee are considered important.[132] Third, no guidance on the scope of review under GCIV has been developed.[133] This is in contrast to the ICCPR and ECHR, for example, where the relevant provisions have been interpreted as requiring review of both the legality of detention and its compliance with the Covenant and Convention more generally.[134] Finally, as explained in section 2.3.2, POWs are not entitled to challenge their internment before any review body under IHL.

It is clear, therefore, that, notwithstanding their shared purpose, the review procedures under IHL and IHRL are fundamentally different, with the former leaving far more discretion to the detaining power. This difference is a result of the role of military necessity in IHL, reserving greater areas to the discretion of states in light of the exceptional circumstances.[135] That IHL is designed specifically for armed conflict, whereas IHRL is designed primarily for 'ordinary' situations,

---

[126] *Prosecutor v Zejnil Delalić et al* (Trial Judgment) ICTY-96-21 (16 November 1998) [580]–[581].
[127] *Prosecutor v Zejnil Delalić et al* (Appeals Judgment) ICTY-96-21-A (20 February 2001) [329].
[128] See above, text to nn 105–7.
[129] JS Pictet (ed), *Commentary to Geneva Convention IV Relative to the Protection of Civilian Persons in Time of War* (ICRC, Geneva 1958) 260; Pejic (n 58) 386; Chatham House and ICRC (n 71) 15.
[130] See above, text to nn 99–104.   [131] See arts 43 and 78 GCIV.
[132] See above, text to nn 108–14.   [133] See the discussion in section 2.3.1.1.
[134] See above, text to nn 115–17.
[135] N Prud'homme, 'Lex Specialis: Oversimplifying a More Complex and Multifaceted Relationship?' (2007) 40 Isr L Rev 355, 360–61.

was explained above as the reason also for the different approaches taken to the standard for detention.[136]

4.2.4 Periodic review

Chapter 2 demonstrated that IHL requires periodic review of civilian internment in international armed conflicts.[137] As explained, the purpose of this is to re-examine the original determination that internment is necessary in light of changing circumstances; it thus helps to enforce the requirement that no person be interned 'for a longer time than the security of the Detaining State demands'.[138] As with initial review, periodic review does not extend to POWs, by virtue of the assumption that their status as enemy combatants renders their internment a necessity for the duration of hostilities.[139] Chapter 3, furthermore, demonstrated that, once again, treaty law is silent on this in non-international conflicts and customary IHL cannot be said to have extended the requirement of periodic review to such situations.

Nothing in the text of the human rights treaties provides specifically for periodic review of detention, independent of *habeas corpus* review. However, jurisprudence has confirmed that IHRL too requires periodic review at 'reasonable intervals' in certain circumstances, for example where the original basis for detention may cease to apply. The HRC, for instance, has held that Article 9(4) ICCPR, in certain cases, requires periodic review:

> The Committee observes...that every decision to keep a person in detention should be open to review periodically so that the grounds justifying the detention can be assessed. In any event, detention should not continue beyond the period for which the State can provide appropriate justification.[140]

This interpretation of the *habeas* provisions seems appropriate. First, none of the human rights treaties suggests that review may occur only once. Instead, each refers simply to the right of the individual to 'take proceedings', 'petition', or to have 'recourse' to a court, without suggesting that this is limited to an initial review.[141] Second, interpreting the *habeas* provisions so as to require periodic review helps to ensure no person is interned for longer than is justified, thus upholding the object and purpose of these provisions, that is, to enforce the prohibition of arbitrary detention.

Finally, it is noteworthy that the HRC's case law above involved administrative immigration detention.[142] In such cases, where the end-point of detention is

---

[136] See section 4.2.1. [137] Arts 43 and 78 GCIV. See section 2.3.1.2.
[138] Pictet, *GCIV* (n 129) 261; *Delalić* (n 126) [581]. [139] See section 2.3.2
[140] *A v Australia* (n 53) [9.4]. Similarly, see *C v Australia* (n 115) [8.3]; HRC (n 38) [12]. The ECtHR has taken the same view: *Luberti v Italy*, App No 9019/80, Judgment, 23 February 1984, [31]; *Bezicheri v Italy*, App No 11400/85, Judgment, 25 October 1989, [20]; *Assenov and others v Bulgaria*, App No 24760/94, Judgment, 28 October 1998, [162]; *Lebedev v Russia*, App No 4493/04, Judgment, 25 October 2007, [78]–[79]; ECtHR, *Guide on Article 5* (n 42) [187].
[141] See, eg, arts 5(4) ECHR and 9(4) ICCPR. [142] See above at n 140.

undefined, the need for periodic review is clear given its importance in ensuring that detention does not become arbitrary. This need similarly exists with the kind of detention with which this book deals (internment), and thus the same rationale as justifies the need for periodic review in immigration detention also applies here.

4.2.5 Release from detention

As shown in section 2.4.1, civilian internees in international armed conflicts must be released once the reasons justifying their internment cease and, if not before, at the cessation of hostilities.[143] That release must occur when the reasons cease was explained as an essential aspect of the rule that internment only occur where necessary for security.[144] The obligation regarding POWs, on the other hand, is merely to release when hostilities cease, for the reasons necessitating their internment are assumed to co-exist with hostilities.[145] Chapter 3 argued that the same obligation to release where the justifications cease applies also in non-international conflicts, based on its inseparability from the basic prohibition of internment that is not necessary as a result of the conflict.[146]

Although there is no explicit provision in the human rights treaties defining the point of release, jurisprudence has addressed this. Thus, the HRC has held that, '[i]n order to avoid a characterization of arbitrariness, detention should not continue beyond the period for which the State party can provide appropriate justification'.[147] The requirement of release where the justification ceases is therefore similarly considered inherent to the prohibition of arbitrariness. Given that the prohibition of arbitrary detention lies at the heart of all of the key human rights treaties,[148] and given that the need for *continued* justification is inherent to this basic norm, the requirement that detainees be released where the reasons justifying their detention cease must apply under each of these treaty regimes.

An important point must be noted here which differentiates IHRL from IHL: certain human rights bodies are particularly sceptical of prolonged, indefinite detention.[149] This is in contrast to IHL, where indefinite detention is an inherent part of internment for security reasons. The ECtHR, whilst apparently not considering indefinite detention itself to be unlawful, addresses the matter in the context of its proportionality assessment. Thus, in highlighting the need for proportionality between the importance of the purpose that detention serves and

---

[143] Arts 132(1) and 133(1) GCIV. [144] See section 2.4.1 [145] See section 2.4.2.
[146] See section 3.3.2.
[147] *Baban v Australia* (n 115) [7.2]. Similarly, see *C v Australia* (n 115) [8.2]; HRC (n 38) [15].
[148] See section 4.2.1.
[149] Pejic (n 58) 382–3; A de Zayas, 'Human Rights and Indefinite Detention' (2005) 87 IRRC 15. See, eg, IACiHR, 'Annual Report: 1976', OAS Doc. OEA/Ser.L/V/II.40, Doc. 5 corr. 1 of 7 June 1977, Section II, Part II; UN Commission on Human Rights, Report of the Working Group on Arbitrary Detention, E/CN.4/2004/3, 15 December 2003, [60]; UN Working Group on Arbitrary Detention, *Obaidullah v United States*, A/HRC/WGAD/2013/10, 12 June 2013, [24]; HRC (n 38) [15].

the importance of the right to liberty, the Court has held that the 'duration of the detention is a relevant factor in striking such a balance'.[150] As detention becomes increasingly prolonged, therefore, one might reasonably argue that the burden required to justify its continuation should be increasingly high.[151] We will return to this issue in chapter 7.

4.2.6 Conclusions on the rules under IHRL

The above sections have explored the categories of procedural rules applicable to detention under IHRL. As demonstrated, similarities exist between those rules and the rules applicable to internment in international armed conflicts under IHL. However, it has also been shown that these rules differ in fundamental respects. Most importantly, regarding review, IHRL is more stringent than IHL in its requirement of *court* rather than *administrative* review. In addition, human rights jurisprudence has developed detailed rules to govern these review proceedings. Moreover, IHRL appears far more sceptical of prolonged, indefinite detention than IHL, with the potential that, the longer it continues, the more likely it is to be labelled as 'arbitrary'.

It was noted at the outset of this chapter that the goal of the remainder of this book is to consider the degree to which IHRL addresses the gaps left in this area by IHL. Whilst it was shown in section 4.1 that IHRL as a body of law continues prima facie to apply in armed conflict, the actual operation of the human rights rules on detention in non-international armed conflict remains to be examined in chapters 5 and 6. Before that, section 4.3 will conclude this chapter with an examination of the customary status of the rules explored above.

4.3 The Procedural Rules Applicable to Detention under Customary International Law

An examination of the extent to which customary international law contains procedural rules applicable to detention, and more specifically whether the treaty rules explored in section 4.2 have crystallized as custom, is necessary for three reasons. First, not all states are party to the general human rights treaties discussed in the previous sections, raising the question of what rules of international law, if any, apply to detentions by such states.[152] Second, whether IHRL obligations

---

[150] *Saadi v UK* (n 50) [70].   [151] HRC (n 38) [15].

[152] This is particularly pertinent for states not party to the ICCPR and in parts of the world that have no regional human rights conventions, such as China (which has signed but not ratified the ICCPR) and certain southeast Asian nations including Myanmar, Bhutan, Malaysia, and Brunei: <https://treaties.un.org/pages/viewdetails.aspx?src=treaty&mtdsg_no=iv-4&chapter=4&lang=en> accessed 4 August 2015. Indeed, Myanmar, for example, has, since it gained independence in 1948, been embroiled in internal armed conflicts: Human Rights Watch (Report), 'Untold Miseries: Wartime

derive from treaties or general international law may impact on the effect of those obligations in domestic law, for many states adopt a dualist approach to treaties (requiring transposition into municipal law) and a monist approach to general international law (not requiring transposition).[153] If transposition is necessary, an individual will not be able to invoke the specific right in domestic courts unless such transposition occurs.[154] Finally, the particular source from which these rules are derived may affect their binding nature vis-à-vis non-state armed groups party to non-international armed conflicts. As will be discussed in section 6.3, whereas human rights treaties are generally considered to bind only states, certain customary norms bind both states and non-state groups alike.

In section 3.3, an examination of what was termed 'customary IHL' was carried out, meaning practice and *opinio iuris* relating to internment specifically in (non-international) armed conflict. The purpose of this was to explore whether the distinction between international and non-international armed conflicts has been eliminated at the level of custom with respect to the procedural regulation of internment, in a similar manner to other areas of IHL. It was shown that no such conclusion can be made, but that there was a basic customary rule applicable in non-international armed conflicts prohibiting internment that is not actually necessary as a result of the conflict. This section is now concerned with customary international law generally, based on practice and *opinio iuris* in all situations. It will be shown that the general rule prohibiting arbitrary deprivation of liberty has crystallized as custom and that contained within this norm is the obligation to release where the reasons justifying detention cease. It will then be argued, however, that the other procedural rules of IHRL explored in this chapter, namely, the obligation to give reasons and the right to *habeas corpus*, cannot so clearly be said to be part of customary international law, given the difficulty in demonstrating an *opinio iuris* to that effect.

4.3.1 The prohibition of arbitrary deprivation of liberty

Regarding the arbitrary deprivation of liberty prohibition, it is worth repeating an earlier quote from chapter 3. There, the International Committee of the Red Cross (ICRC) Study on *Customary International Humanitarian Law* was relied upon, which concluded that 'all States have legislation specifying the grounds on which a person may be detained'.[155] Whilst the specific reasons for detention were

---

Abuses and Forced Displacement in Burma's Kachin State' (20 March 2012) <http://www.hrw.org/reports/2012/03/20/untold-miseries> accessed 4 August 2015. Whether any other rules of international law might apply in such situations, other than the minimal standards in IHL, must, therefore, be examined.

[153] B Simma and P Alston, 'The Sources of Human Rights Law: Custom, *Jus Cogens*, and General Principles' (1988–9) 12 Australian YB Intl L 82, 85–6; T Meron, *Human Rights and Humanitarian Norms as Customary Law* (OUP, Oxford 1989) 4–6.

[154] See, eg, *Medellin v Texas* (n 123).

[155] J-M Henckaerts and L Doswald-Beck, *Customary International Humanitarian Law Volume I: Rules* (CUP, Cambridge 2005) 347.

noted to vary across states,[156] this constitutes widespread practice in favour of the view that detention must be based on pre-determined grounds, and it may be considered to demonstrate a general rejection of a right to detain arbitrarily. Indeed, this legislation is supported by constant reassertions by states in a vast range of different fora regarding the protection of the right to liberty.[157] This extensive practice in domestic law is in addition to the widespread practice of states ratifying the IHRL instruments discussed in this chapter, containing the procedural rules explored above.[158]

It is accepted that both national legislation and treaty ratification constitute legitimate forms of state practice for the purpose of determining the existence of customary international law.[159] However, such practice can only lead to the crystallization of customary rules where accompanied by *opinio iuris*.[160] Proving the existence of *opinio iuris* in this area is complicated by the very fact that the rules under discussion *are* codified in widely ratified treaties; the practice referred

---

[156] Ibid.

[157] See, eg, HRC, 'Fifth Periodic Report: Finland', CCPR/C/FIN/2003/5, 24 July 2003, [131]–[134] (setting out the strict limitations on the deprivation of liberty under Finnish law); HRC, 'Fifth Periodic Report: Poland', CCPR/C/POL/2004/5, 26 January 2004, [157] (setting out the right to liberty under Polish law); HRC, 'Third Periodic Report: Azerbaijan', CCPR/C/AZE/3, 10 December 2007, [37] (stating the limited grounds on which persons may be detained under Azerbaijani law); Nepal, 'His Majesty's Government's Commitment on the Implementation of Human Rights and International Humanitarian Law', 26 March 2004, [3]–[10], annexed to International Commission of Jurists, *Nepal: The Rule of Law Abandoned* (ICJ, Geneva 2005) (committing to uphold the key aspects of the right to liberty); UN Secretary-General, 'Report on Information Submitted by Governments Pursuant to Sub-Commission Res 7 (XXVII) of 20 August 1974', E/CN.4/Sub.2/1990/20, 19 July 1990, [2], [11], and [15], (stating that the Human Rights Commission of the Philippines had confirmed that every person residing in the Philippines had the right not to be detained unlawfully), cited in J-M Henckaerts and L Doswald-Beck, *Customary International Humanitarian Law Volume II: Practice* (CUP, Cambridge 2005) 2338 [2627]; Sri Lanka, Statement by the President of Sri Lanka, 'Directions Issued by Her Excellency the President, Commander-in-Chief of the Armed Forces and Minister of Defence', Colombo, 31 July 1997, [1]–[6] (stating that any detention must be in accordance with the law and proper procedure), cited in ICRC, Customary IHL Database: Practice Relating to Rule 99 Deprivation of Liberty (British Red Cross/ICRC) <https//www.icrc.org/customary-ihl/eng/docs/v2_rul_rule99> accessed 4 August 2015; United Kingdom, 'Government Response to the Intelligence and Security Committee's Report on Rendition', Cm 7172, July 2007, 8 (confirming that 'the UK opposes any form of deprivation of liberty that amounts to placing a detained person outside the protection of the law'), cited in ICRC, Customary IHL Database: Practice Relating to Rule 99 Deprivation of Liberty (British Red Cross/ICRC) <https//www.icrc.org/customary-ihl/eng/docs/v2_rul_rule99> accessed 4 August 2015.

[158] As of 4 August 2015, there are 168 parties to the ICCPR, forty seven parties to the ECHR, twenty-three parties to the ACHR, fifty-three parties to the ACHPR, and thirteen parties to the ArCHR (including Palestine).

[159] See, eg, M Akehurst, 'Custom as a Source of International Law' (1974–5) 47 BYIL 1, 8–9, and 43–4; International Law Commission (ILC), Second Report on Identification of Customary International Law by Michael Wood, Special Rapporteur, A/CN.4/672, 22 May 2014, Draft Conclusion 7.

[160] ILC, Third Report on Identification of Customary International Law by Michael Wood, Special Rapporteur, A/CN.4/682, 27 March 2015, [34] ('...whatever the role that a treaty may play vis-à-vis customary international law...in order for the existence in customary international law of a rule found in a written text to be established, the rule must find support in external instances of practice coupled with acceptance as law').

4.3 Rules under Customary International Law

to above (eg national legislation), it might therefore be argued, is merely reflective of those states' *conventional* obligations, rather than any belief as to the content of *customary* law.[161] It is submitted, however, that these difficulties can be overcome so as to demonstrate that customary international law prohibits the arbitrary deprivation of liberty in all situations. In this regard, both the practice of states not party to the general human rights treaties, together with certain UN practice, is important.[162] Regarding the former, judicial and legislative practice of certain states not party to the ICCPR and the regional human rights treaties that suggests a rejection of unfettered detention power supports the proposition that the arbitrary deprivation of liberty is prohibited by custom.[163] As the practice of states not party to one of the general human rights treaties, there is no question of this arising from any conventional obligations, and it is, therefore, especially important as practice contributing to the formation of a customary rule.[164]

Regarding UN practice, particularly resolutions of the Security Council and the General Assembly, this constitutes an important source of the collective practice and *opinio iuris* of those states supporting specific resolutions.[165] Especially relevant here are resolutions relating to detention that refer to the international obligations, first, of states not party to the key human rights treaties, and, second,

---

[161] RR Baxter, 'Treaties and Custom' (1970) 129 *RdC* 27, 64 ('as the number of parties to a treaty increases, it becomes more difficult to demonstrate what is the state of customary international law dehors the treaty') and ibid, 73 ('[a]s the express acceptance of the treaty increases, the number of states not parties whose practice is relevant diminishes. There will be less scope for the development of international law dehors the treaty'); ILC, Third Report (n 160) [41].

[162] Similarly, see UN Working Group on Arbitrary Detention, 'Deliberation No 9 Concerning the Definition and Scope of Arbitrary Deprivation of Liberty under Customary International Law' in UN Human Rights Council, 'Report of the Working Group on Arbitrary Detention', A/HRC/22/44, 24 December 2012, [43].

[163] See, eg, Myanmar, *Defence Services Act* (1959), s 49(a) (providing for the punishment of 'any person subject to this law who...unnecessarily detains a person in arrest or confinement'), cited in Henckaerts, *Vol II* (n 157) 2335 [2594]; Malaysia, High Court (Kuala Lumpur), *Malek* case, Judgment, 18 October 2007, [18] (stating that '[t]he preservation of the personal liberty of the individual is a sacred universal value of all civilized nations and is enshrined in the Universal Declaration of Human Rights'), cited in ICRC, Customary IHL Database (n 157); China, *Constitution*, 1982, as amended in 2004, Art 37 ('[f]reedom of the person of citizens of the People's Republic of China is inviolable. No citizen may be arrested except with the approval or by decision of a people's procuratorate or by decision of a people's courts...Unlawful detention or deprivation or restriction of citizen's freedom of the person by other means is prohibited'), cited in ICRC, Customary IHL Database (n 157); Cooperation Council for the Arab States of the Gulf, 13th Session, Abu Dhabi, 21–3 December 1992, Final Communique, annexed to Letter dated 24 December 1992 from the UAE to the UN Secretary-General, UN Doc A/47/845-S/25020, 30 December 1992, 6 ('arbitrary arrests represent a total contravention of all the Charters, Law and Conventions of the International Community of Nations'—the UAE, Qatar, and Bahrain were all members of the Cooperation Council for the Arab States of the Gulf at this time and did not have any human rights treaty obligations prohibiting the arbitrary deprivation of liberty), cited in ICRC, Customary IHL Database (n 157).

[164] Similarly, see T Meron, 'Revival of Customary Humanitarian Law' (2005) 99 AJIL 817, 833.

[165] *Case Concerning Military and Paramilitary Activities in and Against Nicaragua (Nicaragua v United States)* [1986] ICJ Rep 14, [188] (employing UN resolutions as evidence of the *opinio iuris* of those states supporting them); *Legality of Nuclear Weapons* (n 14) [70] (recognizing that in certain cases UNGA resolutions can constitute evidence of *opinio iuris*); MD Öberg, 'The Legal Effects of Resolutions of the UN Security Council and General Assembly in the Jurisprudence of the ICJ' (2006) 16 EJIL 879, 898.

of states in general (ie without regard to particular states' treaty obligations). The former demonstrate a belief amongst those states supporting the resolution that, notwithstanding non-ratification of the ICCPR and other human rights treaties, the particular non-state party is bound by a norm of international law prohibiting arbitrary detention; such a norm, absent treaty obligations, must come from general international law.[166] The latter, by not differentiating between those states that are party to particular human rights treaties and those that are not, assume the existence of a rule of general international law prohibiting the arbitrary deprivation of liberty.[167] Together, these two types of resolutions reflect a clear *opinio iuris* supporting the conclusion that arbitrary detention is prohibited under customary international law.

In addition, reference may be made to other sources that evidence an *opinio iuris* supporting the customary prohibition of the arbitrary deprivation of liberty. These come, for example, in the form of executive and judicial statements expressing a general rejection of the right of any state to detain arbitrarily.[168] Moreover,

---

[166] See, eg, the UNSC resolutions on South Africa, condemning arbitrary detentions, before that state ratified the ICCPR: UNSC Res 417 (1977), adopted unanimously, at [3(b)] (demanding '[r]elease [of] all persons imprisoned under arbitrary security laws and all those detained for their opposition to *apartheid*'); UNSC Res 473 (1980), adopted unanimously, at preamble (referring to the 'inalienable human and political rights as set forth in the Charter of the United Nations and the Universal Declaration of Human Rights', Art 9 of the latter prohibiting arbitrary detention); UNSC Res 569 (1985), adopted by thirteen votes to none with two abstentions (United Kingdom and United States) at [2] ('[s]*trongly* condemns the mass arbitrary arrests and detentions recently carried out by the Pretoria Government'). See also resolutions on Myanmar, condemning arbitrary detentions: UNGA Res 55/112 (2001), without vote, at [4] ('[d]*eplores* the continued violations of human rights in Myanmar, including…mass arrests'); UNGA Res 67/233 (2012), without vote, at [6] ('[e]*xpresses* concern about remaining human rights violations, including arbitrary detention'); UNGA Res 66/230 (2011), 83-21-39, at [9] ('[e]*xpresses grave concern* at the continuing practice of arbitrary detention…and urges the Government of Myanmar to undertake without further delay a full, transparent, effective, impartial and independent investigation into all reports of human rights violations'). See also UNGA Res 40/161 A (1985), at [1]–[3] (condemning arbitrary detentions of Arabs by Israel and demanding their release, before Israel had ratified the ICCPR).

[167] See, eg, UNGA Res 61/171 (2006), without vote, at [8] ('*[o]pposes* any form of deprivation of liberty that amounts to placing a detained person outside the protection of the law, and urges States to respect the safeguards concerning the liberty, security and dignity of the person'); UNGA Res 62/159 (2007), without vote, at preamble ('[n]*oting with concern* measures that can undermine human rights and the rule of law, such as the detention of persons suspected of acts of terrorism in the absence of a legal basis for detention and due process guarantees, the deprivation of liberty that amounts to placing a detained person outside the protection of the law…, the illegal deprivation of liberty and transfer of individuals suspected of terrorist activities'); UNGA Res 59/199 (2004), 186-0-0, at [3] ('…*urges* States to ensure, in particular, that no one within their jurisdiction is, because of their religion or belief, deprived of the right to life, liberty and security of person…and the right not to be arbitrarily arrested or detained'); UNGA Res 61/161 (2006), without vote, at [4(f)] (urges states 'to ensure that no one within their jurisdiction is deprived of the right to life, liberty or security of person because of religion or belief and that no one is subjected to…arbitrary arrest or detention on that account').

[168] See, eg, *A and others v Secretary of State for the Home Department* [2002] EWCA Civ 1502, [130]; United Kingdom, 'Government Response to the Intelligence and Security Committee's Report on Rendition', Cm 7172, July 2007 at 8 (confirming that 'the UK opposes any form of deprivation of liberty that amounts to placing a detained person outside the protection of the law'), cited in ICRC, Customary IHL Database (n 157); *Kemal Mehinovic et al v Nikola Vuckovic* (2002) 198 F Supp 2d 1322 (US District Ct for the Northern District of Georgia), 1349 (finding arbitrary

the UN Working Group on Arbitrary Detention, in a 2012 deliberation, similarly concluded that customary international law prohibits arbitrary deprivations of liberty.[169] Indeed, in its *Tehran Hostages* judgment, the ICJ clearly expressed its view that '[w]rongfully to deprive human beings of their freedom...is in itself manifestly incompatible with the principles of the Charter of the United Nations, as well as with fundamental principles enunciated in the Universal Declaration of Human Rights'.[170] Finally, this conclusion is supported by the American Law Institute's (ALI) authoritative *Restatement (Third) of the Foreign Relations Law of the United States*, which declares that '[a] state violates [customary] international law if, as a matter of state policy, it practices, encourages, or condones... prolonged arbitrary detention'.[171] Louis Henkin invoked the ALI's statement of customary human rights norms as an example of a new form of customary law, which emerges on the basis of 'common consensus' rather than practice and *opinio iuris*.[172] However, this section has demonstrated that the traditional tools of custom do in fact point to a prohibition of the arbitrary deprivation of liberty. Indeed, evidence of contrary practice does not undermine this finding, for the references above, for example to UN resolutions, confirm that such contrary practice is treated as a violation of international law and not as a negation of the customary rule.[173]

The content of this customary prohibition, however, is not entirely clear, for many of the references above, particularly the UN resolutions invoked as evidence of *opinio iuris*, do not elaborate on what constitutes 'arbitrariness' here.[174] The ordinary meaning of the term would suggest notions of an unrestrained 'exercise of will', of 'uncontrolled power or authority', as well as being 'uncertain', 'varying', or 'at the discretion or option of any one'.[175] As demonstrated in section 4.2.1, the notion of arbitrariness has been heavily elaborated by human rights bodies. Indeed, it is to this jurisprudence that a number of the authorities cited above refer in giving content to the customary prohibition of arbitrary detention. This was the approach, for example, of the UN Working Group on Arbitrary Detention, which, after concluding that arbitrary detention is prohibited under custom, drew on human rights treaties and case law to demonstrate that the prohibition covers detentions that are both illegal and arbitrary in the broader sense of the HRC.[176]

---

detention to be prohibited under customary international law; as noted in chapter 3, whilst this judgment has been subjected to subsequent negative treatment, the basic proposition referred to here has not, as such, been overturned: see chapter 3, n 158).

[169] UN Working Group on Arbitrary Detention, 'Deliberation No 9' (n 162).
[170] *Case Concerning United States Diplomatic and Consular Staff in Tehran (United States of America v Iran)* [1980] ICJ Rep 3, [91].
[171] ALI, *Restatement (Third): The Foreign Relations Law of the United States, Vol II* (ALI, St Paul 1987) 161, s 702(e). The US Supreme Court in *Sosa v Alvarez-Machain*, 542 U.S. 692 (2004) at 737 appeared to accept this.
[172] L Henkin, 'Human Rights and State "Sovereignty"' (1995/6) 25 Ga J Intl & Comp L 31, 35–9.
[173] Similarly, see *Nicaragua* (n 165) [186].
[174] See, eg, UNSC Res 569 (1985) [2]; UNGA Res 40/161 A (1985) [1]–[3].
[175] *Oxford English Dictionary* (Online) <http://www.oed.com/> accessed 4 August 2015.
[176] UN Working Group on Arbitrary Detention (n 162) [61]–[63].

Similarly, the ALI in its *Restatement (Third) of the Foreign Relations Law of the United States* confirmed that prolonged detention would be arbitrary, and thus in violation of the customary norm, where it is either unlawful or unjust.[177] The ICTY has adopted the same approach in its jurisprudence on the crime against humanity of imprisonment.[178] In interpreting the content of this underlying crime, the Trial Chamber has held that 'any form of arbitrary physical deprivation of liberty of an individual may constitute imprisonment under Article 5(e)'.[179] The Tribunal then looked to IHRL to give content to this prohibition, stressing the need for both a legal basis and non-arbitrariness in the broader sense.[180] On the one hand, by drawing on the jurisprudence of human rights treaty bodies in elaborating the customary rule, these approaches could be criticized on the basis that it is not clear how states not party to the relevant treaties could be bound by that jurisprudence. However, given that these elaborations of the notion of arbitrariness are consistent with that term's ordinary meaning, it is submitted that this is an appropriate approach to giving content to the customary norm.[181]

A final word should be said on the relationship between the general customary rule elaborated here and the specific 'customary IHL' rule found to exist for non-international armed conflicts in chapter 3. As here, it was shown in chapter 3 that the practice establishing the customary IHL rule in the context of non-international armed conflicts was similarly abstract, referring either to arbitrary or unlawful deprivation of liberty.[182] However, whereas in this chapter it was argued that the content of the general customary rule might reasonably be drawn from human rights treaty law, it was argued in chapter 3 that the content of the specific customary IHL rule should be drawn from IHL treaty law, which was shown to prohibit internment that is not actually necessary as a result of the conflict. On the one hand, one might read these two rules as simply two applications of the same customary rule prohibiting arbitrary deprivation of liberty, which is interpreted differently depending on whether it is applied in an armed conflict or in other situations. Indeed, that we are faced with two apparently separate customary rules is partly a result of the approach taken in this book, where 'customary IHL' was explored before a more general survey of customary international law was carried out.[183] On the other hand, one might read these two customary rules

---

[177] ALI (n 171) 164.

[178] The ICTY has jurisdiction over the crime against humanity of imprisonment under its statute: Statute of the International Criminal Tribunal for the former Yugoslavia, adopted by UNSC Res 827 (1993), amended by UNSC Res 1877 (2009), Art 5(e).

[179] *Prosecutor v Milorad Krnojelac* (Trial Judgment) IT-97-25-T, 15 March 2002, [112]. Similarly, see ECCC, Case File 001/18-07-2007/ECCC/TC, *KAING Guek Eav alias Duch*, Trial Judgment, 26 July 2010, [347] ('[i]mprisonment refers to the arbitrary deprivation of an individual's liberty without due process of law').

[180] *Krnojelac* (n 179) [114] and fn 346. Similarly, see *KAING Guek Eav alias Duch* (n 179) [348]; *Prosecutor v Ntagerura et al* (Trial Judgment) ICTR-99-46T (25 February 2004) [702].

[181] See Akehurst (n 159) 51 ('... treaty rules which merely add precision to customary law are very likely to be accepted as customary rules in the future').

[182] Section 3.3.1.

[183] This approach was justified in the *chapeau* of section 3.3, and the reader is referred there to avoid repetition.

as entirely separate, based on separate practice and *opinio iuris*. To a large extent, we need not occupy ourselves with such questions, and both interpretations are reasonable. However, the present author favours the second reading, since it was shown in chapter 3 that common Article 3, which itself is widely recognized as having passed into the corpus of general international law, may be read as prohibiting internment that is not actually necessary as a result of the conflict.

4.3.2 Release where the justifications cease

As was shown to be the case in both chapters 2 and 3 regarding IHL,[184] as well as in section 4.2.5 regarding human rights treaty law, the arbitrary deprivation of liberty prohibition in customary international law may similarly be considered to contain within it a requirement that detention only persist for so long as it is lawful and non-arbitrary. To repeat a quote from the HRC regarding the same rule in treaty law, '[i]n order to avoid a characterization of arbitrariness, detention should not continue beyond the period for which the State party can provide appropriate justification'.[185]

4.3.3 Reasons for detention and *habeas corpus*

The customary status of the other procedural rules applicable to detention under the human rights treaties is less certain, at least when applying the traditional test for custom. The ICRC in its customary humanitarian law Study, when discussing the prohibition of arbitrary detention, also notes that both the right to be informed of the reasons for one's detention and the right to *habeas corpus* are 'part of the domestic law of most, if not all, States in the world'.[186] Similarly, as demonstrated in sections 4.2.2 and 4.2.3, these requirements have been codified in widely ratified treaties.

However, as noted above, this fact of widespread ratification, whilst constituting relevant state practice, can undermine claims as to the existence of custom, given the difficulty in separating practice adopted pursuant to treaty obligations from practice pursuant to customary obligations.[187] Whilst this complication was resolved regarding the arbitrary detention prohibition by referring to UN resolutions that reflected a collective *opinio iuris* as to the customary character of that prohibition, no such reference is available here. This is because those resolutions tend to remain abstract, making reference only to arbitrary detentions without going into further detail regarding other procedural rights, such as the right to *habeas corpus*.[188] In addition, whilst states not party to human rights treaties adopt

---

[184] See sections 2.4 and 3.3.2. [185] *Baban v Australia* (n 115) [7.2].
[186] Henckaerts, *Vol I* (n 155) 350–1. [187] See above at text to n 161.
[188] See, eg, UNGA Res 66/230 (2011) [9] ('[e]xpresses grave concern at the continuing practice of arbitrary detention…'); UNGA Res 61/161 (2006) [4(f)] (urging states not to subject anyone to 'arbitrary arrest or detention').

domestic laws requiring that reasons be given to detainees and access to *habeas corpus* be provided, this practice may not necessarily be a result of a belief that it is required under general international law.[189] As a result, it is difficult to demonstrate an *opinio iuris* to the effect that these rights form part of the corpus of customary international law.

Space prevents a full discussion of the possibility of these rights constituting general principles of law in the sense of Article 38(1)(c) of the ICJ Statute. In any event, it is not clear that a different conclusion would be reached. On one view, 'if all the principal domestic legal systems employ the same rule of law, that rule is a general principle of law'.[190] However, it is difficult to see why the fact of uniformity of domestic legal systems with respect to a certain matter should necessarily entail normative consequences under general international law, in the absence of evidence of *opinio iuris* amongst states.[191] Simply because domestic legal systems align with regard to the regulation of a particular issue does not necessarily mean that a rule of international law thereby forms; rather, it may be that international law remains entirely silent on the matter.

None of the above is intended as a definite answer to the question of the customary status of the rights to know the reasons for one's detention and to *habeas corpus*, however. Indeed, there is practice in support of the customary status of these rights from both states[192] and international bodies.[193] Similarly, the rights to know the reasons for one's detention and to *habeas corpus* feature amongst those principles that have been included in 'soft law' codifications of minimum humanitarian standards.[194] This is a very positive development, given the importance, as

---

[189] See, eg, Malaysia, *Malek* (n 163) [11], (noting that the Federal Constitution requires that the person arrested be informed of the grounds of his arrest); Myanmar, *Defence Services Act* (n 163) s 49(a).

[190] J Charney, 'Universal International Law' (1993) 87 AJIL 529, 535.

[191] Ibid, 535–6. Though this may not be essential for all general principles: see, eg, AV Lowe, *International Law* (OUP, Oxford 2007) 87–8 (structural principles considered essential to the functioning of any legal system, eg, estoppel and *pacta sunt servanda*); A Verdross, 'Les principes généraux du droit dans la jurisprudence internationale' (1935) 52 *RdC* 191, 204–6 (on a natural law theory of general principles).

[192] See, eg, HCJ 7607/05, *Jamal Mustafa Yusef 'Abdullah (Hussin) v Commander of IDF Forces in the West Bank* (2005) 8 YIHL 443 (Israel Supreme Court) [9] ('...judicial review [of detention is]... required under the principles of customary international law'); *R (Abbasi) v Secretary of State for Foreign and Commonwealth Affairs & Secretary of State for the Home Department* [2002] EWCA Civ 1598, [107]; *Re Khodorkovskiy*, Case No KAS06-129, Russian Supreme Court (Cassation Chamber), 133 ILR 365 (finding the UN Body of Principles, which includes the rights to know the reasons for one's detention and the right to *habeas corpus*, to constitute custom).

[193] See, eg, UN Human Rights Council Res 6/4, 28 September 2007, [5(d)] (calling on all states to provide detainees with access to a court to challenge the legality of their detention); UN Commission on Human Rights Res 2004/39, 19 April 2004, [3(c)] (calling on all states to respect and promote the right to *habeas corpus*); UN Working Group on Arbitrary Detention, Deliberation No 9 (n 162) [47]; *Obaidullah v United States* (n 149) [35].

[194] See, eg, Declaration of Minimum Humanitarian Standards Adopted by an Expert Meeting Convened by the Institute for Human Rights, Abo Akademi University, Turku, Finland, 2 December 1990, Art 4(3) (*habeas corpus*); UN Body of Principles for the Protection of All Persons Under Any Form of Detention or Imprisonment, 1988, GA Res 43/173, 9 December 1988, Principle 10 (requiring that reasons be given to detainees) and Principle 32 (*habeas corpus*).

noted throughout this chapter, of both of these rights in enforcing the prohibition of arbitrary detention. Indeed, that the right not to be deprived of one's liberty arbitrarily could only truly be effective where *habeas corpus* is provided and where the reasons for detention are given offers a strong argument that the basic customary rule includes such procedural safeguards.[195] This finds some support from the ECtHR's case law, which makes clear its view that procedural safeguards such as *habeas corpus* are an essential element in protecting the basic right to liberty and 'an important measure of protection against arbitrary behaviour and incommunicado detention'.[196]

Furthermore, theories of custom that, whilst reflecting actual jurisprudential practice in many cases, depart somewhat from the traditional account of the dual requirements of state practice and *opinio iuris*, would likely find these rights as constituting custom. For example, Frederic Kirgis' conception of the dual requirements as operating on a 'sliding scale', allowing an abundance of one to compensate for a lack of the other, would certainly enable one to conclude that these additional procedural rights are of a customary character.[197] Similarly, Anthea Roberts' use of a Dworkinian interpretive method, in which she advocates a balancing of 'fit' and 'substance' when assessing the existence of custom based on the collected data (ie practice, evidence of *opinio iuris*, academic commentary), would also offer strong support for finding the other procedural rules to constitute custom.[198] This is especially so, for Roberts' theory specifically calls for the incorporation of ethical considerations at the 'substance' stage of the calculus, and it is clear that, with respect to the rules under examination, such considerations are especially persuasive.[199] The consequence is that '[t]he best interpretation is the one that makes the practice appear in the best light, judged according to the substantive aspirations of the legal system'.[200] These alternative theories of custom are yet to receive general, explicit endorsement in judicial or state practice. For that reason, relying on them to found a customary rule may at times be counter-productive, especially here where the considerable amount of state practice supporting the customary character of the right to know the reasons for one's

---

[195] HRC (n 38) [12] ('[a]side from judicially imposed sentences for a fixed period of time, the decision to keep a person in any form of detention is arbitrary if it is not subject to periodic re-evaluation of the justification for continuing the detention'); *Krnojelac* (n 179) [115] (fn 347); *Ntagerura* (n 180) [702].

[196] *Brannigan* (n 104) [61]–[65] (on the importance of procedural safeguards such as *habeas corpus* when examining the proportionality of derogation from Art 5(3) ECHR); *A and others v UK* (n 41) [184] (on the necessity of providing adequate safeguards against abuse in order for derogation from Art 5(1) ECHR to be permissible); *Aksoy* (n 114) [79]–[84] (endorsing *Brannigan* and stating that 'the absence of any realistic possibility of being brought before a court to test the legality of the detention meant that he was left completely at the mercy of those holding him'); *Lawless* (n 61) [37] (on the importance of procedural safeguards, such as the Detention Commission, for ensuring proportionality of derogation from Art 5 ECHR).

[197] FL Kirgis, 'Custom on a Sliding Scale' (1987) 81 AJIL 146.

[198] A Roberts, 'Traditional and Modern Approaches to Customary International Law: A Reconciliation' (2001) 95 AJIL 757.

[199] Ibid, 781.   [200] Ibid, 771.

detention and the right to *habeas corpus* is at least accompanied by *some opinio iuris*. At the very least, it can confidently be said that these developments demonstrate an emerging consensus as to the customary status of these rights.

4.4 Conclusions

This chapter has explored the procedural rules applicable to detention under IHRL. Section 4.1 began by demonstrating that IHRL continues prima facie to apply in armed conflict, including non-international armed conflicts. This was a necessary preliminary issue to address in order to demonstrate that IHRL is relevant to the scope of this research. Section 4.2 then examined the procedural rules applicable to detention under IHRL. Whilst various similarities were shown to exist with the equivalent rules under IHL applicable in international armed conflicts, there are a number of important differences between the two, which reflect the more permissive nature of IHL. These differences were said to result in large part from the fact that IHL was designed to apply solely in states of emergency, that is, armed conflict, whereas IHRL was designed to be of general application at all times. As a result, IHL grants significant concessions to states under the name of military necessity, in contrast to IHRL. Moreover, IHRL has benefited from far greater elaboration by human rights treaty bodies, whereas IHL has only recently come to be interpreted by international criminal tribunals.

The final section (4.3) then considered the customary status of the IHRL rules, arguing that, whilst custom certainly prohibits arbitrary detention in all situations, the customary status of the other rules explored in section 4.2 is less clear. However, that arbitrary detention is prohibited by customary international law is an important finding, given that a number of states remain non-parties to the general human rights treaties. Moreover, as will be demonstrated in section 6.3, the customary status of this prohibition has an important bearing on its binding nature vis-à-vis non-state armed groups.

Having discussed the relevant rules under IHRL, a number of complex questions arise regarding their application in non-international armed conflict. Whilst section 4.1 confirmed that IHRL continues prima facie to apply in armed conflict, the operation of the specific rules on detention in non-international armed conflicts can, in practice, be affected by a number of factors. First, the degree to which the application and interpretation of the human rights rules explored in this chapter are affected by other applicable rules of international law must be addressed, for example whether applicable IHL might affect the content of these rules in non-international conflicts. Second, states parties to the various human rights treaties may, in specific non-international conflicts, wish to derogate from the rules on detention; the extent to which this is permissible must be considered. Third, even where states do not derogate, the particular human rights examined may be capable of a more general 'reading down' so as to take account of the extraordinary situation in a non-international armed conflict; the degree to which this is possible also requires consideration. Fourth, whether non-state

4.4 Conclusions

armed groups that are party to non-international conflicts are equally bound by these IHRL rules when interning is important, given the scarcity of relevant rules under IHL. Finally, the degree to which IHRL regulates detentions carried out by states when operating extra-territorially, in support of a 'host' state, must be considered, given that many non-international conflicts now take this form.[201] These issues all go to the heart of the relevance of the human rights rules discussed in this chapter for non-international armed conflicts, and it is to these that we now turn in chapters 5 and 6. In particular, chapter 5 will consider the first issue, that is, the impact of IHL on these human rights rules, whilst chapter 6 will consider the remaining four issues.

---

[201] As examples, see Iraq (section 5.2.2.1) and Afghanistan (section 5.2.2.2).

5
Detention and the Relationship between IHL and IHRL

The previous chapter examined the procedural rules applicable to detention under international human rights law (IHRL). It was shown in section 4.1 that IHRL, prima facie, continues to apply in armed conflict. However, the concluding section (4.4) noted five factors that might affect the actual operation of those rules in non-international armed conflicts,[1] and the present chapter seeks to address the first factor listed there, that is, the impact of other applicable rules of international law. In particular, this chapter will explore the interaction in non-international armed conflict between the IHRL rules on detention and the minimal international humanitarian law (IHL) rules discussed in chapter 3. The first section below analyses the general relationship between IHL and IHRL as developed in the International Court of Justice's (ICJ) jurisprudence, and it considers how this might help in understanding the interplay between these regimes with respect to detention in armed conflict. Section 5.2 then explores the detention practices of states in specific non-international armed conflicts. This practice will demonstrate the clear support for the view that states' IHRL obligations continue fully to regulate their detention operations in non-international armed conflicts, applying in parallel with applicable rules of IHL.

5.1 The Relationship between IHL and IHRL

The relationship between IHL and IHRL has been the subject of significant academic debate, and it remains one of the most contested issues in the contemporary regulation of armed conflict.[2] It not only divides commentators[3] and

---

[1] The five factors are: the application of other rules of international law (ie IHL); derogation; the possibility that, even without derogation, some of the rights may be capable of being 'read down' to account for the exigencies of the situation; the binding nature of the rules vis-à-vis non-state armed groups; the applicability of the rules to detentions by states in extraterritorial military operations.

[2] For just a few of the many pieces of scholarship on this, see, eg, L Doswald-Beck and S Vité, 'International Humanitarian Law and Human Rights Law' (1993) IRRC 94; R Provost, *International Human Rights and Humanitarian Law* (CUP, Cambridge 2002); C Droege, 'Elective Affinities? Human Rights and Humanitarian Law' (2008) 90 IRRC 501; O Ben-Naftali, *International Humanitarian Law and International Human Rights Law* (OUP, Oxford 2011); R Kolb and G Gaggioli (eds), *Research Handbook on Human Rights and Humanitarian Law* (Edward Elgar, Cheltenham 2013). See also the symposia on this topic in (2007) 40 Isr L Rev 306–660; (2009) 14 JCSL 441–527.

[3] The various positions taken sit as different points along a spectrum, but one might crudely categorize them as follows: towards the one end, seeing a minimal role for human rights law in armed

states,[4] but it is also a subject that has seen individual states alter their views over relatively short spaces of time.[5] It is well known that in any instance of legal interpretation, one often sees the interpretive solution reached to be in line with the particular interpreter's own subjectivities.[6] This same correlation is clearly visible in the debates on the interaction between IHL and IHRL.[7] For example, as explained in chapter 1, for states increasingly engaged in international military operations, positing IHL as the *lex specialis* to IHRL in an exclusionary sense, 'offers the advantage of applying...a targeting and detention regime that is appreciably more permissive than that under international human rights law'.[8]

In many ways, the debates on this subject arise as a result of different viewpoints on where the balance between humanitarian and military considerations in armed conflict ought to lie, and, as one would expect, we see the constant movement between apologist and utopian positioning.[9] Here especially, legal principles are often invoked as a basis not only for justifying particular interpretive outcomes but as decisive considerations that exclude any other solution.[10] This is especially

---

conflict (eg, MJ Dennis, 'Non-Application of Civil and Political Rights Treaties Extraterritorially During Times of International Armed Conflict' (2007) 40 Isr L Rev 453; MA Hansen, 'Preventing the Emasculation of Warfare: Halting the Expansion of Human Rights Law Into Armed Conflict' (2007) 194 Mil L Rev 1); approaching the centre of the spectrum, considering human rights law as relevant in armed conflict but, in certain situations, submitting to IHL (L Doswald-Beck, 'The Right to Life in Armed Conflict: Does International Humanitarian Law Provide All the Answers?' (2006) 88 IRRC 881; D Kretzmer, 'Rethinking Application of IHL in Non-International Armed Conflicts' (2009) 42 Isr L Rev 8); towards the other end, seeing human rights law and IHL as equally applicable and relevant in armed conflict (eg, W Abresch, 'A Human Rights Law of Internal Armed Conflict: The European Court of Human Rights in Chechnya' (2005) 16 EJIL 741; M Milanović, 'Norm Conflicts, International Humanitarian Law, and Human Rights Law' in O Ben-Naftali (ed), *International Humanitarian Law and International Human Rights Law* (OUP, Oxford 2011)).

[4] See, eg, PC Tange, 'Netherlands State Practice' (2006) 37 NYIL 233, 336 (on the Netherlands' critique of US Guantanamo policy, stating that human rights law and IHL apply in parallel).

[5] Compare the US views in 'Response of the United States of Request for Precautionary Measures—Detainees in Guantanamo Bay, Cuba' (2002) 41 ILM 1015 and HRC, 'Fourth Periodic Report: United States of America', CCPR/C/USA/4, 22 May 2012, [506]–[507]. Compare the UK's arguments in ECtHR, *Al-Jedda v United Kingdom*, App No 27021/08, Judgment (Grand Chamber), 7 July 2011 and *Serdar Mohammed v Ministry of Defence* [2014] EWHC 1369 (QB).

[6] J Stone, 'Fictional Elements in Treaty Interpretation: A Study in the International Judicial Process' (1954) 1 Sydney L Rev 334; M Koskenniemi, *From Apology to Utopia: The Structure of International Legal Argument* (reissue with new epilogue, CUP, Cambridge 2005) 340–1.

[7] D Stephens, 'Blurring the Lines: The Interpretation, Discourse and Application of the Law of Armed Conflict' (2009) 12 YIHL 85.

[8] C Kress, 'Some Reflections on the International Legal Framework Governing Transnational Armed Conflicts' (2010) 15 JCSL 245, 260–1.

[9] M Milanović, 'The Lost Origins of Lex Specialis: Rethinking the Relationship between Human Rights and International Humanitarian Law,' in J Ohlin (ed), *Theoretical Boundaries of Armed Conflict and Human Rights* (CUP, Cambridge, forthcoming) 2 <http://papers.ssrn.com/sol3/papers.cfm?abstract_id=2463957> accessed 4 August 2015.

[10] Similar reasoning has been well explored in international legal literature from various perspectives: see, eg, M Craven et al, 'We Are Teachers of International Law' (2004) 17 Leiden J Intl L 17; M Koskenniemi, 'What is International Law For?' in M Koskenniemi, *The Politics of International Law* (Hart, Oxford 2011); J d'Aspremont, *Formalism and the Sources of International Law: A Theory of the Ascertainment of Legal Rules* (OUP, Oxford 2011). See also Koskenniemi (n 6) 339 (fn 102) ('it

so with respect to the way in which the ICJ's few brief references to IHL as the *lex specialis* have been invoked by certain states wishing to be judged only according to the less restrictive rules of IHL.[11] Thus, the United States has argued that 'international humanitarian law, as the *lex specialis* of armed conflict, is the controlling body of law with regard to the conduct of hostilities and the protection of war victims'.[12] Canada has similarly taken the view that 'international humanitarian law is the *lex specialis* in factual situations of armed conflict and therefore the controlling body of law in armed conflict'.[13] The United Kingdom has also stated that 'it is the United Kingdom's position that international humanitarian law is the *lex specialis* in situations of armed conflict'.[14] These states invoke the ICJ's jurisprudence on this subject as authority for holding that IHL as a body of law constitutes the *lex specialis* relative to IHRL, thereby modifying or displacing the latter. Certain commentators adopt similar views, albeit to different degrees, viewing IHL as the *lex specialis* and *necessarily* modifying or displacing inconsistent rules of IHRL.[15]

The use of the *lex specialis* maxim as a basis for reconciling IHL and IHRL has been criticized by a number of commentators.[16] Indeed, Marko Milanović has demonstrated that the notion of *lex specialis* only came into mainstream thinking with respect to IHL and IHRL following the ICJ's first reference to this in the *Nuclear Weapons* Advisory Opinion.[17] The present chapter, however, does not wish to take issue with the reliance that has been placed here on the *lex specialis* maxim as such, for whilst it may not have been advanced commonly as a basis for rationalizing the relationship between IHL and IHRL until relatively

is not really that the "canons" [of interpretation], once chosen, would be determining... The solution seems more connected to the "philosophies" or evaluations—while reference to a canon only adds apparent neutrality to the choice').

[11] The ICJ's case law is discussed in detail in section 5.1 below.
[12] Human Rights Committee (HRC), 'Observations of the United States of America on the Human Rights Committee's Draft General Comment 35: Article 9', 10 June 2014, [20] <http://www.ohchr.org/EN/HRBodies/CCPR/Pages/DGCArticle9.aspx> accessed 5 August 2015.
[13] HRC, 'Draft General Comment No. 35, Article 9: Liberty and Security of Person, Comments by the Government of Canada', 6 October 2014, [11] <http://www.ohchr.org/EN/HRBodies/CCPR/Pages/DGCArticle9.aspx> accessed 5 August 2015.
[14] HRC, 'Observations by the Government of the United Kingdom of Great Britain and Northern Ireland on draft General Comment 35 on Article 9 of the International Covenant on Civil and Political Rights (ICCPR) – liberty and security of person' (undated), [21(b)] <http://www.ohchr.org/EN/HRBodies/CCPR/Pages/DGCArticle9.aspx> accessed 5 August 2015.
[15] See, eg, Dennis (n 3); J Pejic, 'Conflict Classification and the Law Applicable to Detention and the Use of Force' in E Wilmshurst (ed), *International Law and the Classification of Conflicts* (OUP, Oxford 2012).
[16] V Gowlland-Debbas, 'The Right to Life and Genocide: the Court and International Public Policy', in L Boisson de Chazournes and P Sands (ed), *International Law, the International Court of Justice and Nuclear Weapons* (CUP, Cambridge 1999); A Lindroos, 'Addressing Norm Conflicts in a Fragmented Legal System: The Doctrine of *Lex Specialis*' (2005) 74 Nordic J Intl L 27 (on the various problems with applying the *lex specialis* maxim in international law generally); Milanović (n 3) 113–16 (arguing that there is no evidence that *lex specialis* can operate to resolve actual conflicts between IHL and IHRL rules).
[17] Milanović (n 9).

recently, it is a technique that is well known to international law, and it need not, therefore, necessarily be excluded here.[18] Rather, the aim is to consider the relationship between IHL and IHRL, and the ICJ's jurisprudence on this, from the perspective of general international law, drawing by analogy from other areas in which similar conflicts arise. It is submitted that this perspective provides a rich normative environment that can help us understand how competing legal norms interact in international law. It is this normative background that is entirely omitted from those accounts of the relationship between IHL and IHRL cited above.[19] The consequence is a significant misunderstanding of the *lex specialis* maxim and the interaction between distinct legal rules in international law. By examining this issue not in isolation but within public international law more generally, this chapter will demonstrate that the relationship between IHL and IHRL is far more nuanced than those accounts above suggest. In particular, it will be shown that the various presumptions on which the above accounts rest (that the *lex specialis* maxim is *always* decisive as a consideration in reconciling IHL and IHRL, and that the consequence is that IHRL is *necessarily* displaced or modified) are unsupported by international law. However, that is not to say that we are left as a result in a legal grey area, for, as will be demonstrated, there is a clear default legal position that one always has to fall back on, that is, the parallel application of IHL and IHRL.

5.1.1 The ICJ's case law

As noted in chapter 4,[20] the traditional bifurcation of IHL and IHRL has now entirely fallen away with the clear consensus that IHRL continues, prima facie, to apply to the actions of states in the context of armed conflict, alongside IHL.[21] The question of IHRL's interaction with IHL has, consequently, arisen. This raises few problems where the particular issue under consideration is regulated either by just one of the two bodies of law or by both bodies in the same way.[22] However, for those issues on which the two lay down different standards, such as detention and the use of force, where IHL is more permissive than IHRL, one is faced with the question of how these regimes interact.[23]

---

[18] See discussion below in section 5.1.1. See also CW Jenks, 'The Conflict of Law-Making Treaties' (1953) 30 BYIL 401, 446 (referring to treaties on the law of war as one of the few uncontroversial examples of *leges speciales*).

[19] See above at text to nn 12–14.   [20] See section 4.1.

[21] Parts of this section were originally published in L Hill-Cawthorne, 'Just Another Case of Treaty Interpretation? Reconciling Humanitarian Law and Human Rights Law in the ICJ' in M Andenas and E Bjorge (eds), *A Farewell to Fragmentation: Reassertion and Convergence in International Law* (CUP, Cambridge 2015).

[22] For an example of the former, see the IHL rules on the right of prisoners of war to elect a prisoners' representative: arts 79–81 GCIII. For an example of the latter, see *Case Concerning Armed Activities on the Territory of the Congo (DRC v Uganda)* (Judgment) [2005] ICJ Rep 168, discussed below at text to nn 32–4.

[23] It was shown throughout chapter 4 that IHL is more permissive than IHRL regarding the procedural regulation of internment in both international armed conflicts and, especially, non-international conflicts, where there is a dearth of IHL rules.

The ICJ has discussed the relationship between IHL and IHRL on three occasions, in two advisory opinions and one contentious case.[24] Despite some differences, its methodology has generally remained consistent. This comprised a two-stage test. First, the Court confirmed the continued applicability of IHRL in armed conflict, alongside IHL, subject to permissible derogation.[25] There are then three possible results of such parallel application:

...some rights may be exclusively matters of international humanitarian law; others may be exclusively matters of human rights law; yet others may be matters of both these branches of international law.[26]

The second stage of the Court's analysis was to consider cases falling within this third category, that is, where the facts raise issues under both IHL and IHRL.[27] In the *Nuclear Weapons* Advisory Opinion, the Court was concerned specifically with the interpretation of the human right not arbitrarily to be deprived of one's life under Article 6 of the International Covenant on Civil and Political Rights (ICCPR) during armed conflict. Given that this was a 'hard case' (where IHL and IHRL lay down different standards), the Court considered the relationship between the relevant IHL and IHRL rules:

The test of what is an arbitrary deprivation of life...falls to be determined by the applicable *lex specialis,* namely, the law applicable in armed conflict which is designed to regulate the conduct of hostilities. Thus whether a particular loss of life, through the use of a certain weapon in warfare, is to be considered an arbitrary deprivation of life contrary to Article 6 of the Covenant, can only be decided by reference to the law applicable in armed conflict and not deduced from the terms of the Covenant itself.[28]

The Court thus rationalized the relationship between the human right to life and the rules on the conduct of hostilities under IHL by interpreting the content of the 'open' human right not *arbitrarily* to be deprived of one's life with reference to the IHL rules, on the grounds that these were designed specifically for application in armed conflict. Hence, if a particular deprivation of life is in accordance with applicable IHL, it is non-arbitrary under IHRL and, thus, also compatible with that body of law.[29] Indeed, the Court had a number of interpretive techniques that it could have applied here to reach the same result, and its use of the *lex specialis* maxim was not strictly necessary. For example, the same result might

---

[24] *Legality of the Threat or Use of Nuclear Weapons,* Advisory Opinion [1996] ICJ Rep 226, [25]; *Legal Consequences of the Construction of a Wall in the Occupied Palestinian Territory,* Advisory Opinion [2004] ICJ Rep 136, [106]; *DRC v Uganda* (n 22) [216].
[25] *Nuclear Weapons* (n 24) [25]; *Israeli Wall* (n 24) [106]; *DRC v Uganda* (n 22) [216].
[26] *Israeli Wall* (n 24) [106].
[27] *Nuclear Weapons* (n 24) [25]; *Israeli Wall* (n 24) [106]. The Court did not need to address this in *DRC v Uganda* (n 22) given the facts at issue: see below, text to nn 32–4.
[28] *Nuclear Weapons* (n 24) [25].
[29] D Akande, 'Nuclear Weapons, Unclear Law? Deciphering the *Nuclear Weapons* Advisory Opinion of the International Court' (1998) 68 BYIL 165, 175 ('[t]he recognition of the applicability of the right to life during war and armed conflict did not therefore create any new substantive right which the victim would not already possess under international humanitarian law').

have been reached by invoking Article 31(3)(c) of the Vienna Convention on the Law of Treaties (VCLT), which calls for reference to be made to other 'relevant rules of international law applicable in the relations between the parties'.[30] Even more simply, the Court might have made a similar *renvoi* to IHL by treating the rules on the conduct of hostilities as constituting the ordinary or special meaning of 'arbitrary' in the specific context of an armed conflict.[31]

The ICJ's two-step analysis in *Nuclear Weapons* therefore involved, first, affirming the applicability of Article 6 ICCPR to deprivations of life in the context of armed conflict and, second, enquiring into the relationship between that provision and applicable IHL. Importantly, in the two other instances in which the ICJ addressed this issue, the Court made it clear that the secondary question regarding the relationship between these two bodies of law need not always be answered in practice. Thus, in both *Israeli Wall* and *DRC v Uganda*, the Court applied provisions of IHL and IHRL in parallel to the same facts, finding violations of both, without regard to the effect of IHL on the content of specific norms of IHRL.[32] In *DRC v Uganda*, many of the issues arising under the right to life comprised systematic attacks against the civilian population.[33] It is clear that such acts constitute violations of both IHL (assuming the particular civilians targeted do not directly participate in hostilities) and IHRL, and the Court simply applied both humanitarian law and human rights law to the same facts and concluded that provisions of both were violated (including Article 6(1) ICCPR on the right to life and Article 51 API on the obligation not to make civilians the object of attack), without suggesting that the applicability of one body of law necessarily affected the interpretation of the other.[34]

Where the Court did seek to reconcile IHL and IHRL, it relied on the *lex specialis* nature of the former.[35] As noted above, its invocation of the principle of *lex specialis* has been the subject of criticism on various grounds.[36] A full discussion of these criticisms is unnecessary for the present enquiry. Rather, it is submitted that the Court's approach is best understood as an application of well-established methods of treaty interpretation, drawing on a principle that has a long historical

---

[30] On Art 31(3)(c) generally, see C McLachlan, 'The Principle of Systemic Integration and Article 31(3)(c) of the Vienna Convention' (2005) 54 ICLQ 279. Indeed, the European Court of Human Rights relied, in part, on Art 31(3)(c) in its finding in *Hassan v United Kingdom*, App No 29750/09, Judgment (Grand Chamber), 16 September 2014 at [102], discussed below.

[31] Arts 31(1) and 31(4) VCLT. Similarly, M Paparinskis, 'Investment Treaty Interpretation and Customary Investment Law' in C Brown and K Miles (eds), *Evolution in Investment Treaty Law and Arbitration* (CUP, Cambridge 2011) 78 (making the same point in the context of investment treaty interpretation); J Pauwelyn, *Conflict of Norms in Public International Law: How WTO Law Relates to Other Rules of International Law* (CUP, Cambridge 2003) 260 (and in the context of interpreting the World Trade Organization (WTO) agreements).

[32] *Israeli Wall* (n 24) [134]; *DRC v Uganda* (n 22) [217]–[220].

[33] *DRC v Uganda* (n 22) [206].   [34] Ibid, [219].

[35] *Nuclear Weapons* (n 24) [25]; *Israeli Wall* (n 24) [106].

[36] See, eg, L Doswald-Beck, 'International Humanitarian Law and the International Court of Justice on the Legality of the Threat or Use of Nuclear Weapons' (1997) 35 IRRC 316; Gowlland-Debbas (n 16); Lindroos (n 16).

pedigree in international law as an interpretive maxim.[37] This is most clear in the *Nuclear Weapons* opinion, where the ICJ employed IHL to interpret IHRL in the specific context. This was possible given the 'open' nature of the human right at issue (the prohibition of *arbitrary* deprivation of life) and the context in which it was being applied (armed conflict). As with any other principle of treaty interpretation, the key objective sought in invoking the *lex specialis* maxim is to ascertain the common (objective) intentions of the states parties.[38] Joost Pauwelyn describes the policy behind the principle in the following way:

> Consequently, much like *lex posterior* – which is based on the view that the 'latest expression of state consent' ought to prevail – the principle of *lex specialis* is but a consequence of the contractual freedom of states, grounded in the idea that the 'most closest [*sic*], detailed, precise or strongest expression of state consent', as it relates to a particular circumstance, ought to prevail. Both Art. 30 [of the VCLT] and the *lex specialis* principle thus attempt to answer one and the same question, namely: which of the two norms in conflict is the 'current expression of state consent'?[39]

Simply put, the *lex specialis* principle points to certain factual considerations that can help approximate the common intentions of the parties, that is, if states have developed a detailed set of rules to apply in a particular situation, one might validly

---

[37] M Akehurst, 'The Hierarchy of the Sources of International Law' (1974–5) 47 BYIL 273, 273 ('*lex specialis* is nothing more than a rule of interpretation'); Report of the Study Group of the International Law Commission, 'Fragmentation of International Law: Difficulties Arising from the Diversification and Expansion of International Law', Finalized by Martti Koskenniemi, 13 April 2006, A/CN.4/L.682, 34–5 ('[t]he principle that special law derogates from general law is a widely accepted maxim of legal interpretation'); 'Fragmentation of International Law', 36 ('[t]he idea that special enjoys priority over general has a long pedigree in international jurisprudence as well'). There is much case law applying *lex specialis*: see, eg, *The Mavrommatis Palestine Concessions*, PCIJ Ser A, No 2 (1924) 31; *Case Concerning the Continental Shelf (Tunisia/Libyan Arab Jamahiriya)* [1982] ICJ Rep 38, [24]; *Case concerning the Gabčíkovo-Nagymaros Project (Hungary/Slovakia)* [1997] ICJ Rep 76, [132].

[38] Commentaries confirm that this is a fundamental goal of treaty interpretation generally: GG Fitzmaurice, 'The Law and Procedure of the International Court of Justice 1951–54: Treaty Interpretation and Certain Other Treaty Points' (1951) 28 BYIL 1, 3; A McNair, *The Law of Treaties* (OUP, Oxford 1961) 365; MS McDougal, HD Lasswell, and JC Miller, *The Interpretation of International Agreements and World Public Order: Principles of Content and Procedure* (New Haven Press, New Haven 1967) xvi; Sir H Lauterpacht, *The Development of International Law by the International Court* (CUP, Cambridge 1982) 27; A Clapham, *Brierly's Law of Nations* (7th edn, OUP, Oxford 2012) 349; E Bjorge, *The Evolutionary Interpretation of Treaties* (OUP, Oxford 2014). Jurisprudence also confirms the centrality of the common intentions of states parties in interpreting treaties: *Reservations to the Convention on the Prevention and Punishment of the Crime of Genocide* (Advisory Opinion) [1951] ICJ Rep 15, 23; *Interpretation of the Air Transport Services Agreement between the United States of America and France* (1963) 16 RIAA 5, 47; WTO, Appellate Body Report, *EC—Computer Equipment*, WT/DS62/AB/R, WT/DS67/AB/R, WT/DS68/AB/R, 5 June 1998 [93]; *Kasikili/Sedudu Island (Botswana/Namibia)* (Judgment) [1999] ICJ Rep 1045, 1114 (Opinion of Judge Higgins).

[39] Pauwelyn (n 31) 388 (note that when Pauwelyn speaks of the principle of *lex specialis*, he refers to its stronger form as a conflict resolution device, looking at the kind of conflict avoidance through consistent interpretation that can be seen in the *Nuclear Weapons* opinion separately). Also confirming that the principle of *lex specialis* seeks to give effect to the intentions of the state parties, see McNair (n 38) 219; Akehurst (n 37) 273; Lindroos (n 16) 36; G Verdirame, 'Human Rights in Wartime: A Framework for Analysis' [2008] EHRLR 689, 700.

infer an intention that such rules constitute the principal legal standards against which their conduct is to be judged in such a situation. As Martti Koskenniemi explained in his report on fragmentation:

> When a 'hard' case does emerge, then it is the role of *lex specialis* to point to a set of considerations with practical relevance: the immediate accessibility and contextual sensitivity of the standard. Now these may not be decisive considerations. They may be overweighed by countervailing ones. Reasoning about such considerations, though impossible to condense in determining rules or techniques, should not, however, be understood as arbitrary. The reasoning may be the object of criticism and whether it prevails will depend on how it succeeds in condensing what may be called, for instance, the 'genuine shared expectations of the parties, within the limits established by overriding community objectives'.[40]

Importantly, as this quote demonstrates, the notion of *lex specialis* has no independent, normative content itself, either in the sense of being capable of indicating which norm is special and which general, or in the sense of determining alone the legal solution to be reached.[41] Rather, it operates as one factual element in that process of balancing numerous considerations that is at the heart of treaty interpretation:[42] 'shared expectations' or 'common intention' is the goal, and in seeking this we are not 'finding' such common intention but rather examining a plethora of different factors in order to attempt to condense or approximate such agreement.[43]

Before moving on, it is clear already that those statements cited above that consider IHL as necessarily the *lex specialis* in armed conflict, resulting in it being the 'controlling body of law', are too simplistic and are not consistent with the function of the *lex specialis* maxim in public international law.[44] It is too often assumed that merely because IHL regulates a particular issue, IHRL must *necessarily* give way.[45]

---

[40] 'Fragmentation of International Law' (n 37) 48–9, quoting McDougal et al (n 38) 83.
[41] Lindroos (n 16) 66.
[42] Pauwelyn (n 31) 388 ('[i]n sum, they [*lex posterior* and *lex specialis*] are more factual/subjective elements in the assessment of contractual freedom and state consent than absolute legal norms in their own right'). The same point was made by Jenks with respect to each conflict resolution device provided by international law: Jenks (n 18) 450 ('...none of them [principles of norm conflict resolution] can be regarded as absolute in character but all may afford useful clues to legislative intention...').
[43] McNair (n 38) 366 ('[t]he process of interpretation, rightly conceived, cannot be regarded as a mere mechanical one of drawing inevitable meanings from the words in a text, or of searching for and discovering some preexisting specific intention of the parties with respect to every situation arising under a treaty...In most instances interpretation involves giving a meaning to a text—not just any meaning which appeals to the interpreter, to be sure, but a meaning which, in the light of the text under consideration and of all the concomitant circumstances of the particular case at hand, appears in his considered judgment to be one which is logical, reasonable, and most likely to accord with and to effectuate the larger general purpose which the parties desired the treaty to serve').
[44] See above at text to nn 12–14.
[45] See, eg, J Pejic (n 15) (implying that, since the IHL rules on the conduct of hostilities apply in non-international armed conflicts under custom, they constitute the *lex specialis*); S Sivakumaran, *The Law of Non-International Armed Conflict* (OUP, Oxford 2012) 98 ('...it is not immediately clear why international human rights law *should* regulate non-international armed conflict. Direct regulation of non-international armed conflict through international human rights law is premised

The above discussion confirms that the relevance and effect of the *lex specialis* maxim is far more nuanced than these accounts suggest, and it cannot alone be decisive; rather, it is subject to other (potentially countervailing) considerations that might provide a more reasonable approximation of the common, objective intentions of the states parties, leading to an alternative interpretive outcome. Indeed, the same is true for the other mechanisms provided by international law to avoid and resolve norm conflict, such as *lex posterior* and Article 31(3)(c) VCLT.[46] This demonstrates that, contrary to what is suggested by those accounts above, examining the interaction between IHL and IHRL requires, first, looking at individual norms rather than entire legal regimes,[47] and, second, even at the level of individual norms, taking into account other relevant considerations that may help approximate party intentions.

The following sections will now seek to apply the above observations on the general relationship between IHL and IHRL to the specific case of detention. This will be examined first in the context of international armed conflicts. It is important to emphasize that the goal there is not to conclude definitively on the relationship between the IHL and IHRL rules on detention in such situations. Rather, it more modestly seeks to introduce the various possibilities open to us, which will then enable us to move on in the subsequent section to the central enquiry of this book, that is, detention in non-international armed conflict.

5.1.2 Detention in international armed conflict

The ICJ's case law usefully confirms the appropriate methodology for determining the application and content of parallel human rights and humanitarian law norms in particular situations. As demonstrated, the Court's starting point was that both IHL and IHRL apply in full in situations of armed conflict. This is consistent with the clear trend in practice supporting the prima facie application of states' international human rights obligations in armed conflict, alongside IHL.[48] It is also consistent with the text of the human rights treaties, which not

---

on the idea that there is a lack of content and specificity on the part of international humanitarian law... However, this premise is open to challenge').

[46] See Jenks (n 18) 407 ('[n]o particular principle or rule can be regarded as of absolute validity. There are a number of principles and rules which must be weighed and reconciled in the light of the circumstances of the particular case'); 'Fragmentation of International Law' (n 37) [410] ('there [is] nothing automatic or mechanical about this process... Whether a rule's speciality or generality should be decisive, or whether priority should be given to the earlier or to the later rule depended on such aspects as the will of the parties, the nature of the instruments and their object and purpose as well as what would be a reasonable way to apply them with minimal disturbance to the operation of the legal system').

[47] In *Israeli Wall*, the Court implied that IHL *as a body of law*, as opposed to specific norms, was *lex specialis* to IHRL: *Israeli Wall* (n 24) [106]. This approach has been criticized, and instead it has been argued that determinations as to what is special and general should be made at the level of norms, rather than legal regimes: see, eg, Lindroos (n 16) 42; Milanović (n 3) 98–101.

[48] See section 4.1. Indeed, as noted there, the United States, traditionally sceptical of this trend, appears more recently to have accepted this premise: HRC, 'Fourth Periodic Report: United States of America' (n 5) [506]–[507].

only contain no provisions limiting their application to peacetime, but moreover confirm their continued application in states of emergency (including armed conflict) by specifically including derogation clauses.[49] Indeed, as was shown in chapter 4, it is clear from the *travaux* of these derogation provisions that many of the drafters of the human rights treaties assumed that they would apply in armed conflict absent derogation, including to those issues for which IHL was designed.[50] Consequently, regarding internment in armed conflict, the default legal position is that all relevant rules of IHRL apply in full, alongside applicable IHL. The secondary question then arises as to the extent to which the application or content of the relevant IHRL rules are affected in the specific situation.[51] The ICJ made it clear that such modification could potentially occur in one of two principal ways:[52] first, a state may derogate from the relevant treaty provisions, subject to the conditions for permissible derogation; second, human rights rules might be interpreted with reference to applicable IHL as the *lex specialis*, where, as argued above, that appears consistent with the common intentions of the states parties. Where neither of these applies, one falls back on the default position of the parallel application of all relevant rules of IHL and IHRL.[53]

The possibility of derogation from the human rights treaty rules on detention will be examined in chapter 6.[54] This chapter focuses on the second option above, that is, the degree to which the content or application of the human rights treaty rules on detention are subject to applicable IHL in situations of armed conflict. In so doing, it must be asked whether the ICJ's interpretive approach could be invoked here to rationalize the relationship between the IHL and IHRL rules on detention in international and non-international armed conflicts. The Court's jurisprudence confirms that the *lex specialis* maxim might be useful in resolving certain apparent conflicts between IHL and IHRL, where the IHRL norm is sufficiently 'open' to allow for interpretation consistent with the relevant IHL norm.[55] Indeed, as noted above, other interpretive principles that permit one to draw on the normative environment when interpreting a treaty provision could equally have led to the same result.[56] The norm with which the Court was dealing in the *Nuclear Weapons* opinion allowed this: when applying the Article 6 ICCPR prohibition of arbitrary deprivation of life, what is 'arbitrary' can depend on the circumstances and, in armed conflict, can be determined by reference to the IHL

---

[49] See, eg, Art 4 ICCPR; Art 15 ECHR.   [50] See section 4.1.
[51] Certain commentators have suggested that IHRL might, in some instances, be considered the *lex specialis*, which should then affect the interpretation of applicable IHL: see, eg, Droege (n 2) 536. The present argument avoids having to consider this by taking as its starting point the *full* application of the ordinary IHRL rules (alongside applicable rules of IHL), unless they can be modified to suit the specific situation.
[52] *Nuclear Weapons* (n 24) [25]; *Israeli Wall* (n 24) [106].
[53] See above at text to n 25. On the ICJ case law confirming that the same acts can constitute violations of both IHL and IHRL, see above at text to nn 32–4.
[54] There we will also examine, among other things, the degree to which the IHRL rules might more generally be 'read down' to take account of the extraordinary situation in a non-international armed conflict, without the need for derogation and without regard to IHL as such.
[55] Similarly, see Milanović (n 3) 106.   [56] See above at text to nn 30–1.

rules on the conduct of hostilities. This might be considered a valid assumption of the intentions of the states parties to the ICCPR, given that they have developed detailed IHL rules in this area. Moreover, the problems associated with different states parties to different multilateral treaties, which might otherwise render more complicated a *renvoi* to extraneous sources when interpreting a treaty,[57] are avoided in this area due to the universal ratification of the Geneva Conventions and their generally accepted status as embodying customary international law.

As chapter 4 showed, a similar arbitrariness standard features in the provisions on detention in most of the general human rights treaties.[58] The same possibility of consistent interpretation therefore appears available with regard to the prohibition of arbitrary deprivation of liberty under human rights treaties and the internment regimes applicable in international armed conflict under IHL. Thus, what is an arbitrary deprivation of liberty under Article 9(1) ICCPR could be determined by reference to the grounds applicable to internment under GCIII and GCIV.[59] The consequence would be that, where a person is interned in accordance with GCIII or GCIV, it would not be arbitrary in the sense of Article 9(1) ICCPR.[60] Moreover, as noted in section 3.1, the law of international armed conflict provides a legal basis to intern in such situations, which could satisfy the requirement of legality in Article 9(1) ICCPR. However, such consistent interpretation appears more difficult regarding certain other procedural rules under IHRL. In particular, it was shown in chapter 4 that a major difference between IHL and IHRL in this area concerns review of detention: whereas GCIV permits administrative review, IHRL requires court review.[61] According to its text and as elaborated in chapter 4, this rule of IHRL requiring 'court' review of detention does not appear susceptible to interpretation consistent with the GCIV rules requiring less stringent forms of review, and to apply GCIV as the *lex specialis* would seem to require modifying if not setting aside the IHRL rule.[62] Indeed, this would especially be the case when attempting

---

[57] WTO, *European Communities—Measures Affecting the Approval and Marketing of Biotech Products* (29 September 2006) WT/DS291/R, WT/DS292/R, WT/DS293/R, [7.68]-[7.70] (requiring that extraneous rules of international law be applicable in the relations between *all* the states parties to the WTO agreements in order for the former to be relevant under Art 31(3)(c) VCLT for interpreting the latter).

[58] See, eg, Art 9(1) ICCPR; Art 7(3) of the American Convention on Human Rights (ACHR); Art 6 of the African Charter on Human and Peoples' Rights (ACHPR); Art 14(1) of the Arab Charter of Human Rights (ArCHR).

[59] Similarly, see Milanović (n 3) 114.

[60] W Kälin, 'Human Rights Law Relating to Arbitrary Detention During Armed Conflict: The Covenant on Civil and Political Rights and its Relationship with International Humanitarian Law' in The University Centre for International Humanitarian Law, 'Expert Meeting on the Supervision of the Lawfulness of Detention During Armed Conflict' (Geneva, 24–25 July 2004) 31–2 <http://www.geneva-academy.ch/docs/expert-meetings/2004/4rapport_detention.pdf> accessed 5 August 2015; S Marks and A Clapham, *International Human Rights Lexicon* (OUP, Oxford 2005) 75; N Rodley and M Pollard, *The Treatment of Prisoners under International Law* (3rd edn OUP, Oxford 2009) 490; HCJ 3239/02, *Mar'ab et al v IDF Commander of Judea and Samaria et al*, 57(2) PD 349, [21] (Israel).

[61] Compare, eg Art 9(4) ICCPR and Art 78 GCIV.

[62] Similarly, see Milanović (n 3) 117–18. As noted, the degree to which the IHRL rules can be 'read down' will be explored in chapter 6.

to reconcile IHRL with the GCIII internment regime, which contains no requirement of the review of prisoner of war (POW) internment,[63] or with the detention standard in Article 5(1) of the European Convention on Human Rights (ECHR), which contains a closed list of permissible grounds for detention, rather than an open arbitrariness standard.[64] Whilst going further in attempting to reconcile IHL and IHRL than the ICJ has done, there is some support for such approaches. In this respect, Martti Koskenniemi has noted two different manifestations of the *lex specialis* principle:

There are two ways in which law may take account of the relationship of a particular rule to general one. A particular rule may be considered an *application* of a general standard in a given circumstance... Or it may be considered as a *modification, overruling* or a *setting aside* of the latter.[65]

The second notion of *lex specialis* suggests that a special rule can indeed have the effect of modifying or displacing a general rule.[66] Whilst some are sceptical that the *lex specialis* maxim is capable of having such an effect,[67] the displacement or modification approach appears to be the view of those states noted above that see IHL as the 'controlling body of law' relative to IHRL.[68] This same approach is supported by certain state practice with regard specifically to the IHL and IHRL rules on detention in international armed conflicts. For example, POWs and civilians interned according to GCIII and GCIV are often not afforded the right to *habeas corpus*, with the IHL internment regimes instead being treated as the *lex specialis* to the exclusion of the IHRL rules. This is the approach taken in the UK Ministry of Defence's *Manual on the Law of Armed Conflict,* which views IHL as operating so as to exclude POWs from exercising the right to *habeas corpus*.[69] Similarly, during the initial international armed conflict in Iraq following the 2003 invasion, coalition forces detained three categories of persons, all of whom were considered to be governed exclusively by IHL: POWs (governed solely by GCIII), security detainees, and those that committed offences against coalition forces (both of which were governed by Article 78 GCIV alone).[70] Certain

---

[63] See section 2.3.2.
[64] However, as discussed below, the ECtHR did in *Hassan* interpret Art 5(1) ECHR in a manner that left room for the GCIV internment regime: see below at text to nn 80–9.
[65] 'Fragmentation of International Law' (n 37) 49.
[66] Indeed, for Pauwelyn, the correct function of the principle of *lex specialis* is as a principle of norm conflict resolution, where one norm *prevails* over another, rather than as a principle of treaty interpretation in the manner in which it was invoked by the ICJ in *Nuclear Weapons*: Pauwelyn (n 31) 247.
[67] Milanović (n 3) 115–16.   [68] See above at text to nn 12–14.
[69] UK Ministry of Defence, *Manual on the Law of Armed Conflict* (OUP, Oxford 2004) section 8.115.1, citing *R v Superintendent of Vine Street Police Station, ex p Liebmann* [1916] 1 KB 268 and *R v Bottrill, ex p Kuechenmeister* [1947] KB 41. See more generally HRC (n 14) [21(b)]. Although, in *Secretary of State for Foreign and Commonwealth Affairs and another (Appellants) v Yunus Rahmatullah* [2012] UKSC 48, at [41], the Supreme Court extended the writ (as a matter of domestic law) 'as of right' to an internee abroad protected by GCIV so long as they were under the control of the addressee of the writ. The same principle would appear to apply to POWs.
[70] MN Schmitt, 'Iraq (2003 onwards)' in E Wilmshurst (ed), *International Law and the Classification of Conflicts* (OUP, Oxford 2012) 375. Similarly, see HCJ 7015/02 and 7019/02, *Ajuri*

international institutions also support this approach. For example, the ICRC appears to take the view that civilian internment in international armed conflicts is regulated by GCIV alone, without the requirement of *habeas corpus*.[71] Moreover, in a 2006 UN report on Guantanamo detainees, the *lex specialis* nature of the GCIII rules on POW internment was acknowledged.[72] Certain commentators also seem to share this view. For example, regarding POW internment, Jelena Pejic notes:

> It is generally uncontroversial that the Third Geneva Convention provides a sufficient legal basis for POW internment... The detaining State is not obliged to provide review, judicial or other, of the lawfulness of POW internment as long as active hostilities are ongoing...[73]

The above examples might be read as suggesting that IHL *displaces* inconsistent IHRL. The alternative approach, referred to in the quote above from Koskenniemi's fragmentation report, is to treat this as a variation on the ICJ's interpretive approach in its *Nuclear Weapons* opinion, that is, not as displacement of IHRL but rather modification thereof. This has been the approach of the Inter-American Commission on Human Rights (IACiHR) and the European Court of Human Rights (ECtHR), both of which have read into their respective treaties the grounds and procedures applicable to internment in international armed conflicts under IHL.[74] Whichever approach one prefers, however, it must be remembered that *lex specialis* plays no normative role itself but, rather, simply points to certain factual elements to be taken into account in approximating the common intentions of the states parties.[75] The validity in any given case of a claim that a particular rule must be interpreted according to an extraneous rule, or that one rule displaces the other, will thus depend on the reasonableness of the claim that this represents the common intentions of the states parties. Thus, where the parties collectively intend for a rule of IHL to *set aside* or *modify* an otherwise applicable rule of IHRL, then this may arguably be the result, and, so the argument

---

and others v IDF Commander in the West Bank, IDF Commander in the Gaza Strip and others [2002] 125 ILR 537 (Israeli Supreme Court) [17] (referring to Art 78 GCIV as the *lex specialis* to the right to liberty).

[71] J Pejic, 'Procedural Principles and Safeguards for Internment/Administrative Detention in Armed Conflict and Other Situations of Violence' (2005) 87 IRRC 375, 386–7.

[72] UN Commission on Human Rights, 'Situation of Detainees at Guantanamo Bay', E/CN.4/2006/120, 27 February 2006, [19].

[73] Pejic (n 15) 87. Similarly, see G Gaggioli and R Kolb, 'A Right to Life in Armed Conflicts? The Contribution of the European Court of Human Rights' (2007) 37 Isr YB Hum Rts 115, 123 (fn 38); LM Olson, 'Practical Challenges of Implementing the Complementarity between International Humanitarian and Human Rights Law—Demonstrated by the Procedural Regulation of Internment in Non-International Armed Conflict' (2009) 40 Case W Res J Intl L 437, 454; Rodley and Pollard (n 60) 490; Sivakumaran (n 45) 90.

[74] *Coard et al v United States*, Report No 109/99, 29 September 1999 [45]–[59]; *Hassan v UK* (n 30) [96]–[107].

[75] Whilst the ECtHR did not rely on *lex specialis* as such, its approach was interpretive, and thus the common intentions of the states parties remains the test against which any particular interpretation must be judged: see below at text to n 80–9.

goes, one might infer such an intention from the fact that states have developed a detailed legal regime under IHL to apply in the specific situation. As part of this interpretive process, however, one must take account of other evidence of the intentions of the states parties, which may undermine the claim that there is a consensus that IHRL is to give way to IHL.[76]

A far more detailed exploration of state practice would, therefore, be needed to offer a definitive conclusion on the relationship between the IHL and IHRL rules on detention in the context of *international* armed conflicts, which is beyond the scope of the present study. What has been demonstrated thus far is that there is no *necessity* of reconciliation between diverging rules in international law.[77] Where no clear common intention to the contrary can be demonstrated, one falls back on the default position of the parallel application of both IHL and IHRL.[78] In such cases, any 'choice' between the different obligations will then be a political one, and the state can either adhere to the more demanding standard, thereby complying with both sets of obligations, or the less demanding standard and face the consequences that follow under the law of state responsibility for the breach of its other obligation. It is certainly the case that, with regard to the conduct of armed conflict in particular, there is a need for a workable legal framework that balances humanitarian and military considerations. However, in the case of IHL and IHRL, states still have the option of derogating from their human rights treaty obligations should they wish to invoke IHL. Indeed, requiring states to derogate from IHRL, rather than forcing a reconciliation of IHL and IHRL where this is not a reasonable interpretation of the common intention of the states parties, would seem consistent with the notion that the obligation to reconcile international obligations rests principally with the state that has consented to them.[79]

---

[76] There is, for example, contrary practice that suggests IHRL continues to regulate in full detentions in international armed conflict: see, eg, the derogation by Azerbaijan dated 16 April 1993 from, inter alia, Art 9 ICCPR as a result of the conflict with Armenia, suggesting that that provision otherwise applied in full: <https://treaties.un.org/pages/viewdetails.aspx?chapter=4&src=treaty&mtdsg_no=iv-4&lang=en> accessed 5 August 2015; *Rahmatullah* (n 69) (applying *habeas corpus* in an international armed conflict, albeit as a domestic law writ). See also IACiHR, 'Report on Terrorism and Human Rights', OEA/Ser.L/V/II.116 Doc. 5 rev. 1 corr., 22 October 2002, ch III [143] and [146]; UN Assistance Mission for Iraq, 'Human Rights Report: 1 April – 30 June 2007', [72] <http://www.ohchr.org/Documents/Countries/IQ/HRReportAprJun2007EN.pdf> accessed 5 August 2015; UN Working Group on Arbitrary Detention (UNWGAD), 'United Nations Basic Principles and Guidelines on Remedies and Procedures on the Right of Anyone Deprived of their Liberty to Bring Proceedings before a Court', A/HRC/30/xx (unedited version), 4 May 2015, [45]–[48]; L Doswald-Beck, *Human Rights in Times of Conflict and Terrorism* (OUP, Oxford 2011) 279; Rodley and Pollard (n 60) 491.

[77] *Southern Bluefin Tuna* case (*Australia and New Zealand/Japan*) (Jurisdiction and Admissibility) UNRIAA vol XXIII (2004) [52] ('...it is a commonplace of international law and State practice for more than one treaty to bear upon a particular dispute. There is no reason why a given act of a State may not violate its obligations under more than one treaty'); 'Fragmentation of International Law' (n 37) [42]; Pauwelyn (n 31) 419–22.

[78] Recognizing this default position enables one to avoid the problem frequently highlighted with relying on party intentions to resolve norm conflicts, that is, that rarely will one find a common intention on the matter: Jenks (n 18) 425–6; Milanović (n 3) 115–16. The answer in such cases will be to uphold this default position.

[79] *Nada v Switzerland*, App No 10593/08, Judgment (Grand Chamber), 12 September 2012, [197].

Before moving on, it should be noted that the ECtHR's interpretive approach in *Hassan v United Kingdom*, referred to above, does, to a certain extent, demonstrate a more nuanced approach to these issues than much of the practice referred to in the preceding sections.[80] In this case, the Court relied on Articles 31(3)(b) and (c) VCLT in reading into Article 5 ECHR the grounds and review mechanisms found in GCIV.[81] Regarding Article 31(3)(c), it must be emphasized that this tool, like *lex specialis*, is not a 'panacea for all instances of regime conflict'.[82] Indeed, its limits have been emphasized elsewhere, such that to invoke Article 31(3)(c) requires examining not simply what constitutes a 'relevant' rule of international law but also what weight should be accorded to any such rule and why.[83] The Court in *Hassan* went some way towards recognizing this, as it did not simply submit Article 5 ECHR to the more permissive treaty standards in GCIII and GCIV. Rather, its approach to this relationship was more symbiotic, seen in its interpretation of the requirement of a 'court' in Article 5(4). It began its assessment by noting the permitted use of a 'competent body' under Article 78 GCIV for the purposes of carrying out initial and periodic reviews.[84] It then stated:

Whilst it might not be practicable, in the course of an international armed conflict, for the legality of detention to be determined by an independent 'court' in the sense generally required by Article 5 § 4... nonetheless, if the Contracting State is to comply with its obligations under Article 5 § 4 in this context, the 'competent body' should provide sufficient guarantees of impartiality and fair procedure to protect against arbitrariness.[85]

Thus, by virtue of the continued operation of Article 5(4) in the background, the Court required more from the 'competent body' than the text of Article 43 or 78 GCIV does. It is unclear, however, the degree to which it would have been as willing to reconcile Article 5(4) ECHR with the complete absence of any review procedure under the GCIII internment regime.[86]

Importantly, and to emphasize the point made throughout this section, the Court did not simply rely on Article 31(3)(c), but also invoked Article 31(3)(b) VCLT, referring to the subsequent practice of the states parties to the ECHR, according to which none had considered it necessary to derogate in order to access the more permissive rules under IHL in international armed conflicts.[87] This practice, the Court concluded, 'could be taken as establishing their agreement' that Article 5 ECHR does not preclude the permitted forms of internment under GCIII and GCIV.[88] The Court thus made clear that the common intentions of the

---

[80] *Hassan v UK* (n 30).   [81] *Hassan v UK* (n 30) [96]–[107].
[82] D Pulkowski, *The Law and Politics of International Regime Conflict* (OUP, Oxford 2014) 292.
[83] See, eg, *Case Concerning Oil Platforms (Islamic Republic of Iran v United States of America)* [2003] ICJ Rep 161, Separate Opinion of Judge Higgins; *Case Concerning Certain Questions of Mutual Assistance in Criminal Matters (Djibouti v France)* [2008] ICJ Rep 177, [112]–[114]; 'Fragmentation of International Law' (n 37) [419]; Pauwelyn (n 31) 254; Paparinskis (n 31) 73; Pulkowski (n 82) 287–93.
[84] *Hassan v UK* (n 30) [106].   [85] Ibid.
[86] *Hassan v UK* (n 30), Partly Dissenting Opinion of Judges Spano, Nicolaou, Bianku, and Kalaydjieva, [5].
[87] *Hassan v UK* (n 30) [101].   [88] Ibid.

5.1 The Relationship between IHL and IHRL

states parties remained the decisive consideration. Unfortunately, the Court was rather unreflective in its actual application of this test, for the lack of derogations does not necessarily support the view that Article 5 ECHR is considered to yield to IHL. The absence of derogations in such situations may well be underpinned more by states' continued attempts to avoid conceding the extraterritoriality of the Convention than any view as to the relationship between IHL and IHRL.[89] Whilst more nuanced than many other accounts of the relationship between IHL and IHRL, the reasoning in the *Hassan* judgment is, therefore, not without its flaws. Of course, the political context within which the Court was operating may well have played a role in its approach and conclusions here.

5.1.3 Detention in non-international armed conflict

The section above considered the relationship between the internment regimes applicable in international armed conflicts under IHL and the human rights rules on detention. Whilst there is some contrary practice, it was shown that a number of states and commentators take the view that the IHL rules operate as the 'controlling body of law', either displacing or modifying the IHRL rules. The question now to be addressed is whether one could reasonably adopt a similar interpretation with regard to internment in *non-international* armed conflict. The difficulty with making such an argument is that, unlike in international armed conflicts, IHL contains no detailed procedural rules applicable to internment in non-international conflicts. It was shown above that many consider the fact that states have developed specific internment regimes in international armed conflicts to evidence an intention that those regimes prevail over IHRL. However, chapter 3 demonstrated that the only relevant rule applicable in non-international armed conflict is to be found in the humane treatment principle in common Article 3, which can be interpreted as prohibiting internment that is not, or no longer, necessary as a result of the conflict. (This was also shown to exist under custom.)[90] One cannot infer from these minimal rules an intention amongst states that IHRL is to be set aside here.

This notwithstanding, there remains considerable disagreement amongst states, international bodies, and commentators regarding the role of IHRL in such situations. The example referred to in the introduction to this book illustrates this well. In noting the scarcity of applicable IHL rules in this area, the United States sought to draw on the law of international armed conflict in developing an internment regime to govern its conflict with al-Qaeda, considered by that state to be non-international in character.[91] Indeed, the United States has stated more generally that:

...international humanitarian law is the *lex specialis* in both international and non-international armed conflicts, including with respect to detention... [Consequently]

---

[89] *Hassan*, Dissenting Opinion (n 86) [12].   [90] See section 3.2.1 and 3.3.

[91] 'Respondents' Memorandum Regarding the Government's Detention Authority Relative to Detainees Held at Guantanamo Bay', *In Re: Guantanamo Bay Detainee Litigation*, Misc No 08-442 (TFH) (DDC 13 March 2009) 1 <http://www.justice.gov/opa/documents/memo-re-det-auth.pdf> accessed 5 August 2015. On this practice, see section 5.2.3.1.

in both international and non-international armed conflicts, a State may detain enemy combatants consistent with the law of armed conflict until the end of hostilities. Similarly... it would be incorrect to state that there is a 'right to take proceedings before a court to enable the court to decide without delay on the lawfulness of detention' in all cases'.[92]

The UK, Canadian, and Australian governments all appear recently to have endorsed the view that IHL modifies or displaces the rules on detention under IHRL in non-international armed conflicts.[93] The HRC, as well as other UN bodies, on the other hand, considers the relevant legal framework governing detention in non-international armed conflict, in the absence of clear IHL rules, to be Article 9 ICCPR.[94] This disagreement illustrates well the point made at the outset of this chapter, that the particular approach taken to the relationship between IHL and IHRL is heavily affected by the identity of the relevant authority making the claim, with certain states keen to preserve their operational discretion by endorsing the displacement or modification approach. Commentators similarly disagree here. Louise Doswald-Beck, for example, states that, since IHL is virtually silent in this area, 'human rights law applies without any possible contradiction'.[95] Jelena Pejic is critical of such suggestions, however, arguing that they do 'not reflect the reality of warfare' and that 'what is essentially being said is that armed conflict must be conducted according to rules primarily developed to be applied in time of peace. This result is surely untenable as it ignores the critical differences between war and peace.'[96]

This disagreement renders it necessary to consider how, notwithstanding the absence of detailed IHL rules, IHL might nonetheless still be considered the *lex specialis* with respect to detention in non-international armed conflicts so as effectively to displace the IHRL rules. This requires considering an alternative interpretive approach, the theory of which will be discussed in the following paragraphs and the practical application of which will be the subject of the remaining sections of this chapter. According to this approach, one might

---

[92] HRC (n 12) [21]–[22].
[93] *Serdar Mohammed and others v Secretary of State for Defence; Yanus Rahmatllah & the Iraqi Civilian Claimants v Ministry of Defence and Foreign & Commonwealth Office* [2015] EWCA Civ 843, [109] (on the UK government's view that IHL displaces or modifies Art 5 ECHR in non-international armed conflict); HRC (n 13) [11]–[13] (on the Canadian view that IHL governs detentions in all armed conflicts, allowing detention of 'enemy combatants' for the duration of hostilities without judicial review); UNWGAD, 'Australia Permanent Mission to the UN Geneva: Australian Response to UN Working Group on Arbitrary Detention's Draft Principles and Guidelines on remedies and procedures on the right of anyone deprived of his or her liberty', Note 23/2015, 17 March 2015, [9] (suggesting that the Copenhagen Principles embody the governing legal standards for detention in non-international armed conflicts) <http://www.ohchr.org/EN/HRBodies/CCPR/Pages/DGCArticle9.aspx> accessed 5 August 2015.
[94] HRC, 'Concluding Observations: United States of America', UN Doc CCPR/C/US/CO/3/Rev.1, 18 December 2006, [18]; UN Commission on Human Rights, 'Situation of Detainees at Guantanamo Bay' (n 72) [24]; HRC, General Comment No 35: Article 9 (Liberty and security of person), CCPR/C/FC/35, 16 December 2014, [66].
[95] Doswald-Beck (n 76) 277. See also Droege (n 2) 535–6. [96] Pejic (n 15) 94.

5.1 The Relationship between IHL and IHRL

perceive the lack of an IHL internment regime for non-international armed conflicts not as a gap, which then leaves IHRL intact, but rather a space within which states intentionally preserved their discretion, to enable them to tailor their approaches according to the circumstances. Laura Olson, for example, has cautioned against unreflectively applying human rights law to fill apparent gaps in IHL, using the example of the absence in GCIII of review mechanisms for challenging the necessity of POW internment; such silence, it is argued, arises not from a gap in the law but, rather, the assumption that POW internment is necessary *ipso facto* for the duration of hostilities.[97] Applying the human right to *habeas corpus* to fill this apparent gap, so the argument goes, would be inconsistent with this assumption.[98]

One might make a similar argument here, treating the broad discretion left by IHL in this area as intentional and excluding or modifying otherwise applicable rules of IHRL.[99] There are, however, certain caveats that one should bear in mind. First, Olson's argument calls for a consideration of the reason underpinning an apparent 'gap' in IHL. Whilst this is useful for the example of POW internment review, the absence of any procedural rules applicable in non-international conflicts under IHL does not benefit from the same principled basis. In particular, it was shown in chapter 1 that IHL's distinction between international and non-international armed conflicts arises from historical considerations regarding the scope of international law and concerns for preserving state sovereignty.[100] Such considerations, however, were shown to be anachronistic in light of subsequent developments in international law.

Second, Olson's approach of referring to IHRL as 'filling gaps' in IHL implies a different starting point to that adopted here, whereby IHL is considered to apply to the exclusion of human rights law, with the latter applying only where appropriate to fill gaps in the former. As explained above, the approach adopted here takes as its starting point the continued application of IHRL in armed conflict alongside IHL. The presumption, therefore, is that any internment carried out by a state is to be judged according to the relevant human rights rules, in addition to the minimal rules of IHL. That presumption is rebutted only where it can be established that there is a common intention amongst the states parties to the relevant human rights treaty that IHRL should give way to IHL. However, in the absence of a detailed internment regime under IHL for non-international armed conflicts, which might otherwise indicate such a shared intention, this would have to be

---

[97] Olson (n 73) 454. See section 2.3.2.
[98] Olson (n 73) 454. Similarly, see Sivakumaran (n 45) 92. For the same interpretive approach being applied in other areas of international law, see M Wood, 'The International Tribunal for Law of the Sea and General International Law' (2007) 22 Intl J Marine & Coastal L 351, 361; Paparinskis (n 31) 77.
[99] This is essentially the approach in R Goodman, 'Authorization versus Regulation of Detention in Non-International Armed Conflicts' (2015) 91 Intl L Stud 155 (arguing that the scope of such discretion is to be determined by analogy to what is permitted and prohibited under the law of international armed conflict).
[100] See sections 1.1 and 1.3.1.

found solely in their (subsequent) practice.[101] When practice does not confirm such a shared intention, the presumption holds, and the ordinarily applicable rules of IHRL continue to regulate detentions alongside IHL. Where this is the case, were a state arbitrarily to intern in a non-international armed conflict, it would violate both IHRL and IHL. As demonstrated above, jurisprudence confirms that the same facts can lead to violations of both IHL and IHRL, without the former necessarily affecting the latter.[102]

A few words should be said about the above interpretive approach. According to this approach, subsequent state practice could be invoked as evidence of a common intention amongst states parties to a human rights treaty that a provision is effectively inapplicable in a situation to which it otherwise appears fully applicable. Similarly to what was said above regarding the application of the IHRL rules in *international* armed conflict, the approach here could be understood in different ways. On the one hand, it might be seen as an interpretation of either the substantive human right (eg Article 5(1) ECHR) or the relevant provision on jurisdiction (eg Article 1 ECHR), whereby a caveat on their non-application or modification for detentions in the context of non-international armed conflicts is read into the text. On the other hand, it might be seen as a form of norm conflict resolution, whereby the human rights rules are displaced by the discretion established under IHL in this area, the latter operating in a sense as the *lex specialis*. Both approaches raise some conceptual problems.[103] These, however, need not detain us here, for regardless of which understanding one follows, their validity must in any event be judged against the reasonableness with which one can claim that they represent the objective intentions of the states parties as reflected in their practice.[104] Based on this, the following sections will examine state practice in specific non-international armed conflicts to consider whether it can be said to convey a shared intention amongst states that the procedural rules on detention by which they are bound under IHRL are modified or displaced in such contexts.

---

[101] Art 31(3)(b) VCLT. Subsequent practice is constantly invoked as an important indication of the parties' intentions: *Kasikili/Sedudu Island (Botswana/Namibia)* [1999] ICJ Rep 1045, [49]; GG Fitzmaurice, 'The Law and Procedure of the International Court of Justice: Treaty Interpretation and Certain Other Treaty Points' (1951) 28 BYIL 1, 20; McNair (n 38) 424; A Aust, *Modern Treaty Law and Practice* (2nd edn, CUP, Cambridge 2007) 241; R Gardiner, *Treaty Interpretation* (OUP, Oxford 2012) 225; J-M Sorel and VB Eveno, '1969 Vienna Convention, Article 31: General Rule of Intepretation' in O Corten and P Klein (ed), *The Vienna Conventions on the Law of Treaties: A Commentary, Volume I* (OUP, Oxford 2011) 826.

[102] *Israeli Wall* (n 24) [134]; *DRC v Uganda* (n 22) [217]–[220]. Similarly, see African Commission on Human and Peoples' Rights (ACiHPR), *DRC v Burundi, Uganda and Rwanda*, Communication No 227/99 (2003), [79]–[80].

[103] For example, regarding the interpretive approach, to the extent that this is considered to involve a use of subsequent practice to modify treaties in the strict sense, it might be objected to as a controversial interpretive method: see, eg, the discussion of the various views on this in ILC, 'Second Report on Subsequent Agreements and Subsequent Practice in Relation to the Interpretation of Treaties by Georg Nolte, Special Rapporteur', A/CN.4/671, 26 March 2014, [115]–[142]. On the other hand, the norm conflict resolution approach is intuitively problematic as it suggests a silence in one regime can displace rules in another regime.

[104] See above at text to nn 75–6 for the same point being made regarding the operation of the human rights rules in international armed conflicts.

5.1 The Relationship between IHL and IHRL 163

It will be shown that no such intention can be discerned, leaving the presumption of the full application of IHRL intact.

A final point must be noted before moving on to an examination of state practice. Subsequent practice can only contribute to the interpretation of a treaty where that practice establishes the agreement of the states parties collectively, for otherwise no *common* intention could be derived therefrom.[105] If anything, the burden of demonstrating that subsequent practice represents the *collective* agreement of the states parties must be even higher when using that practice to interpret human rights treaties, due to their nature as 'community interests' or truly 'multilateral obligations', supplementing the historically bilateralist international legal order.[106] By this is meant that human rights treaty obligations cannot be broken down into a web of reciprocal relationships; rather, they are obligations *erga omnes (partes)*, owed equally by each state party to every other state party (as well as to individuals within their jurisdiction).[107] In the words of the ICJ:

All the other States parties have a common interest in compliance with these obligations by the State. That common interest implies that the obligations in question are owed by any State party to all the other States parties to the Convention.[108]

This particular structure of human rights obligations suggests that 'arguments for a restrictive interpretation based on party intentions [where everything else points to a broader interpretation] should be viewed quite a bit more sceptically and subjected to more rigorous evidentiary standards than in the cases of merely reciprocal obligations'.[109] Consequently, it is submitted that *all* states parties would have to acquiesce *clearly* in the practice establishing that certain provisions of a human rights treaty are inapplicable in a situation to which they otherwise appear

---

[105] Aust (n 101) 243; Gardiner (n 101) 236–7.
[106] The language employed borrows from B Simma, 'From Bilateralism to Community Interest in International Law' (1994) 250 *Recueil des Cours* 217, 242–3, J Crawford, 'Multilateral Rights and Obligations in International Law' (2006) 319 *Recueil des Cours* 325, and L-A Sicilianos, 'The Classification of Obligations and the Multilateral Dimension of the Relations of International Responsibility' (2002) 13 EJIL 1127.
[107] On the *erga omnes/erga omnes partes* nature of human rights obligations generally, see *Case Concerning The Barcelona Traction, Light and Power Company, Limited (Belgium v Spain)*, Second Phase, Judgment [1970] ICJ Rep 3, [33]–[34]; *Application of the Convention on the Prevention and Punishment of the Crime of Genocide (Bosnia and Herzegovina v Yugoslavia)*, Preliminary Objections, Judgment [1996] ICJ Rep 595, [31]; *Prosecutor v Anto Furundzija*, Trial Judgment, IT-95-17/1-T (10 December 1998) [151]; *Questions Relating to the Obligation to Prosecute or Extradite (Belgium v Senegal)*, Judgment [2012] ICJ Rep 422, [68]; ILC, 'Third Report on State Responsibility, by Mr James Crawford, Special Rapporteur' (2000) Doc A/CN.4/507 and Add. 1-4, [106(b)].
[108] *Belgium v Senegal* (n 107) [68].
[109] J Arato, 'Accounting for Difference in Treaty Interpretation Over Time' in A Bianchi, D Peat, and M Windsor (eds), *Interpretation in International Law* (OUP, Oxford 2015) 223 (fn 69). Arguing similarly that the use of subsequent practice to interpret human rights treaties might raise different considerations from the interpretation of other treaties, but on the basis of the conferral of third party rights rather than the structure of the inter-state obligations, see J Alvarez, 'Limits of Change by Way of Subsequent Agreements and Practice' in G Nolte (ed), *Treaties and Subsequent Practice* (OUP, Oxford 2013) 126; A Roberts, 'Power and Persuasion in Investment Treaty Interpretation: The Dual Role of States' (2010) 104 AJIL 179.

applicable; there can be no mere presumption that other states parties accept the practice as a legitimate interpretation of the treaty provision. Were it otherwise the case, certain states parties would effectively be able to 'contract out' through practice and agree amongst themselves to apply less protective rules, which would then potentially violate the rights of the other states parties (as well as the individuals directly affected). This would clearly be the case regarding detention in non-international armed conflict, given that the default legal position was shown to be the parallel application of IHL and IHRL, based on the treaty texts, their *travaux* and practice.[110] Indeed, a useful analogy might be drawn here to the customary rules on modification of multilateral treaties, which prohibit *inter se* modifications between certain of the states parties only, where the structure of obligations are such as would affect the rights of all other states parties to the treaty.[111]

The threshold for rebutting the presumption that human rights law regulates detentions in non-international conflicts is therefore high.[112] Indeed, the same condition must apply with respect to the role of human rights law in the context of *international* armed conflicts, such that the practice in favour of modifying or displacing human rights to make room for IHL must reflect the intention of *every* state party to the relevant human rights treaty. However, the fact that states have developed specific internment regimes for international armed conflicts strengthens the argument that such a shared intention exists (though, as noted above, this is still not unequivocal). The absence of such specifically developed internment regimes for non-international armed conflicts means that state practice alone would need to demonstrate clearly a shared intention to this effect. It is to an examination of relevant state practice that we now turn in the following sections.

5.2 State Practice in Specific Non-International Armed Conflicts

This section will explore state practice regarding detention in specific non-international armed conflicts. It will be shown that no clear intention as to the inapplicability of the relevant IHRL rules can be inferred; rather, practice demonstrates a broad recognition that those rules regulate detentions in relation to non-international armed conflicts.

---

[110] See above at text to nn 48–50.
[111] Art 41(1)(b)(i) VCLT; *The Oscar Chinn Case*, PCIJ Series A/B, No 63, 1934, Separate Opinion of M Schücking; Pauwelyn (n 31) 53 ('[a]n *inter se* modification to a multilateral treaty is, in principle, only permissible when such modification relates to obligations *of the reciprocal type*'); Pauwelyn (n 31) 309 (giving the example of human rights treaties as comprising obligations *erga omnes partes* that, by this nature, preclude *inter se* modification amongst only some of the states parties).
[112] 'Fragmentation of International Law' (n 37) [385] ('...the interest in the distinction [between reciprocal and non-bilateralizable obligations] lay in the manner that conflicts between treaties were to be dealt with – the more "absolute" type of obligation being less easily derogated from by "modification" or *lex posterior*').

The conflicts are divided into three categories: traditional non-international conflicts (ie conflicts between states and non-state armed groups that are confined to the territory of the relevant state); extraterritorial non-international conflicts (ie non-international conflicts in which the 'host' state is supported by a foreign state); and transnational armed conflicts (conflicts between states and non-state armed groups that transcend the boundaries of a single state). For some of these examples, their status as non-international armed conflicts is controversial. However, for present purposes, it is sufficient that the state(s) whose practice is under scrutiny considered it a non-international armed conflict or did not object to that characterization. The conflicts have been selected on the basis of their geographical spread, contemporaneity, and the amount of publicly-available information regarding detention practices. The detention regimes applied by the states are explored in detail, as these will be drawn on in chapter 7 when discussing the potential future development of the law of non-international armed conflict in this area.

5.2.1 Traditional non-international armed conflicts

5.2.1.1 Colombia

That the conflicts waged in Colombia since the 1960s, in particular those between the government on the one hand and the *Feurzas Armadas Revolucionarias de Colombia* (FARC) and *Ejército de Liberación* (ELN) on the other, constitute non-international armed conflicts has been widely acknowledged, including by the Colombian President and Supreme Court.[113] Commentators too have recognized this and suggested that APII applied in the mid-1990s when hostilities reached their peak.[114]

In this context, recent detention practice of the Colombian government is illuminating. In January 2008 a new system of detention became applicable under Colombian law generally, and this follows a purely human rights, criminal law-approach to the procedural regulation of detention, applicable even to detentions carried out in relation to the non-international conflicts.[115] Under this system, a person must be taken before a judge within thirty six hours of being detained to verify the legality of detention and check that their rights have been respected.[116] If declared valid, formal charges must be brought and a criminal trial must take place within ninety days.[117] *Habeas corpus* is available for alleged cases of arbitrary detention.[118] The armed forces are not empowered to execute arrest warrants;

---

[113] F Szesnat and A Bird, 'Colombia' in E Wilmshurst (ed), *International Law and the Classification of Conflicts* (OUP, Oxford 2012) 215.
[114] Szesnat and Bird (n 113) 227.
[115] Human Rights Council, 'Report of the Working Group on Arbitrary Detention: Addendum, Mission to Colombia (1 to 10 October 2008)', A/HRC/10/21/Add.3, 16 February 2009, [22]–[33].
[116] Ibid, [26].   [117] Ibid, [33].   [118] Ibid, [32].

instead, prosecutors who are so authorized should accompany the armed forces to conflict zones.[119]

The above notwithstanding, the HRC and UNWGAD have noted that, in practice, mass arbitrary arrests continued to be prevalent in Colombia even after these new laws were introduced.[120] These problems aside, it is clear that the legal regime governing conflict-related detentions is modelled on the human rights law framework for criminal detention, rather than the IHL model of administrative detention.[121] Consequently, persons are often detained on charges of rebellion or terrorism.[122] Importantly for our purposes, this was not merely a policy-based decision but, rather, a consequence of Colombia's assumption that its conflict-related detention operations continued to be governed by its IHRL obligations. This is confirmed by Colombia's derogation from particular paragraphs of Article 9 ICCPR at numerous points throughout the 1990s as a result of the conflicts, demonstrating its recognition that, absent derogation, detention operations remained fully regulated by that provision.[123]

The practice of Colombia is also enlightening in that it confirms that a human rights-based framework for detention is suitable for non-international conflicts, with the in-built facility of derogation employed where necessary to broaden the state's powers. This is especially important given that, in other areas, notably the use of force, Colombia considers it necessary to revert to an IHL framework in developing applicable rules.[124] Indeed, this reliance on IHRL is true not only for states employing a purely criminal law-based approach to detention, as with Colombia, but also where the state adopts an internment regime. This was the case, for example, regarding the United Kingdom during the 'Troubles' in Northern Ireland, in which it adopted an internment regime by derogating from Article 5 ECHR, demonstrating that IHRL, by providing for derogation, is not necessarily ill-suited for such situations.[125] The extent to which states can validly derogate from the IHRL rules on detention is explored in detail in section 6.1.

---

[119] Ibid, [59] (noting also that, in practice, these rules have been breached). A new law that granted arrest and detention powers to the military was previously declared unconstitutional by the Colombian Constitutional Court: see US State Department, 'Country Reports: Colombia' (2004), s 1(g).
[120] HRC, Concluding Observations: Colombia, CCPR/C/COL/CO/6, 4 August 2010, [20]; Human Rights Council (n 115) [63].
[121] Similarly, see Szesnat and Bird (n 113) 240.
[122] Human Rights Council (n 115) [74]. The US State Department reports that, during 2011 alone, Colombia held more than 1,920 detainees accused of 'rebellion' or 'aiding and abetting insurgence' and that there is a tendency for lengthy pre-trial detentions: US State Department, 'Country Reports: Colombia' (2011), ss 1(e) and 1(d).
[123] See, eg, derogation from Art 9(3) dated 29 May 1994; derogation from Art 9 dated 21 March 1996; derogation from Art 9(1) dated 18 June 1996: <https://treaties.un.org/pages/viewdetails.aspx?chapter=4&src=treaty&mtdsg_no=iv-4&lang=en> accessed 6 August 2015.
[124] C von der Groeben, 'The Conflict in Colombia and the Relationship between Humanitarian Law and Human Rights Law in Practice: Analysis of the New Operational Law of the Colombian Armed Forces' (2011) 16 JCSL 141.
[125] See section 6.1.2 for the relevant case law. Whilst the United Kingdom did not regard this situation as an armed conflict to which IHL applied, commentators have argued that, in fact, it

5.2.1.2 Sri Lanka

The non-international armed conflict between the central Sri Lankan government and the Liberation Tigers of Tamil Eelam (LTTE) that lasted for three decades ended in May 2009, and in August 2011 the government lifted its twenty-eight-year-long state of emergency.[126] This notwithstanding, persons allegedly affiliated with the LTTE continued to be detained under the 1979 Prevention of Terrorism Act (PTA).[127] More generally, '[t]housands of people continued to be held in relation to the former armed conflict at temporary and permanent places of detention around the country, and arrests continued'.[128]

The ICRC reported that those detained as part of the conflict included both 'security detainees' and 'former LTTE fighters who had surrendered to the security forces'.[129] Regarding the legal basis for detention, the ICRC confirmed that alleged LTTE fighters were detained under both emergency regulations and the PTA.[130] Under the emergency regulations adopted several years before the end of the conflict, any person 'acting in any manner prejudicial to the national security or to the maintenance of public order, or to the maintenance of essential services' could be detained for up to eighteen months.[131] Whilst such persons should have been presented before a magistrate within thirty days, the courts had no authority to order release, a power left to the executive.[132]

In addition to the emergency regulations, Sri Lanka's PTA permits administrative detention, '[w]here the Minister has reason to believe or suspect that any person is connected with or concerned in any unlawful activity'.[133] Such persons may be detained for a maximum of eighteen months.[134] The PTA excludes courts from reviewing detention orders.[135] Instead, an advisory board, established by the President and comprising at least three members, considers representations made by the detainee or a person on their behalf.[136] To enable such representations to be made, the detainee is to be informed of the 'unlawful activity in connection with

---

did reach the threshold of a non-international armed conflict: S Haines, 'Northern Ireland: 1968–1998' in E Wilmshurst (ed), *International Law and the Classification of Conflicts* (OUP, Oxford 2012) 130–5.

[126] ICRC, 'Sri Lanka' in ICRC, *Annual Report 2011* (ICRC, May 2012) 245. Sri Lanka recognized this as a non-international armed conflict: Sri Lankan Ministry of Defence, 'Humanitarian Operation: Factual Analysis July 2006 – May 2009' (Ministry of Defence, July 2011) 2 [8].

[127] ICRC (n 126). Similarly, see Human Rights Watch, 'Sri Lanka: "Bait and Switch" on Emergency Law' (7 September 2011) <http://www.hrw.org/news/2011/09/07/sri-lanka-bait-and-switch-emergency-law> accessed 6 August 2015; Sri Lanka, 'Detention – Emergency Regulations – Admissibility of Confessions by a Police Officer' (2011) 17 Asian YBIL 301.

[128] ICRC (n 126) 248.

[129] ICRC, 'Sri Lanka' in ICRC, *Annual Report 2008* (ICRC, May 2009) 212.

[130] ICRC, 'Sri Lanka' in ICRC, *Annual Report 2009* (ICRC, May 2010) 228.

[131] Human Rights Watch, *Legal Limbo: The Uncertain Fate of Detained LTTE Suspects in Sri Lanka* (HRW, New York 2010) 17.

[132] Ibid, 18.

[133] Prevention of Terrorism Act 1979, s 9(1) <http://www.sangam.org/FACTBOOK/PTA1979.htm> accessed 6 August 2015.

[134] Ibid, s 9(1).   [135] Ibid, s 13(2).   [136] Ibid, ss 13(2) and (3).

which' the detention order was made.[137] The board has no power to order release but merely advises the Minister.[138]

The administrative detention regimes under the emergency regulations and the PTA appear incompatible with what ordinarily is required under IHRL, particularly given the absence of judicial review of the legality of detention.[139] The PTA, in particular, seems closer to the GCIV internment regimes applicable in international conflicts, using an administrative body to review detentions. However, both regimes fall short of what would be required under GCIV (were that applicable), as interpreted by the International Criminal Tribunal for the Former Yugoslavia (ICTY), given that the review bodies do not have the power to order release.[140]

It might be inferred from this that Sri Lanka considered its obligations under Article 9 ICCPR to be inapplicable to detentions related to the non-international conflict. However, such an inference cannot validly be made as Sri Lanka derogated from particular paragraphs of Article 9 throughout the conflict, clearly indicating its recognition that that provision was otherwise applicable.[141] As with Colombia, therefore, Sri Lanka operated on the assumption that its IHRL obligations applied in full, utilizing derogation to broaden the scope of permissible action. Indeed, international bodies judged Sri Lanka's detention operations against the IHRL standards, criticizing it for transgressing those rules.[142]

5.2.1.3 Nepal

Nepal's decade-long non-international armed conflict between the government and the Communist Party of Nepal-Maoist (CPN-M) began in February 1996 when the CPN-M launched its 'people's war' with a view to overthrowing the existing government.[143] In May 2006, CPN-M declared a general ceasefire, with a comprehensive peace plan signed by both sides in November of that year.[144] The parties involved in the conflict, as well as external observers, acknowledged that this constituted a non-international armed conflict to which common Article 3 applied.[145]

---

[137] Ibid, s 13(2).   [138] Ibid, s 13(3).   [139] See section 4.2.3.
[140] *Prosecutor v Zejnil Delalić et al* (Appeals Judgment) ICTY-96-21-A (20 February 2001) [329].
[141] See, eg, derogation from Art 9(3) on 18 May 1983, ended on 11 January 1989; derogation from Art 9(2) on 20 June 1989, ended on 4 September 1994; derogation from Arts 9(2) and 9(3) on 30 May 2000, ended on 2 May 2010: <https://treaties.un.org/pages/viewdetails.aspx?chapter=4&src=treaty&mtdsg_no=iv-4&lang=en> accessed 6 August 2015.
[142] See, eg, HRC, 'Concluding Observations: Sri Lanka', CCPR/CO/79/LKA, 1 December 2003, [13]; Human Rights Watch (n 131) 3, 20–1.
[143] PJC Schimmelpenninck van der Oije, 'International Humanitarian Law from a Field Perspective – Case Study: Nepal' (2006) 9 YIHL 394, 396.
[144] Ibid, 401.
[145] Ibid, 404; UN Office of the High Commissioner for Human Rights (OHCHR), *Nepal Conflict Report: An Analysis of Conflict-Related Violations of International Human Rights Law and International Humanitarian Law between February 1996 and 21 November 2006* (OHCHR, Geneva 2012) 63–4.

Internment was permitted via two routes under Nepalese law. First, soon after fighting began, the government reactivated the Public Security (2nd Amendment) Act 1991 (PSA) which permitted preventive detention for up to twelve months on the grounds of 'the interest of the common people'.[146] The Act purported to exclude judicial review of detention orders.[147] However, the non-derogable constitutional writ of *habeas corpus* was held to prevail over the Act, allowing such orders to be challenged.[148] Second, the Terrorist and Disruptive Activities (Control and Punishment) Act 2002 provided, inter alia, for preventive detention for up to ninety days 'upon appropriate grounds for believing that a person has to be stopped from doing anything that may cause a terrorist and disruptive act'.[149] This was subsequently replaced by the Terrorist and Disruptive Activities (Control and Punishment) Ordinance 2004 (TADO), which extended the period of lawful preventive detention to up to one year, to be authorized by a civilian authority, usually the Chief District Officer (CDO).[150] However, '[c]redible reports suggest that CDOs sign detention orders under TADO without any serious consideration of the necessity of the detention'.[151] As with the PSA, TADO sought to exclude judicial review of detention.[152] This notwithstanding, the legality of arrests pursuant to TADO was frequently challenged before the Supreme Court and Appellate Courts.[153] At the adoption of the ceasefire agreement in 2006, most persons held under the PSA and TADO were released.[154]

The internment regimes under the PSA and TADO left considerable discretion to the detaining authorities and sought to exclude any form of review (judicial or otherwise) of the decision to detain. Whilst the Nepalese courts responded to this by asserting their jurisdiction to hear *habeas* claims, it is likely that the grounds for detention under the PSA and TADO were too vague to satisfy the IHRL standard.[155] It is clear, however, that Nepal considered the ICCPR to apply to these detentions notwithstanding the conflict. Thus, Nepal derogated from certain provisions of the ICCPR, indicating its belief that that treaty continued to apply during the conflict.[156] None of these derogations, however, involved Article 9 ICCPR, and, although Nepal declared a number of states of emergency, pursuant to which

---

[146] Schimmelpenninck van der Oije (n 143) 396.   [147] OHCHR (n 145) 153.
[148] Ibid.
[149] UN Commission on Human Rights, 'Report of the Working Group on Involuntary or Enforced Disappearances: Mission to Nepal', E/CN.4/2005/65/Add.1, 28 January 2005, [45].
[150] Ibid.   [151] Ibid, [47].   [152] OHCHR (n 145) 154 (fn 502).
[153] OHCHR (n 145) 154. Similarly, see HRC, 'Second Periodic Reports of States Parties: Nepal', CCPR/C/NPL/2, 8 June 2012, [110] ('[d]uring the period of emergency, the SC [Supreme Court] received about 200 petitions of habeas corpus, and, in over 60 of them it issued orders requiring the security forces and the Government to release the detainees').
[154] ICRC, 'Nepal' in ICRC, *Annual Report 2006* (ICRC, May 2007) 191.
[155] On the need for certainty in the grounds for detention under the IHRL standard, see, eg, *Medvedyev and others v France*, App No 3394/03, Judgment, Grand Chamber, 29 March 2010, [80]; HRC, General Comment No 35: Article 9 (Liberty and security of person), CCPR/C/GC/35, 16 December 2014, [22].
[156] See, eg, its derogations dated 8 March 2002, 16 February 2005, and 29 March 2005, none of which specifically derogates from Art 9 ICCPR: see <https://treaties.un.org/pages/viewdetails.aspx?chapter=4&src=treaty&mtdsg_no=iv-4&lang=en> accessed 6 August 2015.

it suspended the constitutional right not preventively to be detained, it explicitly stated that it was not suspending the right to *habeas corpus*, leaving its domestic courts to continue to exercise their powers of review.[157] Importantly, the Supreme Court of Nepal itself emphasized that the right to liberty, and with it the right to *habeas corpus*, as a matter of international law under Article 9 ICCPR, applied to persons that disappeared during the non-international armed conflict.[158] That Article 9 ICCPR applied to Nepal's detentions in relation to its non-international conflict was also confirmed by international bodies, which consistently reviewed its practices in light of that provision.[159]

5.2.1.4 Democratic Republic of the Congo

The detention practices of the various parties to the conflicts waged within the Democratic Republic of the Congo (DRC) over the last two decades are reflective of the lack of legal clarity in this area. In contrast to the preceding examples of state practice, this section will demonstrate that in the DRC no detention regime was developed during these conflicts. Rather, individuals were detained arbitrarily without even the façade of procedural safeguards. It will also be shown, however, that the DRC's practice demonstrates an assumption that the IHRL rules on detention applied fully, and there was no suggestion that the existence of non-international conflicts led to a setting aside of those rules.

Given the complexity of the various conflicts involving the DRC, it is useful to refer to the study by Louise Arimatsu on the character of those conflicts in which she divides them into four distinct periods: the period preceding the outbreak of the First Congo War (Spring 1993 to Summer 1996); the First Congo War (July 1996 to Summer 1998); the Second Congo War (August 1998 to July 2003); and the period since the end of the Second Congo War and the establishment of the transitional government.[160] During each period, various conflicts involving different parties were waged on the territory of the DRC, including non-international armed conflicts between the incumbent *de jure* government and non-state armed groups.[161] Regarding detentions carried out by government and non-state forces, Arimatsu notes:

During the conflicts, the State authority, under both Mobutu and Kabila, claimed sweeping powers of detention on the grounds of 'reasons of security' with little concern for

---

[157] See, eg, its derogation dated 29 March 2005, which specifically states that it has not derogated from *habeas corpus*: <https://treaties.un.org/pages/viewdetails.aspx?chapter=4&src=treaty&mtdsg_no=iv-4&lang=en> accessed 6 August 2015. The right to *habeas corpus* is specifically non-derogable under the Constitution: see UN Commission on Human Rights (n 149) [15].
[158] *Rabindra Prasad Dhakal on Behalf of Rajendra Prasad Dhakal v Government of Nepal, Ministry of Home Affairs and others* (Divisional Bench of the Supreme Court of Nepal), 1 June 2002 (2008) 14 Asian YBIL 191–2.
[159] See, eg, UN Commission on Human Rights (n 149) [37]–[50]; OHCHR (n 145) 153.
[160] L Arimatsu, 'The Democratic Republic of Congo: 1993–2010' in E Wilmshurst (ed), *International Law and the Classification of Conflicts* (OUP, Oxford 2012) 147–8.
[161] Ibid.

integrating procedural guarantees or for complying with minimum standards on the conditions of detention. The right to detain was also asserted by rebel groups during the Second Congo War which was clearly at odds with both domestic law and human rights law since neither envisages the right of non-state actors to detain.[162]

Space prevents a full discussion of detention practices during each conflict period. However, practices during the latter two periods are indicative of the general issues here. Thus, during the Second Congo War,[163] the UN Special Rapporteur on the DRC noted that there were a number of different armed conflicts, of varying characters, on the territory of the DRC, including non-international conflicts between the government of the DRC on the one hand and the *Rassemblement Congolais pour la Démocratie* (RCD) and *Mouvement national pour la libération du Congo* (MLC) rebel groups on the other.[164] Reports of arbitrary detentions carried out by the DRC government during this period were common.[165] Indeed, the UN Special Rapporteur referred to the right to liberty as 'one of the least respected rights' in the DRC during this period and that '[p]olitical leaders, activists, union leaders, journalists, soldiers, students, traditional chiefs, priests and pastors, attorneys acting in their professional capacity and refugees are constantly being arrested for no apparent reason'.[166] Whilst often no justification was given for detentions, '[t]he reason most often cited [was] collusion with the rebels'.[167] The Special Rapporteur examined the legality of these detentions against the IHRL standards, criticizing, for example, the failure of the government to take all detainees promptly before a judge to determine the legality of their detention.[168]

The final period in Aritmatsu's study followed the establishment of the transitional government and the fighting thereafter between the government on the one hand and the *Congrès national pour la défense du peuple* (CNDP) and *Forces démocratiques de libération du Rwanda* (FDLR) rebel groups on the other.[169] This has been treated by both Kinshasa and external observers as constituting a non-international armed conflict.[170] Once again, reports of arbitrary detentions by the government during this period were widespread and condemned by the international community.[171] As with all previous periods, the standards against which

---

[162] Ibid, 199–200.   [163] On this period, see ibid, 167–85.
[164] UN General Assembly, 'Report of the Special Rapporteur on the Situation of Human Rights in the Democratic Republic of the Congo pursuant to General Assembly Resolution 53/160 and Commission on Human Rights Resolution 1999/56', A/54/361, 17 September 1999, [20]. Although there was no clear indication of Kinshasa's view of the character of the conflicts during this period, it seems that they operated on the assumption that those involving the MLC and RCD constituted non-international armed conflicts: Arimatsu (n 160) 172.
[165] See, eg, UN Security Council, 'Second Report of the Secretary-General on United Nations Mission in the Democratic Republic of the Congo', S/2000/330, 18 April 2000, [55].
[166] 'Report of the Special Rapporteur' (n 164) [50].   [167] Ibid.   [168] Ibid.
[169] On this period, see Arimatsu (n 160) 185–96.
[170] See ibid, 189; Amnesty International, 'Written Submission to the Human Rights Council', A/HRC/S-8/NGO/1, 27 November 2008; UN Security Council, 'Presidential Statement on the Situation Concerning the DRC', S/PRST/2008/38, 21 October 2008.
[171] See, eg, UNGA Res 58/196 (2004) [2(e)] (on human rights in the DRC, condemning arbitrary detentions as a violation); Human Rights Council, 'Report of the High Commissioner on the Situation of Human Rights and the Activities of Her Office in the Democratic Republic of the Congo', A/HRC/10/58, 1 March 2009, [39]–[44]; Human Rights Council, 'Third Joint Report of

these detentions were judged were those under IHRL. The HRC, for example, in its concluding observations on the DRC, whilst acknowledging the existence of a non-international armed conflict,[172] nonetheless required that all deprivations of liberty meet the stipulations under Article 9 ICCPR.[173] It criticized the practice of lengthy detentions without warrant or trial,[174] as well as arbitrary detentions by the government security forces.[175]

The detentions carried out by the DRC in relation to these conflicts were, therefore, constantly reviewed by external observers against the ordinarily applicable rules of IHRL. It is clear that the DRC's detention practices did not satisfy these requirements, most notably due to the absence of clear, reasonable grounds for detention and the lack of judicial review.[176] Indeed, such detentions would also fail to comply with the less demanding GCIV rules.[177] Importantly for our purposes, the DRC nonetheless recognized that IHRL continued to govern its detention operations. In its periodic report to the HRC, the DRC noted that it had made no derogation nor declared any state of emergency, concluding that, 'the Democratic Republic of the Congo remained under an ordinary law regime'.[178] There was no suggestion, therefore, that the DRC's detention practices during these non-international conflicts were not subject to the procedural rules under IHRL.

5.2.1.5 Conclusions on traditional non-international armed conflicts

The preceding sections have all discussed the detention practices of states involved in traditional (internal) non-international armed conflicts. As explained in section 5.1.3, in order to rebut the presumption that IHRL applies to detentions in relation to non-international conflicts, a clear, general practice excluding their application or modifying their content would have to be demonstrated. The above practice has, in fact, shown the opposite to be true: states and international bodies have consistently operated in a manner that suggests the presumption remains. Of particular value in demonstrating this are the examples of states that have specifically derogated from Article 9 ICCPR as a result of a non-international armed conflict, confirming their view that that provision would apply in full but for the derogation. Indeed, there are many other examples, in addition to those explored

---

Seven United Nations Experts on the Democratic Republic of the Congo', A/HRC/16/68, 3 March 2011, [9].

[172] HRC, 'Concluding Observations: Democratic Republic of the Congo', CCPR/C/COD/CO/3, 26 April 2006, [13].
[173] Ibid, [19].   [174] Ibid.   [175] Ibid, [23].
[176] On these requirements under IHRL, see sections 4.2.1 and 4.2.3. On the DRC's non-compliance, see, eg, Amnesty International, 'DRC: Deadly Alliances in Congolese Forests', 3 December 1997, AFR 62/033/1997, 27–31; 'Report of the Special Rapporteur' (n 164) [50]; HRC (n 172) [13].
[177] See, eg, the requirement that civilian internment be necessary for security reasons and subject to periodic review in arts 42–3 and 78 GCIV. See sections sections 2.2.1 and 2.3.1.
[178] HRC, 'Third Periodic Report: Democratic Republic of the Congo', CCPR/C/COD/2005/3, 3 May 2005, [59].

5.2 State Practice in Non-Intl Armed Conflicts 173

in detail above, evidencing such a view, for example, where states have derogated from Article 9 ICCPR during what is arguably a non-international armed conflict,[179] have emphasized that they have *not* derogated in such a situation as evidence of their adherence to ordinary legal standards,[180] or more generally have not sought to exclude the application of the human rights rules on detention during non-international armed conflicts when they might have been expected to were that a legally valid option.[181] Practice does not, therefore, support the positions of those few states, cited above, that take the opposite view that IHL operates as the *lex specialis* in this area, modifying or displacing the human rights rules.[182] Indeed, those views were expressed in response to draft reports by both the UN Working Group on Arbitrary Detention and the HRC in which the applicability of the human rights rules on detention to non-international armed conflicts was reiterated; it is noteworthy that none of the other states that submitted comments objected to that claim.[183]

The following sections will now consider examples of non-international armed conflicts in which states operate outside their territory. It will be shown that,

---

[179] See, eg, derogations by Algeria on 19 June 1991 and 14 February 1992 from, inter alia, Art 9(3) ICCPR; derogations by Nicaragua from, inter alia, Art 9 ICCPR dated 8 June 1984, 1 August 1984, and 22 August 1984; derogation by Bahrain from, inter alia, Art 9 ICCPR dated 28 April 2011; derogations by Peru from, inter alia, Art 9 ICCPR dated 19 December 1984 and 19 March 1992 <https://treaties.un.org/pages/viewdetails.aspx?chapter=4&src=treaty&mtdsg_no=iv-4&lang=en> accessed 6 August 2015.

[180] See, eg, HRC, 'Consideration of Reports Submitted by States Parties under Article 40 of the Covenant, Initial Reports of States Parties: Djibouti', CCPR/C/CJI/1, 13 July 2012, [68] ('[d]espite the serious events that have threatened the nation, such as the civil war during the 1990s and the recent conflict with Eritrea, successive Governments have never declared a state of emergency within the meaning of article 4 of the Covenant and have always striven to honour the principles of republican law and uphold democracy throughout the territory and at all times').

[181] See, eg, HRC, Communication No 1439/2005, CCPR/C/90/D/1439/2005, 16 August 2007 (concerning the administrative detention by Algeria of a suspected member of an armed group, Algeria did not raise any claim that IHL governed or justified the detention, relying instead on domestic emergency laws; the HRC concluded that there were violations of arts 9(1) and (3) ICCPR); Human Rights Council, 2nd Report of the Independent International Commission of Inquiry, 22 February 2012, A/HRC/19/69, Annex II (containing a Note Verbale from the Syrian Arab Republic, raising no objections to the Commission's use of IHRL as a framework for judging the situation in Syria, but rather objecting to the Commission's non-application of that same framework to armed opposition groups); HRC, 'Second Periodic Report: The Philippines', CCPR/C/PHL/2002/2, 18 September 2002, [653] (confirming that detention operations by the armed forces of the Philippines in internal security situations are governed by human rights law).

[182] See above at text to nn 12–14.

[183] See, eg, HRC, 'Observations of Ireland on the draft General Comment No 35, Article 9: Liberty and security of person', 30 May 2014 and HRC, 'Japan's Comments on the draft General Comment No 35 on Article 9 of the International Covenant on Civil and Political Rights' (undated) <http://www.ohchr.org/EN/HRBodies/CCPR/Pages/DGCArticle9.aspx> accessed 6 August 2015; UNWGAD, 'Germany's comments on the "Draft Principles and Guidelines on remedies and procedures on: The right of anyone deprived of his or her liberty by arrest or detention to bring proceedings before a court without delay, in order that the court may decide without delay on the lawfulness of his or her detention and order his or her release if the detention is not lawful"' (undated) and UNWGAD, 'Permanent Mission of Greece Geneva: Note Verbale', Ref No 6171.71/13/550, 31 March 2015 <http://www.ohchr.org/EN/HRBodies/CCPR/Pages/DGCArticle9.aspx> accessed 5 August 2015.

whilst the application of the IHRL rules on detention in such situations is more controversial, it still cannot be said that the presumption of the full applicability of IHRL is displaced.

5.2.2 Extraterritorial non-international armed conflicts

5.2.2.1 Iraq (from 2003)

The initial invasion of Iraq by coalition forces in March 2003 and the subsequent military occupation constituted an international armed conflict.[184] However, following the establishment of an interim Iraqi government and handover of sovereign authority by the occupying powers in June 2004, the coalition forces operated within Iraq with the consent of the newly-established government fighting an armed conflict against insurgents; as a result, the conflict thereafter was non-international in character, a classification accepted by those involved.[185] The detention practice following this change is therefore of direct relevance to the present enquiry.

Following the transition from international to non-international armed conflict, the number of persons detained by the multi-national forces in Iraq (MNF-I) increased considerably, with 4,000 recorded in Spring 2004 and 11,350 one year later.[186] At their height in 2007, coalition forces were detaining over 26,000 persons.[187] Following the June 2004 transition, the legal basis for detention shifted from that provided by GCIII and GCIV to Security Council Resolution (SCR) 1546.[188] This empowered MNF-I 'to take all necessary measures to contribute to the maintenance of security and stability in Iraq', which was elaborated in a letter from US Secretary of State Colin Powell, annexed to the Resolution, as including 'internment where this is necessary for imperative reasons of security'.[189] This language was clearly based on the grounds established by Article 78 GCIV for

---

[184] See Schmitt (n 70) 358–67.
[185] Ibid, 368–9 (confirming that both US and UK officials accepted this classification); *HM, RM, HF v the Secretary of State for the Home Department* [2012] UKUT 409 (IAC), [36] and *Regina v Gul* [2012] EWCA Crim 280, [20] (noting the UK government's acceptance that the situation in Iraq constituted a non-international armed conflict). Also confirming this change in the classification of the conflict, see: UNSC Res 1546 (2004); ICRC, 'Iraq post 28 June 2004: protecting persons deprived of freedom remains a priority' (5 August 2004) <http://www.icrc.org/eng/resources/documents/misc/63kkj8.htm> accessed 6 August 2015. Although cf AE Wall, 'Civilian Detentions in Iraq' in MN Schmitt and J Pejic (eds), *International Law and Armed Conflict: Exploring the Faultlines* (Brill, The Hague 2007) 421–2 (arguing that the conflict remained international in character).
[186] B Graham, 'US to Expand Prison Facilities in Iraq', *Washington Post* (10 May 2005) A15, cited in Wall (n 185) 414.
[187] BJ Bill, 'Detention Operations in Iraq: A View from the Ground' in RA Pedrozo (ed), *The War in Iraq: A Legal Analysis* (2010) (Vol 86, US Naval War College International Law Studies) 411.
[188] Thus, the United Kingdom relied on UNSC Res 1546 (2004) as the legal basis for its internment of Al-Jedda: *Al-Jedda* (n 5) [16]. The authorizations provided for in SCR 1546 were renewed by subsequent SCRs: see, eg, UNSC Res 1637 (2005); UNSC Res 1723 (2006); UNSC Res 1790 (2007).
[189] UNSC Res 1546 (2004), Annex.

5.2 State Practice in Non-Intl Armed Conflicts 175

civilian internment in occupied territory, which was the applicable regime preceding the transition. Indeed, Michael Schmitt noted that 'the transition had little practical influence on operational matters for US forces'.[190] However, following expiration of Security Council authorization in December 2008, any detentions by coalition forces had to be authorized by the Iraqi government in accordance with domestic Iraqi criminal law and human rights law.[191] As noted by Brian Bill, 'the Security Agreement [between Iraq and the United States following expiration of UN authorization] moved away from the "imperative threat" administrative internment model to one that is based on criminal detention overseen by the Iraqi judiciary'.[192]

In elaborating the 'imperative reasons of security' standard in SCR 1546, guidance was issued to coalition forces, and the following non-exhaustive list of examples where this standard would be satisfied has been offered:

…attacks on Coalition Forces; interference with the mission accomplishment or movement of Coalition Forces; entering or attempting to enter a restricted area; illegal weapons possession; or committing, attempting, conspiring, threatening or soliciting another to commit/aid/abet the commission of a serious crime against Coalition Forces. Additionally, members of terrorist organizations or insurgent groups known to carry out attacks on Coalition Forces could also be detained for imperative reasons of security.[193]

Whilst the 'imperative reasons of security' standard is taken from the conduct-based civilian internment regimes in GCIV, the final sentence of the above quote implies that members of armed groups could be detained solely on the basis of that membership. Moreover, '[o]fficially, individuals could be detained for their intelligence value for no more than 72 hours; however, anecdotal evidence suggested that longer intelligence detentions were common'.[194] It was argued in chapter 2 that both status-based internment and internment on the basis of intelligence value are incompatible with the GCIV standards, and, given that SCR 1546 sought to extend that standard to the non-international conflict in Iraq, these practices should be seen equally as incompatible with the internment authority established by that resolution.[195]

The procedures for internment review during the non-international conflict phase were similarly based on GCIV.[196] On 27 June 2004, the Coalition Provisional Authority (CPA) issued a revised version of the review process elaborating the new authorization for internment under SCR 1546.[197] That memorandum

---

[190] Schmitt (n 70) 379. Similarly, see *R (on the application of Al-Jedda) (FC) (Appellant) v Secretary of State for Defence (Respondent)* [2007] UKHL 58, [32].
[191] Schmitt (n 70) 379 (also noting the problems that arose as a result).
[192] Bill (n 187) 416–7. Similarly, see D Webber, 'Preventive Detention in the Law of Armed Conflict: Throwing Away the Key?' (2012) 6 J Nat Sec L & Ply 167, 194.
[193] Wall (n 185) 430–1.   [194] Ibid, 431.   [195] Section 2.2.1.
[196] Bill (n 187) 416.
[197] CPA Memorandum No 3 (Revised), CPA/MEM/27 June 2004/03, available at <http://www.iraqcoalition.org/regulations/20040627_CPAMEMO_3_Criminal_Procedures__Rev_.pdf> accessed 6 August 2015.

required, inter alia, that any detainee held for longer than seventy-two hours have their detention reviewed within seven days, with periodic reviews at least every six months.[198] Furthermore, it stated that no internee could be held for longer than imperative reasons of security demand, and any person must either be released or transferred to Iraqi criminal jurisdiction within eighteen months.[199] Where, for imperative reasons of security, it was considered that internment should last longer than eighteen months, an application was required to the Joint Detention Committee, comprising senior representatives of the MNF, interim Iraqi government and the UK ambassador.[200]

More detailed rules were elaborated by individual coalition members. For US detainees, for example, a military magistrate reviewed the case of those held for more than seventy-two hours to determine whether a reasonable basis existed for believing they posed an imperative threat to security.[201] However, release could only be ordered by the MNF-I Deputy Commanding General for Detention Operations.[202] If detention continued, the detainee's case was considered for criminal prosecution in Iraq.[203] If the facts justifying internment did not constitute a criminal offence under Iraqi law, or if there was insufficient evidence, the detainee was forwarded to the Combined Review and Release Board (CRRB), comprising nine members (three MNF-I officers from the military police, military intelligence and a judge advocate, and six representatives from the Iraqi government); this performed an initial appeal of the magistrate's decision within ninety days and six-monthly periodic reviews thereafter, to determine whether the detainee was considered an imperative threat to security.[204] The MNF-I Deputy Commanding General for Detention Operations had the final say on release, although 'CRRB recommendations to release were followed over 99% of the time'.[205]

The CRRB was criticized for the brevity of its consideration of cases, spending 'no more than a couple of minutes on each'.[206] Detainees also had no right to appear.[207] These deficiencies led to the creation of the Multi-National Force Review Committee (MNFRC), which performed periodic reviews: 'The single biggest innovation was that the detainee was to appear before the board and participate in the hearing.'[208] The procedures for Article 5 GCIII tribunals were applied to the MNFRC by analogy, comprising three members (a senior officer presiding, with one of the other members being a 'senior enlisted person').[209] The detainee could raise any evidence they wished, make a statement, and challenge the evidence against them.[210] The board then voted by majority on whether it considered them an imperative threat to security.[211] The final say over release remained with the Deputy Commanding General for Detention Operations.[212] The MNFRC process was continually refined, for example, by offering personal representatives (to assist but not advocate) to certain detainees appearing before the Committee (especially juvenile detainees), following an ICRC recommendation.[213]

[198] Ibid, ss 6(1)–(3). [199] Ibid, s 6(5). [200] Ibid, s 6(6).
[201] Wall (n 185) 433. [202] Ibid, 431. [203] Ibid, 433. [204] Ibid, 433–4.
[205] Ibid, 434. [206] Ibid, 436. [207] Bill (n 187) 428. [208] Ibid.
[209] Ibid, 430. [210] Ibid, 431. [211] Ibid. [212] Ibid. [213] Ibid, 433–4.

The US' internment regime was clearly modelled on that for civilian internees applicable in international armed conflict.[214] Thus, internment was permitted for 'imperative reasons of security' and was subject to initial and periodic administrative review. This analogy to GCIV was similarly the approach taken by other coalition members.[215] That said, the reviewing authorities, such as the CRRB, would not satisfy the GCIV requirements, according to the ICTY's interpretation, as they did not have the power to order release.[216] Nonetheless, the analogy was clearly drawn to the internment regimes applicable under IHL in international armed conflicts, rather than the more protective (judicial) procedures under IHRL. For the United States, IHRL was not 'the controlling body of law' with respect to its detention operations in Iraq.[217] The United States had previously taken the view that its international human rights obligations prima facie apply neither extraterritorially nor in armed conflict.[218] The extraterritoriality of the human rights rules on detention will be explored in section 6.2, and it will be shown there that practice confirms the continued application of those rules when states detain persons outside their territory. Regarding application in armed conflict, as already explained, the US' view has since concretized into an acceptance of the prima facie applicability of IHRL in armed conflict, subject to IHL as the *lex specialis*.[219] This is precisely the question under consideration in this chapter, and it was explained above that, if state practice is to establish that a human rights treaty provision does not apply in situations to which it appears applicable, there must be clear acceptance by all other states parties, and only then can the default legal position of the parallel application of IHL and IHRL be said to have been rebutted.[220] It is clear from the preceding sections on practice in traditional non-international armed conflicts that the fact that a situation reaches the threshold of a non-international armed conflict does not itself affect the application of a state's human rights treaty obligations. Even if that is accepted, however, it might nonetheless be argued that in the context of *extraterritorial* non-international armed conflicts, a different conclusion should be reached.[221] Indeed, it is particularly in such contexts that certain other states noted above, such as the United Kingdom and Australia, have recently advanced the claim that IHL operates as

---

[214] Ibid, 416.
[215] See, eg, the details of the UK's internment regime in Iraq, discussed in *Al-Jedda* (n 5) at [11]–[13].
[216] *Delalić* (n 140) [329].   [217] See above at text to n 12.
[218] See, eg, HRC, 'Third Periodic Reports of States Parties Due in 2003: United States of America', CCPR/C/USA/3, 28 November 2005, [130]; P Alston, J Morgan-Foster, and W Abresch, 'The Competence of the UN Human Rights Council and its Special Procedures in Relation to Armed Conflicts: Extrajudicial Executions in the "War on Terror"' (2008) 19 EJIL 183, 185–90.
[219] HRC, 'Fourth Periodic Report: United States of America' (n 5) [506]–[507].
[220] See section 5.1.3.
[221] ICRC, Strengthening International Humanitarian Law, Protecting Persons Deprived of their Liberty: Thematic Consultation of Government Experts on Grounds and Procedures for Internment and Detainee Transfers, Montreux, Switzerland, 20–22 October 2014, 11–12 (noting that internment is more likely in an extraterritorial setting than in a conflict at home); *Serdar Mohammed* (n 93) [167]–[173] (noting this possibility).

the *lex specialis* with regard to detention in non-international armed conflict.[222] Moreover, like the United States, other coalition forces in Iraq did not derogate from their human rights treaty obligations notwithstanding that they too adopted internment regimes, including the United Kingdom.[223] States have never derogated with respect to military operations abroad, and this has been claimed to indicate a general consensus that human rights treaties do not apply generally in such situations.[224]

However, practice of other states in the context of extraterritorial non-international armed conflicts does not support these views, but instead confirms the continued relevance of IHRL. Germany, for example, has made explicit its view that, for persons detained by their armed forces in military operations abroad, human rights treaty obligations, including the ICCPR and ECHR, continue to apply.[225] Moreover, amongst those troop-contributing nations to MNF-I, practice of certain states other than the United States also supports the view that their human rights treaty obligations are applicable in such situations. The Netherlands, for example, has explicitly clarified, with respect to extraterritorial military operations, that 'in addition to the rules of international humanitarian law, international human rights norms – insofar as they cannot be suspended in emergency situations – should also apply without restriction during armed conflicts' and that 'the undeniable importance of keeping potential combatants away from the battlefield cannot entail that detainees are held for an unlimited period and without due process'.[226] Furthermore, the United Kingdom's claims referenced above regarding the overruling or setting aside of Article 9 ICCPR in non-international armed conflicts are in fact a recent change from its previous position. Thus, the United Kingdom previously confirmed that the ICCPR

---

[222] See, eg, *Serdar Mohammed* (n 93); UNWGAD, 'Australia Permanent Mission to the UN Geneva' (n 93) [9].
[223] *Al-Jedda* (n 5) [11]–[13] (describing the UK's internment regime in Iraq).
[224] Dennis (n 3) 477.
[225] Germany, Bundestag, Reply by the Federal Government to the Minor Interpellation by the Members Winfried Nachtwei, Alexander Bonde, Volker Beck (Cologne), further Members and the Parliamentary Group Bündnis 90/Die Grünen—BT-Drs 16/6174, Basic Law and international law in deployments abroad of the Federal Armed Forces: treatment of Persons Taken into Custody, BT-Drs 16/6282, 29 August 2007, 5–13 (for persons detained in military operations abroad, 'the existing international law obligations of the Federal Republic of Germany, such as Geneva Convention III, the International Covenant on Civil and Political Rights (ICCPR) or the European Convention for the Protection of Human Rights (ECHR) as well as constitutional law parameters are implemented'), cited in ICRC, Customary IHL Database: Practice Relating to Rule 99 Deprivation of Liberty (British Red Cross/ICRC) <https://www.icrc.org/customary-ihl/eng/docs/v2_rul_rule99> accessed 6 August 2015. Similarly, see Human Rights Council, 'Report of the Working Group on UPR: United Kingdom', 23 May 2008, A/HRC/8/25, [33] (Switzerland) ('[w]ith regard to the armed forces of the United Kingdom abroad, it [Switzerland] noted the report of the United Kingdom that its obligations on human rights "may" apply and that the applicable provisions of the ECHR need to be qualified to take into account decisions of Security Council resolutions under Chapter VII of the United Nations Charter. Switzerland recommended that the United Kingdom consider that any person detained by armed forces is under the jurisdiction of that State, which should respect its obligations concerning the human rights of such individuals').
[226] Tange, 'Netherlands State Practice' (n 4) 336.

applied to detainees held abroad in military detention.[227] Moreover, in *Al-Jedda v UK*, regarding the UK's detention practices in Iraq, the government did not dispute the prima facie applicability of Article 5 ECHR to detentions conducted in the context of the non-international armed conflict there; its arguments, rather, were based solely on the attribution of the internment to the UN and the relevance of Article 103 of the UN Charter.[228] At no point, however, did the United Kingdom suggest that the character of the situation as an extraterritorial non-international armed conflict affected the application of Article 5 ECHR. Such arguments are, instead, a recent innovation in the UK's *opinio iuris*, and, at the time of writing, remain under appeal before English courts.[229] As argued above, the structure of human rights treaty obligations are such that the minimum standards they prescribe enjoy greater protection against attempts to lower them compared with reciprocal obligations.[230] Consequently, for the US' practice, as well as the UK's more recent practice, to be considered valid, one would need to demonstrate its acceptance by other states parties to the ICCPR and ECHR, which, it is clear, cannot at present be met.

It is finally to be noted that international bodies have confirmed that the detention operations of coalition forces in Iraq, including the United States, were regulated in full by those states' international human rights obligations.[231] It cannot, therefore, be concluded that practice in Iraq rebuts the presumption that the IHRL rules on detention applied to the non-international armed conflict there.

5.2.2.2 *Afghanistan (post-2001)*

With the US-led invasion into Afghanistan in October 2001, an international armed conflict began between the coalition forces on the one hand and Afghanistan (with the Taliban as the *de facto* government) on the other.[232] However, by most accounts, the conflict subsequently became non-international in character, following the holding of the Loya Jirga in Kabul and the establishment of the Afghan Transitional Government in June 2002.[233] This characterization has been accepted by the states involved.[234]

---

[227] HRC, 'Information Received from UK on the Implementation of the Concluding Observations', CCPR/C/GBR/CO/6/Add.1, 3 November 2009, [24].

[228] *Al-Jedda* (n 5) is discussed in detail in section 6.1.2.

[229] At the time of writing, the UK government's claims here have been rejected both at first instance and in the Court of Appeal: see *Serdar Mohammed* (n 5); *Serdar Mohammed* (n 93).

[230] See above at text to nn 109–12.

[231] UNSC, Report of Secretary-General Pursuant to Paragraph 30 of Resolution 1546 (2004), S/2005/373, 7 June 2005, [72]; HRC, 'Concluding Observations of the Human Rights Committee: United States of America', CCPR/C/USA/CO/3, 15 September 2006, [18]; UN Assistance Mission for Iraq (n 76) [72]; *Al-Jedda* (n 5).

[232] A Cole, 'Legal Issues in Forming the Coalition' in M Schmitt (ed), *The War in Afghanistan: A Legal Analysis* (2009) (Vol 85, US Naval War College International Law Studies).

[233] R Geiß and M Siegrist, 'Has the Armed Conflict in Afghanistan Affected the Rules on the Conduct of Hostilities?' (2011) 93 IRRC 11, 13–14.

[234] F Hampson, 'Afghanistan 2001–2010' in E Wilmshurst (ed), *International Law and the Classification of Conflicts* (OUP, Oxford 2012) 255 (noting that this has been accepted by the United

Amongst the coalition states, the US operated the most developed internment regime in Afghanistan. The legal basis for detention during the non-international armed conflict phase varied depending on whether it was part of Operation Enduring Freedom (OEF) or the International Security Assistance Force (ISAF). Operations in the context of ISAF arguably derived their authority (including the authority to detain for ninety-six hours) from Security Council resolutions and agreement with the Afghan government,[235] though, as noted in section 3.1, the vague 'all necessary measures' typical of Chapter VII resolutions could be problematic for complying with the human rights requirement of a legal basis to detain.[236] This is in contrast to SCR 1546, which explicitly referred to 'internment for imperative reasons of security' in the context of Iraq.[237] Regarding operations outside the context of ISAF, as Stephane Ojeda notes, there was no clear legal basis for detentions by states, given the absence of Security Council authorization or clear agreement with the Afghan authorities.[238] Whilst certain states have relied on either IHL[239] or the general right of self-defence under Article 51 of the Charter of the United Nations (UNC)[240] as providing a legal basis to intern in Afghanistan, it was demonstrated in section 3.1 that these claims find insufficient support under international law.

The grounds for detention applied by the United States were re-stated in a July 2010 memo, which confirmed that those subject to detention were persons who:

...planned, authorized, committed, or aided the terrorist attacks that occurred on September 11, 2001, and persons who harboured those responsible for those attacks...

Kingdom, the United States, and Germany); *GS (Existence of Internal Armed Conflict) Afghanistan v Secretary of State for the Home Department*, CG [2009] UKAIT 00010, cited in Hampson, ibid and *Regina v Gul* (n 185) [20] (the UK government stating its view that a non-international armed conflict exists in Afghanistan).

[235] UNSC Res 1707 (2006), [2]; PC Tange, 'Netherlands State Practice' (2009) 40 NYIL 249, 326; *Serdar Mohammed* (n 5) [218] (on the UK's position that relevant SCRs authorized detention in Afghanistan). Similarly, see C Greenwood, 'International Law Framework for the Treatment of Persons Detained in Afghanistan by Canadian Forces', [18], Report submitted to the Federal Court of Canada in *Amnesty International Canada and British Columbia Civil Liberties Association v Chief of the Defence Staff for the Canadian Forces, Minister of National Defense and Attorney-General of Canada*, Judgment, 12 March 2008, [2008] FC 336; MC Waxman, 'The Law of Armed Conflict and Detention Operations in Afghanistan' in MN Schmitt (ed), *The War in Afghanistan: A Legal Analysis* (2009) (Vol 85, US Naval War College International Law Studies) 345; S Ojeda, 'US Detention of Taliban Fighters: Some Legal Considerations' in MN Schmitt (ed), *The War in Afghanistan: A Legal Analysis* (2009) (Vol 85, US Naval War College International Law Studies) 365.

[236] Though see *Serdar Mohammed* (n 5) [218]–[219] (the first instance judge accepting that the authorization of 'all necessary measures' in SCRs did permit ISAF to capture rather than kill enemies, but rejecting that this also provided a legal basis for long-term detention). Cf the view of the Court of Appeal that the SCRs were, in principle, sufficient to authorize long-term detention: *Serdar Mohammed* (n 93) [143]–[148].

[237] See section 5.2.2.1.

[238] Ojeda (n 235) 365; *Serdar Mohammed* (n 93). Cf JA Bovarnick, 'Detainee Review Boards in Afghanistan: From Strategic Liability to Legitimacy' [June 2010] The Army Lawyer 9, 22.

[239] See, eg, the UK's arguments in *Serdar Mohammed* (n 5) [232] (relying on IHL as providing a legal basis to detain in non-international armed conflict).

[240] See, eg, United States, Speech by the Legal Advisor, US Department of State, 'The Obama Administration and International Law', ASIL, Washington, DC, 25 March 2010 <http://www.state.gov/s/l/releases/remarks/139119.htm> accessed 30 July 2015.

[and] persons who were part of, or substantially supported, Taliban or al-Qaida forces or associated forces that are engaged in hostilities against the United States or its coalition partners, including any person who has committed a belligerent act, or has directly supported hostilities, in aid of such enemy armed forces.[241]

As with the detention standard in Iraq, this contains both conduct and status-based elements.[242] Moreover, it appears heavily focused on past behaviour rather than present or future security threat, on which the IHL internment regimes applicable in international armed conflicts are premised.[243] Whilst past behaviour may be relevant in considering present or future threat, undue focus on this risks internment being retributive rather than preventive, which in turn increases the possibility of indefinite detention. Where detention is considered necessary in response to past acts, the criminal justice system should be used.[244]

Internment review was carried out by various administrative boards established and replaced by the United States over time.[245] Each comprised a board of military officers reviewing the detainee's status without the detainee present or able to make submissions.[246] By 2006 all cases were taken before an Enemy Combatant Review Board (ECRB), comprising five officers, within seventy-five days.[247] The ECRB would recommend to the commanding general by majority vote whether the individual should continue to be detained.[248] Where detention continued, the ECRB performed six-monthly periodic reviews.[249]

In September 2009, the Obama Administration introduced a new system for detainee review at Bagram (now Parwan) airbase, known as Detainee Review Boards (DRBs).[250] Under the DRB process, detainees were to receive 'timely notice' of the facts justifying internment.[251] Within sixty days they were to be given an initial review, to be repeated thereafter every six months.[252] DRBs consisted of three officers, and 'no board members will be among those directly involved in the detainee's capture or transfer'.[253] Detainees had personal representatives (PRs) whose job it was to present the facts in the most favourable light for the detainee.[254] Both hearsay and classified evidence were admissible, the latter discussed in closed session which the detainee could not attend and shown to the PR who was not allowed to discuss it with the detainee.[255] During

---

[241] Memorandum from Robert Harward, Vice Admiral, US Navy, Deputy Commander, Detention Operations, US Department of Defense, to US Military Forces Conducting Detention Operations in Afghanistan (July 19, 2010) 2, cited in Human Rights First, *Detained and Denied in Afghanistan: How to Make U.S. Detention Comply with the Law* (Human Rights First, New York, May 2011) 10 (fn 45).
[242] This approach will be evaluated in chapter 7 when discussing the *lex ferenda*.
[243] See section 2.2.   [244] Pejic (n 71) 381.   [245] Human Rights First (n 241) 7.
[246] Ibid.   [247] Waxman (n 235) 350.   [248] Ibid.   [249] Ibid.
[250] Hampson (n 234) 269.
[251] US Department of Defense, 'Memorandum for US Military Forces Conducting Detention Operations in Afghanistan: Detainee Review Board Policy Memorandum' (11 July 2010) 6 [11] <http://www.politico.com/pdf/PPM205_bagrambrfb.pdf> accessed 6 August 2015.
[252] Ibid, 2 [7].   [253] Ibid, 3 [9a] and 3 [9a(4)].   [254] Ibid, 4–5 [9e].
[255] Ibid, 8 [12i(6)] and 7 [12h].

unclassified sessions, the detainee was permitted to attend and present evidence, including witnesses.[256] The DRB used a 'preponderance of the evidence standard' and determined, first, 'whether the criteria for internment are met' and, if so, 'whether internment is necessary to mitigate the threat posed by the detainee, by taking into account the detainee's potential for rehabilitation, reconciliation, and eventual reintegration into society'.[257] However, the 'Commander [of Detention Operations in Afghanistan], or his designee, [was] the [final] approval authority for the transfer or release of detainees in Afghanistan'.[258]

As in Iraq, the US' internment regime in Afghanistan was clearly modelled on GCIV rather than IHRL.[259] This is demonstrated most clearly by the initial and periodic administrative review procedures for internees.[260] However, whilst certain features of the DRB process went further than would be required under GCIV (eg by providing a PR and the right to call witnesses), once again, the absence of a power to order release by the DRB would fall short of GCIV, were that Convention applicable as law.[261] As with its position regarding Iraq, the United States took the view that IHRL was inapplicable to its detention operations in the non-international armed conflict in Afghanistan, given its rejection of the extraterritorial application of human rights treaties and its view regarding the *lex specialis* nature of IHL generally in armed conflict.[262] Moreover, it is in the particular context of the non-international armed conflict in Afghanistan that the UK's views have changed in the manner described above, such that now it too considers IHL to be the *lex specialis* with respect to detention, modifying or displacing applicable IHRL.[263] It was demonstrated above, however, that the practice of other states does not support this view of IHRL as being inapplicable to detentions in the context of extraterritorial non-international armed conflicts.[264] Indeed, in the context of Afghanistan, other members of the coalition, particularly those party to the ECHR, were reluctant to intern, due to their concern that they would be held responsible for violating Article 5 ECHR; they consequently held individuals for security reasons only up to ninety-six hours, after which they would either be transferred to a coalition partner (the United States or Afghanistan) or released.[265] The same approach

---

[256] Ibid, 7 [12h] and [12i].   [257] Ibid, 2 [6c] and 8 [12n].   [258] Ibid, 11 [13a].
[259] Waxman (n 235) 348–9.
[260] Section 1024 of the National Defense Authorization Act 2012, HR 1540, introduced a new rule that persons not entitled to the constitutional writ of *habeas corpus* must have a status determination by a military judge. US federal courts rejected *habeas* jurisdiction over Bagram detainees and, as such, s 1024 applied to them: *Fadi Al Maqaleh et al v Robert Gates et al*, 605 F.3d 84 (2010) (DC Cir Ct).
[261] *Delalić* (n 140) [329].   [262] Hampson (n 234) 265–6.
[263] *Serdar Mohammed* (n 93) [109].   [264] See above at text to nn 225–9.
[265] S Pomper, 'Human Rights Obligations, Armed Conflict and Afghanistan: Looking Back Before Looking Ahead' in MN Schmitt (ed), *The War in Afghanistan: A Legal Analysis* (2009) (International Law Studies, Vol 85) 535; Hampson (n 234) 271. In 2009, the United Kingdom departed from the ISAF policy of ninety-six hours and introduced a policy of holding certain persons beyond this point for logistical or intelligence reasons, and it was this that sparked the *Serdar Mohammed* litigation: see *Serdar Mohammed* (n 5) [46]–[53].

can be seen in other extraterritorial non-international armed conflicts, such as France's support of the Malian government against certain armed groups in the North, during which France did not intern captured persons, but rather handed them over to the Malian authorities for the purpose of prosecution.[266] More generally, other coalition members made clear their view that IHRL applied to detainees held in Afghanistan.[267] Indeed, international bodies have consistently criticized the US' detention operations in Afghanistan for their failure to comply with IHRL.[268] The Afghan government similarly does not appear to dispute the applicability of IHRL to its detention operations in the non-international conflict; the problem, rather, lies with implementation of and adherence to those rules.[269] Indeed, 'Afghan law does not appear to permit indefinite detention for national security reasons', with only the criminal justice system officially available.[270] Once again, therefore, the practice of those few states which suggests the non-applicability of human rights law to detentions in extraterritorial non-international armed conflicts does not find clear support from other states.

5.2.2.3 Conclusions on extraterritorial non-international armed conflicts

The above sections confirm that, whilst there is some practice endorsing the view that IHRL does not regulate detentions in the context of extraterritorial non-international conflicts, other practice supports the default position of the parallel application of IHL and IHRL. Given that that default position was shown only to be rebutted where one could infer a clear agreement to that effect amongst all states parties to the relevant human rights treaties, the conclusion must be that the default position accurately reflects existing international law.

Before moving on to the final category of so-called 'transnational armed conflicts', the relevance of the Copenhagen Process to this discussion should briefly

---

[266] See *French Forces Detain Suspects in Mali U.N. Attack*, Reuters, 19 October 2014 <http://www.reuters.com/article/2014/10/19/us-mali-un-idUSKCN0I80OH20141019> accessed 24 June 2015; B Chesney, 'What Happens to Captured Persons in Mali?', *Lawfare* Blog, 1 May 2013 <http://www.lawfareblog.com/what-happens-captured-persons-mali> accessed 24 June 2015.

[267] See, eg, Germany, Bundestag (n 225) 5–13 (in response to a question on the applicable protections for persons detained in the context of OEF and ISAF: '...the protection of human rights has always been and is a formative element especially also of the Federal Armed Forces' deployments abroad').

[268] See, eg, UN Commission on Human Rights, 'Situation of Detainees at Guantanamo Bay' (n 72) [24]; Human Rights First (n 241) 13–19.

[269] Hampson (n 234) 272.

[270] Webber (n 192) 190; G Rona, 'Is There a Way Out of the Non-International Armed Conflict Detention Dilemma?' (2015) 91 Intl L Stud 32, 51. That said, with the end of official US military operations and the handover of detainees from the United States to Afghanistan, it does appear that certain persons continued to be held by Afghanistan outside the criminal justice system on the basis of executive decision: Regional Policy Institute, 'Remaking Bagram: The Creation of an Afghan Internment Regime and the Divide over US Detention Power' (Open Society Foundations, 6 September 2012).

be considered. The states involved in the Copenhagen Process set out principles and guidelines to regulate detention in international military operations, which included, inter alia, extraterritorial non-international armed conflicts.[271] As noted in chapter 3, these were clearly based on the GCIV internment regime rather than human rights standards, evidenced, for example, by the initial and periodic administrative review procedures.[272] The fact of a multilateral process in which procedural rules on detention are set out for these situations might be thought to buttress the argument referred to above, that, even if human rights law operates as the governing regime in internal non-international conflicts, it might be different in *extraterritorial* non-international armed conflicts. Indeed, in its response to the draft report of the UN Working Group on Arbitrary Detention, in which the applicability of Article 9 ICCPR to detentions in non-international armed conflicts was affirmed,[273] Australia explicitly stated that the Copenhagen Principles reflect its view of the governing standards applicable to detention in such situations, implying that they consider IHRL to be set aside (or modified) here.[274]

However, as explained in chapter 3, the Copenhagen Principles themselves make clear throughout that they are not intended to affect the legal obligations of states nor to reflect the *opinio iuris* of the participating states.[275] Moreover, it is here again that the nature of human rights treaties as comprising obligations *erga omnes partes* is important, as it reminds us that, for the Copenhagen Principles to reflect an authoritative interpretation of the applicability of IHRL in extraterritorial non-international armed conflicts, all states parties to the relevant human rights treaties would have to acquiesce. The practice noted above of states such as Germany and the Netherlands, both of whom participated in the Copenhagen Process, makes clear the continued importance of human rights law and thus confirms that no such agreement to displace or modify those rules can be said to exist.[276] It is important in this respect that no similar point with regard to the Copenhagen Principles, or the application of the human rights rules on detention in extraterritorial non-international conflicts more generally, was raised in any other state response to the UN Working Group's draft report.[277]

---

[271] 'The Copenhagen Process on the Handling of Detainees in International Military Operations, The Copenhagen Process: Principles and Guidelines' (October 2012) (hereinafter 'Copenhagen Principles') and 'Chairman's Commentary to the Copenhagen Process: Principles and Guidelines' (hereinafter 'Chairman's Commentary') <http://um.dk/en/-/media/UM/English-site/Documents/Politics-and-diplomacy/Copenhangen%20Process%20Principles%20and%20Guidelines.pdf> accessed 2 August 2015.
[272] See Copenhagen Principles (n 271) Principle 12.
[273] UNWGAD (n 76) [45]–[48] (for the wording on this in the final report).
[274] UNWGAD, 'Australia Permanent Mission to the UN Geneva' (n 93) [9].
[275] Copenhagen Principles (n 271) preambular [2]; Chairman's Commentary (n 271) [16.2].
[276] See above at text to nn 225–9.   [277] See, eg, those state responses cited above at n 183.

5.2.3 Transnational armed conflicts

5.2.3.1 US conflict with al-Qaeda

The US' conflict with al-Qaeda, although concentrated mostly in Afghanistan since 9/11, has included operations conducted in Pakistan, Yemen, and Somalia.[278] Whilst the legal nature of the hostilities between the United States and al-Qaeda has always been the subject of controversy,[279] US courts and the Obama Administration consider them to constitute a single, global non-international armed conflict.[280] The US' detention practice is, therefore, relevant to the present enquiry.

Beyond the detention of persons in Afghanistan and Iraq, the majority of those detained as part of this conflict were held by the US Department of Defense at the US Naval Base in Guantánamo Bay, Cuba. As will become clear, the procedural frameworks gradually adopted by the United States to govern these detentions, as with those in Iraq and Afghanistan, have been based on the IHL regimes applicable in international armed conflicts. Regarding the legal basis and grounds for detention, both the Bush and Obama Administrations relied on Congress' September 2001 authorization to the President

> ...to use all necessary and appropriate force against those nations, organizations, or persons he determines planned, authorized, committed, or aided the terrorist attacks that occurred on September 11, 2001, or harbored such organizations or persons, in order to prevent any future acts of international terrorism against the United States by such nations, organizations or persons.[281]

The US Supreme Court has held that this is a sufficient legal basis for detentions in the conflict with al-Qaeda (as a matter of domestic law).[282] However, given the extraterritorial nature of this conflict, whether this could also constitute a legal basis for detentions for *international law* purposes, and more specifically IHRL, is more controversial. Ordinarily, to exercise extraterritorial jurisdiction, a state would need to demonstrate a jurisdictional link to those individuals covered, lest

---

[278] S Shane, M Mazzetti and RF Worth, 'Secret Assault on Terrorism Widens on Two Continents', *The New York Times* (15 August 2010), A1.
[279] N Lubell, 'The War (?) Against Al-Qaeda' in E Wilmshurst (ed), *International Law and the Classification of Conflicts* (OUP, Oxford 2012) 428. See discussion in section 1.2.1.
[280] On the Obama Administration's view, see US Department of Justice, White Paper, 'Lawfulness of a Lethal Operation Directed Against a U.S. Citizen Who is a Senior Operational Leader of Al-Qa'ida or An Associated Force' (undated; made public on 4 February 2013) 3 <http://msnbcmedia.msn.com/i/msnbc/sections/news/020413_DOJ_White_Paper.pdf> accessed 6 August 2015. On the US courts' view, see *Gherebi v Obama*, 609 F Supp 2d 43 (DDC 2009) 57 (fn 8); *Hamlily v Obama*, 616 F Supp 2d 63 (DDC 2009) 73.
[281] Authorization for Use of Military Force (AUMF), Pub. L. 107–40, 115 Stat 224 (18 September 2001) s 2(a). The Obama Administration considers this to be the legal basis for detentions in the conflict with al-Qaeda: see 'Respondents' Memorandum' (n 91) 1. Since 9/11, the AUMF has controversially been invoked to justify military operations and detentions in a broad range of circumstances: S Vladeck, 'Detention After the AUMF' (2014) 82 Fordham L Rev 2189.
[282] *Hamdi v Rumsfeld*, 542 US 507, 519 (2004) (US Supreme Court).

it infringe the sovereignty of the 'host' state.[283] Whilst space prevents a detailed discussion of this issue, it is conceivable that such a jurisdictional link could be established on the basis of the protective principle,[284] though the requirement under IHRL that the legal basis for detention be clear and predictable may well not be met, particularly where the host state's own laws do not provide for detention in comparable circumstances.[285] However, it may also be the case that, in an extraterritorial non-international armed conflict, where the host state consents to the presence of the assisting state, the host state also consents to detention operations by the assisting state, effectively delegating to the latter whatever detention powers it itself has under its domestic law.[286]

Pursuant to its domestic law authorization under the AUMF, the Obama Administration applied the same detention standard in its conflict with al-Qaeda as that noted above for Afghanistan.[287] As noted, that standard contains both conduct and status-based elements. The problems posed by such an approach will be discussed in section 7.2 when considering how the law might best develop in this area.

Regarding the review procedures for Guantanamo detainees, these were developed over time, in light of domestic US case law. Following the decisions of the Supreme Court in June 2004 in *Rasul v Bush* and *Hamdi v Rumsfeld*,[288] the government established Combatant Status Review Tribunals (CSRTs), which played the role of an initial review procedure,[289] although they could be reconvened subsequently should new information come to light.[290] The tribunals were 'composed of three neutral commissioned officers not involved in the capture, detention or interrogation of the detainee'.[291] Each detainee was given a Personal Representative (PR) of officer rank that assisted them throughout the process.[292] The detainee could attend all open sessions of the CSRT, which did not include sessions involving deliberation and voting or evidence 'that would compromise national security if held in the open'.[293] Only the CSRT and PR, but not the detainees themselves, could see classified evidence.[294] The detainee could call witnesses and question those called by the Tribunal.[295] The CSRT decided by majority whether, by a preponderance of the evidence, the detainee was an enemy combatant (the standard of detention originally employed by the Bush Administration).[296] The decision

---

[283] AV Lowe, 'Jurisdiction' in M Evans (ed), *International Law* (2nd edn, OUP, Oxford 2006) 340–2.
[284] W Estey, 'The Five Bases of Extraterritorial Jurisdiction and the Failure of the Presumption Against Extraterritoriality' (1997) 21 Hastings Intl & Comp L Rev 177, 199–204.
[285] See section 4.2.1 on the need for a clear and predictable legal basis to detain.
[286] Applying a similar argument in a different context, see D Akande, 'The Jurisdiction of the International Criminal Court over Nationals of Non-Parties: Legal Basis and Limits' (2003) 1 JICJ 618.
[287] For the detention standard, see above at text to n 241. Applying this standard to the conflict with al-Qaeda see 'Respondents' Memorandum' (n 91) 2.
[288] *Rasul v Bush*, 542 US 466 (2004); *Hamdi* (n 282).
[289] US Department of Defense, 'Combatant Status Review Tribunal (CSRT) Process at Guantanamo' (July 2007) 1.
[290] Ibid, 2.   [291] Ibid.   [292] Ibid, 3.   [293] Ibid.   [294] Ibid, 4 and 5.
[295] Ibid, 3.
[296] Ibid, 3 and 4. For the purposes of CSRT proceedings, 'enemy combatant' was defined as 'an individual who was part of or supporting Taliban or al Qaida forces or associated forces that are engaged in hostilities against the United States or its coalition partners. This includes any person

was then forwarded to the Director of the CSRT who could either approve it or return the file to the CSRT for reconsideration.[297]

If detention continued, it 'would be authorized indefinitely subject to an annual review to assess the continued detention justification'.[298] This annual review was conducted by an Administrative Review Board (ARB), which would examine whether the detainee continued to pose a threat and whether any other reasons may have justified continued detention, such as intelligence value.[299] The composition and procedures of the ARBs were similar to the CSRTs.[300] The recommendation of the ARB was passed on to the Deputy US Secretary of Defense who had the final say over release or continued detention.[301]

The Obama Administration revised the review procedures in March 2011 and established Periodic Review Boards (PRBs).[302] PRBs comprise senior US government officials and carry out an initial review of the detention.[303] The procedures are similar to the CSRT procedures and include provision of a PR (a military officer) who advocates on behalf of the detainee and challenges the government's evidence, as well as the right of the detainee to argue before the PRB, call witnesses, and have access to all evidence, except where withholding is 'necessary to protect national security'.[304] The standard against which continued detention is judged is that it must be 'necessary to protect against a continuing significant threat to the security of the United States'.[305] The final decision on release or continued detention rests with the Secretary of Defence.[306] For those that remain

---

who has committed a belligerent act or has directly supported hostilities in aid of enemy armed forces': Deputy Secretary of Defense, 'Memorandum for Secretaries of the Military Departments, Chairman of the Joint Chiefs of Staff, Under Secretary of Defense for Policy: Implementation for Combatant Status Review Tribunal Procedures for Enemy Combatants Detained at U.S. Naval Base Guantanamo Bay, Cuba' (14 July 2006) 1 (encl 1).

[297] Deputy Secretary of Defense, 'CSRT Procedures', ibid, 9 (encl 1).

[298] GS Corn and PA Chickris, 'Unprivileged Belligerents, Preventive Detention, and Fundamental Fairness: Rethinking the Review Tribunal Representation Model' (2012) 11 Santa Clara J Intl L 115, 144.

[299] Deputy Secretary of Defense, 'Memorandum for Secretaries of the Military Departments, Chairman of the Joint Chiefs of Staff, Under Secretary of Defense for Policy: Revised Implementation of Administrative Review Procedures for Enemy Combatants Detained at U.S. Naval Base Guantanamo Bay, Cuba' (14 July 2006) 2.

[300] For an overview of the ARB procedures, see generally Deputy Secretary of Defense, 'ARB Procedures', ibid.

[301] Ibid, 6 (encl 3).

[302] Executive Order 13,567 (7 March 2011), 'Periodic Review of Individuals Detained at Guantanamo Bay Naval Station Pursuant to the Authorization for Use of Military Force'.

[303] Ibid, s 9(b).

[304] US Department of Defense, 'Memorandum for Secretaries of the Military Departments et al: Implementing Guidelines for Periodic Review of Detainees Held at Guantanamo Bay per Executive Order 13567' (reissue 4 November 2013) 10, 13, 15–17 <https://fas.org/irp/doddir/dod/dtm-12-005.pdf> accessed 6 August 2015.

[305] Ibid, 6. The National Defense Authorization Act 2012 (n 260) at s 1023(b)(1) states that 'the purpose of the periodic review process is not to determine the legality of any detainee's law of war detention, but to make discretionary determinations whether or not a detainee represents a continuing threat to the security of the United States'.

[306] National Defense Authorization Act 2012 (n 260) s 1023(b)(2). Similarly, see US Department of Defense, 'Executive Order 13567' (n 304) 18.

in detention, continued assessments of the feasibility of prosecution must be made.[307] This same procedure is then repeated on a triennial basis.[308] In addition, every six months, each detainee is subjected to a file review by the PRB, whereby the information on each is reviewed, with the detainee permitted to make written submissions; where 'a significant question is raised' as to the necessity of detention, a full PRB is then convened.[309]

It is clear that the US' detention models have consistently been based on those applicable in international armed conflicts under IHL. Interestingly, whilst the availability of initial and periodic administrative review procedures mirror the requirements under GCIV, the specific procedures adopted by the CSRT were based on the procedures applied by Article 5 GCIII tribunals under domestic US law.[310] As in Iraq and Afghanistan, the United States has taken the view that its detention operations in the conflict with al-Qaeda are not governed by IHRL.[311] However, once again, this view is not shared by other states. Indeed, a significant number of states have criticized the Guantánamo detention facility, emphasized the applicability of IHRL to detainees held there, and called for its closure.[312] As Anthony Dworkin notes, 'objections to Guantánamo were based above all on...the sweeping and often arbitrary nature of American decisions about whom to detain'.[313] More generally, the US' practice of treating its military engagements with al-Qaeda as an armed conflict, governed by IHL alone, is at odds with the approach of other states. The United Kingdom, for example, responded to the 9/11 attacks by derogating from Article 5 ECHR and adopting the Anti-Terrorism, Crime and Security Act 2001, providing for administrative detention, demonstrating its view that Article 5 ECHR was otherwise fully applicable.[314]

---

[307] Executive Order 13,567 (n 302) s 6.   [308] Ibid, s 3(b).   [309] Ibid, s 3(c).
[310] US Department of Defense, 'CSRT Process' (n 289) 1. On Art 5 GCIII, see section 2.3.2.
[311] UN Commission on Human Rights, 'Letter dated 14 April 2003 from the Chief of Section, Political and Specialized Agencies, of the Permanent Mission of the United States of America to the United Nations Office at Geneva Addressed to the Secretariat of the Commission on Human Rights', UN Doc E/CN.4/2003/G/80, 22 April 2003, 4–5.
[312] See, eg, *Abbasi v Secretary of State for Foreign and Commonwealth Affairs et al* [2002] EWCA Civ 1598, [107]; *Canada (Justice) v Khadr* [2008] 2 SCR 125 (Canadian Supreme Court) [24]–[25]. See also Tange, 'Netherlands State Practice' (n 4) 336; JR Crook (ed), 'Contemporary Practice of the United States Relating to International Law' (2006) 100 AJIL 690, 709; K Kaikobad and others, 'United Kingdom Materials on International Law, Part Six: VIII (Human rights and fundamental freedoms)' (2007) 78 BYIL 737, 752–5; P Rowe, 'Correspondents' Reports: United Kingdom' (2007) 10 YIHL 445, 452; T Desch, 'Correspondents' Reports: Austria' (2009) 12 YIHL 466, 470; UN Human Rights Council, 'Report of the Working Group on the Universal Periodic Review: United States of America', A/HRC/16/11, 4 January 2011, [11], [27], [39], [40], [41], [51], [92.58], [92.136], [92.137], [92.155], [92.156], [92.157], [92.158], [92.159], [92.160] (statements and recommendations by, respectively, Russia, Republic of Korea, Libya, the United Kingdom, France, Spain, Iran, Democratic People's Republic of Korea, Cuba, Venezuela, Egypt and Ireland, China, Sudan, Viet Nam, and Switzerland).
[313] A Dworkin, 'Beyond the "War on Terror": Towards a New Transatlantic Framework for Counterterrorism' (European Council on Foreign Relations Policy Brief, ECFR/13) (May 2009) 6 <http://ecfr.3cdn.net/1e18727eafdddcceb7_81m6ibwez.pdf> accessed 6 August 2015.
[314] See, eg, UK House of Lords, Statement by the Parliamentary Under-Secretary of State, Home Office, *Hansard*, HL, vol 645, cols 1291–94 (11 March 2003) cited in ICRC, Customary IHL

Finally, as in Iraq and Afghanistan, the US' detention practices here have been scrutinized by numerous international bodies, all of which apply the IHRL rules on detention as the relevant standards.[315]

It should lastly be noted that, in addition to the above administrative procedures, Guantánamo detainees are now also entitled to the domestic writ of *habeas corpus* in US courts, following a series of US Supreme Court judgments.[316] Interestingly, the United States relied on these judgments in response to the HRC's concluding observations, in which the latter had called on the United States to extend the right to *habeas corpus* in Article 9(4) ICCPR to Guantánamo detainees.[317] It is noteworthy, however, that the Circuit Court for the District of Columbia has suggested that such *habeas* petitions require only a minimal scope of review, undermining the degree to which they satisfy Article 9(4) ICCPR.[318]

5.3 Conclusions on State Practice

It was argued in section 5.1.3 that the default legal position regarding detentions in relation to non-international conflicts is that they are regulated both by the minimal rules of IHL explored in chapter 3 and the more detailed human rights rules explored in chapter 4; this presumption arises from the text and *travaux* of human rights treaties, as well as the broad acceptance that IHRL, prima facie, applies in armed conflict. This presumption was then said to be rebuttable either where the state derogates or, potentially, where it can be established that the states parties to the relevant human rights treaties collectively intend for their human rights obligations not to apply or to be modified in such situations. In international armed conflicts, there is some support for inferring such an intention

---

Database (n 225); comparing US and UK approaches here, see RH Wagstaff, *Terror Detentions and the Rule of Law: US and UK Perspectives* (OUP, New York 2014). Similarly, see HRC, 'Fifth Periodic Report: Canada', CCPR/C/CAN/2004/5, 18 November 2004, [61]–[68] (discussing new counter-terrorism laws introduced in light of 9/11, which were based on pre-existing criminal law detention powers).

[315] See, eg, UN Commission on Human Rights (n 72) [24]; HRC (n 231) [18]; UN Human Rights Council, 'Report of the Special Rapporteur on the Promotion and Protection of Human Rights and Fundamental Freedoms While Countering Terrorism: Mission to the United States of America', A/HRC/6/17/Add.3 (22 November 2007) [14]; UN Working Group on Arbitrary Detention, *Obaidullah v United States*, A/HRC/WGAD/2013/10, 12 June 2013.

[316] The key cases were: *Rasul* (n 288); *Hamdan v Rumsfeld*, 548 US 557 (2006); *Boumediene et al v Bush et al*, 553 US 723 (2008). Congressional attempts to overrule these failed: see, eg, Pub L No 109–148, 119 Stat 2680 (2005), at § 1005(e) (the Detainee Treatment Act 2005); Pub L No 109–366, 120 Stat 2600 (2006), §§ 7(a)(1) & (b) (Military Commissions Act 2006).

[317] HRC (n 231) [569]–[572].

[318] See, eg, *Al-Bihani v Obama*, 590 F.3d 866 (2010) (DC Cir Ct) (holding, inter alia, a burden-shifting 'preponderance of the evidence' standard to be sufficient for proving the necessary threat, whilst also suggesting that such a standard was not necessarily required constitutionally). On this case law generally, see B Wittes, RM Chesney, and L Reynolds, *The Emerging Law of Detention 2.0: The Guantánamo Habeas Cases as Lawmaking* (Brookings Institution, 2012). On the requirements of Article 9(4) ICCPR, see section 4.2.3.

from the fact that states have developed internment regimes specifically for those situations, suggesting that it is primarily against those that their conduct is to be judged.[319] In non-international armed conflicts, however, no internment regime exists under IHL from which one might derive a similar intention. This notwithstanding, there remains considerable disagreement over the applicability of IHRL here. In light of this disagreement, it was considered how else one might derive a common intention amongst the states parties that a human rights treaty provision does not apply in non-international armed conflict. It was suggested that one might arguably derive such an intention from the subsequent practice of the states parties, and hence the above sections examined state practice in a number of non-international conflicts. In so doing, it was shown that practice does not establish a shared intention as to the inapplicability of the IHRL rules here. Rather, the opposite appears to be true. Thus, the examples of traditional non-international armed conflicts made clear that the states involved operated on the presumption that their human rights obligations continued to apply fully to their detention operations. Regarding the examples of extraterritorial and transnational non-international conflicts, there was admittedly clear practice from the United States that their human rights obligations did not regulate its detention practices. However, this was countered by other states, including coalition partners, which were of the view that IHRL continued to govern detentions. Finally, it was also shown that, whilst the United Kingdom, Australia, and Canada appear recently to have adopted a view similar to that of the United States, such that the human right to liberty is modified or displaced in the context of non-international armed conflicts, these views remain too embryonic and unsupported by other states to be considered valid interpretations of existing law.

The general practice explored above thus confirms that those claims that IHRL does not apply to detention in the context of non-international armed conflicts are legally untenable. The nature of human rights obligations as non-bilateralizable or *erga omnes partes* means that those states that reject the applicability of IHRL in such situations violate not only the rights of those they detain but also the rights of all other states parties under relevant human rights treaties (eg the ECHR and ICCPR). It was demonstrated that this structure of the inter-state obligations under human rights treaties provides an additional safeguard against the watering down of human rights standards by a few states *inter se*. All states parties would need to accept unequivocally an interpretation of a human rights treaty that appeared to reduce its applicability or protection. In the absence of such consensus, the default position stands, with the consequence that the same facts (eg an unnecessary detention by a state of a civilian in a non-international armed conflict) may lead to violations of both IHRL and IHL, as has been recognized in jurisprudence.[320]

---

[319] It must be reiterated, however, that the present book does not take a final position on this.
[320] ACiHPR, *DRC v Burundi, Uganda and Rwanda* (n 102) [79]–[80]; *Israeli Wall* (n 24) [134]; *DRC v Uganda* (n 22) [217]–[220].

5.3 Conclusions on State Practice

It was recognized at the outset of this chapter that the approach taken to the relationship between IHL and IHRL is often heavily contingent on the position of the particular interpreter; states engaged in extraterritorial military operations are keen to invoke IHL as the *lex specialis* so as to exploit its more permissive standards, whereas persons or organizations with a human rights-based mandate seek to advocate the highest standards as the applicable legal regime. For commentators, this relationship goes to the heart of the balance between humanitarian considerations and military necessity; where one locates oneself along that spectrum affects one's approach to this relationship. The consequence has been an intractable debate, in which it is difficult to have a voice without some accusation of bias. The present chapter sought to move away from this by making clear its goal at the outset: to assess the relationship between IHL and IHRL from the perspective of general international law, employing traditional methods of treaty interpretation and conflict resolution and relying on the common intentions of the states parties as the decisive consideration in the interpretive process. The importance of examining subsequent state practice arose from the fact that it is from here, more than from most other sources, that we can often distil some sense of intention. This enabled us to examine in detail the extent to which traditional techniques in international law validated the various interpretive positions that have been advanced for addressing the relationship between IHL and IHRL in the area of detention. It has been shown that those techniques cannot be relied upon to justify the exclusion of human rights obligations relating to detention from non-international armed conflict.

6
The Practical Application of IHRL to Detention in Non-International Armed Conflict

The previous chapter demonstrated that the international human rights law (IHRL) rules on detention fully apply to detentions in relation to non-international armed conflicts, alongside the minimal rules of international humanitarian law (IHL) explored in chapter 3. That is not the end of the discussion, however, for a number of complex questions regarding how these human rights rules operate in practice in non-international armed conflicts must now be answered. Indeed, the question of the practical application of IHRL in armed conflict is often omitted, with accounts focusing instead on the abstract relationship between IHL and IHRL. If a workable body of law is to be determined, one that is capable realistically of regulating armed conflict, such questions of practicability must be addressed; this chapter seeks to fill this void. It begins in section 6.1 with an examination of the extent to which the exigencies of the situation may be taken into account in interpreting the specific content of the rules, drawing on the jurisprudence of the human rights treaty bodies. Whilst the general content of these rules was discussed in chapter 4, the focus here is on what these rules demand from states in the kinds of emergency situations that are the subject of the present enquiry, both with and without derogation.

The remaining sections will then discuss two further complex issues regarding the practical application of these human rights rules: their extraterritorial application and their binding nature vis-à-vis non-state armed groups. Whilst it will be demonstrated in section 6.2 that states continue to be held responsible under IHRL for detentions they conduct abroad, section 6.3 will highlight the limitations regarding the application of these rules to non-state groups. Given the absence of detailed IHL rules in this area that bind armed groups, this demonstrates a major shortcoming of the current *lex lata*, offering an opportunity to discuss how this might be remedied in the concluding chapter.

6.1 The Practice of Human Rights Treaty Bodies

This section will focus on the practice of human rights treaty bodies and their application of the IHRL rules on detention to situations constituting non-international armed conflicts. Their practice is important for several reasons. First, as the authoritative interpreters of the treaties, their jurisprudence has strong persuasive value.[1] Second, the case law offers an opportunity to explore how the human rights rules are applied in practice and, more specifically, the extent to which they may be modified to take account of the exigencies of the situation. In so doing, three lines of enquiry are explored in the subsections to follow: first, does the particular treaty body apply the treaty rules on detention in full to detentions in relation to non-international armed conflicts? As part of this line of enquiry, reference will be made to the treaty bodies' jurisprudence on the relationship between IHL and IHRL. The goal here is to consider whether the practice of the treaty bodies confirms the conclusions made in the previous chapter. Second, if so, can those rules be 'read down' so as to take account of the exigencies of the situation (outside the context of derogation)? Third, to what extent is derogation from the procedural rules on detention permitted? It will be shown that, whilst the treaty bodies unanimously answer the first line of enquiry affirmatively (confirming the conclusions made in the previous chapter), their approaches to the second and third differ considerably. A proposal for reconciling their approaches will then be made in section 6.1.5.

Before examining these three lines of enquiry, a brief introduction to the notion of derogation should be made. With the exception of the African Charter on Human and Peoples' Rights (ACHPR), each of the human rights treaties referenced in this book provides for derogation

[i]n time of public emergency which threatens the life of the nation and the existence of which is officially proclaimed... to the extent strictly required by the exigencies of the situation, provided that such measures are not inconsistent with [the state's] other obligations under international law.[2]

Given that a 'public emergency' would arguably exist where the threshold for a non-international armed conflict has been reached,[3] and given that the procedural rules applicable to detention are not explicitly listed as non-derogable,[4] one is

---

[1] *Case Concerning Ahmadou Sadio Diallo (Republic of Guinea v Democratic Republic of Congo)*, Merits Judgment [2010] ICJ Rep 639, [66]–[68]; S Ghandhi, 'Human Rights and the International Court of Justice: The *Ahmadou Sadio Diallo* Case' (2011) 11 HRLR 527, 533–8; N Rodley, 'The International Court of Justice and Human Rights Treaty Bodies' in M Andenas and E Bjorge (eds), *A Farewell to Fragmentation: Reassertion and Convergence in International Law* (CUP, Cambridge 2015) 94–6.

[2] Art 4(1) of the International Covenant on Civil and Political Rights (ICCPR); Art 15(1) of the European Convention on Human Rights (ECHR); Art 27(1) of the American Convention on Human Rights (ACHR); Art 4(1) of the Arab Charter of Human Rights ArCHR.

[3] It may be that a non-international conflict that is limited to one part of the country could not justify derogating measures applicable throughout the whole country: *Greek* case (1969) 12 YB 1, [153] (European Commission on Human Rights); ECtHR, *Sakik and others v Turkey*, App Nos 23878/94, 23879/94, 23880/94, 23881/94, 23882/94, 23883/94, Judgment, 26 November 1997, [39].

[4] Art 4(2) ICCPR; Art 15(2) ECHR; Art 27(2) ACHR; Art 4(2) ArCHR.

faced with the question of whether these rules are in fact capable of addressing the silence of IHL in this area. However, it must be borne in mind that the derogation provisions place important limits on the extent of permissible derogation, most importantly by restricting it to the 'extent strictly required by the exigencies of the situation'. This requires that *both* the general derogation *and* each measure adopted pursuant thereto are not only necessary to respond to the threat but also proportionate to that end, that is, the least rights-restrictive option.[5] More generally, derogating measures 'must be of an exceptional and temporary nature'.[6] With that in mind, we can now turn to the practice of the human rights treaty bodies regarding our three lines of enquiry.

6.1.1 Human Rights Committee (HRC)

Regarding our initial line of enquiry, it is first to be noted that the HRC's approach to the general relationship between IHL and IHRL appears to leave no room for the claim that Article 9 ICCPR does not apply in full in non-international armed conflicts. The HRC has opined that:

…the Covenant applies also in situations of armed conflict to which the rules of international humanitarian law are applicable. While, in respect of certain Covenant rights, more specific rules of international humanitarian law may be specially relevant for the purposes of the interpretation of Covenant rights, both spheres of law are complementary, not mutually exclusive.[7]

Based on this, there seems to be scope for the HRC to invoke IHL as an interpretive aid in the same sense as the International Court of Justice (ICJ) in the *Nuclear Weapons* Advisory Opinion,[8] that is, what is an 'arbitrary' deprivation of life in Article 6 ICCPR might be interpreted with a *renvoi* to IHL.[9] However, given the emphasis by the HRC that IHL and IHRL are 'complementary, not mutually exclusive',[10] there would appear to be no room for the argument that the minimal IHL rules applicable to internment in non-international conflicts (discussed in chapter 3) set aside Article 9 ICCPR. This is confirmed by its jurisprudence, in which it has consistently applied Article 9 ICCPR in full to

---

[5] HRC, General Comment No 29: States of Emergency (Article 4), CCPR/C/21/Rev.1/Add.11, 31 August 2001, [4]; R Higgins, 'Derogations under Human Rights Treaties' (1976) 48 BYIL 281, 282–3.
[6] HRC, General Comment No 29 (n 5) [2].
[7] HRC, General Comment No 31: The Nature of the General Legal Obligation Imposed on States Parties to the Covenant, CCPR/C/21/Rev.1/Add.13, 26 May 2004, [11]. Similarly, see HRC, Report of 7 Special Rapporteurs: Mission to Lebanon and Israel (7–14 September 2006), UN Doc A/HRC/2/7, 2 October 2006, [16].
[8] *Legality of the Threat or Use of Nuclear Weapons*, Advisory Opinion [1996] ICJ Rep 226, [25].
[9] W Kälin, 'Universal Human Rights Bodies and International Humanitarian Law' in R Kolb and G Gaggioli (eds), *Research Handbook on Human Rights and Humanitarian Law* (Edward Elgar, Cheltenham 2013) 444.
[10] The HRC makes this point in particular with regard to the rules on detention in HRC, General Comment No 35: Article 9 (Liberty and Security of Person), CCPR/C/GC/35, 16 December 2014, [64].

detentions in relation to non-international armed conflicts.[11] Indeed, other international bodies too have applied Article 9 ICCPR in full to detentions in non-international conflicts.[12]

Given this, the second line of enquiry requires consideration of the extent to which Article 9 ICCPR might be 'read down' to take account of the exigencies of such situations. The goal here is to consider what the relevant treaty rules require in situations of emergency where the state has *not* derogated. The HRC's jurisprudence on states of emergency (outside the context of derogation) suggests that there is very limited scope for reading down Article 9. For example, the Committee held that the Combatant Status Review Tribunals (CSRT) and Administrative Review Board (ARB) procedures for Guantánamo detainees did not satisfy Article 9(4) due, inter alia, to 'their lack of independence from the executive branch and the army… [and the] restrictions on the rights of detainees to have access to all proceedings and evidence'; it concluded that the United States must ensure that all detainees are:

…entitled to proceedings before a court to decide, without delay, on the lawfulness of their detention or order their release. Due process, independence of the reviewing courts from the executive branch and the army, access of detainees to counsel of their choice and to all proceedings and evidence, should be guaranteed in this regard.[13]

Moreover, in the context of Israel's administrative detention practices, the HRC confirmed, notwithstanding the security situation, the importance of informing detainees promptly and in sufficient detail of the reasons for their detention (Article 9(2) ICCPR) and providing them with legal counsel in order to challenge the legality of their detention.[14]

---

[11] See, eg, *Sarma v Sri Lanka*, CCPR/C/78/D/950/2000, 31 July 2003, [9.3]; HRC, 'Concluding Observations: Sri Lanka', CCPR/CO/79/LKA, 1 December 2003, [13]; HRC, Concluding Observations: Colombia, CCPR/CO/80/COL, 26 May 2004, [9]; HRC, 'Concluding Observations: Democratic Republic of the Congo', CCPR/C/COD/CO/3, 26 April 2006, [19]; HRC, 'Concluding Observations: United States of America', CCPR/C/US/CO/3/Rev.1, 18 December 2006, [18]; HRC, Concluding Observations: United Kingdom, CCPR/C/GBR/CO/6, 30 July 2008, [14]; *Traoré v Côte d'Ivoire*, CCPR/C/103/D/1759/2008, 17 January 2011, [7.5]; *Maharjan v Nepal*, CCPR/C/105/D/1863/2009, 2 August 2012, [8.6].

[12] UN Commission on Human Rights, 'Situation of Detainees at Guantanamo Bay', E/CN.4/2006/120, 27 February 2006, [24]; UN Assistance Mission for Iraq, 'Human Rights Report: 1 April–30 June 2007', [72] <http://www.ohchr.org/Documents/Countries/IQ/HRReportAprJun2007EN.pdf> accessed 7 August 2015; Human Rights Council, 'Report of the Independent International Commission of Inquiry on the Syrian Arab Republic', UN Doc A/HRC/21/50, 15 August 2012, [63]–[73]; UN Working Group on Arbitrary Detention, *Obaidullah v United States*, A/HRC/WGAD/2013/10, 12 June 2013.

[13] HRC, 'Concluding Observations of the Human Rights Committee: United States of America', CCPR/C/USA/CO/3, 15 September 2006, [18]. Similarly, see UN Commission on Human Rights, 'Report of the Working Group on Involuntary or Enforced Disappearances: Mission to Nepal', E/CN.4/2005/65/Add.1, 28 January 2005, [45]–[50].

[14] HRC, 'Concluding Observations: Israel' CCPR/CO/78/ISR, 21 August 2003, [12]–[13]; HRC, 'Concluding Observations: Israel' CCPR/C/ISR/CO/3, 3 September 2010, [7].

The procedural safeguards in Articles 9(2) and (4) ICCPR are, therefore, interpreted strictly.[15] However, the HRC has held the arbitrariness standard in Article 9(1) itself to be context-sensitive: 'The existence and nature of a public emergency which threatens the life of the nation may…be relevant to a determination of whether a particular arrest or detention is arbitrary'.[16] The HRC's approach is, therefore, to take the state of emergency into account in the initial determination of the arbitrariness of the detention, with little room for the subsequent procedural safeguards, such as *habeas corpus*, to be read down in light of the situation.

This apparently strict approach is mirrored in the HRC's jurisprudence regarding our third line of enquiry, on the possibility of derogation from Article 9 ICCPR. The Committee has held both the prohibition of arbitrary detention and the right to *habeas corpus* to be non-derogable. The former is considered non-derogable on the basis that violations thereof are said to violate 'humanitarian law or peremptory norms of international law',[17] whilst the non-derogability of *habeas corpus* is said to arise from its role in protecting other, explicitly non-derogable rights.[18] Other bodies, too, consider these rights to be non-derogable under the ICCPR.[19]

The present author's view of the HRC's approach to the second and third lines of enquiry will be addressed in section 6.1.5. Before that, however, the approaches of the other treaty bodies must first be considered.

6.1.2 European Court of Human Rights (ECtHR)

Regarding our first line of enquiry, as was noted in the previous chapter, the ECtHR has drawn on IHL explicitly for the purposes of interpreting the ECHR, reading into Article 5 ECHR the more permissive internment regime provided for in GCIV.[20] This, however, was in the context of an international armed conflict, and the Court has never explicitly applied IHL over the ECHR in non-international armed conflicts. However, certain commentators have argued that the ECtHR has drawn on the more permissive principles of IHL when applying the ECHR in situations appearing to constitute non-international armed conflicts.[21] This suggests

---

[15] Though note HRC, General Comment No 35 (n 10) [45] (the 'court' in Art 9(4) 'should ordinarily be a court within the judiciary. Exceptionally, for some forms of detention, legislation may provide for proceedings before a specialized tribunal, which must be established by law and must either be independent of the executive and legislative branches or enjoy judicial independence in deciding legal matters in proceedings that are judicial in nature').

[16] HRC, General Comment No 35 (n 10) [66]. Although note UN Commission on Human Rights (n 13) [45]–[50] (demonstrating the impermissibility of vague security grounds as a basis for detention).

[17] HRC, General Comment No 29 (n 5) [11]. [18] Ibid, [16].

[19] See, eg, UN Working Group on Arbitrary Detention (UNWGAD), 'Deliberation No 9 Concerning the Definition and Scope of Arbitrary Deprivation of Liberty under Customary International Law' in Human Rights Council, 'Report of the Working Group on Arbitrary Detention', A/HRC/22/44, 24 December 2012, [47]–[51].

[20] *Hassan v United Kingdom*, App No 29750/09, Judgment (Grand Chamber), 16 September 2014.

[21] See, eg, HJ Heintze, 'On the Relationship between Human Rights Law Protection and International Humanitarian Law' (2004) 86 IRRC 789; C Droege, 'Elective Affinities? Human Rights and Humanitarian Law' (2008) 90 IRRC 501; P Leach, 'The Chechen Conflict: Analysing

that the Court might be willing to set aside (or at least read down) Article 5 ECHR in such situations. Commentators have made such claims regarding the Turkish and Chechen cases,[22] for example, arguing that the Court's references to the IHL requirement of minimizing incidental loss of civilian life suggests an acceptance of the targeting of 'opposition forces... even in the absence of an immediate threat'.[23]

However, it must be noted that 'the degree of force used against [opposition forces] directly was not considered' in these cases.[24] Indeed, a number of commentators argue that, notwithstanding implicit references in these cases to IHL, the Court continued to apply the normal ECHR standards.[25] It is submitted that this is the more accurate reading of the Court's approach here. Thus, in *Ergi v Turkey*, whilst the Court did make reference to the need for the state to avoid 'incidental loss to civilian life', it also confirmed that all force must be proportionate to the aims in Article 2(2) ECHR and that operations be planned accordingly.[26] No inference can therefore be made that lethal force against non-civilians was lawful; indeed, the evidence was inconclusive as to the presence of 'non-civilians'.[27] Moreover, in *Isayeva et al v Russia* and *Isayeva v Russia*, the government made no claim to be exercising any right under IHL, but rather argued that its actions were justified under Article 2(2)(a) ECHR, in response to alleged force by armed groups.[28] Whilst the Court referred to the need to minimize civilian injury,[29] it also confirmed that *any* lethal force must be necessary to achieve one of the purposes in Article 2(2) ECHR and proportionate to that end.[30] Indeed, in *Isayeva*, after stating that the state's actions may have fallen under Article 2(2)(a) by virtue of the presence of non-state armed groups, the Court held that it exceeded what was permitted by that provision.[31] The Court thus made no suggestion in any of

---

the Oversight of the European Court of Human Rights' [2008] EHRLR 732, 734; N Melzer, *Targeted Killings in International Law* (OUP, Oxford 2008) 391; A Orakhelashvili, 'The Interaction between Human Rights and Humanitarian Law: Fragmentation, Conflict, Parallelism, or Convergence' (2008) 19 EJIL 161; E Tamura, 'The *Isayeva* Cases of the European Court of Human Rights: The Application of International Humanitarian Law and Human Rights Law in Non-International Armed Conflicts' (2011) 10 Chinese J Intl L 129.

[22] *Ergi v Turkey*, App No 23818/94, Judgment (Merits), 28 July 1998; *Isayeva v Russia*, App No 57950, Judgment (Merits), 24 February 2005; *Isayeva, Yusupova and Bazayeva v Russia*, App Nos 57947/00, 57948/00, and 57949/00, Judgment (Merits), 24 February 2005.

[23] Droege (n 21) 533. Referring to the IHL requirement, see, eg, *Ergi v Turkey* (n 22) [79].

[24] L Doswald-Beck, 'The Right to Life in Armed Conflict: Does International Humanitarian Law Provide all the Answers?' (2006) 86 IRRC 881, 884.

[25] See, eg, W Abresch 'A Human Rights Law of Internal Armed Conflict: The European Court of Human Rights in Chechnya' (2005) 16 EJIL 741; C Byron, 'A Blurring of the Boundaries: The Application of International Humanitarian Law by Human Rights Bodies' (2007) 47 Va J Intl L 839, 851–6; F Hampson, 'The Relationship between International Humanitarian Law and Human Rights Law From the Perspective of a Human Rights Treaty Body' (2008) 90 IRRC 549, 561; L Moir, 'The European Court of Human Rights and International Humanitarian Law' in R Kolb and G Gaggioli (eds), *Research Handbook on Human Rights and Humanitarian Law* (Edward Elgar, Cheltenham 2013) 481–6.

[26] *Ergi v Turkey* (n 22) [79], citing *McCann and others v UK*, App No 18984/91, Judgment (Merits), 17 September 1995, [148]–[150].

[27] *Ergi v Turkey* (n 22) [80].   [28] *Isayeva et al* (n 22) [160]; *Isayeva* (n 22) [170].
[29] *Isayeva et al* (n 22) [177].   [30] Ibid, [169]–[171]; *Isayeva* (n 22) [172]–[178].
[31] *Isayeva* (n 22) [191].

these cases that certain actions that would otherwise have been unlawful under Article 2 ECHR were considered lawful by virtue of the application of IHL.

This also holds true for Article 5 ECHR in non-international armed conflicts. Importantly for our first line of enquiry, the ECtHR addressed a case of internment by the United Kingdom in the context of the non-international armed conflict in Iraq, applying Article 5(1) ECHR as the governing standard.[32] It was explained in chapter 4 that this provision lists the exhaustive grounds on which detention may be based and, in so doing, does not include preventive, security detention; derogation is therefore necessary for internment to be lawful.[33] In *Al-Jedda v UK*, the petitioner had been interned by the United Kingdom on the basis that it was 'necessary for imperative reasons of security' in accordance with Security Council Resolution (SCR) 1546.[34] The applicant complained that this was in violation of Article 5(1) ECHR, not being based on any of the grounds listed therein.[35] The United Kingdom made two alternative arguments in response: first, that Al-Jedda's detention was attributable to the UN and not, therefore, within the UK's jurisdiction according to Article 1 ECHR; second, that the detention was based on SCR 1546, which, by virtue of Article 103 of the UN Charter, displaced the obligations under Article 5(1) ECHR.[36] The Court found in favour of Al-Jedda, rejecting the UK's first claim on the basis that the UN did not exercise the requisite level of control for a holding of attribution.[37] Regarding the UK's second claim, it held that, since SCR 1546 did not create an 'obligation' to intern, there was no conflict between that resolution and the UK's obligations under Article 5(1) ECHR; Article 103 of the UN Charter was thus inapplicable, leaving Article 5(1) ECHR intact.[38] Importantly, Al-Jedda was interned in October 2004, when the armed conflict in Iraq was of a non-international character.[39] The Court nonetheless made clear that Article 5(1) ECHR fully applied unless explicitly set aside by a binding SCR,[40] or through derogation.[41] Whilst the Court did not address the applicability of the other paragraphs of Article 5 ECHR, its reasoning would seem to apply to those equally, including Article 5(2) requiring that reasons be given to the detainee and Article 5(4) requiring *habeas corpus*. Consequently, for states party to the ECHR that have neither derogated from Article 5 ECHR nor had that provision explicitly set aside by a SCR, any detentions carried out as part of a non-international armed conflict (whether at home or abroad) remain

---

[32] *Al-Jedda v United Kingdom*, App No 27021/08, Judgment (Grand Chamber), 7 July 2011. The following discussion of *Al-Jedda* was originally published in L Hill-Cawthorne, 'The Copenhagen Principles on the Handling of Detainees: Implications for the Procedural Regulation of Internment' (2013) 18 JCSL 481.
[33] Section 4.2.1.   [34] *Al-Jedda* (n 32) [11] and [16].   [35] Ibid, [59].
[36] Ibid, [60]. Art 103 of the UN Charter reads: 'In the event of a conflict between the obligations of the Members of the United Nations under the present Charter and their obligations under any other international agreement, their obligations under the present Charter shall prevail.'
[37] Ibid, [74]–[86].   [38] Ibid, [97]–[110].
[39] ICRC, 'Iraq post 28 June 2004: protecting persons deprived of freedom remains a priority' (5 August 2004) <http://www.icrc.org/eng/resources/documents/misc/63kkj8.htm> accessed 7 August 2015. See discussion in section 5.2.2.1.
[40] *Al-Jedda* (n 32) [102].   [41] Ibid, [99].

fully regulated by that provision, regardless of applicable IHL.[42] It should finally be noted that the distinction between the Court's approaches in *Hassan v UK* and *Al-Jedda v UK* rests on principled grounds: whereas in *Hassan*, the Court was faced with an international armed conflict, in which it considered that the existence of detailed procedural rules in IHL, together with state practice, necessitated its openness to reading Article 5 ECHR in conformity with IHL, in *Al-Jedda*, the Court was faced with a non-international armed conflict, in which, as the previous chapters have confirmed, there exists neither detailed IHL rules on detention nor clear supporting state practice on the inapplicability of IHRL. Though certain aspects of the *Hassan* judgment are open to criticism,[43] it is clear that, to the extent that it might be considered valid, its reasoning is limited to international armed conflicts.

Having confirmed that the ECtHR applies Article 5 ECHR in full to detentions in non-international armed conflicts, the second line of enquiry requires considering the possibility of reading down the Article 5 ECHR requirements to take account of the exigencies of such situations. The ECtHR addressed this issue in *Ireland v UK*, in which it had to examine the conformity of the UK's internment regime in Northern Ireland with the Convention.[44] The first part of the judgment sheds light on our enquiry into the degree to which the Article 5 requirements can be read down outside the context of derogation. The Court held that the UK's internment regime was incompatible with Article 5 ECHR, not falling into any of the grounds for permissible detention listed in Article 5(1); for any internment to be lawful under the Convention, derogation from Article 5(1) would be necessary.[45] In addition, the fact that, 'in general, [internees] were simply told that the arrest was made pursuant to the emergency legislation and they were given no further details' violated Article 5(2).[46] Finally, the review procedures under the emergency legislation, which consisted of an advisory committee and commissioners, were held not to satisfy Article 5(4) on several grounds.[47] First, the advisory committee could only recommend, but not order, release.[48] Second, neither the advisory committee nor the commissioners afforded 'the fundamental guarantees inherent in the notion of "court"'.[49] Regarding the

---

[42] The judgment was criticized by some for its refusal to take account of IHL: see, eg, J Pejic, 'The European Court of Human Rights' *Al-Jedda* Judgment: The Oversight of International Humanitarian Law' (2011) 93 IRRC 837, 850. However, the United Kingdom did not raise any IHL-based argument as such, in contrast to its argument in *Hassan v UK* (n 20).

[43] See the analysis in section 5.1.2.

[44] *Ireland v UK*, App No 5310/71, Judgment (Merits), 18 January 1978. Whilst the Court read down Article 5 ECHR in *Hassan v UK* (n 20), this was a consequence of its view on the interaction between that provision and the law of international armed conflict. It is not therefore directly relevant to our second line of enquiry, which concerns the possibility of reading down (outside the context of derogation) the IHRL rules on detention to take account of the exigencies of the situation generally, rather than as a specific result of applicable rules of IHL.

[45] *Ireland v UK* (n 44) [194]–[196].   [46] Ibid, [198].   [47] Ibid, [200].

[48] Ibid, [200]. Similarly, see *A and others v UK*, App No 3455/05, Judgment (Grand Chamber), 19 February 2009, [202] ('[t]he reviewing "court" must not have merely advisory functions but must have the competence to "decide" the "lawfulness" of the detention and to order release if the detention is unlawful').

[49] *Ireland v UK* (n 44) [200].

advisory committee, comprising a judge and two laymen, detainees had no legal right to appear, to be legally represented, to challenge the grounds for internment, or to call or examine witnesses.[50] Regarding the commissioners, the Court held these not to satisfy Article 5(4), inter alia, because only the Chief Constable or Secretary of State could refer a case to them; detainees could not refer their case themselves.[51] Moreover, the availability of the common law writ of *habeas corpus* also failed to satisfy Article 5(4) as the scope of review was insufficiently wide.[52] Specifically, courts could intervene only if there had been:

> ...bad faith, absence of a genuine suspicion, improper motive or failure to comply either with the statutory procedures or with such principles of the common law as were held not to be excluded by the language of the Regulation; however, they could not in general enquire into the reasonableness or fairness of the suspicion or of the decision to exercise the power.[53]

This jurisprudence confirms that, even in situations of emergency, the reasons for detention must be sufficiently detailed and there must be review of a sufficiently wide scope by a judicial body with the power to order release, offering fundamental guarantees, including the right to legal representation and to call and examine witnesses. It should be noted, however, that the ECtHR has shown some willingness to take account of security concerns in certain aspects of *habeas* proceedings. Thus, it has confirmed that, whilst the reviewing court must have access to all the evidence,[54] certain evidence can be withheld from the detainee so long as most of that relied upon was open to the detainee and sufficiently precise.[55]

Our third line of enquiry concerns the extent to which states parties can derogate from Article 5 ECHR. The ECtHR seems to take a different approach to the HRC here, which, it will be remembered, considers Article 9 ICCPR non-derogable. It was on this issue that the Court focused in the second part of its *Ireland v UK* judgment, holding that the UK's derogation from Article 5 was permissible.[56] It first confirmed that the Troubles in Northern Ireland constituted a 'public emergency threatening the life of the nation'.[57] It then went on to hold that, given the growth in violence in the region, derogation from Article 5(1) ECHR and the introduction of internment could not be said to go beyond what was 'strictly required by the exigencies of the situation'.[58] Furthermore, the Court concluded that the derogations from Articles 5(2) and (4) ECHR equally complied with this proportionality requirement.[59] It considered the existence of review procedures particularly relevant in holding that the United Kingdom had not gone beyond what was necessary: 'the advisory committee...afforded,

---

[50] Ibid, [84]. Similarly, see *Chahal v UK*, App No 22414/93, Judgment (Grand Chamber), 15 November 1996, [130]–[131] (found a violation of Art 5(4) as the advisory panel, chaired by a judge, did not have the authority to order release, the individual had no right to legal representation and they were given only an outline of the national security case against them).
[51] *Ireland v UK* (n 44) [200]. [52] Ibid, [200]. [53] Ibid, [82] and [84].
[54] *Chahal v UK* (n 50) [130]–[131]. [55] *A and others* (n 48) [220].
[56] *Ireland v UK* (n 44) [202]–[224]. [57] Ibid, [205]. [58] Ibid, [212]–[214].
[59] Ibid, [215]–[221].

notwithstanding its non-judicial character, a certain measure of protection that cannot be discounted'.[60] Procedures for the review of detention were, therefore, a necessary condition for the validity of derogation from Article 5.[61]

The ECtHR's jurisprudence thus suggests that states may validly derogate from Article 5 ECHR, although the Court will judge the necessity and proportionality of such derogation, in part, on the presence of safeguards. This is in contrast to the HRC, discussed above. The ECtHR has more recently confirmed the permissibility of derogating from Article 5(1) for the purposes of introducing internment.[62] However, regarding derogation from Articles 5(2) and (4), the age of the above cases must be acknowledged, and whether they would be decided in the same way today remains to be seen.[63] Given the subsequent developments in the jurisprudence of other human rights treaty bodies in favour of the non-derogability of the procedural rules on detention, the ECtHR may follow suit, particularly given the requirement in Article 15 ECHR that any derogation be compatible with the state's other obligations under international law. It is noteworthy in this regard that, though concerned not with derogation but rather the relationship between Article 5 ECHR and IHL, the Court's *Hassan* judgment highlighted the importance it places on adequate procedural safeguards, such that, even in an international armed conflict, 'if the Contracting State is to comply with its obligations under Article 5 § 4 in this context, the "competent body" [under GCIV] should provide sufficient guarantees of impartiality and fair procedure to protect against arbitrariness'.[64] As noted, a proposal for moving forward in this area will be discussed in section 6.1.5, after examining the jurisprudence of the remaining treaty bodies.

6.1.3 Inter-American institutions

The Inter-American Commission (IACiHR) and Court (IACtHR) of Human Rights have applied IHL as the *lex specialis* when interpreting the ACHR and American Declaration on the Rights and Duties of Man (ADRDM), both in a similar manner as the ICJ in its *Nuclear Weapons* Advisory Opinion and, at times, going beyond that.[65] Thus, in *Abella v Argentina*, the Commission applied the

---

[60] Ibid, [218]–[219]. It is also noteworthy that amendments to the internment regime made in August 1973 included the requirement that 'the Secretary of State had to refer to a commissioner the case of anyone held under a detention order for one year since the making of the order or for six months since the last review': ibid, [88]. This mirrors the periodic review provisions in GCIV: see section 2.3.1.2.

[61] Similarly, see *Lawless v Ireland (No 3)*, App No 332/57, Judgment (Plenary), 1 July 1961, [37]; *Brannigan and McBride v UK*, App Nos 14553/89 and 14554/89, Judgment (Merits), 25 May 1993, [66]; *Aksoy v Turkey*, App No 21987/93, Judgment (Merits), 18 December 1996, [83]; *A and others* (n 48) [184].

[62] *A and others v UK* (n 48).

[63] L Doswald-Beck, *Human Rights in Times of Conflict and Terrorism* (OUP, Oxford 2011) 97.

[64] *Hassan v UK* (n 20) [106].

[65] CM Cerna, 'The History of the Inter-American's System's Jurisprudence as Regards Situations of Armed Conflict' (2011) 2 J Intl Humanitarian Legal Studies 3.

IHL rules on the conduct of hostilities when interpreting the right to life under the ACHR, concluding that the targeting of non-state fighters was not a violation of the ACHR or IHL, as such individuals, by virtue of their direct participation in hostilities, were lawful targets under the latter.[66] The Commission therefore applied IHL as the governing standard in a similar manner to the ICJ, without also considering whether the IHRL requirements of necessity and proportionality had been met. Moreover, the Commission has applied IHL as the *lex specialis* when considering the procedural regulation of detention in *international* armed conflicts, reading the relevant human rights rules so as make room for the GCIV internment regime.[67]

The IACtHR has similarly held that IHL 'may be taken into consideration as elements for the interpretation of the American Convention'.[68] It has been suggested that it remains unclear as to how the Court would treat a case where interpreting the ACHR through the lens of IHL would have the effect of lowering the protections that otherwise would be afforded by the former.[69] However, it is certainly clear that the Court is unwilling to accept preliminary objections by states that their conduct cannot be judged against the ACHR, howsoever interpreted, where IHL applies.[70]

---

[66] *Juan Carlos Abella v Argentina*, Report No 55/97, 18 November 1997, [178]. Similarly, see *Franklin Guillermo Aisalla Molina (Ecuador v Colombia)*, Inter-State Petition IP-02 (Admissibility), Report No 112/10, 21 October 2010, [113]–[126]. Note that the IACtHR later held that neither it nor the Commission is competent to rule on state compliance with IHL: *Las Palmeras v Colombia*, Judgment (Preliminary Objections), IACtHR (Ser C) No 67 (2000).

[67] Its jurisprudence is a little mixed here: see, eg, *Coard et al v United States*, Report No 109/99, 29 September 1999 [45]–[59] (interpreting the requirements of Art XXV ADRDM, including the right to *habeas corpus*, in light of Art 78 GCIV); *Detainees in Guantanamo Bay, Cuba: Request for Precautionary Measures* (13 March 2002) ('[i]n certain circumstances, however, the test for evaluating the observance of a particular right, such as the right to liberty, in a situation of armed conflict may be distinct from that applicable in time of peace. In such situations, international law, including the jurisprudence of this Commission, dictates that it may be necessary to deduce the applicable standard by reference to international humanitarian law as the applicable *lex specialis*'). Though see also IACiHR, 'Report on Terrorism and Human Rights', OEA/Ser.L/V/II.116 Doc. 5 rev. 1 corr., 22 October 2002, ch III [142]–[143] (suggesting that the procedural rights under IHRL are *set aside* in the case of POW internment, whereas in the case of civilian internment 'minimum standards of human rights law require that detention review proceedings [under GCIV] comply with the rules of procedural fairness', including impartiality and legal representation); *Djamel Ameziane v United States*, Report No 17/12, Admissibility Decision, 20 March 2012, [28] ('[a]lthough international humanitarian law is the *lex specialis* for determining states' obligations in such situations [armed conflict], in certain circumstances, its norms may not provide sufficient protection for the rights of the persons affected').

[68] *Las Palmeras* (n 66) [32]; *Bámaca Velásquez v Guatemala*, Judgment, IACtHR (Series C) No 70 (2000) [209]; *Serrano-Cruz Sisters v El Salvador*, Judgment (Preliminary Objections), IACtHR (Series C) No 118 (2004) [119]. See also the extensive references to IHL for the purposes of interpreting various rights in the ACHR in *Case of the Santo Domingo Massacre v Colombia*, Judgment, IACtHR (Series C) No 259 (2012).

[69] C McCarthy, 'Human Rights and the Laws of War under the American Convention on Human Rights' [2008] EHRLR 762, 778; G Oberleitner, *Human Rights in Armed Conflict: Law, Practice, Policy* (CUP, Cambridge 2015) 294.

[70] *Case of the Santo Domingo Massacre v Colombia* (n 68) [16]–[26]; *Case of Rodríguez Vera et al (The Disappeared from the Palace of Justice) v Colombia*, Judgment, IACtHR (Series C) No 287 (2014) [38]–[39].

6.1 Practice of Human Rights Treaty Bodies

The above confirms that the inter-American institutions are generally willing to draw on IHL as an aid for interpreting the ACHR and ADRDM. However, when faced with detentions by a state in the context of *non-international* armed conflicts, they have applied Articles 7 ACHR and XXV ADRDM in full, without regard to IHL. Thus, in a 2011 admissibility decision regarding an armed confrontation between Colombian forces and rebels, both parties, as well as the IACiHR, accepted Article 7 ACHR as the governing standard for detentions by the state of alleged members of non-state groups.[71] Similarly, the IACtHR, in *Bámaca Velásquez v Guatemala*, held Article 7 ACHR to have been infringed as a result of the state's detention and disappearance of a member of a non-state group party to a non-international conflict: 'Although this is a case of the detention of a guerrilla during an internal conflict..., the detainee should have been ensured the guarantees that exist under the rule of law, and been submitted to a legal proceeding.'[72] Importantly, in the same case the Court considered that the IHL rules applicable in non-international armed conflicts can be utilized when interpreting certain provisions of the ACHR.[73] It clearly did not, however, feel that this could be done with regard to the legality of detention, for which it relied entirely on the framework provided by Article 7 ACHR.

Having confirmed that both the Commission and Court apply the human rights treaty rules on detention in non-international conflicts, the second line of enquiry regarding the possibility of reading down the requirements of these rules must be considered. The IACiHR addressed the extent to which Article XXV ADRDM can be read down in *Coard et al v United States*,[74] concerning the US invasion and occupation of Grenada, which both parties in the case recognized as an international armed conflict.[75] The Commission had to consider the legality of detentions by the US, and it applied Article XXV, interpreting it with reference to Article 78 GCIV.[76] Interestingly, the Commission considered Article XXV and Article 78 as 'largely in accord',[77] interpreting their requirements symbiotically:

...pursuant to the terms of the Fourth Geneva Convention and the American Declaration, [the requirement of *habeas corpus*] could have been accomplished through the establishment of an expeditious judicial or board (quasi-judicial) review process carried out by United States agents with the power to order the production of the person concerned, and release in the event the detention contravened applicable norms or was otherwise unjustified.[78]

---

[71] *Luis and Leonardo Caizales Dogenesama v Colombia*, Report No 152/11, 2 November 2011, especially at [22]–[23] and [50]. Similarly, see *Extrajudicial Executions and Forced Disappearances of Persons (Peru)*, Report No 101/01, 11 October 2001, [216]–[225]; *James Zapata Valencia and Jose Heriberto Ramirez Llanos v Colombia*, Report No 79/11, 21 July 2011, [123]–[131].

[72] *Bámaca Velásquez v Guatemala* (n 68) [143] (footnotes omitted). Similarly, see *Case of Ituango Massacres v Colombia*, Judgment, IACtHR (Series C) No 148 (2006), [139]–[153]; *Case of J v Peru*, Judgment, IACtHR, 27 November 2013, [125]–[172]; *Case of Rodríguez Vera et al (The Disappeared from the Palace of Justice) v Colombia* (n 70) [397]–[416].

[73] *Bámaca Velásquez v Guatemala* (n 68) [209].   [74] *Coard et al v United States* (n 67).
[75] Ibid, [44].   [76] Ibid, [45]–[59].   [77] Ibid, [55].   [78] Ibid, [58].

Whilst the Commission seems to defer to Article 78 GCIV in that it does not require that a *court* carry out the review, it goes further than this provision in requiring that the reviewing authority have the power to 'order the production of the person concerned, and release in the event that detention' is unlawful.[79]

The Commission, therefore, made clear that, for the purposes of *habeas corpus* under Article XXV ADRDM, a 'quasi-judicial' board consisting of US agents with the power to order the production of the detainee and release would suffice. This suggests that the formal requirements of *habeas corpus* could be read down so as to require an administrative, as opposed to judicial, review. Whilst the Commission in that case was faced with the question of the interaction between the law of international armed conflict and IHRL, invoking Article 78 GCIV as the *lex specialis*,[80] its reasoning would extend to situations where Article 78 GCIV does not apply as a matter of law (including non-international armed conflicts), as it considered its interpretation to be consistent with Article XXV generally, making clear that, where Article 78 GCIV and Article XXV 'provide levels of protection which are distinct, the Commission is bound by its Charter-based mandate to give effect to the normative standard which best safeguards the rights of the individual'.[81] In extraordinary situations, therefore, the Commission is clearly willing to read down what is normally required by Article XXV ADRDM.

The IACtHR has implied that it is less willing to do this. Whilst the Court has not had the opportunity to elaborate on the specific procedural safeguards required under Article 7(6) ACHR (on *habeas corpus*),[82] it has emphasized the *judicial* character of *habeas corpus*, stating in its advisory opinion on *Habeas Corpus in Emergency Situations* that '[i]mplicit in this... is the active involvement of an independent and impartial judicial body having the power to pass on the lawfulness of measures adopted in a state of emergency'.[83] It is unclear how to reconcile this emphasis on an independent, judicial body to review the lawfulness of detention with the IACiHR's acceptance in *Coard v US* of a board of (non-judicial) US agents, and it remains to be seen how this jurisprudence will develop in the future.

Finally, regarding the third line of enquiry, the Commission and Court have held the following procedural rules to be non-derogable under the inter-American system: the requirement of a legal basis for detention, the right to be informed of the reasons for detention, the right to legal counsel, and the right to *habeas corpus*

---

[79] As noted, the International Criminal Tribunal for the Former Yugoslavia (ICTY) has interpreted Art 43 GCIV as requiring that the reviewing authority have the power to order release: *Prosecutor v Zejnil Delalić et al* (Appeals Judgment) ICTY-96-21-A (20 February 2001) [329].

[80] *Coard et al v US* (n 67) [42]. [81] Ibid.

[82] B Farrell, 'The Right to Habeas Corpus in the Inter-American Human Rights System' (2010) 33 Suff Transnat L Rev 197, 219–20.

[83] *Habeas Corpus in Emergency Situations (Arts. 27(2) and 7(6) of the American Convention on Human Rights)*, Advisory Opinion OC-8/87, IACtHR (Series A) No 8 (1987), [30]. Similarly, *Durand and Ugarte v Peru*, Judgment, IACtHR (Series C) No 68 (2000), [93]–[110].

and periodic review.[84] Of course, the Commission's willingness to read down these rules might reduce the need for derogation. We will come back to this in section 6.1.5.

6.1.4 African Commission on Human and Peoples' Rights (ACiHPR)

Pursuant to our first line of enquiry, the Commission's jurisprudence on the general relationship between IHL and IHRL has tended to mirror the ICJ's approach in *DRC v Uganda*,[85] simply noting violations of both IHL and IHRL, without exploring the relationship between the two.[86] This was the case, for example, in *DRC v Burundi, Uganda and Rwanda*, in which the Commission found the respondent states responsible for, inter alia, killings and rapes in violation of GCIV, API, and the ACHPR.[87]

The Commission has not, therefore, shown any willingness to interpret the ACHPR in accordance with IHL, let alone to set aside its provisions in favour of the latter. This is demonstrated by its jurisprudence on the procedural rules on detention in Article 6 ACHPR. As noted in chapter 4, whilst Article 6 is very general, without a number of the specific rights found in other human rights treaties (such as *habeas corpus*), the Commission has elaborated on its specific content.[88] This has been done most fully in its *Principles and Guidelines on the Right to a Fair Trial and Legal Assistance in Africa*.[89] In common with the other treaty bodies, the ACiHPR has applied Article 6 ACHPR, as developed in its jurisprudence and in the *Principles and Guidelines*, to detentions by states in relation to situations that likely reach the level of a non-international armed conflict.[90]

---

[84] See, eg, *Habeas Corpus in Emergency Situations* (n 83); *Judicial Guarantees in States of Emergency (Arts. 27(2), 25 and 8 of the American Convention on Human Rights)*, Advisory Opinion OC-9/87, IACtHR (Series A) No 9 (1987); *Case of Osorio Rivera and Family Members v Peru*, Judgment, IACtHR (Series C) No 274 (2013) [120]; IACiHR, 'Report on Terrorism and Human Rights' (n 67) Ch III [126]–[127] and [139].
[85] *Case Concerning Armed Activities on the Territory of the Congo (DRC v Uganda)* (Judgment) [2005] ICJ Rep 168, [217]–[220].
[86] DL Tehindrazanarivelo, 'The African Union and International Humanitarian Law' in R Kolb and G Gaggioli (eds), *Research Handbook on Human Rights and Humanitarian Law* (Edward Elgar, Cheltenham 2013) 508–12.
[87] Communication No 227/99 (2003), [79]–[80].
[88] Art 6 reads: 'Every individual shall have the right to liberty and to the security of his person. No one may be deprived of his freedom except for reasons and conditions previously laid down by law. In particular, no one may be arbitrarily arrested or detained.'
[89] ACiHPR, *Principles and Guidelines on the Right to a Fair Trial and Legal Assistance in Africa*, adopted at 33rd session in Niamey, Niger, 29 May 2003, preamble <http://www.achpr.org/instruments/principles-guidelines-right-fair-trial/> accessed 7 August 2015.
[90] See, eg, *Commission nationale des droits de l'Homme et des libertés v Chad*, Communication No 74/92 (1995), [23]–[26]; *Constitutional Rights Project, Civil Liberties Organisation and Media Rights Agenda v Nigeria*, Communication Nos 140/94, 141/94, and 145/95 (1999), [50]–[51]; *Huri—Laws v Nigeria*, Communication No 225/98 (2000), [42]–[44]; *Kazeem Aminu v Nigeria*, Communication No 205/97 (2000), [21]; *Amnesty International and others v Sudan*, Communication Nos 48/90, 50/91, 52/91, and 89/93 (2003), [58]–[60]; *Sudan Human Rights Organisation & Centre on Housing Rights and Evictions (COHRE) v Sudan*, Communication Nos 279/03 and 296/05 (2009), [169]–[179].

This takes us to our second line of enquiry, on the possibility of reading down the requirements of Article 6 ACHPR to take account of the exigencies of an internal conflict. Much of the Commission's case law on Article 6 has dealt with flagrant breaches, leaving little need to go into detail regarding what is and what is not permitted under that provision. It has, however, demonstrated a clear concern with ensuring that states of emergency are not invoked as a basis for undermining the object and purpose of Article 6. In *Amnesty International v Sudan*, for example, it found a violation of Article 6 due to the vague grounds for detention and the absence of an independent review under a 1989 emergency decree providing for the detention of anyone 'suspected of being a threat to political or economic security'.[91] More specifically, a violation of the right to *habeas corpus* was found because 'appeal in the case of arrest lies to the body whose president orders the arrest'.[92] Furthermore, in *Huri—Laws v Nigeria*, the Commission found a violation of Article 6 for the detention of two persons under the 1984 State Security (Detention of Persons) Decree on the grounds that reasons were not given for their detentions and neither was given a fair hearing to challenge their detention.[93] The Commission's jurisprudence therefore confirms that the requirements that persons only be detained on reasonable and foreseeable grounds, that reasons be given for a detention, and that detainees be given an independent, judicial review are the minimum safeguards demanded by Article 6 ACHPR.

Regarding our third line of enquiry, the Commission has confirmed that derogation from Article 6 ACHPR is not permissible, given the absence of a derogation provision in the Charter.[94] Thus, 'even a situation of... war... cannot be cited as justification by the State violating or permitting violations of the African Charter'.[95] The focus in much of the jurisprudence has been on the non-derogability of *habeas corpus*. Thus, in its *Principles and Guidelines*, the Commission states that '[n]o circumstances whatever must [*sic*] be invoked as a justification for denying the right to habeas corpus, amparo or similar procedures'.[96] In *Constitutional Rights Project and Civil Liberties Organisation v Nigeria*, the Commission rejected Nigeria's plea that state security necessitated the suspension of *habeas corpus* on the basis that '[i]t is dangerous for the protection of human rights for the executive branch of government to operate without such checks as the judiciary can usefully perform'.[97] Like the HRC and the inter-American institutions, the ACiHPR, therefore, does not permit derogation from the procedural rules applicable to detention.

---

[91] *Amnesty International v Sudan* (n 90) [58]–[60].
[92] Ibid, [60]. Similarly, see *Constitutional Rights Project et al v Nigeria* (n 90) [20] (stressing the need for independence from the executive).
[93] *Huri—Laws v Nigeria* (n 90) [42]–[44].
[94] *Commission nationale des droits de l'Homme et des libertés v Chad* (n 90) [23]–[26].
[95] *DRC v Burundi, Rwanda and Uganda* (n 87) 65.
[96] *Principles and Guidelines* (n 89) Principle M.5(e). Similarly, see ibid, Principle R.
[97] *Constitutional Rights Project et al v Nigeria* (n 90) [33].

6.1.5 Conclusions on treaty body practice: a proposal for reconciling their approaches

The practice of the human rights treaty bodies regarding our first line of enquiry unanimously confirms the conclusions in chapter 5: the IHRL rules on detention continue to apply fully to detentions carried out in relation to non-international armed conflicts. As such, there is no 'displacing' of states' international human rights obligations in this area by IHL. The recent contrary practice of a few states was shown to be too embryonic and insufficiently supported by other states to rebut the presumption of parallel application of IHL and IHRL. Rather, as demonstrated in section 5.2 and confirmed in the sections above, states generally justify their detention practices in non-international conflicts (whether criminal or administrative) 'through' IHRL, by either derogating from the treaty provisions with which such practices conflict or by seeking to read down what is required by those provisions.[98]

The validity of such justifications was the subject of the second and third lines of enquiry explored above, which addressed the practical application of these rules by human rights treaty bodies and, in particular, the extent to which they can be modified to take account of the exigencies of the situation. There was shown to be less agreement amongst treaty bodies here. First, there seems to be disagreement between the ECtHR and the other treaty bodies regarding the derogability of the procedural rules on detention. Whereas the HRC, ACiHPR, and inter-American institutions take the view that many or all of these rules are non-derogable, the ECtHR's jurisprudence suggests that states may derogate from each of the rules, so long as procedural safeguards remain in place. To some extent, this difference is inevitable given the different structure of Article 5 ECHR compared with the other treaties. In particular, whereas the other treaties prohibit 'arbitrary' detention, leaving states free to implement internment regimes that are not 'arbitrary', Article 5(1) ECHR gives an exhaustive list of permissible grounds for detention, none of which allows for preventive, security detention. For states party to the ECHR, therefore, derogation is necessary in order to adopt internment regimes.[99] Regarding derogation from the other paragraphs of Article 5 ECHR, it was noted that the age of the Court's case law in this area leaves some doubt as to the approach it would take today.

Second, the treaty bodies have explored the extent to which the procedural rules on detention may more generally be 'read down' to take account of the exigencies of the situation, outside the context of derogation and without relying on IHL and *lex specialis*-based arguments. The goal here was to assess what the minimum requirements of these provisions are, for only then can their operability in non-international armed conflict be assessed. The HRC, ECtHR, IACtHR, and ACiHPR have all highlighted aspects of these rules that they consider incapable of being read down. In particular, whilst the existence of a public emergency may

---

[98] See, eg, the examples of Colombia and Sri Lanka in section 5.2.1.
[99] *Ireland v UK* (n 44) [194]–[196]; *A and others* (n 48) [172].

be relevant in assessing the 'arbitrariness' of a detention,[100] the grounds on which it is based must not be vague.[101] Moreover, the reasons for detention must be conveyed promptly to detainees in sufficient detail.[102] Finally, judicial review must be available, which provides an independent and impartial review of a sufficiently wide scope of the reasonableness of detention and which has the power to order release.[103] As part of this review, the detainees must be given legal counsel, as well as have the right to appear, call witnesses, and view the evidence against them.[104]

The IACiHR seems to depart from the other treaty bodies here. In particular, it has suggested that a 'quasi-judicial' board of government agents would suffice for the purposes of *habeas corpus*.[105] The Commission did, however, emphasize that the purpose of this board is to ensure that detention is not left to the sole discretion of a state agent, and that it must have the power to order production of the person concerned and their release.[106] Notwithstanding its view of the non-derogability of these rules, therefore, the Commission seems to allow for the kind of detention regimes adopted by states in armed conflicts by reading down the requirements of the rules on detention. As noted, it remains unclear how to reconcile this with the IACtHR's jurisprudence.[107]

There are, therefore, important differences between the approaches of the treaty bodies with regard both to derogation from the IHRL rules on detention and the extent to which those rules may be read down. To move forward, a uniform approach to these issues is desirable, not least because many states are party to more than one of these treaties. It is submitted that an appropriate compromise can be found by relying on the object and purpose of these rules to interpret the extent to which they can be read down. As emphasized both in chapters 2 and 3 regarding IHL and in chapter 4 regarding IHRL, these procedural rules serve the common purpose of ensuring that no person is arbitrarily deprived of their liberty, thereby providing a check on the executive's detention powers.[108] When considering the extent to which the exigencies of a situation can be taken into account to interpret the IHRL rules, this underlying object and purpose must be given weight.[109]

---

[100] HRC, General Comment No 35 (n 10) [66].
[101] UN Commission on Human Rights (n 13) [45]–[50]; *Amnesty International v Sudan* (n 90) [58]–[60].
[102] *Ireland v UK* (n 44) [198]; HRC, 'Concluding Observations: Israel', 21 August 2003 (n 14) [12]–[13]; *Huri—Laws v Nigeria* (n 90) [42]–[44].
[103] HRC (n 13) [18]; *Ireland v UK* (n 44) [200]; *A and others* (n 48) [202]; *Chahal v UK* (n 50) [130]–[131]; *Habeas Corpus in Emergency Situations* (n 83) [30]; *Amnesty International v Sudan* (n 90) [60].
[104] HRC (n 13) [18]; *Ireland v UK* (n 44) [200]; *A and others* (n 48) [216]–[217].
[105] *Coard et al v United States* (n 67) [58].   [106] Ibid.
[107] *Habeas Corpus in Emergency Situations* (n 83) [30].
[108] Confirming that this is the *raison d'être* of the IHL provisions, see, eg *Prosecutor v Zejnil Delalić et al* (Trial Judgment) ICTY-96-21 (16 November 1998) [580]; HCJ 7015/02 and 7019/02, *Ajuri and others v IDF Commander in the West Bank, IDF Commander in the Gaza Strip and others* [2002] 125 ILR 537, [29]. Confirming the same for the IHRL provisions: *Tibi v Ecuador*, Judgment, IACtHR (Series C) No 114 (2004), [129]; ECtHR, *Guide on Article 5: Right to Liberty and Security* (Council of Europe/ECtHR 2012), [1]; HRC, General Comment No 35 (n 10) [41].
[109] This is in accordance with customary rules on treaty interpretation, codified in Art 31(1) of the Vienna Convention on the Law of Treaties (VCLT).

This approach can also then help to determine the extent to which derogation from these rules should be permissible. It is submitted that, where the exigencies of the situation render it necessary to derogate, the state should be able to do so, but only to a limited extent. It is conceded that this is in contrast to the views of the HRC, IACiHR, IACtHR, and ACiHPR, which, as noted, consider some or all of these procedural rules to be non-derogable. However, the concerns of those treaty bodies that lead them to prohibit derogation can be addressed by limiting the extent of permissible derogation. First, it must be remembered that derogation does not leave the state's actions unregulated; derogation must be shown to be 'strictly required by the exigencies of the situation'.[110] It is here that the necessity and proportionality requirements are found, that is, derogation, and the individual measures adopted pursuant thereto, are permitted only where necessary, and no more than is necessary, to respond to the emergency.[111] Second, and following on from the first point, only those rules that are incapable of being interpreted so as to take account of the exigencies of a situation should be considered derogable, for it is only from those rules that derogation could be *necessary*. The approach advocated here will now be demonstrated with reference to each procedural rule.

First, regarding the arbitrary deprivation of liberty prohibition, as the HRC has noted, what is 'arbitrary' in a particular situation is necessarily context-dependent, and the existence of a non-international armed conflict may be taken into account in making this determination.[112] Given the openness of this norm, it is submitted that derogation therefrom should be impermissible, as the kinds of necessity-based considerations that are provided for via derogation can be factored into the arbitrariness standard itself; consequently, it could never be necessary to derogate.[113] As noted in chapter 4, contained within this norm is also the requirement of release where the reasons justifying detention cease; this too must be considered non-derogable, for detention beyond the point for which it is justified can never be necessary.[114] Indeed, as explained in chapter 4, the arbitrary detention prohibition does not, as such, prevent a state from adopting an internment regime.[115] However, as noted by the ACiHPR and UN Commission on Human Rights, even in extraordinary situations (eg where there is a threat to state security), the legal grounds on which detention are based must not be overly vague, lest they be open to abuse so as to undermine the very purpose of the arbitrary detention prohibition.[116] It is also worth repeating here that, as demonstrated in chapter 3, IHL does not provide a legal basis to intern in non-international armed conflicts;

---

[110] See, eg, Art 4 ICCPR; Art 15 ECHR. See also UN Commission on Human Rights, 'The Siracusa Principles on the Limitation and Derogation Provisions in the International Covenant on Civil and Political Rights', E/CN.4/1985/4, 28 September 1984, [54] ('[t]he principle of strict necessity shall be applied in an objective manner').
[111] See above at text to n 5. [112] HRC, General Comment No 35 (n 10) [66].
[113] UNWGAD, Deliberation No 9 (n 19) [47]–[51]. [114] Section 4.2.5.
[115] Section 4.2.1.1.
[116] UN Commission on Human Rights (n 13) [45]–[50]; *Amnesty International v Sudan* (n 90) [58]–[60].

to do so lawfully, states must therefore find such a basis (and a sufficiently detailed one) elsewhere, for example in domestic law or a SCR.[117]

The different structure of Article 5(1) ECHR means this approach cannot be applied to that provision. Thus, given the closed list of permissible grounds for detention in Article 5(1) ECHR, where it is necessary to adopt an internment regime, the state must derogate. As demonstrated, the right to derogate for these purposes has been recognized by the ECtHR.[118]

Second, in a similar manner to the basic arbitrariness standard, the requirement that the reasons for detention be given to the detainee may, to an extent, be interpreted so as to take account of the exigencies of the situation. Thus, certain evidence might reasonably be withheld from the detainee for national security reasons, so long as the undisclosed evidence does not form the majority of evidence against them.[119] Moreover, regarding the requirement that reasons be conveyed 'promptly', a slightly longer delay than normal might be acceptable where the situation is such as to make immediate disclosure to the detainee impossible.[120] It is submitted, however, that, when interpreting the extent to which this right can be read down, its object and purpose must be borne in mind. Thus, the reasons given for detention must always be sufficiently detailed to serve their purpose of providing the necessary factual and legal information so as to enable the detainee to challenge their detention.[121] To hold otherwise would effectively be to extinguish the right to *habeas corpus*. It is also because of this fundamental role of the right to know the reasons for one's detention that it should never be considered derogable.[122] As a result, subject to the limited degree to which the right can be read down, it is submitted that detainees should in all circumstances be informed of the reasons for their detention so as to enable them to challenge it.

The third procedural rule under IHRL, relating to review of detention, differs from the previous two, in that it leaves little scope for any possible reading down. Thus, the relevant provisions require *court* review of the legality of detention.[123] Given this, it is submitted that this right should be interpreted strictly, with little room for taking account of the exigencies of the situation. Thus, the review, both initial and periodic, should be by an ordinary court, that is, a judicial body, fully independent of the executive and the parties, with the power to order the production of the person concerned and release.[124] These proceedings should offer essential judicial guarantees, including the right to appear, to be legally represented, and to call and challenge witnesses.[125] This interpretation is consistent with the object and purpose of *habeas corpus*, which, as noted, is to protect against arbitrary

---

[117] Section 3.1.   [118] *Ireland v UK* (n 44) [212]–[214]; *A and others* (n 48).
[119] *A and others* (n 48) [220].
[120] *Kerr v UK*, App No 40451/98, Admissibility Decision, 7 December 1999.
[121] HRC, General Comment No 35 (n 10) [25]; *Kerr v UK* (n 120); *Van der Leer v Netherlands*, App No 11509/85, Judgment, 21 February 1990, [28].
[122] Similarly, see IACiHR, 'Report on Terrorism and Human Rights' (n 67) Ch III [139].
[123] See, eg, Art 9(4) ICCPR; Art 5(4) ECHR.
[124] Human rights treaty bodies generally take the same view: see above, text to n 103.
[125] See above, text to n 104.

6.1 Practice of Human Rights Treaty Bodies

detention and provide a check on the detention power of the executive;[126] the most effective means of doing so is for an independent judiciary to be charged with this task. It is for this reason that the proposed strict interpretation is considered preferable to the possibility of reading down the notion of a 'court' to allow for an administrative review within the military infrastructure.

Given that the right to *habeas corpus* cannot be interpreted to take account of the exigencies of the situation, however, it is submitted that it should be seen as derogable, but only to a limited extent. Here, the jurisprudence of the ECtHR is useful, for whilst the Court has not held *habeas corpus* to be non-derogable, it has made clear that procedural safeguards must always remain in place.[127] In *Ireland v UK*, the existence of such safeguards was treated by the Court as important evidence that the United Kingdom had not gone beyond what was 'strictly required by the exigencies of the situation' (the proportionality assessment).[128] Thus, where it is actually necessary, and no more than is necessary, a state should be able to derogate from the right to *habeas corpus* so as to allow a body other than an ordinary court to review, initially and periodically, the legality and reasonableness of detention. In order to comply with the necessity and proportionality requirements, however, the basic object and purpose of this right should be preserved, and the reviewing body (which, if not a judge, should be comprised of more than one person) should always be independent of the authority that initiated the detention and should have the power to order release where the detention is found to be unlawful or unreasonable.[129] This should ensure that, whilst the reviewing body may not be outside the executive or military (in the same sense as the ordinary judiciary), it is still sufficiently impartial in the specific case to satisfy the purpose of review, that is, to provide a check on the exercise of detention power. Moreover, derogation must be temporary, such that full *habeas* review should resume as soon as possible.[130] These limits on the right to derogate, it is submitted, would address the concerns of those human rights bodies that consider *habeas corpus* to be non-derogable, whilst promoting the idea that *court* review of detention should always be the norm, with any other forms of review only being permissible in the most extraordinary circumstances. Indeed, a similar approach was followed by experts when adopting the 'Siracusa Principles on the Limitation and Derogation Provisions in the International Covenant on Civil and Political Rights'.[131]

It must finally be noted that certain commentators have questioned whether providing *habeas* review in non-international armed conflict is practicable, particularly

---

[126] *Tibi v Ecuador* (n 108) [129]; *Constitutional Rights Project et al v Nigeria* (n 90) [33]; *Khudyakova v Russia*, App No 13476/04, Judgment, 8 January 2009, [93]; HRC, General Comment No 35 (n 10) [41].

[127] See above, text to nn 56–61.   [128] *Ireland v UK* (n 44) [218]–[219].

[129] These basic requirements have similarly been read into the review provisions in GCIV: see section 2.3.1.

[130] HRC, General Comment No 29 (n 5) [2].

[131] UN Commission on Human Rights, 'The Siracusa Principles' (n 110) [70(d)] ('[w]here persons are detained without charge, the need for their continued detention shall be considered periodically by an independent review tribunal').

given the large numbers of persons often detained in such situations.[132] Indeed, this problem was acknowledged by the US Supreme Court in *Boumediene v Bush*.[133] The impracticability of court review, however, should not be assumed. Indeed, an *amicus* brief by Israeli military and academic experts to the courts in *Boumediene* refuted claims that judicial review of detention in the US' conflict with al-Qaeda would be infeasible, drawing on Israel's experience, in which it provides *habeas corpus* review to the many more it holds as security detainees.[134] The approach advocated above would allow for derogation from *habeas* review where there is a genuine necessity to depart from this ordinary requirement, whilst continuing to ensure impartial review of detention, without assuming such a necessity exists simply because the threshold for a non-international armed conflict has been reached.

We will return to the proposals made above in the concluding chapter, when discussing how the law here might best develop. Before that, however, two final issues regarding the practical application of IHRL here must be addressed. First, IHRL is viewed by some as applicable only within a state's territory and not to its operations abroad, a view which would result in the human rights rules applying only in traditional, internal non-international armed conflicts. Second, traditional interpretations of IHRL consider it as binding only on states, in contrast to IHL, which binds both states and non-state groups party to non-international armed conflicts.[135] This interpretation poses a particular challenge to the ability of IHRL to regulate detention in non-international conflicts. The final two sections will explore these remaining issues of applicability for the human rights rules on detention.

6.2 Extraterritorial Application of IHRL

It has been shown that the procedural rules applicable to detention under IHRL continue to apply fully, subject to permissible derogation, in non-international armed conflicts. This is confirmed in the practice both of states and human rights treaty bodies. Sections 5.2.2 and 5.2.3 explored state practice in extraterritorial non-international armed conflicts and transnational armed conflicts between a state and non-state armed group. What differentiates these from 'traditional' non-international conflicts is that they involve states operating extraterritorially. It was shown that the United States took the view that IHRL was not applicable in these situations, in part due to their extraterritorial

---

[132] See, eg, M Sassòli and LM Olson, 'The Relationship between International Humanitarian and Human Rights Law Where It Matters: Admissible Killing and Internment of Fighters in Non-International Armed Conflicts' (2008) 90 IRRC 599, 622.

[133] *Boumediene et al v Bush et al*, 553 US 723 (2008), 770.

[134] Brief of *Amici Curiae* Specialists in Israeli Military Law and Constitutional Law in Support of Petititioners, *Boumediene et al v Bush et al*, On Writs of Certiorari to the United States Court of Appeals for the District of Columbia Circuit.

[135] On the binding nature of IHL for non-state groups, see section 3.4.

character.[136] The present section will demonstrate that, contrary to this view, state responsibility continues to be invoked under human rights treaties for detention operations abroad. This is especially important given that, as shown in the examples of Iraq and Afghanistan,[137] many non-international armed conflicts are now of this type.

The focus in this section is on the practice of international and regional bodies and the extent to which they have applied the relevant treaty rules on detention extraterritorially. Reasons of space, however, prevent a detailed evaluation of this practice. Indeed, in discussing the extraterritorial application of the IHRL rules on detention, this section falls within a much broader debate concerning the extraterritoriality of human rights treaties generally, and it would not be possible to make a meaningful contribution to that well-developed literature within the limited space available.[138] Rather, the purpose here is the much more modest one of demonstrating that, in practice, states are held responsible under IHRL for their detention operations abroad.

Before exploring treaty body practice, the clauses of the key human rights treaties regarding their scope of application must be noted. The treaties discussed in this book may be divided into three categories for this purpose. The first category comprises the ECHR, ACHR, and ArCHR, all of which specify that they apply within each state party's 'jurisdiction'.[139] As shown below, this has been interpreted to include both control over territory and control over individuals abroad. The second category comprises the ICCPR, which has an apparently narrower scope of application, applying 'to all individuals within its territory *and* subject to its jurisdiction'.[140] Whilst this has been interpreted so as to restrict the ICCPR's application to the sovereign territory of states parties,[141] the HRC and ICJ have held that it should be interpreted as requiring the application of the

---

[136] See, eg, HRC, 'Third Periodic Report: United States of America', CCPR/C/USA/3, 28 November 2005, 109–11. For academic support of such a view, see MJ Dennis, 'Non-Application of Civil and Political Rights Treaties Extraterritorially During Times of International Armed Conflict' (2007) 40 Isr L Rev 453. Similarly appearing to reject the extraterritoriality of the ICCPR, see UNWGAD, 'Comments by the Government of Canada: Working Group on Arbitrary Detention's Draft Principles and Guidelines' (Ottawa, 28 April 2015) [4] <http://www.ohchr.org/EN/Issues/Detention/Pages/DraftBasicPrinciples.aspx> accessed 7 August 2015.

[137] On these, see sections 5.2.2.1 and 5.2.2.2.

[138] See, eg, T Meron, 'Extraterritoriality of Human Rights Treaties' (1995) 89 AJIL 78; F Coomans and M Kamminga (eds), *Extraterritorial Application of Human Rights Treaties* (Intersentia, Oxford 2004); S Borelli, 'Casting Light on the Legal Black Hole: International Law and Detentions Abroad in the "War on Terror"' (2005) 87 IRRC 39; M Gondek, 'Extraterritorial Application of the European Convention on Human Rights: Territorial Focus in the Age of Globalization?' (2005) 52 NILR 349; A Roberts, 'Transformative Military Occupation: Applying the Laws of War and Human Rights' (2006) 100 AJIL 580; R Wilde, 'Triggering State Obligations Extraterritorially: The Spatial Test in Certain Human Rights Treaties' (2007) 40 Isr L Rev 503; Dennis (n 136); M Milanović, *Extraterritorial Application of Human Rights Treaties: Law, Principles, and Policy* (OUP, Oxford 2011); K da Costa, *The Extraterritorial Application of Selected Human Rights Treaties* (Martinus Nijhoff, The Hague 2012).

[139] Art 1 ECHR; Art 1(1) ACHR; Art 3(1) ArCHR.

[140] Art 2(1) ICCPR (my emphasis).

[141] See, eg, HRC (n 136) 109–11; HRC, 'Second Periodic Report: Israel', CCPR/C/ISR/2001/2, 4 December 2001, [8]; Dennis (n 136).

Covenant *both* in state party territory *and* extraterritorially where they exercise jurisdiction.[142] The third category comprises the ACHPR and ADRDM, neither of which has any clause restricting their scope of application. Consequently, the ICJ, ACiHPR, and IACiHR have been free to apply the ACHPR and ADRDM to the actions of states parties outside their territory.[143]

Each treaty has, therefore, been applied to the conduct of states parties outside their territory where they exercise jurisdiction. It remains to be shown in what circumstances states are considered to exercise 'jurisdiction' and whether the situations with which this enquiry is concerned fall within these circumstances. In his study on the extraterritorial application of human rights treaties, Marko Milanović demonstrates that human rights jurisprudence has developed two key models of 'jurisdiction', the 'spatial model', requiring effective territorial control, and the 'personal model…based on various forms of state authority and control over individuals'.[144] The spatial model is the higher threshold to meet and would only cover detentions abroad in a territory[145] over which the detaining state exercises effective control.[146]

The personal model offers a broader basis on which all persons detained by a state abroad would be protected by the latter's human rights treaty obligations. The personal basis for jurisdiction has been applied to determine the extraterritorial application of the ICCPR,[147] ECHR,[148] ACHR,[149] and

[142] HRC, *Lopez Burgos v Uruguay*, CCPR/C/13/D/52/1979, 29 July 1981, [12.1]–[12.3]; *Legal Consequences of the Construction of a Wall in the Occupied Palestinian Territory*, Advisory Opinion [2004] ICJ Rep 136 [107]–[111]; *DRC v Uganda* (n 85) [219].

[143] *Coard et al v United States* (n 67) [37]; *DRC v Burundi, Rwanda and Uganda* (n 87) [79]–[80]; *DRC v Uganda* (n 85) [219]. On the extraterritoriality of the ACHPR, compare C Anyangwe 'Obligations of State Parties to the African Charter on Human and Peoples' Rights' (1998) 10 African J Intl & Comp L 625, 627 and TS Bulto, 'Patching the "Legal Black Hole": The Extraterritorial Reach of States' Human Rights Duties in the African Human Rights System' (2011) 27 South African J Hum Rts 249. On the extraterritoriality of the ADRDM, see RK Goldman, 'Extraterritorial application of the human rights to life and personal liberty, including *habeas corpus*, during situations of armed conflict' in R Kolb and G Gaggioli, *Research Handbook on Human Rights and Humanitarian Law* (Edward Elgar, Cheltenham 2013) 111.

[144] Milanović (n 138) 118.

[145] An alternative reading of the spatial model views it as control over *areas* or *places*, which might cover detention centres abroad: *Al-Saadoon and Mufdhi v United Kingdom*, Admissibility Decision, App No 61498/08, 30 June 2009, [88].

[146] The Court of Appeal and House of Lords, for example, both concluded that, given the level of insurgency in Basra, the United Kingdom lacked effective control over that territory for the purposes of the ECHR, notwithstanding its status under IHL as an occupying power: *R (Al-Skeini and others) v Secretary of State for Defence (The Redress Trust and others intervening)* [2005] EWCA Civ 1609, [124] (per Lord Justice Brooke); *R (Al-Skeini and others) v Secretary of State for Defence (The Redress Trust and others intervening)* [2007] UKHL 26, [83] (per Lord Rodger).

[147] *Lopez Burgos v Uruguay* (n 142) [12.1]–[12.3]; *Celiberti de Casariego v Uruguay*, CCPR/C/OP/1, 29 July 1981, [10.1]–[10.3]; HRC, General Comment No 31 (n 7) [10].

[148] *Issa v Turkey*, App No 31821/96, Judgment, 16 November 2004, [71]; *Ocalan v Turkey*, App No 46221/99, Judgment (Grand Chamber), 12 May 2005, [91]; *Al-Skeini and others v UK*, App No 55721/07, Judgment (Grand Chamber), 7 July 2011, [137]. It is noteworthy that these cases came after the Court's suggested limitation of the ECHR to its *espace juridique*: see *Bankovic v United Kingdom*, App No 52207/99, Admissibility Decision, 12 December 2001, [75] and [80].

[149] *Franklin Guillermo Aisalla Molina* (n 66) [91].

ADRDM.[150] The ECtHR Grand Chamber explained the personal model as follows:

It is clear that, whenever the State through its agents exercises control and authority over an individual, and thus jurisdiction, the State is under an obligation under Article 1 to secure to that individual the rights and freedoms under Section 1 of the Convention that are relevant to the situation of that individual.[151]

The requirement of the exercise of 'control and authority over an individual' would clearly be met where a state detains an individual abroad. In the ECtHR's language, the rules 'that are relevant to the situation' would then apply, which, in the case of detention, include the procedural rules under the relevant human rights treaty. Indeed, human rights bodies have consistently held that individuals detained abroad fall within the detaining state's jurisdiction for the purposes of the relevant treaty provisions; this has been the case with the HRC,[152] ECtHR,[153] and IACiHR.[154]

Thus, when states detain individuals abroad in the context of a non-international armed conflict, they remain bound by the procedural rules on detention under those human rights treaties to which they are party.[155] Indeed, as was noted in chapter 5, whilst the United States took the view that its detention operations in the conflicts in Iraq and Afghanistan were not regulated by their human rights treaty obligations, other states have taken the contrary view, accepting the application of their human rights obligations when detaining abroad.[156]

---

[150] *Coard et al v United States* (n 67) [37]; *Alejandre v Cuba*, Report No 86/99, 29 September 1999, [25]. See, however, Goldman (n 143) 111 (suggesting that the ACHR and ADRDM would not extend beyond the Western Hemisphere).

[151] *Al-Skeini* (n 148) [137].

[152] *Lopez-Burgos v Uruguay* (n 142) [12.1]; *Celiberti v Uruguay* (n 147) [10.1]; HRC (n 13) [18]; HRC, General Comment No 35 (n 10) [65].

[153] *Ocalan v Turkey* (n 148) [91]; *Al-Saadoon* (n 145) [87]–[88]; *Medvedyev and others v France*, App No 3394/03, Judgment (Grand Chamber), 29 March 2010, [66]–[67]; *Al-Jedda* (n 32) [85] and [75]; *Al-Skeini* (n 148) [136].

[154] *Coard et al v United States* (n 67) [37].

[155] Similarly, see G Verdirame, 'Human Rights in Wartime: A Framework for Analysis' (2010) 6 EHRLR 689, 698. The discussion here has focused on states' negative obligations. Jurisprudence suggests that the extent to which a state is bound by its positive obligations to protect individuals from arbitrary detention by non-state actors (including armed groups) abroad will likely depend on *territorial* control: *Loizidou v Turkey*, App No 15318/89, Judgment (Preliminary Objections), 23 February 1995, [62]; *Bankovic* (n 148) [70]; *DRC v Uganda* (n 85) [179].

[156] See, eg, HRC, 'Information Received from the United Kingdom of Great Britain and Northern Ireland on the Implementation of the Concluding Observations of the Human Rights Committee', CCPR/C/GBR/CO/6/Add.1, 3 November 2009, [24] ('[w]e are prepared to accept that the UK's obligations under the ICCPR could in principle apply to persons taken into custody by UK forces and held in military detention facilities outside the UK. However, any such decision would need to be made in the light of the specific circumstances and facts prevailing at the time'). This acceptance has been reiterated even since the UK's change in position regarding the relevance of IHRL for detentions in non-international armed conflict: HRC, 'Observations by the Government of the United Kingdom of Great Britain and Northern Ireland on draft General Comment 35 on Article 9 of the International Covenant on Civil and Political Rights (ICCPR) – liberty and security of person' (undated), [27]–[28] <http://www.ohchr.org/EN/HRBodies/CCPR/Pages/DGCArticle9.

6.2.1 Extraterritorial derogation from human rights treaties

Several key arguments have now been presented in this book. First, states remain bound in full by their IHRL obligations when interning individuals in the context of a non-international armed conflict. Second, concerns related to military necessity can adequately be addressed through derogation from certain of those obligations. Third, those IHRL obligations also apply where states detain persons in extraterritorial non-international armed conflicts. The question remains, therefore, as to whether it is, in principle, permissible to derogate from human rights treaty obligations due to a state voluntarily participating in a non-international armed conflict abroad (where there is no tangible *internal* threat to the state). This question arises since the language of the derogation clauses in human rights treaties appears focused on an internal threat to a state, referring to a 'public emergency which threatens the life of the nation'.[157] Indeed, states have never derogated from their human rights treaty obligations in respect of situations abroad with no domestic threat, and this has been suggested as evidence that extraterritorial derogation is not permissible.[158]

Whilst this issue is yet to be settled in jurisprudence, the present author is of the view that derogation should be permissible with respect to extraterritorial situations. A number of arguments warrant this conclusion. First, as argued by Marko Milanović, the absence of extraterritorial derogations by states cannot be said to evidence a shared view as to their impermissibility; rather, this is equally likely to be a result of the attempts by certain states not to concede the general extraterritorial application of human rights treaties.[159] Second, if the substantive rights are accepted as being capable of applying extraterritorially where the state exercises jurisdiction, there is no principled reason for not also accepting that the derogation clause can extend extraterritorially; indeed, given that the derogation clause is designed to account for situations of necessity, it would seem that its application should be coterminous with the application of the substantive rights.[160] Third, though the language of the derogation clauses implies the need for an internal existential threat to the state before derogation would be permissible, they have been interpreted as having a broader scope, and applying them extraterritorially would follow this trend.[161] For these reasons, it is submitted that derogation from

---

aspx> accessed 5 August 2015. See further references to other states in support of the extraterritoriality of the IHRL rules on detention in sections 5.2.2.1 and 5.2.2.2.

[157] See, eg, Art 4(1) ICCPR.

[158] *R (Al-Jedda) v Secretary of State for Defence* [2007] UKHL 58, [38] (Lord Bingham); *R (Smith) v Secretary of State for Defence*, [2010] UKSC 29, [57]; *R (Smith and others) v The Ministry of Defence*, [2013] UKSC 41, [59]–[60]; Goldman (n 143) 114.

[159] M Milanović, 'Extraterritorial Derogations from Human Rights Treaties in Armed Conflict' in N Bhuta (ed), *The Frontiers of Human Rights: Extraterritoriality and its Challenges* (Collected Courses of the Academy of European Law, OUP, Oxford, forthcoming) 3–4 <http://papers.ssrn.com/sol3/papers.cfm?abstract_id=2447183> accessed 4 August 2015.

[160] *Serdar Mohammed v Ministry of Defence* [2014] EWHC 1369 (QB) [155]–[156].

[161] Milanović (n 159) 17–18; H Krieger, 'After Al-Jedda: Detention, Derogation, and an Enduring Dilemma,' (2011) 50 Mil L & L War Rev 419, 436; R Wilde, 'The Extraterritorial Application of

6.3 Human Rights Obligations of Non-State Armed Groups

certain human rights treaty provisions with respect to military operations abroad should not per se be considered impermissible.[162]

Chapters 5 and 6 have thus far examined the extent to which IHRL regulates detentions by *states* in non-international armed conflict. It has been shown that the relevant rules fully apply to detentions by states in relation to non-international conflicts, thereby helping to address an issue left open by IHL. However, the extent to which IHRL also regulates detentions by non-state armed groups in non-international conflicts remains to be examined. This question falls within a broader debate regarding the human rights obligations of non-state actors generally.[163] Whilst a detailed discussion of this issue is beyond the scope of the present book, it will be shown that there is an emerging consensus that IHRL binds non-state groups in certain situations, although it remains to be seen whether this will come to be universally accepted. However, in many other situations, only persons detained by the state will benefit from the protections under IHRL. This is notwithstanding the frequency with which non-state groups detain persons in non-international conflicts.[164] Moreover, even if it is accepted that these human rights rules bind armed groups, a number of difficulties arise in applying those rules to them. Consequently, it will be shown that IHRL alone is not sufficient to protect victims of non-international conflicts from arbitrary deprivations of liberty.[165]

It was traditionally thought that IHRL binds only *states* and could not also bind non-state actors.[166] In recent years, however, this traditional view has been challenged in both doctrine and practice.[167] Both the Security Council and

---

International Human Rights Law on Civil and Political Rights' in S Sheeran and N Rodley (eds), *Routledge Handbook of International Human Rights Law* (Routledge, Abingdon 2013) 654–5.

[162] Though not addressing this, the ECtHR in *Al-Jedda* (n 32) at [100] did imply that it considers extraterritorial derogations to be, in principle, permissible. However, see also K de Costa, *The Extraterritorial Application of Selected Human Rights Treaties* (Brill, Leiden 2013) 135–6 (on various *practical* difficulties that states might encounter in making a case that derogation is lawful with respect to extraterritorial military operations).

[163] See, eg, P Alston, *Non-State Actors and Human Rights* (OUP, Oxford 2005); A Clapham, *Human Rights Obligations of Non-State Actors* (OUP, Oxford 2006).

[164] See section 3.4 for examples.

[165] Similarly, see J Pejic, 'Conflict Classification and the Law Applicable to Detention and the Use of Force' in E Wilmshurst (ed), *International Law and the Classification of Conflicts* (OUP, Oxford 2012) 90–1.

[166] See, eg, *Prosecutor v Dragoljub Kunarac et al* (Trial Judgment) IT-96-23-T and IT-96-23/1-T (22 February 2001) [470]; L Zegveld, *The Accountability of Armed Opposition Groups in International Law* (CUP, Cambridge 2002) 38–55; L Moir, *The Law of Internal Armed Conflict* (CUP, Cambridge 2002) 194.

[167] Certain commentators consider IHRL to bind non-state groups in non-international armed conflict: D Fleck, 'Humanitarian Protection Against Non-State Actors' in JA Frowein et al (eds), *Verhandeln für den Frieden—Negotiating for Peace: Liber Amicorum Tono Eitel* (Springer, Berlin 2003); C Tomuschat, 'The Applicability of Human Rights Law to Insurgent Movements' in H Fischer et al (eds), *Krisensicherung und Humanitärer Schutz—Crisis Management and Humanitarian*

General Assembly, for example, have called for adherence to IHL *and* IHRL by both states and non-state groups in non-international conflicts.[168] Christian Tomuschat argues that, in these resolutions, the Security Council and General Assembly are purporting to state the law as it currently stands.[169] Other bodies, too, have assumed that IHRL creates obligations for non-state armed groups.[170]

Notwithstanding the above trend, it remains unclear as to the basis of obligation of non-state groups in these situations. The statements by the General Assembly and Security Council, for example, make little or no reference to the basis or source of obligations.[171] However, though various grounds have been advanced for the binding nature of IHRL vis-à-vis non-state groups, the view that they are bound where they exercise territorial control 'has attracted the most support and represents, by some margin, the predominant view to date'.[172] Indeed, practice of UN and other bodies endorses this view that non-state groups are bound by IHRL where they control territory.[173]

Protection: Festschrift für Dieter Fleck (BWV, Berlin 2004); A Clapham, 'Human Rights Obligations of Non-State Actors in Conflict Situations' (2006) 88 IRRC 491.

[168] See, eg, UNGA Res 67/262 (2012) [2] (Syria); UNSC Res 1834 (2008) preambular [4] (Chad); UNSC Res 1814 (2008) [16] (Somalia); UNSC Res 1464 (2003) [7] (Côte d'Ivoire); UNSC Res 1468 (2003) [2], UNSC Res 1417 (2002) [4], and UNGA Res 53/160 (1998) [4] (DRC); UNGA Res 57/230 (2002) [3(b)], and UNGA Res 54/182 (1999) [3(a)] (Sudan); UNSC Res 1213 (1998) [7] (Angola); UNGA Res 48/153 (1993) [4] (the former Yugoslavia).

[169] Tomuschat (n 167) 586.

[170] See, eg, *Institut de Droit International*, 'The Application of International Humanitarian Law and Fundamental Human Rights in Armed Conflicts, in which Non-State Entities are Parties' (Session of Berlin—1999), Art II <http://www.idi-iil.org/idiE/resolutionsE/1999_ber_03_en.PDF> accessed 7 August 2015; UN Commission on Human Rights, 'Extrajudicial, Summary or Arbitrary Executions: Report of the Special Rapporteur, Philip Alston: Mission to Sri Lanka', UN Doc E/CN.4/2006/53/Add.5, 27 March 2006, [26]; Human Rights Council, 'Human Rights in Palestine and Other Occupied Arab Territories: Report of the United Nations Fact-Finding Mission on the Gaza Conflict', A/HRC/12/48, 25 September 2009, [305]; *Informe de la Comisión para el Esclarecimiento Histórico, Guatemala Momoria del Silencio*, Vol I, 1999, 46 [20], cited and translated in J-M Henckaerts and C Wiesener, 'Human Rights Obligations of Non-State Armed Groups: A Possible Contribution from Customary International Law?' in R Kolb and G Gaggioli, *Research Handbook on Human Rights and Humanitarian Law* (Edward Elgar, Cheltenham 2013) 152.

[171] See, eg, UNGA Res 67/262 (2012) [2] (Syria) (referring generally to 'human rights abuses' and 'violations of international humanitarian law' by anti-government armed groups); UNSC Res 1834 (2008) preambular [4] (Chad) (referring to 'serious violations of human rights and international humanitarian law' by armed groups).

[172] S Sivakumaran, *The Law of Non-International Armed Conflict* (OUP, Oxford 2012) 96, citing, eg, NS Rodley, 'Can Armed Opposition Groups Violate Human Rights?' in KE Mahoney and P Mahoney (eds), *Human Rights in the Twenty-First Century: A Global Challenge* (Martinus Nijhoff, Dordrecht 1993); Zegveld (n 166) 148–51; C Ryngaert, 'Human Rights Obligations of Armed Groups' [2008] RBDI 355. Similarly, see Tomuschat (n 167) 588; JA Hessbruegge, 'Human Rights Violations Arising from the Conduct of Non-State Actors' (2005) 11 Buff Hum Rghts L Rev 21, 40–1.

[173] See, eg, UN Commission on Human Rights, Mission to Sri Lanka (n 170) [26]; UN Commission on Human Rights, 'Extrajudicial, Summary or Arbitrary Executions: Report of the Special Rapporteur, Philip Alston', E/CN.4/2005/7, 22 December 2004, [76]; Human Rights Council, Mission on the Gaza Conflict (n 170) [305] and [1369]; UN Secretary-General, 'Report of the Secretary-General's Panel of Experts on Accountability in Sri Lanka' (31 March 2011) [188] <http://www.refworld.org/docid/4db7b23e2.html> accessed 7 August 2015; Human Rights Council, 'Report of the International Commission of Inquiry to Investigate All Alleged Violations of International Human Rights Law in the Libyan Arab Jamahiriya', UN Doc A/HRC/17/44,

6.3 Human Rights and Non-State Groups

Even if this is accepted, it remains to be seen what the source of the obligations is (eg treaty or custom) in such situations. There is no reason in principle why human rights treaties could not bind non-state actors (including armed groups) in addition to states parties. It was shown in chapter 3 that, where states parties intend a treaty to bind individuals, then this can be the result.[174] However, whilst it was shown that such an intention is clear regarding IHL treaties, the same cannot be said for human rights treaties, as neither their text nor subsequent practice demonstrates a clear intention that they bind non-state armed groups. Indeed, the text suggests that they bind states parties alone.[175]

It has been suggested that non-state groups in control of territory could be bound by the human rights treaty obligations of the state with sovereign authority over that territory based on the HRC's view regarding state succession: 'once the people are accorded the protection of the rights under the [ICCPR], such protection devolves with territory'.[176] However, there are two problems with this argument. First, it is not clear that this *sui generis* approach to state succession has, or indeed will, crystallize as a customary norm.[177] Second, even were it so to crystallize, the focus remains on *state* succession, and there is no suggestion that the same principle applies where *non-state* actors control territory within a single, existing state.

It is submitted that the more plausible source of human rights obligations of non-state armed groups is custom. As chapter 4 demonstrated, the arbitrary deprivation of liberty prohibition under the general human rights treaties has crystallized as a customary rule.[178] It was explained in section 3.4.3 that customary international law can bind non-state armed groups. As the ICJ made clear in the *Reparations* case, what constitutes an actor with international legal personality, and with rights and duties derived therefrom (including under custom), varies depending on the needs of the international community.[179] Particularly where

---

1 June 2011, [72]; Human Rights Council, 'Report of the Independent International Commission of Inquiry on the Syrian Arab Republic', UN Doc A/HRC/21/50, 16 August 2012, 47, Annex II [10].

[174] See section 3.4.2.

[175] See, eg, Art 2(1) ICCPR ('[e]ach *State party*...') (my emphasis); Art 1 ECHR ('[t]he High Contracting Parties shall secure...'); Art 1(1) ACHR ('[t]he State Parties to this Convention undertake...'). Although note the 'duties' contained in ACHPR, Part I, ch II.

[176] On the HRC's view, see HRC, General Comment No 26: Continuity of Obligations, CCPR/C/21/Rev.1/Add.8/Rev.1, 8 December 1997, [4]. Similarly, see MT Kamminga, 'State Succession in Respect of Human Rights Treaties' (1996) 7 EJIL 469; R Müllerson, 'The Continuity and Succession of States, by Reference to the Former USSR and Yugoslavia' (1993) 42 ICLQ 473. Applying this to the case of non-state armed groups in control of territory, see Tomuschat (n 167) 588; A Cullen and S Wheatley, 'The Human Rights of Individuals in *De Facto* Regimes under the European Convention on Human Rights' (2013) 13 HRLR 691, 717–23.

[177] MN Shaw, *International Law* (6th edn, CUP, Cambridge 2008) 984. Though the issue of succession depends on the nature of the treaty and the circumstances surrounding succession, the traditional view is that newly created states emerge free from most of the conventional obligations of the former sovereigns: DP O'Connell, *State Succession in Municipal and International Law: Volume II* (CUP, Cambridge 1967) 88. The main exceptions to this lie with boundary and territorial treaties: see Vienna Convention on Succession of States in Respect of Treaties, 1946 UNTS 3 (adopted 23 August 1978, entered into force 6 November 1996), arts 11 and 12.

[178] Section 4.3.1.

[179] *Advisory Opinion Concerning Reparation for Injuries Suffered in the Service of the United Nations (Reparations)* [1949] ICJ Rep 174, 178.

non-state groups control territory, a clear need arises for them to be bound by customary human rights norms, lest their territorial control create a gap in the protection afforded to individuals. Such a gap could arise as the state's positive obligation to protect individuals from arbitrary detention by non-state actors may not extend to insurgent-held territory, due to the absence of the requisite degree of control for such obligations to apply.[180] Given the very general terms in which the UN and other bodies referred to above speak when discussing the human rights obligations of non-state armed groups, and in particular the absence of any reference to particular treaties, there is a strong argument that it is customary human rights norms which they have in mind.[181] As such, non-state groups in control of territory should be considered bound by the customary human rights rule prohibiting arbitrary deprivations of liberty.

Finally, it is to be noted that non-state armed groups may become bound by additional human rights norms through their consent. As noted in chapter 3 regarding IHL, such consent is commonly expressed through either unilateral declarations or bilateral agreements between the relevant state and non-state group.[182] Certain non-state groups have used both avenues to commit themselves to honour additional human rights norms.[183] Indeed, a number of unilateral and bilateral commitments incorporate the procedural rules on detention under IHRL. For example, in the 2011 Manual issued by the National Transitional Council (NTC) in Libya, a purely IHRL-model was adopted for all detainees other than 'fighters', requiring release unless held on criminal charges and tried before a court in accordance with the Libyan criminal code.[184] Similarly, the 1990 San José agreement between the government of El Salvador and the *Frente Farabundo Martí para la Liberación Nacional* (FMLN) contained a number of procedural rules relating to detention that mirror those under IHRL.[185] As such, the agreement demands from both sides that individual liberty be respected,[186] that individuals be arrested 'only if ordered by the competent authority in writing and in accordance with the law',[187] that anyone arrested be informed of the reasons for the arrest,[188] that detainees be ensured the right to assistance from legal

---

[180] Milanović (n 138) 106–7. Although cf the ECtHR's approach in *Case of Ilascu and others v Moldova and Russia*, App No 48787/99, Judgment (Grand Chamber), 8 July 2004, [322]–[352].

[181] See references above at n 171. See also Human Rights Council, 'Report of the Independent International Commission of Inquiry on the Syrian Arab Republic', UN Doc A/HRC/21/50, 16 August 2012, 47, Annex II [10] (referring specifically to customary IHRL as binding non-state armed groups).

[182] Section 3.4.

[183] Sivakumaran (n 172) 107–51. See, eg, Political Programme of the Ogaden National Liberation Front (Ethiopia); Appeal of the Communist Party of Nepal (Maoist), 16 March 2004, both cited in Sivakumaran (n 172) 123.

[184] Manual, National Transitional Council, Libya (19 May 2011) <http://www.ejiltalk.org/ wp-content/uploads/2011/08/Final-Libyan-LOAC-Guidelines-17-May-2011.ppt> accessed 7 August 2015.

[185] For the text of the agreement, see 'Document 9: Note Verbale dated 14 August 1990 from El Salvador transmitting test of the Agreement on Human Rights signed at San José, Costa Rica, on 26 July 1990 between the Government of El Salvador and the *Frente Farabundo Martí para la Liberación Nacional* (FMLN), A/44/971-S/21541, 16 August 1990' in UN, *The United Nations and El Salvador: 1990–1995* (The UN Blue Book Series Volume IV, 1995) 107–9.

[186] Ibid, Art 2, *chapeau*.   [187] Ibid, Art 2(b).   [188] Ibid, Art 2(c).

counsel,[189] and that '[t]he fullest possible support shall be given to ensuring the effectiveness of the remedies of *amparo* and *habeas corpus*'.[190]

6.3.1 Concluding remarks: the inadequacy of IHRL

As noted at the outset, it has not been the purpose of this section to engage in a detailed analysis of the extent to which IHRL binds non-state actors generally; such an endeavour is beyond the scope of this book. Rather, the aim has been to explore those situations in which non-state armed groups might be bound by the IHRL rules on detention. In so doing, it has been shown that there is an emerging consensus in favour of the binding status of IHRL for non-state groups that control territory.[191] This leaves a considerable proportion of detainees (ie those held by non-state groups that do not control territory) without protection under IHRL. Moreover, it was argued that even those non-state groups in control of territory appear to be bound only by customary human rights norms. Chapter 4 demonstrated that, regarding the procedural regulation of detention, only the basic prohibition of arbitrary deprivations of liberty can confidently be said to have crystallized as custom (though, as noted in chapter 4, there are strong arguments that the other relevant rules are also customary). As a result, the dearth of procedural rules under IHL applicable to internment in non-international armed conflicts cannot be considered to be remedied by IHRL, given these limitations on its binding nature for non-state groups.

What is more, applying even the basic customary human rights prohibition of arbitrary deprivations of liberty to non-state groups creates problems. In particular, because the human rights rules were developed for states, they may not be appropriate for regulating detentions by non-state groups. For example, as shown in chapter 4, the prohibition of arbitrary deprivations of liberty requires, inter alia, that all detentions have a legal basis.[192] Non-state armed groups, however, can point to no such legal basis. Chapter 3 demonstrated that IHL provides no legal basis to intern in non-international armed conflicts,[193] and domestic law generally permits only state authorities to detain, treating detentions by non-state actors as illegal.[194] In consequence, applying the IHRL rules on detention to non-state armed groups could result in all detentions carried out by such groups,

---

[189] Ibid, Art 2(e).
[190] Ibid, Art 4. Similarly, see Comprehensive Agreement on Respect for Human Rights and International Humanitarian Law between the Government of the Republic of the Philippines and the National Democratic Front of the Philippines (signed 16 March 1998 in The Hague, Netherlands), Part III, Art 2(5) <http://www.incore.ulst.ac.uk/services/cds/agreements/pdf/phil8.pdf> accessed 7 August 2015.
[191] If control of territory is the defining criterion, then arguably the LTTE in north and east Sri Lanka, FARC in Colombia, and the Sudan People's Liberation Movement in south Sudan would each have been bound by customary human rights law: Sivakumaran (n 172) 98.
[192] Section 4.2.1.   [193] Section 3.1.
[194] LM Olson, 'Practical Challenges of Implementing the Complementarity between International Humanitarian and Human Rights Law—Demonstrated by the Procedural Regulation of Internment in Non-International Armed Conflict' (2009) 40 Case W Res J Intl L 437, 452.

regardless of any apparent necessity on security grounds, being violations of the customary human rights norm prohibiting arbitrary detentions. IHRL would, therefore, fail to regulate detentions carried out by such groups effectively, risking non-compliance.[195] We will return to this issue in chapter 7.

It is therefore clear that relying on IHRL alone to regulate internment in non-international conflicts provides insufficient protection for individuals. There remains considerable doubt over the extent to which those rules bind non-state armed groups and thus protect persons detained by them. Moreover, even where non-state groups may be considered bound (such as where they control territory), the state-centric nature of the rules arguably makes them inappropriate for regulating the actions of such groups. This leaves the current law in a deficient state and raises the question of how it should be developed. It is to this question that we now turn in the concluding chapter.

---

[195] Ibid, 453; D Casalin, 'Taking Prisoners: Reviewing the International Humanitarian Law Grounds for Deprivation of Liberty by Armed Opposition Groups' (2011) 93 IRRC 743.

PART IV
DEVELOPING THE LAW

7

Conclusion

Developing an Internment Regime for Non-International Armed Conflicts

The preceding chapters explored the current *lex lata* regarding the procedural regulation of internment in non-international armed conflict. This chapter will now conclude the book with a proposal for how the law in this area might be developed. In so doing, the approach taken is to *build upon* the current law as elaborated in the previous chapters, rather than replace it with a new legal regime.

It should be noted at the outset that the proposals made here are not intended to form the basis for a new treaty, for such multilateralism in this area is unlikely in the near future. Instead, it is suggested that these proposals form the basis for policies of non-governmental organizations that work with those involved in non-international armed conflicts, as well as inform the decisions of international courts and tribunals that are faced with such matters. First and foremost, this would include the International Committee of the Red Cross (ICRC), which in 2011 included on its agenda the formulating of new guidance on detention in non-international armed conflict.[1] Second, organizations such as Geneva Call work directly with non-state armed groups in encouraging the adoption of deeds of commitment. Whilst originally aimed at obtaining commitments on adherence to the ban on anti-personnel mines, it has since expanded to include commitments on the protection of women and children in armed conflict.[2] Organizations of this nature provide an essential avenue for involving non-state armed groups in the norm-creation process, thus increasing the legitimacy and compliance-pull of any resulting rules.[3] It is submitted that the proposals below would form an appropriate starting point for a deed of commitment relating to the procedural rights of internees. Finally, given that

---

[1] 31st International Conference of the Red Cross and Red Crescent 2011, Resolution 1: Strengthening Legal Protection for Victims of Armed Conflict; ICRC, 'Detention in Non-International Armed Conflict: The ICRC's Work on Strengthening Legal Protection' (21 April 2015) <www.icrc.org/eng/what-we-do/other-activities/development-ihl/strengthening-legal-protection-ihl-detention.htm> accessed 7 August 2015.

[2] See <http://www.genevacall.org> accessed 7 August 2015.

[3] See generally A Roberts and S Sivakumaran, 'Lawmaking by Non-State Actors: Engaging Armed Groups in the Creation of International Humanitarian Law' (2012) 37 YJIL 107.

the proposals are intended to build upon the current *lex lata*, they might also usefully form a reference point for human rights bodies (including UN and treaty bodies) in considering the extent to which derogation from human rights relating to detention is permissible and, more generally, the application of those rules in non-international armed conflicts.

7.1 Building on the Current Law

It has been demonstrated that the current *lex lata* regarding internment in non-international armed conflicts is derived from both international humanitarian law (IHL) and international human rights law (IHRL). Thus, chapter 3 argued that both conventional and customary IHL prohibit internment in non-international conflicts where it is not actually necessary as a result of the conflict.[4] Moreover, chapter 5 showed that the far more detailed rules under IHRL continue to apply fully, absent derogation, in non-international conflicts, alongside this basic IHL norm.

However, these IHRL rules are limited in two respects. First, section 4.3 noted that not all states are party to one of the general human rights treaties, leaving detentions by such states regulated at the international level only by those rules of human rights law that are of a customary nature (in addition to the basic IHL rule). Second, section 6.3 demonstrated that, whilst there is a growing acknowledgement that IHRL binds non-state armed groups in certain circumstances (eg where they control territory), the source of such obligations currently appears limited to custom. As with those detained by states not party to a human rights treaty, therefore, those held by non-state armed groups are similarly protected at most by only customary IHRL and the basic IHL rule. This is of particular concern as it was shown that only the basic prohibition of the arbitrary deprivation of liberty in IHRL can confidently be said to have crystallized as custom.[5] Consequently, those detained by states without human rights treaty obligations and by armed groups do not appear to enjoy the other procedural safeguards applicable under human rights treaties, such as the right to *habeas corpus*.[6] Moreover, it was also shown that applying even that basic IHRL prohibition of arbitrary detention to non-state groups is problematic, given its genesis in the law applicable to states. The current *lex lata* cannot, therefore, be considered adequate to protect persons interned in non-international armed conflicts.

---

[4] See sections 3.2.1 and 3.3.   [5] See section 4.3.

[6] It should be reiterated that the claim is *not* that the right to *habeas corpus* is not protected under customary law; rather, it is merely that, of the procedural rules under human rights law explored in the present book, only the basic prohibition of arbitrary detention can be said *without any doubt* to exist under custom. Indeed, it was shown that there is practice supporting the customary status of the right to *habeas corpus*. However, the existence of even some doubt here poses the risk of uncontrolled discretion of parties to non-international armed conflicts.

7.1.1 Eliminate the distinction between categories of armed conflict?

In response to the lack of clear, adequate rules in this area, certain commentators have advocated extending (all or parts of) the internment regimes applicable under IHL in international armed conflicts to non-international conflicts.[7] Indeed, chapter 5 demonstrated that states party to non-international armed conflicts have often adopted internment regimes that mirror those under GCIII and GCIV.[8] Similarly, this was shown to be the approach taken in the Copenhagen Principles on the Handling of Detainees in International Military Operations, which advocate a series of procedural rules to apply in extraterritorial non-international armed conflicts that are clearly based on the GCIV internment regime.[9] These approaches can be seen as part of the general trend in favour of the elimination of the distinction between international and non-international armed conflicts. Chapter 1 demonstrated that the basis for this distinction in the traditional limitation of international law to inter-state matters no longer applies, given the emergence of intra-state structures of obligation.[10] Moreover, the sovereignty arguments often raised in favour of preserving what remains of the distinction were shown to be valid only for certain issues; such arguments cannot justify the exclusion of the procedural rules applicable to internment from non-international armed conflicts.[11]

However, it was also shown that, more recently, the preservation of the distinction between categories of armed conflict has been advocated on humanitarian grounds.[12] It has long been recognized that victims of non-international conflicts require protection under international law,[13] and the traditional means by which this was achieved was to draw on the rules of IHL originally applicable

---

[7] See, eg, Chatham House and ICRC, 'Meeting Summary: Procedural Safeguards for Security Detention in Non-International Armed Conflict', London, 22–3 September 2008, 4–6, 16 <http://www.chathamhouse.org/sites/files/chathamhouse/public/Research/International%20Law/il220908summary.pdf> accessed 7 August 2015; B Oswald, 'Detention of Civilians on Military Operations: Reasons for and Challenges to Developing a Special Law of Detention' (2008) 32 Melb UL Rev 524, 548–9; M Sassòli and LM Olson, 'The Relationship between International Humanitarian Law and Human Rights Law Where it Matters: Admissible Killing and Internment of Fighters in Non-International Armed Conflicts' (2008) 90 IRRC 599, 623–7; J Pejic, 'Conflict Classification and the Law Applicable to Detention and the Use of Force' in Elizabeth Wilmshurst (ed), *International Law and the Classification of Conflicts* (Oxford University Press 2012) 95–6; E Debuf, *Captured in War: Lawful Internment in Armed Conflict* (Editions A Pedone/Hart, Paris/Oxford 2013) 502–14.

[8] See, eg, sections 5.2.1.2 (Sri Lanka) and 5.2.2.1 (Iraq).

[9] 'The Copenhagen Process on the Handling of Detainees in International Military Operations, The Copenhagen Process: Principles and Guidelines' (October 2012) (hereinafter 'Copenhagen Principles') and 'Chairman's Commentary to the Copenhagen Process: Principles and Guidelines' (hereinafter 'Chairman's Commentary') <http://um.dk/en/~/media/UM/English-site/Documents/Politics-and-diplomacy/Copenhangen%20Process%20Principles%20and%20Guidelines.pdf> accessed 2 August 2015.

[10] Section 1.1. [11] Section 1.3.1. [12] See section 1.3.2.

[13] JS Pictet (ed), *Commentary to Geneva Convention IV Relative to the Protection of Civilian Persons in Time of War* (ICRC, Geneva 1958) 27 (noting a draft convention on civil wars at the 1912 International Red Cross Conference).

in international armed conflicts only.[14] However, alongside these developments emerged IHRL, applicable to the state's actions vis-à-vis those within its jurisdiction. These rules are more protective than IHL, illustrated by the procedural regulation of internment.[15] As demonstrated in chapters 4 and 5, the IHRL rules on detention continue to apply in non-international armed conflicts, such that extending the GCIII and GCIV internment regimes to those situations could, through claims that they operate as the *lex specialis*, serve to *undermine* these protections under IHRL.[16] For this reason, it is submitted that eliminating the distinction between international and non-international armed conflicts in this area, and applying the GCIII and GCIV internment regimes to the latter as the *lex specialis*, would be a regressive step—not only are those regimes much more permissive than IHRL, but, as chapter 2 demonstrated, the IHL rules also leave a number of issues unanswered, resulting in considerable discretion for the detaining power. Moreover, it was also shown in chapter 6 that the IHRL rules on detention are capable, through contextual interpretation and a (limited) right to derogate, of taking account of the kinds of necessity-based concerns of states that commonly arise in armed conflict.

7.1.2 Developing an internment regime for non-international armed conflicts

Whilst the distinction between types of armed conflict in this area should, therefore, be retained, the internment regimes applicable in international armed conflicts can nonetheless be drawn on in developing a regime for non-international conflicts. This is the approach taken in the present chapter, and the proposal made here is to build upon the current *lex lata*.[17]

---

[14] See, eg, *Prosecutor v Duško Tadić* (Decision on the Defence Motion for Interlocutory Appeal on Jurisdiction) ICTY-94-1 (2 October 1995) [127]. Commentators, too, have advocated this approach: A Duxbury, 'Drawing Lines in the Sand – Characterising Conflicts for the Purposes of Teaching International Humanitarian Law' (2007) 8 MJIL 259, 268; E Crawford, 'Unequal Before the Law: The Case for the Elimination of the Distinction between International and Non-International Armed Conflicts' (2007) 20 LJIL 441; K Mastorodimos, 'The Character of the Conflict in Gaza: Another Argument Towards Abolishing the Distinction between International and Non-International Armed Conflicts' (2010) 12 ICLR 437.

[15] This was demonstrated throughout chapter 4.

[16] Similarly, see D Kretzmer, 'Rethinking Application of IHL in Non-International Armed Conflicts' (2009) 42 Isr L Rev 8.

[17] Others too have recognized the need for developments to build on, rather than replace, existing law: see, eg, University Centre for International Humanitarian Law, 'Expert Meeting on the Supervision of the Lawfulness of Detention During Armed Conflict', Graduate Institute of International Studies, Geneva, 24–5 July 2004, 41; J Pejic, 'Procedural Principles and Safeguards for Internment/Administrative Detention in Armed Conflict and Other Situations of Violence' (2005) 87 IRRC 375; T Davidson and K Gibson, 'Experts Meeting on Security Detention Report' (2009) 40 Case W Res J Intl L 323, 340–42; JB Bellinger and VM Padmanabhan, 'Detention Operations in Contemporary Conflicts: Four Challenges for the Geneva Conventions and Other Existing Law' (2011) 105 AJIL 201.

7.1 Building on Current Law

Before setting out the proposals, a few observations on the relationship between the current law and the proposed internment regime are warranted. First, an internment regime designed specifically for non-international armed conflicts would help to address the shortcomings with the current *lex lata* outlined above. Thus, it would develop the minimum rules applicable to internment in non-international conflicts by both states not party to one of the general human rights treaties, as well as non-state armed groups. The regime would build upon the current international legal norms applicable to these actors, which, as noted, currently comprise only the basic IHL rule prohibiting unnecessary internment, as well as the customary human rights prohibition of arbitrary deprivations of liberty.

In addition, the internment regime would also provide guidance to states that are party to one or more of the general human rights treaties by setting out the minimum humanitarian standards applicable. Such guidance is necessary to give clarity to the operation of conventional human rights obligations in non-international conflicts and, in particular, the extent to which those obligations can be 'read down' or derogated from. Chapters 5 and 6 showed a clear practice amongst states and human rights treaty bodies that IHRL regulates detentions in relation to non-international conflicts.[18] The treaty bodies diverge, however, in their approaches to the possibility of reading down and/or derogating from the IHRL rules on detention.[19] A compromise between these different approaches was proposed in section 6.1.5, which advocated emphasizing the object and purpose of these rules when interpreting their minimum requirements. It was argued there that the prohibition of arbitrary deprivation of liberty and the requirement that reasons be given are sufficiently open to allow for the exigencies of the situation to be taken into account. Consequently, it was suggested that derogation from these rules is impermissible.[20] The exception here is Article 5(1) of the European Convention on Human Rights (ECHR), from which derogation is necessary in order to introduce an internment regime.[21]

Like Article 5(1) ECHR, it was shown that the right to *habeas corpus* in each of the human rights treaties does not appear open to the same reading down as the basic prohibition of 'arbitrary' detention. It was therefore argued that, in keeping with their text and object and purpose, the *habeas* provisions should be applied strictly even in non-international armed conflicts. Thus, *habeas corpus* requires independent, *judicial* review of detention, with the usual fundamental guarantees applying.[22] Where it is actually necessary, however, to depart from

---

[18] See sections 5.2 (on state practice) and 6.1 (on human rights treaty body practice).
[19] Compare, eg, sections 6.1.1 (Human Rights Committee (HRC)), 6.1.2 (European Court of Human Rights (ECtHR)), and 6.1.3 (inter-American institutions).
[20] Similarly, see HRC, General Comment No 29: States of Emergency (Article 4), CCPR/C/21/Rev.1/Add.11, 31 August 2001, [11]; Inter-American Commission on Human Rights (IACiHR), 'Report on Terrorism and Human Rights', OEA/Ser.L/V/II.116 Doc. 5 rev. 1 corr., 22 October 2002, ch III [127].
[21] *A and others v UK*, App No 3455/05, Judgment (Grand Chamber), 19 February 2009, [172].
[22] Similarly, see *Ireland v UK*, App No 5310/71, Judgment (Merits), 18 January 1978, [200]; HRC, 'Concluding Observations: United States of America', CCPR/C/USA/CO/3, 15 September 2006, [18].

these standards, it was argued that derogation should be permitted, albeit to a limited extent. In particular, it was shown that the necessity and proportionality requirements could limit derogation from *habeas corpus* by requiring, at a minimum, that an alternative review body be established that is independent at least from the specific authority that ordered detention, impartial and that has the power to order release.

The internment regime proposed in this chapter would elaborate these *minimum* standards that must be applied by states with conventional human rights obligations, as interpreted above. For example, the internment standard would be defined in a manner that is compliant with the IHRL prohibition of arbitrary detention. Moreover, where it is necessary and proportionate to derogate from *habeas corpus*, the internment regime would clarify the minimum procedures that the state must offer for their derogation to be valid. It must be emphasized that this regime is intended to comprise *minimum* rules; in a specific case, derogation from *habeas corpus*, for example, may only be permitted to a more limited extent. For non-state armed groups and states without human rights treaty obligations, however, the proposed regime would constitute the generally applicable rules in non-international armed conflicts, building upon the basic norms that currently apply to these actors.

As noted, in developing this internment regime, the IHL regimes applicable in international armed conflicts may be drawn on, with the proviso that we learn from the shortcomings of those rules and their development in doctrine and practice.[23] The sections below will now elaborate on the provisions of the proposed internment regime. Section 7.2 will demonstrate the inappropriateness of drawing by analogy from GCIII, whilst section 7.3 will argue that GCIV provides a useful starting point here.

7.2 Analogizing to GCIII

It will be remembered from chapter 2 that GCIII permits status-based internment for the duration of hostilities, with no review of the necessity of internment.[24] The examples of state practice in chapter 5 demonstrate that certain states have similarly interned persons in non-international armed conflicts on the basis of status, specifically membership of non-state armed groups.[25] Indeed, the Commentary to the Copenhagen Principles takes the view that '[a] person may be detained [eg] for…belonging to an enemy organised armed group'.[26] Moreover, armed groups in non-international armed conflicts have also detained members of state armed forces.[27] Based on this practice, it might be argued that we should draw

---

[23] See the discussion on this throughout chapter 2.   [24] Arts 21 and 118 GCIII.
[25] See, eg, sections 5.2.1.2 (Sri Lanka) and 5.2.2.2 (Afghanistan).
[26] Chairman's Commentary (n 9) [1.3].
[27] See, eg, 'Report of the Independent International Fact-Finding Mission on the Conflict in Georgia: Volume II', September 2009, 360–2 (South Ossetian forces detaining Georgian armed forces).

by analogy from GCIII in developing an internment regime for non-international conflicts.[28]

However, it is submitted that the GCIII internment regime could not appropriately be transplanted to non-international conflicts. In particular, the two elements of that regime (internment on the basis of status and for the duration of hostilities) pose significant problems when applied to non-international conflicts. Regarding status-based internment, whilst IHL does, to an extent, recognize different statuses of person in non-international armed conflicts,[29] the absence of a clearly defined status of 'combatant', to which a status-based internment regime could apply, poses problems, particularly regarding the non-state side.[30] Without this, differentiating between 'combatants' and 'civilians' becomes problematic, raising the possibility of arbitrary, indefinite internment of civilians.[31] Moreover, it is important to differentiate between the 'armed forces' and the civilian (political or humanitarian) elements of non-state armed groups, for it is only the former for whom the label 'combatant' might be appropriate.[32] However, 'the informal and clandestine structures of most organized armed groups and the elastic nature of membership render it particularly difficult to distinguish between a non-State party to the conflict and its armed forces'.[33]

Attempts have, however, been made to define membership of non-state armed forces. In its *Guidance on Direct Participation in Hostilities*, the ICRC suggested that members of non-state armed groups may be targeted on the basis of status, akin to combatant targeting in international armed conflict.[34] The ICRC adopted a functional test for membership of armed groups.[35] Thus, those performing a 'continuous combat function' are said to constitute members of the non-state armed forces.[36] In pertinent part:

...individuals whose continuous function involves the preparation, execution, or command of acts or operations amounting to direct participation in hostilities are assuming a continuous combat function.[37]

---

[28] ICRC, Strengthening International Humanitarian Law, Protecting Persons Deprived of their Liberty: Thematic Consultation of Government Experts on Grounds and Procedures for Internment and Detainee Transfers, Montreux, Switzerland, 20–22 October 2014, 18 (noting that some experts considered a status-based approach to internment in non-international armed conflicts to be appropriate).
[29] N Melzer, *Interpretive Guidance on the Notion of Direct Participation in Hostilities under International Humanitarian Law* (ICRC, Geneva 2009) (hereinafter 'ICRC Guidance') 28 (noting that the wording of common Art 3 and APII demonstrates that civilians, armed forces, and organized armed groups 'are mutually exclusive categories also in non-international armed conflict').
[30] JK Kleffner, 'From "Belligerents" to "Fighters" and Civilians Directly Participating in Hostilities – On the Principle of Distinction in Non-International Armed Conflicts One Hundred Years After the Second Hague Peace Conference' (2007) 54 NILR 315, 321.
[31] Ibid, 323. [32] ICRC Guidance (n 29) 32; Sassòli and Olson (n 7) 607–8.
[33] ICRC Guidance (n 29) 33. [34] Ibid, 27.
[35] Ibid, 32–3; N Melzer, 'Keeping the Balance between Military Necessity and Humanity: A Response to Four Critiques of the ICRC's Interpretive Guidance on the Notion of Direct Participation in Hostilities' (2010) 42 NYU J Intl L & Pol 831, 839. Similarly, see Sassòli and Olson (n 7) 623.
[36] ICRC Guidance (n 29) 33. [37] ICRC Guidance (n 29) 34.

This approach has been criticized for being too narrow.[38] A more liberal test for membership, also based on function, has been advocated by the Obama Administration and the DC district court in the *habeas corpus* cases involving Guantánamo detainees.[39] In defining membership, Judge Walton in *Gherebi v Obama* held that '"persons who receive and execute orders" from the enemy's "command structure" can be considered members of the enemy's armed forces'.[40] The DC court's more liberal definition, compared to the ICRC's, is seen in Judge Walton's point that 'armed forces' is wider than 'fighters' (those performing a 'continuous combat function') and that the key issue is whether the individual receives and carries out orders from the 'enemy force's combat apparatus'.[41]

In addition to the difficulty with defining membership, identifying persons who fall within those definitions also presents problems. Whilst certain non-state forces, such as the *Fuerzas Armadas Revolucionarias de Colombia* (FARC) in Colombia, the Liberation Tigers of Tamil Eelam (LTTE) in Sri Lanka and the Kosovo Liberation Army, have been known to distinguish themselves,[42] making the determination of membership more objective, these are within the minority.[43] Absent an objectively identifiable emblem or uniform, the detaining power would be required to make a determination of each individual's function. Identifying an individual as a member of a non-state armed group will thus often involve a significant degree of discretion. Indeed, it is the discretion exercised when interning civilians, which explains GCIV's requirement of review.[44] Chapter 2 explained, however, that GCIII does not provide an equivalent review for prisoners of war (POWs).[45] Extending the GCIII internment regime thus raises the possibility of error without any chance of rectification via review, risking arbitrary detention on the mistaken belief that individuals are members of non-state armed forces. This would contravene both the basic IHL rule applicable in non-international armed conflicts (prohibiting internment that is not necessary as a result of the war), as well as the prohibition of arbitrary deprivations of liberty in customary human rights law. Drawing on GCIII would, therefore, undermine the current *lex lata* which, as noted, should be built upon, rather than replaced.

---

[38] K Watkin, 'Opportunity Lost: Organized Armed Groups and the ICRC "Direct Participation in Hostilities" Interpretive Guidance' (2010) 42 NYU J Intl L & Pol 641, 676.

[39] Respondents' Memorandum Regarding the Government's Detention Authority Relative to Detainees Held at Guantanamo Bay, *In Re: Guantanamo Bay Detainee Litigation*, Misc No 08-442 (TFH) (DDC 13 March 2009) 6–7 <http://www.justice.gov/opa/documents/memo-re-det-auth.pdf> accessed 7 August 2015; *Hamlily v Obama*, 616 F Supp 2d 63 (DDC 2009) 75.

[40] *Gherebi v Obama*, 609 F Supp 2d 43 (DDC 2009) 68, citing CA Bradley and JL Goldsmith, 'Congressional Authorization and the War on Terrorism' (2005) 118 Harv L Rev 2047, 2114–5; *Hamlily* (n 39) 75.

[41] *Gherebi* (n 40) 69.

[42] Kleffner (n 30) 334 (fn 90); Watkin (n 38) 678; UK Ministry of Defence, *The Manual of the Law of Armed Conflict* (OUP, Oxford 2004) 143 (fn 25).

[43] Kleffner (n 30) 334; ICRC Guidance (n 29) 32–3; Sassòli and Olson (n 7) 609; *A and B v State of Israel*, Crim A 3261/08 (11 June 2008) (Israeli Supreme Court) 23.

[44] Arts 43 and 78 GCIV. See section 2.3.1.   [45] Section 2.3.2.

7.2 Analogizing to GCIII

The other aspect of the GCIII internment regime—internment for the duration of hostilities—poses further problems in non-international armed conflicts. The Obama Administration and the DC courts, for example, argued that members of al-Qaeda may be interned for the duration of hostilities.[46] Chapter 2 explained that the philosophy underpinning this rule in international armed conflicts is that combatants are assumed to pose the threat of returning to the battlefield until hostilities cease.[47] It must be borne in mind, however, that both customary human rights and humanitarian law applicable in non-international conflicts require release of *all* internees as soon as the reasons justifying internment cease, lest internment become arbitrary.[48] The difficulty here is that 'the informal… structures of most organized armed groups and the elastic nature of membership' means that those initially interned as 'members' may not continue to be so for the duration of hostilities.[49] As with membership, functional criteria may be sufficient to constitute *de facto* withdrawal from non-state forces. As the ICRC notes, '[d]isengagement from an organized armed group…[may] be expressed through conclusive behaviour, such as a lasting physical distancing from the group'.[50] The internee in such a case may no longer pose the threat of rejoining hostilities. An example of this arose in *Basardh v Obama*, part of the Guantanamo *habeas* litigation, in which Judge Huvelle acknowledged that the detainee had ostracized himself from al-Qaeda, through his well-publicized cooperation with the US authorities, to such an extent as to no longer constitute a member of that group.[51] Detention for the duration of hostilities was thus unnecessary.

The above concern is exacerbated by the indeterminacy in the point at which hostilities cease in non-international armed conflicts, raising the chances of extremely prolonged detention.[52] Indeed, this could be problematic for compliance with the customary human rights prohibition of arbitrary deprivation of liberty, given the trend referred to in chapter 4 whereby human rights bodies are increasingly sceptical of prolonged, indefinite detention.[53] Moreover, it is for this reason that applying the GCIII internment regime to govern detentions by non-state armed groups of regular state forces would also be problematic, notwithstanding that that regime was designed primarily with state forces in mind.[54] The indeterminacy in the point at which hostilities cease in

---

[46] *Hamlily* (n 39) 70.   [47] Section 2.4.2.
[48] See sections 3.3.2 (IHL) and 4.3.2 (IHRL).   [49] ICRC Guidance (n 29) 33.
[50] Ibid, 72.
[51] *Basardh v Obama*, 612 F Supp 2d 30 (DDC 2009). Cf *Awad v Obama*, 608 F 3d 1 (DC Cir 2010) 18.
[52] Similarly, see *In re Guantanamo Detainee Cases*, 355 F Supp 2d 443 (DDC 2005) 465–6; cf *Al-Bihani v Obama and others* [2010] 140 ILR 716 (DC Cir) 727; CA Bradley and JL Goldsmith, 'Congressional Authorization and the War on Terrorism' (2004–5) 118 Harv L Rev 2047, 2124–5; Sassòli and Olson (n 7) 624; MC Waxman, 'The Structure of Terrorism Threats and the Laws of War' (2010) 20 Duke J Comp & Intl L 429, 452–4; Bellinger & Padmanabhan (n 17) 228–33.
[53] See section 4.2.5.
[54] Y Dinstein, *The Conduct of Hostilities under the Law of International Armed Conflict* (2nd edn CUP, Cambridge 2010) 41.

many non-international armed conflicts would make applying the GCIII rule on release particularly difficult.

In light of the above, it is submitted that the GCIII internment regime is inappropriate for application in non-international armed conflict. The next section will demonstrate how GCIV might be useful here.

7.3 Analogizing to GCIV

By being premised on individual *conduct* as opposed to *status*, the GCIV internment regime offers a more useful framework from which we may draw inspiration, as it helps to address the concerns raised above. For example, as demonstrated in chapter 2, GCIV permits internment only for so long as it is necessary for security, based on *individual* threat, thus avoiding the concern that persons could be held beyond this point (and thus arbitrarily) were the assumption under GCIII of internment for the duration of hostilities extended to non-international armed conflicts.[55] Similarly, initial and periodic review of the necessity of internment as required by GCIV could help to provide a check on any discretion that might be exercised by the detaining authority.[56]

GCIV is therefore a useful starting point in developing an internment regime for non-international conflicts. Each category of procedural rules under GCIV will now be considered for application in non-international conflicts, drawing on the criticisms and elaborations of those rules discussed in chapter 2. Their ability to satisfy and enforce the current *lex lata*, and thus to build upon that framework, will be the principal frame of reference.

7.3.1 Standard for internment

The standard for internment must be such as to satisfy the current minimum *lex lata* applicable in non-international conflicts, comprising both IHL's prohibition of internment that is not actually necessary as a result of the conflict,[57] as well as the customary human rights prohibition of arbitrary deprivation of liberty.[58] This is especially important, given that both of these norms were said to be non-derogable and to bind all parties in non-international conflicts, states and non-state groups alike.[59] In light of this, the Article 42(1) GCIV standard, permitting internment 'only if the security of the Detaining Power makes it absolutely necessary', seems more appropriate than the Article 78(1) GCIV standard, which, as

---

[55] Art 132(1) GCIV. See section 2.4.1.
[56] Arts 43(1) and 78(2) GCIV. See section 2.3.1. [57] Section 3.2.1.
[58] Section 4.3.1.
[59] On non-derogability of the human rights rule, see section 6.1.5. On the binding nature of these rules for non-state groups, see sections 3.4 (IHL) and 6.3 (IHRL). It was noted in section 6.3, however, that the customary human rights prohibition of arbitrary deprivations of liberty currently appears to bind non-state groups in control of territory only. By contrast, the IHL norm applies to any group that is a party to a non-international armed conflict.

7.3 Analogizing to GCIV

explained in chapter 2, is partly subjective, in that it permits internment where the 'Occupying Power *considers* it necessary, for imperative reasons of security'.[60] Indeed, as chapter 3 demonstrated, Article 27(4) GCIV, on which the basic IHL norm applicable in non-international armed conflicts was said to be based, requires that measures of security (eg internment) *actually* be necessary as a result of the conflict.[61] Similarly, the IHRL prohibition of arbitrary detention requires that any detention *actually* be necessary, and no more than is necessary, for the legitimate purpose sought.[62] The objective standard in Article 42(1) GCIV therefore seems more appropriate for non-international conflicts than the standard in Article 78(1) GCIV. Moreover, the decision on internment should be taken at a high level of command to allow for consideration of its actual necessity as soon as possible after the initial capture.[63] It should be repeated here that there is an 'assumption [in IHRL] that the criminal justice system is able to deal with persons suspected of representing a danger to State security'; internment can only be employed where *actually* necessary to address the security threat, which includes the requirement that the criminal justice system cannot contain that threat.[64]

Chapter 2, however, demonstrated that the GCIV standards, particularly the 'security' prong, leave significant discretion to the detaining power. This could be problematic since human rights jurisprudence confirms that, as part of the arbitrary deprivation of liberty prohibition, the grounds for detention must be 'clearly defined' and 'foreseeable in application'.[65] Whilst the Article 42(1) GCIV standard could fail to satisfy this requirement, this can be mitigated in a number of ways, all of which have been discussed in the previous chapters. First, as noted above, the prohibition of arbitrary deprivation of liberty in IHRL is sufficiently open to take account of the exigencies of a non-international conflict; the situation can thus affect what qualifies as 'arbitrary'.[66] For example, whilst internment where 'the security of the Detaining Power makes it absolutely necessary' might, in ordinary situations, be considered too vague, the existence of a non-international armed conflict could be such as to allow this less specific standard, along with the elaborations of it noted below. The standard must not, however, be so broad as to allow detention to be entirely within the discretion of the detaining authority.[67]

---

[60] See section 2.2.1. [61] See section 3.2.1.
[62] HRC, *A v Australia*, CCPR/C/59/D/560/93, 3 April 1997, [9.2]; Inter-American Court of Human Rights (IACtHR), *Chaparro Alvarez and Lapo Iniguez v Ecuador*, Judgment, IACtHR (Series C) No 170 (2007) [93]; ECtHR, *Saadi v UK*, App No 13229/03, Judgment, 29 January 2008, [70].
[63] Similarly, see Chatham House and ICRC (n 7) 6; ICRC, Strengthening International Humanitarian Law (n 28) 20–3.
[64] Pejic (n 17) 380; Chatham House and ICRC (n 7) 5; ICRC, Strengthening International Humanitarian Law (n 28) 10–12. See section 4.2.1.1.
[65] ECtHR, *Medvedyev and others v France*, App No 3394/03, Judgment (Grand Chamber), 29 March 2010, [80]. Similarly, see IACiHR, *Dayra María Levoyer Jiménez v Ecuador*, Report No 66/01, 14 June 2001, [37]; ACiHPR, *Amnesty International and others v Sudan*, Communication Nos 48/90, 50/91, 52/91, and 89/93 (2003), [58]–[60].
[66] HRC, General Comment No 35: Article 9 (Liberty and security of person), CCPR/C/FC/35, 16 December 2014, [66].
[67] *Amnesty International v Sudan* (n 65) [58]–[60]. Similarly, see Chatham House and ICRC (n 7) 8 (warning that, whilst the internment standard in Colin Powell's annexed letter to UNSC Res

Second, we can draw on elaborations of this standard in doctrine and practice. Thus, chapter 2 demonstrated that practice has endorsed the view that, to satisfy the GCIV internment standards, 'the party must have good reason to think that the person concerned, by his activities, knowledge or qualifications, represents a real threat to its present or future security'.[68] More specifically, '[s]ubversive activity...or actions...of direct assistance to an opposing party' may satisfy the standard if the detaining authority 'has *serious and legitimate reasons* to think that they may seriously prejudice its security by means such as sabotage or espionage'.[69] It was argued in section 2.2.1 that further defining *in abstracto* the situations that may be considered security threats necessitating internment would risk being either under- or over-inclusive. In a specific situation, however, by making known to the population in advance the kinds of actions that would constitute a security threat justifying internment, the vagueness of the Article 42(1) GCIV standard can be mitigated.[70]

Third, we can learn from other areas of international law in which state security may be invoked as a basis for departing from the ordinary rules. For example, chapter 2 noted that the International Court of Justice (ICJ), the ECtHR, and the European Court of Justice (ECJ) have all addressed national security claims of states by treating separately the two issues of national security and necessity, with the result that, whilst deference is given to the state in defining what constitutes a threat to its security, the necessity element is an objective standard susceptible to judicial review.[71] As the necessity requirement in Article 42(1) GCIV is objective (cf Article 78(1) GCIV), it offers a reasonable counterbalance to the discretion left to the detaining authority under the security element of the internment standard. As will be shown below, this necessity element can then be utilized by the reviewing body as an objective check on detention authority.

Fourth, we can also draw on the *limits* of the GCIV detention authority that have been developed.[72] For example, the following characteristics, by themselves, are considered insufficient to render internment necessary for security reasons: nationality or alignment with the opposing party;[73] being of military age;[74]

1546 (2004) is arguably sufficient, a UNSC Res authorizing simply 'all necessary measures' probably would not be).

[68] *Prosecutor v Zejnil Delalić et al* (Trial Judgment) ICTY-96-21 (16 November 1998) [577]. This standard was originally included in Pictet, *GCIV* (n 13) 257–8. The standard has been adopted for international conflicts in UK Ministry of Defence, *Manual* (n 42) at 230.

[69] *Delalić* (n 68) [576].

[70] In *Steel and others v UK*, App 24838/94, Judgment, 23 September 1998, at [54], the ECtHR emphasized that the legal basis for detention must be sufficiently detailed so as to enable individuals to know what the consequences of their actions will be.

[71] D Akande and S Williams, 'International Adjudication on National Security Issues: What Role for the WTO?' (2003) 43 Va J Intl L 365, 382–3 and 396–8.

[72] See section 2.2.1.

[73] *Delalić* (n 68) [577]; *Prosecutor v Zejnil Delalić et al* (Appeals Judgment) ICTY-96-21-A (20 February 2001) [327]; *Prosecutor v Dario Kordić and Mario Čerkez* (Trial Judgment) ICTY-95-14/2-T (26 February 2001) [284]; EECC, *Civilians Claims, Ethiopia's Claim 5 (Ethiopia/Eritrea)*, Partial Award, 17 December 2004, 135 ILR 427, [102]–[104]; Pictet, *GCIV* (n 13) 258; UK Ministry of Defence, *Manual* (n 42) 230.

[74] *Delalić* (n 68) [577]; *Kordić and Čerkez* (n 73) [284]; Pictet, *GCIV* (n 13) 258.

possessing intelligence;[75] and following particular political or religious opinions or practices.[76] These limits help to ensure that nobody is unnecessarily or arbitrarily interned in contravention of IHL and IHRL. In addition, as section 2.2.1 demonstrated, jurisprudence has confirmed that GCIV permits internment only where the *individual* poses a threat necessitating internment; alleged membership of a particular group, by itself, is insufficient.[77] It was also acknowledged, however, that internment on the basis of membership of particular groups and the need for an individual threat are not necessarily inconsistent. Rather, as discussed by the Israeli Supreme Court, the particular role of the individual within the group must be considered to determine whether that role is such as to render the *individual* a security threat.[78] The same approach can be applied in non-international armed conflicts, which should help to protect against the risks posed by extending pure status-based internment to non-state armed groups, discussed above.[79]

Finally, as noted in section 6.3.1, the requirement of a legal basis for detention, which forms part of the customary human rights prohibition of arbitrary deprivation of liberty, poses particular difficulties in non-international armed conflicts, given the absence of such a legal basis in applicable IHL.[80] Whilst the legal basis for internments by the *state* will often be found in domestic law, the absence of a legal basis for *non-state* armed groups could result in any detention by them violating the customary human rights prohibition of arbitrary deprivation of liberty, even if arguably necessary for security.[81] In the absence of an internment regime being adopted in law for non-international armed conflicts, in which such a legal basis might be included, one solution to this might be to consider decrees adopted by non-state armed groups as, in certain circumstances, capable of providing the legal basis for their detentions. Indeed, non-state groups, particularly those in control of territory, have been known to adopt legislation pertaining to the activities within the territory they control.[82] On the one hand, such decrees would fall short of what is normally required of a legal basis for detention. As the UN Working Group on Arbitrary Detention has stated, such a law should either

---

[75] *Hamdi et al v Rumsfeld et al*, 542 US 507 (2004), 521 (US Supreme Court); Pejic (n 17) 380; Chatham House and ICRC (n 7) 5; Davidson and Gibson (n 17) 343–4.

[76] Y Sandoz, C Swinarski and B Zimmerman (eds), *Commentary on the Additional Protocols of 8 June 1977 to the Geneva Conventions of 12 August 1949* (ICRC/Martinus Nijhoff, Geneva 1987) 871; Israel, MOJ, Fact Sheet on Administrative Detention (2003) 3, cited in Debuf (n 7) 406.

[77] *Delalić* (n 68) [578]; *Kordić and Čerkez* (n 73) [285]; *Prosecutor v Milorad Krnojelac* (Trial Judgment) ICTY-97-25 (15 March 2002) [123]; Pictet, *GCIV* (n 13) 258; Pejic (n 17) 381.

[78] *A and B v Israel* (n 43) [21].

[79] This compromise should help to address the concerns raised by both those advocating a status-based approach to internment in non-international armed conflicts and those advocating an individual threat-based approach: ICRC, Strengthening International Humanitarian Law (n 28) 18–19.

[80] On the absence of such a legal basis, see section 3.1.

[81] LM Olson, 'Practical Challenges of Implementing the Complementarity between International Humanitarian and Human Rights Law—Demonstrated by the Procedural Regulation of Internment in Non-International Armed Conflict' (2009) 40 Case W Res J Intl L 437, 451–3.

[82] See, eg, Communist Party of Nepal-Maoist, Public Legal Code 2060 (2003/04); LTTE, Tamil Eelam Child Protection Act (Act No 3 of 2006), cited in S Sivakumaran, *The Law of Non-International Armed Conflict* (OUP, Oxford 2012) 140.

have been adopted through a democratic process or developed in long-standing practice by an independent judiciary.[83] Decrees of armed groups would clearly fail to meet this. On the other hand, where they are sufficiently clear and reflect a collective decision, they might offer sufficient notice to those within the territory controlled by the group of the kind of activity deemed prejudicial to security and thus which could lead to internment.

7.3.2 Reasons for internment

Like the arbitrary deprivation of liberty prohibition, it was argued that the IHRL requirement that the reasons for detention be given to the detainee should also be considered non-derogable, since the right is a *sine qua non* to availing oneself effectively of the right to *habeas corpus*; indeed, the right was also shown to be sufficiently open to take account of the exigencies of the situation.[84] IHL similarly requires that reasons be given to civilian internees in international armed conflicts.[85] Such a rule should therefore be incorporated into an internment regime for non-international armed conflicts.[86]

That the exigencies of a situation may be factored into this requirement will mean that its application could be affected in practice. Thus, as described in section 6.1.5, it may be justified to have a short delay before which the reasons are conveyed to the internee, for example, because their safety necessitates that they are taken from the zone of hostilities to a detention facility.[87] Moreover, certain details regarding the factual basis for detention or the evidence concerning the detainee may reasonably be withheld from them where necessary for security reasons.[88] However, the object and purpose of this right indicate that the information given must always be sufficiently detailed so as to allow the detainee to challenge the grounds on which they are detained.[89] The review body (on which see below) should have the power to examine the necessity of withholding information from the internee on security grounds.[90]

---

[83] UN Commission on Human Rights, Report of the Working Group on Arbitrary Detention, E/CN.4/2005/6, 1 December 2004, [54(a)].
[84] See section 6.1.5.   [85] Art 75(3) API.
[86] Similarly, see Copenhagen Principles (n 9) Principle 7; Pejic (n 17) 384; Body of Principles for the Protection of All Persons under Any Form of Detention or Imprisonment, 1988, UNGA Res 43/173, 9 December 1988, Principle 10.
[87] See Chatham House and ICRC (n 7) at 13, where it notes that certain experts considered that an appropriate balance between an internee's rights and the necessities of the situation might be a phased release of information, with more general reasons given at the point of capture and more detailed reasons given at the initial review stage.
[88] See, eg, the discussion in section 6.1.2 on the ECtHR's case law here: *A and others* (n 21) [220] (confirming that withholding evidence from the detainee, but not from the court, for security reasons is acceptable so long as most of the evidence relied upon is open to the detainee and sufficiently detailed). Similarly, see Chatham House and ICRC (n 7) 10.
[89] HRC, General Comment No 35 (n 66) [25]; ECtHR, *Van der Leer v Netherlands*, App No 11509/85, Judgment, 21 February 1990, [28]; *Juan Humberto Sanchez v Honduras*, Judgment, IACtHR (Ser C) No 99 (2003), [82]. Similarly, see Chatham House and ICRC (n 7) 11.
[90] Chatham House and ICRC (n 7) 13 (noting Israeli practice, where the court could order that evidence be declassified).

7.3.3 Review of internment

It was argued in section 6.1.5 that the human rights treaty provisions on *habeas corpus* should not be read down to permit non-judicial forms of review.[91] However, it was also argued that the right to *habeas corpus* should be seen as derogable to a limited extent, such that, where it is necessary and proportionate to do so, a state should be permitted temporarily to derogate from the requirement of *court* review of detention and instead provide an alternative method of review.[92] Nonetheless, the review body should always be independent of the authority that ordered detention and should have the power to order release where detention is found to be unlawful or unnecessary. This, it was argued, would enforce the basic rule in IHRL that no person be deprived of their liberty arbitrarily.

This alternative form of review should be elaborated in an internment regime for non-international armed conflicts, so as to highlight the minimum procedures that must be provided by states when derogating from *habeas corpus* under a human rights treaty. In addition, this minimum review mechanism would provide a much-needed safeguard for detainees held by states not party to a human rights treaty and by non-state armed groups in non-international armed conflicts. This review mechanism might reasonably be modelled on the initial and periodic review procedures in Article 43(1) GCIV, which provides for review of internment 'as soon as possible by an appropriate court or administrative board' as well as bi-annual periodic review by the same body. Indeed, similar approaches have been advocated in various fora when developing minimum humanitarian standards.[93]

Chapter 2, however, noted that the GCIV provisions on review are vague and leave considerable discretion to the detaining authority.[94] It is important that the same level of discretion is not extended to non-international armed conflicts, lest the arbitrary detention prohibition in IHRL, as well as the IHL prohibition of internment that is not necessary as a result of the conflict, be undermined. To address this, we can draw on the elaborations of Article 43(1) GCIV that were shown in chapter 2 to have been developed in doctrine and practice. First, the reference to administrative 'board' confirms that the decision cannot rest with a single person.[95] Furthermore, given the complex legal questions that arise in such proceedings, it would be preferable if at least one of the members was a lawyer with expertise in humanitarian or human rights law or a judge.[96] Second, the reviewing authority must operate impartially and independently from the authority that

---

[91] Whilst the other human rights treaty bodies took the same view, the IACiHR was shown to differ here: *Coard et al v United States*, Report No 109/99, 29 September 1999, [58].

[92] This approach was accepted by the ECtHR: *Ireland v UK* (n 22) [218]–[219].

[93] Body of Principles (n 86) Principle 32(1); UN Commission on Human Rights, 'The Siracusa Principles on the Limitation and Derogation Provisions in the International Covenant on Civil and Political Rights', E/CN.4/1985/4, 28 September 1984, [70(d)]. The Turku Declaration appears to borrow from the less defined review procedures in Art 78 GCIV: Declaration of Minimum Humanitarian Standards Adopted by an Expert Meeting Convened by the Institute for Human Rights, Abo Akademi University, Turku, Finland, 2 December 1990, Art 11.

[94] See section 2.3.1.   [95] Pictet, *GCIV* (n 13) 260; Pejic (n 17) 387.

[96] Similarly, see Chatham House and ICRC (n 7) 17.

ordered detention.⁹⁷ This, at a minimum, requires that the review tribunal be independent of the chain of command that ordered the detention, if not fully outside the military or executive.⁹⁸ Third, the review authority must examine the actual necessity of internment for protecting against the stated security threat. Thus, as noted above, internment is permitted under Article 42(1) GCIV only where it is absolutely necessary for reasons of security. Whilst the security element leaves discretion to the detaining authority, the necessity element offers an objective benchmark against which the reviewing authority can judge the internment.⁹⁹ Moreover, as part of this review, the board should consider whether the individual can be transferred to the criminal justice system.¹⁰⁰ This was the practice, for example, of the United States in Iraq.¹⁰¹ Fourth, the authority must have the power to order release, binding on the detaining authority.¹⁰² Fifth, the burden of proof must rest on the detaining authority to demonstrate that internment is actually necessary, and no more than is necessary, to protect against the stated security threat.¹⁰³

Sixth, the initial review should be conducted as soon as possible after the initial capture; in particular contexts, this may require a slight delay, for example, when a detainee is taken from the zone of hostilities, but it cannot be delayed without reasonable justification.¹⁰⁴ Moreover, periodic review should be provided at least every six months, as required in GCIV, although more frequent periodic review should be available where possible, as its purpose is to ensure release where the reasons justifying detention no longer apply; it thus serves to enforce the basic prohibition in IHL of unnecessary internment, binding on all parties to non-international conflicts.¹⁰⁵ The UK's *Joint Doctrine Publication on Captured Persons*, for example, requires initial review within forty-eight hours and periodic review no less frequently than every twenty-eight days.¹⁰⁶ Where the resources of the detaining authority do not permit this, an alternative might be to provide

---

⁹⁷ Pictet, *GCIV* (n 13) 260; Pejic (n 17) 386–7; Chatham House and ICRC (n 7) 15.
⁹⁸ Similarly, see ICRC, Strengthening International Humanitarian Law (n 28) 28; UK Ministry of Defence, *Joint Doctrine Publication 1-10: Captured Persons (CPERS)* (3rd edn, MOD, 2015) Annex 1B [1B3]. The Copenhagen Principles, although requiring impartiality, do not require independence from the chain of command: Copenhagen Principles (n 9) Principle 12.
⁹⁹ See above, text to n 71.
¹⁰⁰ It was noted that there is human rights practice promoting the use of criminal proceedings over administrative detention: see, eg, Pejic (n 17) 380–1. For the non-state side, transfer to the criminal jurisdiction may not be possible, however.
¹⁰¹ AE Wall, 'Civilians Detentions in Iraq' in MN Schmitt and J Pejic (eds), *International Law and Armed Conflict: Exploring the Faultlines* (Brill, The Hague 2007) 433.
¹⁰² *Delalić* (n 73) [329]; ICRC, Strengthening International Humanitarian Law (n 28) 29. The Copenhagen Principles do not require this: compare, eg, the statement that it 'may be appropriate' for the reviewing authority in cases of penal detention to have the power to order release, with the absence of any such reference with regard to the reviewing authority in cases of security detention: Chairman's Commentary (n 9) [13.2].
¹⁰³ *Delalic* (n 73) [329]; HCJ 466/86, *Abu Bakr v Judge of the Military Court in Schechem*, 40(3) PD 649, 650–1 (Israeli Supreme Court), cited in Y Dinstein, *The International Law of Belligerent Occupation* (CUP, Cambridge 2009) 176.
¹⁰⁴ ICRC, Strengthening International Humanitarian Law (n 28) 25.
¹⁰⁵ Pictet, *GCIV* (n 13) 261.   ¹⁰⁶ UK Ministry of Defence (n 98) Annex 1B [1B5].

a file review between full periodic reviews, as is the practice of the United States regarding Guantánamo detainees.[107] Additionally, periodic review should be performed whenever new information regarding an internee comes to light.[108]

Finally, the specific procedures adopted by the review body should be conducive to allowing the internee to present their case as strongly as possible. As such, internees should have personal representatives to advise them,[109] as well as the ability to make oral and written statements and to call and challenge witnesses.[110] As demonstrated in chapter 5, such procedures have, to varying degrees, been adopted by states in certain non-international armed conflicts.[111]

It is suggested that the above rules also form the framework for detention review bodies set up by non-state armed groups party to non-international armed conflicts, in addition to states. It might be objected that these would be unrealistic for non-state armed groups, who will often have far fewer resources than the state. The capacity to apply and enforce these rules will certainly vary from one group to the next. However, it should be noted that it is not necessarily the case that non-state groups would be unable to comply. Indeed, many such groups, particularly those in control of territory, have established court systems.[112] What is more, the rules above do not impose impossible burdens on the detaining authorities, and they could be framed in a sufficiently flexible way as to ensure their practicability without compromising on the principles that underpin them.

7.3.4 Release

The requirement of release where the reasons justifying detention cease was shown in chapter 4 to be inherent in the customary human rights prohibition of the arbitrary deprivation of liberty.[113] This requirement was also shown in chapter 3 to be part of IHL's basic prohibition of internment that is not necessary as a result of the conflict, applicable in non-international armed conflict.[114] As such, all parties to non-international conflicts, both states and non-state groups alike,

---

[107] Executive Order 13,567 (7 March 2011), 'Periodic Review of Individuals Detained at Guantanamo Bay Naval Station Pursuant to the Authorization for Use of Military Force', s 3(c).

[108] Similarly, see Chairman's Commentary (n 9) [12.3]; ICRC, Strengthening International Humanitarian Law (n 28) 26–7.

[109] Similarly see Body of Principles (n 86) Principle 17; Expert Meeting on the Supervision of the Lawfulness of Detention During Armed Conflict, University Centre for International Humanitarian Law, Geneva, 24–5 July 2004, 44 (noting that, whilst it may not be practicable to provide a lawyer immediately at capture, once removed from the battlefield and taken to a detention centre, a lawyer should be provided); Pejic (n 17) 388; Chatham House and ICRC (n 7) 14.

[110] Similarly see Pejic (n 17) 389; Chatham House and ICRC (n 7) 15.

[111] See, eg, the discussion of the Multi-National Force Review Committee in Iraq in BJ Bill, 'Detention Operations in Iraq: A View from the Ground' in RA Pedrozo (ed), *The War in Iraq: A Legal Analysis* (2010) (Vol 86, US Naval War College International Law Studies) 428–34.

[112] S Sivakumaran, 'Courts of Armed Opposition Groups: Fair Trials or Summary Justice?' (2009) 7 JICJ 489.

[113] See section 4.3.2. Similarly, see HRC, *C v Australia*, CCPR/C/76/D/900/1999, 28 October 2002, [8.2]; HRC, *Baban et al v Australia*, CCPR/C/78/D/1014/2001, 18 September 2003, [7.2].

[114] See section 3.3.2.

are required under custom to release internees where the reasons justifying their internment cease. Any internment regime for non-international conflicts must, therefore, include such a norm.[115] As such, the relevant rule in GCIV, requiring release where the reasons cease and, if not before, when hostilities cease, may be transplanted to non-international armed conflicts.[116]

An important caveat must be noted, however. Section 4.2.5 explained that certain human rights bodies appear sceptical of potentially prolonged, indefinite detention.[117] On the one hand, the indefinite nature of detention is an inherent feature of internment during armed conflict, and if the law is to be effective here, it cannot prohibit internment for the reason that it does not have a pre-determined end-point.[118] However, this scepticism of IHRL towards prolonged, indefinite detention could nonetheless be useful here in protecting detainees from arbitrary deprivations of liberty. To that end, it is submitted that, the longer detention continues, the more burdensome it should be on the detaining power to justify it before the review body.[119] Indeed, the principle of proportionality as developed in human rights jurisprudence is particularly useful here. Thus, the ECtHR has confirmed that:

…a balance must be struck between the importance in a democratic society of securing the immediate fulfilment of the obligation in question and the importance of the right to liberty…The duration of the detention is a relevant factor in striking such a balance.[120]

As detention continues, the proportionality balance should therefore shift in favour of release, requiring increasingly convincing evidence that continued internment is necessary.

7.4 Concluding Remarks

The proposals above recommend drawing by analogy from the GCIV internment regimes and the developments thereof in doctrine and practice. Importantly, it was made clear that the distinction between international and non-international armed conflicts in this area should not simply be eliminated, with the GCIII and GCIV internment regimes being extended to non-international conflicts,

---

[115] Similarly, see Pejic (n 17) 382–3; Copenhagen Principles (n 9) Principle 4.2.
[116] Arts 132(1) and 133(1) GCIV.
[117] IACiHR, 'Annual Report: 1976', OAS Doc. OEA/Ser.L/V/II.40, Doc. 5 corr. 1 of 7 June 1977, Section II, Part II; UN Commission on Human Rights, Report of the Working Group on Arbitrary Detention, E/CN. 4/2004/3, 15 December 2003, [60]; UN Working Group on Arbitrary Detention, *Obaidullah v United States*, A/HRC/WGAD/2013/10, 12 June 2013, [24]; HRC, General Comment No 35 (n 66) [15].
[118] This is confirmed by practice acknowledging that internment is not necessarily inconsistent with IHRL: see section 4.2.1.1.
[119] Similarly, see CFH 7048/97, *Anonymous v Minister of Defence*, 54(1) PD 721 (Israeli Supreme Court) [25]; HRC, General Comment No 35 (n 66) [15].
[120] *Saadi v UK* (n 62) [70].

7.4 Concluding Remarks

lest the current legal protections afforded to those detained in such situations be undermined. Instead, it was suggested that the current *lex lata* be built upon, with GCIV as our starting point, ensuring that the proposed internment regime complies with the basic customary rules of IHL and IHRL, which earlier chapters showed bind all parties in non-international conflicts.[121] Thus, the proposed regime offers a framework, currently lacking in the law, to states without conventional human rights obligations and to non-state armed groups, giving content to their basic obligations under IHL and customary human rights law. In addition, for the majority of states with human rights treaty obligations, the proposals are intended as minimum humanitarian standards that states can apply 'through' their IHRL obligations (eg via derogation).

It is submitted that the approach above represents an appropriate balance between military necessity and humanitarian concerns, for internment is permitted but only where subject to strict safeguards. Importantly, as noted, derogation, for example from *habeas corpus*, cannot be an automatic measure once a non-international armed conflict has come into existence; rather, it is permitted to a limited extent only where *actually* necessary, and no more than is necessary, in the prevailing circumstances.[122] Indeed, the practice of Colombia, discussed in section 5.2.1.1, demonstrates that internment need not be necessary in a non-international conflict, and instead the criminal model of detention could sufficiently respond to threats to state security. Similarly, the practice of Israel confirms that, whilst the introduction of internment may be necessary, derogation from *habeas corpus* need not be.[123]

IHL, however, is premised on a different presumption, that is, 'that the existence of an armed conflict automatically invokes a certain "basic level" of military necessity.'[124] It is this presumption that explains IHL's more permissive approach to internment, relative to IHRL.[125] Were the distinction between the two categories of armed conflict eliminated in this area, those more permissive IHL rules might then be argued to apply as the *lex specialis* in non-international conflicts, effectively undermining the more protective human rights treaty norms that already bind most states.[126] The more permissive IHL rules on internment would

---

[121] The exception, as noted, is that customary human rights law appears, presently, to be binding on non-state armed groups only where they control territory: section 6.3.

[122] See, eg, Art 4(1) ICCPR; Art 15(1) ECHR; HRC, General Comment No 29: States of Emergency (Article 4), CCPR/C/21/Rev.1/Add.11, 31 August 2001, [4]; R Higgins, 'Derogations under Human Rights Treaties' (1976) 48 BYIL 281, 282–3.

[123] Brief of *Amici Curiae* Specialists in Israeli Military Law and Constitutional Law in Support of Petitioners, *Boumediene et al v Bush et al*, On Writs of Certiorari to the United States Court of Appeals for the District of Columbia Circuit. This is discussed in section 6.1.5.

[124] R Geiß, 'Military Necessity: A Fundamental "Principle" Fallen into Oblivion' (2008) 2 ESIL Proc 554, 559. Similarly, see WG Downey Jr, 'The Law of War and Military Necessity' (1953) 47 AJIL 251, 256–60 (arguing that military necessity in IHL leads to a presumption that one can, inter alia, target and capture members of the enemy armed forces).

[125] This was demonstrated throughout chapter 4.

[126] This notion of *lex specialis* was discussed regarding internment in international armed conflict in section 5.1.2.

then become the governing legal standards, regardless of whether it was actually necessary in the prevailing circumstances to depart from the stricter human rights standards. The approach advocated here allows us to move away from this presumption and preserve the ordinary law regime (IHRL), so long as it is not actually necessary to depart therefrom.[127]

Of course, for non-state armed groups and for states not party to a human rights treaty, the proposed regime would form the principal applicable norms in any situation reaching the level of a non-international armed conflict. Unlike states with conventional human rights obligations, no derogation would be necessary for them to 'access' this regime. It may be argued that this approach is inappropriate, as it would require non-state armed groups to adhere to less restrictive rules than states that have *not* derogated from their human rights treaty obligations. However, such differentiated obligations arise not from any inequality under IHL,[128] but rather from the voluntary assumption of stricter obligations under human rights treaties by most states, which in turn would restrict their ability to 'access' the more permissive internment regime. As demonstrated in section 5.2, states generally already accept the application of IHRL in these situations, and, in so doing, many resort to derogation in order to broaden their discretion. From the perspective of states with human rights treaty obligations, the proposed regime would offer greater clarity regarding minimum humanitarian standards where they do derogate. Moreover, given the current lack of rules applicable to non-state armed groups and to states without human rights treaty obligations, the proposed regime would offer an important development on the current law.

---

[127] This approach is based on a more general proposal by the present author for developing the law of non-international armed conflict: L Hill-Cawthorne, 'The Role of Necessity in International Humanitarian and Human Rights Law' (2014) 47 Isr L Rev 225.

[128] On the importance of equality of belligerents under IHL for compliance, see Sassòli and Olson (n 7) 609–10; F Bugnion, '*Jud Ad Bellum, Jus In Bello* and Non-International Armed Conflicts' (2003) 6 YIHL 167; C Greenwood, 'Historical Development and Legal Basis' in Dieter Fleck (ed), *The Handbook of International Humanitarian Law* (2nd edn OUP, Oxford 2008) 10–11. Cf G Blum, 'On a Differential Law of War' (2011) 52 Harv Intl LJ 163.

Select Bibliography

BOOKS AND CHAPTERS

Akande, D, 'Classification of Armed Conflicts: Relevant Legal Concepts' in E Wilmshurst (ed), *International Law and the Classification of Conflicts* (OUP, Oxford 2012)

Alston, P, *Non-State Actors and Human Rights* (OUP, Oxford 2005)

Alvarez, J, 'Limits of Change by Way of Subsequent Agreements and Practice' in G Nolte (ed), *Treaties and Subsequent Practice* (OUP, Oxford 2013)

Arai-Takahashi, Y, *The Law of Occupation: Continuity and Change of International Humanitarian Law, and its Interaction with International Human Rights Law* (Martinus Nijhoff, Leiden 2009)

Arato, J, 'Accounting for Difference in Treaty Interpretation Over Time' in A Bianchi, D Peat, and M Windsor (eds), *Interpretation in International Law* (OUP, Oxford 2015)

Arimatsu, L, 'The Democratic Republic of Congo: 1993–2010' in E Wilmshurst (ed), *International Law and the Classification of Conflicts* (OUP, Oxford 2012)

Aust, A, *Modern Treaty Law and Practice* (2nd edn, CUP, Cambridge 2007)

Baxter, RR, 'Ius in Bellow Interno: The Present and Future Law' in JN Moore (ed), *Law and Civil War in the Modern World* (The Johns Hopkins University Press, Baltimore 1974)

Ben-Naftali, O, *International Humanitarian Law and International Human Rights Law* (OUP, Oxford 2011)

Berman, F, 'Jurisdiction: The State' in P Capps et al (eds), *Asserting Jurisdiction: International and European Legal Perspectives* (Hart, Portland, Oregon 2003)

Best, G, *War and Law since 1945* (OUP, Oxford 1994)

Bethlehem, D, 'The Methological Framework of the Study' in E Wilmhurst and S Breau (eds), *Perspectives on the ICRC Study on Customary International Humanitarian Law* (CUP, Cambridge 2007)

Bill, BJ, 'Detention Operations in Iraq: A View from the Ground' in RA Pedrozo (ed), *The War in Iraq: A Legal Analysis* (2010) (Vol 86, US Naval War College International Law Studies)

Bjorge, E, *The Evolutionary Interpretation of Treaties* (OUP, Oxford 2014)

Borelli, S and Olleson, S, 'Obligations Relating to Human Rights and Humanitarian Law' in J Crawford, A Pellet, and S Olleson (eds), *The Law of International Responsibility* (OUP, Oxford 2010)

Burgorgue-Larsen, L and De Torres, AU, *The Inter-American Court of Human Rights: Case Law and Commentary* (OUP, Oxford 2011)

Carlson, SN and Gisvold, G, *Practical Guide to the International Covenant on Civil and Political Rights* (Transnational, Ardsley 2003)

Castren, E, *Civil War* (Suomalainen Tiedeakatemia, Helsinki 1966)

Clapham, A, *Human Rights Obligations of Non-State Actors* (OUP, Oxford 2006)

Clapham, A, *Brierly's Law of Nations* (7th edn, OUP, Oxford 2012)

Cole, A, 'Legal Issues in Forming the Coalition' in M Schmitt (ed), *The War in Afghanistan: A Legal Analysis* (2009) (Vol 85, US Naval War College International Law Studies)

Coomans, F and Kamminga, M (eds), *Extraterritorial Application of Human Rights Treaties* (Intersentia, Oxford 2004)

Crawford, E, *The Treatment of Combatants and Insurgents under the Law of Armed Conflict* (OUP, Oxford 2010)
Crawford, J, *Brownlie's Principles of Public International Law* (8th edn, OUP, Oxford 2012)
da Costa, K, *The Extraterritorial Application of Selected Human Rights Treaties* (Martinus Nijhoff 2012)
D'Amato, AA, *The Concept of Custom in International Law* (Cornell University Press, Ithaca 1971)
d'Aspremont, J, *Formalism and the Sources of International Law: A Theory of the Ascertainment of Legal Rules* (OUP, Oxford 2011)
Danilenko, GM, *Law-Making in the International Community* (Martinus Nijhoff, Dordrecht 1993)
Debuf, E, *Captured in War: Lawful Internment in Armed Conflict* (Editions Pedone/Hart, Paris/Oxford 2013)
Dinstein, Y, 'Right to Life, Physical Integrity, and Liberty' in L Henkin (ed), *The International Bill of Rights: the Covenant on Civil and Political Rights* (Columbia University Press, New York 1981)
Dinstein, Y, *The International Law of Belligerent Occupation* (CUP, Cambridge 2009)
Dinstein, Y, 'Terrorism and Afghanistan' in MN Schmitt (ed), *The War in Afghanistan: A Legal Analysis* (2009) (Vol 85, US Naval War College International Law Studies)
Dinstein, Y, *The Conduct of Hostilities under the Law of International Armed Conflict* (2nd edn, CUP, Cambridge 2010)
Doswald-Beck, L, 'Implementation of International Humanitarian Law in Future Wars' in MN Schmitt and LC Green (eds), *The Law of Armed Conflict: Into the Next Millennium* (International Law Studies Vol 71, Naval War College, Newport 1998)
Doswald-Beck, L, *Human Rights in Times of Conflict and Terrorism* (OUP, Oxford 2011)
Draper, GIAD, *The Red Cross Conventions* (Stevens & Sons, London 1958)
Draper, GIAD, 'Humanitarian Law and Human Rights' in MA Meyer and H McCoubrey (eds), *Reflections on Law and Armed Conflicts* (Kluwer, The Hague 1998)
Falk, RA, 'Janus Tormented: The International Law of Internal War' in JN Rosenau (ed), *International Aspects of Civil Strife* (Princeton University Press, Princeton 1964)
Fischer, H, 'Protection of Prisoners of War' in D Fleck (ed), *The Handbook of International Humanitarian Law* (2nd edn, OUP, Oxford 2008)
Fitzmaurice, M, 'The Practical Working of the Law of Treaties' in MD Evans (ed), *International Law* (2nd edn, OUP, Oxford 2006)
Fleck, D, 'Humanitarian Protection Against Non-State Actors' in JA Frowein et al (eds), *Verhandeln für den Frieden—Negotiating for Peace: Liber Amicorum Tono Eitel* (Springer, Berlin 2003)
Fleck, D, 'The Law of Non-International Armed Conflict' in D Fleck (ed), *The Handbook of International Humanitarian Law* (3rd edn, OUP, Oxford 2013)
Franck, TM, *The Power of Legitimacy Among Nations* (OUP, Oxford 1990)
Gardam, J, *Necessity, Proportionality and the Use of Force by States* (CUP, Cambridge 2004)
Gardiner, R, *Treaty Interpretation* (OUP, Oxford 2008)
Gasser, H-P and Dörmann, K, 'Protection of the Civilian Population' in D Fleck (ed), *The Handbook of International Humanitarian Law* (3rd edn, OUP, Oxford 2013)
Goodman, R, 'Rationales for Detention: Security Threats and Intelligence Value' in MN Schmitt (ed), *The War in Afghanistan: A Legal Analysis* (2009) (Vol 85, US Naval War College International Law Studies)
Gowlland-Debbas, V, 'The Right to Life and Genocide: the Court and International Public Policy' in L Boisson de Chazournes and P Sands (eds), *International Law, the International Court of Justice and Nuclear Weapons* (CUP, Cambridge 1999)

Green, LC, *The Contemporary Law of Armed Conflict* (Melland Schill Studies in International Law, 3rd edn, Manchester University Press, Manchester 2008)

Greenwood, C, 'The Law of War (International Humanitarian Law)' in MD Evans (ed), *International Law* (2nd edn, OUP, Oxford 2006)

Greenwood, C, 'Historical Development and Legal Basis' in D Fleck (ed), *The Handbook of International Humanitarian Law* (2nd edn, OUP, Oxford 2008)

Greenwood, C, 'Scope of Application of Humanitarian Law' in D Fleck (ed), *The Handbook of International Humanitarian Law* (2nd edn, OUP, Oxford 2008)

Hafner, G, 'Subsequent Agreements and Practice: Between Interpretation, Informal Modification, and Formal Amendment' in G Nolte (ed), *Treaties and Subsequent Practice* (OUP, Oxford 2013)

Haines, S, 'Northern Ireland: 1968–1998' in E Wilmshurst (ed), *International Law and the Classification of Conflicts* (OUP, Oxford 2012)

Hall, WE, *A Treatise on International Law* (3rd edn, Clarendon Press, Oxford 1890)

Hampson, F, 'Fundamental Guarantees' in E Wilmshurst and S Breau (eds), *Perspectives on the ICRC Study on Customary International Humanitarian Law* (CUP, Cambridge 2007)

Hampson, F, 'Other Areas of Customary Law in Relation to the Study' in E Wilmshurst and S Breau (eds), *Perspectives on the ICRC Study on Customary International Humanitarian Law* (CUP, Cambridge 2007)

Henckaerts, J-M and Doswald-Beck, L, *Customary International Humanitarian Law Volume I: Rules* (CUP, Cambridge 2005)

Henckaerts, J-M and Doswald-Beck, L, *Customary International Humanitarian Law Volume II: Practice* (CUP, Cambridge 2005)

Henckaerts, J-M and Wiesener, C, 'Human Rights Obligations of Non-State Armed Groups: A Possible Contribution from Customary International Law?' in R Kolb and G Gaggioli (eds), *Research Handbook on Human Rights and Humanitarian Law* (Edward Elgar, Cheltenham 2013)

Henderson, I, *The Contemporary Law of Targeting: Military Objectives, Proportionality and Precautions in Attack under Additional Protocol I* (Martinus Nijhoff, Leiden 2009)

Higgins, AP (ed), *Hall's Treatise on International Law* (8th edn, Clarendon Press, Oxford 1924)

Hill-Cawthorne, L, 'Just Another Case of Treaty Interpretation? Reconciling Humanitarian Law and Human Rights Law in the ICJ' in M Andenas and E Bjorge (eds), *From Fragmentation to Convergence in International Law* (CUP, Cambridge 2015)

Ipsen, K, 'Combatants and Non-Combatants' in D Fleck (ed), *The Handbook of International Humanitarian Law* (2nd edn, OUP, Oxford 2008)

Jachec-Neale, A, 'Status and Treatment of Prisoners of War and Other Persons Deprived of Their Liberty' in E Wilmshurst and S Breau (eds), *Perspectives on the ICRC Study on Customary International Humanitarian Law* (CUP, Cambridge 2007)

Jennings, R and Watts, A, *Oppenheim's International Law, Volume I: Peace* (9th edn, OUP, Oxford 1992)

Jinks, D, 'International Human Rights Law in Times of Armed Conflict' in A Clapham and P Gaeta (eds), *The Oxford Handbook of International Law in Armed Conflict* (OUP, Oxford 2014)

Joseph, S, Schultz, J, and Castan, M, *The International Covenant on Civil and Political Rights: Cases, Materials, and Commentary* (paperback edn, 2nd edn, OUP, Oxford 2005)

Kalin, W, 'Universal Human Rights Bodies and International Humanitarian Law' in R Kolb and G Gaggioli (eds), *Research Handbook on Human Rights and Humanitarian Law* (Edward Elgar, Cheltenham 2013)

Koskenniemi, M, *From Apology to Utopia: The Structure of International Legal Argument* (CUP, Cambridge 2005)

Koskenniemi, M, 'What is International Law For?' in M Koskenniemi, *The Politics of International Law* (Hart, Oxford 2011)

Krähenmann, S, 'Protection of Prisoners in Armed Conflict' in D Fleck (ed), *The Handbook of International Humanitarian Law* (3rd edn, OUP, Oxford 2013)

Kramer, AR, 'Prisoners in the First World War' in S Scheipers (ed), *Prisoners in War* (OUP, Oxford 2010)

Levie, HS, *Prisoners of War in International Armed Conflict* (1978) (Vol 59, US Naval War College International Law Studies)

Lauterpacht, H, *Oppenheim's International Law, A Treatise: Volume II, Disputes, War and Neutrality* (5th edn, Longman's, Green & Co, London 1935)

Lauterpacht, H, *Oppenheim's International Law, A Treatise: Volume II, War and Neutrality* (6th edn, Longman's, Green & Co, London 1940)

Lauterpacht, H, *Recognition in International Law* (CUP, Cambridge 1947)

Lauterpacht, H, *Oppenheim's International Law, A Treatise: Volume II, Disputes, War and Neutrality* (7th edn, Longhams, London 1952)

Lauterpacht, H, *International Law and Human Rights* (unaltered reprint of 1950 edition by Stevens & Sons Ltd, Archon Books, 1968)

Lauterpacht, H, *The Development of International Law by the International Court* (reissue, CUP, Cambridge 1982)

Lauterpacht, H, *The Function of Law in the International Community* (reissue with foreword and introduction, OUP, Oxford 2011)

Lowe, AV, 'Jurisdiction' in M Evans (ed), *International Law* (2nd edn, OUP, Oxford 2006)

Lubell, N, *Extraterritorial Use of Force Against Non-State Actors* (OUP, Oxford 2010)

Lubell, N, 'The War (?) Against Al-Qaeda' in E Wilmshurst (ed), *The Classification of Conflicts in International Law* (OUP, Oxford 2012)

Marks, S and Clapham, A, *International Human Rights Lexicon* (OUP, Oxford 2005)

McDougal, MS, Lasswell, HD, and Miller, JC, *The Interpretation of International Agreements and World Public Order: Principles of Content and Procedure* (New Haven Press, New Haven 1967)

McNair, A, *The Law of Treaties* (OUP, Oxford 1961)

Melzer, N, *Targeted Killing in International Law* (Oxford Monographs in International Law, OUP, Oxford 2008)

Meron, T, *Human Rights and Humanitarian Norms as Customary Law* (OUP, Oxford 1989)

Meron, T, *The Humanization of International Law* (The Hague Academy of International Law, Martinus Nijhoff, The Hague 2006)

Mettraux, G, *International Crimes and the Ad Hoc Tribunals* (OUP, Oxford 2005)

Milanović, M, *Extraterritorial Application of Human Rights Treaties: Law, Principles, and Policy* (OUP, Oxford 2011)

Milanović, M, 'Norm Conflicts, International Humanitarian Law, and Human Rights Law' in O Ben-Naftali (ed), *International Humanitarian Law and International Human Rights Law* (OUP, Oxford 2011)

Milanović, M, 'The Lost Origins of Lex Specialis: Rethinking the Relationship between Human Rights and International Humanitarian Law' in J Ohlin (ed), *Theoretical Boundaries of Armed Conflict and Human Rights* (CUP, Cambridge 2016, forthcoming)

Milanović, M, 'Extraterritorial Derogations from Human Rights Treaties in Armed Conflict' in N Bhuta (ed), *The Frontiers of Human Rights: Extraterritoriality and its Challenges* (Collected Courses of the Academy of European Law, OUP, Oxford, forthcoming)

Modirzadeh, NK, 'The Dark Sides of Convergence: A Pro-Civilian Critique of the Extraterritorial Application of Human Rights Law in Armed Conflict' in RA Pedrozo (ed), *The War in Iraq: A Legal Analysis* (2010) (Vol 86, US Naval War College International Law Studies)
Moir, L, *The Law of Internal Armed Conflict* (CUP, Cambridge 2002)
Moir, L, 'The European Court of Human Rights and International Humanitarian Law' in R Kolb and G Gaggioli (eds), *Research Handbook on Human Rights and Humanitarian Law* (Edward Elgar, Cheltenham 2013)
Moore, JB, *History and Digest of the International Arbitrations to which the United States has been a Party: Volume IV* (Government Printing Office, Washington 1898)
Neff, SC, *War the Law of Nations: A General History* (CUP, Cambridge 2005)
Neff, SC, 'Prisoners of War in International Law: The Nineteenth Century' in S Scheipers (ed), *Prisoners in War* (OUP, Oxford 2010)
Nijman, JE, 'Minorities and Majorities' in B Fassbender and A Peters (eds), *The Oxford Handbook of the History of International Law* (OUP, Oxford 2012)
Nolte, G, 'Subsequent Practice as a Means of Interpretation in the Jurisprudence of the WTO Appellate Body' in E Cannizzaro (ed), *The Law of Treaties Beyond the Vienna Convention* (OUP, Oxford 2011)
O'Connell, DP, *State Succession in Municipal and International Law: Volume II* (CUP, Cambridge 1967)
Ojeda, S, 'US Detention of Taliban Fighters: Some Legal Considerations' in MN Schmitt (ed), *The War in Afghanistan: A Legal Analysis* (2009) (Vol 85, US Naval War College International Law Studies)
Oppenheim, L, *International Law, A Treatise: Volume II, War and Neutrality* (Longmans, Green & Co, London 1906)
Ovey, C and White, RCA, *Jacobs & White: The European Convention on Human Rights* (4th edn, OUP, Oxford 2006)
Paparinskis, M, 'Investment Treaty Interpretation and Customary Investment Law' in C Brown and K Miles (eds), *Evolution in Investment Treaty Law and Arbitration* (CUP, Cambridge 2011)
Paparinskis, M, *The International Minimum Standard and Fair and Equitable Treatment* (OUP, Oxford 2013)
Parlett, K, *The Individual in the International Legal System* (CUP, Cambridge 2011)
Pauwelyn, J, *Conflict of Norms in Public International Law: How WTO Law Relates to Other Rules of International Law* (CUP, Cambridge 2003)
Pejic, J, 'Status of Armed Conflicts' in E Wilmshurst and SC Breau (eds), *Perspectives on the ICRC Study on Customary International Humanitarian Law* (CUP, Cambridge 2007)
Pejic, J, 'Conflict Classification and the Law Applicable to Detention and the Use of Force' in E Wilmshurst (ed), *International Law and the Classification of Conflicts* (OUP, Oxford 2012)
Phillimore, R, *Commentaries upon International Law: Volume III* (T & JW Johnson & Co, Philadelphia 1857)
Pictet, JS (ed), *Commentary to Geneva Convention I for the Amelioration of the Condition of the Wounded and Sick in Armed Forces in the Field* (ICRC, Geneva 1952)
Pictet, JS (ed), *Commentary to Geneva Convention IV Relative to the Protection of Civilian Persons in Time of War* (ICRC, Geneva 1958)
Pictet, JS (ed), *Commentary to Geneva Convention II for the Amelioration of the Condition of Wounded, Sick and Shipwrecked Members of Armed Forces at Sea* (ICRC, Geneva 1960)

Pictet, JS (ed), *Commentary to Geneva Convention III Relative to the Treatment of Prisoners of War* (ICRC, Geneva 1960)

Pictet, JS, *Development and Principles of International Humanitarian Law* (Martinus Nijhoff, Dordrecht 1985)

Pomper, S, 'Human Rights Obligations, Armed Conflict and Afghanistan: Looking Back Before Looking Ahead' in MN Schmitt (ed), *The War in Afghanistan: A Legal Analysis* (2009) (International Law Studies, Vol 85)

Provost, R, *International Human Rights and Humanitarian Law* (CUP, Cambridge 2002)

Pulkowski, D, *The Law and Politics of International Regime Conflict* (OUP, Oxford 2014)

Risius, G, 'Prisoners of War in the United Kingdom' in P Rowe (ed), *The Gulf War 1990–91 in International and English Law* (Routledge, Oxford 1993)

Roberts, A and Guelff, R, *Documents on the Laws of War* (3rd edn, OUP, Oxford 2000)

Rodley, NS, 'Can Armed Opposition Groups Violate Human Rights?' in KE Mahoney and P Mahoney (eds), *Human Rights in the Twenty-First Century* (Martinus Nijhoff 1993)

Rodley, NS, 'The International Court of Justice and Human Rights Treaty Bodies' in M Andenas and E Bjorge (eds), *A Farewell to Fragmentation: Reassertion and Convergence in International Law* (CUP, Cambridge 2015)

Rodley, NS and Pollard, M, *The Treatment of Prisoners under International Law* (3rd edn, OUP, Oxford 2009)

Roth, AH, *The Minimum Standard of International Law Applied to Aliens* (AW Sijthoff's Uitgeversmaatschappij NV, Leiden 1949)

Roxburgh, R, *Oppenheim's International Law, A Treatise: Volume II, War and Neutrality* (3rd edn, Longman's, Green & Co, London 1921)

Sandoz, Y, Swinarski, C, and Zimmerman, B (eds), *Commentary on the Additional Protocols of 8 June 1977 to the Geneva Conventions of 12 August 1949* (ICRC/Martinus Nijhoff, Geneva 1987)

Sassòli, M, '*Ius ad Bellum and Ius in Bello*—The Separation between the Legality of the Use of Force and Humanitarian Rules to be Respected in Warfare: Crucial or Outdated' in MN Schmitt and J Pejic (eds), *International Law and Armed Conflict: Exploring the Faultlines* (Martinus Nijhoff, Leiden 2007)

Sassòli, M and Bouvier, A, *How Does Law Protect in War?: Cases, Documents and Teaching Materials on Contemporary Practice in International Humanitarian Law, Volumes I & II* (ICRC, Geneva 1999)

Scheipers, S (ed), *Prisoners in War* (OUP, Oxford 2010)

Schmitt, MN, 'Iraq (2003 onwards)' in E Wilmshurst (ed), *International Law and the Classification of Conflicts* (OUP, Oxford 2012)

Schwarzenberger, G, *A Manual of International Law* (Stevens & Sons, London 1947)

Scobbie, I, 'The Approach to Customary International Law in the Study' in E Wilmhurst and S Breau (eds), *Perspectives on the ICRC Study on Customary International Humanitarian Law* (CUP, Cambridge 2007)

Shah, S, 'Administration of Justice' in D Moeckli, S Shah, and S Sivakumaran (eds), *International Human Rights Law* (OUP, Oxford 2010)

Shaw, MN, *International Law* (CUP, Cambridge 2012)

Sivakumaran, S, *The Law of Non-International Armed Conflict* (OUP, Oxford 2012)

Solis, GD, *The Law of Armed Conflict: International Humanitarian Law in War* (CUP, Cambridge 2010)

Sorel, JM and Eveno, VB, '1969 Vienna Convention, Article 31: General Rule of Intepretation' in O Corten and P Klein (ed), *The Vienna Conventions on the Law of Treaties: A Commentary, Volume I* (OUP, Oxford 2011)

Szesnat, F and Bird, A, 'Colombia' in E Wilmshurst (ed), *The Classification of Conflicts in International Law* (OUP, Oxford 2012)

Tehindrazanarivelo, DL, 'The African Union and International Humanitarian Law' in R Kolb and G Gaggioli (eds), *Research Handbook on Human Rights and Humanitarian Law* (Edward Elgar, Cheltenham 2013)

Thirlway, H, *The Sources of International Law* (OUP, Oxford 2014)

Thornberry, P, *International Law and the Rights of Minorities* (OUP, Oxford 1991)

Tomuschat, C, 'The Applicability of Human Rights Law to Insurgent Movements' in H Fischer et al (eds), *Krisensicherung und Humanitärer Schutz – Crisis Management and Humanitarian Protection: Festschrift für Dieter Fleck* (BWV, Berlin 2004)

Vance, J (ed), *Encyclopedia of Prisoners of War and Internment* (2nd edn, Grey House Publishing, Inc, Millerton, NY 2006)

Wagstaff, RH, *Terror Detentions and the Rule of Law: US and UK Perspectives* (OUP, New York 2014)

Wall, AE, 'Civilian Detentions in Iraq' in MN Schmitt and J Pejic (eds), *International Law and Armed Conflict: Exploring the Faultlines* (Brill, The Hague 2007)

Walsh, B, 'Detention and Deportation of Foreign Nationals in the United Kingdom during the Gulf Conflict' in P Rowe (ed), *The Gulf War 1990–91 in International and English Law* (Routledge, Oxford 1993)

Walzer, M, *Just and Unjust Wars: A Moral Argument with Historical Illustrations* (3rd edn, Basic Books, New York 2000)

Warbrick, C, 'States and Recognition and International Law' in MD Evans (ed), *International Law* (2nd edn, OUP, Oxford 2006)

Waxman, MC, 'The Law of Armed Conflict and Detention Operations in Afghanistan' in MN Schmitt (ed), *The War in Afghanistan: A Legal Analysis* (2009) (Vol 85, US Naval War College International Law Studies)

Westlake, J, *Chapters on the Principles of International Law* (CUP, Cambridge 1894)

Westlake, J, *International Law Part II: War* (CUP, Cambridge 1907)

White, RCA and Ovey, C, *Jacobs, White & Ovey: The European Convention on Human Rights* (5th edn, OUP, Oxford 2010)

Wilde, R, 'The Extraterritorial Application of International Human Rights Law on Civil and Political Rights' in S Sheeran and N Rodley (eds), *Routledge Handbook of International Human Rights Law* (Routledge, Abingdon 2013)

Wittes, B, Chesney, RM, and Reynolds, L, *The Emerging Law of Detention 2.0: The Guantánamo Habeas Cases as Lawmaking* (Brookings Institution, 2012)

Wolfke, K, *Custom in Present International Law* (2nd edn, Martinus Nijhoff 1993)

Zegveld, L, *The Accountability of Armed Opposition Groups in International Law* (CUP, Cambridge 2002

ARTICLES

Abresch, W, 'A Human Rights Law of Internal Armed Conflict: The European Court of Human Rights in Chechnya' (2005) 16 EJIL 741

Akande, D, 'Nuclear Weapons, Unclear Law? Deciphering the *Nuclear Weapons* Advisory Opinion of the International Court' (1998) 68 BYIL 165

Akande, D, 'The Jurisdiction of the International Criminal Court over Nationals of Non-Parties: Legal Basis and Limits' (2003) 1 JICJ 618

Akande, D, 'Clearing the Fog of War? The ICRC's Interpretive Guidance on Direct Participation in Hostilities' (2010) 59 ICLQ 180

Select Bibliography

Akande, D and Williams, S, 'International Adjudication on National Security issues: What Role for the WTO?' (2003) 43 Va J Intl L 365

Akehurst, M, 'The Hierarchy of the Sources of International Law' (1974–5) 47 BYIL 273

Akehurst, M, 'Custom as a Source of International Law' (1975) 47 BYIL 1

Aldrich, GH, 'The Laws of Wars on Land' (2000) 84 AJIL 42

Aldrich, GH, 'Customary International Humanitarian Law—An Interpretation on Behalf of the International Committee of the Red Cross' (2005) 76 BYIL 503

Alston, P, Morgan-Foster, J, and Abresch, W, 'The Competence of the UN Human Rights Council and its Special Procedures in Relation to Armed Conflicts: Extrajudicial Executions in the "War on Terror"' (2008) 19 EJIL 183

Anyangwe, C, 'Obligations of State Parties to the African Charter on Human and Peoples' Rights' (1998) 10 African J Intl & Comp L 625

Aughey, S and Sari, A, 'Targeting and Detention in Non-International Armed Conflict: *Serdar Mohammed* and the Limits of Human Rights Convergence' (2015) 91 Intl L Stud 60

Barnsby, RE, 'Yes We Can: The Authority to Detain as Customary International Law' (2009) 202 Mil L Rev 53

Bartels, R, 'Timelines, Borderlines and Conflicts: The Historical Evolution of the Legal Divide between International and Non-International Armed Conflicts' (2009) 91 IRRC 35

Baxter, RR, 'So-Called "Unprivileged Belligerency": Spies, Guerrillas, and Saboteurs' (1951) 28 BYIL 323

Baxter, RR, 'Treaties and Custom' (1970) 129 Recueil des Cours 27

Bell, C, 'Peace Agreements: Their Nature and Legal Status' (2006) 100 AJIL 373

Bellinger III, JB and Haynes II, WJ, 'A US Government Response to the International Committee of the Red Cross Study *Customary International Humanitarian Law*' (2007) 89 IRRC 443

Bellinger III, JB and Padmanabhan, VM, 'Detention Operations in Contemporary Conflicts: Four Challenges for the Geneva Conventions and Other Existing Law' (2011) 105 AJIL 201

Bentwich, N, 'International Law as Applied by England in the War: The Treatment of Alien Enemies' (1915) 9 AJIL 642

Berman, F, 'Treaty "Interpretation" in a Judicial Context' (2004) Yale J Intl L 315

Berman, F, 'The UN Charter and the Use of Force' (2006) 10 SYBIL 9

Berman, N, 'Privileging Combat? Contemporary Conflict and the Legal Construction of War' (2004) 43 Colum J Transnatl L 1

Blum, G, 'On a Differential Law of War' (2011) 52 Harv Intl LJ 163

Boelart-Suominen, S, 'Grave Breaches, Universal Jurisdiction and Internal Armed Conflict: Is Customary Law Moving Towards a Uniform Mechanism for all Armed Conflicts?' (2000) 5 JCSL 63

Bongard, P and Somer, J, 'Monitoring Armed Non-State Actor Compliance with Humanitarian Norms: A Look at International Mechanisms and the Geneva Call *Deed of Commitment*' (2011) 93 IRRC 673

Borchard, E, 'The Access of Individuals to International Courts' (1930) 24 AJIL 359

Borelli, S, 'Casting Light on the Legal Black Hole: International Law and Detentions Abroad in the 'War on Terror"' (2005) 87 IRRC 39

Bothe, M, 'Article 3 and Protocol II: Case Studies of Nigeria and El Salvador' (1982) 31 Am U L Rev 899

Bovarnick, JA, 'Detainee Review Boards in Afghanistan: From Strategic Liability to Legitimacy' [June 2010] The Army Lawyer 9

Bradley, CA and Goldsmith, JL, 'Congressional Authorization and the War on Terrorism' (2004–5) 118 Harv L Rev 2047
Brandon, M, 'Legal Control over Resident Enemy Aliens in Time of War in the United States and in the United Kingdom' (1950) 44 AJIL 382
Brilmayer, L, 'From "Contract" to "Pledge": The Structure of International Human Rights Agreements' (2007) 77 BYIL 163
Brooks, RE, 'War Everywhere: Rights, National Security Law, and the Law of Armed Conflict in the Age of Terror' (2004) 153 U Pa L Rev 675
Bugnion, F, '*Jud Ad Bellum, Jus In Bello* and Non-International Armed Conflicts' (2003) 6 YIHL 167
Bulto, TS, 'Patching the "Legal Black Hole": The Extraterritorial Reach of States' Human Rights Duties in the African Human Rights System' (2011) 27 South African J Hum Rts 249
Byron, C, 'Armed Conflicts: International or Non-International?' (2001) 6 JCSL 63
Byron, C, 'A Blurring of the Boundaries: The Application of International Humanitarian Law by Human Rights Bodies' (2007) 47 Va J Intl L 839
Callen, J, 'Unlawful Combatants and the Geneva Conventions' (2004) 44 Va J Intl L 1025
Carnahan, BM, 'Lincoln, Lieber and the Laws of War: The Origins and Limits of the Principle of Military Necessity' (1998) 92 AJIL 213
Carvin, S, 'Caught in the Cold: International Humanitarian Law and Prisoners of War During the Cold War' (2006) 11 JCSL 67
Casalin, D, 'Taking Prisoners: Reviewing the International Humanitarian Law Grounds for Deprivation of Liberty by Armed Opposition Groups' (2011) 93 IRRC 743
Cassese, A, 'The Status of Rebels Under the 1977 Geneva Protocol on Non-International Armed Conflicts' (1981) 30 ICLQ 416
Cassese, A, 'The Geneva Protocols of 1977 on the Humanitarian Law of Armed Conflict and Customary International Law' (1984) UCLA Pacific Basin LJ 55
Cassese, A, 'The Special Court and International Law: The Decision Concerning the Lomé Agreement Amnesty' (2004) 2 JICJ 1130
Cerna, CM, 'The History of the Inter-American's System's Jurisprudence as Regards Situations of Armed Conflict' (2011) 2 J Intl Humanitarian Legal Studies 3
Cerone, J, 'Jurisdiction and Power: The Intersection of Human Rights Law & The Law of Non-International Armed Conflict in an Extraterritorial Context' (2007) 40 Isr L Rev 396
Charney, J, 'Universal International Law' (1993) 87 AJIL 529
Chesney, RM, 'Leaving Guantanamo: The Law of International Detainee Transfers' (2006) 40 U Rich L Rev 657
Chesney, RM, 'Iraq and the Military Detention Debate: Firsthand Perspectives from the Other War, 2003–2010' (2011) 51 Va J Intl L 549
Clapham, A, 'Human Rights Obligations of Non-State Actors in Conflict Situations' (2006) 88 IRRC 491
Cohn, EJ, 'Legal Aspects of Internment' (1941) 4 MLR 200
Corn, GS, 'Filling the Void: Providing a Framework for the Legal Regulation of the Military Component of the War on Terror Through Application of Basic Principles of the Law of Armed Conflict' (2006) 12 ILSA J Intl & Comp L 481
Corn, GS, 'Enemy Combatants and Access to *Habeas Corpus*: Questioning the Validity of the Prisoner of War Analogy' (2007) 5 Santa Clara J Intl L 236
Corn, GS, 'Hamdan, Lebanon, and the Regulation of Armed Conflict: The Need to Recognise a Hybrid Category of Armed Conflict' (2007) 40 Vand J Transnat L 295

Corn, GS and Jensen, ET, 'Transnational Armed Conflict: A "Principled" Approach to the Regulation of Counter-Terror Combat Operations' (2009) 42 Isr L Rev 42

Corn, GS, and Chickris, PA, 'Unprivileged Belligerents, Preventive Detention, and Fundamental Fairness: Rethinking the Review Tribunal Representation Model' (2012) 11 Santa Clara J Intl L 115

Craven, M et al, 'We Are Teachers of International Law' (2004) 17 Leiden J Intl L 17

Crawford, E, 'Unequal before the Law: The Case for the Elimination of the Distinction between International and Non-International Armed Conflicts' (2007) 20 LJIL 441

Crawford, J, 'Multilateral Rights and Obligations in International Law' (2006) 319 *Recueil des Cours* 325

Crook, JR (ed), 'Contemporary Practice of the United States Relating to International Law' (2006) 100 AJIL 690

Cullen, A, and Wheatley, S, 'The Human Rights of Individuals in *De Facto* Regimes under the European Convention on Human Rights' (2013) 13 HRLR 691

D'Amato, AA, 'Trashing Customary International Law' (1987) 81 AJIL 101

Danilenko, GM, 'The Theory of International Customary Law' (1988) 31 GYIL 9

Davidson, T and Gibson, K, 'Experts Meeting on Security Detention Report' (2009) 40 Case W Res J Intl L 323

de Schutter, B, and Van Der Wyngaert, C, 'Coping with Non-International Armed Conflicts: The Borderline Between National and International Law' (1983) 13 Ga J Intl & Comp L 279

de Zayas, A, 'Human Rights and Indefinite Detention' (2005) 87 IRRC 15

Deeks, A, 'Administrative Detention in Armed Conflict' (2009) 40 Case W Res J Intl L 403

Dennis, MJ, 'Application of Human Rights Treaties Extraterritorially in Times of Armed Conflict and Military Occupation' (2005) 99 AJIL 119

Dennis, MJ, 'Non-Application of Civil and Political Rights Treaties Extraterritorially During Times of International Armed Conflict' (2007) 40 Isr L Rev 453

Dingwall, J, 'Unlawful Confinement as a War Crime: The Jurisprudence of the Yugoslav Tribunal and the Common Core of International Humanitarian Law Applicable to Contemporary Armed Conflicts' (2004) 9 JCSL 133

Dörmann, K, 'The Legal Situation of "Unlawful/Unprivileged Combatants"' (2003) 85 IRRC 45

Doswald-Beck, L, 'International Humanitarian Law and the International Court of Justice on the Legality of the Threat or Use of Nuclear Weapons' (1997) 35 IRRC 316

Doswald-Beck, L, 'The Right to Life in Armed Conflict: Does International Humanitarian Law Provide all the Answers?' (2006) 86 IRRC 881

Doswald-Beck, L and Vité, S, 'International Humanitarian Law and Human Rights Law' (1993) IRRC 94

Downey Jr, WG, 'The Law of War and Military Necessity' (1953) 47 AJIL 251

Draper, GIAD, 'The Geneva Conventions of 1949' (1965) 114 *Recueil des Cours* 59

Draper, GIAD, 'The Relationship between the Human Rights Regime and the Law of Armed Conflicts' (1971) 1 Isr Ybk Human Rights 191

Droege, C, 'The Interplay between International Humanitarian Law and International Human Rights Law in Situations of Armed Conflict' (2007) 40 Isr L Rev 310

Droege, C, '"In truth the leitmotiv": the Prohibition of Torture and Other Forms of Ill-treatment in International Humanitarian Law' (2007) 89 IRRC 515

Droege, C, 'Elective Affinities? Human Rights and Humanitarian Law' (2008) 90 IRRC 501

Droege, C, 'Transfers of Detainees: Legal Framework, *Non-Refoulement* and Contemporary Challenges' (2008) 90 IRRC 669

Dumberry, P, 'Incoherent and Ineffective: The Concept of Persistent Objector Revisited' (2010) 59 ICLQ 779

Duxbury, A, 'Drawing Lines in the Sand – Characterising Conflicts for the Purposes of Teaching International Humanitarian Law' (2007) 8 MJIL 259

Elder, DA, 'The Historical Background of Common Article 3 of the Geneva Conventions of 1949' (1979) 11 Case W Res J Intl L 37

Estey, W, 'The Five Bases of Extraterritorial Jurisdiction and the Failure of the Presumption Against Extraterritoriality' (1997) 21 Hastings Intl & Comp L Rev 177

Farrell, B, 'The Right to Habeas Corpus in the Inter-American Human Rights System' (2010) 33 Suff Transnat L Rev 197

Fenrick, WJ, 'ICRC Guidance on Direct Participation in Hostilities' (2009) 12 YIHL 287

Ferraro, T, 'The Applicability and Application of International Humanitarian Law to Multinational Forces' (2013) 95 IRRC 561

Fitzmaurice, GG, 'The Law and Procedure of the International Court of Justice: Treaty Interpretation and Certain Other Treaty Points' (1951) 28 BYIL 1

Fitzmaurice, GG, 'The Law and Procedure of the International Court of Justice 1951–4: Treaty Interpretation and Other Treaty Points' (1957) 33 BYIL 203

Fortin, K, 'Complementarity between the ICRC and the United Nations and International Humanitarian Law and International Human Rights Law, 1948–1968' (2012) 94 IRRC 1433

Gaggioli, G and Kolb, R, 'A Right to Life in Armed Conflicts? The Contribution of the European Court of Human Rights' (2007) 37 Isr YB Human Rights 115

Garner, JW, 'Treatment of Enemy Aliens: Measures in Respect to Personal Liberty' (1918) 12 AJIL 27

Garraway, C, 'The Use and Abuse of Military Manuals' (2004) 7 YIHL 425

Gasser, H-P, 'Agora: The U.S. Decision Not to Ratify Protocol I to the Geneva Conventions on the Protection of War Victims' (1987) 81 AJIL 910

Gehring, RW, 'Loss of Civilian Protections under the Fourth Geneva Convention and Protocol I' (1980) 19 MLLWR 11

Geiß, R, 'Asymmetric conflict structures' (2006) 88 IRRC 757

Geiß, R, 'Military Necessity: A Fundamental "Principle" Fallen into Oblivion' (2008) 2 ESIL Proc 554

Geiß, R and Siegrist, M, 'Has the Armed Conflict in Afghanistan Affected the Rules on the Conduct of Hostilities?' (2011) 93 IRRC 11

Ghandhi, S, 'Human Rights and the International Court of Justice: The *Ahmadou Sadio Diallo* Case' (2011) 11 HRLR 527

Gillard, E-C, 'There's No Place Like Home: States' Obligations in Relation to Transfers of Persons' (2008) 90 IRRC 703

Gleditsch, NP et al, 'Armed Conflict 1946–2001: A New Dataset' (2002) 39 J of Peace Research 615

Gondek, M, 'Extraterritorial Application of the European Convention on Human Rights: Territorial Focus in the Age of Globalization?' (2005) 52 NILR 349

Goodman, R, 'The Detention of Civilians in Armed Conflict' (2009) 103 AJIL 48

Goodman, R, 'The Power to Kill or Capture Enemy Combatants' (2013) 24 EJIL 819

Goodman, R, 'Authorization versus Regulation of Detention in Non-International Armed Conflicts' (2015) 91 Intl L Stud 155

Goodman, R and Jinks, D, 'International Law, U.S. War Powers and the Global War on Terrorism' (2005) 118 Harvard L Rev 2653

Greenwood, CJ, 'The Concept of War in Modern International Law' (1987) 36 ICLQ 283

Greenwood, CJ, 'International Humanitarian Law and the *Tadic* Case' (1996) 7 EJIL 265

Greenwood, CJ, 'International Law and the "War Against Terrorism"' (2002) 78 Intl Affairs 301

Gutteridge, JAC, 'The Repatriation of Prisoners of War' (1953) 2 ICLQ 207

Hakimi, M, 'International Standards for Detaining Terrorism Suspects: Moving Beyond the Armed Conflict-Criminal Divide' (2009) 40 Case W Res J Intl L 593

Hampson, F, 'The Geneva Conventions and the Detention of Civilians and Alleged Prisoners of War' [1991] PL 507

Hampson, F, 'The Relationship between International Humanitarian Law and Human Rights Law From the Perspective of a Human Rights Treaty Body' (2008) 90 IRRC 549

Hansen, MA, 'Preventing the Emasculation of Warfare: Halting the Expansion of Human Rights Law Into Armed Conflict' (2007) 194 Mil L Rev 1

Hathaway, O, 'Do Human Rights Treaties Make a Difference?' (2002) 11 Yale LJ 1935

Heintze, HJ, 'On the Relationship Between Human Rights Law Protection and International Humanitarian Law' (2004) 86 IRRC 789

Henckaerts, J-M, '*Customary International Humanitarian Law*: A Response to US Comments' (2007) 89 IRRC 473

Henkin, L, 'Human Rights and State "Sovereignty"' (1995/6) 25 Ga J Intl & Comp L 31

Hershey, AS, 'Treatment of Enemy Aliens' (1918) 12 AJIL 156

Hessbruegge, JA, 'Human Rights Violations Arising from the Conduct of Non-State Actors' (2005) 11 Buff Hum Rghts L Rev 21

Higgins, R, 'Derogations under Human Rights Treaties' (1976) 48 BYIL 281

Hill-Cawthorne, L, 'The Copenhagen Principles on the Handling of Detainees: Implications for the Procedural Regulation of Internment' (2013) 18 JCSL 481

Hill-Cawthorne, L, 'The Role of Necessity in International Humanitarian and Human Rights Law' (2014) 47 Isr L Rev 225

Hill-Cawthorne, L, 'Humanitarian Law, Human Rights Law and the Bifurcation of Armed Conflict' (2015) 64 ICLQ 293

Hudson, MO, 'The Central American Court of Justice' (1932) 26 AJIL 759

Jenks, CW, 'The Conflict of Law-Making Treaties' (1953) 30 BYIL 401

Jinks, D, 'The Declining Significance of POW Status' (2004) 45 Harvard Intl LJ 367

Junod, S, 'Additional Protocol II: History and Scope' (1983) 33 Am U L Rev 29

Kaikobad, K et al, 'United Kingdom Materials on International Law, Part Six: VIII (Human rights and fundamental freedoms)' (2007) 78 BYIL 737

Kalshoven, F, 'A Colombian View on Protocol II' (1998) 1 YIHL 262

Kamminga, MT, 'State Succession in Respect of Human Rights Treaties' (1996) 7 EJIL 469

Kirgis Jr, FL, 'Custom on a Sliding Scale' (1987) 81 AJIL 146

Kleffner, JK, 'From "Belligerents" to "Fighters" and Civilians Directly Participating in Hostilities – On the Principle of Distinction in Non-International Armed Conflicts One Hundred Years After the Second Hague Peace Conference' (2007) 54 NILR 315

Kleffner, JK, 'Section IX of the ICRC Interpretive Guidance on Direct Participation in Hostilities: The End of Jus in Bello Proportionality as We Know It?' (2012) 45 Isr L Rev 35

Kolb, R, 'The Relationship between International Humanitarian Law and Human Rights Law: A Brief History of the 1948 Universal Declaration of Human Rights and the 1949 Geneva Conventions' (1998) 38 IRRC 409

Kolb, R, 'Selected Problems in the Theory of Customary International Law' (2003) 50 NYIL 119

Koskenniemi, M, 'The Politics of International Law—20 Years Later' (2009) 20 EJIL 7

Kress, C, 'Some Reflections on the International Legal Framework Governing Transnational Armed Conflicts' (2010) 15 JCSL 245

Kretzmer, D, 'Targeted Killing of Suspected Terrorists: Extra-Judicial Executions or Legitimate Means of Defence?' (2005) 16 EJIL 171

Kretzmer, D, 'Rethinking Application of IHL in Non-International Armed Conflicts' (2009) 42 Isr L Rev 8

Krieger, H, 'A Conflict of Norms: The Relationship Between Humanitarian Law and Human Rights Law in the ICRC Customary Law Study' (2006) 11 JCSL 265

Krieger, H, 'After Al-Jedda: Detention, Derogation, and an Enduring Dilemma,' (2011) 50 Mil L & L War Rev 419

Lauterpacht, H, 'The Universal Declaration of Human Rights' (1948) 25 BYIL 354

Lauterpacht, H, 'The Problem of the Revision of the Law of War' (1952) 29 BYIL 360

Leach, P, 'The Chechen Conflict: Analysing the Oversight of the European Court of Human Rights' [2008] EHRLR 732

Levie, HS, 'Legal Aspects of the Continued Detention of the Pakistani Prisoners of War by India' (1973) 67 AJIL 512

Lindroos, A, 'Addressing Norm Conflicts in a Fragmented Legal System: The Doctrine of Lex Specialis' (2005) 74 Nordic J Intl L 27

Lopez, L, 'Uncivil Wars: The Challenge of Applying International Humanitarian Law to Internal Armed Conflicts' (1994) 69 NYU L Rev 916

Lubell, N and Derejko, N, 'A Global Battlefield? Drones and the Geographical Scope of Armed Conflict' (2013) 11 JICJ 65

Mačák, K, 'Needle in a Haystack? Locating the Legal Basis for Detention in Non-International Armed Conflict' (2015) IYHR (forthcoming)

Marcoux Jr, L, 'Protection from Arbitrary Arrest and Detention under International Law' (1982) 5 Boston College Intl & Comp L Rev 345

Mastorodimos, K, 'The Character of the Conflict in Gaza: Another Argument Towards Abolishing the Distinction between International and Non-International Armed Conflicts' (2010) 12 ICLR 437

McCarthy, C, 'The Paradox of the International Law of Military Occupation: Sovereignty and the Reformation of Iraq' (2005) 10 JCSL 43

McCarthy, C, 'Human Rights and the Laws of War under the American Convention on Human Rights' [2008] EHRLR 762

McLachlan, C, 'The Principle of Systemic Integration and Article 31(3)(c) of the Vienna Convention' (2005) 54 ICLQ 279

Melzer, N, 'Keeping the Balance between Military Necessity and Humanity: A Response to Four Critiques of the ICRC's Interpretive Guidance on the Notion of Direct Participation in Hostilities' (2010) 42 NYU J Intl L & Pol 831

Meron, T, 'The Geneva Conventions as Customary Law' (1987) 81 AJIL 361

Meron, T, 'Application of Humanitarian Law in Noninternational Armed Conflicts' (1991) 85 ASIL Proceedings 83

Meron, T, 'International Criminalization of Internal Atrocities' (1995) 89 AJIL 554

Meron, T, 'Extraterritoriality of Human Rights Treaties' (1995) 89 AJIL 78

Meron, T, 'Classification of Armed Conflict in the Former Yugoslavia: *Nicaragua*'s Fallout' (1998) 92 AJIL 236

Meron, T, 'The Humanization of Humanitarian Law' (2000) 94 AJIL 239

Meron, T, 'Revival of Customary Humanitarian Law' (2005) 99 AJIL 817

Milanović, M, 'A Norm Conflict Perspective on the Relationship between International Humanitarian Law and Human Rights Law' (2009) 14 JCSL 459

Milanović, M, 'Is the Rome Statute Binding on Individuals? (And Why We Should Care)' (2011) 9 JICJ 25

Milanović, M and Papic, T, 'As Bad As It Gets: The European Court of Human Rights' *Behrami and Saramati* Decision and General International Law' (2009) 58 ICLQ 267

Müllerson, R, 'The Continuity and Succession of States, by Reference to the Former USSR and Yugoslavia' (1993) 42 ICLQ 473

Müllerson, R, 'International Humanitarian Law in Internal Conflicts' (1997) 2 JACL 109

Murray, C, 'The 1977 Geneva Protocols and Conflict in Southern Africa' (1984) 33 ICLQ 262

Murray, D, 'How International Humanitarian Law Treaties Bind Non-State Armed Groups' (2015) 20 JCSL 101

Ni Aolain, F, 'The No Gaps Approach to Parallel Application in the Context of the War on Terror' (2007) 40 Isr L Rev 563

Öberg, MD, 'The Legal Effects of Resolutions of the UN Security Council and General Assembly in the Jurisprudence of the ICJ' (2006) 16 EJIL 879

Olson, LM, 'Practical Challenges of Implementing the Complementarity between International Humanitarian and Human Rights Law—Demonstrated by the Procedural Regulation of Internment in Non-International Armed Conflict' (2009) 40 Case W Res J Intl L 437

Olson, LM, 'Guantánamo Habeas Review: Are the D.C. District Court's Decisions Consistent with IHL Internment Standards?' (2009) 42 Case W Res J Intl L 197

Orakhelashvili, A, 'The Interaction between Human Rights and Humanitarian Law: Fragmentation, Conflict, Parallelism, or Convergence' (2008) 19 EJIL 161

Oswald, B, 'The Law on Military Occupation: Answering the Challenges of Detention During Contemporary Peace Operations?' (2007) 8 Melb J Intl L 311

Oswald, B, 'Detention of Civilians on Military Operations: Reasons for and Challenges to Developing a Special Law of Detention' (2008) 32 Melb UL Rev 524

Parks, WH, 'Part IX of the ICRC's "Direct Participation in Hostilities": No Mandate, No Expertise and Legally Incorrect' (2010) 42 NYU J Intl L & Pol 769

Paust, JJ, 'Executive Plans and Authorizations to Violate International Law Concerning Treatment and Interrogation of Detainees' (2005) 43 Colum J Transnatl L 811

Pearlstein, DN, 'Avoiding an International Law Fix for Terrorist Detention' (2008) 41 Creighton L Rev 663

Pejic, J, 'Procedural Principles and Safeguards for Internment/Administrative Detention in Armed Conflict and Other Situations of Violence' (2005) 87 IRRC 375

Pejic, J, 'The European Court of Human Rights' *Al-Jedda* Judgment: The Oversight of International Humanitarian Law' (2011) 93 IRRC 837

Pejic, J, 'The Protective Scope of Common Article 3: More Than Meets the Eye' (2011) 93 IRRC 189

Prud'homme, N, '*Lex Specialis*: Oversimplifying a More Complex and Multifaceted Relationship?' (2007) 40 Isr L Rev 356

Reisman, WM, 'Application of Humanitarian Law in Noninternational Armed Conflicts' (1991) 85 ASIL Proc 83

Roberts, A, 'Transformative Military Occupation: Applying the Laws of War and Human Rights' (2006) 100 AJIL 580

Roberts, AE, 'Traditional and Modern Approaches to Customary International Law: A Reconciliation' (2001) 95 AJIL 757

Roberts, AE, 'Power and Persuasion in Investment Treaty Interpretation: The Dual Role of States' (2010) 104 AJIL 179

Roberts, AE and Sivakumaran, S, 'Lawmaking by Non-State Actors: Engaging Armed Groups in the Creation of International Humanitarian Law' (2012) 37 YJIL 107

Roberts, GB, 'The New Rules for Waging War: The Case Against Ratification of Additional Protocol I' (1985–6) 26 Va J Intl L 109

Rona, G, 'An Appraisal of US Practice Relating to "Enemy Combatants"' (2007) 10 YIHL 232

Rona, G, 'Is There a Way Out of the Non-International Armed Conflict Detention Dilemma?' (2015) 91 Intl L Stud 32

Rondeau, S, 'Participation of Armed Groups in the Development of the Law Applicable to Armed Conflicts' (2011) 93 IRRC 649

Rowe, P, 'Is There a Right to Detain Civilians by Foreign Armed Forces During a Non-International Armed Conflict' (2011) 61 ICLQ 697

Ryngaert, C, 'Human Rights Obligations of Armed Groups' [2008] RBDI 355

Sassòli, M, 'The Status of Persons Held in Guantánamo under International Humanitarian Law' (2004) 2 JICJ 96

Sassòli, M, 'Taking Armed Groups Seriously: Ways to Improve Compliance with International Humanitarian Law' (2010) 1 J Intl Human L Studies 12

Sassòli, M and Olson, LM, 'The Relationship between International Humanitarian Law and Human Rights law Where it Matters: Admissible Killing and Internment of Fighters in Non-International Armed Conflicts' (2008) 90 IRRC 599

Schabas, BA, '*Lex Specialis*? Belt and Suspenders? The Parallel Operation of Human Rights Law and the Law of Armed Conflict, and the Conundrum of *Jus Ad Bellum*' (2007) 40 Isr L Rev 592

Schimmelpenninck van der Oije, PJC, 'International Humanitarian Law from a Field Perspective – Case Study: Nepal' (2006) 9 YIHL 394

Schindler, D, 'The Different Types of Armed Conflicts According to the Geneva Conventions and Protocols' (1979) 163 Recueil des Cours 133

Schloemann, HL and Ohlhoff, S, '"Constitutionalization" and Dispute Settlement in the WTO: National Security as an Issue of Competence' (1999) 93 AJIL 424

Schmitt, MN, 'The Interpretive Guidance on the Notion of Direct Participation in Hostilities: A Critical Analysis' (2010) 1 Harv Nat Sec J 5

Schmitt, MN, 'Military Necessity and Humanity in International Humanitarian Law: Preserving the Delicate Balance' (2010) 50 Va J Intl L 795

Schöndorf, RS, 'Extra-State Armed Conflicts: Is there a Need for a New Legal Regime?' (2004) 37 NYU J Intl L & Pol 1

Schwelb, E, 'Crimes Against Humanity' (1946) 23 BYIL 178

Scobbie, I, 'Principle or Pragmatics? The Relationship between Human Rights Law and the Laws of Armed Conflict' (2009) 14 JCSL 449

Sicilianos, L-A, 'The Classification of Obligations and the Multilateral Dimension of the Relations of International Responsibility' (2002) 13 EJIL 1127

Simma, B, 'Self-Contained Regimes' (1985) 16 Neth YB Intl L 111

Simma, B, 'From Bilateralism to Community Interest in International Law' (1994) 250 Recueil des Cours 217

Simma, B and Alston, P, 'The Sources of Human Rights Law: Custom, Jus Cogens, and General Principles' (1988–9) 12 Australian YB Intl L 82

Simma, B, and Pulkowski, D, 'Of Planets and the Universe: Self-Contained Regimes in International Law' (2006) 17 EJIL 483

Sivakumaran, S, 'Binding Armed Opposition Groups' (2006) 55 ICLQ 369

Sivakumaran, S, 'Re-Envisaging the International Law of Internal Armed Conflict' (2011) 22 EJIL 219

Sivakumaran, S, 'Lessons from the Law of Armed Conflict from Commitments of Armed Groups: Identification of Legitimate Targets and Prisoners of War' (2011) 93 IRRC 463
Sofaer, AD, 'The Rationale for the United States Decision' (1988) 82 AJIL 784
Solf, WA, 'The Status of Combatants in Non-International Armed Conflicts Under Domestic Law and Transnational Practice' (1983) 33 Am U L Rev 53
Solf, WA, 'Problems with the Application of Norms Governing Interstate Armed Conflict to Non-International Armed Conflict' (1983) 13 Ga J Intl & Comp L 291
Solis, G, 'Targeted Killing and the Law of Armed Conflict' (2007) 60 NWCR 127
Stein, TL, 'The Approach of the Different Drummer: The Principle of the Persistent Objector in International Law' (1985) 26 Harv Intl LJ 457
Stephens, D, 'Blurring the Lines: The Interpretation, Discourse and Application of the Law of Armed Conflict' (2009) 12 YIHL 85
Stewart, JG, 'Towards a Single Definition of Armed Conflict in International Humanitarian Law: A Critique of Internationalized Armed Conflict' (2003) 85 IRRC 313
Steyn, J, 'Guantanamo Bay: The Legal Black Hole' (2004) 53 ICLQ 1
Stone, J, 'Fictional Elements in Treaty Interpretation: A Study in the International Judicial Process' (1954) 1 Sydney L Rev 334
Stone, R, 'American-German Conference on Prisoners of War' (1919) 13 AJIL 406
Suter, K, 'An Inquiry into the Meaning of the Phrase "Human Rights in Armed Conflicts"' (1976) 15 *Revue de Droit Pénal Militaire et de Droit de la Guerre* 393
Taft IV, WH, 'The Law of Armed Conflict After 9/11: Some Salient Features' (2003) 28 Yale J Intl L 319
Tamura, E, 'The *Isayeva* Cases of the European Court of Human Rights: The Application of International Humanitarian Law and Human Rights Law in Non-International Armed Conflicts' (2011) 10 Chinese J Intl L 129
Treves, T, 'The UN Body of Principles for the Protection of Detained or Imprisoned Persons' (1990) 84 AJIL 578
Verdirame, G, 'Human Rights in Wartime: A Framework for Analysis' [2008] EHRLR 689
Vité, S, 'Typology of Armed Conflicts in International Humanitarian Law: Legal Concepts and Actual Situations' (2009) 91 IRRC 69
von der Groeben, C, 'The Conflict in Colombia and the Relationship between Humanitarian Law and Human Rights Law in Practice: Analysis of the New Operational Law of the Colombian Armed Forces' (2011) 16 JCSL 141
von Glahn, G, 'The Protection of Human Rights in Armed Conflicts' (1971) 1 Isr Ybk Human Rights 208
Warbrick, C, 'United Kingdom Materials on International Law' (2007) 78 BYIL 752
Watkin, K, 'Controlling the Use of Force: A Role for Human Rights Norms in Contemporary Armed Conflict' (2004) 98 AJIL 1
Watkin, K, 'Opportunity Lost: Organized Armed Groups and the ICRC "Direct Participation in Hostilities" Interpretive Guidance' (2010) 42 NYU J Intl L & Pol 641
Watts, S, 'Reciprocity and the Law of War' (2009) 50 Harvard Intl LJ 365
Waxman, MC, 'Administrative Detention of Terrorists: Why Detain and Detain Whom?' (2009) 3 J Nat Sec L & Ply 1
Waxman, MC, 'The Structure of Terrorism Threats and the Laws of War' (2010) 20 Duke J Comp & Intl L 429
Webber, D, 'Preventive Detention in the Law of Armed Conflict: Throwing Away the Key?' (2012) 6 J Nat Sec L & Ply 167
Wilde, R, 'Triggering State Obligations Extraterritorially: The Spatial Test in Certain Human Rights Treaties' (2007) 40 Isr L Rev 503

Willmott, D, 'Removing the Distinction Between International and Non-International Armed Conflict in the *Rome Statute of the International Criminal Court*' (2004) 5 MJIL 196

Winkler, T, 'The Copenhagen Process on Detainees: A Necessity' (2010) 78 Nordic J Intl L 489

Wood, M, 'The International Tribunal for Law of the Sea and General International Law' (2007) 22 Intl J Marine & Coastal L 351

Yingling, RT and Ginnane, RW, 'The Geneva Conventions of 1949' (1952) 46 AJIL 393

Yoo, J, 'Transferring Terrorists' (2004) 79 Notre Dame L Rev 1183

UN DOCUMENTS

Final Act of the International Conference on Human Rights, UN Doc A/Conf.32/41, 22 April–13 May 1968

Human Rights Committee, 'Concluding Observations: Australia', UN Doc A/55/40 (2000)

Human Rights Committee, 'Concluding Observations: Colombia', CCPR/CO/80/COL, 26 May 2004

Human Rights Committee, 'Concluding Observations: Colombia', CCPR/C/COL/CO/6, 4 August 2010

Human Rights Committee, 'Concluding Observations: Democratic Republic of the Congo', CCPR/C/COD/CO/3, 26 April 2006

Human Rights Committee, 'Concluding Observations: Israel', CCPR/CO/78/ISR, 21 August 2003

Human Rights Committee, 'Concluding Observations: Israel', CCPR/C/ISR/CO/3, 3 September 2010

Human Rights Committee, 'Concluding Observations: Sri Lanka', CCPR/CO/79/LKA, 1 December 2003

Human Rights Committee, 'Concluding Observations: Trinidad and Tobago', CCPR/CO/70/TTO, 10 November 2000

Human Rights Committee, 'Concluding Observations: United Kingdom', CCPR/C/GBR/CO/6, 30 July 2008

Human Rights Committee, 'Concluding Observations: United States of America', CCPR/C/USA/CO/3, 15 September 2006

Human Rights Committee, 'Concluding Observations: United States of America', CCPR/C/US/CO/3/Rev.1, 18 December 2006

Human Rights Committee, 'Draft General Comment No 35: Article 9', CCPR/C/107/R.3, 28 January 2013

Human Rights Committee, 'Fifth Periodic Report: Canada', CCPR/C/CAN/2004/5, 18 November 2004

Human Rights Committee, 'Fifth Periodic Report: Finland', CCPR/C/FIN/2003/5, 24 July 2003

Human Rights Committee, 'Fifth Periodic Report: Poland', CCPR/C/POL/2004/5, 26 January 2004

Human Rights Committee, 'Fourth Periodic Report: United States of America', CCPR/C/USA/4, 22 May 2012

Human Rights Committee, 'General Comment No 8: Right to Liberty and Security of Persons', 30 June 1982

Human Rights Committee, 'General Comment No 26: Continuity of Obligations', CCPR/C/21/Rev.1/Add.8/Rev.1, 8 December 1997

Human Rights Committee, 'General Comment No 29: States of Emergency (Article 4)', CCPR/C/21/Rev.1/Add.11, 31 August 2001

Human Rights Committee, 'General Comment No 31: The Nature of the General Legal Obligation Imposed on States Parties to the Covenant', CCPR/C/21/Rev.1/Add.13, 26 May 2004

Human Rights Committee, 'General Comment No 35: Article 9 (Liberty and security of person)', CCPR/C/GC/35, 10 December 2014

Human Rights Committee, 'Information Received from the United Kingdom of Great Britain and Northern Ireland on the Implementation of the Concluding Observations of the Human Rights Committee', CCPR/C/GBR/CO/6/Add.1, 3 November 2009

Human Rights Committee, 'Periodic Report of States Parties: Australia', CCPR/C/AUS/5, 19 February 2008

Human Rights Committee, 'Second Periodic Report: Israel', CCPR/C/ISR/2001/2, 4 December 2001

Human Rights Committee, 'Second Periodic Report: Nepal', CCPR/C/NPL/2, 8 June 2012

Human Rights Committee, 'Selected Decisions of the Human Rights Committee under the Optional Protocol: Volume II' (1985), CCPR/C/OP/1

Human Rights Committee, 'Third Periodic Report: Azerbaijan', CCPR/C/AZE/3, 10 December 2007

Human Rights Committee, 'Third Periodic Report: Democratic Republic of the Congo', CCPR/C/COD/2005/3, 3 May 2005

Human Rights Committee, 'Third Periodic Report: United States of America', CCPR/C/USA/3, 28 November 2005

Human Rights Council, 'Human Rights in Palestine and Other Occupied Arab Territories: Report of the United Nations Fact-Finding Mission on the Gaza Conflict', A/HRC/12/48, 25 September 2009

Human Rights Council, 'Report of 7 Special Rapporteurs: Mission to Lebanon and Israel (7–14 September 2006)', A/HRC/2/7, 2 October 2006

Human Rights Council, 'Report of the High Commissioner on the Situation of Human Rights and the Activities of Her Office in the Democratic Republic of the Congo', A/HRC/10/58, 1 March 2009

Human Rights Council, 'Report of the Independent International Commission of Inquiry on the Syrian Arab Republic', UN Doc A/HRC/21/50, 16 August 2012

Human Rights Council, 'Report of the International Commission of Inquiry to Investigate All Alleged Violations of International Human Rights Law in the Libyan Arab Jamahiriya', UN Doc A/HRC/17/44, 1 June 2011

Human Rights Council, 'Report of the Special Rapporteur on Extrajudicial, Summary or Arbitrary Executions, Philip Alston: Study on Targeted Killings', A/HRC/14/24/Add.6, 28 May 2010

Human Rights Council, 'Report of the Special Rapporteur on the Promotion and Protection of Human Rights and Fundamental Freedoms While Countering Terrorism: Mission to the United States of America', A/HRC/6/17/Add.3 (22 November 2007)

Human Rights Council, 'Report of the Working Group on Arbitrary Detention: Addendum, Mission to Colombia (1 to 10 October 2008)', A/HRC/10/21/Add.3, 16 February 2009

Human Rights Council, 'Report of the Working Group on the Universal Periodic Review: United States of America', A/HRC/16/11, 4 January 2011

Human Rights Council, 'Arbitrary Detention', Res 6/4, 28 September 2007

Human Rights Council, 'Third Joint Report of Seven United Nations Experts on the Democratic Republic of the Congo', A/HRC/16/68, 3 March 2011

Human Rights Council, 'Universal Periodic Review: United States of America', UN Doc A/HRC/WG.6/9/USA/1, 23 August 2010

'Report of the International Commission of Inquiry on Darfur to the Secretary-General', S/2005/60, 1 February 2005

UN Assistance Mission for Iraq, 'Human Rights Report: 1 April—30 June 2007'

UN Commission on Human Rights, 'Extrajudicial, Summary or Arbitrary Executions: Report of the Special Rapporteur, Philip Alston', E/CN.4/2005/7, 22 December 2004

UN Commission on Human Rights, 'Extrajudicial, Summary or Arbitrary Executions: Report of the Special Rapporteur, Philip Alston: Mission to Sri Lanka', UN Doc E/CN.4/2006/53/Add.5, 27 March 2006

UN Commission on Human Rights, 'Letter dated 14 April 2003 from the Chief of Section, Political and Specialized Agencies, of the Permanent Mission of the United States of America to the United Nations Office at Geneva Addressed to the Secretariat of the Commission on Human Rights', UN Doc E/CN.4/2003/G/80, 22 April 2003

UN Commission on Human Rights, 'Report on the Situation of Human Rights in the Democratic Republic of the Congo, Submitted by the Special Rapporteur, Mr. Roberto Garretón, in Accordance with Commission on Human Rights Resolution 2000/15', E/CN.4/2001/40, 1 February 2001

UN Commission on Human Rights, 'Report of the Working Group on Arbitrary Detention', E/CN. 4/2004/3, 15 December 2003

UN Commission on Human Rights, 'Report of the Working Group on Arbitrary Detention', E/CN.4/2006/7, 12 December 2005

UN Commission on Human Rights, 'Report of the Working Group on Involuntary or Enforced Disappearances: Mission to Nepal', E/CN.4/2005/65/Add.1, 28 January 2005

UN Commission on Human Rights, Arbitrary Detention, Res 2004/39, 19 April 2004

UN Commission on Human Rights, 'Situation of Detainees at Guantanamo Bay', E/CN.4/2006/120, 27 February 2006

UN Commission on Human Rights, 'Situation of Human Rights in Sudan', E/CN. 4/1994/48, 1 February 1994

UN Commission on Human Rights, 'The Siracusa Principles on the Limitation and Derogation Provisions in the International Covenant on Civil and Political Rights', E/CN.4/1985/4, 28 September 1984

UN Department of Economic and Social Affairs, 'Study of the Right of Everyone to be Free from Arbitrary Arrest, Detention and Exile', UN Doc E/CN 4/826 Rev 1 (1964)

UN General Assembly, 'Report of the Special Rapporteur on the Situation of Human Rights in the Democratic Republic of the Congo Pursuant to General Assembly Resolution 53/160 and Commission on Human Rights Resolution 1999/56', A/54/361, 17 September 1999

UN Office of the High Commissioner for Human Rights, *Nepal Conflict Report: An Analysis of Conflict-Related Violations of International Human Rights Law and International Humanitarian Law between February 1996 and 21 November 2006* (OHCHR, Geneva 2012)

UN Secretary-General, 'Report on Information Submitted by Governments Pursuant to Sub-Commission Res 7 (XXVII) of 20 August 1974', E/CN.4/Sub.2/1990/20, 19 July 1990

UN Security Council, 'Presidential Statement on the Situation Concerning the DRC', S/PRST/2008/38, 21 October 2008

UN Security Council, 'Report of Secretary-General Pursuant to Paragraph 30 of Resolution 1546 (2004)', S/2005/373, 7 June 2005

UN Security Council, 'Second Report of the Secretary-General on United Nations Mission in the Democratic Republic of the Congo', S/2000/330, 18 April 2000

UN Security Council, Statement by the President of the Security Council, S/PRST/2013/15, 2 October 2013

UN Security Council, 'Verbatim Record, Statement by Bangladesh (16 November 1992)', UN Doc S/PV.3137

UN Working Group on Arbitrary Detention, 'Deliberation No 9 Concerning the Definition and Scope of Arbitrary Deprivation of Liberty under Customary International Law' in Human Rights Council, 'Report of the Working Group on Arbitrary Detention', A/HRC/22/44, 24 December 2012

UN Working Group on Arbitrary Detention, 'Fact Sheet 26', <http://www.ohchr.org/Documents/Publications/FactSheet26en.pdf> accessed 19 April 2012

UN Working Group on Arbitrary Detention, 'United Nations Basic Principles and Guidelines on Remedies and Procedures on the Right of Anyone Deprived of their Liberty to Bring Proceedings before a Court', A/HRC/30/xx (unedited version), 4 May 2015

INTERNATIONAL LAW COMMISSION (ILC) DOCUMENTS

Guiding Principles Applicable to Unilateral Declarations of States Capable of Creating Legal Obligations with Commentaries Thereto [2006] Ybk of the ILC, Volume II, Part II

Provisional Summary Record of the 3225th Meeting (17 July 2014), A/CN.4/SR.3225, 18 September 2014

Report of the International Law Commission (ILC) to the General Assembly on its Second Session, 5 June–29 July 1950, Document A/1316 [1950] Ybk of the ILC, Vol II

Report of the Study Group of the International Law Commission, 'Fragmentation of International Law: Difficulties Arising from the Diversification and Expansion of International Law', Finalized by Martti Koskenniemi, 13 April 2006, A/CN.4/L.682

Report of the Work of its Sixty-Sixth Session (5 May to 6 June and 7 July to 8 August 2014), Official Records, Sixty-Ninth Session, Supp No 10 (A/69/10)

Second Report on Identification of Customary International Law by Michael Wood, Special Rapporteur, A/CN4/ 672, 22 May 2014

Second Report on Subsequent Agreements and Subsequent Practice in Relation to the Interpretation of Treaties by Georg Nolte, Special Rapporteur, A/CN.4/671, 26 March 2014

MILITARY DOCTRINE

Canada, Joint Doctrine Manual: Law of Armed Conflict at the Operational and Tactical Levels (Office of the Judge Advocate General, Ottawa, 2001)

Canada, Prisoner of War Status Determination Regulations, SOR/ 91-134, 25 January 1991

Judge Advocate General (Canada), Law of Armed Conflict at the Operational and Tactical Levels (Office of the Judge Advocate General, Ottawa 2001)

Netherlands Ministry of Defence, Netherlands Defence Doctrine (2013)

UK Ministry of Defence, Joint Doctrine Publication 1-10: Captured Persons (CPERS) (3rd edn, Ministry of Defence, Shrivenham 2015)
UK Ministry of Defence, Joint Doctrine Publication 1-10: Prisoners of War, Internees and Detainees (Ministry of Defence, Shrivenham 2006)
UK Ministry of Defence, The Manual of the Law of Armed Conflict (OUP, Oxford 2004)
United States Army Field Manual, FM 27-10: The Law of Land Warfare (Department of the Army, Washington, DC 1956)
United States Army Judge Advocate General's Legal Center and School, Law of Armed Conflict Deskbook (Charlottesville 2014)
United States Army Regulation 190–8, Enemy Prisoners of War, Retained Personnel, Civilian Internees and Other Detainees (Departments of the Army, Navy, Air Force and Marine Corps, Washington, DC 1997)
The White House (Office of the Press Secretary), 'Fact Sheet: New Actions on Guantanamo and Detainee Policy' (7 March 2011)

AFRICAN COMMISSION ON HUMAN AND PEOPLES' RIGHTS DOCUMENTS

Principles and Guidelines on the Right to a Fair Trial and Legal Assistance in Africa, adopted at 33rd session in Niamey, Niger, 29 May 2003

INTER-AMERICAN COMMISSION ON HUMAN RIGHTS (IACIHR) DOCUMENTS

IACiHR, 'Annual Report: 1976', OAS Doc. OEA/Ser.L/V/II.40, Doc. 5 corr. 1 of 7 June 1977
IACiHR, 'Report on Terrorism and Human Rights', OEA/Ser.L/V/II.116 Doc. 5 rev. 1 corr., 22 October 2002
IACiHR, 'Third Report on the Human Rights Situation in Colombia' (26 February 1999) OEA/Ser.L/V/II.102 Doc 9 rev 1

TRAVAUX PRÉPARATOIRES OF KEY IHL TREATIES

Conference of Government Experts on the Reaffirmation and Development of International Humanitarian Law Applicable in Armed Conflicts, Volume V: Protection of Victims of Non-International Armed Conflicts (ICRC, Geneva 1971)
Final Record of the Diplomatic Conference of Geneva of 1949: Vol I (ICRC, 1963)
Final Record of the Diplomatic Conference of Geneva of 1949: Vol II, Section A (ICRC, 1963)
Final Record of the Diplomatic Conference of Geneva of 1949: Vol II, Section B (ICRC, 1963)
Final Record of the Diplomatic Conference of Geneva of 1949: Vol III (ICRC, 1963)
Official Records of the Diplomatic Conference on the Reaffirmation and Development of International Humanitarian Law Applicable in Armed Conflicts (Geneva 1974–77): Volume V (Federal Political Department, Bern 1978)
Official Records of the Diplomatic Conference on the Reaffirmation and Development of International Humanitarian Law Applicable in Armed Conflicts, Geneva (1974–1977): Volume VII (Federal Political Department, Bern 1978)

Official Records of the Diplomatic Conference on the Reaffirmation and Development of International Humanitarian Law Applicable in Armed Conflicts, Geneva (1974–1977): Volume VIII (Federal Political Department, Bern 1978)

Remarks and Proposals Submitted by the International Committee of the Red Cross: Documents for the Consideration of Governments Invited by the Swiss Federal Council to Attend the Diplomatic Conference at Geneva (April 21, 1949) (ICRC, Geneva 1949)

Report on the Work of the Conference of Government Experts for the Study of the Conventions for the Protection of War Victims: Geneva, April 14–26, 1947 (ICRC, Geneva 1947)

NON-GOVERNMENTAL AND CIVIL SOCIETY ORGANIZATIONS

American Law Institute, *Restatement (Third): The Foreign Relations Law of the United States, Vol II* (ALI, St Paul 1987)

Amnesty International, 'DRC: Deadly Alliances in Congolese Forests', 3 December 1997, AFR 62/033/1997, 27–31

Human Rights Watch, *Legal Limbo: The Uncertain Fate of Detained LTTE Suspects in Sri Lanka* (HRW, New York 2010)

Human Rights Watch (Report), 'Untold Miseries: Wartime Abuses and Forced Displacement in Burma's Kachin State' (20 March 2012)

Human Rights Watch, 'Sri Lanka: "Bait and Switch" on Emergency Law' (7 September 2011)

Human Rights Watch, 'Up in Flames: Humanitarian Law Violations and Civilian Victims in the Conflict Over South Ossetia', 1-56432-427-3 (January 2009)

Institut de Droit International, 'The Application of International Humanitarian Law and Fundamental Human Rights in Armed Conflicts, in which Non-State Entities are Parties' (Session of Berlin –1999)

International Commission of Jurists, *Nepal: The Rule of Law Abandoned* (ICJ, Geneva 2005)

International Committee of the Red Cross, 'Internment in Armed Conflict: Basic Rules and Challenges' (Opinion Paper, Nov 2014)

International Committee of the Red Cross, 'Nepal' in ICRC, *Annual Report 2006* (ICRC, May 2007)

International Committee of the Red Cross, Report of the 31st International Conference of the RedCross and Red Crescent, 'IHL and the Challenges of Contemporary Armed Conflicts', October 2011

International Committee of the Red Cross, *Report on the Practice of Colombia* (1998)

International Committee of the Red Cross, *Report on the Practice of France* (1999)

International Committee of the Red Cross, *Report on the Practice of India* (1997)

International Committee of the Red Cross, *Report on the Practice of Nigeria* (1997)

International Committee of the Red Cross, *Report on US Practice* (1997)

International Committee of the Red Cross, 'Sri Lanka' in ICRC, *Annual Report 2008* (ICRC, May 2009)

International Committee of the Red Cross, 'Sri Lanka' in ICRC, *Annual Report 2009* (ICRC, May 2010)

International Committee of the Red Cross, 'Sri Lanka' in ICRC, *Annual Report 2011* (ICRC, May 2012)

International Committee of the Red Cross, Strengthening Legal Protection for Persons Deprived of their Liberty in Relation to Non-International Armed Conflict, Regional Consultations 2012–13: Background Paper (undated)

OTHER MULTILATERAL DOCUMENTS

African Parliamentary Conference on International Humanitarian Law for the Protection of Civilians during Armed Conflict, Niamey, 18–20 February 2002, Final Declaration

Cooperation Council for the Arab States of the Gulf, 13th Session, Abu Dhabi, 21–3 December 1992, Final Communique, annexed to Letter dated 24 December 1992 from the UAE to the UN Secretary-General, UN Doc A/47/845-S/25020, 30 December 1992

'The Copenhagen Process on the Handling of Detainees in International Military Operations, The Copenhagen Process: Principles and Guidelines' with Chairman's Commentary (October 2012)

Declaration of Minimum Humanitarian Standards Adopted by an Expert Meeting Convened by the Institute for Human Rights, Abo Akademi University, Turku, Finland, 2 December 1990

'Report of the Independent International Fact-Finding Mission on the Conflict in Georgia: Volume II', September 2009

AGREEMENTS BETWEEN STATES AND NON-STATE ARMED GROUPS

Abidjan Peace Agreement between the Government of Sierra Leone and the Revolutionary United Front (30 November 1996)

Comprehensive Agreement on Respect for Human Rights and International Humanitarian Law between the Government of the Republic of the Philippines and the National Democratic Front of the Philippines (signed 16 March 1998 in The Hague, Netherlands)

Darfur Peace Agreement between the Government of the Sudan, the Sudan Liberation Movement/Army and the Justice and Equality Movement (done at Abuja, Nigeria, 5 May 2006)

'Document 9: Note Verbale dated 14 August 1990 from El Salvador transmitting test of the Agreement on Human Rights signed at San José, Costa Rica, on 26 July 1990 between the Government of El Salvador and the Frente Farabundo Martí para la Liberación Nacional (FMLN), A/44/971-S/21541, 16 August 1990' in UN, The United Nations and El Salvador: 1990–1995 (The UN Blue Book Series Volume IV, 1995)

Peace Accords between the Government of Angola and UNITA (Bicesse Accords), annexed to Letter dated 17 May 1991 from the Chargé d'affaires a.i. of the Permanent Mission of Angola to the UN addressed to the UN Secretary General, UN Doc S/22609 (17 May 1991)

UNILATERAL ACTS OF NON-STATE ARMED GROUPS

Communist Party of Nepal-Maoist, Public Legal Code 2060 (2003/04)
LTTE, Tamil Eelam Child Protection Act (Act No 3 of 2006)
Manual, National Transitional Council, Libya (19 May 2011)
Political Programme of the Ogaden National Liberation Front (Ethiopia)

COALITION PROVISIONAL AUTHORITY (IRAQ)

Coalition Provisional Authority, Memorandum No 3 (Revised), CPA/MEM/27, June 2004/03

OTHER DOMESTIC DOCUMENTS

Australia Permanent Mission to the UN Geneva, Australian Response to UN Working Group on Arbitrary Detention's Draft Principles and Guidelines on remedies and procedures on the right of anyone deprived of his or her liberty, Note 23/2015, 17 March 2015

The Baha Mousa Public Inquiry, 'Closing Submissions on Modules 1– 3 on Behalf of the Ministry of Defence', 25 June 2010

Human Rights Committee, 'Draft General Comment No. 35, Article 9: Liberty and Security of Person, Comments by the Government of Canada', 6 October 2014

Human Rights Committee, 'Japan's Comments on the draft General Comment No 35 on Article 9 of the International Covenant on Civil and Political Rights' (undated)

Human Rights Committee, 'Observations by the Government of the United Kingdom of Great Britain and Northern Ireland on draft General Comment 35 on Article 9 of the International Covenant on Civil and Political Rights (ICCPR) – liberty and security of person' (undated)

Human Rights Committee, 'Observations of Ireland on the draft General Comment No 35, Article 9: Liberty and security of person', 30 May 2014

Human Rights Committee, 'Observations of the United States of America on the Human Rights Committee's Draft General Comment 35: Article 9', 10 June 2014

Koh, HH, 'The Obama Administration and International Law', Remarks at the Annual Meeting of ASIL, Washington, DC, 25 March 2010

UN Working Group on Arbitrary Detention, 'Germany's comments on the "Draft Principles and Guidelines on remedies and procedures on: The right of anyone deprived of his or her liberty by arrest or detention to bring proceedings before a court without delay, in order that the court may decide without delay on the lawfulness of his or her detention and order his or her release if the detention is not lawful"' (undated)

UN Working Group on Arbitrary Detention, 'Permanent Mission of Greece Geneva: Note Verbale', Ref No 6171.71/ 13/ 550, 31 March 2015

US Department of Justice White Paper, 'Lawfulness of a Lethal Operation Directed Against a U.S. Citizen Who is a Senior Operational Leader of Al-Qa'ida or An Associated Force' (undated; made public on 4 February 2013)

Index

Additional Protocols to Geneva Conventions *see* API (Additional Protocol I), Geneva Conventions 1949; APII (Additional Protocol II), Geneva Conventions 1949
Administrative Review Board (ARB) 195
Afghanistan
　Afghan Transitional Government 179
　Detainee Review Boards 181, 182
　International Security Assistance Force 180
　non-international armed conflict (post-2001) 179–183
　Operation Enduring Freedom 180
African Charter on Human and People's Rights (ACHPR) 193, 214
　Article 6 205, 206
African Commission on Human and People's Rights (AciHPRR) 205–206
　Principles and Guidelines on the Right to a Fair Trial and Legal Assistance in Africa 205, 206
African Parliamentary Union
　conference of 2002 78
Algeria, National Liberation Army 26
al-Qaeda
　classification of US conflict with 21
　status under IHL 38
　US detention practices 185–189
American Convention on Human Rights (ACHR) 114–115, 203
American Declaration on the Rights and Duties of Man (ADRDM) 114, 201, 203, 204, 214
　Article XXV 203, 204
amnesties 27
API (Additional Protocol I), Geneva Conventions 1949
　adoption 16–17
　armed forces, defined 35
　combatant/POW status 34, 35, 48
　refusal by some states to ratify 36
　review of internment 57, 58
　status under custom 36–37
APII (Additional Protocol II), Geneva Conventions 1949
　adoption 16–17
　binding on non-state armed groups 100–103
　field of application 83–84
　Martens Clause 85
　regulation of internment 69, 70, 77, 83–85
　release of detainees 97
　scope of application 17
　substantive provisions 17

armed conflicts
　distinction between international and non-international *see* distinction between international and non-international armed conflicts
　international *see* international armed conflict
　non-international *see* non-international armed conflict
　transnational, between states and non-state armed groups 5, 20, 89, 183
Article 3 common to Geneva Conventions 13, 15, 16
　adoption 16
　context 15, 23
　and emergence of human rights law 15
　binding on non-state armed groups 100–103
　as 'Convention in miniature' 80
　and diplomatic conference of 1949 15, 25
　drafting history 15–16, 80
　humane treatment principle 76, 79, 80, 82, 84
　preamble to Geneva Conventions, based on 16
　regulation of internment 69, 76–83

Bangladesh
　release of detainees, public calls for 96
belligerency doctrine, customary international law 13

ceasefire agreements, release of internees 95
Charter of United Nations (UNC)
　Article 2 16
　Article 51 180
　Article 103 179, 198
　and common Article 3 15
　legal basis for internment, in non-international armed conflict 75
civil war
　belligerency doctrine 13
　insurgency doctrine 13
civilians, internment in international armed conflict
　definition of 'civilian' in Additional Protocol I 49
　definition of 'civilian' in GCIV 37
　release 59–60
　review 51–56
　　initial 51–55
　　periodic 56
　standard for internment 39

Colombia
arbitrary deprivation of liberty in 2, 78
Constitutional Court 93
detention practices in the Colombian conflict 165–166
ELN (*Ejército de Liberación*) 165
FARC (*Feurzas Armadas Revolucionarias de Colombia*) 99, 165, 232
Combatant Status Review Tribunals (CSRTs) 186, 187, 187, 195
combatants
internment in international armed conflict
Article 5 GCIII tribunals 56–57
Article 45(1) API tribunals 57–58
civilians compared 34
definition of 'combatant' in GCIII 34–37
historical position 47–48
release 60–62
review 56–59
standard for internment 47–51
'unlawful combatants' 37–39
Combined Review and Release Board (CRRB) 176, 177
common Article 3 *see* Article 3 common to Geneva Conventions
Communist Party of Nepal-Maoist (CPN-M), Nepal 168
compulsory military service
First World War 39
Convention on the Prevention and Punishment of the Crime of Genocide (1948) 14
Convention on the Prohibition of the Development, Production and Stockpiling of Bateriological (Biological) and Toxin Weapons and on their Destruction (1975) 17
Convention on the Prohibition of the Development, Production, Stockpiling and Use of Chemical Weapons and on their Destruction (1997) 17
Convention on the Prohibition of the Use, Stockpiling, Production and Transfer of Anti-Personnel Mines and on the Destruction (199) 17
Copenhagen Principles on the Handling of Detainees in International Military Operations 87, 88, 88–89, 184, 227, 230
customary international humanitarian law
see also customary humanitarian law
binding non-state armed groups 104–105
defining 'customary IHL' 85–87
internment in non-international armed conflict 85–98
end-point of internment 95–98
prohibition of arbitary deprivation of liberty 90–91

legal basis to intern in non-international armed conflict 70
Rule 99 of the ICRC Study 94
Rule 128C of the ICRC Study 96, 97

Darfur Peace Agreement (2006) 95
Democratic Republic of Congo (DRC)
Congo Wars 170, 171
Congrès national pour la défense du peuple (CNDP) 171
detention practices in the DRC conflicts 170–172
Forces démocratiques de libération du Rwanda (FDLR) 171
Mouvement national pour la libération du Congo (MLC) 171
Rassemblement Congolais pour la Democratie (RCD) 99, 171
derogation
see also 'Siracusa Principles on the Limitation and Derogation Provisions in the International Covenant on Civil and Political Rights'
from ECHR Article 5 200, 201, 229
extraterritorial derogation from human rights treaties 216–217
from internal review (*habeas corpus*) 230
Detainee Review Boards (DRBs), Afghanistan 181, 182
detention
see also internment
and distinction between international and non-international armed conflicts 85–91, 94
of enemy aliens 40
under international human rights law *see* detention under IHRL
post-9/11 US practices 38, 43
and relationship between IHL and IHRL 112, 144–190
detention under IHRL 111–127
applicability in armed conflict 111–116
arbitrary arrest or detention 117
defined 120
indefinite detention 126
initial review (*habeas corpus*) 124–127
liberty, right to 117
obligations to give reasons for detention 122–124
procedural rules under human rights treaties 116–127
standard for detention 117–122
diplomatic conference of 1949 15, 24
and Article 5 GCIV 62
Burmese delegation 15, 26
and common Article 3 15, 25
internment review 54
sovereignty concerns 24
and United Kingdom 19

Index

diplomatic conference of 1974–77 20, 25, 26, 113
  Pakistani delegation 26
  sovereignty concerns 23, 24
distinction between international and non-international armed conflicts 1, 11–30
  Additional Protocols, implications for 16–17
  common Article 3, implications for 16
  consequences 1
  convergence of law of international and non-international armed conflict 86, 87
  criticisms 11, 19–22, 24, 30
    humanitarian problems 21–22
    pragmatic problems 19–21
  detention, with respect to 85–91, 94
    whether to eliminate 227–228
  historical basis 11, 11–18, 23, 33
  ICTY on 22
  inter-state focus of international law 13
  in nineteenth century 13
  post-war developments 14
  prior to Geneva Conventions of 1949 11–13
  reasons for preserving 11, 18, 22–29, 30
    humanitarian concerns 27–29
    sovereignty concerns 23–27
DRC *see* **Democratic Republic of Congo (DRC)**

El Salvador 220
enemy aliens, historical position regarding detention of 39–40
Enemy Combatant Review Board (ECRB), Afghanistan 181
European Convention on Human Rights (ECHR) 114, 117
  application of Article 5 in non-international armed conflict 198–199
  derogation from Article 5 200–201
  incompatibility of internment with Article 5 121
European Court of Human Rights (ECtHR) 45, 119–120, 156, 196–201
  application of European Convention on Human Rights 114, 121
  initial review (*habeas corpus*) 124, 125
  promptness standard, detention 123
  and reasons for detention 123
European Court of Justice (ECJ) 45
extraterritoriality
  application of IHRL 212–217
  derogation from human rights treaties 216–217

FARC (*Feurzas Armadas Revolucionarias de Colombia*) 99, 232

FMLN (*Frente Farabundo Martí para la Liberación Nacional*) 220
France
  release of detainees, public calls for 96
  and sovereignty concerns 23

GCI (Geneva Convention for the Amelioration of the Condition of the Wonded and Sick in Armed Forces in the Field), 1949 12
  see also Geneva Conventions (1949)
GCII (Geneva Convention for the Amelioration of the Condition of the Wounded, Sick and Shipwrecked Members of the Armed Forces), 1949 11
  see also Geneva Conventions (1949)
GCIII (Geneva Convention Relative to the Treatment of Prisoners of War), 1949 11
  see also Geneva Conventions (1949)
  analogizing to GCIII in non-international armed conflict 230–234
  combatant/POW status 34, 35, 36, 37, 48
  detention authorized by GCIII 48, 68
GCIV (Geneva Convention Relative to the Protection of Civilian Persons in Time of War), 1949 11
  see also Geneva Conventions (1949)
  analogizing to GCIV in non-international armed conflict 234–242
  Article 4 35, 37, 38
  Article 5 37, 38, 57, 58, 62
  civilian status 37, 39, 40–41
  detention authorized by 68
  drafting 40
  humane treatment principle 81
  as *lex specialis* 154
  limitations on application 37
  review of internment 54, 56–57
  standards of internment 44–45, 235, 236
  unlawful confinement as grave breach of 39
General Agreement on Tariffs and Trade (GATT), national security exceptions 45
General Assembly of United Nations 113, 218
Geneva Conventions (1949)
  see also GCI (Geneva Convention for the Amelioration of the Condition of the Wonded and Sick in Armed Forces in the Field), 1949; GCII (Geneva Convention for the Amelioration of the Condition of the Wounded, Sick and Shipwrecked Members of the Armed Forces), 1949; GCIII (Geneva Convention Relative to the Treatment of Prisoners of War), 1949; GCIV (Geneva Convention Relative to the Protection of Civilian Persons in Time of War), 1949

Geneva Conventions (1949) (*cont.*):
  adoption 11
  common Article 3 *see* Article 3 common to Geneva Conventions
  'non-effect' clause 25
  preamble, common Article 3 based on 16
Guantánamo Bay, Cuba 38, 156, 185, 186, 188, 189
guerilla warfare, POW framework 36, 58

habeas corpus (initial review)
  access and Guantanamo detainees 3
  adversarial proceedings 127
  and African Charter of Human Rights 205
  and American Convention on Human Rights 204
  derogation from 230
  detention under IHRL 124–127
    nature and procedures of review body 127
    'without delay' 124–125
  ECtHR, jurisprudence 124
Haiti, arbitrary deprivation of liberty in 2
hostage taking, proscribed act 46
Human Rights Committee (HRC) 3, 119, 121, 122, 194–196
  on Colombia 166
  Concluding Observations on Australia 127
  Concluding Observations on Trinidad and Tobago 119
  and detention in non-international armed conflict 160
  non-arbitrariness requirement, interpretation 121
  and reasons for detention 123
human rights treaties
  see also international human rights law (IHRL)
  as embodying obligations *erga omnes partes* 163
  interpretation 163
  procedural rules applicable to detention under 116–127
  treaty bodies *see* human rights treaty bodies
human rights treaty bodies
  extent of binding character of decisions 7
  jurisprudence 7
  practice in cases of detention in non-international armed conflict 192–212
    African Commission on Human and People's Rights 205–206
    European Court of Human Rights 196–201
    Human Rights Committee 194–196
    Inter-American institutions 201–205
    proposal for reconciling approaches 207–212
humane treatment principle
  and Additional Protocol II 84
  common Article 3 76, 79, 80, 82, 84
  content 81
  necessity, notion of 81
  non-derogable nature 81
  relationship to internment 81

ICJ *see* International Court of Justice (ICJ)
ICRC *see* International Committee of Red Cross (ICRC)
ICRC Customary International Humanitarian Law Study 17, 18, 90–91, 92, 93
  criticism 90, 92
ICTY *see* International Criminal Tribunal for the former Yugoslavia (ICTY)
IHL *see* international humanitarian law (IHL)
IHRL *see* international human rights law (IHRL)
immunity
  combatant
    compliance with IHL 36
    extending to non-international conflicts 24, 26–27
  domestic law violations, amnesties for 27
India
  release of detainees, public calls for 96
insurgency doctrine, customary international law 13
Inter-American Commission on Human Rights (IACiHR) 78, 114, 156, 201
Inter-American Court of Human Rights (IACtHR) 114, 120, 125, 201, 202, 203
international armed conflicts
  convergence with law of non-international armed conflict 86, 87
  detention and the relationship between IHL and IHRL 152–159
  internment *see* internment, international armed conflict
  and non-international armed conflict, distinction *see* distinction between international and non-international armed conflicts
International Committee of Red Cross (ICRC)
  access to detainees 6
  on Additional Protocol I 36
  Customary International Humanitarian Law Study (2005) *see* ICRC Customary International Humanitarian Law Study
  Guidance on Direct Participation in Hostilities 231
  on internment in non-international armed conflict 69, 78
  and protection of detainees in non-international conflicts 4–5

Index

International Conference on the Reaffirmation and Development of International Humanitarian Law *see* diplomatic conference of 1974–77
International Court of Justice (ICJ)
  and binding nature of common Article 3 and APII for non-state armed groups 101
  custom, approach to 8
  on the relationship between IHL and IHRL 147–152
International Covenant on Civil and Political Rights (ICCPR) 3, 115, 148
  Article 9 160, 170, 172, 173, 178, 184, 189, 194, 195, 196
International Criminal Court, jurisdiction 103
International Criminal Tribunal for the former Yugoslavia (ICTY)
  on civilian internment 42
  on distinction between international and non-international armed conflicts 17, 22
  standards for internment 45, 45, 46
  on State-sovereignty vs human-being-oriented approach 22
international human rights law (IHRL)
  applicability in armed conflict 28, 111–116
  detention and lawfulness requirement 118, 119, 121
  detention and non-arbitrariness requirement 118, 119, 121
  extraterritorial application 212–217
  historical developments 14
  lethal force, use of 73
  relationship with IHL 112, 144–164
international humanitarian law (IHL)
  binding nature, for non-state armed groups 99–107
  customary *see* customary international humanitarian law
  internment in international armed conflict under *see* internment, international armed conflict
  internment in non-international armed conflict *see* internment, non-international armed conflict
  relationship with IHRL 112, 144–164
International Security Assistance Force (ISAF), Afghanistan 180
internment
  see also detention and relationship between IHL and IHRL; detention in non-international armed conflict, practical application of rules; detention under IHRL; internment, international armed conflict; internment, non-international armed conflict
  defined 1

internment, international armed conflict 33–65
  'belligerent nexus,' need for 47
  burden of proof 55
  discretion of detaining power 52
  grounds for civilian internment 41
  and Israeli Supreme Court 41, 43, 44, 53, 237
  limits on states' internment authority 45–46, 47
  parameters of internment authority under IHL 43–44
  release of detainees 59–62
    civilians 59–60
    combatants 60–62
  review 51–59
    civilians 34–56
    combatants 56–59
  standard 39–51
    civilians 39–47
    combatants 47–51
internment, non-international armed conflict 66–108
  conventional humanitarian law, procedural rules under
    Additional Protocol II 69, 83–85
    common Article 3 69, 76–83
  customary humanitarian law, procedural rules under 85–98
    conclusions 98
    end-point of internment 95–98
    prohibition of arbitrary deprivation of liberty 91–95
  legal basis 66–76, 101
  and non-state armed groups *see* non-state (armed) groups
internment committee, United Kingdom 40
Iraq (2003 onwards)
  coalition forces, detentions by 175
  Coalition Provisional Authority (CPA) 175
  Combined Review and Release Board 176, 177
  Multi-National Force Review Committee 176
Israel
  application of IHRL in armed conflict 114
  Supreme Court 41, 43, 44, 53, 237

Korean War 61

lex specialis
  different meanings 155
  GCIII internment regime 155
  GCIV internment regime 154, 155
  international humanitarian law as 146, 149, 153, 160, 173, 182, 202
Liberation Tigers of Tamil Eelam (LTTE) 167

Libya
  criminal code 220
  National Transitional Council (NTC) 220

Mali, arbitrary deprivation of liberty in 2
Martens Clause, in APII 85
military manuals 45, 91, 93
  in ICRC Study 92, 93
military necessity principle 79, 83
Multi-National Force Review Committee (MNFRC), Iraq 176
multi-national forces, detention practices
  Afghanistan 2
  Iraq 2, 174, 178

National Liberation Army
  Algeria 26
National Transitional Council (NTC), Libya 220
nationality principle, and binding non-state groups 103
necessity
  in GCIV 236
  general internment of resident enemy aliens 40
  and humane treatment 81
  of internment under GCIV 83
  military necessity principle 79, 83
  reasonableness standard 83
Nepal
  arbitrary deprivation of liberty in 2
  Communist Party of Nepal-Maoist (CPN-M), Nepal 168
  non-international armed conflict 168–170
  Public Security (2nd Amendment) Act 1991 (PSA) 169
  Terrorist and Disruptive Activities (Control and Punishment) Act 2002 169
  Terrorist and Disruptive Activities (Control and Punishment) Ordinance 2004 (TADO) 169
non-arbitrariness requirement
  international human rights law 118–119, 121
non-international armed conflict
  convergence with law of international armed conflict 87
  definitions 5
  gaps in current law 3
  internment see internment, non-international armed conflict
  internment *de lege ferenda* 228–230
non-refoulement, importance in contemporary armed conflicts 6
non-state (armed) groups
  bilateral agreements with states 106
  binding nature of IHL for 99–107
  binding nature of IHRL for 217–221
  versus non-state armed forces/fighters 1

status under domestic law 26
unilateral declarations by 106
Northern Ireland
  The Troubles in constituting a public emergency 200
  UK internment regime 199

Obama Administration 185, 186, 187, 232, 233
Operation Enduring Freedom (OEF) 180
opinio iuris
  and Copenhagen Principles 88
  customary humanitarian law 93
  evidence 8
  sources 8

pacta sunt servanda principle, application of IHL treaties 99
pacta tertiis rule, extension to non-state groups 102
Peace Accords between the Government of Angola and UNITA (Bicesse Accords) 95
Periodic Review Boards (PRBs) 187, 188
Personal Representatives (PRs) for detainees 176, 181, 186, 187
Philippines
  release of detainees, public calls for 96
POWs (prisoners of war), internment in international armed conflict
  categories of persons to be treated as POWs 35, 50
  definition of POWs 35
  and GCIII 232
  guerilla warfare within POW framework 36, 58
  internment standard 47, 48
  release 60, 97
  status 34–37
  qualification for 49–50
Prevention of Terrorism Act (PTA), 1979 (Sri Lanka) 167
prisoners of war *see* POWs (prisoners of war), internment in international armed conflict
procedural rules/regulation
  definition 4

release of detainees
  analogizing to GCIV in non-international armed conflict 241–242
  ceasefire agreements 95
  cessation of active hostilities 60, 97
  under IHL, in international armed conflict 59–62
    civilians 59–60
    combatants 60–62
  internment under IHL, non-international armed conflict 95–98

review of internment
  analogizing to GCIV in non-international armed conflict 239–241
  under IHL in international armed conflict
    civilians 51–56
    combatants 56–59
    composition of review bodies 53
    initial review 51–52
    periodic review 56, 98
    timing of 53

San José agreement (1990) 220
Security Council, United Nations
  and binding nature of common Article 3 and APII for non-state armed groups 101
  and continued relevance of IHRL during armed conflict 113
  and non-state groups 218
  resolutions 75, 89, 121, 174, 175, 198
'Siracusa Principles on the Limitation and Derogation Provisions in the International Covenant on Civil and Political Rights' 209, 211
South Ossetia conflict (2008) 99
Spain, civil war and belligerency doctrine 13
Sri Lanka
  detention practice 167–168
  Liberation Tigers of Tamil Eelam (LTTE) 167, 232
state practice, sources 8
Syria, arbitrary deprivation of liberty in 2

Taliban
  as *de facto* government 179
  and laws of war 3
  status 38
Tehran International Conference on Human Rights (1968) 113
territoriality principle
  and binding non-state groups 103

transfer issues, importance in contemporary armed conflicts 6
transnational armed conflicts 5, 20
  US conflict with al-Qaeda 185–189

United Kingdom
  authority to detain enemy aliens 40
  and ICRC Study 94
  incorporation of treaties 101
  internment policy
    international armed conflict 40
    non-international armed conflict 71, 72
  Joint Doctrine Publication on Captured Persons 54, 240
  Manual of the Law of Armed Conflict 155
  Northern Ireland, internment regime 199
United Nations (UN)
  Charter *see* Charter of United Nations
  General Assembly *see* General Assembly of United Nations
  and non-international armed conflict 5
  Security Council *see* Security Council, United Nations
United States
  Afghanistan, detention operations 180
  al-Qaeda, conflict with 2, 159–160
  detention operations 72, 185–189
  on the application of IHRL in armed conflict 114
  Iraq, detention operations 176–177
Universal Declaration of Human Rights (1948) 112
  adoption 14
'unlawful combatants' 37–38
'unprivileged belligerents' *see* 'unlawful combatants'

'war on terror,' and 'unlawful combatants' 38
Working Group on Arbitrary Detention (UNWGAD) 118, 166, 173

Printed and bound by CPI Group (UK) Ltd, Croydon, CR0 4YY